ST/SG/AC.10/1/Rev.23 (Vol.II)

Recommendations on the

TRANSPORT OF DANGEROUS GOODS

Model Regulations

Volume II

Twenty-third revised edition

UNITED NATIONS
New York and Geneva, 2023

© 2023 United Nations
All rights reserved worldwide

Requests to reproduce excerpts or to photocopy should be addressed to the Copyright Clearance Center at copyright.com.

All other queries on rights and licenses, including subsidiary rights, should be addressed to:

United Nations Publications
405 East 42nd Street, S-09FW001
New York, NY 10017
United States of America

Email: permissions@un.org
website: https://shop.un.org

The designations employed and the presentation of the material in this publication do not imply the expression of any opinion whatsoever on the part of the Secretariat of the United Nations concerning the legal status of any country, territory, city or area, or of its authorities, or concerning the delimitation of its frontiers or boundaries.

United Nations publication issued by the United Nations Economic Commission for Europe.

ST/SG/AC.10/1/Rev.23 (Vol. II)

ISBN: 978-92-1-139221-0
eISBN: 978-92-1-001905-7

ISSN: 1014-5753
eISSN: 2412-0820

Sales number: E.23.VIII.3

Complete set of two volumes.
Volumes I and II not to be sold separately.

TABLE OF CONTENTS

VOLUME II

	Page
ANNEX: MODEL REGULATIONS ON THE TRANSPORT OF DANGEROUS GOODS (cont'd)	1

			Page
Part 4	**PACKING AND TANK PROVISIONS**		3
	Chapter 4.1	Use of packagings, including intermediate bulk containers (IBCs) and large packagings	5
		4.1.1 General provisions for the packing of dangerous goods in packagings, including IBCs and large packagings	5
		4.1.2 Additional general provisions for the use of IBCs	10
		4.1.3 General provisions concerning packing instructions	10
		4.1.4 List of packing instructions	14
		4.1.5 Special packing provisions for goods of Class 1	117
		4.1.6 Special packing provisions for goods of Class 2	118
		4.1.7 Special packing provisions for organic peroxides (Division 5.2) and self-reactive substances of Division 4.1	120
		4.1.8 Special packing provisions for infectious substances of Category A (Division 6.2, UN Nos. 2814 and 2900)	122
		4.1.9 Special packing provisions for radioactive material	123
	Chapter 4.2	Use of portable tanks and multiple-element gas containers (MEGCs)	127
		4.2.1 General provisions for the use of portable tanks for the transport of substances of Class 1 and Classes 3 to 9	127
		4.2.2 General provisions for the use of portable tanks for the transport of non-refrigerated liquefied gases and chemicals under pressure	131
		4.2.3 General provisions for the use of portable tanks for the transport of refrigerated liquefied gases	133
		4.2.4 General provisions for the use of multiple-element gas containers (MEGCs)	134
		4.2.5 Portable tank instructions and special provisions	135
		4.2.6 Transitional measures	149
	Chapter 4.3	Use of bulk containers	151
		4.3.1 General provisions	151
		4.3.2 Additional provisions applicable to bulk goods of Divisions 4.2, 4.3, 5.1, 6.2 and Classes 7 and 8	152

TABLE OF CONTENTS (cont'd)

VOLUME II

			Page
Part 5	**CONSIGNMENT PROCEDURES**		155
	Chapter 5.1 General provisions		157
	5.1.1	Application and general provisions	157
	5.1.2	Use of overpacks	157
	5.1.3	Empty packagings	157
	5.1.4	Mixed packing	157
	5.1.5	General provisions for Class 7	158
	Chapter 5.2 Marking and labelling		163
	5.2.1	Marking	163
	5.2.2	Labelling	167
	Chapter 5.3 Placarding and marking of cargo transport units and bulk containers		179
	5.3.1	Placarding	179
	5.3.2	Marking	181
	Chapter 5.4 Documentation		183
	5.4.1	Dangerous goods transport information	183
	5.4.2	Container/vehicle packing certificate	189
	5.4.3	Emergency response information	190
	5.4.4	Retention of dangerous goods transport information	190
	Chapter 5.5 Special provisions		193
	5.5.1	*(Deleted)*	193
	5.5.2	Special provisions applicable to fumigated cargo transport units (UN 3359)	193
	5.5.3	Special provisions applicable to packages and cargo transport units containing substances presenting a risk of asphyxiation when used for cooling or conditioning purposes (such as dry ice (UN 1845) or nitrogen, refrigerated liquid (UN 1977) or argon, refrigerated liquid (UN 1951) or nitrogen)	195
	5.5.4	Dangerous goods in equipment in use or intended for use during transport	198
Part 6.	**REQUIREMENTS FOR THE CONSTRUCTION AND TESTING OF PACKAGINGS, INTERMEDIATE BULK CONTAINERS (IBCs), LARGE PACKAGINGS, PORTABLE TANKS, MULTIPLE-ELEMENT GAS CONTAINERS (MEGCs) AND BULK CONTAINERS**		199
	Chapter 6.1 Requirements for the construction and testing of packagings		201
	6.1.1	General	201
	6.1.2	Code for designating types of packagings	202
	6.1.3	Marking	204
	6.1.4	Requirements for packagings	208
	6.1.5	Test requirements for packagings	218

TABLE OF CONTENTS (cont'd)

VOLUME II

			Page
Chapter 6.2		Requirements for the construction and testing of pressure receptacles, aerosol dispensers, small receptacles containing gas (gas cartridges) and fuel cell cartridges containing liquefied flammable gas	225
	6.2.1	General requirements	225
	6.2.2	Requirements for UN pressure receptacles	232
	6.2.3	Requirements for non-UN pressure receptacles	256
	6.2.4	Requirements for aerosol dispensers, small receptacles containing gas (gas cartridges) and fuel cell cartridges containing liquefied flammable gas	257
Chapter 6.3		Requirements for the construction and testing of packagings for Division 6.2 infectious substances of Category A (UN Nos. 2814 and 2900)	261
	6.3.1	General	261
	6.3.2	Requirements for packagings	261
	6.3.3	Code for designating types of packagings	261
	6.3.4	Marking	261
	6.3.5	Test requirements for packagings	262
Chapter 6.4		Requirements for the construction, testing and approval of packages for radioactive material and for the approval of such material	267
	6.4.1	*(Reserved)*	267
	6.4.2	General requirements	267
	6.4.3	Additional requirements for packages transported by air	268
	6.4.4	Requirements for excepted packages	268
	6.4.5	Requirements for industrial packages	268
	6.4.6	Requirements for packages containing uranium hexafluoride	270
	6.4.7	Requirements for Type A packages	270
	6.4.8	Requirements for Type B(U) packages	272
	6.4.9	Requirements for Type B(M) packages	273
	6.4.10	Requirements for Type C packages	274
	6.4.11	Requirements for packages containing fissile material	274
	6.4.12	Test procedures and demonstration of compliance	278
	6.4.13	Testing the integrity of the containment system and shielding and evaluating criticality safety	279
	6.4.14	Target for drop tests	279
	6.4.15	Test for demonstrating ability to withstand normal conditions of transport	279
	6.4.16	Additional tests for Type A packages designed for liquids and gases	281
	6.4.17	Tests for demonstrating ability to withstand accident conditions in transport	281
	6.4.18	Enhanced water immersion test for Type B(U) and Type B(M) packages containing more than 10^5 A2 and Type C packages	282
	6.4.19	Water leakage test for packages containing fissile material	282
	6.4.20	Tests for Type C packages	282
	6.4.21	Tests for packagings designed to contain uranium hexafluoride	283
	6.4.22	Approvals of package designs and materials	283
	6.4.23	Applications and approvals for radioactive material transport	284
	6.4.24	Transitional measures for Class 7	294

TABLE OF CONTENTS (cont'd)

VOLUME II

			Page
Chapter 6.5		Requirements for the construction and testing of intermediate bulk containers	297
	6.5.1	General requirements	297
	6.5.2	Marking	300
	6.5.3	Construction requirements	303
	6.5.4	Testing, certification and inspection	304
	6.5.5	Specific requirements for IBCs	305
	6.5.6	Test requirements for IBCs	312
Chapter 6.6		Requirements for the construction and testing of large packagings	321
	6.6.1	General	321
	6.6.2	Code for designating types of large packagings	321
	6.6.3	Marking	322
	6.6.4	Specific requirements for large packagings	323
	6.6.5	Test requirements for large packagings	326
Chapter 6.7		Requirements for the design, construction, inspection and testing of portable tanks and multiple-element gas containers (MEGCs)	331
	6.7.1	Application and general requirements	331
	6.7.2	Requirements for the design, construction, inspection and testing of portable tanks intended for the transport of substances of Class 1 and Classes 3 to 9	331
	6.7.3	Requirements for the design, construction, inspection and testing of portable tanks intended for the transport of non-refrigerated liquefied gases	350
	6.7.4	Requirements for the design, construction, inspection and testing of portable tanks intended for the transport of refrigerated liquefied gases	364
	6.7.5	Requirements for the design, construction, inspection and testing of multiple-element gas containers (MEGCs) intended for the transport of non-refrigerated gases	377
Chapter 6.8		Requirements for the design, construction, inspection and testing of bulk containers	385
	6.8.1	Definitions	385
	6.8.2	Application and general requirements	385
	6.8.3	Requirements for the design, construction, inspection and testing of freight containers used as BK1 or BK2 bulk containers	385
	6.8.4	Requirements for the design, construction and approval of BK1 and BK2 bulk containers other than freight containers	386
	6.8.5	Requirements for the design, construction, inspection and testing of flexible bulk containers BK3	387
Chapter 6.9		Requirements for the design, construction, inspection and testing of portable tanks with shells made of fibre reinforced plastics (FRP) materials	393
	6.9.1	Application and general requirements	393
	6.9.2	Requirements for the design, construction, inspection and testing of FRP portable tanks	393

TABLE OF CONTENTS (cont'd)

VOLUME II

	Page
Part 7 PROVISIONS CONCERNING TRANSPORT OPERATIONS	407
Chapter 7.1 Provisions concerning transport operations by all modes of transport	409
7.1.1 Application, general provisions and loading requirements	409
7.1.2 Segregation of dangerous goods	411
7.1.3 Special provisions applicable to the transport of explosives	411
7.1.4 Special provisions applicable to the transport of gases	413
7.1.5 Special provisions applicable to the transport of self-reactive substances of Division 4.1, organic peroxides of Division 5.2 and substances stabilized by temperature control (other than self-reactive substances and organic peroxides)	413
7.1.6 *(Reserved)*	416
7.1.7 Special provisions applicable to the transport of Division 6.1 (toxic) and Division 6.2 (infectious) substances	416
7.1.8 Special provisions applicable to the transport of radioactive material	417
7.1.9 Reporting of accidents or incidents involving dangerous goods in transport	420
7.1.10 Retention of dangerous goods transport information	421
Chapter 7.2 Modal provisions	423
7.2.1 Application and general provisions	423
7.2.2 Special provisions applicable to the transport of portable tanks on vehicles	423
7.2.3 Special provisions applicable to the transport of radioactive material	423
7.2.4 Security provisions for transport by road, rail and inland waterway	424
TABLE OF CORRESPONDENCE between paragraphs, tables and figures in the 2018 edition of the IAEA Regulations for the Safe Transport of Radioactive Material and the twenty-third revised edition of the Recommendations on the Transport of Dangerous Goods	425

Annex

Model Regulations on the

TRANSPORT OF DANGEROUS GOODS
(cont'd)

PART 4

PACKING AND TANK PROVISIONS

CHAPTER 4.1

USE OF PACKAGINGS, INCLUDING INTERMEDIATE BULK CONTAINERS (IBCs) AND LARGE PACKAGINGS

4.1.1   General provisions for the packing of dangerous goods in packagings, including IBCs and large packagings

NOTE: For the packing of goods of Class 2, Division 6.2 and Class 7, the general provisions of this section only apply as indicated in 4.1.8.2 (Division 6.2, UN Nos. 2814 and 2900), 4.1.9.1.5 (Class 7) and in the applicable packing instructions of 4.1.4 (P201, P207 and LP02 for Class 2 and P620, P621, P622, IBC620, LP621 and LP622 for Division 6.2).

4.1.1.1   Dangerous goods shall be packed in good quality packagings, including IBCs and large packagings, which shall be strong enough to withstand the shocks and loadings normally encountered during transport, including transshipment between cargo transport units and between cargo transport units and warehouses as well as any removal from a pallet or overpack for subsequent manual or mechanical handling. Packagings, including IBCs and large packagings, shall be constructed and closed so as to prevent any loss of contents when prepared for transport which may be caused under normal conditions of transport, by vibration, or by changes in temperature, humidity or pressure (resulting from altitude, for example). Packagings, including IBCs and large packagings, shall be closed in accordance with the information provided by the manufacturer. No dangerous residue shall adhere to the outside of packages, IBCs and large packagings during transport. These provisions apply, as appropriate, to new, reused, reconditioned or remanufactured packagings, and to new, reused, repaired or remanufactured IBCs, and to new, reused or remanufactured large packagings.

4.1.1.2   Parts of packagings, including IBCs and large packagings, which are in direct contact with dangerous goods:

- (a)   Shall not be affected or significantly weakened by those dangerous goods;

- (b)   Shall not cause a dangerous effect e.g. catalysing a reaction or reacting with the dangerous goods; and

- (c)   Shall not allow permeation of the dangerous goods that could constitute a danger under normal conditions of transport.

Where necessary, they shall be provided with a suitable inner coating or treatment.

4.1.1.3   Unless otherwise provided elsewhere in these Regulations, each packaging, including IBCs and large packagings, except inner packagings, shall conform to a design type successfully tested in accordance with the requirements of 6.1.5, 6.3.5, 6.5.6 or 6.6.5, as applicable.

However, IBCs manufactured before 1 January 2011 and conforming to a design type which has not passed the vibration test of 6.5.6.13 or which was not required to meet the criteria of 6.5.6.9.5 (d) at the time it was subjected to the drop test, may still be used.

4.1.1.3.1   Packagings, including IBCs and large packagings, may conform to one or more than one successfully tested design type and may bear more than one mark.

4.1.1.4   When filling packagings, including IBCs and large packagings, with liquids, sufficient ullage (outage) shall be left to ensure that neither leakage nor permanent distortion of the packaging occurs as a result of an expansion of the liquid caused by temperatures likely to occur during transport. Unless specific requirements are prescribed, liquids shall not completely fill a packaging at a temperature of 55 °C. However, sufficient ullage shall be left in an IBC to ensure that at the mean bulk temperature of 50 °C it is not filled to more than 98 % of its water capacity.

4.1.1.4.1   For air transport, packagings intended to contain liquids shall also be capable of withstanding a pressure differential without leakage as specified in the international regulations for air transport.

4.1.1.5   Inner packagings shall be packed in an outer packaging in such a way that, under normal conditions of transport, they cannot break, be punctured or leak their contents into the outer packaging. Inner packagings containing liquids shall be packed with their closures upward and placed within outer packagings consistent with the orientation marks prescribed in 5.2.1.7 of these Regulations. Inner packagings that are liable to break or be punctured easily, such as those made of glass, porcelain or stoneware or of certain plastics materials, etc., shall be secured in outer packagings with suitable cushioning material. Any leakage of the contents shall not substantially impair the protective properties of the cushioning material or of the outer packaging.

4.1.1.5.1   Where an outer packaging of a combination packaging or a large packaging has been successfully tested with different types of inner packagings, a variety of such different inner packagings may also be assembled in this outer packaging or large packaging. In addition, provided an equivalent level of performance is maintained, the following variations in inner packagings are allowed without further testing of the package:

    (a)   Inner packagings of equivalent or smaller size may be used provided:

        (i)   The inner packagings are of similar design to the tested inner packagings (e.g. shape - round, rectangular, etc.);

        (ii)   The material of construction of the inner packagings (glass, plastics, metal, etc.) offers resistance to impact and stacking forces equal to or greater than that of the originally tested inner packaging;

        (iii)   The inner packagings have the same or smaller openings and the closure is of similar design (e.g. screw cap, friction lid, etc.);

        (iv)   Sufficient additional cushioning material is used to take up void spaces and to prevent significant movement of the inner packagings; and

        (v)   Inner packagings are oriented within the outer packaging in the same manner as in the tested package.

    (b)   A lesser number of the tested inner packagings, or of the alternative types of inner packagings identified in (a) above, may be used provided sufficient cushioning is added to fill the void space(s) and to prevent significant movement of the inner packagings.

4.1.1.5.2   Use of supplementary packagings within an outer packaging (e.g. an intermediate packaging or a receptacle inside a required inner packaging) additional to what is required by the packing instructions is authorized provided all relevant requirements are met, including those of 4.1.1.3, and, if appropriate, suitable cushioning is used to prevent movement within the packaging.

4.1.1.6   Dangerous goods shall not be packed together in the same outer packaging or in large packagings, with dangerous or other goods if they react dangerously with each other and cause:

    (a)   Combustion and/or evolution of considerable heat;

    (b)   Evolution of flammable, toxic or asphyxiant gases;

    (c)   The formation of corrosive substances; or

    (d)   The formation of unstable substances.

4.1.1.7   The closures of packagings containing wetted or diluted substances shall be such that the percentage of liquid (water, solvent or phlegmatizer) does not fall below the prescribed limits during transport.

4.1.1.7.1	Where two or more closure systems are fitted in series on an IBC, that nearest to the substance being carried shall be closed first.

4.1.1.8	Where pressure may develop in a package by the emission of gas from the contents (as a result of temperature increase or other causes), the packaging or IBC may be fitted with a vent provided that the gas emitted will not cause danger on account of its toxicity, its flammability or the quantity released, for example.

A venting device shall be fitted if dangerous overpressure may develop due to normal decomposition of substances. The vent shall be so designed that, when the packaging or IBC is in the attitude in which it is intended to be transported, leakages of liquid and the penetration of foreign substances are prevented under normal conditions of transport.

4.1.1.8.1	Liquids may only be filled into inner packagings which have an appropriate resistance to internal pressure that may be developed under normal conditions of transport.

4.1.1.8.2	Venting of the package is not permitted for air transport.

4.1.1.9	New, remanufactured or reused packagings, including IBCs and large packagings, or reconditioned packagings and repaired or routinely maintained IBCs shall be capable of passing the tests prescribed in 6.1.5, 6.3.5, 6.5.6 or 6.6.5, as applicable. Before being filled and handed over for transport, every packaging, including IBCs and large packagings, shall be inspected to ensure that it is free from corrosion, contamination or other damage and every IBC shall be inspected with regard to the proper functioning of any service equipment. Any packaging, which shows signs of reduced strength as compared with the approved design type shall no longer be used or shall be so reconditioned, that it is able to withstand the design type tests. Any IBC which shows signs of reduced strength as compared with the tested design type shall no longer be used or shall be so repaired or routinely maintained that it is able to withstand the design type tests.

4.1.1.10	Liquids shall be filled only into packagings, including IBCs, which have an appropriate resistance to the internal pressure that may develop under normal conditions of transport. Packagings and IBCs marked with the hydraulic test pressure prescribed in 6.1.3.1 (d) and 6.5.2.2.1, respectively shall be filled only with a liquid having a vapour pressure:

(a)	Such that the total gauge pressure in the packaging or IBC (i.e. the vapour pressure of the filling substance plus the partial pressure of air or other inert gases, less 100 kPa) at 55 °C, determined on the basis of a maximum degree of filling in accordance with 4.1.1.4 and a filling temperature of 15 °C, will not exceed two thirds of the marked test pressure; or

(b)	At 50 °C less than four sevenths of the sum of the marked test pressure plus 100 kPa; or

(c)	At 55 °C less than two thirds of the sum of the marked test pressure plus 100 kPa.

IBCs intended for the transport of liquids shall not be used to carry liquids having a vapour pressure of more than 110 kPa (1.1 bar) at 50 °C or 130 kPa (1.3 bar) at 55 °C.

**Examples of required marked test pressures for packagings,
including IBCs, calculated as in 4.1.1.10 (c)**

UN No.	Name	Class	Packing group	V_{p55} (kPa)	$V_{p55} \times 1.5$ (kPa)	($V_{p55} \times 1.5$) minus 100 (kPa)	Required minimum test pressure gauge under 6.1.5.5.4 (c) (kPa)	Minimum test pressure (gauge) to be marked on the packaging (kPa)
2056	Tetrahydrofuran	3	II	70	105	5	100	100
2247	n-Decane	3	III	1.4	2.1	-97.9	100	100
1593	Dichloromethane	6.1	III	164	246	146	146	150
1155	Diethyl ether	3	I	199	299	199	199	250

NOTE 1: *For pure liquids the vapour pressure at 55 °C (V_{p55}) can often be obtained from scientific tables.*

NOTE 2: *The table refers to the use of 4.1.1.10 (c) only, which means that the marked test pressure shall exceed 1.5 times the vapour pressure at 55 °C less 100 kPa. When, for example, the test pressure for n-decane is determined according to 6.1.5.5.4 (a), the minimum marked test pressure may be lower.*

NOTE 3: *For diethyl ether the required minimum test pressure under 6.1.5.5.5 is 250 kPa.*

4.1.1.11   Empty packagings, including IBCs and large packagings, that have contained a dangerous substance shall be treated in the same manner as is required by these Regulations for a filled packaging, unless adequate measures have been taken to nullify any hazard.

4.1.1.12   Every packaging as specified in chapter 6.1 intended to contain liquids shall successfully undergo a suitable leakproofness test. This test is part of a quality assurance programme as stipulated in 6.1.1.4 which shows the capability of meeting the appropriate test level indicated in 6.1.5.4.3:

(a) Before it is first used for transport;

(b) After remanufacturing or reconditioning of any packaging, before it is re-used for transport.

For this test the packaging need not have its closures fitted. The inner receptacle of a composite packaging may be tested without the outer packaging, provided the test results are not affected. This test is not necessary for inner packagings of combination packagings or large packagings.

4.1.1.13   Packagings, including IBCs, used for solids which may become liquid at temperatures likely to be encountered during transport shall also be capable of containing the substance in the liquid state.

4.1.1.14   Packagings, including IBCs, used for powdery or granular substances shall be siftproof or shall be provided with a liner.

4.1.1.15   For plastics drums and jerricans, rigid plastics IBCs and composite IBCs with plastics inner receptacles, unless otherwise approved by the competent authority, the period of use permitted for the transport of dangerous substances shall be five years from the date of manufacture of the receptacles, except where a shorter period of use is prescribed because of the nature of the substance to be transported.

NOTE: *For composite IBCs the period of use refers to the date of manufacture of the inner receptacle.*

4.1.1.16   Where ice is used as a coolant it shall not affect the integrity of the packaging.

4.1.1.17 *Explosives, self-reactive substances and organic peroxides*

Unless specific provision to the contrary is made in these Regulations, the packagings, including IBCs and large packagings, used for goods of Class 1, self-reactive substances of Division 4.1 and organic peroxides of Division 5.2 shall comply with the provisions for the medium danger group (packing group II).

4.1.1.18 *Use of salvage packagings and large salvage packagings*

4.1.1.18.1　Damaged, defective, leaking or non-conforming packages, or dangerous goods that have spilled or leaked may be transported in salvage packagings mentioned in 6.1.5.1.11 and 6.6.5.1.9. This does not prevent the use of a larger size packaging or large packaging of appropriate type and performance level and under the conditions of 4.1.1.18.2 and 4.1.1.18.3.

4.1.1.18.2　Appropriate measures shall be taken to prevent excessive movement of the damaged or leaking packages within a salvage packaging. When the salvage packaging contains liquids, sufficient inert absorbent material shall be added to eliminate the presence of free liquid.

4.1.1.18.3　Appropriate measures shall be taken to ensure that there is no dangerous build up of pressure.

4.1.1.19 *Use of salvage pressure receptacles*

4.1.1.19.1　In the case of damaged, defective, leaking or non-conforming pressure receptacles, salvage pressure receptacles according to 6.2.3 may be used.

NOTE:　*A salvage pressure receptacle may be used as an overpack in accordance with 5.1.2. When used as an overpack, marks shall be in accordance with 5.1.2.1 instead of 5.2.1.3.*

4.1.1.19.2　Pressure receptacles shall be placed in salvage pressure receptacles of suitable size. More than one pressure receptacle may be placed in the same salvage pressure receptacle only if the contents are known and do not react dangerously with each other (see 4.1.1.6). In this case the total sum of water capacities of the placed pressure receptacles shall not exceed 3 000 litres. Measures shall be taken to prevent movement of the pressure receptacles within the salvage pressure receptacle e.g. by partitioning, securing or cushioning.

4.1.1.19.3　A pressure receptacle may only be placed in a salvage pressure receptacle if:

(a) The salvage pressure receptacle is in accordance with 6.2.3.5 and a copy of the approval certificate is available;

(b) Parts of the salvage pressure receptacle which are, or are likely to be in direct contact with the dangerous goods will not be affected or weakened by those dangerous goods and will not cause a dangerous effect (e.g. catalyzing reaction or reacting with the dangerous goods); and

(c) The contents of the contained pressure receptacle(s) are limited in pressure and volume so that if totally discharged into the salvage pressure receptacle, the pressure in the salvage pressure receptacle at 65 °C will not exceed the test pressure of the salvage pressure receptacle (for gases, see packing instruction in P200 (3) in 4.1.4.1). The reduction of the useable water capacity of the salvage pressure receptacle, e.g. by any contained equipment and cushioning, shall be taken into account.

4.1.1.19.4　The proper shipping name, the UN Number preceded by the letters "UN" and label(s) as required for packages in chapter 5.2 applicable to the dangerous goods inside the contained pressure receptacle(s) shall be applied to the salvage pressure receptacle for transport.

4.1.1.19.5　Salvage pressure receptacles shall be cleaned, purged and visually inspected internally and externally after each use. They shall be periodically inspected and tested in accordance with 6.2.1.6 at least once every five years.

4.1.2 Additional general provisions for the use of IBCs

4.1.2.1 When IBCs are used for the transport of liquids with a flash point of 60 °C (closed-cup) or lower, or of powders liable to dust explosion, measures shall be taken to prevent a dangerous electrostatic discharge.

4.1.2.2 Every metal, rigid plastics and composite IBC shall be inspected and tested, as relevant, in accordance with 6.5.4.4 or 6.5.4.5:

- Before it is put into service;

- Thereafter at intervals not exceeding two and a half and five years, as appropriate; and

- After the repair or remanufacture, before it is re-used for transport.

An IBC shall not be filled and offered for transport after the date of expiry of the last periodic test or inspection. However, an IBC filled prior to the date of expiry of the last periodic test or inspection may be transported for a period not to exceed three months beyond the date of expiry of the last periodic test or inspection. In addition, an IBC may be transported after the date of expiry of the last periodic test or inspection:

(a) After emptying but before cleaning, for purposes of performing the required test or inspection prior to refilling; and

(b) Unless otherwise approved by the competent authority, for a period not to exceed six months beyond the date of expiry of the last periodic test or inspection in order to allow the return of dangerous goods or residues for proper disposal or recycling. Reference to this exemption shall be entered in the transport document.

4.1.2.3 IBCs of type 31HZ2 shall be filled to at least 80 % of the volume of the outer casing and always be carried in closed cargo transport units.

4.1.2.4 Except for routine maintenance of metal, rigid plastics, composite and flexible IBCs performed by the owner of the IBC, whose State and name or authorized symbol is durably marked on the IBC, the party performing routine maintenance shall durably mark the IBC near the manufacturer's UN design type mark to show:

(a) The State in which the routine maintenance was carried out; and

(b) The name or authorized symbol of the party performing the routine maintenance.

4.1.3 General provisions concerning packing instructions

4.1.3.1 Packing instructions applicable to dangerous goods of Classes 1 to 9 are specified in 4.1.4. They are subdivided depending on the type of packagings to which they apply:

- 4.1.4.1 for packagings other than IBCs and large packagings; these packing instructions are designated by an alphanumeric code comprising the letter "P";

- 4.1.4.2 for IBCs; these are designated by an alphanumeric code comprising the letters "IBC";

- 4.1.4.3 for large packagings; these are designated by an alphanumeric code comprising the letters "LP".

Generally, packing instructions specify that the general provisions of 4.1.1, 4.1.2 and/or 4.1.3, as appropriate, are applicable. They may also require compliance with the special provisions of sections 4.1.5, 4.1.6, 4.1.7, 4.1.8 or 4.1.9 when appropriate. Special packing provisions may also be specified in the packing instruction for individual substances or articles. They are also designated by an alphanumeric code comprising the letters:

"PP" for packagings other than IBCs and large packagings
"B" for IBCs
"L" for large packagings.

Unless otherwise specified, each packaging shall conform to the applicable requirements of part 6. Generally packing instructions do not provide guidance on compatibility and the user should not select a packaging without checking that the substance is compatible with the packaging material selected (e.g. most fluorides are unsuitable for glass receptacles). Where glass receptacles are permitted in the packing instructions porcelain, earthenware and stoneware packagings are also allowed.

4.1.3.2 Column 8 of the dangerous goods list shows for each article or substance the packing instruction(s) that shall be used. Column 9 indicates the special packing provisions applicable to specific substances or articles.

4.1.3.3 Each packing instruction shows, where applicable, the acceptable single and combination packagings. For combination packagings, the acceptable outer packagings, inner packagings and when applicable the maximum quantity permitted in each inner or outer packaging, are shown. Maximum net mass and maximum capacity are as defined in 1.2.1. Where packagings which need not meet the requirements of 4.1.1.3 (e.g., crates, pallets, etc.) are authorized in a packing instruction or the special provisions named in the dangerous goods list, these packagings are not subject to the mass or volume limits generally applicable to packagings conforming to the requirements of chapter 6.1, unless otherwise indicated in the relevant packing instruction or special provision.

4.1.3.4 The following packagings shall not be used when the substances being transported are liable to become liquid during transport:

Packagings

Drums: 1D and 1G
Boxes: 4C1, 4C2, 4D, 4F, 4G and 4H1
Bags: 5L1, 5L2, 5L3, 5H1, 5H2, 5H3, 5H4, 5M1 and 5M2
Composite packagings: 6HC, 6HD2, 6HG1, 6HG2, 6HD1, 6PC, 6PD1, 6PD2, 6PG1, 6PG2 and 6PH1

Large packagings

Flexible plastics: 51H (outer packaging)

IBCs

For substances of packing group I: All types of IBCs;

For substances of packing groups II and III:

Wooden: 11C, 11D and 11F
Fibreboard: 11G
Flexible: 13H1, 13H2, 13H3, 13H4, 13H5, 13L1, 13L2, 13L3, 13L4, 13M1 and 13M2
Composite: 11HZ2 and 21HZ2.

4.1.3.5 Where the packing instructions in this chapter authorize the use of a particular type of packaging (e.g. 4G; 1A2), packagings bearing the same packaging identification code followed by the letters "V", "U" or "W" marked in accordance with the requirements of part 6 (e.g. 4GV, 4GU or 4GW; 1A2V, 1A2U or 1A2W) may also be used under the same conditions and limitations applicable to the use of that type of packaging according to the relevant packing instructions. For example, a combination packaging marked with the packaging code "4GV" may be used whenever a combination packaging marked "4G" is authorized, provided the requirements in the relevant packing instruction regarding types of inner packagings and quantity limitations are respected.

4.1.3.6 *Pressure receptacles for liquids and solids*

4.1.3.6.1   Unless otherwise indicated in these Regulations, pressure receptacles conforming to:

(a)   The applicable requirements of chapter 6.2; or

(b)   The national or international standards on the design, construction, testing, manufacturing and inspection, as applied by the country in which the pressure receptacles are manufactured, provided that the provisions of 4.1.3.6 and 6.2.3.3 are met;

are authorized for the transport of any liquid or solid substance other than explosives, thermally unstable substances, organic peroxides, self-reactive substances, substances where significant pressure may develop by evolution of chemical reaction and radioactive material (unless permitted in 4.1.9).

This sub-section is not applicable to the substances mentioned in 4.1.4.1, packing instruction P200, table 3.

4.1.3.6.2   Every design type of pressure receptacle shall be approved by the competent authority of the country of manufacture or as indicated in chapter 6.2.

4.1.3.6.3   Unless otherwise indicated, pressure receptacles having a minimum test pressure of 0.6 MPa shall be used.

4.1.3.6.4   Unless otherwise indicated, pressure receptacles may be provided with an emergency pressure relief device designed to avoid bursting in case of overfill or fire accidents.

Pressure receptacle valves shall be designed and constructed in such a way that they are inherently able to withstand damage without release of the contents or shall be protected from damage which could cause inadvertent release of the contents of the pressure receptacle, by one of the methods as given in 4.1.6.1.8 (a) to (e).

4.1.3.6.5   The level of filling shall not exceed 95 % of the capacity of the pressure receptacle at 50 °C. Sufficient ullage (outage) shall be left to ensure that the pressure receptacle will not be liquid full at a temperature of 55 °C.

4.1.3.6.6   Unless otherwise indicated pressure receptacles shall be subjected to a periodic inspection and test every 5 years. The periodic inspection shall include an external examination, an internal examination or alternative method as approved by the competent authority, a pressure test or equivalent effective non-destructive testing with the agreement of the competent authority including an inspection of all accessories (e.g. tightness of valves, emergency relief valves or fusible elements). Pressure receptacles shall not be filled after they become due for periodic inspection and test but may be transported after the expiry of the time limit. Pressure receptacle repairs shall meet the requirements of 4.1.6.1.11.

4.1.3.6.7   Prior to filling, the filler shall perform an inspection of the pressure receptacle and ensure that the pressure receptacle is authorized for the substances to be transported and that the provisions of these Regulations have been met. Shut-off valves shall be closed after filling and remain closed during transport. The consignor shall verify that the closures and equipment are not leaking.

4.1.3.6.8   Refillable pressure receptacles shall not be filled with a substance different from that previously contained unless the necessary operations for change of service have been performed.

4.1.3.6.9   Marking of pressure receptacles for liquids and solids according to 4.1.3.6 (not conforming to the requirements of chapter 6.2) shall be in accordance with the requirements of the competent authority of the country of manufacturing.

4.1.3.7 Packagings or IBCs not specifically authorized in the applicable packing instruction shall not be used for the transport of a substance or article unless specifically approved by the competent authority and provided:

(a) The alternative packaging complies with the general requirements of this part;

(b) When the packing instruction indicated in the Dangerous Goods List so specifies, the alternative packaging meets the requirements of part 6;

(c) The competent authority determines that the alternative packaging provides at least the same level of safety as if the substance were packed in accordance with a method specified in the particular packing instruction indicated in the Dangerous Goods List; and

(d) A copy of the competent authority approval accompanies each consignment or the transport document includes an indication that alternative packaging was approved by the competent authority.

NOTE: *The competent authorities granting such approvals should take action to amend these Model Regulations to include the provisions covered by the approval as appropriate.*

4.1.3.8 *Unpackaged articles other than Class 1 articles*

4.1.3.8.1 Where large and robust articles cannot be packaged in accordance with the requirements of chapters 6.1 or 6.6 and they have to be transported empty, uncleaned and unpackaged, the competent authority may approve such transport. In doing so the competent authority shall take into account that:

(a) Large and robust articles shall be strong enough to withstand the shocks and loadings normally encountered during transport including trans-shipment between cargo transport units and between cargo transport units and warehouses, as well as any removal from a pallet for subsequent manual or mechanical handling;

(b) All closures and openings shall be sealed so that there can be no loss of contents which might be caused under normal conditions of transport, by vibration, or by changes in temperature, humidity or pressure (resulting from altitude, for example). No dangerous residue shall adhere to the outside of the large and robust articles;

(c) Parts of large and robust articles, which are in direct contact with dangerous goods:

(i) shall not be affected or significantly weakened by those dangerous goods; and

(ii) shall not cause a dangerous effect e.g. catalysing a reaction or reacting with the dangerous goods;

(d) Large and robust articles containing liquids shall be stowed and secured to ensure that neither leakage nor permanent distortion of the article occurs during transport;

(e) They shall be fixed in cradles or crates or other handling devices in such a way that they will not become loose during normal conditions of transport.

4.1.3.8.2 Unpackaged articles approved by the competent authority in accordance with the provisions of 4.1.3.8.1 shall be subject to the consignment procedures of part 5. In addition the consignor of such articles shall ensure that a copy of any such approval is transported with the large and robust articles.

NOTE: *A large and robust article may include flexible fuel containment systems, military equipment, machinery or equipment containing dangerous goods above the limited quantity thresholds.*

4.1.4 List of packing instructions

4.1.4.1 Packing instructions concerning the use of packagings (except IBCs and large packagings)

P001		PACKING INSTRUCTION (LIQUIDS)		P001
The following packagings are authorized provided that the general provisions of **4.1.1** and **4.1.3** are met:				
		Maximum capacity/net mass (see 4.1.3.3)		
		Packing group I	Packing group II	Packing group III
Combination packagings				
Inner packagings	Outer packagings			
Glass 10 *l* Plastics 30 *l* Metal 40 *l*	**Drums** steel (1A1, 1A2) aluminium (1B1, 1B2) other metal (1N1, 1N2) plastics (1H1, 1H2) plywood (1D) fibre (1G)	250 kg 250 kg 250 kg 250 kg 150 kg 75 kg	400 kg 400 kg 400 kg 400 kg 400 kg 400 kg	400 kg 400 kg 400 kg 400 kg 400 kg 400 kg
	Boxes steel (4A) aluminium (4B) other metal (4N) natural wood (4C1, 4C2) plywood (4D) reconstituted wood (4F) fibreboard (4G) expanded plastics (4H1) solid plastics (4H2)	250 kg 250 kg 250 kg 150 kg 150 kg 75 kg 75 kg 60 kg 150 kg	400 kg 400 kg 400 kg 400 kg 400 kg 400 kg 400 kg 60 kg 400 kg	400 kg 400 kg 400 kg 400 kg 400 kg 400 kg 400 kg 60 kg 400 kg
	Jerricans steel (3A1, 3A2) aluminium (3B1, 3B2) plastics (3H1, 3H2)	120 kg 120 kg 120 kg	120 kg 120 kg 120 kg	120 kg 120 kg 120 kg
Single packagings				
Drums steel, non-removable head (1A1) steel, removable head (1A2) aluminium, non-removable head (1B1) aluminium, removable head (1B2) other metal, non-removable head (1N1) other metal, removable head (1N2) plastics, non-removable head (1H1) plastics, removable head (1H2)		250 *l* 250 *l* [a] 250 *l* 250 *l* [a] 250 *l* 250 *l* [a] 250 *l* 250 *l* [a]	450 *l* 450 *l* 450 *l* 450 *l* 450 *l* 450 *l* 450 *l* 450 *l*	450 *l* 450 *l* 450 *l* 450 *l* 450 *l* 450 *l* 450 *l* 450 *l*
Jerricans steel, non-removable head (3A1) steel, removable head (3A2) aluminium, non-removable head (3B1) aluminium, removable head (3B2) plastics, non-removable head (3H1) plastics, removable head (3H2)		60 *l* 60 *l* [a] 60 *l* 60 *l* [a] 60 *l* 60 *l* [a]	60 *l* 60 *l* 60 *l* 60 *l* 60 *l* 60 *l*	60 *l* 60 *l* 60 *l* 60 *l* 60 *l* 60 *l*

[a] *Only substances with a viscosity more than 200 mm^2/s are permitted.*

Cont'd on next page

P001	PACKING INSTRUCTION (LIQUIDS) *(cont'd)*			P001
		Maximum capacity/Net mass (see 4.1.3.3)		
		Packing group I	Packing group II	Packing group III
Single packagings *(cont'd)*				
Composite packagings				
plastics receptacle in steel or aluminium or plastics drum (6HA1, 6HB1, 6HH1)		250 *l*	250 *l*	250 *l*
plastics receptacle in fibre or plywood drum (6HG1, 6HD1)		120 *l*	250 *l*	250 *l*
plastics receptacle in steel or aluminium crate or box or plastic receptacle in wooden, plywood, fibreboard or solid plastics box (6HA2, 6HB2, 6HC, 6HD2, 6HG2 or 6HH2)		60 *l*	60 *l*	60 *l*
glass receptacle in steel, aluminium, fibre, plywood, expanded plastics or solid plastics drum (6PA1, 6PB1, 6PG1, 6PD1, 6PH1 or 6PH2) or in steel, aluminium, wooden or fibreboard box or in a wickerwork hamper (6PA2, 6PB2, 6PC, 6PG2 or 6PD2)		60 *l*	60 *l*	60 *l*

Pressure receptacles, provided that the general provisions of 4.1.3.6 are met.

Special packing provisions:

PP1 For UN Nos. 1133, 1210, 1263 and 1866 and for adhesives, printing inks, printing ink related materials, paints, paint related materials and resin solutions which are assigned to UN 3082, metal or plastics packagings for substances of packing groups II and III in quantities of 5 litres or less per packaging are not required to meet the performance tests in chapter 6.1 when transported:

   (a) In palletized loads, a pallet box or unit load device, e.g. individual packagings placed or stacked and secured by strapping, shrink or stretch-wrapping or other suitable means to a pallet. For sea transport, the palletized loads, pallet boxes or unit load devices shall be firmly packed and secured in closed cargo transport units; or

   (b) As an inner packaging of a combination packaging with a maximum net mass of 40 kg.

PP2 For UN 3065, wooden barrels with a maximum capacity of 250 litres and which do not meet the provisions of chapter 6.1 may be used.

PP4 For UN 1774, packagings shall meet the packing group II performance level.

PP5 For UN 1204, packagings shall be so constructed that explosion is not possible by reason of increased internal pressure. Gas cylinders and gas receptacles shall not be used for these substances.

PP10 For UN 1791, packing group II, the packaging shall be vented.

PP31 For UN 1131, packagings shall be hermetically sealed.

PP33 For UN 1308, packing groups I and II, only combination packagings with a maximum gross mass of 75 kg are allowed.

PP81 For UN 1790 with more than 60 % but not more than 85 % hydrogen fluoride and UN 2031 with more than 55 % nitric acid, the permitted use of plastics, drums and jerricans as single packagings shall be two years from their date of manufacture.

PP93 For UN Nos. 3532 and 3534, packagings shall be designed and constructed to permit the release of gas or vapour to prevent a build-up of pressure that could rupture the packagings in the event of loss of stabilization.

| P002 | PACKING INSTRUCTION (SOLIDS) | | | P002 |

The following packagings are authorized provided that the general provisions of **4.1.1** and **4.1.3** are met:

		Maximum net mass (see 4.1.3.3)		
		Packing group I	Packing group II	Packing group III
Combination packagings				
Inner packagings	**Outer packagings**			
Glass 10 kg	**Drums**			
Plastics [a] 50 kg	steel (1A1, 1A2)	400 kg	400 kg	400 kg
Metal 50 kg	aluminium (1B1, 1B2)	400 kg	400 kg	400 kg
Paper [a, b, c] 50 kg	other metal (1N1, 1N2)	400 kg	400 kg	400 kg
Fibre [a, b, c] 50 kg	plastics (1H1, 1H2)	400 kg	400 kg	400 kg
	plywood (1D)	400 kg	400 kg	400 kg
	fibre (1G)	400 kg	400 kg	400 kg
	Boxes			
	steel (4A)	400 kg	400 kg	400 kg
	aluminium (4B)	400 kg	400 kg	400 kg
	other metal (4N)	400 kg	400 kg	400 kg
	natural wood (4C1)	250 kg	400 kg	400 kg
	natural wood with sift proof walls (4C2)	250 kg	400 kg	400 kg
	plywood (4D)	250 kg	400 kg	400 kg
	reconstituted wood (4F)	125 kg	400 kg	400 kg
	fibreboard (4G)	125 kg	400 kg	400 kg
	expanded plastics (4H1)	60 kg	60 kg	60 kg
	solid plastics (4H2)	250 kg	400 kg	400 kg
	Jerricans			
	steel (3A1, 3A2)	120 kg	120 kg	120 kg
	aluminium (3B1, 3B2)	120 kg	120 kg	120 kg
	plastics (3H1, 3H2)	120 kg	120 kg	120 kg
Single packagings				
Drums				
steel (1A1 or 1A2[d])		400 kg	400 kg	400 kg
aluminium (1B1 or 1B2[d])		400 kg	400 kg	400 kg
metal, other than steel, or aluminium (1N1 or 1N2[d])		400 kg	400 kg	400 kg
plastics (1H1 or 1H2[d])		400 kg	400 kg	400 kg
fibre (1G)[e]		400 kg	400 kg	400 kg
plywood (1D)[e]		400 kg	400 kg	400 kg

[a] *These inner packagings shall be siftproof.*

[b] *These inner packagings shall not be used when the substances being transported may become liquid during transport (see 4.1.3.4).*

[c] *Paper and fibre inner packagings shall not be used for substances of packing group I.*

[d] *These packagings shall not be used for substances of packing group I that may become liquid during transport (see 4.1.3.4).*

[e] *These packagings shall not be used when the substances being transported may become liquid during transport (see 4.1.3.4).*

Cont'd on next page

P002	PACKING INSTRUCTION (SOLIDS) *(cont'd)*		P002
	Maximum net mass (see 4.1.3.3)		
	Packing group I	Packing group II	Packing group III
Single packagings *(cont'd)*			
Jerricans			
Steel (3A1 or 3A2[d])	120 kg	120 kg	120 kg
Aluminium (3B1 or 3B2[d])	120 kg	120 kg	120 kg
plastics (3H1 or 3H2[d])	120 kg	120 kg	120 kg
Boxes			
steel (4A)[e]	Not allowed	400 kg	400 kg
aluminium (4B)[e]	Not allowed	400 kg	400 kg
other metal (4N)[e]	Not allowed	400 kg	400 kg
natural wood (4C1)[e]	Not allowed	400 kg	400 kg
plywood (4D)[e]	Not allowed	400 kg	400 kg
reconstituted wood (4F)[e]	Not allowed	400 kg	400 kg
natural wood with sift proof walls (4C2)[e]	Not allowed	400 kg	400 kg
fibreboard (4G)[e]	Not allowed	400 kg	400 kg
solid plastics (4H2)[e]	Not allowed	400 kg	400 kg
Bags			
bags (5H3, 5H4, 5L3, 5M2)[e]	Not allowed	50 kg	50 kg
Composite packagings			
plastics receptacle in steel, aluminium, plywood, fibre or plastics drum (6HA1, 6HB1, 6HG1[e], 6HD1[e], or 6HH1)	400 kg	400 kg	400 kg
plastics receptacle in steel or aluminium crate or box, wooden box, plywood box, fibreboard box or solid plastics box (6HA2, 6HB2, 6HC, 6HD2[e], 6HG2[e] or 6HH2)	75 kg	75 kg	75 kg
glass receptacle in steel, aluminium, plywood or fibre drum (6PA1, 6PB1, 6PD1[e] or 6PG1[e]) or in steel, aluminium, wooden or fibreboard box or in wickerwork hamper (6PA2, 6PB2, 6PC, 6PG2[e], or 6PD2[e]) or in expanded or solid plastics packaging (6PH1 or 6PH2[e])	75 kg	75 kg	75 kg

Pressure receptacles, provided that the general provisions of 4.1.3.6 are met.

Special packing provisions:

PP7   For UN 2000, celluloid may be transported unpacked on pallets, wrapped in plastic film and secured by appropriate means, such as steel bands as a full load in closed cargo transport units. Each pallet shall not exceed 1000 kg.

PP8   For UN 2002, packagings shall be so constructed that explosion is not possible by reason of increased internal pressure. Gas cylinders and gas receptacles shall not be used for these substances.

PP9   For UN Nos. 3175, 3243 and 3244, packagings shall conform to a design type that has passed a leakproofness test at the packing group II performance level. For UN 3175 the leakproofness test is not required when the liquids are fully absorbed in solid material contained in sealed bags.

PP11   For UN 1309, packing group III, and UN 1362, 5H1, 5L1 and 5M1 bags are allowed if they are overpacked in plastic bags and are wrapped in shrink or stretch wrap on pallets.

PP12   For UN Nos. 1361, 2213 and 3077, 5H1, 5L1 and 5M1 bags are allowed when transported in closed cargo transport units.

[d]   *These packagings shall not be used for substances of packing group I that may become liquid during transport (see 4.1.3.4).*

[e]   *These packagings shall not be used when the substances being transported may become liquid during transport (see 4.1.3.4).*

Cont'd on next page

P002	PACKING INSTRUCTION (SOLIDS) *(cont'd)*	P002

Special packing provisions *(cont'd)*:

PP13 For articles classified under UN 2870, only combination packagings meeting the packing group I performance level are authorized.

PP14 For UN Nos. 2211, 2698 and 3314, packagings are not required to meet the performance tests in chapter 6.1.

PP15 For UN Nos. 1324 and 2623, packagings shall meet the packing group III performance level.

PP20 For UN 2217, any siftproof, tearproof receptacle may be used.

PP30 For UN 2471, paper or fibre inner packagings are not permitted.

PP34 For UN 2969 (as whole beans), 5H1, 5L1 and 5M1 bags are permitted.

PP37 For UN Nos. 2590 and 2212, 5M1 bags are permitted. All bags of any type shall be transported in closed cargo transport units or be placed in closed rigid overpacks.

PP38 For UN 1309, packing group II, bags are permitted only in closed cargo transport units.

PP84 For UN 1057, rigid outer packagings meeting the packing group II performance level shall be used. The packagings shall be designed and constructed and arranged to prevent movement, inadvertent ignition of the devices or inadvertent release of flammable gas or liquid.

PP85 For UN Nos. 1748, 2208, 2880, 3485, 3486 and 3487, if bags are used as single packagings they should be adequately separated to allow for the dissipation of heat. For transport by sea, bags are not allowed as single packagings.

PP92 For UN Nos. 3531 and 3533, packagings shall be designed and constructed to permit the release of gas or vapour to prevent a build-up of pressure that could rupture the packagings in the event of loss of stabilization.

P003	PACKING INSTRUCTION	P003

Dangerous goods shall be placed in suitable outer packagings. The packagings shall meet the provisions of **4.1.1.1, 4.1.1.2, 4.1.1.4, 4.1.1.8** and **4.1.3** and be so designed that they meet the construction requirements of **6.1.4**. Outer packagings constructed of suitable material, and of adequate strength and design in relation to the packaging capacity and its intended use, shall be used. Where this packing instruction is used for the transport of articles or inner packagings of combination packagings the packaging shall be designed and constructed to prevent inadvertent discharge of articles during normal conditions of transport.

Special packing provisions:

PP16 For UN 2800, batteries shall be protected from short circuit within the packagings.

PP17 For UN 2037, packages shall not exceed 55 kg net mass for fibreboard packagings or 125 kg net mass for other packagings.

PP18 For UN 1845, packagings shall be designed and constructed to permit the release of carbon dioxide gas to prevent a build-up of pressure that could rupture the packagings.

PP19 For UN Nos. 1327, 1364, 1365, 1856 and 3360 transport as bales is authorized.

PP20 For UN Nos. 1363, 1386, 1408 and 2793 any siftproof, tearproof receptacle may be used.

PP32 UN Nos. 2857 and 3358 and robust articles consigned under UN 3164 may be transported unpackaged, in crates or in appropriate overpacks.

NOTE: The packagings authorized may exceed a net mass of 400 kg (see 4.1.3.3).

PP90 For UN Nos. 3506 and 3554, sealed inner liners or bags of strong leak-proof and puncture resistant material impervious to mercury or gallium, as appropriate, which will prevent escape of the substance from the package irrespective of the position or the orientation of the package shall be used. For air transport additional requirements may apply.

PP91 For UN 1044, large fire extinguishers may also be transported unpackaged provided that the requirements of 4.1.3.8.1 (a) to (e) are met, the valves are protected by one of the methods in accordance with 4.1.6.1.8 (a) to (d) and other equipment mounted on the fire extinguisher is protected to prevent accidental activation. For the purpose of this special packing provision, "large fire extinguishers" means fire extinguishers as described in indents (c) to (e) of special provision 225 of chapter 3.3.

PP96 For UN 2037 waste gas cartridges transported in accordance with special provision 327, the packagings shall be adequately ventilated to prevent the creation of dangerous atmospheres and the build-up of pressure.

P004	**PACKING INSTRUCTION**	P004

This instruction applies to UN Nos. 3473, 3476, 3477, 3478 and 3479.

(1) For fuel cell cartridges, provided that the general provisions of **4.1.1.1, 4.1.1.2, 4.1.1.3, 4.1.1.6** and **4.1.3** are met:

    Drums (1A2, 1B2, 1N2, 1H2, 1D, 1G);

    Boxes (4A, 4B, 4N, 4C1, 4C2, 4D, 4F, 4G, 4H1, 4H2);

    Jerricans (3A2, 3B2, 3H2).

Packagings shall conform to the packing group II performance level.

(2) For fuel cell cartridges packed with equipment: strong outer packagings which meet the general provisions of **4.1.1.1, 4.1.1.2, 4.1.1.6** and **4.1.3**.

When fuel cell cartridges are packed with equipment, they shall be packed in inner packagings or placed in the outer packaging with cushioning material or divider(s) so that the fuel cell cartridges are protected against damage that may be caused by the movement or placement of the contents within the outer packaging.

The equipment shall be secured against movement within the outer packaging.

For the purpose of this packing instruction, "equipment" means apparatus requiring the fuel cell cartridges with which it is packed for its operation.

(3) For fuel cell cartridges contained in equipment: strong outer packagings which meet the general provisions of **4.1.1.1, 4.1.1.2, 4.1.1.6** and **4.1.3**.

Large robust equipment (see 4.1.3.8) containing fuel cell cartridges may be transported unpackaged. For fuel cell cartridges contained in equipment, the entire system shall be protected against short circuit and inadvertent operation.

NOTE: *The packagings authorized in (2) and (3) may exceed a net mass of 400 kg (see 4.1.3.3).*

P005	**PACKING INSTRUCTION**	P005

This instruction applies to UN Nos. 3528, 3529 and 3530.

If the engine or machinery is constructed and designed so that the means of containment containing the dangerous goods affords adequate protection, an outer packaging is not required.

Dangerous goods in engines or machinery shall otherwise be packed in outer packagings constructed of suitable material, and of adequate strength and design in relation to the packaging capacity and its intended use, and meeting the applicable requirements of 4.1.1.1, or they shall be fixed in such a way that they will not become loose during normal conditions of transport, e.g. in cradles or crates or other handling devices.

NOTE: *The packagings authorized may exceed a net mass of 400 kg (see 4.1.3.3).*

In addition, the manner in which means of containment are contained within the engine or machinery, shall be such that under normal conditions of transport, damage to the means of containment containing the dangerous goods is prevented; and in the event of damage to the means of containment containing liquid dangerous goods, no leakage of the dangerous goods from the engine or machinery is possible (a leakproof liner may be used to satisfy this requirement).

Means of containment containing dangerous goods shall be so installed, secured or cushioned as to prevent their breakage or leakage and so as to control their movement within the engine or machinery during normal conditions of transport. Cushioning material shall not react dangerously with the content of the means of containment. Any leakage of the contents shall not substantially impair the protective properties of the cushioning material.

Additional requirement:

Other dangerous goods (e.g. batteries, fire extinguishers, compressed gas accumulators or safety devices) required for the functioning or safe operation of the engine or machinery shall be securely mounted in the engine or machine.

P006	PACKING INSTRUCTION	P006

This instruction applies to UN Nos. 3537, 3538, 3540, 3541, 3546, 3547 and 3548.

(1) The following packagings are authorized, provided that the general provisions of **4.1.1** and **4.1.3** are met:

Drums (1A2, 1B2, 1N2, 1H2, 1D, 1G);

Boxes (4A, 4B, 4N, 4C1, 4C2, 4D, 4F, 4G, 4H1, 4H2);

Jerricans (3A2, 3B2, 3H2)

Packagings shall conform to the packing group II performance level.

(2) In addition, for robust articles the following packagings are authorized:

Strong outer packagings constructed of suitable material and of adequate strength and design in relation to the packaging capacity and its intended use. The packagings shall meet the provisions of 4.1.1.1, 4.1.1.2, 4.1.1.8 and 4.1.3 in order to achieve a level of protection that is at least equivalent to that provided by chapter 6.1. Articles may be transported unpackaged or on pallets when the dangerous goods are afforded equivalent protection by the article in which they are contained.

NOTE: The packagings authorized may exceed a net mass of 400 kg (see 4.1.3.3).

(3) Additionally, the following conditions shall be met:

(a) Receptacles within articles containing liquids or solids shall be constructed of suitable materials and secured in the article in such a way that, under normal conditions of transport, they cannot break, be punctured or leak their contents into the article itself or the outer packaging;

(b) Receptacles containing liquids with closures shall be packed with their closures correctly oriented. The receptacles shall in addition conform to the internal pressure test provisions of 6.1.5.5;

(c) Receptacles that are liable to break or be punctured easily, such as those made of glass, porcelain or stoneware or of certain plastics materials shall be properly secured. Any leakage of the contents shall not substantially impair the protective properties of the article or of the outer packaging;

(d) Receptacles within articles containing gases shall meet the requirements of section 4.1.6 and chapter 6.2 as appropriate or be capable of providing an equivalent level of protection as packing instructions P200 or P208;

(e) Where there is no receptacle within the article, the article shall fully enclose the dangerous substances and prevent their release under normal conditions of transport.

(4) Articles shall be packed to prevent movement and inadvertent operation during normal conditions of transport.

(5) Articles containing pre-production prototype lithium cells or batteries when these prototypes are transported for testing or production runs of not more than 100 lithium cells or batteries that are of a type that have not met the testing requirements of the *Manual of Tests and Criteria*, part III, sub-section 38.3 shall in addition meet the following:

(a) Packagings shall conform to the requirements in paragraph (1) of this packing instruction;

(b) Appropriate measures shall be taken to minimize the effects of vibration and shocks and prevent movement of the article within the package that may lead to damage and a dangerous condition during transport. When cushioning material is used to meet this requirement it shall be non-combustible and electrically non-conductive;

(c) Non-combustibility of the cushioning material shall be assessed according to a standard recognized in the country where the packaging is designed or manufactured;

(d) The article may be transported unpackaged under conditions specified by the competent authority. Additional conditions that may be considered in the approval process include, but are not limited to:

(i) The article shall be strong enough to withstand the shocks and loadings normally encountered during transport, including trans-shipment between cargo transport units and between cargo transport units and warehouses as well as any removal from a pallet for subsequent manual or mechanical handling; and

(ii) The article shall be fixed in cradles or crates or other handling devices in such a way that it will not become loose during normal conditions of transport.

P010	PACKING INSTRUCTION	P010

The following packagings are authorized, provided that the general provisions of **4.1.1** and **4.1.3** are met:

		Maximum capacity/net mass (see 4.1.3.3)
Combination packagings		
Inner packagings	**Outer packagings**	
Glass 1 *l* Steel 40 *l*	**Drums** steel (1A1, 1A2) plastics (1H1, 1H2) plywood (1D) fibre (1G)	 400 kg 400 kg 400 kg 400 kg
	Boxes steel (4A) natural wood (4C1, 4C2) plywood (4D) reconstituted wood (4F) fibreboard (4G) expanded plastics (4H1) solid plastics (4H2)	 400 kg 400 kg 400 kg 400 kg 400 kg 60 kg 400 kg
Single packagings		
Drums steel, non-removable head (1A1)		450 *l*
Jerricans steel, non-removable head (3A1)		60 *l*
Composite packagings plastics receptacle in steel drums (6HA1)		250 *l*
Steel pressure receptacles, provided that the general provisions of 4.1.3.6 are met.		

P099	PACKING INSTRUCTION	P099

Only packagings which are approved by the competent authority for these goods may be used (see **4.1.3.7**). A copy of the competent authority approval shall accompany each consignment or the transport document shall include an indication that the packaging was approved by the competent authority.

P101	PACKING INSTRUCTION	P101

Only packagings which are approved by the competent authority may be used. The distinguishing sign used on vehicles in international road traffic[a] of the country for which the authority acts, shall be marked on the transport documents as follows:

"Packaging approved by the competent authority of... "

[a] *Distinguishing sign of the State of registration used on motor vehicles and trailers in international road traffic, e.g. in accordance with the Geneva Convention on Road Traffic of 1949 or the Vienna Convention on Road Traffic of 1968.*

P110(a)	PACKING INSTRUCTION	P110(a)

The following packagings are authorized, provided that the general packing provisions of **4.1.1**, **4.1.3** and special packing provisions of **4.1.5** are met:

Inner packagings	Intermediate packagings	Outer packagings
Bags 　plastics 　textile, plastic coated or lined 　rubber 　textile, rubberised 　textile **Receptacles** 　wood	**Bags** 　plastics 　textile, plastic coated or lined 　rubber 　textile, rubberized **Receptacles** 　plastics 　metal 　wood	**Drums** 　steel (1A1, 1A2) 　metal, other than steel or aluminium 　　(1N1, 1N2) 　plastics (1H1, 1H2)

Additional requirements:

1. The intermediate packagings shall be filled with water saturated material such as an anti-freeze solution or wetted cushioning.

2. Outer packagings shall be filled with water saturated material such as an anti-freeze solution or wetted cushioning. Outer packagings shall be constructed and sealed to prevent evaporation of the wetting solution, except for UN 0224 when carried dry.

P110(b)	PACKING INSTRUCTION	P110(b)

The following packagings are authorized, provided that the general packing provisions of **4.1.1**, **4.1.3** and special packing provisions of **4.1.5** are met:

Inner packagings	Intermediate packagings	Outer packagings
Receptacles 　metal 　wood 　rubber, conductive 　plastics, conductive **Bags** 　rubber, conductive 　plastics, conductive	**Dividing partitions** 　metal 　wood 　plastics 　fibreboard	**Boxes** 　natural wood, sift-proof wall (4C2) 　plywood (4D) 　reconstituted wood (4F)

Special packing provision:

PP42　For UN Nos. 0074, 0113, 0114, 0129, 0130, 0135 and 0224, the following conditions shall be met:

　(a)　Inner packagings shall not contain more than 50 g of explosive substance (quantity corresponding to dry substance);

　(b)　Compartments between dividing partitions shall not contain more than one inner packaging, firmly fitted; and

　(c)　The outer packaging may be partitioned into up to 25 compartments.

| P111 | PACKING INSTRUCTION | P111 |

The following packagings are authorized, provided that the general packing provisions of **4.1.1**, **4.1.3** and special packing provisions of **4.1.5** are met:

Inner packagings	Intermediate packagings	Outer packagings

Bags
  paper, waterproofed
  plastics
  textile, rubberized
Receptacles
  wood
Sheets
  plastics
  textile, rubberized
	Not necessary	**Boxes**
		  steel (4A)
		  aluminium (4B)
		  other metal (4N)
		  natural wood, ordinary (4C1)
		  natural wood, sift-proof (4C2)
		  plywood (4D)
		  reconstituted wood (4F)
		  fibreboard (4G)
		  plastics, expanded (4H1)
		  plastics, solid (4H2)
		Drums
		  steel (1A1, 1A2)
		  aluminium (1B1, 1B2)
		  other metal (1N1, 1N2)
		  plywood (1D)
		  fibre (1G)
		  plastics (1H1, 1H2)

Special packing provision:

PP43 For UN 0159, inner packagings are not required when metal (1A1, 1A2, 1B1, 1B2, 1N1 or 1N2) or plastics (1H1 or 1H2) drums are used as outer packagings.

P112(a)	PACKING INSTRUCTION (Solid wetted, 1.1D)	P112(a)

The following packagings are authorized, provided that the general packing provisions of **4.1.1**, **4.1.3** and special packing provisions of **4.1.5** are met:

Inner packagings	Intermediate packagings	Outer packagings

Bags
   paper, multiwall, water-resistant
   plastics
   textile
   textile, rubberised
   woven plastics
Receptacles
   metal
   plastics
   wood
	Bags
	   plastics
	   textile, plastic coated or lined
	Receptacles
	   metal
	   plastics
	   wood
		Boxes
		   steel (4A)
		   aluminium (4B)
		   other metal (4N)
		   natural wood, ordinary (4C1)
		   natural wood, sift-proof (4C2)
		   plywood (4D)
		   reconstituted wood (4F)
		   fibreboard (4G)
		   plastics, expanded (4H1)
		   plastics, solid (4H2)
		Drums
		   steel (1A1, 1A2)
		   aluminium (1B1, 1B2)
		   other metal (1N1, 1N2)
		   plywood (1D)
		   fibre (1G)
		   plastics (1H1, 1H2)

Additional requirement:

   Intermediate packagings are not required if leakproof removable head drums are used as the outer packaging.

Special packing provisions:

PP26   For UN Nos. 0004, 0076, 0078, 0154, 0219 and 0394, packagings shall be lead free.

PP45   For UN Nos. 0072 and 0226, intermediate packagings are not required.

P112(b)	PACKING INSTRUCTION (Solid dry, other than powder 1.1D)	P112(b)

The following packagings are authorized, provided that the general packing provisions of **4.1.1**, **4.1.3** and special packing provisions of **4.1.5** are met:

Inner packagings	Intermediate packagings	Outer packagings

Bags
  paper, kraft
  paper, multiwall, water-resistant
  plastics
  textile
  textile, rubberised
  woven plastics
	Bags (for UN 0150 only)
	  plastics
	  textile, plastic coated or lined
		Bags
		  woven plastics, sift-proof (5H2)
		  woven plastics, water-resistant (5H3)
		  plastics, film (5H4)
		  textile, sift-proof (5L2)
		  textile, water-resistant (5L3)
		  paper, multiwall, water-resistant (5M2)
		Boxes
		  steel (4A)
		  aluminium (4B)
		  other metal (4N)
		  natural wood, ordinary (4C1)
		  natural wood, sift-proof (4C2)
		  plywood (4D)
		  reconstituted wood (4F)
		  fibreboard (4G)
		  plastics, expanded (4H1)
		  plastics, solid (4H2)
		Drums
		  steel (1A1, 1A2)
		  aluminium (1B1, 1B2)
		  other metal (1N1, 1N2)
		  plywood (1D)
		  fibre (1G)
		  plastics (1H1, 1H2)

Special packing provisions:

PP26   For UN Nos. 0004, 0076, 0078, 0154, 0216, 0219 and 0386, packagings shall be lead free.

PP46   For UN 0209, bags, sift-proof (5H2) are recommended for flake or prilled TNT in the dry state and a maximum net mass of 30 kg.

PP47   For UN 0222 inner packagings are not required when the outer packaging is a bag.

P112(c)	PACKING INSTRUCTION (Solid dry powder 1.1D)	P112(c)

The following packagings are authorized, provided that the general packing provisions of **4.1.1**, **4.1.3** and special packing provisions of **4.1.5** are met:

Inner packagings	Intermediate packagings	Outer packagings

Bags
    paper, multiwall, water-resistant
    plastics
    woven plastics
Receptacles
    fibreboard
    metal
    plastics
    wood
	Bags
	    paper, multiwall, water-resistant with inner lining plastics
	Receptacles
	    metal
	    plastics
	    wood
		Boxes
		    steel (4A)
		    aluminium (4B)
		    other metal (4N)
		    natural wood, ordinary (4C1)
		    natural wood, sift-proof (4C2)
		    plywood (4D)
		    reconstituted wood (4F)
		    fibreboard (4G)
		    plastics, solid (4H2)
		Drums
		    steel (1A1, 1A2)
		    aluminium (1B1, 1B2)
		    other metal (1N1, 1N2)
		    plywood (1D)
		    fibre (1G)
		    plastics (1H1, 1H2)

Additional requirements:

1. Inner packagings are not required if drums are used as the outer packaging.
2. The packaging shall be sift-proof.

Special packing provision:

PP26 For UN Nos. 0004, 0076, 0078, 0154, 0216, 0219 and 0386, packagings shall be lead free.

PP46 For UN 0209, bags, sift-proof (5H2) are recommended for flake or prilled TNT in the dry state and a maximum net mass of 30 kg.

PP48 For UN 0504, metal packagings shall not be used. Packagings of other material with a small amount of metal, for example metal closures or other metal fittings such as those mentioned in 6.1.4, are not considered metal packagings.

P113	PACKING INSTRUCTION	P113
\multicolumn{3}{l	}{The following packagings are authorized, provided that the general packing provisions of **4.1.1**, **4.1.3** and special packing provisions of **4.1.5** are met:}

Inner packagings	Intermediate packagings	Outer packagings

Bags
    paper
    plastics
    textile, rubberised
Receptacles
    fibreboard
    metal
    plastics
    wood
	Not necessary	**Boxes**
		    steel (4A)
		    aluminium (4B)
		    other metal (4N)
		    natural wood, ordinary (4C1)
		    natural wood, sift-proof walls (4C2)
		    plywood (4D)
		    reconstituted wood (4F)
		    fibreboard (4G)
		    plastics, solid (4H2)
		Drums
		    steel (1A1, 1A2)
		    aluminium (1B1, 1B2)
		    other metal (1N1, 1N2)
		    plywood (1D)
		    fibre (1G)
		    plastics (1H1, 1H2)

Additional requirement:
   The packaging shall be sift-proof.

Special packing provisions:

PP49   For UN Nos. 0094 and 0305, no more than 50 g of substance shall be packed in an inner packaging.

PP50   For UN 0027, inner packagings are not necessary when drums are used as the outer packaging.

PP51   For UN 0028, paper kraft or waxed paper sheets may be used as inner packagings.

P114(a)	PACKING INSTRUCTION (Solid wetted)	P114(a)

The following packagings are authorized, provided that the general packing provisions of **4.1.1**, **4.1.3** and special packing provisions of **4.1.5** are met:

Inner packagings	Intermediate packagings	Outer packagings

Bags
  plastics
  textile
  woven plastics
Receptacles
  metal
  plastics
  wood
	Bags
	  plastics
	  textile, plastics coated or lined
	Receptacles
	  metal
	  plastics
	Dividing partitions
	  wood
		Boxes
		  steel (4A)
		  metal, other than steel or aluminium (4N)
		  natural wood, ordinary (4C1)
		  natural wood, sift-proof walls (4C2)
		  plywood (4D)
		  reconstituted wood (4F)
		  fibreboard (4G)
		  plastics, solid (4H2)
		Drums
		  steel (1A1, 1A2)
		  aluminium (1B1, 1B2)
		  other metal (1N1, 1N2)
		  plywood (1D)
		  fibre (1G)
		  plastics (1H1, 1H2)

Additional requirement:

    Intermediate packagings are not required if leakproof removable head drums are used as the outer packaging.

Special packing provisions:

PP26   For UN Nos. 0077, 0132, 0234, 0235 and 0236, packagings shall be lead free.

PP43   For UN 0342, inner packagings are not required when metal (1A1, 1A2, 1B1, 1B2, 1N1 or 1N2) or plastics (1H1 or 1H2) drums are used as outer packagings.

P114(b)	PACKING INSTRUCTION (Solid dry)	P114(b)

The following packagings are authorized, provided that the general packing provisions of **4.1.1**, **4.1.3** and special packing provisions of **4.1.5** are met:

Inner packagings	Intermediate packagings	Outer packagings

Bags
  paper, kraft
  plastics
  textile, sift-proof
  woven plastics, sift-proof
Receptacles
  fibreboard
  metal
  paper
  woven plastics, sift-proof
  wood
  plastics
	Not necessary	**Boxes**
		  natural wood, ordinary (4C1)
		  natural wood, sift-proof walls (4C2)
		  plywood (4D)
		  reconstituted wood (4F)
		  fibreboard (4G)
		Drums
		  steel (1A1, 1A2)
		  aluminium (1B1, 1B2)
		  other metal (1N1, 1N2)
		  plywood (1D)
		  fibre (1G)
		  plastics (1H1, 1H2)

Special packing provisions:

PP26 For UN Nos. 0077, 0132, 0234, 0235 and 0236, packagings shall be lead free.

PP48 For UN Nos. 0508 and 0509, metal packagings shall not be used. Packagings of other material with a small amount of metal, for example metal closures or other metal fittings such as those mentioned in 6.1.4, are not considered metal packagings.

PP50 For UN Nos. 0160, 0161 and 0508, inner packagings are not necessary if drums are used as the outer packaging.

PP52 For UN Nos. 0160 and 0161, when metal drums (1A1, 1A2, 1B1, 1B2, 1N1 or 1N2) are used as the outer packaging, metal packagings shall be so constructed that the risk of explosion, by reason of increase internal pressure from internal or external causes is prevented.

| P115 | PACKING INSTRUCTION | P115 |

The following packagings are authorized, provided that the general packing provisions of **4.1.1**, **4.1.3** and special packing provisions of **4.1.5** are met:

Inner packagings	Intermediate packagings	Outer packagings
Receptacles plastics wood	**Bags** plastics in metal receptacles **Drums** metal **Receptacles** wood	**Boxes** natural wood, ordinary (4C1) natural wood, sift-proof walls (4C2) plywood (4D) reconstituted wood (4F) **Drums** steel (1A1, 1A2) aluminium (1B1, 1B2) other metal (1N1, 1N2) plywood (1D) fibre (1G) plastics (1H1, 1H2)

Special packing provisions:

PP45 For UN 0144, intermediate packagings are not required.

PP53 For UN Nos. 0075, 0143, 0495 and 0497, when boxes are used as the outer packaging, inner packagings shall have taped screw cap closures and be not more than 5 litres capacity each. Inner packagings shall be surrounded with non-combustible absorbent cushioning materials. The amount of absorbent cushioning material shall be sufficient to absorb the liquid contents. Metal receptacles shall be cushioned from each other. Net mass of propellant is a limited to 30 kg for each package when outer packagings are boxes.

PP54 For UN Nos. 0075, 0143, 0495 and 0497, when drums are used as the outer packaging and when intermediate packagings are drums, they shall be surrounded with non-combustible cushioning material in a quantity sufficient to absorb the liquid contents. A composite packaging consisting of a plastic receptacle in a metal drum may be used instead of the inner and intermediate packagings. The net volume of propellant in each package shall not exceed 120 litres.

PP55 For UN 0144, absorbent cushioning material shall be inserted.

PP56 For UN 0144, metal receptacles may be used as inner packagings.

PP57 For UN Nos. 0075, 0143, 0495 and 0497, bags shall be used as intermediate packagings when boxes are used as outer packagings.

PP58 For UN Nos. 0075, 0143, 0495 and 0497, drums shall be used as intermediate packagings when drums are used as outer packagings.

PP59 For UN 0144, fibreboard boxes (4G) may be used as outer packagings.

PP60 For UN 0144, aluminium drums (1B1 and 1B2) and metal, other than steel or aluminium, drums (1N1 and 1N2) shall not be used.

P116	PACKING INSTRUCTION	P116

The following packagings are authorized, provided that the general packing provisions of **4.1.1**, **4.1.3** and special packing provisions of **4.1.5** are met:

Inner packagings	Intermediate packagings	Outer packagings

Bags
    paper, water and oil resistant
    plastics
    textile, plastic coated or lined
    woven plastics, sift-proof
Receptacles
    fibreboard, water-resistant
    metal
    plastics
    wood, sift-proof
Sheets
    paper, water-resistant
    paper, waxed
    plastics
	Not necessary	**Bags**
		    woven plastics (5H1, 5H2, 5H3)
		    paper, multiwall, water-resistant (5M2)
		    plastics, film (5H4)
		    textile, sift-proof (5L2)
		    textile, water-resistant (5L3)
		Boxes
		    steel (4A)
		    aluminium (4B)
		    other metal (4N)
		    natural wood, ordinary (4C1)
		    natural wood, sift-proof walls (4C2)
		    plywood (4D)
		    reconstituted wood (4F)
		    fibreboard (4G)
		    plastics, solid (4H2)
		Drums
		    steel (1A1, 1A2)
		    aluminium (1B1, 1B2)
		    other metal (1N1, 1N2)
		    plywood (1D)
		    fibre (1G)
		    plastics (1H1, 1H2)
		Jerricans
		    steel (3A1, 3A2)
		    plastics (3H1, 3H2)

Special packing provisions:

PP61 For UN Nos. 0082, 0241, 0331 and 0332, inner packagings are not required if leakproof removable head drums are used as the outer packaging.

PP62 For UN Nos. 0082, 0241, 0331 and 0332, inner packagings are not required when the explosive is contained in a material impervious to liquid.

PP63 For UN 0081, inner packagings are not required when contained in rigid plastics which is impervious to nitric esters.

PP64 For UN 0331, inner packagings are not required when bags (5H2), (5H3) or (5H4) are used as outer packagings.

PP65 *Deleted.*

PP66 For UN 0081, bags shall not be used as outer packagings.

| P130 | PACKING INSTRUCTION | P130 |

The following packagings are authorized, provided that the general packing provisions of **4.1.1**, **4.1.3** and special packing provisions of **4.1.5** are met:

Inner packagings	Intermediate packagings	Outer packagings

Not necessary	Not necessary	**Boxes**
		  steel (4A)
		  aluminium (4B)
		  other metal (4N)
		  natural wood, ordinary (4C1)
		  natural wood, sift-proof walls (4C2)
		  plywood (4D)
		  reconstituted wood (4F)
		  fibreboard (4G)
		  plastics, expanded (4H1)
		  plastics, solid (4H2)
		Drums
		  steel (1A1, 1A2)
		  aluminium (1B1, 1B2)
		  other metal (1N1, 1N2)
		  plywood (1D)
		  fibre (1G)
		  plastics (1H1, 1H2)

Special packing provision:

PP67 The following applies to UN Nos. 0006, 0009, 0010, 0015, 0016, 0018, 0019, 0034, 0035, 0038, 0039, 0048, 0056, 0137, 0138, 0168, 0169, 0171, 0181, 0182, 0183, 0186, 0221, 0243, 0244, 0245, 0246, 0254, 0280, 0281, 0286, 0287, 0297, 0299, 0300, 0301, 0303, 0321, 0328, 0329, 0344, 0345, 0346, 0347, 0362, 0363, 0370, 0412, 0424, 0425, 0434, 0435, 0436, 0437, 0438, 0451, 0488, 0502 and 0510: Large and robust explosives articles, normally intended for military use, without their means of initiation or with their means of initiation containing at least two effective protective features, may be carried unpackaged. When such articles have propelling charges or are self-propelled, their ignition systems shall be protected against stimuli encountered during normal conditions of transport. A negative result in test series 4 on an unpackaged article indicates that the article can be considered for transport unpackaged. Such unpackaged articles may be fixed to cradles or contained in crates or other suitable handling devices.

NOTE: The packagings authorized may exceed a net mass of 400 kg (see 4.1.3.3).

P131	PACKING INSTRUCTION	P131

The following packagings are authorized, provided that the general packing provisions of **4.1.1**, **4.1.3** and special packing provisions of **4.1.5** are met:

Inner packagings	Intermediate packagings	Outer packagings

Bags
    paper
    plastics
Receptacles
    fibreboard
    metal
    plastics
    wood
Reels
	Not necessary	**Boxes**
		    steel (4A)
		    aluminium (4B)
		    other metal (4N)
		    natural wood, ordinary (4C1)
		    natural wood, sift-proof walls (4C2)
		    plywood (4D)
		    reconstituted wood (4F)
		    fibreboard (4G)
		    plastics, solid (4H2)
		Drums
		    steel (1A1, 1A2)
		    aluminium (1B1, 1B2)
		    other metal (1N1, 1N2)
		    plywood (1D)
		    fibre (1G)
		    plastics (1H1, 1H2)

Special packing provision:
PP68   For UN Nos. 0029, 0267 and 0455, bags and reels shall not be used as inner packagings.

P132(a)	PACKING INSTRUCTION (Articles consisting of closed metal, plastics or fibreboard casings that contain a detonating explosive, or consisting of plastics-bonded detonating explosives)	P132(a)

The following packagings are authorized, provided that the general packing provisions of **4.1.1**, **4.1.3** and special packing provisions of **4.1.5** are met:

Inner packagings	Intermediate packagings	Outer packagings

Not necessary	Not necessary	**Boxes**
		    steel (4A)
		    aluminium (4B)
		    other metal (4N)
		    wood, natural, ordinary (4C1)
		    wood, natural, sift-proof walls (4C2)
		    plywood (4D)
		    reconstituted wood (4F)
		    fibreboard (4G)
		    plastics, solid (4H2)

P132(b)	PACKING INSTRUCTION (Articles without closed casings)	P132(b)

The following packagings are authorized, provided that the general packing provisions of **4.1.1**, **4.1.3** and special packing provisions of **4.1.5** are met:

Inner packagings	Intermediate packagings	Outer packagings

Receptacles
   fibreboard
   metal
   plastics
   wood
Sheets
   paper
   plastics
	Not necessary	**Boxes**
		   steel (4A)
		   aluminium (4B)
		   other metal (4N)
		   natural wood, ordinary (4C1)
		   natural wood, sift-proof walls (4C2)
		   plywood (4D)
		   reconstituted wood (4F)
		   fibreboard (4G)
		   plastics, solid (4H2)

P133	PACKING INSTRUCTION	P133

The following packagings are authorized, provided that the general packing provisions of **4.1.1**, **4.1.3** and special packing provisions of **4.1.5** are met:

Inner packagings	Intermediate packagings	Outer packagings

Receptacles
   fibreboard
   metal
   plastics
   wood
Trays, fitted with dividing partitions
   fibreboard
   plastics
   wood
	Receptacles
	   fibreboard
	   metal
	   plastics
	   wood
		Boxes
		   steel (4A)
		   aluminium (4B)
		   other metal (4N)
		   natural wood, ordinary (4C1)
		   natural wood, sift-proof walls (4C2)
		   plywood (4D)
		   reconstituted wood (4F)
		   fibreboard (4G)
		   plastics, solid (4H2)

Additional requirement:

   Receptacles are only required as intermediate packagings when the inner packagings are trays.

Special packing provision:

PP69   For UN Nos. 0043, 0212, 0225, 0268 and 0306, trays shall not be used as inner packagings.

P134	PACKING INSTRUCTION	P134
\multicolumn{3}{l	}{The following packagings are authorized, provided that the general packing provisions of **4.1.1**, **4.1.3** and special packing provisions of **4.1.5** are met:}

Inner packagings	Intermediate packagings	Outer packagings

Bags
  water-resistant
Receptacles
  fibreboard
  metal
  plastics
  wood
Sheets
  fibreboard, corrugated
Tubes
  fibreboard
	Not necessary	**Boxes**
		  steel (4A)
		  aluminium (4B)
		  other metal (4N)
		  natural wood, ordinary (4C1)
		  natural wood, sift-proof walls (4C2)
		  plywood (4D)
		  reconstituted wood (4F)
		  fibreboard (4G)
		  plastics, expanded (4H1)
		  plastics, solid (4H2)
		Drums
		  steel (1A1, 1A2)
		  aluminium (1B1, 1B2)
		  other metal (1N1, 1N2)
		  plywood (1D)
		  fibre (1G)
		  plastics (1H1, 1H2)

P135	PACKING INSTRUCTION	P135
\multicolumn{3}{l	}{The following packagings are authorized, provided that the general packing provisions of **4.1.1**, **4.1.3** and special packing provisions of **4.1.5** are met:}

Inner packagings	Intermediate packagings	Outer packagings

Bags
  paper
  plastics
Receptacles
  fibreboard
  metal
  plastics
  wood
Sheets
  paper
  plastics
	Not necessary	**Boxes**
		  steel (4A)
		  aluminium (4B)
		  other metal (4N)
		  natural wood, ordinary (4C1)
		  natural wood, sift-proof walls (4C2)
		  plywood (4D)
		  reconstituted wood (4F)
		  fibreboard (4G)
		  plastics, expanded (4H1)
		  plastics, solid (4H2)
		Drums
		  steel (1A1, 1A2)
		  aluminium (1B1, 1B2)
		  other metal (1N1, 1N2)
		  plywood (1D)
		  fibre (1G)
		  plastics (1H1, 1H2)

| P136 | PACKING INSTRUCTION | P136 |

The following packagings are authorized, provided that the general packing provisions of **4.1.1**, **4.1.3** and special packing provisions of **4.1.5** are met:

Inner packagings	Intermediate packagings	Outer packagings

Bags
  plastics
  textile
Boxes
  fibreboard
  plastics
  wood
Dividing partitions in the outer packagings
	Not necessary	**Boxes**
		  steel (4A)
		  aluminium (4B)
		  other metal (4N)
		  natural wood, ordinary (4C1)
		  natural wood, sift-proof walls (4C2)
		  plywood (4D)
		  reconstituted wood (4F)
		  fibreboard (4G)
		  plastics, solid (4H2)
		Drums
		  steel (1A1, 1A2)
		  aluminium (1B1, 1B2)
		  other metal (1N1, 1N2)
		  plywood (1D)
		  fibre (1G)
		  plastics (1H1, 1H2)

| P137 | PACKING INSTRUCTION | P137 |

The following packagings are authorized, provided that the general packing provisions of **4.1.1**, **4.1.3** and special packing provisions of **4.1.5** are met:

Inner packagings	Intermediate packagings	Outer packagings

Bags
  plastics
Boxes
  fibreboard
  wood
Tubes
  fibreboard
  metal
  plastics
Dividing partitions in the outer packagings
	Not necessary	**Boxes**
		  steel (4A)
		  aluminium (4B)
		  other metal (4N)
		  natural wood, ordinary (4C1)
		  natural wood, sift-proof walls (4C2)
		  plywood (4D)
		  reconstituted wood (4F)
		  fibreboard (4G)
		  plastics, solid (4H2)
		Drums
		  steel (1A1, 1A2)
		  aluminium (1B1, 1B2)
		  other metal (1N1, 1N2)
		  plywood (1D)
		  fibre (1G)
		  plastics (1H1, 1H2)

Special packing provision:

PP70 For UN Nos. 0059, 0439, 0440 and 0441, when the shaped charges are packed singly, the conical cavity shall face downwards and the package shall be marked as illustrated in figures 5.2.3 or 5.2.4. When the shaped charges are packed in pairs, the conical cavities shall face inwards to minimize the jetting effect in the event of accidental initiation.

P138	PACKING INSTRUCTION	P138

The following packagings are authorized, provided that the general packing provisions of **4.1.1**, **4.1.3** and special packing provisions of **4.1.5** are met:

Inner packagings	Intermediate packagings	Outer packagings

Bags
   plastics
	Not necessary	**Boxes**
		   steel (4A)
		   aluminium (4B)
		   other metal (4N)
		   natural wood, ordinary (4C1)
		   natural wood, sift-proof walls (4C2)
		   plywood (4D)
		   reconstituted wood (4F)
		   fibreboard (4G)
		   plastics, solid (4H2)
		Drums
		   steel (1A1, 1A2)
		   aluminium (1B1, 1B2)
		   other metal (1N1, 1N2)
		   plywood (1D)
		   fibre (1G)
		   plastics (1H1, 1H2)

Additional requirement:
   If the ends of the articles are sealed, inner packagings are not necessary.

P139	PACKING INSTRUCTION	P139

The following packagings are authorized, provided that the general packing provisions of **4.1.1**, **4.1.3** and special packing provisions of **4.1.5** are met:

Inner packagings	Intermediate packagings	Outer packagings

Bags
   plastics
Receptacles
   fibreboard
   metal
   plastics
   wood
Reels
Sheets
   paper
   plastics
	Not necessary	**Boxes**
		   steel (4A)
		   aluminium (4B)
		   other metal (4N)
		   natural wood, ordinary (4C1)
		   natural wood, sift-proof walls (4C2)
		   plywood (4D)
		   reconstituted wood (4F)
		   fibreboard (4G)
		   plastics, solid (4H2)
		Drums
		   steel (1A1, 1A2)
		   aluminium (1B1, 1B2)
		   other metal (1N1, 1N2)
		   plywood (1D)
		   fibre (1G)
		   plastics (1H1, 1H2)

Special packing provisions:

PP71   For UN Nos. 0065, 0102, 0104, 0289 and 0290, the ends of the detonating cord shall be sealed, for example, by a plug firmly fixed so that the explosive cannot escape. The ends of flexible detonating cord shall be fastened securely.

PP72   For UN Nos. 0065 and 0289, inner packagings are not required when they are in coils.

P140	PACKING INSTRUCTION	P140

The following packagings are authorized, provided that the general packing provisions of **4.1.1**, **4.1.3** and special packing provisions of **4.1.5** are met:

Inner packagings	Intermediate packagings	Outer packagings

Bags
  plastics
Receptacles
  wood
Reels
Sheets
  paper, kraft
  plastics
	Not necessary	**Boxes**
		  steel (4A)
		  aluminium (4B)
		  other metal (4N)
		  natural wood, ordinary (4C1)
		  natural wood, sift-proof walls (4C2)
		  plywood (4D)
		  reconstituted wood (4F)
		  fibreboard (4G)
		  plastics, solid (4H2)
		Drums
		  steel (1A1, 1A2)
		  aluminium (1B1, 1B2)
		  other metal (1N1, 1N2)
		  plywood (1D)
		  fibre (1G)
		  plastics (1H1, 1H2)

Special packing provisions:

PP73 For UN 0105, no inner packagings are required if the ends are sealed.

PP74 For UN 0101, the packaging shall be sift-proof except when the fuse is covered by a paper tube and both ends of the tube are covered with removable caps.

PP75 For UN 0101, steel, aluminium or other metal boxes or drums shall not be used.

P141	PACKING INSTRUCTION	P141

The following packagings are authorized, provided that the general packing provisions of **4.1.1**, **4.1.3** and special packing provisions of **4.1.5** are met:

Inner packagings	Intermediate packagings	Outer packagings

Receptacles
  fibreboard
  metal
  plastics
  wood
Trays, fitted with dividing partitions
  plastics
  wood
Dividing partitions in the outer packagings
	Not necessary	**Boxes**
		  steel (4A)
		  aluminium (4B)
		  other metal (4N)
		  natural wood, ordinary (4C1)
		  natural wood, sift-proof walls (4C2)
		  plywood (4D)
		  reconstituted wood (4F)
		  fibreboard (4G)
		  plastics, solid (4H2)
		Drums
		  steel (1A1, 1A2)
		  aluminium (1B1, 1B2)
		  other metal (1N1, 1N2)
		  plywood (1D)
		  fibre (1G)
		  plastics (1H1, 1H2)

P142	PACKING INSTRUCTION	P142

The following packagings are authorized, provided that the general packing provisions of **4.1.1**, **4.1.3** and special packing provisions of **4.1.5** are met:

Inner packagings	Intermediate packagings	Outer packagings

Bags
  paper
  plastics
Receptacles
  fibreboard
  metal
  plastics
  wood
Sheets
  paper
Trays, fitted with dividing partitions
  plastics
	Not necessary	**Boxes**
		  steel (4A)
		  aluminium (4B)
		  other metal (4N)
		  natural wood, ordinary (4C1)
		  natural wood, sift-proof walls (4C2)
		  plywood (4D)
		  reconstituted wood (4F)
		  fibreboard (4G)
		  plastics, solid (4H2)
		Drums
		  steel (1A1, 1A2)
		  aluminium (1B1, 1B2)
		  other metal (1N1, 1N2)
		  plywood (1D)
		  fibre (1G)
		  plastics (1H1, 1H2)

P143	PACKING INSTRUCTION	P143

The following packagings are authorized, provided that the general packing provisions of **4.1.1**, **4.1.3** and special packing provisions of **4.1.5** are met:

Inner packagings	Intermediate packagings	Outer packagings

Bags
  paper, kraft
  plastics
  textile
  textile, rubberized
Receptacles
  fibreboard
  metal
  plastics
  wood
Trays, fitted with dividing partitions
  plastics
  wood
	Not necessary	**Boxes**
		  steel (4A)
		  aluminium (4B)
		  other metal (4N)
		  natural wood, ordinary (4C1)
		  natural wood, sift-proof walls (4C2)
		  plywood (4D)
		  reconstituted wood (4F)
		  fibreboard (4G)
		  plastics, solid (4H2)
		Drums
		  steel (1A1, 1A2)
		  aluminium (1B1, 1B2)
		  other metal (1N1, 1N2)
		  plywood (1D)
		  fibre (1G)
		  plastics (1H1, 1H2)

Additional requirement:

    Instead of the above inner and outer packagings, composite packagings (6HH2) (plastic receptacle with outer solid box) may be used.

Special packing provision:

PP76   For UN Nos. 0271, 0272, 0415 and 0491, when metal packagings are used, metal packagings shall be so constructed that the risk of explosion, by reason of increase in internal pressure from internal or external causes is prevented.

| P144 | PACKING INSTRUCTION | P144 |

The following packagings are authorized, provided that the general packing provisions of **4.1.1**, **4.1.3** and special packing provisions of **4.1.5** are met:

Inner packagings	Intermediate packagings	Outer packagings

Receptacles
    fibreboard
    metal
    plastics
    wood
Dividing partitions in the outer packagings
	Not necessary	**Boxes**
		    steel (4A)
		    aluminium (4B)
		    other metal (4N)
		    natural wood, ordinary (4C1) with metal liner
		    plywood (4D) with metal liner
		    reconstituted wood (4F) with metal liner
		    plastics, expanded (4H1)
		    plastics, solid (4H2)
		Drums
		    steel (1A1, 1A2)
		    aluminium (1B1, 1B2)
		    other metal (1N1, 1N2)
		    plastics (1H1, 1H2)

Special packing provision:

PP77   For UN Nos. 0248 and 0249, packagings shall be protected against the ingress of water. When water-activated contrivances are transported unpackaged, they shall be provided with at least two independent protective features which prevent the ingress of water.

NOTE: The packagings authorized may exceed a net mass of 400 kg (see 4.1.3.3).

| P200 | PACKING INSTRUCTION | P200 |

For pressure receptacles, the general packing requirements of **4.1.6.1** shall be met. In addition, for MEGCs, the general requirements of **4.2.4** shall be met.

Cylinders, tubes, pressure drums, bundles of cylinders constructed as specified in chapter 6.2 and MEGCs constructed as specified in 6.7.5 are authorised for the transport of a specific substance when specified in the following tables. For some substances the special packing provisions may prohibit a particular type of cylinder, tube, pressure drum or bundle of cylinders.

(1) Pressure receptacles containing toxic substances with an LC_{50} less than or equal to 200 ml/m³ (ppm) as specified in the table shall not be equipped with any pressure relief device. Pressure relief devices shall be fitted on pressure receptacles used for the transport of UN 1013 carbon dioxide and UN 1070 nitrous oxide. Other pressure receptacles shall be fitted with a pressure relief device if specified by the competent authority of the country of use. The type of pressure relief device, the set to discharge pressure and relief capacity of pressure relief devices, if required, shall be specified by the competent authority of the country of use.

(2) The following three tables cover compressed gases (table 1), liquefied and dissolved gases (table 2) and substances not in Class 2 (table 3). They provide:

    (a) The UN number, name and description, and classification of the substance;

    (b) The LC_{50} for toxic substances;

    (c) The types of pressure receptacles authorised for the substance, shown by the letter "X";

    (d) The maximum test period for periodic inspection of the pressure receptacles.

    NOTE: For pressure receptacles which make use of composite materials, the maximum test period shall be 5 years. The test period may be extended to that specified in tables 1 and 2 (i.e. up to 10 years), if approved by the competent authority of the country of use.

    (e) The minimum test pressure of the pressure receptacles;

    (f) The maximum working pressure of the pressure receptacles for compressed gases (where no value is given, the working pressure shall not exceed two thirds of the test pressure) or the maximum filling ratio(s) dependent on the test pressure(s) for liquefied and dissolved gases;

    (g) Special packing provisions that are specific to a substance.

(3) In no case shall pressure receptacles be filled in excess of the limit permitted in the following requirements.

    (a) For compressed gases, the working pressure shall be not more than two thirds of the test pressure of the pressure receptacles. Restrictions to this upper limit on working pressure are imposed by (5), special packing provision "o". In no case shall the internal pressure at 65 °C exceed the test pressure;

    (b) For high pressure liquefied gases, the filling ratio shall be such that the settled pressure at 65 °C does not exceed the test pressure of the pressure receptacles.

    The use of test pressures and filling ratios other than those in the table is permitted, except where (5), special packing provision "o" applies, provided that:

    (i) the criterion of (5), special packing provision "r" is met when applicable; or

    (ii) the above criterion is met in all other cases.

    For high pressure liquefied gases and gas mixtures for which relevant data are not available, the maximum filling ratio (*FR*) shall be determined as follows:

$$FR = 8.5 \times 10^{-4} \times d_g \times P_h$$

where:

    FR = maximum filling ratio

    d_g = gas density (at 15 °C, 1 bar)(in g/l)

    P_h = minimum test pressure (in bar)

Cont'd on next page

If the density of the gas is unknown, the maximum filling ratio shall be determined as follows:

$$FR = \frac{P_h \times MM \times 10^{-3}}{R \times 338}$$

where:

FR = maximum filling ratio

P_h = minimum test pressure (in bar)

MM = molecular mass (in g/mol)

$R = 8.31451 \times 10^{-2}$ bar·l/mol·K (gas constant)

For gas mixtures, the average molecular mass is to be taken, taking into account the volumetric concentrations of the various components;

(c) For low pressure liquefied gases, the maximum mass of contents per litre of water capacity shall equal 0.95 times the density of the liquid phase at 50 °C; in addition, the liquid phase shall not fill the pressure receptacle at any temperature up to 60 °C. The test pressure of the pressure receptacle shall be at least equal to the vapour pressure (absolute) of the liquid at 65 °C, minus 100 kPa (1 bar).

For low pressure liquefied gases and gas mixtures for which relevant data are not available, the maximum filling ratio shall be determined as follows:

$$FR = (0.0032 \times BP - 0.24) \times d_1$$

where:

FR = maximum filling ratio

BP = boiling point (in Kelvin)

d_1 = density of the liquid at boiling point (in kg/l);

(d) For UN 1001, acetylene, dissolved, and UN 3374 acetylene, solvent free, see (5), special packing provision "p".

(e) For liquefied gases charged with compressed gases, both components – the liquefied gas and the compressed gas – have to be taken into consideration in the calculation of the internal pressure in the pressure receptacle.

The maximum mass of contents per litre of water capacity shall not exceed 0.95 times the density of the liquid phase at 50 °C; in addition, the liquid phase shall not completely fill the pressure receptacle at any temperature up to 60 °C.

When filled, the internal pressure at 65 °C shall not exceed the test pressure of the pressure receptacles. The vapour pressures and volumetric expansions of all substances in the pressure receptacles shall be considered. When experimental data is not available, the following steps shall be carried out:

(i) Calculation of the vapour pressure of the liquefied gas and of the partial pressure of the compressed gas at 15 °C (filling temperature);

(ii) Calculation of the volumetric expansion of the liquid phase resulting from the heating from 15 °C to 65 °C and calculation of the remaining volume for the gaseous phase;

(iii) Calculation of the partial pressure of the compressed gas at 65 °C considering the volumetric expansion of the liquid phase;

NOTE: *The compressibility factor of the compressed gas at 15 °C and 65 °C shall be considered.*

(iv) Calculation of the vapour pressure of the liquefied gas at 65 °C;

(v) The total pressure is the sum of the vapour pressure of the liquefied gas and the partial pressure of the compressed gas at 65 °C;

(vi) Consideration of the solubility of the compressed gas at 65 °C in the liquid phase;

The test pressure of the pressure receptacle shall not be less than the calculated total pressure minus 100 kPa (1 bar).

If the solubility of the compressed gas in the liquid phase is not known for the calculation, the test pressure can be calculated without taking the gas solubility (sub-paragraph (vi)) into account.

Cont'd on next page

| P200 | PACKING INSTRUCTION *(cont'd)* | P200 |

(4) The filling of pressure receptacles shall be carried out by qualified staff using appropriate equipment and procedures.

The procedures should include checks of:

(a) The conformity of receptacles and accessories with these Regulations;

(b) Their compatibility with the product to be transported;

(c) The absence of damage which might affect safety;

(d) Compliance with the degree or pressure of filling, as appropriate;

(e) Marks and identification.

These requirements are deemed to be met if the following standards are applied:

ISO 10691:2004: Gas cylinders – Refillable welded steel cylinders for liquefied petroleum gas (LPG) – Procedures for checking before, during and after filling.

ISO 11372:2011: Gas cylinders – Acetylene cylinders – Filling conditions and filling inspection

ISO 11755:2005: Gas cylinders – Cylinder bundles for compressed and liquefied gases (excluding acetylene) – Inspection at time of filling

ISO 13088:2011 + Amd 1:2020: Gas cylinders – Acetylene cylinder bundles – Filling conditions and filling inspection

ISO 24431:2016: Gas cylinders – Seamless, welded and composite cylinders for compressed and liquefied gases (excluding acetylene) – Inspection at time of filling

(5) Special packing provisions:

Material compatibility

a: Aluminium alloy pressure receptacles shall not be used.

b: Copper valves shall not be used.

c: Metal parts in contact with the contents shall not contain more than 65 % copper.

d: When steel pressure receptacles or composite pressure receptacles with steel liners are used, only those bearing the "H" mark in accordance with 6.2.2.7.4 (p) are permitted.

Requirements for toxic substances with an LC_{50} less than or equal to 200 ml/m^3 (ppm)

k: Valve outlets shall be fitted with pressure retaining gas-tight plugs or caps having threads that match those of the valve outlets.

Each cylinder within a bundle shall be fitted with an individual valve that shall be closed during transport. After filling, the manifold shall be evacuated, purged and plugged.

Bundles containing UN 1045 Fluorine, compressed, may be constructed with isolation valves on groups of cylinders not exceeding 150 litres total water capacity instead of isolation valves on every cylinder.

Cylinders and individual cylinders in a bundle shall have a test pressure greater than or equal to 200 bar and a minimum wall thickness of 3.5 mm for aluminium alloy or 2 mm for steel. Individual cylinders not complying with this requirement shall be transported in a rigid outer packaging that will adequately protect the cylinder and its fittings and meeting the packing group I performance level. Pressure drums shall have a minimum wall thickness as specified by the competent authority.

Pressure receptacles shall not be fitted with a pressure relief device.

Cylinders and individual cylinders in a bundle shall be limited to a maximum water capacity of 85 litres.

Each valve shall be capable of withstanding the test pressure of the pressure receptacle and be connected directly to the pressure receptacle by either a taper thread or other means which meets the requirements of ISO 10692-2:2001.

Each valve shall either be of the packless type with non-perforated diaphragm, or be of a type which prevents leakage through or past the packing.

Each pressure receptacle shall be tested for leakage after filling.

Cont'd on next page

P200   **PACKING INSTRUCTION** *(cont'd)*   **P200**

Gas specific provisions

l: UN 1040 ethylene oxide may also be packed in hermetically sealed glass or metal inner packagings suitably cushioned in fibreboard, wooden or metal boxes meeting the packing group I performance level. The maximum quantity permitted in any glass inner packaging is 30 g, and the maximum quantity permitted in any metal inner packaging is 200 g. After filling, each inner packaging shall be determined to be leak-tight by placing the inner packaging in a hot water bath at a temperature, and for a period of time, sufficient to ensure that an internal pressure equal to the vapour pressure of ethylene oxide at 55 °C is achieved. The maximum net mass in any outer packaging shall not exceed 2.5 kg.

m: Pressure receptacles shall be filled to a working pressure not exceeding 5 bar.

n: Cylinders and individual cylinders in a bundle shall contain not more than 5 kg of the gas. When bundles containing UN 1045 fluorine, compressed are divided into groups of cylinders in accordance with special packing provision "k" each group shall contain not more than 5 kg of the gas.

o: In no case shall the working pressure or filling ratio shown in the table be exceeded.

p: For UN 1001 acetylene, dissolved and UN 3374 acetylene, solvent free: cylinders shall be filled with a homogeneous monolithic porous material; the working pressure and the quantity of acetylene shall not exceed the values prescribed in the approval or in ISO 3807-1:2000, ISO 3807-2:2000 or ISO 3807:2013, as applicable.

     For UN 1001 acetylene, dissolved: cylinders shall contain a quantity of acetone or suitable solvent as specified in the approval (see ISO 3807-1:2000, ISO 3807-2:2000 or ISO 3807:2013, as applicable); cylinders fitted with pressure relief devices or manifolded together shall be transported vertically.

     The test pressure of 52 bar applies only to cylinders fitted with a fusible plug.

q: Valve outlets of pressure receptacles for pyrophoric gases or flammable mixtures of gases containing more than 1 % of pyrophoric compounds shall be fitted with gas-tight plugs or caps. When these pressure receptacles are manifolded in a bundle, each of the pressure receptacles shall be fitted with an individual valve that shall be closed during transport, and the outlet of the manifold valve shall be fitted with a pressure retaining gas-tight plug or cap. Gas-tight plugs or caps shall have threads that match those of the valve outlets.

r: The filling ratio of this gas shall be limited such that, if complete decomposition occurs, the pressure does not exceed two thirds of the test pressure of the pressure receptacle.

ra: This gas may also be packed in capsules under the following conditions:

     (a)   The mass of gas shall not exceed 150 g per capsule;

     (b)   The capsules shall be free from faults liable to impair the strength;

     (c)   The leakproofness of the closure shall be ensured by an additional device (cap, crown, seal, binding, etc.) capable of preventing any leakage of the closure during transport;

     (d)   The capsules shall be placed in an outer packaging of sufficient strength. A package shall not weigh more than 75 kg.

s: Aluminium alloy pressure receptacles shall be:

     (a)   Equipped only with brass or stainless steel valves; and

     (b)   Cleaned in accordance with ISO 11621:1997 and not contaminated with oil.

t: (a)   The wall thickness of pressure receptacles shall be not less than 3 mm.

     (b)   Prior to transport it shall be ensured that the pressure has not risen due to potential hydrogen generation.

Cont'd on next page

| P200 | **PACKING INSTRUCTION** *(cont'd)* | P200 |

Periodic inspection

u: The interval between periodic tests may be extended to 10 years for aluminium alloy pressure receptacles when the alloy of the pressure receptacle has been subjected to stress corrosion testing as specified in ISO 7866:2012 + Cor 1:2014.

v: The interval between periodic inspections for steel cylinders may be extended to 15 years if approved by the competent authority of the country of use.

Requirements for N.O.S. descriptions and for mixtures

z: The construction materials of the pressure receptacles and their accessories shall be compatible with the contents and shall not react to form harmful or dangerous compounds therewith.

The test pressure and filling ratio shall be calculated in accordance with the relevant requirements of (3).

Toxic substances with an LC_{50} less than or equal to 200 ml/m³ shall not be transported in tubes, pressure drums or MEGCs and shall meet the requirements of special packing provision "k". However, UN 1975 nitric oxide and dinitrogen tetroxide mixture may be transported in pressure drums.

For pressure receptacles containing pyrophoric gases or flammable mixtures of gases containing more than 1 % pyrophoric compounds, the requirements of special packing provision "q" shall be met.

The necessary steps shall be taken to prevent dangerous reactions (i.e. polymerisation or decomposition) during transport. If necessary, stabilisation or addition of an inhibitor shall be required.

Mixtures containing UN 1911 diborane, shall be filled to a pressure such that, if complete decomposition of the diborane occurs, two thirds of the test pressure of the pressure receptacle shall not be exceeded.

Mixtures containing UN 2192 germane, other than mixtures of up to 35 % germane in hydrogen or nitrogen or up to 28 % germane in helium or argon, shall be filled to a pressure such that, if complete decomposition of the germane occurs, two thirds of the test pressure of the pressure receptacle shall not be exceeded.

Mixtures of fluorine and nitrogen with a fluorine concentration below 35 % by volume may be filled in pressure receptacles up to a maximum allowable working pressure for which the partial pressure of fluorine does not exceed 31 bar (absolute).

$$working\ pressure\ (bar) < \frac{31}{x_f} - 1$$

where:

x_f = fluorine concentration in % by volume/100.

Mixtures of fluorine and inert gases with a fluorine concentration below 35 % by volume may be filled in pressure receptacles up to a maximum allowable working pressure for which the partial pressure of fluorine does not exceed 31 bar (absolute), additionally taking the coefficient of nitrogen equivalency in accordance with ISO 10156:2017 into account when calculating the partial pressure.

$$working\ pressure\ (bar) < \frac{31}{x_f}(x_f + K_k \times x_k) - 1$$

where:

x_f = fluorine concentration in % by volume/100;

K_k = coefficient of equivalency of an inert gas relative to nitrogen (coefficient of nitrogen equivalency);

x_k = inert gas concentration in % by volume/100.

However, the working pressure for mixtures of fluorine and inert gases shall not exceed 200 bar. The minimum test pressure of pressure receptacles for mixtures of fluorine and inert gases equals 1.5 times the working pressure or 200 bar, with the greater value to be applied.

Cont'd on next page

P200	PACKING INSTRUCTION *(cont'd)*											P200
Table 1: COMPRESSED GASES											
UN No.	Name and description	Class or Division	Subsidiary hazards	LC_{50} (ml/m³)	Cylinders	Tubes	Pressure drums	Bundles of cylinders	MEGCs	Test period (years)	Test pressure (bar)	Maximum working pressure[a] (bar)	Special packing provisions
1002	AIR, COMPRESSED	2.2			X	X	X	X	X	10			
1006	ARGON, COMPRESSED	2.2			X	X	X	X	X	10			
1016	CARBON MONOXIDE, COMPRESSED	2.3	2.1	3 760	X	X	X	X	X	5			u
1023	COAL GAS, COMPRESSED	2.3	2.1		X	X	X	X	X	5			
1045	FLUORINE, COMPRESSED	2.3	5.1, 8	185	X			X		5	200	30	a, k, n, o
1046	HELIUM, COMPRESSED	2.2			X	X	X	X	X	10			
1049	HYDROGEN, COMPRESSED	2.1			X	X	X	X	X	10			d
1056	KRYPTON, COMPRESSED	2.2			X	X	X	X	X	10			
1065	NEON, COMPRESSED	2.2			X	X	X	X	X	10			
1066	NITROGEN, COMPRESSED	2.2			X	X	X	X	X	10			
1071	OIL GAS, COMPRESSED	2.3	2.1		X	X	X	X	X	5			
1072	OXYGEN, COMPRESSED	2.2	5.1		X	X	X	X	X	10			s
1612	HEXAETHYL TETRAPHOSPHATE AND COMPRESSED GAS MIXTURE	2.3			X	X	X	X	X	5			z
1660	NITRIC OXIDE, COMPRESSED	2.3	5.1, 8	115	X			X		5	225	33	k, o
1953	COMPRESSED GAS, TOXIC, FLAMMABLE, N.O.S.	2.3	2.1	≤ 5 000	X	X	X	X	X	5			z
1954	COMPRESSED GAS, FLAMMABLE, N.O.S	2.1			X	X	X	X	X	10			z
1955	COMPRESSED GAS, TOXIC, N.O.S.	2.3		≤ 5 000	X	X	X	X	X	5			z
1956	COMPRESSED GAS, N.O.S.	2.2			X	X	X	X	X	10			z
1957	DEUTERIUM, COMPRESSED	2.1			X	X	X	X	X	10			d
1964	HYDROCARBON GAS MIXTURE, COMPRESSED, N.O.S	2.1			X	X	X	X	X	10			z
1971	METHANE, COMPRESSED or NATURAL GAS, COMPRESSED with high methane content	2.1			X	X	X	X	X	10			

[a] *Where the entries are blank, the working pressure shall not exceed two thirds of the test pressure.*

Cont'd on next page

P200	PACKING INSTRUCTION *(cont'd)*												P200
Table 1: COMPRESSED GASES													
UN No.	Name and description	Class or Division	Subsidiary hazards	LC_{50} (ml/m³)	Cylinders	Tubes	Pressure drums	Bundles of cylinders	MEGCs	Test period (years)	Test pressure (bar)	Maximum working pressure[a] (bar)	Special packing provisions
2034	HYDROGEN AND METHANE MIXTURE, COMPRESSED	2.1			X	X	X	X	X	10			d
2190	OXYGEN DIFLUORIDE, COMPRESSED	2.3	5.1, 8	2.6	X			X		5	200	30	a, k, n, o
3156	COMPRESSED GAS, OXIDIZING, N.O.S.	2.2	5.1		X	X	X	X	X	10			z
3303	COMPRESSED GAS, TOXIC, OXIDIZING, N.O.S.	2.3	5.1	≤ 5 000	X	X	X	X	X	5			z
3304	COMPRESSED GAS, TOXIC, CORROSIVE, N.O.S.	2.3	8	≤ 5 000	X	X	X	X	X	5			z
3305	COMPRESSED GAS, TOXIC, FLAMMABLE, CORROSIVE, N.O.S.	2.3	2.1, 8	≤ 5 000	X	X	X	X	X	5			z

[a] *Where the entries are blank, the working pressure shall not exceed two thirds of the test pressure.*

Cont'd on next page

P200	PACKING INSTRUCTION (cont'd)										P200
Table 2: LIQUEFIED GASES AND DISSOLVED GASES											
UN No.	Name and description	Class or Division	Subsidiary hazards	LC_{50} (ml/m³)	Cylinders	Tubes	Pressure drums	Bundles of cylinders	MEGCs	Test period (years)	Test pressure (bar)	Filling ratio	Special packing provisions
1001	ACETYLENE, DISSOLVED	2.1			X			X		10	60		c, p
											52		c, p
1005	AMMONIA, ANHYDROUS	2.3	8	4 000	X	X	X	X	X	5	29	0.54	b
1008	BORON TRIFLUORIDE	2.3	8	864	X	X	X	X	X	5	225	0.715	a
											300	0.86	a
1009	BROMOTRIFLUORO-METHANE (REFRIGERANT GAS R 13B1)	2.2			X	X	X	X	X	10	42	1.13	
											120	1.44	
											250	1.60	
1010	BUTADIENES, STABILIZED (1,2-butadiene), or	2.1			X	X	X	X	X	10	10	0.59	
	BUTADIENES, STABILIZED (1,3-butadiene), or	2.1			X	X	X	X	X	10	10	0.55	
	BUTADIENES AND HYDROCARBON MIXTURE, STABILIZED, containing more than 20 % butadienes	2.1			X	X	X	X	X	10			v, z
1011	BUTANE	2.1			X	X	X	X	X	10	10	0.52	v
1012	BUTYLENE (butylenes mixture), or	2.1			X	X	X	X	X	10	10	0.50	z
	BUTYLENE (1-butylene), or	2.1			X	X	X	X	X	10	10	0.53	
	BUTYLENE (cis-2-butylene), or	2.1			X	X	X	X	X	10	10	0.55	
	BUTYLENE (trans-2 butylene)	2.1			X	X	X	X	X	10	10	0.54	
1013	CARBON DIOXIDE	2.2			X	X	X	X	X	10	190	0.68	
											250	0.76	
1017	CHLORINE	2.3	5.1, 8	293	X	X	X	X	X	5	22	1.25	a
1018	CHLORODIFLUORO-METHANE (REFRIGERANT GAS R 22)	2.2			X	X	X	X	X	10	27	1.03	
1020	CHLOROPENTA-FLUOROETHANE (REFRIGERANT GAS R 115)	2.2			X	X	X	X	X	10	25	1.05	
1021	1-CHLORO-1,2,2,2-TETRAFLUOROETHANE (REFRIGERANT GAS R 124)	2.2			X	X	X	X	X	10	11	1.20	
1022	CHLOROTRIFLUORO-METHANE (REFRIGERANT GAS R 13)	2.2			X	X	X	X	X	10	100	0.83	
											120	0.90	
											190	1.04	
											250	1.11	
1026	CYANOGEN	2.3	2.1	350	X	X	X	X	X	5	100	0.70	u
1027	CYCLOPROPANE	2.1			X	X	X	X	X	10	18	0.55	
1028	DICHLORODIFLUORO-METHANE (REFRIGERANT GAS R 12)	2.2			X	X	X	X	X	10	16	1.15	
1029	DICHLOROFLUORO-METHANE (REFRIGERANT GAS R 21)	2.2			X	X	X	X	X	10	10	1.23	
1030	1,1-DIFLUOROETHANE (REFRIGERANT GAS R 152a)	2.1			X	X	X	X	X	10	16	0.79	
1032	DIMETHYLAMINE, ANHYDROUS	2.1			X	X	X	X	X	10	10	0.59	b
1033	DIMETHYL ETHER	2.1			X	X	X	X	X	10	18	0.58	

Cont'd on next page

P200 PACKING INSTRUCTION (cont'd)

Table 2: LIQUEFIED GASES AND DISSOLVED GASES

UN No.	Name and description	Class or Division	Subsidiary hazards	LC_{50} (ml/m³)	Cylinders	Tubes	Pressure drums	Bundles of cylinders	MEGCs	Test period (years)	Test pressure (bar)	Filling ratio	Special packing provisions
1035	ETHANE	2.1			X	X	X	X	X	10	95	0.25	
											120	0.30	
											300	0.40	
1036	ETHYLAMINE	2.1			X	X	X	X	X	10	10	0.61	b
1037	ETHYL CHLORIDE	2.1			X	X	X	X	X	10	10	0.80	a, ra
1039	ETHYL METHYL ETHER	2.1			X	X	X	X	X	10	10	0.64	
1040	ETHYLENE OXIDE, or ETHYLENE OXIDE WITH NITROGEN up to a total pressure of 1 MPa (10 bar) at 50 °C	2.3	2.1	2 900	X	X	X	X	X	5	15	0.78	l
1041	ETHYLENE OXIDE AND CARBON DIOXIDE MIXTURE with more than 9 % ethylene oxide but not more than 87 %	2.1			X	X	X	X	X	10	190	0.66	
											250	0.75	
1043	FERTILIZER AMMONIATING SOLUTION with free ammonia	2.2			X		X	X		5			b, z
1048	HYDROGEN BROMIDE, ANHYDROUS	2.3	8	2 860	X	X	X	X	X	5	60	1.51	a, d
1050	HYDROGEN CHLORIDE, ANHYDROUS	2.3	8	2 810	X	X	X	X	X	5	100	0.30	a, d
											120	0.56	a, d
											150	0.67	a, d
											200	0.74	a, d
1053	HYDROGEN SULPHIDE	2.3	2.1	712	X	X	X	X	X	5	48	0.67	d, u
1055	ISOBUTYLENE	2.1			X	X	X	X	X	10	10	0.52	
1058	LIQUEFIED GASES, non-flammable, charged with nitrogen, carbon dioxide or air	2.2			X	X	X	X	X	10			z
1060	METHYLACETYLENE AND PROPADIENE MIXTURE, STABILIZED, or	2.1			X	X	X	X	X	10			c, z
	METHYLACETYLENE AND PROPADIENE MIXTURE, STABILIZED (Propadiene with 1 % to 4 % methylacetylene)	2.1			X	X	X	X	X	10	22	0.52	c
1061	METHYLAMINE, ANHYDROUS	2.1			X	X	X	X	X	10	13	0.58	b
1062	METHYL BROMIDE	2.3		850	X	X	X	X	X	5	10	1.51	a
1063	METHYL CHLORIDE (REFRIGERANT GAS R 40)	2.1			X	X	X	X	X	10	17	0.81	a
1064	METHYL MERCAPTAN	2.3	2.1	1 350	X	X	X	X	X	5	10	0.78	d, u
1067	DINITROGEN TETROXIDE (NITROGEN DIOXIDE)	2.3	5.1, 8	115	X		X	X		5	10	1.30	k
1069	NITROSYL CHLORIDE	2.3	8	35	X			X		5	13	1.10	k

Cont'd on next page

P200	PACKING INSTRUCTION (cont'd)											P200
Table 2: LIQUEFIED GASES AND DISSOLVED GASES												
UN No.	Name and description	Class or Division	Subsidiary hazards	LC$_{50}$ (ml/m³)	Cylinders	Tubes	Pressure drums	Bundles of cylinders	MEGCs	Test period (years)	Test pressure (bar)	Filling ratio	Special packing provisions
1070	NITROUS OXIDE	2.2	5.1		X	X	X	X	X	10	180	0.68	
											225	0.74	
											250	0.75	
1075	PETROLEUM GASES, LIQUEFIED	2.1			X	X	X	X	X	10			v, z
1076	PHOSGENE	2.3	8	5	X		X	X		5	20	1.23	a, k
1077	PROPYLENE	2.1			X	X	X	X	X	10	27	0.43	
1078	REFRIGERANT GAS, N.O.S.	2.2			X	X	X	X	X	10			z
1079	SULPHUR DIOXIDE	2.3	8	2 520	X	X	X	X	X	5	12	1.23	
1080	SULPHUR HEXAFLUORIDE	2.2			X	X	X	X	X	10	70	1.06	
											140	1.34	
											160	1.38	
1081	TETRAFLUORO-ETHYLENE, STABILIZED	2.1			X	X	X	X	X	10	200		m, o
1082	TRIFLUOROCHLORO-ETHYLENE, STABILIZED (Refrigerant gas R 1113)	2.3	2.1	2 000	X	X	X	X	X	5	19	1.13	u
1083	TRIMETHYLAMINE, ANHYDROUS	2.1			X	X	X	X	X	10	10	0.56	b
1085	VINYL BROMIDE, STABILIZED	2.1			X	X	X	X	X	10	10	1.37	a
1086	VINYL CHLORIDE, STABILIZED	2.1			X	X	X	X	X	10	12	0.81	a
1087	VINYL METHYL ETHER, STABILIZED	2.1			X	X	X	X	X	10	10	0.67	
1581	CHLOROPICRIN AND METHYL BROMIDE MIXTURE	2.3		850	X	X	X	X	X	5	10	1.51	a
1582	CHLOROPICRIN AND METHYL CHLORIDE MIXTURE	2.3			X	X	X	X	X	5	17	0.81	a
1589	CYANOGEN CHLORIDE, STABILIZED	2.3	8	80	X			X		5	20	1.03	k
1741	BORON TRICHLORIDE	2.3	8	2 541	X	X	X	X	X	5	10	1.19	a
1749	CHLORINE TRIFLUORIDE	2.3	5.1, 8	299	X	X	X	X	X	5	30	1.40	a
1858	HEXAFLUORO-PROPYLENE (REFRIGERANT GAS R 1216)	2.2			X	X	X	X	X	10	22	1.11	
1859	SILICON TETRAFLUORIDE	2.3	8	922	X	X	X	X	X	5	200	0.74	a
											300	1.10	a
1860	VINYL FLUORIDE, STABILIZED	2.1			X	X	X	X	X	10	250	0.64	a
1911	DIBORANE	2.3	2.1	80	X			X		5	250	0.07	d, k, o
1912	METHYL CHLORIDE AND METHYLENE CHLORIDE MIXTURE	2.1			X	X	X	X	X	10	17	0.81	a
1952	ETHYLENE OXIDE AND CARBON DIOXIDE MIXTURE with not more than 9 % ethylene oxide	2.2			X	X	X	X	X	10	190	0.66	
											250	0.75	
1958	1,2-DICHLORO-1,1,2,2-TETRAFLUOROETHANE (REFRIGERANT GAS R 114)	2.2			X	X	X	X	X	10	10	1.30	

Cont'd on next page

P200	PACKING INSTRUCTION (cont'd)											P200
Table 2: LIQUEFIED GASES AND DISSOLVED GASES												
UN No.	Name and description	Class or Division	Subsidiary hazards	LC_{50} (ml/m³)	Cylinders	Tubes	Pressure drums	Bundles of cylinders	MEGCs	Test period (years)	Test pressure (bar)	Filling ratio	Special packing provisions
1959	1,1-DIFLUORO-ETHYLENE (REFRIGERANT GAS R 1132a)	2.1			X	X	X	X	X	10	250	0.77	
1962	ETHYLENE	2.1			X	X	X	X	X	10	225	0.34	
											300	0.38	
1965	HYDROCARBON GAS MIXTURE, LIQUEFIED, N.O.S.	2.1			X	X	X	X	X	10			v, z
1967	INSECTICIDE GAS, TOXIC, N.O.S.	2.3			X	X	X	X	X	5			z
1968	INSECTICIDE GAS, N.O.S.	2.2			X	X	X	X	X	10			z
1969	ISOBUTANE	2.1			X	X	X	X	X	10	10	0.49	v
1973	CHLORODIFLUORO-METHANE AND CHLOROPENTA-FLUOROETHANE MIXTURE with fixed boiling point, with approximately 49 % chlorodifluoromethane (REFRIGERANT GAS R 502)	2.2			X	X	X	X	X	10	31	1.01	
1974	CHLORODIFLUORO-BROMOMETHANE (REFRIGERANT GAS R 12B1)	2.2			X	X	X	X	X	10	10	1.61	
1975	NITRIC OXIDE AND DINITROGEN TETROXIDE MIXTURE (NITRIC OXIDE AND NITROGEN DIOXIDE MIXTURE)	2.3	5.1, 8	115	X		X	X		5			k, z
1976	OCTAFLUOROCYCLO-BUTANE (REFRIGERANT GAS RC 318)	2.2			X	X	X	X	X	10	11	1.32	
1978	PROPANE	2.1			X	X	X	X	X	10	23	0.43	v
1982	TETRAFLUORO-METHANE (REFRIGERANT GAS R 14)	2.2			X	X	X	X	X	10	200	0.71	
											300	0.90	
1983	1-CHLORO-2,2,2-TRIFLUOROETHANE (REFRIGERANT GAS R 133a)	2.2			X	X	X	X	X	10	10	1.18	
1984	TRIFLUOROMETHANE (REFRIGERANT GAS R 23)	2.2			X	X	X	X	X	10	190	0.88	
											250	0.96	
2035	1,1,1-TRIFLUORO-ETHANE (REFRIGERANT GAS R 143a)	2.1			X	X	X	X	X	10	35	0.73	
2036	XENON	2.2			X	X	X	X	X	10	130	1.28	
2044	2,2-DIMETHYLPROPANE	2.1			X	X	X	X	X	10	10	0.53	
2073	AMMONIA SOLUTION, relative density less than 0.880 at 15 °C in water, with more than 35 % but not more than 40 % ammonia	2.2			X	X	X	X	X	5	10	0.80	b
	AMMONIA SOLUTION, relative density less than 0.880 at 15 °C in water, with more than 40 % but not more than 50 % ammonia	2.2			X	X	X	X	X	5	12	0.77	b
2188	ARSINE	2.3	2.1	178	X			X		5	42	1.10	d, k

Cont'd on next page

P200 PACKING INSTRUCTION (cont'd)

Table 2: LIQUEFIED GASES AND DISSOLVED GASES

UN No.	Name and description	Class or Division	Subsidiary hazards	LC_{50} (ml/m³)	Cylinders	Tubes	Pressure drums	Bundles of cylinders	MEGCs	Test period (years)	Test pressure (bar)	Filling ratio	Special packing provisions
2189	DICHLOROSILANE	2.3	2.1, 8	314	X	X	X	X	X	5	10	0.90	a
											200	1.08	a
2191	SULPHURYL FLUORIDE	2.3		3 020	X	X	X	X	X	5	50	1.10	u
2192	GERMANE	2.3	2.1	620	X	X	X	X	X	5	250	0.064	d, q, r
2193	HEXAFLUOROETHANE (REFRIGERANT GAS R 116)	2.2			X	X	X	X	X	10	200	1.13	
2194	SELENIUM HEXAFLUORIDE	2.3	8	50	X			X		5	36	1.46	k
2195	TELLURIUM HEXAFLUORIDE	2.3	8	25	X			X		5	20	1.00	k
2196	TUNGSTEN HEXAFLUORIDE	2.3	8	218	X	X	X	X	X	5	10	3.08	a
2197	HYDROGEN IODIDE, ANHYDROUS	2.3	8	2 860	X	X	X	X	X	5	23	2.25	a, d
2198	PHOSPHORUS PENTAFLUORIDE	2.3	8	261	X	X	X	X	X	5	200	0.90	
											300	1.25	
2199	PHOSPHINE	2.3	2.1	20	X			X		5	225	0.30	d, k, q
											250	0.45	d, k, q
2200	PROPADIENE, STABILIZED	2.1			X	X	X	X	X	10	22	0.50	
2202	HYDROGEN SELENIDE, ANHYDROUS	2.3	2.1	51	X			X		5	31	1.60	k
2203	SILANE	2.1			X	X	X	X	X	10	225	0.32	q
											250	0.36	q
2204	CARBONYL SULPHIDE	2.3	2.1	1 700	X	X	X	X	X	5	30	0.87	u
2417	CARBONYL FLUORIDE	2.3	8	360	X	X	X	X	X	5	200	0.47	
											300	0.70	
2418	SULPHUR TETRAFLUORIDE	2.3	8	40	X			X		5	30	0.91	a, k
2419	BROMOTRIFLUORO-ETHYLENE	2.1			X	X	X	X	X	10	10	1.19	
2420	HEXAFLUOROACETONE	2.3	8	470	X	X	X	X	X	5	22	1.08	
2421	NITROGEN TRIOXIDE	2.3	5.1, 8	57	X			X		5			k
2422	OCTAFLUOROBUT-2-ENE (REFRIGERANT GAS R 1318)	2.2			X	X	X	X	X	10	12	1.34	
2424	OCTAFLUOROPROPANE (REFRIGERANT GAS R 218)	2.2			X	X	X	X	X	10	25	1.04	
2451	NITROGEN TRIFLUORIDE	2.2	5.1		X	X	X	X	X	10	200	0.50	
2452	ETHYLACETYLENE, STABILIZED	2.1			X	X	X	X	X	10	10	0.57	c
2453	ETHYL FLUORIDE (REFRIGERANT GAS R 161)	2.1			X	X	X	X	X	10	30	0.57	
2454	METHYL FLUORIDE (REFRIGERANT GAS R 41)	2.1			X	X	X	X	X	10	300	0.63	
2455	METHYL NITRITE	2.2											
2517	1-CHLORO-1,1-DIFLUOROETHANE (REFRIGERANT GAS R 142b)	2.1			X	X	X	X	X	10	10	0.99	
2534	METHYLCHLORO-SILANE	2.3	2.1, 8	2 810	X	X	X	X	X	5			z
2548	CHLORINE PENTAFLUORIDE	2.3	5.1, 8	122	X			X		5	13	1.49	a, k

Cont'd on next page

P200	PACKING INSTRUCTION (cont'd)											P200
Table 2: LIQUEFIED GASES AND DISSOLVED GASES												
UN No.	Name and description	Class or Division	Subsidiary hazards	LC$_{50}$ (ml/m³)	Cylinders	Tubes	Pressure drums	Bundles of cylinders	MEGCs	Test period (years)	Test pressure (bar)	Filling ratio	Special packing provisions
2599	CHLOROTRIFLUORO-METHANE AND TRIFLUOROMETHANE AZEOTROPIC MIXTURE with approximately 60 % chlorotrifluoromethane (REFRIGERANT GAS R 503)	2.2			X	X	X	X	X	10	31 42 100	0.12 0.17 0.64	
2601	CYCLOBUTANE	2.1			X	X	X	X	X	10	10	0.63	
2602	DICHLORODIFLUORO-METHANE AND DIFLUOROETHANE AZEOTROPIC MIXTURE with approximately 74 % dichlorodifluoromethane (REFRIGERANT GAS R 500)	2.2			X	X	X	X	X	10	22	1.01	
2676	STIBINE	2.3	2.1	178	X			X		5	200	0.49	k, r
2901	BROMINE CHLORIDE	2.3	5.1, 8	290	X	X	X	X	X	5	10	1.50	a
3057	TRIFLUOROACETYL CHLORIDE	2.3	8	10	X		X	X		5	17	1.17	k
3070	ETHYLENE OXIDE AND DICHLORODIFLUORO-METHANE MIXTURE with not more than 12.5 % ethylene oxide	2.2			X	X	X	X	X	10	18	1.09	
3083	PERCHLORYL FLUORIDE	2.3	5.1	770	X	X	X	X	X	5	33	1.21	u
3153	PERFLUORO (METHYL VINYL ETHER)	2.1			X	X	X	X	X	10	20	0.75	
3154	PERFLUORO (ETHYL VINYL ETHER)	2.1			X	X	X	X	X	10	10	0.98	
3157	LIQUEFIED GAS, OXIDIZING, N.O.S.	2.2	5.1		X	X	X	X	X	10			z
3159	1,1,1,2-TETRAFLUORO-ETHANE (REFRIGERANT GAS R 134a)	2.2			X	X	X	X	X	10	18	1.05	
3160	LIQUEFIED GAS, TOXIC, FLAMMABLE, N.O.S.	2.3	2.1	≤ 5 000	X	X	X	X	X	5			z
3161	LIQUEFIED GAS, FLAMMABLE, N.O.S.	2.1			X	X	X	X	X	10			z
3162	LIQUEFIED GAS, TOXIC, N.O.S.	2.3		≤ 5 000	X	X	X	X	X	5			z
3163	LIQUEFIED GAS, N.O.S.	2.2			X	X	X	X	X	10			z
3220	PENTAFLUOROETHANE (REFRIGERANT GAS R 125)	2.2			X	X	X	X	X	10	49 35	0.95 0.87	
3252	DIFLUOROMETHANE (REFRIGERANT GAS R 32)	2.1			X	X	X	X	X	10	48	0.78	
3296	HEPTAFLUORO-PROPANE (REFRIGERANT GAS R 227)	2.2			X	X	X	X	X	10	13	1.21	
3297	ETHYLENE OXIDE AND CHLOROTETRA-FLUOROETHANE MIXTURE with not more than 8.8 % ethylene oxide	2.2			X	X	X	X	X	10	10	1.16	
3298	ETHYLENE OXIDE AND PENTAFLUOROETHANE MIXTURE with not more than 7.9 % ethylene oxide	2.2			X	X	X	X	X	10	26	1.02	

Cont'd on next page

P200	PACKING INSTRUCTION *(cont'd)*												P200
Table 2: **LIQUEFIED GASES AND DISSOLVED GASES**													
UN No.	Name and description	Class or Division	Subsidiary hazards	LC_{50} (ml/m³)	Cylinders	Tubes	Pressure drums	Bundles of cylinders	MEGCs	Test period (years)	Test pressure (bar)	Filling ratio	Special packing provisions
3299	ETHYLENE OXIDE AND TETRAFLUOROETHANE MIXTURE with not more than 5.6 % ethylene oxide	2.2			X	X	X	X	X	10	17	1.03	
3300	ETHYLENE OXIDE AND CARBON DIOXIDE MIXTURE with more than 87 % ethylene oxide	2.3	2.1	More than 2 900	X	X	X	X	X	5	28	0.73	
3307	LIQUEFIED GAS, TOXIC, OXIDIZING, N.O.S.	2.3	5.1	≤ 5 000	X	X	X	X	X	5			z
3308	LIQUEFIED GAS, TOXIC, CORROSIVE, N.O.S.	2.3	8	≤ 5 000	X	X	X	X	X	5			z
3309	LIQUEFIED GAS, TOXIC, FLAMMABLE, CORROSIVE, N.O.S.	2.3	2.1, 8	≤ 5 000	X	X	X	X	X	5			z
3310	LIQUEFIED GAS, TOXIC, OXIDIZING, CORROSIVE, N.O.S.	2.3	5.1, 8	≤ 5 000	X	X	X	X	X	5			z
3318	AMMONIA SOLUTION, relative density less than 0.880 at 15 °C in water, with more than 50 % ammonia	2.3	8		X	X	X	X	X	5			b
3337	REFRIGERANT GAS R 404A	2.2			X	X	X	X	X	10	36	0.82	
3338	REFRIGERANT GAS R 407A	2.2			X	X	X	X	X	10	32	0.94	
3339	REFRIGERANT GAS R 407B	2.2			X	X	X	X	X	10	33	0.93	
3340	REFRIGERANT GAS R 407C	2.2			X	X	X	X	X	10	30	0.95	
3354	INSECTICIDE GAS, FLAMMABLE, N.O.S	2.1			X	X	X	X	X	10			z
3355	INSECTICIDE GAS, TOXIC, FLAMMABLE, N.O.S.	2.3	2.1		X	X	X	X	X	5			z
3374	ACETYLENE, SOLVENT FREE	2.1			X			X		5	60		c, p
											52		c, p
3553	DISILANE	2.1			X	X	X	X		10	225	0.39	q

Cont'd on next page

P200	PACKING INSTRUCTION *(cont'd)*											P200
Table 3: SUBSTANCES NOT IN CLASS 2												
UN No.	Name and description	Class or Division	Subsidiary hazards	LC_{50} (ml/m³)	Cylinders	Tubes	Pressure drums	Bundles of cylinders	MEGCs	Test period (years)	Test pressure (bar)	Filling ratio	Special packing provisions
1051	HYDROGEN CYANIDE, STABILIZED containing less than 3 % water	6.1	3	40	X			X		5	100	0.55	k
1052	HYDROGEN FLUORIDE, ANHYDROUS	8	6.1	1 307	X		X	X		5	10	0.84	a, t
1745	BROMINE PENTAFLUORIDE	5.1	6.1, 8	25	X		X	X		5	10	b	k
1746	BROMINE TRIFLUORIDE	5.1	6.1, 8	50	X		X	X		5	10	b	k
2495	IODINE PENTAFLUORIDE	5.1	6.1, 8	120	X		X	X		5	10	b	k

b   *A minimum ullage of 8 % by volume is required.*

P201	PACKING INSTRUCTION	P201
This instruction applies to UN Nos. 3167, 3168 and 3169.		

The following packagings are authorized:
(1) Cylinders and gas receptacles conforming to the construction, testing and filling requirements approved by the competent authority.
(2) The following combination packagings provided that the general provisions of **4.1.1** and **4.1.3** are met:
    Outer packagings:
        Drums (1A1, 1A2, 1B1, 1B2, 1N1, 1N2, 1H1, 1H2, 1D, 1G);
        Boxes (4A, 4B, 4N, 4C1, 4C2, 4D, 4F, 4G, 4H1, 4H2);
        Jerricans (3A1, 3A2, 3B1, 3B2, 3H1, 3H2).
    Inner packagings:
    (a) For non-toxic gases, hermetically sealed inner packagings of glass or metal with a maximum capacity of 5 litres per package;
    (b) For toxic gases, hermetically sealed inner packagings of glass or metal with a maximum capacity of 1 litre per package.
Packagings shall conform to the packing group III performance level.		

P202	PACKING INSTRUCTION	P202
	(Reserved)	

P203	**PACKING INSTRUCTION**	P203

This instruction applies to Class 2 refrigerated liquefied gases.

Requirements for closed cryogenic receptacles:

(1) The general requirements of 4.1.6.1 shall be met.

(2) The requirements of chapter 6.2 shall be met.

(3) The closed cryogenic receptacles shall be so insulated that they do not become coated with frost.

(4) Test pressure

Refrigerated liquids shall be filled in closed cryogenic receptacles with the following minimum test pressures:

  (a) For closed cryogenic receptacles with vacuum insulation, the test pressure shall not be less than 1.3 times the sum of the maximum internal pressure of the filled receptacle, including during filling and discharge, plus 100 kPa (1 bar);

  (b) For other closed cryogenic receptacles, the test pressure shall be not less than 1.3 times the maximum internal pressure of the filled receptacle, taking into account the pressure developed during filling and discharge.

(5) Filling

For non-flammable, non-toxic refrigerated liquefied gases the volume of liquid phase at the filling temperature and at a pressure of 100 kPa (1 bar) shall not exceed 98 % of the water capacity of the pressure receptacle.

For flammable refrigerated liquefied gases the gas filled into the receptacle shall remain below the level at which, if the contents were raised to the temperature at which the vapour pressure equalled the opening pressure of the relief valve, the volume of the liquid phase would reach 98 % of the water capacity at that temperature.

(6) Pressure-relief devices

Closed cryogenic receptacles shall be fitted with at least one pressure-relief device.

(7) Compatibility

Materials used to ensure the leakproofness of the joints or for the maintenance of the closures shall be compatible with the contents. In the case of receptacles intended for the transport of oxidizing gases (i.e. with a subsidiary hazard of 5.1), these materials shall not react with these gases in a dangerous manner.

(8) Periodic inspection

The periodic inspection and test frequencies of pressure relief valves in accordance with 6.2.1.6.3 shall not exceed five years.

Requirements for open cryogenic receptacles:

Only the following non oxidizing refrigerated liquefied gases of Division 2.2 may be transported in open cryogenic receptacles: UN Nos. 1913, 1951, 1963, 1970, 1977, 2591, 3136 and 3158. For these gases, when used as a coolant, the requirements of 5.5.3 shall apply.

Open cryogenic receptacles shall be constructed to meet the following requirements:

(1) The receptacles shall be designed, manufactured, tested and equipped in such a way as to withstand all conditions, including fatigue, to which they will be subjected during their normal use and during normal conditions of transport.

(2) The capacity shall be not more than 450 litres.

(3) The receptacle shall have a double wall construction with the space between the inner and outer wall being evacuated (vacuum insulation). The insulation shall prevent the formation of hoar frost on the exterior of the receptacle.

(4) The materials of construction shall have suitable mechanical properties at the service temperature.

(5) Materials which are in direct contact with the dangerous goods shall not be affected or weakened by the dangerous goods intended to be transported and shall not cause a dangerous effect, e.g. catalysing a reaction or reacting with the dangerous goods.

(6) Receptacles of glass double wall construction shall have an outer packaging with suitable cushioning or absorbent materials which withstand the pressures and impacts liable to occur under normal conditions of transport.

Cont'd on next page

P203	PACKING INSTRUCTION *(cont'd)*	P203
Requirements for open cryogenic receptacles *(cont'd)*:		

(7) The receptacle shall be designed to remain in an upright position during transport, e.g. have a base whose smaller horizontal dimension is greater than the height of the centre of gravity when filled to capacity or be mounted on gimbals.

(8) The openings of the receptacles shall be fitted with devices allowing gases to escape, preventing any splashing out of liquid, and so configured that they remain in place during transport.

(9) Open cryogenic receptacles shall bear the following marks permanently affixed e.g. by stamping, engraving or etching:

    (a) The manufacturer's name and address;

    (b) The model number or name;

    (c) The serial or batch number;

    (d) The UN number and proper shipping name of gases for which the receptacle is intended;

    (e) The capacity of the receptacle in litres.

P205	PACKING INSTRUCTION	P205
This instruction applies to UN 3468.		

(1) For metal hydride storage systems, the general packing requirements of 4.1.6.1 shall be met.

(2) Only pressure receptacles not exceeding 150 litres in water capacity and having a maximum developed pressure not exceeding 25 MPa are covered by this packing instruction.

(3) Metal hydride storage systems meeting the applicable requirements for the construction and testing of pressure receptacles containing gas of chapter 6.2 are authorised for the transport of hydrogen only.

(4) When steel pressure receptacles or composite pressure receptacles with steel liners are used, only those bearing the "H" mark, in accordance with 6.2.2.9.2 (j) shall be used.

(5) Metal hydride storage systems shall meet the service conditions, design criteria, rated capacity, type tests, batch tests, routine tests, test pressure, rated charging pressure and provisions for pressure relief devices for transportable metal hydride storage systems specified in ISO 16111:2008 or ISO 16111:2018 and their conformity and approval shall be assessed in accordance with 6.2.2.5.

(6) Metal hydride storage systems shall be filled with hydrogen at a pressure not exceeding the rated charging pressure shown in the permanent mark on the system as specified by ISO 16111:2008 or ISO 16111:2018.

(7) The periodic test requirements for a metal hydride storage system shall be in accordance with ISO 16111:2008 or ISO 16111:2018 and carried out in accordance with 6.2.2.6, and the interval between periodic inspections shall not exceed five years. See 6.2.2.4 to determine which standard is applicable at the time of periodic inspection and test.

P206	PACKING INSTRUCTION	P206

This instruction applies to UN Nos. 3500, 3501, 3502, 3503, 3504 and 3505.

Unless otherwise indicated in these Regulations, cylinders and pressure drums conforming to the applicable requirements of chapter 6.2 are authorized.

(1) The general packing requirements of **4.1.6.1** shall be met.

(2) The maximum test period for periodic inspection shall be 5 years.

(3) Cylinders and pressure drums shall be so filled that at 50 °C the non-gaseous phase does not exceed 95 % of their water capacity and they are not completely filled at 60 °C. When filled, the internal pressure at 65 °C shall not exceed the test pressure of the cylinders and pressure drums. The vapour pressures and volumetric expansion of all substances in the cylinders and pressure drums shall be taken into account.

For liquids charged with a compressed gas both components – the liquid and the compressed gas – have to be taken into consideration in the calculation of the internal pressure in the pressure receptacle. When experimental data is not available, the following steps shall be carried out:

(a) Calculation of the vapour pressure of the liquid and of the partial pressure of the compressed gas at 15 °C (filling temperature);

(b) Calculation of the volumetric expansion of the liquid phase resulting from the heating from 15 °C to 65 °C and calculation of the remaining volume for the gaseous phase;

(c) Calculation of the partial pressure of the compressed gas at 65 °C considering the volumetric expansion of the liquid phase;

NOTE: The compressibility factor of the compressed gas at 15 °C and 65 °C shall be considered.

(d) Calculation of the vapour pressure of the liquid at 65 °C;

(e) The total pressure is the sum of the vapour pressure of the liquid and the partial pressure of the compressed gas at 65 °C;

(f) Consideration of the solubility of the compressed gas at 65 °C in the liquid phase.

The test pressure of the cylinders or pressure drums shall not be less than the calculated total pressure minus 100 kPa (1 bar).

If the solubility of the compressed gas in the liquid phase is not known for the calculation, the test pressure can be calculated without taking the gas solubility (sub-paragraph (f)) into account.

(4) The minimum test pressure shall be in accordance with P200 for the propellant but shall not be less than 20 bar.

Additional requirement:

Cylinders and pressure drums shall not be offered for transport when connected with spray application equipment such as a hose and wand assembly.

Special packing provisions:

PP89 For UN Nos. 3501, 3502, 3503, 3504 and 3505, notwithstanding 4.1.6.1.9 (b), non-refillable cylinders used may have a water capacity in litres not exceeding 1 000 litres divided by the test pressure expressed in bars provided capacity and pressure restrictions of the construction standard comply with clause 1 of ISO 11118:2015 + Amd 1:2019, which limits the maximum capacity to 50 litres.

PP97 For fire extinguishing agents assigned to UN 3500 the maximum test period for periodic inspection shall be 10 years. They may be transported in tubes of a maximum water capacity of 450 *l* conforming to the applicable requirements of chapter 6.2.

P207	PACKING INSTRUCTION	P207

This instruction applies to UN 1950.

The following packagings are authorized, provided that the general provisions of **4.1.1** and **4.1.3** are met:

(a) Drums (1A1, 1A2, 1B1, 1B2, 1N1, 1N2, 1H1, 1H2, 1D, 1G);

   Boxes (4A, 4B, 4N, 4C1, 4C2, 4D, 4F, 4G, 4H1, 4H2).

   Packagings shall conform to the packing group II performance level.

(b) Rigid outer packagings with a maximum net mass as follows:

   Fibreboard: 55 kg

   Other than fibreboard: 125 kg

   The provisions of 4.1.1.3 need not be met.

The packagings shall be designed and constructed to prevent excessive movement of the aerosols and inadvertent discharge during normal conditions of transport.

Special packing provision:

PP87 For UN 1950 waste aerosols transported in accordance with special provision 327, the packagings shall have a means of retaining any free liquid that might escape during transport, e.g. absorbent material. The packagings shall be adequately ventilated to prevent the creation of dangerous atmospheres and the build-up of pressure.

P208	PACKING INSTRUCTION	P208
	This instruction applies to Class 2 adsorbed gases.	

(1) The following packagings are authorized provided the general packing requirements of **4.1.6.1** are met:

    (a) Cylinders constructed as specified in 6.2.2 and in accordance with ISO 11513:2011, ISO 11513:2019, ISO 9809-1:2010 or ISO 9809-1:2019; and

    (b) Cylinders constructed before 1 January 2016 in accordance with 6.2.3 and a specification approved by the competent authorities of the countries of transport and use.

(2) The pressure of each filled cylinder shall be less than 101.3 kPa at 20 °C and less than 300 kPa at 50 °C.

(3) The minimum test pressure of the cylinder shall be 21 bar.

(4) The minimum burst pressure of the cylinder shall be 94.5 bar.

(5) The internal pressure at 65 °C of the filled cylinder shall not exceed the test pressure of the cylinder.

(6) The adsorbent material shall be compatible with the cylinder and shall not form harmful or dangerous compounds with the gas to be adsorbed. The gas in combination with the adsorbent material shall not affect or weaken the cylinder or cause a dangerous reaction (e.g. a catalyzing reaction).

(7) The quality of the adsorbent shall be verified at the time of each fill to assure the pressure and chemical stability requirements of this packing instruction are met each time an adsorbed gas package is offered for transport.

(8) The adsorbent material shall not meet the criteria of any of the Classes or Divisions in these Regulations.

(9) Requirements for cylinders and closures containing toxic gases with an LC_{50} less than or equal to 200 ml/m^3 (ppm) (see table 1) shall be as follows:

    (a) Valve outlets shall be fitted with pressure retaining gas-tight plugs or caps having threads matching those of the valve outlets.

    (b) Each valve shall either be of the packless type with non-perforated diaphragm, or be of a type which prevents leakage through or past the packing.

    (c) Each cylinder and closure shall be tested for leakage after filling.

    (d) Each valve shall be capable of withstanding the test pressure of the cylinder and be directly connected to the cylinder by either a taper-thread or other means which meets the requirements of ISO 10692-2:2001.

Cylinders and valves shall not be fitted with a pressure relief device.

(10) Valve outlets for cylinders containing pyrophoric gases shall be fitted with gas-tight plugs or caps having threads matching those of the valve outlets.

(11) The filling procedure shall be in accordance with annex A of ISO 11513:2011 (applicable until 31 December 2024) or annex A of ISO 11513:2019.

(12) The maximum period for periodic inspections shall be 5 years.

(13) Special packing provisions that are specific to a substance (see table 1).

Material compatibility

    a: Aluminium alloy cylinders shall not be used.

    d: When steel cylinders are used, only those bearing the "H" mark in accordance with 6.2.2.7.4 (p) are permitted.

Gas specific provisions

    r: The filling of this gas shall be limited such that, if complete decomposition occurs, the pressure does not exceed two thirds of the test pressure of the cylinder.

Material compatibility for n.o.s. adsorbed gas entries

    z: The construction materials of the cylinders and their accessories shall be compatible with the contents and shall not react to form harmful or dangerous compounds therewith.

Cont'd on next page

P208	PACKING INSTRUCTION *(cont'd)*				P208
Table 1: ADSORBED GASES					
UN No.	Name and description	Class or Division	Subsidiary hazards	LC_{50} (ml/m^3)	Special packing provisions
3510	ADSORBED GAS, FLAMMABLE, N.O.S.	2.1			z
3511	ADSORBED GAS, N.O.S.	2.2			z
3512	ADSORBED GAS, TOXIC, N.O.S.	2.3		≤ 5000	z
3513	ADSORBED GAS, OXIDIZING, N.O.S.	2.2	5.1		z
3514	ADSORBED GAS, TOXIC, FLAMMABLE, N.O.S.	2.3	2.1	≤ 5000	z
3515	ADSORBED GAS, TOXIC, OXIDIZING, N.O.S.	2.3	5.1	≤ 5000	z
3516	ADSORBED GAS, TOXIC, CORROSIVE, N.O.S.	2.3	8	≤ 5000	z
3517	ADSORBED GAS, TOXIC, FLAMMABLE, CORROSIVE, N.O.S.	2.3	2.1, 8	≤ 5000	z
3518	ADSORBED GAS, TOXIC, OXIDIZING, CORROSIVE, N.O.S.	2.3	5.1, 8	≤ 5000	z
3519	BORON TRIFLUORIDE, ADSORBED	2.3	8	387	a
3520	CHLORINE, ADSORBED	2.3	5.1, 8	293	a
3521	SILICON TETRAFLUORIDE, ADSORBED	2.3	8	450	a
3522	ARSINE, ADSORBED	2.3	2.1	20	d
3523	GERMANE, ADSORBED	2.3	2.1	620	d, r
3524	PHOSPHORUS PENTAFLUORIDE, ADSORBED	2.3	8	190	
3525	PHOSPHINE, ADSORBED	2.3	2.1	20	d
3526	HYDROGEN SELENIDE, ADSORBED	2.3	2.1	2	

P300	PACKING INSTRUCTION	P300
This instruction applies to UN 3064.		
The following packagings are authorized, provided that the general provisions of **4.1.1** and **4.1.3** are met: Combination packagings consisting of inner metal cans of not more than 1 litre capacity each and outer wooden boxes (4C1, 4C2, 4D or 4F) containing not more than 5 litres of solution.		
Additional requirements: 1. Metal cans shall be completely surrounded with absorbent cushioning material. 2. Wooden boxes shall be completely lined with suitable material impervious to water and nitroglycerin.		

P301	PACKING INSTRUCTION	P301

This instruction applies to UN 3165.

The following packagings are authorized, provided that the general provisions of **4.1.1.1**, **4.1.1.2**, **4.1.1.4**, **4.1.1.5**, **4.1.1.6** and **4.1.3** are met:

(1) Aluminium pressure receptacle made from tubing and having welded heads.

Primary containment of the fuel within this receptacle shall consist of a welded aluminium bladder having a maximum internal volume of 46 litres.

The outer receptacle shall have a minimum design gauge pressure of 1 275 kPa and a minimum burst gauge pressure of 2 755 kPa.

Each receptacle shall be leak checked during manufacture and before shipment and shall be found leakproof.

The complete inner unit shall be securely packed in non-combustible cushioning material, such as vermiculite, in a strong outer tightly closed metal packaging which will adequately protect all fittings.

Maximum quantity of fuel per primary containment and package is 42 litres.

(2) Aluminium pressure receptacle.

Primary containment of the fuel within this receptacle shall consist of a welded vapour tight fuel compartment with an elastomeric bladder having a maximum internal volume of 46 litres.

The pressure receptacle shall have a minimum design gauge pressure of 2 680 kPa and a minimum burst pressure of 5 170 kPa.

Each receptacle shall be leak-checked during manufacture and before shipment and shall be securely packed in non-combustible cushioning material such as vermiculite, in a strong outer tightly closed metal packaging which will adequately protect all fittings.

Maximum quantity of fuel per primary containment and package is 42 litres.

P302	PACKING INSTRUCTION	P302

This instruction applies to UN 3269.

The following combination packagings are authorized, provided that the general provisions of **4.1.1** and **4.1.3** are met:

Outer packagings:

Drums (1A1, 1A2, 1B1, 1B2, 1N1, 1N2, 1H1, 1H2, 1D, 1G);

Boxes (4A, 4B, 4N, 4C1, 4C2, 4D, 4F, 4G, 4H1, 4H2);

Jerricans (3A1, 3A2, 3B1, 3B2, 3H1, 3H2);

Inner packagings:

The activator (organic peroxide) shall have a maximum quantity of 125 ml per inner packaging if liquid, and 500 g per inner packaging if solid.

The base material and the activator shall be each separately packed in inner packagings.

The components may be placed in the same outer packaging provided that they will not interact dangerously in the event of a leakage.

Packagings shall conform to the packing group II or III performance level according to the criteria for Class 3 applied to the base material.

P303	PACKING INSTRUCTION	P303

This instruction applies to UN 3555.

The following packagings are authorized, provided that the general provisions of **4.1.1** and **4.1.3** as well as **4.1.5.12** are met:

    Plastics drum non-removeable head (1H1) of maximum capacity 250 *l*.

Additional requirement:

    The packagings shall be transported in an upright position.

Special packing provision:

PP26   For UN 3555, packagings shall be lead free.

P400	PACKING INSTRUCTION	P400

The following packagings are authorized, provided that the general provisions of **4.1.1** and **4.1.3** are met:

(1)   Pressure receptacles, provided that the general provisions of 4.1.3.6 are met. They shall be made of steel and shall be subjected to an initial test and periodic tests every 10 years at a pressure of not less than 1MPa (10 bar) (gauge pressure). During transport, the liquid shall be under a layer of inert gas with a gauge pressure of not less than 20 kPa (0.2 bar).

(2)   Boxes (4A, 4B, 4N, 4C1, 4C2, 4D, 4F or 4G), drums (1A1, 1A2, 1B1, 1B2, 1N1, 1N2, 1D or 1G) or jerricans (3A1, 3A2, 3B1 or 3B2) enclosing hermetically sealed metal cans with inner packagings of glass or metal, with a capacity of not more than 1 litre each, having closures with gaskets. Inner packagings shall have threaded closures or closures physically held in place by any means capable of preventing back-off or loosening of the closure by impact or vibration during transport. Inner packagings shall be cushioned on all sides with dry, absorbent, non-combustible material in a quantity sufficient to absorb the entire contents. Inner packagings shall not be filled to more than 90 % of their capacity. Outer packagings shall have a maximum net mass of 125 kg.

(3)   Steel, aluminium or metal drums (1A1, 1A2, 1B1, 1B2, 1N1 or 1N2), jerricans (3A1, 3A2, 3B1 or 3B2) or boxes (4A, 4B or 4N) with a maximum net mass of 150 kg each with hermetically sealed inner metal cans not more than 4 litre capacity each, with closures fitted with gaskets. Inner packagings shall have threaded closures or closures physically held in place by any means capable of preventing back-off or loosening of the closure by impact or vibration during transport. Inner packagings shall be cushioned on all sides with dry, absorbent, non-combustible material in a quantity sufficient to absorb the entire contents. Each layer of inner packagings shall be separated by a dividing partition in addition to cushioning material. Inner packagings shall not be filled to more than 90 % of their capacity.

Special packing provision:

PP86   For UN Nos. 3392 and 3394, air shall be eliminated from the vapour space by nitrogen or other means.

P401	PACKING INSTRUCTION	P401

The following packagings are authorized, provided that the general provisions of **4.1.1** and **4.1.3** are met:

(1) Pressure receptacles, provided that the general provisions of 4.1.3.6 are met. They shall be made of steel and subjected to an initial test and periodic tests every 10 years at a pressure of not less than 0.6 MPa (6 bar) (gauge pressure). During transport, the liquid shall be under a layer of inert gas with a gauge pressure of not less than 20 kPa (0.2 bar).

(2) Combination packagings:

> Outer packagings:
>
>> Drums (1A1, 1A2, 1B1, 1B2, 1N1, 1N2, 1H1, 1H2, 1D, 1G);
>>
>> Boxes (4A, 4B, 4N, 4C1, 4C2, 4D, 4F, 4G, 4H1, 4H2);
>>
>> Jerricans (3A1, 3A2, 3B1, 3B2, 3H1, 3H2).
>
> Inner packagings:
>
>> Glass, metal or plastics which have threaded closures with a maximum capacity of 1 litre.

Each inner packaging shall be surrounded by inert cushioning and absorbent material in a quantity sufficient to absorb the entire contents.

The maximum net mass per outer packaging shall not exceed 30 kg.

P402	PACKING INSTRUCTION	P402

The following packagings are authorized, provided that the general provisions of **4.1.1** and **4.1.3** are met:

(1) Pressure receptacles, provided that the general provisions of 4.1.3.6 are met. They shall be made of steel and subjected to an initial test and periodic tests every 10 years at a pressure of not less than 0.6 MPa (6 bar) (gauge pressure). During transport, the liquid shall be under a layer of inert gas with a gauge pressure of not less than 20 kPa (0.2 bar).

(2) Combination packagings:

> Outer packagings:
>
>> Drums (1A1, 1A2, 1B1, 1B2, 1N1, 1N2, 1H1, 1H2, 1D, 1G);
>>
>> Boxes (4A, 4B, 4N, 4C1, 4C2, 4D, 4F, 4G, 4H1, 4H2);
>>
>> Jerricans (3A1, 3A2, 3B1, 3B2, 3H1, 3H2).
>
> Inner packagings with a maximum net mass as follows:
>
>> Glass: 10 kg
>>
>> Metal or plastics: 15 kg

Each inner packaging shall be fitted with threaded closures.

Each inner packaging shall be surrounded by inert cushioning and absorbent material in a quantity sufficient to absorb the entire contents.

The maximum net mass per outer packaging shall not exceed 125 kg.

(3) Steel drums (1A1) with a maximum capacity of 250 litres.

(4) Composite packagings consisting of plastics receptacle in a steel or aluminium drum (6HA1 or 6HB1) with a maximum capacity of 250 litres.

P403	PACKING INSTRUCTION	P403
The following packagings are authorized, provided that the general provisions of **4.1.1** and **4.1.3** are met:		

Combination packagings

Inner packagings	Outer packagings	Maximum net mass

Glass 2 kg
Plastic 15 kg
Metal 20 kg
Inner packagings shall be hermetically sealed (e.g. by taping or by threaded closures)
	Drums
	  steel (1A1, 1A2)
	  aluminium (1B1, 1B2)
	  other metal (1N1, 1N2)
	  plastics (1H1, 1H2)
	  plywood (1D)
	  fibre (1G)
	Boxes
	  steel (4A)
	  aluminium (4B)
	  other metal (4N)
	  natural wood (4C1)
	  natural wood with sift proof walls (4C2)
	  plywood (4D)
	  reconstituted wood (4F)
	  fibreboard (4G)
	  expanded plastics (4H1)
	  solid plastics (4H2)
	Jerricans
	  steel (3A1, 3A2)
	  aluminium (3B1, 3B2)
	  plastics (3H1, 3H2)
		
		400 kg
		400 kg
		400 kg
		400 kg
		400 kg
		400 kg
		
		400 kg
		400 kg
		400 kg
		250 kg
		250 kg
		250 kg
		125 kg
		125 kg
		60 kg
		250 kg
		
		120 kg
		120 kg
		120 kg

Single packagings	Maximum net mass

Drums
  steel (1A1, 1A2)
  aluminium (1B1, 1B2)
  metal other than steel or aluminium (1N1, 1N2)
  plastics (1H1, 1H2)
Jerricans
  steel (3A1, 3A2)
  aluminium (3B1, 3B2)
  plastics (3H1, 3H2)
Composite packagings
  plastics receptacle in steel or aluminium drums (6HA1 or 6HB1)
  plastics receptacle in fibre, plastics or plywood drums (6HG1, 6HH1 or 6HD1)
  plastics receptacle in steel, aluminium, wood, plywood, fibreboard or solid plastics boxes (6HA2, 6HB2, 6HC, 6HD2, 6HG2 or 6HH2)
	
	250 kg
	250 kg
	250 kg
	250 kg
	
	120 kg
	120 kg
	120 kg
	
	250 kg
	75 kg
	75 kg

Pressure receptacles, provided that the general provisions of 4.1.3.6 are met.

Special packing provision:
PP83 *Deleted*

P404	PACKING INSTRUCTION	P404

This instruction applies to pyrophoric solids: UN Nos.: 1383, 1854, 1855, 2005, 2008, 2441, 2545, 2546, 2846, 2881, 3200, 3391 and 3393.

The following packagings are authorized, provided that the general provisions of **4.1.1** and **4.1.3** are met:

(1) Combination packagings:

    Outer packagings:

        Drums (1A1, 1A2, 1B1, 1B2, 1N1, 1N2, 1H1, 1H2, 1D, 1G);

        Boxes (4A, 4B, 4N, 4C1, 4C2, 4D, 4F, 4G, 4H2).

    Inner packagings:

        Metal receptacles with a maximum net mass of 15 kg each. Inner packagings shall be hermetically sealed;

        Glass receptacles, with a maximum net mass of 1 kg each, having closures with gaskets, cushioned on all sides and contained in hermetically sealed metal cans.

    Outer packagings shall have a maximum net mass of 125 kg.

    Inner packagings shall have threaded closures or closures physically held in place by any means capable of preventing back-off or loosening of the closure by impact or vibration during transport.

(2) Metal packagings:

    Drums (1A1, 1A2, 1B1, 1B2, 1N1, 1N2);

    Jerricans (3A1, 3A2, 3B1, 3B2).

Maximum gross mass: 150 kg

(3) Composite packagings:

    Plastics receptacle in a steel or aluminium drum (6HA1 or 6HB1).

Maximum gross mass: 150 kg

(4) Pressure receptacles, provided that the general provisions of 4.1.3.6 are met.

Special packing provision:

PP86 For UN Nos. 3391 and 3393, air shall be eliminated from the vapour space by nitrogen or other means.

P405	PACKING INSTRUCTION	P405

This instruction applies to UN 1381.

The following packagings are authorized, provided that the general provisions of **4.1.1** and **4.1.3** are met:

(1) For UN 1381, phosphorus wet:

    (a) Combination packagings

    Outer packagings:

        Boxes (4A, 4B, 4N, 4C1, 4C2, 4D or 4F). Maximum net mass: 75 kg

    Inner packagings:

        (i) hermetically sealed metal cans, with a maximum net mass of 15 kg; or

        (ii) glass inner packagings cushioned on all sides with dry, absorbent, non-combustible material in a quantity sufficient to absorb the entire contents with a maximum net mass of 2 kg; or

    (b) Drums (1A1, 1A2, 1B1, 1B2, 1N1 or 1N2). Maximum net mass: 400 kg

        Jerricans (3A1 or 3B1). Maximum net mass: 120 kg.

These packagings shall be capable of passing the leakproofness test specified in 6.1.5.4 at the packing group II performance level.

(2) For UN 1381, dry phosphorus:

    (a) When fused, drums (1A2, 1B2 or 1N2) with a maximum net mass of 400 kg; or

    (b) In projectiles or hard cased articles when transported without Class 1 components as specified by the competent authority.

P406	PACKING INSTRUCTION	P406

The following packagings are authorized, provided that the general provisions of **4.1.1** and **4.1.3** are met:

(1) Combination packagings

   Outer packagings: (4C1, 4C2, 4D, 4F, 4G, 4H1, 4H2, 1G, 1D, 1H1, 1H2, 3H1 or 3H2)

   Inner packagings: water-resistant packagings.

(2) Plastics, plywood or fibreboard drums (1H2, 1D or 1G) or boxes (4A, 4B, 4N, 4C1, 4D, 4F, 4C2, 4G and 4H2) with a water-resistant inner bag, plastics film lining or water-resistant coating.

(3) Metal drums (1A1, 1A2, 1B1, 1B2, 1N1 or 1N2), plastics drums (1H1 or 1H2), metal jerricans (3A1, 3A2, 3B1 or 3B2), plastics jerricans (3H1 or 3H2), plastics receptacle in steel or aluminium drums (6HA1 or 6HB1), plastics receptacle in fibre, plastics or plywood drums (6HG1, 6HH1 or 6HD1), plastics receptacle in steel, aluminium, wood, plywood, fibreboard or solid plastics boxes (6HA2, 6HB2, 6HC, 6HD2, 6HG2 or 6HH2).

Additional requirements:

1. Packagings shall be designed and constructed to prevent the loss of water or alcohol content or the content of the phlegmatizer.
2. Packagings shall be so constructed and closed so as to avoid an explosive over pressure or pressure build-up of more than 300 kPa (3 bar).
3. The type of packaging and maximum permitted quantity per packaging are limited by the provisions of 2.1.3.6.

Special packing provisions:

PP24 UN Nos. 2852, 3364, 3365, 3366, 3367, 3368 and 3369 shall not be transported in quantities of more than 500 g per package.

PP25 UN 1347 shall not be transported in quantities of more than 15 kg per package.

PP26 For UN Nos. 1310, 1320, 1321, 1322, 1344, 1347, 1348, 1349, 1517, 2907, 3317, 3344 and 3376 packagings shall be lead free.

PP48 For UN 3474, metal packagings shall not be used. Packagings of other material with a small amount of metal, for example metal closures or other metal fittings such as those mentioned in 6.1.4, are not considered metal packagings.

PP78 UN 3370 shall not be transported in quantities of more than 11.5 kg per package.

PP80 For UN Nos. 2907 and 3344, packagings shall meet the packing group II performance level. Packagings meeting the test criteria of packing group I shall not be used.

P407	PACKING INSTRUCTION	P407

This instruction applies to UN Nos. 1331, 1944, 1945 and 2254.

The following packagings are authorized, provided that the general provisions of **4.1.1** and **4.1.3** are met:

Outer packagings:

   Drums (1A1, 1A2, 1B1, 1B2, 1N1, 1N2, 1H1, 1H2, 1D, 1G);

   Boxes (4A, 4B, 4N, 4C1, 4C2, 4D, 4F, 4G, 4H1, 4H2);

   Jerricans (3A1, 3A2, 3B1, 3B2, 3H1, 3H2).

Inner packagings:

   Matches shall be tightly packed in securely closed inner packagings to prevent accidental ignition under normal conditions of transport.

The maximum gross mass of the package shall not exceed 45 kg except for fibreboard boxes which shall not exceed 30 kg.

Packagings shall conform to the packing group III performance level.

Special packing provision:

PP27 UN 1331, Strike-anywhere matches shall not be packed in the same outer packaging with any other dangerous goods other than safety matches or wax Vesta matches, which shall be packed in separate inner packagings. Inner packagings shall not contain more than 700 strike-anywhere matches.

P408	PACKING INSTRUCTION	P408

This instruction applies to UN 3292.

The following packagings are authorized, provided that the general provisions of **4.1.1** and **4.1.3** are met:

(1) For cells:

      Drums (1A2, 1B2, 1N2, 1H2, 1D, 1G);

      Boxes (4A, 4B, 4N, 4C1, 4C2, 4D, 4F, 4G, 4H1, 4H2);

      Jerricans (3A2, 3B2, 3H2).

There shall be sufficient cushioning material to prevent contact between cells and between cells and the internal surfaces of the outer packaging and to ensure that no dangerous movement of the cells within the outer packaging occurs in transport.

Packagings shall conform to the packing group II performance level.

(2) Batteries may be transported unpacked or in protective enclosures (e.g. fully enclosed or wooden slatted crates). The terminals shall not support the weight of other batteries or materials packed with the batteries.

Packagings need not meet the requirements of 4.1.1.3.

NOTE: The packagings authorized may exceed a net mass of 400 kg (see 4.1.3.3).

Additional requirement:

Cells and batteries shall be protected against short circuit and shall be isolated in such a manner as to prevent short circuits.

P409	PACKING INSTRUCTION	P409

This instruction applies to UN Nos. 2956, 3242 and 3251.

The following packagings are authorized, provided that the general provisions of **4.1.1** and **4.1.3** are met:

(1) Fibre drum (1G) which may be fitted with a liner or coating; maximum net mass: 50 kg

(2) Combination packagings: Fibreboard box (4G) with a single inner plastic bag; maximum net mass 50 kg

(3) Combination packagings: Fibreboard box (4G) or fibre drum (1G) with inner plastic packagings each containing a maximum of 5 kg; maximum net mass: 25 kg

P410	PACKING INSTRUCTION		P410

P410	PACKING INSTRUCTION	P410

The following packagings are authorized, provided that the general provisions of **4.1.1** and **4.1.3** are met:

Combination packagings

Inner packagings		Outer packagings	Maximum net mass	
			Packing group II	Packing group III
Glass	10 kg	**Drums**		
Plastics [a]	30 kg	steel (1A1; 1A2)	400 kg	400 kg
Metal	40 kg	aluminium (1B1, 1B2)	400 kg	400 kg
Paper [a, b]	10 kg	other metal (1N1, 1N2)	400 kg	400 kg
Fibre [a, b]	10 kg	plastics (1H1, 1H2)	400 kg	400 kg
		plywood (1D)	400 kg	400 kg
		fibre (1G)[a]	400 kg	400 kg
		Boxes		
		steel (4A)	400 kg	400 kg
		aluminium (4B)	400 kg	400 kg
		other metal (4N)	400 kg	400 kg
		natural wood (4C1)	400 kg	400 kg
		natural wood with sift proof walls (4C2)	400 kg	400 kg
		plywood (4D)	400 kg	400 kg
		reconstituted wood (4F)	400 kg	400 kg
		fibreboard (4G)[a]	400 kg	400 kg
		expanded plastics (4H1)	60 kg	60 kg
		solid plastics (4H2)	400 kg	400 kg
		Jerricans		
		steel (3A1, 3A2)	120 kg	120 kg
		aluminium (3B1, 3B2)	120 kg	120 kg
		plastics (3H1, 3H2)	120 kg	120 kg

Single packagings

	Packing group II	Packing group III
Drums		
steel (1A1 or 1A2)	400 kg	400 kg
aluminium (1B1 or 1B2)	400 kg	400 kg
metal other than steel, or aluminium (1N1 or 1N2)	400 kg	400 kg
plastics (1H1 or 1H2)	400 kg	400 kg
Jerricans		
steel (3A1 or 3A2)	120 kg	120 kg
aluminium (3B1 or 3B2)	120 kg	120 kg
plastics (3H1 or 3H2)	120 kg	120 kg

[a]   *Packagings shall be siftproof.*

[b]   *These inner packagings shall not be used when the substances being transported may become liquid during transport (see 4.1.3.4).*

Cont'd on next page

P410	PACKING INSTRUCTION *(cont'd)*		P410
Single packagings *(cont'd)*		Maximum net mass	
		Packing group II	Packing group III
Boxes			
steel (4A)[c]		400 kg	400 kg
aluminium (4B)[c]		400 kg	400 kg
other metal (4N)[c]		400 kg	400 kg
natural wood (4C1)[c]		400 kg	400 kg
plywood (4D)[c]		400 kg	400 kg
reconstituted wood (4F)[c]		400 kg	400 kg
natural wood with sift proof walls (4C2)[c]		400 kg	400 kg
fibreboard (4G)[c]		400 kg	400 kg
solid plastics (4H2)[c]		400 kg	400 kg
Bags			
bags (5H3, 5H4, 5L3, 5M2)[c,d]		50 kg	50 kg
Composite packagings			
plastics receptacle in steel, aluminium, plywood, fibre or plastics drum (6HA1, 6HB1, 6HG1, 6HD1, or 6HH1)		400 kg	400 kg
plastics receptacle in steel or aluminium crate or box, wooden box, plywood box, fibreboard box or solid plastics box (6HA2, 6HB2, 6HC, 6HD2, 6HG2 or 6HH2)		75 kg	75 kg
glass receptacle in steel, aluminium, plywood or fibre drum (6PA1, 6PB1, 6PD1 or 6PG1) or in steel, aluminium, wooden, wickerwork hamper or fibreboard box (6PA2, 6PB2, 6PC, 6PD2, or 6PG2) or in expanded or solid plastics packaging (6PH1 or 6PH2)		75 kg	75 kg

Pressure receptacles, provided that the general provisions of 4.1.3.6 are met.

Special packing provisions:

PP39   For UN 1378, for metal packagings a venting device is required.

PP40   For UN Nos. 1326, 1352, 1358, 1437 and 1871, and for UN 3182, packing group II, bags are not allowed.

PP83   *Deleted*

[c]   *These packagings shall not be used when the substances being transported may become liquid during transport (see 4.1.3.4).*

[d]   *For packing group II substances, these packagings may only be used when transported in a closed cargo transport unit.*

P411	PACKING INSTRUCTION	P411

This instruction applies to UN 3270.

The following packagings are authorized, provided that the general provisions of **4.1.1** and **4.1.3** are met:
    Drums (1A2, 1B2, 1N2, 1H2, 1D, 1G);
    Boxes (4A, 4B, 4N, 4C1, 4C2, 4D, 4F, 4G, 4H1, 4H2);
    Jerricans (3A2, 3B2, 3H2);
provided that explosion is not possible by reason of increased internal pressure.

The maximum net mass shall not exceed 30 kg.

P412	PACKING INSTRUCTION	P412

This instruction applies to UN 3527

The following combination packagings are authorized, provided that the general provisions of **4.1.1** and **4.1.3** are met:

(1) Outer packagings:

    Drums (1A1, 1A2, 1B1, 1B2, 1N1, 1N2, 1H1, 1H2, 1D, 1G);

    Boxes (4A, 4B, 4N, 4C1, 4C2, 4D, 4F, 4G, 4H1, 4H2)

    Jerricans (3A1, 3A2, 3B1, 3B2, 3H1, 3H2);

(2) Inner packagings:

    (a) The activator (organic peroxide) shall have a maximum quantity of 125 ml per inner packaging if liquid, and 500 g per inner packaging if solid.

    (b) The base material and the activator shall be each separately packed in inner packagings.

The components may be placed in the same outer packaging provided that they will not interact dangerously in the event of a leakage.

Packagings shall conform to the packing group II or III performance level according to the criteria for Division 4.1 applied to the base material.

P500	PACKING INSTRUCTION	P500

This instruction applies to UN 3356.

The following packagings are authorized, provided that the general provisions of **4.1.1** and **4.1.3** are met:
    Drums (1A2, 1B2, 1N2, 1H2, 1D, 1G);
    Boxes (4A, 4B, 4N, 4C1, 4C2, 4D, 4F, 4G, 4H1, 4H2);
    Jerricans (3A2, 3B2, 3H2).

Packagings shall conform to the packing group II performance level.

The generator(s) shall be transported in a package which meets the following requirements when one generator in the package is actuated:

(a) Other generators in the package will not be actuated;

(b) Packaging material will not ignite; and

(c) The outside surface temperature of the completed package shall not exceed 100 °C.

P501	PACKING INSTRUCTION	P501

This instruction applies to UN 2015.

The following packagings are authorized, provided that the general provisions of **4.1.1** and **4.1.3** are met:

Combination packagings	Inner packaging maximum capacity	Outer packaging maximum net mass
Boxes (4A, 4B, 4N, 4C1, 4C2, 4D, 4H2) or drums (1A1, 1A2, 1B1, 1B2, 1N1, 1N2, 1H1, 1H2, 1D) or jerricans (3A1, 3A2, 3B1, 3B2, 3H1, 3H2) with glass, plastics or metal inner packagings	5 *l*	125 kg
Fibreboard boxes (4G) or fibre drums (1G), with plastics or metal inner packagings each in a plastics bag	2 *l*	50 kg
Single packagings		Maximum capacity

Single packagings	Maximum capacity
Drums	
steel (1A1)	250 *l*
aluminium (1B1)	250 *l*
metal other than steel or aluminium (1N1)	250 *l*
plastics (1H1)	250 *l*
Jerricans	
steel (3A1)	60 *l*
aluminium (3B1)	60 *l*
plastics (3H1)	60 *l*
Composite packagings	
plastics receptacle in steel or aluminium drum (6HA1, 6HB1)	250 *l*
plastics receptacle in fibre, plastics or plywood drum (6HG1, 6HH1, 6HD1)	250 *l*
plastics receptacle in steel or aluminium crate or box or plastic receptacle in wood, plywood, fibreboard or solid plastics box (6HA2, 6HB2, 6HC, 6HD2, 6HG2 or 6HH2)	60 *l*
glass receptacle in steel, aluminium, fibre or plywood drum (6PA1, 6PB1, 6PD1 or 6PG1) or in a steel, aluminium, wood or fibreboard box or in wickerwork hamper (6PA2, 6PB2, 6PC, 6PG2 or 6PD2) or in expanded or solid plastics packaging (6PH1 or 6PH2).	60 *l*

Additional requirements:

1. Packagings shall have a minimum ullage of 10 %.
2. Packagings shall be vented.

P502	PACKING INSTRUCTION	P502
The following packagings are authorized, provided that the general provisions of **4.1.1** and **4.1.3** are met:		

Combination packagings		
Inner packagings	**Outer packagings**	**Maximum net mass**
Glass 5 *l* Metal 5 *l* Plastic 5 *l*	**Drums** steel (1A1, 1A2) aluminium (1B1, 1B2) other metal (1N1, 1N2) plywood (1D) fibre (1G) plastics (1H1, 1H2) **Boxes** steel (4A) aluminium (4B) other metal (4N) natural wood (4C1) natural wood with sift proof walls (4C2) plywood (4D) reconstituted wood (4F) fibreboard (4G) expanded plastics (4H1) solid plastics (4H2)	 125 kg 125 kg 125 kg 125 kg 125 kg 125 kg 125 kg 125 kg 125 kg 125 kg 125 kg 125 kg 125 kg 125 kg 60 kg 125 kg
Single packagings		**Maximum capacity**
Drums steel (1A1) aluminium (1B1) plastics (1H1) **Jerricans** steel (3A1) aluminium (3B1) plastics (3H1) **Composite packagings** plastics receptacle in steel or aluminium drum (6HA1, 6HB1) plastics receptacle in fibre, plastics or plywood drum (6HG1, 6HH1, 6HD1) plastics receptacle in steel or aluminium crate or box or plastics receptacle in wood, plywood, fibreboard or solid plastics box (6HA2, 6HB2, 6HC, 6HD2, 6HG2 or 6HH2) glass receptacle in steel, aluminium, fibre or plywood drum (6PA1, 6PB1, 6PD1 or 6PG1) or in a steel, aluminium, wood or fibreboard box or in wickerwork hamper (6PA2, 6PB2, 6PC, 6PG2 or 6PD2) or in expanded or solid plastics packaging (6PH1 or 6PH2).		 250 *l* 250 *l* 250 *l* 60 *l* 60 *l* 60 *l* 250 *l* 250 *l* 60 *l* 60 *l*
Special packing provision:		
PP28 For UN 1873, parts of packagings which are in direct contact with perchloric acid shall be constructed of glass or plastics.		

P503	PACKING INSTRUCTION	P503
The following packagings are authorized, provided that the general provisions of **4.1.1** and **4.1.3** are met:		
Combination packagings		

Inner packagings		**Outer packagings**	**Maximum net mass**
Glass	5 kg	**Drums**	
Metal	5 kg	steel (1A1, 1A2)	125 kg
Plastic	5 kg	aluminium (1B1, 1B2)	125 kg
		other metal (1N1, 1N2)	125 kg
		plywood (1D)	125 kg
		fibre (1G)	125 kg
		plastics (1H1, 1H2)	125 kg
		Boxes	
		steel (4A)	125 kg
		aluminium (4B)	125 kg
		other metal (4N)	125 kg
		natural wood (4C1)	125 kg
		natural wood with sift proof walls (4C2)	125 kg
		plywood (4D)	125 kg
		reconstituted wood (4F)	125 kg
		fibreboard (4G)	40 kg
		expanded plastics (4H1)	60 kg
		solid plastics (4H2)	125 kg
Single packagings			
Drums			
Metal drums (1A1, 1A2, 1B1, 1B2, 1N1 or 1N2)			250 kg
Fibreboard (1G) or plywood drums (1D) fitted with inner liners			200 kg

P504	PACKING INSTRUCTION	P504
The following packagings are authorized, provided that the general provisions of **4.1.1** and **4.1.3** are met:		
Combination packagings		**Maximum net mass**
(1) Outer packagings: (1A1, 1A2, 1B1, 1B2, 1N1, 1N2, 1H1, 1H2, 1D, 1G, 4A, 4B, 4N, 4C1, 4C2, 4D, 4F, 4G, 4H2) Inner packagings: Glass receptacles with a maximum capacity of 5 litres		75 kg
(2) Outer packagings: (1A1, 1A2, 1B1, 1B2, 1N1, 1N2, 1H1, 1H2, 1D, 1G, 4A, 4B, 4N, 4C1, 4C2, 4D, 4F, 4G, 4H2) Inner packagings: Plastic receptacles with a maximum capacity of 30 litres		75 kg
(3) Outer packagings: 1G, 4F or 4G Inner packagings: Metal receptacles with a maximum capacity of 40 litres		125 kg
(4) Outer packagings: (1A1, 1A2, 1B1, 1B2, 1N1, 1N2, 1H1, 1H2, 1D, 4A, 4B, 4N, 4C1, 4C2, 4D, 4H2) Inner packagings: Metal receptacles with a maximum capacity of 40 litres		225 kg
Single packagings		**Maximum capacity**
Drums		
steel, non-removable head (1A1)		250 l
aluminium, non-removable head (1B1)		250 l
metal other than steel or aluminium, non-removable head (1N1)		250 l
plastics, non-removable head (1H1)		250 l
Jerricans		
steel non-removable head (3A1)		60 l
aluminium non-removable head (3B1)		60 l
plastics non-removable head (3H1)		60 l
Composite packagings		
plastics receptacle in steel or aluminium drum (6HA1, 6HB1)		250 l
plastics receptacle in fibre, plastics or plywood drum (6HG1, 6HH1, 6HD1)		120 l
plastics receptacle in steel or aluminium crate or box or plastic receptacle in wood, plywood, fibreboard or solid plastics box (6HA2, 6HB2, 6HC, 6HD2, 6HG2 or 6HH2)		60 l
glass receptacle in steel, aluminium, fibre or plywood drum (6PA1, 6PB1, 6PD1 or 6PG1) or in a steel, aluminium, wood or fibreboard box or in wickerwork hamper (6PA2, 6PB2, 6PC, 6PG2 or 6PD2) or in expanded or solid plastics packaging (6PH1 or 6PH2).		60 l
Special packing provision:		
PP10 For UN Nos. 2014 and 3149, the packaging shall be vented.		

P505	PACKING INSTRUCTION	P505
This instruction applies to UN 3375		
The following packagings are authorized, provided that the general provisions of **4.1.1** and **4.1.3** are met:		

		Maximum capacity/maximum net mass
Combination packagings		
Inner packagings	**Outer packagings**	
glass 5 *l* plastics 5 *l* metal 5 *l*	**Boxes** aluminium (4B) natural wood, ordinary (4C1) natural wood, sift-proof walls (4C2) plywood (4D) fibreboard (4G) plastics, solid (4H2)	125 kg 125 kg 125 kg 125 kg 125 kg 125 kg
	Drums aluminium, removable head (1B2) fibre (1G) other metal, removable head (1N2) plastics, removable head (1H2) plywood (1D)	125 kg 125 kg 125 kg 125 kg 125 kg
	Jerricans aluminium, removable head (3B2) plastics, removable head (3H2)	125 kg 125 kg
Single packagings		
Drums aluminium (1B1, 1B2) plastics (1H1, 1H2)		250 *l* 250 *l*
Jerricans aluminium (3B1, 3B2) plastics (3H1, 3H2)		60 *l* 60 *l*
Composite packagings plastics receptacle with outer aluminium drum (6HB1) plastics receptacle with outer fibre, plastics or plywood drum (6HG1, 6HH1, 6HD1) plastics receptacle with outer aluminium crate or box or plastics receptacle with outer wooden, plywood, fibreboard or solid plastics box (6HB2, 6HC, 6HD2, 6HG2 or 6HH2) glass receptacle with outer aluminium, fibre or plywood drum (6PB1, 6PG1, 6PD1) or with outer expanded plastics or solid plastics receptacles (6PH1 or 6PH2) or with outer aluminium crate or box or with outer wooden or fibreboard box or with outer wickerwork hamper (6PB2, 6PC, 6PG2 or 6PD2)		250 *l* 250 *l* 60 *l* 60 *l*

P520	PACKING INSTRUCTION	P520

This instruction applies to organic peroxides of Division 5.2 and self-reactive substances of Division 4.1

The packagings listed below are authorized provided that the general provisions of **4.1.1** and **4.1.3** and special provisions of **4.1.7** are met.

The packing methods are designated OP1 to OP8. The packing methods appropriate for the individual currently assigned organic peroxides and self-reactive substances are listed in 2.4.2.3.2.3 and 2.5.3.2.4.

The quantities specified for each packing method are the maximum quantities authorized per package. The following packagings are authorized:

(1) Combination packagings with outer packagings comprising boxes (4A, 4B, 4N, 4C1, 4C2, 4D, 4F, 4G, 4H1 and 4H2), drums (1A1, 1A2, 1B1, 1B2, 1G, 1H1, 1H2 and 1D) and jerricans (3A1, 3A2, 3B1, 3B2, 3H1 and 3H2);

(2) Single packagings consisting of drums (1A1, 1A2, 1B1, 1B2, 1G, 1H1, 1H2 and 1D) and jerricans (3A1, 3A2, 3B1, 3B2, 3H1 and 3H2);

(3) Composite packagings with plastics inner receptacles (6HA1, 6HA2, 6HB1, 6HB2, 6HC, 6HD1, 6HD2, 6HG1, 6HG2, 6HH1 and 6HH2).

The maximum quantities per packaging/package for packing methods OP1 to OP8 are:

	OP1	OP2[a]	OP3	OP4[a]	OP5	OP6	OP7	OP8
Maximum net mass (kg) for solids and for combination packagings (liquid and solid)	0.5	0.5/10	5	5/25	25	50	50	400[b]
Maximum contents in litres for liquids[c]	0.5	-	5	-	30	60	60	225[d]

Additional requirements:

1. Metal packagings, including inner packagings of combination packagings and outer packagings of combination or composite packagings may only be used for packing methods OP7 and OP8;

2. In combination packagings, glass receptacles may only be used as inner packagings with a maximum content of 0.5 kg for solids or 0.5 litre for liquids.

3. In combination packagings, cushioning materials shall not be readily combustible.

4. The packaging of an organic peroxide or self-reactive substance required to bear an "EXPLOSIVE" subsidiary hazard label (Model No.1, see 5.2.2.2.2) shall also comply with the provisions given in 4.1.5.10 and 4.1.5.11.

Special packing provisions:

PP21 For certain self-reactive substances of types B or C (UN Nos. 3221, 3222, 3223, 3224, 3231, 3232, 3233 and 3234), a smaller packaging than that allowed by packing methods OP5 or OP6 respectively shall be used (see 4.1.7 and 2.4.2.3.2.3).

PP22 UN 3241, 2-Bromo-2-nitropropane-1,3-diol, shall be packed in accordance with packing method OP6.

[a] *If two values are given, the first applies to the maximum net mass per inner packaging and the second to the maximum net mass of the complete package.*

[b] *60 kg for jerricans/200 kg for boxes and, for solids, 400 kg in combination packagings with outer packagings comprising boxes (4C1, 4C2, 4D, 4F, 4G, 4H1 and 4H2) and with inner packagings of plastics or fibre with a maximum net mass of 25 kg.*

[c] *Viscous liquids shall be treated as solids when they do not meet the criteria provided in the definition for "liquids" presented in 1.2.1.*

[d] *60 litres for jerricans.*

Cont'd on next page

P520	PACKING INSTRUCTION *(cont'd)*	P520

Special packing provisions: *(Cont'd)*

PP94 Very small amounts of energetic samples of section 2.0.4.3 may be carried under UN Nos. 3223 or 3224, as appropriate, provided that:

    (a) Only combination packaging with outer packaging comprising boxes (4A, 4B, 4N, 4C1, 4C2, 4D, 4F, 4G, 4H1 and 4H2) are used;

    (b) The samples are carried in microtiter plates or multi-titer plates made of plastics, glass, porcelain or stoneware as inner packaging;

    (c) The maximum amount per individual inner cavity does not exceed 0.01 g for solids or 0.01 ml for liquids;

    (d) The maximum net quantity per outer packaging is 20 g for solids or 20 ml for liquids, or in the case of mixed packing the sum of grams and millilitres does not exceed 20; and

    (e) When dry ice or liquid nitrogen is optionally used as a coolant for quality control measures, the requirements of 5.5.3 are complied with. Interior supports shall be provided to secure the inner packagings in their original position. The inner and outer packagings shall maintain their integrity at the temperature of the refrigerant used as well as the temperatures and the pressures which could result if refrigeration were lost.

PP95 Small amounts of energetic samples of section 2.0.4.3 may be carried under UN Nos. 3223 or 3224, as appropriate, provided that:

    (a) The outer packaging consist only of corrugated fibreboard of type 4G having minimum dimensions of 60 cm (length) by 40.5 cm (width) by 30 cm (height) and minimum wall thickness of 1.3 cm;

    (b) The individual substance is contained in an inner packaging of glass or plastics of maximum capacity 30 ml placed in an expandable polyethylene foam matrix of at least 130 mm thickness having a density of 18 ± 1 g/l;

    (c) Within the foam carrier, inner packagings are segregated from each other by a minimum distance of 40 mm and from the wall of the outer packaging by a minimum distance of 70 mm. The package may contain up to two layers of such foam matrices, each carrying up to 28 inner packagings;

    (d) The maximum content of each inner packaging does not exceed 1 g for solids or 1 ml for liquids;

    (e) The maximum net quantity per outer packaging is 56 g for solids or 56 ml for liquids, or in the case of mixed packing the sum of grams and millilitres does not exceed 56; and

    (f) When dry ice or liquid nitrogen is optionally used as a coolant for quality control measures, the requirements of 5.5.3 are complied with. Interior supports shall be provided to secure the inner packagings in their original position. The inner and outer packagings shall maintain their integrity at the temperature of the refrigerant used as well as the temperatures and the pressures which could result if refrigeration were lost.

P600	PACKING INSTRUCTION	P600

This instruction applies to UN Nos. 1700, 2016 and 2017.

The following packagings are authorized, provided that the general provisions of **4.1.1** and **4.1.3** are met:

    Drums (1A1, 1A2, 1B1, 1B2, 1N1, 1N2, 1H1, 1H2, 1D, 1G);

    Boxes (4A, 4B, 4N, 4C1, 4C2, 4D, 4F, 4G, 4H2).

Outer packagings shall meet the packing group II performance level.

Articles shall be individually packaged and separated from each other using partitions, dividers, inner packagings or cushioning material to prevent inadvertent discharge during normal conditions of transport.

Maximum net mass: 75 kg

| P601 | **PACKING INSTRUCTION** | P601 |

The following packagings are authorized provided that the general provisions of **4.1.1** and **4.1.3** are met and the packagings are hermetically sealed:

(1) Combination packagings with a maximum gross mass of 15 kg, consisting of

    (a) one or more glass inner packaging(s) with a maximum net quantity of 1 litre each and filled to not more than 90 % of their capacity; the closure(s) of which shall be physically held in place by any means capable of preventing back-off or loosening by impact or vibration during transport, individually placed in

    (b) metal receptacles together with cushioning and absorbent material sufficient to absorb the entire contents of the glass inner packaging(s), further packed in

    (c) 1A1, 1A2, 1B1, 1B2, 1N1, 1N2, 1H1, 1H2, 1D, 1G, 4A, 4B, 4N, 4C1, 4C2, 4D, 4F, 4G or 4H2 outer packagings.

(2) Combination packagings consisting of metal or plastics inner packagings not exceeding 5 litres in capacity individually packed with absorbent material sufficient to absorb the contents and inert cushioning material in 1A1, 1A2, 1B1, 1B2, 1N1, 1N2, 1H1, 1H2, 1D, 1G, 4A, 4B, 4N, 4C1, 4C2, 4D, 4F, 4G or 4H2 outer packagings with a maximum gross mass of 75 kg. Inner packagings shall not be filled to more than 90 % of their capacity. The closure of each inner packaging shall be physically held in place by any means capable of preventing back-off or loosening of the closure by impact or vibration during transport.

(3) Packagings consisting of:

Outer packagings: Steel or plastics drums (1A1, 1A2, 1H1 or 1H2), tested in accordance with the test requirements in 6.1.5 at a mass corresponding to the mass of the assembled package either as a packaging intended to contain inner packagings, or as a single packaging intended to contain solids or liquids, and marked accordingly.

Inner packagings: Drums and composite packagings (1A1, 1B1, 1N1, 1H1 or 6HA1), meeting the requirements of chapter 6.1 for single packagings), subject to the following conditions:

    (a) The hydraulic pressure test shall be conducted at a pressure of at least 3 bar (gauge pressure);

    (b) The design and production leakproofness tests shall be conducted at a test pressure of 0.30 bar;

    (c) They shall be isolated from the outer drum by the use of inert shock-mitigating cushioning material which surrounds the inner packaging on all sides;

    (d) Their capacity shall not exceed 125 litres; and

    (e) Closures shall be of a screw cap type that are:

        (i) physically held in place by any means capable of preventing back-off or loosening of the closure by impact or vibration during transport; and

        (ii) provided with a cap seal.

    (f) The outer and inner packagings shall be subjected periodically to a leakproofness test according to (b) at intervals of not more than two and a half years; and

    (g) The outer and inner packagings shall bear in clearly legible and durable characters:

        (i) the date (month, year) of the initial testing and the latest periodical test;

        (ii) the name or authorized symbol of the party performing the tests and inspections.

(4) Pressure receptacles, provided that the general provisions of **4.1.3.6** are met. They shall be subjected to an initial test and periodic tests every 10 years at a pressure of not less than 1 MPa (10 bar) (gauge pressure). Pressure receptacles may not be equipped with any pressure relief device. Each pressure receptacle containing a toxic by inhalation liquid with an LC_{50} less than or equal to 200 ml/m^3 (ppm) shall be closed with a plug or valve conforming to the following:

    (a) Each plug or valve shall have a taper-threaded connection directly to the pressure receptacle and be capable of withstanding the test pressure of the pressure receptacle without damage or leakage;

    (b) Each valve shall be of the packless type with non-perforated diaphragm, except that, for corrosive substances, a valve may be of the packed type with an assembly made gas-tight by means of a seal cap with gasket joint attached to the valve body or the pressure receptacle to prevent loss of substance through or past the packing;

    (c) Each valve outlet shall be sealed by a threaded cap or threaded solid plug and inert gasket material;

    (d) The materials of construction for the pressure receptacle, valves, plugs, outlet caps, luting and gaskets shall be compatible with each other and with the contents.

Each pressure receptacle with a wall thickness at any point of less than 2.0 mm and each pressure receptacle which does not have fitted valve protection shall be transported in an outer packaging. Pressure receptacles shall not be manifolded or interconnected.

| P602 | **PACKING INSTRUCTION** | P602 |

The following packagings are authorised provided that the general provisions of **4.1.1** and **4.1.3** are met and the packagings are hermetically sealed:

(1) Combination packagings with a maximum gross mass of 15 kg, consisting of

    (a) one or more glass inner packaging(s) with a maximum net quantity of 1 litre each and filled to not more than 90 % of their capacity; the closure(s) of which shall be physically held in place by any means capable of preventing back-off or loosening by impact or vibration during transport, individually placed in

    (b) metal receptacles together with cushioning and absorbent material sufficient to absorb the entire contents of the glass inner packaging(s), further packed in

    (c) 1A1, 1A2, 1B1, 1B2, 1N1, 1N2, 1H1, 1H2, 1D, 1G, 4A, 4B, 4N, 4C1, 4C2, 4D, 4F, 4G or 4H2 outer packagings.

(2) Combination packagings consisting of metal or plastics inner packagings individually packed with absorbent material sufficient to absorb the contents and inert cushioning material in 1A1, 1A2, 1B1, 1B2, 1N1, 1N2, 1H1, 1H2, 1D, 1G, 4A, 4B, 4N, 4C1, 4C2, 4D, 4F, 4G or 4H2 outer packagings with a maximum gross mass of 75 kg. Inner packagings shall not be filled to more than 90 % of their capacity. The closure of each inner packaging shall be physically held in place by any means capable of preventing back-off or loosening of the closure by impact or vibration during transport. Inner packagings shall not exceed 5 litres in capacity.

(3) Drums and composite packagings (1A1, 1B1, 1N1, 1H1, 6HA1 or 6HH1), subject to the following conditions:

    (a) The hydraulic pressure test shall be conducted at a pressure of at least 3 bar (gauge pressure);

    (b) The design and production leakproofness tests shall be conducted at a test pressure of 0.30 bar; and

    (c) Closures shall be of a screw cap type that are:

        (i) physically held in place by any means capable of preventing back-off or loosening of the closure by impact or vibration during transport; and

        (ii) provided with a cap seal.

(4) Pressure receptacles, provided that the general provisions of 4.1.3.6 are met. They shall be subjected to an initial test and periodic tests every 10 years at a pressure of not less than 1 MPa (10 bar) (gauge pressure). Pressure receptacles may not be equipped with any pressure relief device. Each pressure receptacle containing a toxic by inhalation liquid with an LC_{50} less than or equal to 200 ml/m^3 (ppm) shall be closed with a plug or valve conforming to the following:

    (a) Each plug or valve shall have a taper-threaded connection directly to the pressure receptacle and be capable of withstanding the test pressure of the pressure receptacle without damage or leakage;

    (b) Each valve shall be of the packless type with non-perforated diaphragm, except that, for corrosive substances, a valve may be of the packed type with an assembly made gas-tight by means of a seal cap with gasket joint attached to the valve body or the pressure receptacle to prevent loss of substance through or past the packing;

    (c) Each valve outlet shall be sealed by a threaded cap or threaded solid plug and inert gasket material;

    (d) The materials of construction for the pressure receptacle, valves, plugs, outlet caps, luting and gaskets shall be compatible with each other and with the contents.

Each pressure receptacle with a wall thickness at any point of less than 2.0 mm and each pressure receptacle which does not have fitted valve protection shall be transported in an outer packaging. Pressure receptacles shall not be manifolded or interconnected.

P603	PACKING INSTRUCTION	P603

This instruction applies to UN 3507.

The following packagings are authorized provided that the general provisions of **4.1.1** and **4.1.3** and the special packing provisions of **4.1.9.1.2, 4.1.9.1.4** and **4.1.9.1.7** are met:

Packagings consisting of:

(a) Metal or plastics primary receptacle(s); in

(b) Leakproof rigid secondary packaging(s); in

(c) A rigid outer packaging:

    Drums (1A2, 1B2, 1N2, 1H2, 1D, 1G);

    Boxes (4A, 4B, 4C1, 4C2, 4D, 4F, 4G, 4H1, 4H2);

    Jerricans (3A2, 3B2, 3H2).

Additional requirements:

1. Primary inner receptacles shall be packed in secondary packagings in a way that, under normal conditions of transport, they cannot break, be punctured or leak their contents into the secondary packaging. Secondary packagings shall be secured in outer packagings with suitable cushioning material to prevent movement. If multiple primary receptacles are placed in a single secondary packaging, they shall be either individually wrapped or separated so as to prevent contact between them;

2. The contents shall comply with the provisions of 2.7.2.4.5.2;

3. The provisions of 6.4.4 shall be met.

4. In the case of fissile-excepted material, limits specified in 2.7.2.3.5 shall be met.

P620	PACKING INSTRUCTION	P620

This instruction applies to UN Nos. 2814 and 2900.

The following packagings are authorized provided that the special packing provisions of **4.1.8** are met:

Packagings meeting the requirements of chapter 6.3 and approved accordingly consisting of:

(a) Inner packagings comprising:

    (i) leakproof primary receptacle(s);

    (ii) a leakproof secondary packaging;

    (iii) other than for solid infectious substances, an absorbent material in sufficient quantity to absorb the entire contents placed between the primary receptacle(s) and the secondary packaging; if multiple primary receptacles are placed in a single secondary packaging, they shall be either individually wrapped or separated so as to prevent contact between them;

(b) A rigid outer packaging:

    Drums (1A1, 1A2, 1B1, 1B2, 1N1, 1N2, 1H1, 1H2, 1D, 1G);

    Boxes (4A, 4B, 4N, 4C1, 4C2, 4D, 4F, 4G, 4H1, 4H2);

    Jerricans (3A1, 3A2, 3B1, 3B2, 3H1, 3H2).

The smallest external dimension shall be not less than 100 mm.

Additional requirements:

1. Inner packagings containing infectious substances shall not be consolidated with inner packagings containing unrelated types of goods. Complete packages may be overpacked in accordance with the provisions of 1.2.1 and 5.1.2: such an overpack may contain dry ice. When dry ice or other refrigerants presenting a risk of asphyxiation are used as a coolant, the requirements of 5.5.3 shall apply.

2. Other than for exceptional consignments, e.g. whole organs which require special packaging, the following additional requirements shall apply:

    (a) Substances consigned at ambient temperatures or at a higher temperature. Primary receptacles shall be of glass, metal or plastics. Positive means of ensuring a leakproof seal shall be provided, e.g. a heat seal, a skirted stopper or a metal crimp seal. If screw caps are used, they shall be secured by positive means, e.g., tape, paraffin sealing tape or manufactured locking closure;

    (b) Substances consigned refrigerated or frozen. Ice, dry ice or other refrigerant shall be placed around the secondary packaging(s) or alternatively in an overpack with one or more complete packages marked in accordance with 6.3.3. Interior supports shall be provided to secure secondary packaging(s) or packages in position after the ice or dry ice has dissipated. When dry ice or other refrigerants presenting a risk of asphyxiation are used as a coolant, the requirements of 5.5.3 shall apply. If ice is used, the outer packaging or overpack shall be leakproof. If dry ice is used, the outer packaging or overpack shall permit the release of carbon dioxide gas. The primary receptacle and the secondary packaging shall maintain their integrity at the temperature of the refrigerant used;

    (c) Substances consigned in liquid nitrogen. When liquid nitrogen is used as a coolant, the requirements of 5.5.3 shall apply. Plastics primary receptacles capable of withstanding very low temperature shall be used. The secondary packaging shall also be capable of withstanding very low temperatures, and in most cases will need to be fitted over the primary receptacle individually. Provisions for the consignment of liquid nitrogen shall also be fulfilled. The primary receptacle and the secondary packaging shall maintain their integrity at the temperature of the liquid nitrogen;

    (d) Lyophilized substances may also be transported in primary receptacles that are flame-sealed glass ampoules or rubber-stoppered glass vials fitted with metal seals.

3. Whatever the intended temperature of the consignment, the primary receptacle or the secondary packaging shall be capable of withstanding without leakage an internal pressure producing a pressure differential of not less than 95 kPa. This primary receptacle or secondary packaging shall also be capable of withstanding temperatures in the range -40 °C to +55 °C.

4. Other dangerous goods shall not be packed in the same packaging as Division 6.2 infectious substances unless they are necessary for maintaining the viability, stabilizing or preventing degradation or neutralizing the hazards of the infectious substances. A quantity of 30 ml or less of dangerous goods included in Classes 3, 8 or 9 may be packed in each primary receptacle containing infectious substances. These small quantities of dangerous goods of Classes 3, 8 or 9 are not subject to any additional requirements of these Regulations when packed in accordance with this packing instruction.

5. Alternative packagings for the transport of animal material may be authorized by the competent authority in accordance with the provisions of 4.1.3.7.

P621	PACKING INSTRUCTION	P621
This instruction applies to UN 3291.			

The following packagings are authorized provided that the general provisions of **4.1.1** except 4.1.1.15 and **4.1.3** are met:

(1) Provided that there is sufficient absorbent material to absorb the entire amount of liquid present and the packaging is capable of retaining liquids:

　　Drums (1A1, 1A2, 1B1, 1B2, 1N1, 1N2, 1H1, 1H2, 1D, 1G);

　　Boxes (4A, 4B, 4N, 4C1, 4C2, 4D, 4F, 4G, 4H1, 4H2);

　　Jerricans (3A1, 3A2, 3B1, 3B2, 3H1, 3H2).

Packagings shall conform to the packing group II performance level for solids.

(2) For packages containing larger quantities of liquid:

　　Drums (1A1, 1A2, 1B1, 1B2, 1N1, 1N2, 1H1, 1H2, 1D, 1G);

　　Jerricans (3A1, 3A2, 3B1, 3B2, 3H1, 3H2);

　　Composites (6HA1, 6HB1, 6HG1, 6HH1, 6HD1, 6HA2, 6HB2, 6HC, 6HD2, 6HG2, 6HH2, 6PA1, 6PB1, 6PG1, 6PD1, 6PH1, 6PH2, 6PA2, 6PB2, 6PC, 6PG2 or 6PD2).

Packagings shall conform to the packing group II performance level for liquids.

Additional requirement:

Packagings intended to contain sharp objects such as broken glass and needles shall be resistant to puncture and retain liquids under the performance test conditions in chapter 6.1.

| P622 | PACKING INSTRUCTION | P622 |

This instruction applies to waste of UN 3549 transported for disposal.

The following packagings are authorized provided the general provisions of **4.1.1** and **4.1.3** are met:

Inner packagings	Intermediate packagings	Outer packagings
metal plastics	metal plastics	**Boxes** steel (4A) aluminium (4B) other metal (4N) plywood (4D) fibreboard (4G) plastics, solid (4H2) **Drums** steel (1A2) aluminium (1B2) other metal (1N2) plywood (1D) fibre (1G) plastics (1H2) **Jerricans** steel (3A2) aluminium (3B2) plastics (3H2)

The outer packaging shall conform to the packing group I performance level for solids.

Additional requirements:

1. Fragile articles shall be contained in either a rigid inner packaging or a rigid intermediate packaging.
2. Inner packagings containing sharp objects such as broken glass and needles shall be rigid and resistant to puncture.
3. The inner packaging, the intermediate packaging, and the outer packaging shall be capable of retaining liquids. Outer packagings that are not capable of retaining liquids by design shall be fitted with a liner or suitable measure of retaining liquids.
4. The inner packaging and/or the intermediate packaging may be flexible. When flexible packagings are used, they shall be capable of passing the impact resistance test of at least 165 g according to ISO 7765-1:1988 "Plastics film and sheeting – Determination of impact resistance by the free-falling dart method – Part 1: Staircase methods" and the tear resistance test of at least 480 g in both parallel and perpendicular planes with respect to the length of the bag in accordance with ISO 6383-2:1983 "Plastics – Film and sheeting – Determination of tear resistance – Part 2: Elmendorf method". The maximum net mass of each flexible inner packaging shall be 30kg.
5. Each flexible intermediate packaging shall contain only one inner packaging.
6. Inner packagings containing a small amount of free liquid may be included in intermediate packaging provided that there is sufficient absorbent or solidifying material in the inner or intermediate packaging to absorb or solidify all the liquid content present. Suitable absorbent material which withstands the temperatures and vibrations liable to occur under normal conditions of transport shall be used.
7. Intermediate packagings shall be secured in outer packagings with suitable cushioning and/or absorbent material.

| P650 | **PACKING INSTRUCTION** | P650 |

This instruction applies to UN 3373.

(1) The packaging shall be of good quality, strong enough to withstand the shocks and loadings normally encountered during transport, including transhipment between cargo transport units and between cargo transport units and warehouses as well as any removal from a pallet or overpack for subsequent manual or mechanical handling. Packagings shall be constructed and closed to prevent any loss of contents that might be caused under normal conditions of transport by vibration or by changes in temperature, humidity or pressure.

(2) The packaging shall consist of at least three components:

    (a) a primary receptacle;

    (b) a secondary packaging; and

    (c) an outer packaging

of which either the secondary or the outer packaging shall be rigid.

(3) Primary receptacles shall be packed in secondary packagings in such a way that, under normal conditions of transport, they cannot break, be punctured or leak their contents into the secondary packaging. Secondary packagings shall be secured in outer packagings with suitable cushioning material. Any leakage of the contents shall not compromise the integrity of the cushioning material or of the outer packaging.

(4) For transport, the mark illustrated below shall be displayed on the external surface of the outer packaging on a background of a contrasting colour and shall be clearly visible and legible. The mark shall be in the form of a square set at an angle of 45° (diamond-shaped) with each side having a length of at least 50 mm; the width of the line shall be at least 2 mm and the letters and numbers shall be at least 6 mm high. The proper shipping name "BIOLOGICAL SUBSTANCE, CATEGORY B" in letters at least 6 mm high shall be marked on the outer packaging adjacent to the diamond-shaped mark.

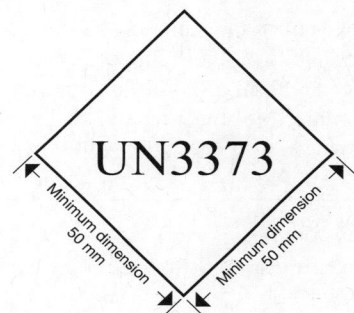

(5) At least one surface of the outer packaging shall have a minimum dimension of 100 mm × 100 mm.

(6) The completed package shall be capable of withstanding a 1.2 m drop in any orientation without leakage from the primary receptacle(s), which shall remain protected by absorbent material, when required, in the secondary packaging.

NOTE: Capability may be demonstrated by testing, assessment or experience.

(7) For liquid substances

    (a) The primary receptacle(s) shall be leakproof;

    (b) The secondary packaging shall be leakproof;

    (c) If multiple fragile primary receptacles are placed in a single secondary packaging, they shall be either individually wrapped or separated to prevent contact between them;

    (d) Absorbent material shall be placed between the primary receptacle(s) and the secondary packaging. The absorbent material shall be in quantity sufficient to absorb the entire contents of the primary receptacle(s) so that any release of the liquid substance will not compromise the integrity of the cushioning material or of the outer packaging; and

    (e) The primary receptacle or the secondary packaging shall be capable of withstanding, without leakage, an internal pressure of 95 kPa (0.95 bar).

NOTE: Capability may be demonstrated by testing, assessment or experience.

Cont'd on next page

P650	PACKING INSTRUCTION *(cont'd)*	P650

(8) For solid substances

    (a) The primary receptacle(s) shall be siftproof;

    (b) The secondary packaging shall be siftproof;

    (c) If multiple fragile primary receptacles are placed in a single secondary packaging, they shall be either individually wrapped or separated to prevent contact between them; and

    (d) If there is any doubt as to whether or not residual liquid may be present in the primary receptacle during transport then a packaging suitable for liquids, including absorbent materials, shall be used.

(9) Refrigerated or frozen specimens: Ice, dry ice and liquid nitrogen

    (a) When dry ice or liquid nitrogen is used as a coolant, the requirements of 5.5.3 shall apply. When used, ice shall be placed outside the secondary packagings or in the outer packaging or an overpack. Interior supports shall be provided to secure the secondary packagings in the original position. If ice is used, the outside packaging or overpack shall be leakproof; and

    (b) The primary receptacle and the secondary packaging shall maintain their integrity at the temperature of the refrigerant used as well as the temperatures and the pressures which could result if refrigeration were lost.

(10) When packages are placed in an overpack, the package marks required by this packing instruction shall either be clearly visible or be reproduced on the outside of the overpack.

(11) Infectious substances assigned to UN 3373 which are packed and marked in accordance with this packing instruction are not subject to any other requirement in these Regulations.

(12) Clear instructions on filling and closing such packages shall be provided by packaging manufacturers and subsequent distributors to the consignor or to the person who prepares the package (e.g. patient) to enable the package to be correctly prepared for transport.

(13) Other dangerous goods shall not be packed in the same packaging as Division 6.2 infectious substances unless they are necessary for maintaining the viability, stabilizing or preventing degradation or neutralizing the hazards of the infectious substances. A quantity of 30 ml or less of dangerous goods included in Classes 3, 8 or 9 may be packed in each primary receptacle containing infectious substances. When these small quantities of dangerous goods are packed with infectious substances in accordance with this packing instruction no other requirements in these Regulations need be met.

Additional requirement:

Alternative packagings for the transport of animal material may be authorized by the competent authority in accordance with the provisions of 4.1.3.7.

P800	**PACKING INSTRUCTION**	**P800**

This instruction applies to UN Nos. 2803 and 2809.

The following packagings are authorized, provided that the general provisions of **4.1.1** and **4.1.3** are met:

(1) Pressure receptacles, provided that the general provisions of 4.1.3.6 are met.

(2) Steel flasks or bottles with threaded closures with a capacity not exceeding 3 l; or

(3) Combination packagings which conform to the following requirements:

    (a) Inner packagings shall comprise glass, metal or rigid plastics intended to contain liquids with a maximum net mass of 15 kg each;

    (b) The inner packagings shall be packed with sufficient cushioning material to prevent breakage;

    (c) Either the inner packagings or the outer packagings shall have inner liners or bags of strong leakproof and puncture-resistant material impervious to the contents and completely surrounding the contents to prevent it from escaping from the package irrespective of its position or orientation;

    (d) The following outer packagings and maximum net masses are authorized:

Outer packaging:	**Maximum net mass**
Drums	
steel (1A1, 1A2)	400 kg
metal, other than steel or aluminium (1N1, 1N2)	400 kg
plastics (1H1, 1H2)	400 kg
plywood (1D)	400 kg
fibre (1G)	400 kg
Boxes	
steel (4A)	400 kg
metal, other than steel or aluminium (4N)	400 kg
natural wood (4C1)	250 kg
natural wood with sift proof walls (4C2)	250 kg
plywood (4D)	250 kg
reconstituted wood (4F)	125 kg
fibreboard (4G)	125 kg
expanded plastics (4H1)	60 kg
solid plastics (4H2)	125 kg

Special packing provision:

PP41 For UN 2803, when it is necessary to transport Gallium at low temperatures in order to maintain it in a completely solid state, the above packagings may be overpacked in a strong, water-resistant outer packaging which contains dry ice or other means of refrigeration. When dry ice or other means of refrigeration presenting a risk of asphyxiation are used as a coolant, the requirements of 5.5.3 shall apply. If a refrigerant is used, all of the above materials used in the packaging of gallium shall be chemically and physically resistant to the refrigerant and shall have impact resistance at the low temperatures of the refrigerant employed. If dry ice is used, the outer packaging shall permit the release of carbon dioxide gas. Interior supports shall be provided to prevent movement after the dissipation of the refrigerant.

P801	PACKING INSTRUCTION	P801
This instruction applies to UN Nos. 2794, 2795 and 3028.		

The following packagings are authorized, provided that the provisions of **4.1.1.1, 4.1.1.2, 4.1.1.6**, and **4.1.3** are met:

(1) Rigid outer packagings, wooden slatted crates or pallets.

   Additionally, the following conditions shall be met:

   (a) Battery stacks shall be in tiers separated by a layer of electrically non-conductive material;

   (b) Battery terminals shall not support the weight of other superimposed elements;

   (c) Batteries shall be packaged or secured to prevent inadvertent movement;

   (d) Batteries shall not leak under normal conditions of transport or appropriate measures shall be taken to prevent the release of electrolyte from the package (e.g. individually packaging batteries or other equally effective methods); and

   (e) Batteries shall be protected against short circuits.

(2) Stainless steel or plastics bins may also be used to transport used batteries.

   Additionally, the following conditions shall be met:

   (a) The bins shall be resistant to the electrolyte that was contained in the batteries;

   (b) The bins shall not be filled to a height greater than the height of their sides;

   (c) The outside of the bins shall be free of residues of electrolyte contained in the batteries;

   (d) Under normal conditions of transport, no electrolyte shall leak from the bins;

   (e) Measures shall be taken to ensure that filled bins cannot lose their content; and

   (f) Measures shall be taken to prevent short circuits (e.g. batteries are discharged, individual protection of the battery terminals, etc.).

NOTE: *The packagings authorized in (1) and (2) may exceed a net mass of 400 kg (see 4.1.3.3).*

P802	PACKING INSTRUCTION	P802

The following packagings are authorized, provided that the general provisions of **4.1.1** and **4.1.3** are met:

(1) Combination packagings

　　Outer packagings: 1A1, 1A2, 1B1, 1B2, 1N1, 1N2, 1H1, 1H2, 1D, 1G, 4A, 4B, 4N, 4C1, 4C2, 4D, 4F, 4G or 4H2; maximum net mass: 75 kg.

　　Inner packagings: glass or plastics; maximum capacity: 10 litres.

(2) Combination packagings

　　Outer packagings: 1A1, 1A2, 1B1, 1B2, 1N1, 1N2, 1H1, 1H2, 1D, 1G, 4A, 4B, 4N, 4C1, 4C2, 4D, 4F, 4G or 4H2; maximum net mass: 125 kg.

　　Inner packagings: metal; maximum capacity: 40 litres

(3) Composite packagings: Glass receptacle in steel, aluminium or plywood drum (6PA1, 6PB1 or 6PD1) or in a steel, aluminium or wood box or in wickerwork hamper (6PA2, 6PB2, 6PC or 6PD2) or in solid plastics packaging (6PH2); maximum capacity: 60 litres.

(4) Steel drums (1A1) with a maximum capacity of 250 litres.

(5) Pressure receptacles, provided that the general provisions of 4.1.3.6 are met.

Special packing provision:

PP79 For UN 1790 with more than 60 % but not more than 85 % hydrogen fluoride, see P001.

P803	PACKING INSTRUCTION	P803

This instruction applies to UN 2028.

The following packagings are authorized, provided that the general provisions of **4.1.1** and **4.1.3** are met:

　　Drums (1A2, 1B2, 1N2, 1H2, 1D, 1G);

　　Boxes (4A, 4B, 4N, 4C1, 4C2, 4D, 4F, 4G, 4H2).

Packagings shall conform to the packing group II performance level.

Articles shall be individually packaged and separated from each other using partitions, dividers, inner packagings or cushioning material to prevent inadvertent discharge during normal conditions of transport.

Maximum net mass: 75 kg.

| P804 | PACKING INSTRUCTION | P804 |

This instruction applies to UN 1744.

The following packagings are authorized provided that the general provisions of **4.1.1** and **4.1.3** are met and the packagings are hermetically sealed:

(1) Combination packagings with a maximum gross mass of 25 kg, consisting of

    (a) one or more glass inner packaging(s) with a maximum capacity of 1.3 litres each and filled to not more than 90 % of their capacity; the closure(s) of which shall be physically held in place by any means capable of preventing back-off or loosening by impact or vibration during transport, individually placed in

    (b) metal or rigid plastics receptacles together with cushioning and absorbent material sufficient to absorb the entire contents of the glass inner packaging(s), further packed in

    (c) 1A1, 1A2, 1B1, 1B2, 1N1, 1N2, 1H1, 1H2, 1D, 1G, 4A, 4B, 4N, 4C1, 4C2, 4D, 4F, 4G or 4H2 outer packagings.

(2) Combination packagings consisting of metal or polyvinylidene fluoride (PVDF) inner packagings, not exceeding 5 litres in capacity individually packed with absorbent material sufficient to absorb the contents and inert cushioning material in 1A1, 1A2, 1B1, 1B2, 1N1, 1N2, 1H1, 1H2, 1D, 1G, 4A, 4B, 4N, 4C1, 4C2, 4D, 4F, 4G or 4H2 outer packagings with a maximum gross mass of 75 kg. Inner packagings shall not be filled to more than 90 % of their capacity. The closure of each inner packaging shall be physically held in place by any means capable of preventing back-off or loosening of the closure by impact or vibration during transport;

(3) Packagings consisting of:

Outer packagings: Steel or plastics drums (1A1, 1A2, 1H1 or 1H2) tested in accordance with the test requirements in 6.1.5 at a mass corresponding to the mass of the assembled package either as a packaging intended to contain inner packagings, or as a single packaging intended to contain solids or liquids, and marked accordingly;

Inner packagings: Drums and composite packagings (1A1, 1B1, 1N1, 1H1 or 6HA1) meeting the requirements of chapter 6.1 for single packagings, subject to the following conditions:

    (a) The hydraulic pressure test shall be conducted at a pressure of at least 300 kPa (3 bar) (gauge pressure);

    (b) The design and production leakproofness tests shall be conducted at a test pressure of 30 kPa (0,3 bar);

    (c) They shall be isolated from the outer drum by the use of inert shock-mitigating cushioning material which surrounds the inner packaging on all sides;

    (d) Their capacity shall not exceed 125 litres;

    (e) Closures shall be of a screw type that are:

        (i) Physically held in place by any means capable of preventing back-off or loosening of the closure by impact or vibration during transport;

        (ii) Provided with a cap seal;

    (f) The outer and inner packagings shall be subjected periodically to an internal inspection and leakproofness test according to (b) at intervals of not more than two and a half years; and

    (g) The outer and inner packagings shall bear in clearly legible and durable characters:

        (i) the date (month, year) of the initial test and the latest periodic test and inspection of the inner packaging; and

        (ii) the name or authorized symbol of the expert performing the tests and inspections;

(4) Pressure receptacles, provided that the general provisions of 4.1.3.6 are met.

    (a) They shall be subjected to an initial test and periodic tests every 10 years at a pressure of not less than 1 MPa (10 bar) (gauge pressure);

    (b) They shall be subjected periodically to an internal inspection and leakproofness test at intervals of not more than two and a half years;

    (c) They may not be equipped with any pressure relief device;

    (d) Each pressure receptacle shall be closed with a plug or valve(s) fitted with a secondary closure device; and

    (e) The materials of construction for the pressure receptacle, valves, plugs, outlet caps, luting and gaskets shall be compatible with each other and with the contents.

P900	PACKING INSTRUCTION	P900

This instruction applies to UN 2216.

The following packagings are authorized, provided that the general provisions of **4.1.1** and **4.1.3** are met:
(1)   Packagings according to P002; or
(2)   Bags (5H1, 5H2, 5H3, 5H4, 5L1, 5L2, 5L3, 5M1 or 5M2) with a maximum net mass of 50 kg.

Fish meal may also be transported unpackaged when it is packed in closed cargo transport units and the free air space has been restricted to a minimum.

P901	PACKING INSTRUCTION	P901

This instruction applies to UN 3316.

The following combination packagings are authorized provided the general provisions of 4.1.1 and 4.1.3 are met:

   Drums (1A1, 1A2, 1B1, 1B2, 1N1, 1N2, 1H1, 1H2, 1D, 1G);

   Boxes (4A, 4B, 4N, 4C1, 4C2, 4D, 4F, 4G, 4H1, 4H2);

   Jerricans (3A1, 3A2, 3B1, 3B2, 3H1, 3H2).

Packagings shall conform to the performance level consistent with the packing group assigned to the kit as a whole (see 3.3.1, special provision 251). Where the kit contains only dangerous goods to which no packing group is assigned, packagings shall meet packing group II performance level.

Maximum quantity of dangerous goods per outer packaging: 10 kg excluding the mass of any carbon dioxide, solid (dry ice) used as a refrigerant.

If dry ice is used as a coolant, the requirements of 5.5.3 shall apply.

Additional requirement:
   Dangerous goods in kits shall be packed in inner packagings which shall be protected from other materials in the kit.

P902	PACKING INSTRUCTION	P902

This instruction applies to UN Nos. 3268 and 3559.

(1)   Packaged articles:

   The following packagings are authorized provided the general provisions of **4.1.1** and **4.1.3** are met:

      Drums (1A2, 1B2, 1N2, 1H2, 1D, 1G);

      Boxes (4A, 4B, 4N, 4C1, 4C2, 4D, 4F, 4G, 4H1, 4H2);

      Jerricans (3A2, 3B2, 3H2).

   Packagings shall conform to the packing group III performance level.

   The packagings shall be designed and constructed so as to prevent movement of the articles and inadvertent operation during normal conditions of transport.

(2)   Unpackaged articles:

   Except for UN 3559, the articles may also be transported unpackaged in dedicated handling devices, vehicles or containers when moved to, from, or between where they are manufactured and an assembly plant including intermediate handling locations.

Additional requirement:
   Any pressure receptacle shall be in accordance with the requirements of the competent authority for the substance(s) contained therein.

P903	PACKING INSTRUCTION	P903

This instruction applies to UN Nos. 3090, 3091, 3480, 3481, 3551 and 3552.

For the purpose of this packing instruction, "equipment" means apparatus for which the cells or batteries will provide electrical power for its operation. The following packagings are authorized provided that the general provisions of **4.1.1** and **4.1.3** are met:

(1) For cells and batteries:

    Drums (1A2, 1B2, 1N2, 1H2, 1D, 1G);

    Boxes (4A, 4B, 4N, 4C1, 4C2, 4D, 4F, 4G, 4H1, 4H2);

    Jerricans (3A2, 3B2, 3H2).

Cells or batteries shall be packed in packagings so that the cells or batteries are protected against damage that may be caused by the movement or placement of the cells or batteries within the packaging.

Packagings shall conform to the packing group II performance level.

(2) In addition, for a cell or a battery with a gross mass of 12 kg or more employing a strong, impact resistant outer casing:

    (a) Strong outer packagings;

    (b) Protective enclosures (e.g., fully enclosed or wooden slatted crates); or

    (c) Pallets or other handling devices.

Cells or batteries shall be secured to prevent inadvertent movement, and the terminals shall not support the weight of other superimposed elements.

Packagings need not meet the requirements of 4.1.1.3.

(3) For cells or batteries packed with equipment:

Packagings conforming to the requirements in paragraph (1) of this packing instruction, then placed with the equipment in an outer packaging; or

Packagings that completely enclose the cells or batteries, then placed with equipment in a packaging conforming to the requirements in paragraph (1) of this packing instruction.

The equipment shall be secured against movement within the outer packaging.

(4) For cells or batteries contained in equipment:

Strong outer packagings constructed of suitable material, and of adequate strength and design in relation to the packaging capacity and its intended use. They shall be constructed in such a manner as to prevent accidental operation during transport. Packagings need not meet the requirements of 4.1.1.3.

Large equipment can be offered for transport unpackaged or on pallets when the cells or batteries are afforded equivalent protection by the equipment in which they are contained.

When intentionally active, devices such as radio frequency identification (RFID) tags, watches and temperature loggers, which are not capable of generating a dangerous evolution of heat, may be transported in strong outer packagings. When active, these devices shall meet defined standards for electromagnetic radiation to ensure that the operation of the device does not interfere with aircraft systems.

(5) For packagings containing both cells or batteries packed with equipment and contained in equipment:

    (a) For cells and batteries, packagings that completely enclose the cells or batteries, then placed with equipment in a packaging conforming to the requirements in paragraph (1) of this packing instruction; or

    (b) Packagings conforming to the requirements in paragraph (1) of this packing instruction, then placed with the equipment in a strong outer packaging constructed of suitable material, and of adequate strength and design in relation to the packaging capacity and its intended use. The outer packaging shall be constructed in such a manner as to prevent accidental operation during transport and need not meet the requirements of 4.1.1.3.

The equipment shall be secured against movement within the outer packaging.

When intentionally active, devices such as radio frequency identification (RFID) tags, watches and temperature loggers, which are not capable of generating a dangerous evolution of heat, may be transported in strong outer packagings. When active, these devices shall meet defined standards for electromagnetic radiation to ensure that the operation of the devices does not interfere with aircraft systems.

NOTE: *The packagings authorized in (2), (4) and (5) may exceed a net mass of 400 kg (see 4.1.3.3).*

Additional requirement:

    Cells or batteries shall be protected against short circuit.

P904	PACKING INSTRUCTION	P904
	This instruction applies to UN 3245.	

The following packagings are authorized:

(1) Packagings meeting the provisions of 4.1.1.1, 4.1.1.2, 4.1.1.4, 4.1.1.8 and 4.1.3 and so designed that they meet the construction requirements of 6.1.4. Outer packagings constructed of suitable material, and of adequate strength and design in relation to the packaging capacity and its intended use, shall be used. Where this packing instruction is used for the transport of inner packagings of combination packagings the packaging shall be designed and constructed to prevent inadvertent discharge during normal conditions of transport.

(2) Packagings, which need not conform to the packaging test requirements of part 6, but conforming to the following:

    (a) An inner packaging comprising:

        (i) primary receptacle(s) and a secondary packaging, the primary receptacle(s) or the secondary packaging shall be leakproof for liquids or siftproof for solids;

        (ii) for liquids, absorbent material placed between the primary receptacle(s) and the secondary packaging. The absorbent material shall be in a quantity sufficient to absorb the entire contents of the primary receptacle(s) so that any release of the liquid substance will not compromise the integrity of the cushioning material or of the outer packaging;

        (iii) if multiple fragile primary receptacles are placed in a single secondary packaging they shall be individually wrapped or separated to prevent contact between them;

    (b) An outer packaging shall be strong enough for its capacity, mass and intended use, and with a smallest external dimension of at least 100 mm.

For transport, the mark illustrated below shall be displayed on the external surface of the outer packaging on a background of a contrasting colour and shall be clearly visible and legible. The mark shall be in the form of a square set at an angle of 45° (diamond-shaped) with each side having a length of at least 50 mm; the width of the line shall be at least 2 mm and the letters and numbers shall be at least 6 mm high.

Additional requirement:

When dry ice or liquid nitrogen is used as a coolant, the requirements of 5.5.3 shall apply. When used, ice shall be placed outside the secondary packagings or in the outer packaging or an overpack. Interior supports shall be provided to secure the secondary packaging in the original position. If ice is used, the outside packaging or overpack shall be leakproof.

P905	PACKING INSTRUCTION	P905

This instruction applies to UN Nos. 3072 and 2990.

Any suitable packaging is authorized, provided that the general provisions of **4.1.1** and **4.1.3** are met, except that packagings need not conform to the requirements of part 6.

NOTE: The packagings authorized may exceed a net mass of 400 kg (see 4.1.3.3).

When the life saving appliances are constructed to incorporate or are contained in rigid outer weatherproof casings (such as for lifeboats), they may be transported unpackaged.

Additional requirements:

1. All dangerous substances and articles contained as equipment within the appliances shall be secured to prevent inadvertent movement and in addition:

    (a) Signal devices of Class 1 shall be packed in plastics or fibreboard inner packagings;

    (b) Gases (Division 2.2) shall be contained in cylinders as specified by the competent authority, which may be connected to the appliance;

    (c) Electric storage batteries (Class 8) and lithium batteries and sodium ion batteries (Class 9) shall be disconnected or electrically isolated and secured to prevent any spillage of liquid; and

    (d) Small quantities of other dangerous substances (for example in Class 3 or Divisions 4.1 and 5.2) shall be packed in strong inner packagings.

2. Preparation for transport and packaging shall include provisions to prevent any accidental inflation of the appliance.

P906	PACKING INSTRUCTION	P906

This instruction applies to UN Nos. 2315, 3151, 3152 and 3432.

The following packagings are authorized, provided that the general provisions of **4.1.1** and **4.1.3** are met:

(1) For liquids and solids containing or contaminated with PCBs, polyhalogenated biphenyls, polyhalogenated terphenyls or halogenated monomethyldiphenylmethanes: Packagings in accordance with P001 or P002, as appropriate.

(2) For transformers and condensers and other articles:

   (a) Packagings in accordance with packing instructions P001 or P002. Articles shall be secured with suitable cushioning material to prevent inadvertent movement during normal conditions of transport; or

   (b) Leakproof packagings which are capable of containing, in addition to the articles, at least 1.25 times the volume of the liquid PCBs, polyhalogenated biphenyls, polyhalogenated terphenyls or halogenated monomethyldiphenylmethanes present in them. There shall be sufficient absorbent material in the packagings to absorb at least 1.1 times the volume of liquid which is contained in the articles. In general, transformers and condensers shall be carried in leakproof metal packagings which are capable of holding, in addition to the transformers and condensers, at least 1.25 times the volume of the liquid present in them.

   NOTE 1: The packagings authorized may exceed a net mass of 400 kg (see 4.1.3.3).

Notwithstanding the above, liquids and solids not packaged in accordance with P001 and P002 and unpackaged transformers and condensers may be transported in cargo transport units fitted with a leakproof metal tray to a height of at least 800 mm, containing sufficient inert absorbent material to absorb at least 1.1 times the volume of any free liquid.

NOTE 2: The packagings authorized may exceed a net mass of 400 kg (see 4.1.3.3).

Additional requirement:

Adequate provisions shall be taken to seal the transformers and condensers to prevent leakage during normal conditions of transport.

P907	**PACKING INSTRUCTION**	P907

This instruction applies to articles such as machinery, apparatus or devices of UN 3363.

If the article is constructed and designed so that the receptacles containing the dangerous goods are afforded adequate protection, an outer packaging is not required. Dangerous goods in an article shall otherwise be packed in outer packagings constructed of suitable material, and of adequate strength and design in relation to the packaging capacity and its intended use, and meeting the applicable requirements of **4.1.1.1**.

Receptacles containing dangerous goods shall conform to the general provisions in 4.1.1, except that 4.1.1.3, 4.1.1.4, 4.1.1.12 and 4.1.1.14 do not apply. For Division 2.2 gases, the inner cylinder or receptacle, its contents and filling ratio shall be to the satisfaction of the competent authority of the country in which the cylinder or receptacle is filled.

In addition, the manner in which receptacles are contained within the article, shall be such that under normal conditions of transport, damage to receptacles containing the dangerous goods is unlikely; and in the event of damage to receptacles containing solid or liquid dangerous goods, no leakage of the dangerous goods from the article is possible (a leakproof liner may be used to satisfy this requirement). Receptacles containing dangerous goods shall be so installed, secured or cushioned as to prevent their breakage or leakage and so as to control their movement within the article during normal conditions of transport. Cushioning material shall not react dangerously with the content of the receptacles. Any leakage of the contents shall not substantially impair the protective properties of the cushioning material.

NOTE: The packagings authorized may exceed a net mass of 400 kg (see 4.1.3.3).

P908	**PACKING INSTRUCTION**	P908

This instruction applies to damaged or defective cells and batteries, including those contained in equipment, of UN Nos. 3090, 3091, 3480, 3481, 3551 and 3552.

The following packagings are authorized provided the general provisions of 4.1.1 and 4.1.3 are met:

For cells and batteries and equipment containing cells and batteries:

    Drums (1A2, 1B2, 1N2, 1H2, 1D, 1G)

    Boxes (4A, 4B, 4N, 4C1, 4C2, 4D, 4F, 4G, 4H1, 4H2)

    Jerricans (3A2, 3B2, 3H2)

Packagings shall conform to the packing group II performance level.

Packagings shall also meet the following requirements:

(a) Each damaged or defective cell or battery or equipment containing such cells or batteries shall be individually packed in inner packaging and placed inside of an outer packaging. The inner packaging or outer packaging shall be leak-proof to prevent the potential release of electrolyte.

(b) Each inner packaging shall be surrounded by sufficient non-combustible and electrically non-conductive thermal insulation material to protect against a dangerous evolution of heat.

(c) Sealed packagings shall be fitted with a venting device when appropriate.

(d) Appropriate measures shall be taken to minimize the effects of vibrations and shocks, prevent movement of the cells or batteries within the package that may lead to further damage and a dangerous condition during transport. Cushioning material that is non-combustible and electrically non-conductive may also be used to meet this requirement.

(e) The non-combustibility of the thermal insulation material and the cushioning material shall be assessed according to a standard recognized in the country where the packaging is designed or manufactured.

For leaking cells or batteries, sufficient inert absorbent material shall be added to the inner or outer packaging to absorb any release of electrolyte.

A cell or battery with a net mass of more than 30 kg shall be limited to one cell or battery per outer packaging.

Additional requirements:

    Cells or batteries shall be protected against short circuit.

P909	PACKING INSTRUCTION	P909

This instruction applies to UN Nos. 3090, 3091, 3480, 3481, 3551 and 3552 transported for disposal or recycling, either packed together with or packed without non-lithium batteries:

(1) Cells and batteries shall be packed in accordance with the following:

    (a) The following packagings are authorized, provided that the general provisions of 4.1.1 and 4.1.3, are met:

        Drums (1A2, 1B2, 1N2, 1H2, 1D, 1G);

        Boxes (4A, 4B, 4N, 4C1, 4C2, 4D, 4F, 4G, 4H2); and

        Jerricans (3A2, 3B2, 3H2).

    (b) Packagings shall conform to the packing group II performance level.

    (c) Metal packagings shall be fitted with an electrically non-conductive lining material (e.g., plastics) of adequate strength for the intended use.

(2) However, lithium ion or sodium ion cells with a watt-hour rating of not more than 20 Wh, lithium ion or sodium ion batteries with a watt-hour rating of not more than 100 Wh, lithium metal cells with a lithium content of not more than 1 g and lithium metal batteries with an aggregate lithium content of not more than 2 g may be packed in accordance with the following:

    (a) In strong outer packaging up to 30 kg gross mass meeting the general provisions of 4.1.1, except 4.1.1.3, and 4.1.3.

    (b) Metal packagings shall be fitted with a electrically non-conductive lining material (e.g., plastics) of adequate strength for the intended use.

(3) For cells or batteries contained in equipment, strong outer packagings constructed of suitable material, and of adequate strength and design in relation to the packaging capacity and its intended use, may be used. Packagings need not meet the requirements of 4.1.1.3. Equipment may also be offered for transport unpackaged or on pallets when the cells or batteries are afforded equivalent protection by the equipment in which they are contained.

(4) In addition, for cells or batteries with a gross mass of 12 kg or more employing a strong, impact resistant outer casing, strong outer packagings constructed of suitable material and of adequate strength and design in relation to the packagings capacity and its intended use, may be used. Packagings need not meet the requirements of 4.1.1.3.

NOTE: The packagings authorized in (3) and (4) may exceed a net mass of 400 kg (see 4.1.3.3).

Additional requirements:

1. Cells and batteries shall be designed or packed to prevent short circuits and the dangerous evolution of heat.
2. Protection against short circuits and the dangerous evolution of heat includes, but is not limited to,

    (a) individual protection of the battery terminals,

    (b) inner packaging to prevent contact between cells and batteries,

    (c) batteries with recessed terminals designed to protect against short circuits, or

    (d) the use of an electrically non-conductive and non-combustible cushioning material to fill empty space between the cells or batteries in the packaging.

3. Cells and batteries shall be secured within the outer packaging to prevent excessive movement during transport (e.g. by using a non-combustible and electrically non-conductive cushioning material or through the use of a tightly closed plastics bag).

| P910 | PACKING INSTRUCTION | P910 |

This instruction applies to UN Nos. 3090, 3091, 3480, 3481, 3551 and 3552 production runs consisting of not more than 100 cells or batteries and to pre-production prototypes of cells or batteries when these prototypes are transported for testing.

The following packagings are authorized provided that the general provisions of 4.1.1 and 4.1.3 are met:

(1) For cells and batteries, including when packed with equipment:

   Drums (1A2, 1B2, 1N2, 1H2, 1D, 1G);

   Boxes (4A, 4B, 4N, 4C1, 4C2, 4D, 4F, 4G, 4H1, 4H2);

   Jerricans (3A2, 3B2, 3H2).

   Packagings shall conform to the packing group II performance level and shall meet the following requirements:

   (a) Batteries and cells, including equipment, of different sizes, shapes or masses shall be packaged in an outer packaging of a tested design type listed above provided the total gross mass of the package does not exceed the gross mass for which the design type has been tested;

   (b) Each cell or battery shall be individually packed in an inner packaging and placed inside an outer packaging;

   (c) Each inner packaging shall be completely surrounded by sufficient non-combustible and electrically non-conductive thermal insulation material to protect against a dangerous evolution of heat;

   (d) Appropriate measures shall be taken to minimize the effects of vibration and shocks and prevent movement of the cells or batteries within the package that may lead to damage and a dangerous condition during transport. Cushioning material that is non-combustible and electrically non-conductive may be used to meet this requirement;

   (e) The non-combustibility of the thermal insulation material and the cushioning material shall be assessed according to a standard recognized in the country where the packaging is designed or manufactured;

   (f) A cell or battery with a net mass of more than 30 kg shall be limited to one cell or battery per outer packaging.

(2) For cells and batteries contained in equipment:

   Drums (1A2, 1B2, 1N2, 1H2, 1D, 1G);

   Boxes (4A, 4B, 4N, 4C1, 4C2, 4D, 4F, 4G, 4H1, 4H2);

   Jerricans (3A2, 3B2, 3H2).

   Packagings shall conform to the packing group II performance level and shall meet the following requirements:

   (a) Equipment of different sizes, shapes or masses shall be packaged in an outer packaging of a tested design type listed above provided the total gross mass of the package does not exceed the gross mass for which the design type has been tested;

   (b) The equipment shall be constructed or packaged in such a manner as to prevent accidental operation during transport;

   (c) Appropriate measures shall be taken to minimize the effects of vibration and shocks and prevent movement of the equipment within the package that may lead to damage and a dangerous condition during transport. When cushioning material is used to meet this requirement it shall be non-combustible and electrically non-conductive; and

   (d) The non-combustibility of the cushioning material shall be assessed according to a standard recognized in the country where the packaging is designed or manufactured.

Cont'd on next page

P910	PACKING INSTRUCTION *(cont'd)*	P910

(3) The equipment or the batteries may be transported unpackaged under conditions specified by the competent authority. Additional conditions that may be considered in the approval process include, but are not limited to:

    (a) The equipment or the battery shall be strong enough to withstand the shocks and loadings normally encountered during transport, including transshipment between cargo transport units and between cargo transport units and warehouses as well as any removal from a pallet for subsequent manual or mechanical handling; and

    (b) The equipment or the battery shall be fixed in cradles or crates or other handling devices in such a way that it will not become loose during normal conditions of transport.

NOTE: The packagings authorized may exceed a net mass of 400 kg (see 4.1.3.3).

Additional requirement:

The cells and batteries shall be protected against short circuit. Protection against short circuits includes, but is not limited to:

    (a) individual protection of the battery terminals,

    (b) inner packaging to prevent contact between cells and batteries,

    (c) batteries with recessed terminals designed to protect against short circuits, or

    (d) the use of an electrically non-conductive and non-combustible cushioning material to fill empty space between the cells or batteries in the packaging.

P911	PACKING INSTRUCTION	P911

This instruction applies to damaged or defective cells and batteries of UN Nos. 3090, 3091, 3480, 3481, 3551 and 3552 liable to rapidly disassemble, dangerously react, produce a flame or a dangerous evolution of heat or a dangerous emission of toxic, corrosive or flammable gases or vapours under normal conditions of transport.

The following packagings are authorized, provided that the general provisions of 4.1.1 and 4.1.3 are met:

For cells and batteries and equipment containing cells and batteries:

    Drums (1A2, 1B2, 1N2, 1H2, 1D, 1G);

    Boxes (4A, 4B, 4N, 4C1, 4C2, 4D, 4F, 4G, 4H1, 4H2);

    Jerricans (3A2, 3B2, 3H2)

The packagings shall conform to the packing group I performance level.

(1) The packaging shall be capable of meeting the following additional performance requirements in case of rapid disassembly, dangerous reaction, production of a flame or a dangerous evolution of heat or a dangerous emission of toxic, corrosive or flammable gases or vapours of the cells or batteries:

    (a) The outside surface temperature of the completed package shall not have a temperature of more than 100 °C. A momentary spike in temperature up to 200 °C is acceptable;

    (b) No flame shall occur outside the package;

    (c) No projectiles shall exit the package;

    (d) The structural integrity of the package shall be maintained

    (e) The packagings shall have a gas management system (e.g. filter system, air circulation, containment for gas, gas tight packaging etc.), as appropriate.

Cont'd on next page

P911	**PACKING INSTRUCTION** *(cont'd)*	P911

(2) The additional packaging performance requirements shall be verified by a test as specified by the competent authority[a].

A verification report shall be available on request. As a minimum requirement, the cell or battery name, the cell or battery number, the mass, type, energy content of the cells or batteries, the packaging identification and the test data according to the verification method as specified by the competent authority shall be listed in the verification report

(3) When dry ice or liquid nitrogen is used as a coolant, the requirements of section 5.5.3 shall apply. The inner packaging and outer packaging shall maintain their integrity at the temperature of the refrigerant used as well as the temperatures and the pressures which could result if refrigeration were lost.

Additional requirement:

Cells or batteries shall be protected against short circuit.

[a] *The following criteria, as relevant, may be considered to assess the performance of the packaging:*

  (a) *The assessment shall be done under a quality management system (as described e.g. in section 2.9.4 (e)) allowing for the traceability of tests results, reference data and characterization models used;*

  (b) *The list of hazards expected in case of thermal runaway for the cell or battery type, in the condition it is transported (e.g. usage of an inner packaging, state of charge (SOC), use of sufficient non-combustible, electrically non-conductive and absorbent cushioning material etc.), shall be clearly identified and quantified; the reference list of possible hazards for cells or batteries (e.g. rapidly disassemble, dangerously react, produce a flame or a dangerous evolution of heat or a dangerous emission of toxic, corrosive or flammable gases or vapours) can be used for this purpose. The quantification of these hazards shall rely on available scientific literature;*

  (c) *The mitigating effects of the packaging shall be identified and characterized, based on the nature of the protections provided and the construction material properties. A list of technical characteristics and drawings shall be used to support this assessment (Density $[kg \cdot m^{-3}]$, specific heat capacity $[J \cdot kg^{-1} \cdot K^{-1}]$, heating value $[kJ \cdot kg^{-1}]$, thermal conductivity $[W \cdot m^{-1} \cdot K^{-1}]$, melting temperature and flammability temperature $[K]$, heat transfer coefficient of the outer packaging $[W \cdot m^{-2} \cdot K^{-1}]$, ...);*

  (d) *The test and any supporting calculations shall assess the result of a thermal run-away of the cell or battery inside the packaging in the normal conditions of transport;*

  (e) *In case the SOC of the cell or battery is not known, the assessment used, shall be done with the highest possible SOC corresponding to the cell or battery use conditions;*

  (f) *The surrounding conditions in which the packaging may be used and transported shall be described (including for possible consequences of gas or smoke emissions on the environment, such as ventilation or other methods) according to the gas management system of the packaging;*

  (g) *The tests or the model calculation shall consider the worst case scenario for the thermal runaway triggering and propagation inside the cell or battery: this scenario includes the worst possible failure in the normal transport condition, the maximum heat and flame emissions for the possible propagation of the reaction;*

  (h) *These scenarios shall be assessed over a period of time long enough to allow all the possible consequences to occur (e.g. 24 hours).*

  (i) *In the case of multiple batteries and multiple items of equipment containing batteries, additional requirements such as the maximum number of batteries and items of equipment, the total maximum energy content of the batteries, and the configuration inside the package, including separations and protections of the parts, shall be considered.*

| P912 | **PACKING INSTRUCTION** *(cont'd)* | P912 |

This instruction applies to UN Nos. 3556, 3557 and 3558.

The vehicle shall be secured in a strong, rigid outer packaging constructed of suitable material, and of adequate strength and design in relation to the packaging capacity and its intended use. It shall be constructed in such a manner as to prevent accidental operation during transport. Packagings need not meet the requirements of 4.1.1.3. The vehicle shall be secured by means capable of restraining the vehicle in the outer packaging to prevent any movement during transport which would change the orientation or cause the battery in the vehicle to be damaged.

Vehicles transported in a packaging may have some parts of the vehicle, other than the battery, detached from its frame to fit into the packaging.

NOTE: *The packagings may exceed a net mass of 400 kg (see 4.1.3.3).*

Vehicles with an individual net mass of 30 kg or more:

(a) may be loaded into crates or secured to pallets;

(b) may be transported unpackaged providing that the vehicle is capable of remaining upright during transport without additional support and the vehicle provides adequate protection to the battery so that no damage to the battery can occur; or

(c) where the vehicles have the potential to topple over during transport (e.g. motor cycles), may be transported unpackaged in a cargo transport unit fitted with the means to prevent toppling in transport, such as by the use of bracing, frames or racking.

4.1.4.2 Packing instructions concerning the use of IBCs

IBC01	PACKING INSTRUCTION	IBC01

The following IBCs are authorized, provided that the general provisions of **4.1.1**, **4.1.2** and **4.1.3** are met:
    Metal (31A, 31B and 31N).

IBC02	PACKING INSTRUCTION	IBC02

The following IBCs are authorized, provided that the general provisions of **4.1.1**, **4.1.2** and **4.1.3** are met:
    Metal (31A, 31B and 31N);
    Rigid plastics (31H1 and 31H2);
    Composite (31HZ1).

Special packing provisions:

B5   For UN Nos. 1791, 2014, 2984 and 3149, IBCs shall be provided with a device to allow venting during transport. The inlet to the venting device shall be sited in the vapour space of the IBC under maximum filling conditions during transport.

B7   For UN Nos. 1222 and 1865, IBCs with a capacity greater than 450 litres are not permitted due to the substance's potential for explosion when transported in large volumes.

B8   The pure form of this substance shall not be transported in IBCs since it is known to have a vapour pressure of more than 110 kPa at 50 °C or 130 kPa at 55 °C.

B15   For UN 2031 with more than 55 % nitric acid, the permitted use of rigid plastics IBCs and of rigid plastics inner receptacles of composite IBCs shall be two years from their date of manufacture.

B16   For UN 3375, IBCs of type 31A and 31N are not allowed without competent authority approval.

IBC03	PACKING INSTRUCTION	IBC03

The following IBCs are authorized, provided that the general provisions of **4.1.1**, **4.1.2** and **4.1.3** are met:
    Metal (31A, 31B and 31N);
    Rigid plastics (31H1 and 31H2);
    Composite (31HZ1 and 31HA2, 31HB2, 31HN2, 31HD2 and 31HH2).

Special packing provisions:

B8   The pure form of this substance shall not be transported in IBCs since it is known to have a vapour pressure of more than 110 kPa at 50 °C or 130 kPa at 55 °C.

B11   Notwithstanding the provisions of the second paragraph of 4.1.1.10, UN 2672 ammonia solution in concentrations not exceeding 25 % may be transported in IBCs.

B19   For UN Nos. 3532 and 3534, IBCs shall be designed and constructed to permit the release of gas or vapour to prevent a build-up of pressure that could rupture the IBCs in the event of loss of stabilization.

IBC04	PACKING INSTRUCTION	IBC04

The following IBCs are authorized, provided that the general provisions of **4.1.1**, **4.1.2** and **4.1.3** are met:
    Metal (11A, 11B, 11N, 21A, 21B, 21N, 31A, 31B and 31N).

Special packing provision:

B1   For packing group I substances, IBCs shall be transported in closed cargo transport units.

IBC05	PACKING INSTRUCTION	IBC05

The following IBCs are authorized, provided that the general provisions of **4.1.1**, **4.1.2** and **4.1.3** are met:
    Metal (11A, 11B, 11N, 21A, 21B, 21N, 31A, 31B and 31N);
    Rigid plastics (11H1, 11H2, 21H1, 21H2, 31H1 and 31H2);
    Composite (11HZ1, 21HZ1 and 31HZ1).

Special packing provisions:

B1   For packing group I substances, IBCs shall be transported in closed cargo transport units.

B2   For solid substances in IBCs other than metal or rigid plastics IBCs, the IBCs shall be transported in closed cargo transport units.

IBC06	PACKING INSTRUCTION	IBC06

The following IBCs are authorized, provided that the general provisions of **4.1.1**, **4.1.2** and **4.1.3** are met:
    Metal (11A, 11B, 11N, 21A, 21B, 21N, 31A, 31B and 31N);
    Rigid plastics (11H1, 11H2, 21H1, 21H2, 31H1 and 31H2);
    Composite (11HZ1, 11HZ2, 21HZ1, 21HZ2 and 31HZ1).

Additional requirement:
    Where the solid may become liquid during transport see 4.1.3.4.

Special packing provisions:

B1   For packing group I substances, IBCs shall be transported in closed cargo transport units.

B2   For solid substances in IBCs other than metal or rigid plastics IBCs, the IBCs shall be transported in closed cargo transport units.

B12   For UN 2907, IBCs shall meet the packing group II performance level. IBCs meeting the test criteria of packing group I shall not be used.

IBC07	PACKING INSTRUCTION	IBC07

The following IBCs are authorized, provided that the general provisions of **4.1.1**, **4.1.2** and **4.1.3** are met:
    Metal (11A, 11B, 11N, 21A, 21B, 21N, 31A, 31B and 31N);
    Rigid plastics (11H1, 11H2, 21H1, 21H2, 31H1 and 31H2);
    Composite (11HZ1, 11HZ2, 21HZ1, 21HZ2 and 31HZ1);
    Wooden (11C, 11D and 11F).

Additional requirements:

1.   Where the solid may become liquid during transport see 4.1.3.4.
2.   Liners of wooden IBCs shall be siftproof.

Special packing provisions:

B1   For packing group I substances, IBCs shall be transported in closed cargo transport units.

B2   For solid substances in IBCs other than metal or rigid plastics IBCs, the IBCs shall be transported in closed cargo transport units.

B18   For UN Nos. 3531 and 3533, IBCs shall be designed and constructed to permit the release of gas or vapour to prevent a build-up of pressure that could rupture the IBCs in the event of loss of stabilization.

B20   UN 3550 may be transported in flexible IBCs (13H3 or 13H4) with siftproof liners to prevent any egress of dust during transport.

IBC08	PACKING INSTRUCTION	IBC08

The following IBCs are authorized, provided that the general provisions of **4.1.1**, **4.1.2** and **4.1.3** are met:
- Metal (11A, 11B, 11N, 21A, 21B, 21N, 31A, 31B and 31N);
- Rigid plastics (11H1, 11H2, 21H1, 21H2, 31H1 and 31H2);
- Composite (11HZ1, 11HZ2, 21HZ1, 21HZ2 and 31HZ1);
- Fibreboard (11G);
- Wooden (11C, 11D and 11F);
- Flexible (13H1, 13H2, 13H3, 13H4, 13H5, 13L1, 13L2, 13L3, 13L4, 13M1 or 13M2).

Additional requirement:
Where the solid may become liquid during transport see 4.1.3.4.

Special packing provisions:

B2 For solid substances in IBCs other than metal or rigid plastics IBCs, the IBCs shall be transported in closed cargo transport units.

B3 Flexible IBCs shall be sift-proof and water-resistant or shall be fitted with a sift-proof and water-resistant liner.

B4 Flexible, fibreboard or wooden IBCs shall be sift-proof and water-resistant or shall be fitted with a sift-proof and water-resistant liner.

B6 For UN Nos. 1327, 1363, 1364, 1365, 1386, 1408, 1841, 2211, 2217, 2793 and 3314, IBCs are not required to meet the IBC testing requirements of chapter 6.5.

B13 For UN Nos. 1748, 2208, 2880, 3485, 3486 and 3487, transport by sea in IBCs is prohibited.

IBC99	PACKING INSTRUCTION	IBC99

Only IBCs which are approved by the competent authority for these goods may be used (see 4.1.3.7). A copy of the competent authority approval shall accompany each consignment or the transport document shall include an indication that the packaging was approved by the competent authority.

IBC100	PACKING INSTRUCTION	IBC100

This instruction applies to UN Nos. 0082, 0222, 0241, 0331 and 0332.

The following IBCs are authorized, provided that the general provisions of 4.1.1, 4.1.2 and 4.1.3 and special provisions of 4.1.5 are met:
- Metal (11A, 11B, 11N, 21A, 21B, 21N, 31A, 31B and 31N);
- Flexible (13H2, 13H3, 13H4, 13L2, 13L3, 13L4 and 13M2);
- Rigid plastics (11H1, 11H2, 21H1, 21H2, 31H1, and 31H2);
- Composite (11HZ1, 11HZ2, 21HZ1, 21HZ2, 31HZ1 and 31HZ2).

Additional requirements:
1. IBCs shall only be used for free-flowing substances.
2. Flexible IBCs shall only be used for solids.

Special packing provisions:

B2 For UN 0222 in IBCs other than metal or rigid plastics IBCs, the IBCs shall be transported in closed cargo transport units.

B3 For UN 0222, flexible IBCs shall be sift-proof and water-resistant or shall be fitted with a sift-proof and water-resistant liner.

B9 For UN 0082, this packing instruction may only be used when the substances are mixtures of ammonium nitrate or other inorganic nitrates with other combustible substances which are not explosive ingredients. Such explosives shall not contain nitroglycerin, similar liquid organic nitrates, or chlorates. Metal IBCs are not authorized.

B10 For UN 0241, this packing instruction may only be used for substances which consist of water as an essential ingredient and high proportions of ammonium nitrate or other oxidizing substances some or all of which are in solution. The other constituents may include hydrocarbons or aluminium powder, but shall not include nitro-derivatives such as trinitrotoluene. Metal IBCs are not authorized.

B17 For UN 0222, metal IBCs are not authorized.

IBC520	PACKING INSTRUCTION				IBC520

This instruction applies to organic peroxides and self-reactive substances of type F.

The IBCs listed below are authorized for the formulations listed, provided that the general provisions of **4.1.1**, **4.1.2** and **4.1.3** and special provisions of **4.1.7.2** are met. The formulations not listed in 2.4.2.3.2.3 or 2.5.3.2.4 but listed below may also be transported packed in accordance with packing method OP8 of packing instruction P520 of 4.1.4.1, with the same control and emergency temperatures, if applicable.

For formulations not listed below, only IBCs which are approved by the competent authority may be used (see 4.1.7.2.2).

UN No.	Organic peroxide	Type of IBC	Maximum quantity (litres)	Control temperature	Emergency temperature
3109	ORGANIC PEROXIDE, TYPE F, LIQUID				
	tert-Butyl cumyl peroxide	31HA1	1 000		
	tert-Butyl hydroperoxide, not more than 72 % with water	31A 31HA1	1 250 1 000		
	tert-Butyl peroxyacetate, not more than 32 % in diluent type A	31A 31HA1	1 250 1 000		
	tert-Butyl peroxybenzoate, not more than 32 % in diluent type A	31A	1 250		
	tert-Butyl peroxy-3,5,5-trimethylhexanoate, not more than 37 % in diluent type A	31A 31HA1	1 250 1 000		
	Cumyl hydroperoxide, not more than 90 % in diluent type A	31HA1	1 250		
	Dibenzoyl peroxide, not more than 42 % as a stable dispersion	31H1	1 000		
	2,5-Dimethyl-2,5-di(tert-butylperoxy)hexane, not more than 52 % in diluent type A	31HA1	1 000		
	Di-tert-butyl peroxide, not more than 52 % in diluent type A	31A 31HA1	1 250 1 000		
	1,1-Di-(tert-butylperoxy)cyclohexane, not more than 37 % in diluent type A	31A	1 250		
	1,1-Di-(tert-butylperoxy)cyclohexane, not more than 42 % in diluent type A	31H1	1 000		
	Dilauroyl peroxide, not more than 42 %, stable dispersion, in water	31HA1	1 000		
	Isopropylcumyl hydroperoxide, not more than 72 % in diluent type A	31HA1	1 250		
	p-Menthyl hydroperoxide, not more than 72 % in diluent type A	31HA1	1 250		
	Peroxyacetic acid, stabilized, not more than 17 %	31H1 31H2 31HA1 31A	1 500 1 500 1 500 1 500		
	3,6,9-Triethyl-3,6,9-trimethyl-1,4,7-triperoxonane, not more than 27 % in diluent type A	31HA1	1 000		
3110	ORGANIC PEROXIDE, TYPE F, SOLID				
	Dicumyl peroxide	31A 31H 31HA1	2 000		

Cont'd on next page

IBC520	PACKING INSTRUCTION *(cont'd)*				IBC520
UN No.	Organic peroxide	Type of IBC	Maximum quantity (litres)	Control temperature	Emergency temperature
3119	**ORGANIC PEROXIDE, TYPE F, LIQUID, TEMPERATURE CONTROLLED**				
	tert-Amyl peroxy-2-ethylhexanoate, not more than 62 % in diluent type A	31HA1	1 000	+15 °C	+20 °C
	tert-Amyl peroxypivalate, not more than 32 % in diluent type A	31A	1 250	+10 °C	+15 °C
	tert-Amyl peroxypivalate, not more than 42 % as a stable dispersion in water	31HA1	1 050	0 °C	+10 °C
	tert-Butyl peroxy-2-ethylhexanoate, not more than 32 % in diluent type B	31HA1 31A	1 000 1 250	+30 °C +30 °C	+35 °C +35 °C
	tert-Butyl peroxyneodecanoate, not more than 32 % in diluent type A	31A	1 250	0 °C	+10 °C
	tert-Butyl peroxyneodecanoate, not more than 42 % stable dispersion, in water	31A	1 250	- 5 °C	+5 °C
	tert-Butyl peroxyneodecanoate, not more than 52 %, stable dispersion, in water	31A	1 250	-5 °C	+5 °C
	tert-Butyl peroxypivalate, not more than 27 % in diluent type B	31HA1 31A	1 000 1 250	+10 °C +10 °C	+15 °C +15 °C
	tert-Butyl peroxypivalate, not more than 42 % in diluent type A	31HA1 31A	1 000 1 250	+10 °C +10 °C	+15 °C +15 °C
	Cumyl peroxyneodecanoate, not more than 52 %, stable dispersion, in water	31A	1 250	- 15 °C	- 5 °C
	Di-(4-tert-butylcyclohexyl) peroxydicarbonate, not more than 42 %, stable dispersion, in water	31HA1	1 000	+30 °C	+35 °C
	Dicetyl peroxydicarbonate, not more than 42 %, stable dispersion, in water	31HA1	1 000	+30 °C	+35 °C
	Dicyclohexylperoxydicarbonate, not more than 42 % as a stable dispersion, in water	31A	1 250	+10 °C	+15 °C
	Di-(2-ethylhexyl) peroxydicarbonate, not more than 62 %, stable dispersion, in water	31A 31HA1	1 250 1000	-20 °C -20 °C	-10 °C -10 °C
	Diisobutyryl peroxide, not more than 28 % as a stable dispersion in water	31HA1 31A	1 000 1 250	-20 °C -20 °C	-10 °C -10 °C
	Diisobutyryl peroxide, not more than 42 % as a stable dispersion in water	31HA1 31A	1 000 1 250	-25 °C -25 °C	-15 °C -15 °C
	Dimyristyl peroxydicarbonate, not more than 42 %, stable dispersion, in water	31HA1	1 000	+15 °C	+20 °C
	Di-(2-neodecanoylperoxyisopropyl) benzene, not more than 42 %, stable dispersion, in water	31A	1 250	-15 °C	-5 °C
	Di-(3,5,5-trimethylhexanoyl) peroxide, not more than 52 % in diluent type A	31HA1 31A	1 000 1 250	+10 °C +10 °C	+15 °C +15 °C
	Di-(3,5,5-trimethylhexanoyl) peroxide, not more than 52 %, stable dispersion, in water	31HA1 31A	1 000 1 250	+10 °C +10 °C	+15 °C +15 °C
	3-Hydroxy-1,1-dimethylbutyl peroxyneodecanoate, not more than 52 %, stable dispersion, in water	31A	1 250	-15 °C	-5 °C
	1,1,3,3-Tetramethylbutyl peroxy-2-ethylhexanoate, not more than 67 %, in diluent type A	31HA1	1000	+15 °C	+20 °C
	1,1,3,3-Tetramethylbutyl peroxyneodecanoate, not more than 52 %, stable dispersion, in water	31A 31HA1	1 250 1 000	-5 °C -5 °C	+5 °C +5 °C
3120	**ORGANIC PEROXIDE, TYPE F, SOLID, TEMPERATURE CONTROLLED**				

Cont'd on next page

IBC520	PACKING INSTRUCTION *(cont'd)*	IBC520

Additional requirements:

1. IBCs shall be provided with a device to allow venting during transport. The inlet to the pressure-relief device shall be sited in the vapour space of the IBC under maximum filling conditions during transport.

2. To prevent explosive rupture of metal IBCs or composite IBCs with complete metal casing, the emergency-relief devices shall be designed to vent all the decomposition products and vapours evolved during self-accelerating decomposition or during a period of not less than one hour of complete fire-engulfment as calculated by the formula in 4.2.1.13.8. The control and emergency temperatures specified in this packing instruction are based on a non-insulated IBC. When consigning an organic peroxide in an IBC in accordance with this instruction, it is the responsibility of the consignor to ensure that:

    (a) the pressure and emergency relief devices installed on the IBC are designed to take appropriate account of the self-accelerating decomposition of the organic peroxide and of fire-engulfment; and

    (b) when applicable, the control and emergency temperatures indicated are appropriate, taking into account the design (e.g. insulation) of the IBC to be used.

IBC620	PACKING INSTRUCTION	IBC620

This instruction applies to UN 3291.

The following IBCs are authorized, provided that the general provisions of **4.1.1**, except 4.1.1.15, **4.1.2** and **4.1.3** are met:

Rigid, leakproof IBCs conforming to the packing group II performance level.

Additional requirements:

1. There shall be sufficient absorbent material to absorb the entire amount of liquid present in the IBC.
2. IBCs shall be capable of retaining liquids.
3. IBCs intended to contain sharp objects such as broken glass and needles shall be resistant to puncture.

4.1.4.3 Packing instructions concerning the use of large packagings

LP01	PACKING INSTRUCTION (LIQUIDS)			LP01

The following large packagings are authorized provided that the general provision of **4.1.1** and **4.1.3** are met:

Inner packagings	Large outer packagings	Packing group I	Packing group II	Packing group III
Glass 10 litre Plastics 30 litre Metal 40 litre	steel (50A) aluminium (50B) metal other than steel or aluminium (50N) rigid plastics (50H) natural wood (50C) plywood (50D) reconstituted wood (50F) rigid fibreboard (50G)	Not allowed	Not allowed	Maximum capacity: 3 m^3

LP02	PACKING INSTRUCTION (SOLIDS)			LP02

The following large packagings are authorized provided that the general provision of **4.1.1** and **4.1.3** are met:

Inner packagings	Large outer packagings	Packing group I	Packing group II	Packing group III
Glass 10 kg Plastics^b 50 kg Metal 50 kg Paper$^{a,\,b}$ 50 kg Fibre$^{a,\,b}$ 50 kg	steel (50A) aluminium (50B) metal other than steel or aluminium (50N) flexible plastics (51H)^c rigid plastics (50H) natural wood (50C) plywood (50D) reconstituted wood (50F) rigid fibreboard (50G)	Not allowed	Not allowed	Maximum capacity: 3 m^3

Special packing provisions:

L2 *Deleted*

L3 For UN Nos. 2208 and 3486, transport by sea in large packagings is prohibited.

^{a} *These packagings shall not be used when the substances being transported may become liquid during transport.*

^{b} *Packagings shall be siftproof.*

^{c} *To be used with flexible inner packagings only.*

LP03	PACKING INSTRUCTION	LP03

This instruction applies to UN Nos. 3537, 3538, 3540, 3541, 3546, 3547 and 3548.

(1) The following large packagings are authorized, provided that the general provisions of **4.1.1** and **4.1.3** are met:

Rigid large packagings conforming to the packing group II performance level made of:

    steel (50A);

    aluminium (50B);

    metal other than steel or aluminium (50N);

    rigid plastics (50H);

    natural wood (50C);

    plywood (50D);

    reconstituted wood (50F);

    rigid fibreboard (50G).

(2) Additionally, the following conditions shall be met:

    (a) Receptacles within articles containing liquids or solids shall be constructed of suitable materials and secured in the article in such a way that, under normal conditions of transport, they cannot break, be punctured or leak their contents into the article itself or the outer packaging;

    (b) Receptacles containing liquids with closures shall be packed with their closures correctly oriented. The receptacles shall in addition conform to the internal pressure test provisions of 6.1.5.5;

    (c) Receptacles that are liable to break or be punctured easily, such as those made of glass, porcelain or stoneware or of certain plastics materials shall be properly secured. Any leakage of the contents shall not substantially impair the protective properties of the article or of the outer packaging;

    (d) Receptacles within articles containing gases shall meet the requirements of section 4.1.6 and chapter 6.2 as appropriate or be capable of providing an equivalent level of protection as packing instructions P200 or P208; and

    (e) Where there is no receptacle within the article, the article shall fully enclose the dangerous substances and prevent their release under normal conditions of transport.

(3) Articles shall be packed to prevent movement and inadvertent operation during normal conditions of transport.

(4) Articles containing pre-production prototype lithium cells or batteries when these prototypes are transported for testing or production runs of not more than 100 lithium cells or batteries that are of a type that have not met the testing requirements of the *Manual of Tests and Criteria*, part III, sub-section 38.3 shall in addition meet the following:

    (a) Packagings shall conform to the requirements in paragraph (1) of this packing instruction;

    (b) Appropriate measures shall be taken to minimize the effects of vibration and shocks and prevent movement of the article within the package that may lead to damage and a dangerous condition during transport. When cushioning material is used to meet this requirement it shall be non-combustible and electrically non-conductive;

    (c) Non-combustibility of the cushioning material shall be assessed according to a standard recognized in the country where the packaging is designed or manufactured.

LP99	PACKING INSTRUCTION	LP99

Only large packagings which are approved by the Competent Authority for these goods may be used (see 4.1.3.7). A copy of the competent authority approval shall accompany each consignment or the transport document shall include an indication that the packaging was approved by the competent authority.

LP101	PACKING INSTRUCTION	LP101

The following large packagings are authorized, provided that the general provisions of **4.1.1** and **4.1.3** and special provisions of **4.1.5** are met:

Inner packagings	Intermediate packagings	Large packagings
Not necessary	Not necessary	steel (50A) aluminium (50B) metal other than steel or aluminium (50N) rigid plastics (50H) natural wood (50C) plywood (50D) reconstituted wood (50F) rigid fibreboard (50G)

Special packing provision:

L1 For UN Nos. 0006, 0009, 0010, 0015, 0016, 0018, 0019, 0034, 0035, 0038, 0039, 0048, 0056, 0137, 0138, 0168, 0169, 0171, 0181, 0182, 0183, 0186, 0221, 0243, 0244, 0245, 0246, 0254, 0280, 0281, 0286, 0287, 0297, 0299, 0300, 0301, 0303, 0321, 0328, 0329, 0344, 0345, 0346, 0347, 0362, 0363, 0370, 0412, 0424, 0425, 0434, 0435, 0436, 0437, 0438, 0451, 0488, 0502 and 0510:

Large and robust explosives articles, normally intended for military use, without their means of initiation or with their means of initiation containing at least two effective protective features, may be carried unpackaged. When such articles have propelling charges or are self-propelled, their ignition systems shall be protected against stimuli encountered during normal conditions of transport. A negative result in test series 4 on an unpackaged article indicates that the article can be considered for transport unpackaged. Such unpackaged articles may be fixed to cradles or contained in crates or other suitable handling devices.

LP102	PACKING INSTRUCTION	LP102

The following large packagings are authorized, provided that the general provisions of **4.1.1** and **4.1.3** and special provisions of **4.1.5** are met:

Inner packagings	Intermediate packagings	Outer packagings

Bags
    water-resistant
 Receptacles
    fibreboard
    metal
    plastics
    wood
 Sheets
    fibreboard, corrugated
 Tubes
    fibreboard
	Not necessary	steel (50A)
		 aluminium (50B)
		 metal other than steel or aluminium (50N)
		 rigid plastics (50H)
		 natural wood (50C)
		 plywood (50D)
		 reconstituted wood (50F)
		 rigid fibreboard (50G)

LP200	PACKING INSTRUCTION	LP200

This instruction applies to UN Nos. 1950 and 2037.

The following large packagings are authorized for aerosols and gas cartridges, provided that the general provisions of **4.1.1** and **4.1.3** are met:

Rigid large packagings conforming to the packing group II performance level, made of:

> steel (50A);
>
> aluminium (50B);
>
> metal other than steel or aluminium (50N);
>
> rigid plastics (50H);
>
> natural wood (50C);
>
> plywood (50D);
>
> reconstituted wood (50F);
>
> rigid fibreboard (50G).

Special packing provision:

L2 The large packagings shall be designed and constructed to prevent dangerous movement and inadvertent discharge during normal conditions of transport. For waste aerosols transported in accordance with special provision 327, the large packagings shall have a means of retaining any free liquid that might escape during transport, e.g. absorbent material. For waste aerosols and waste gas cartridges carried in accordance with special provision 327, the large packagings shall be adequately ventilated to prevent the creation of dangerous atmospheres and the build-up of pressure.

LP621	PACKING INSTRUCTION	LP621

This instruction applies to UN 3291.

The following large packagings are authorized, provided that the general provisions of **4.1.1** and **4.1.3** are met:

(1) For clinical waste placed in inner packagings: Rigid, leakproof large packagings conforming to the requirements of chapter 6.6 for solids, at the packing group II performance level, provided that there is sufficient absorbent material to absorb the entire amount of liquid present and the large packaging is capable of retaining liquids.

(2) For packages containing larger quantities of liquid: Large rigid packagings conforming to the requirements of chapter 6.6, at the packing group II performance level, for liquids.

Additional requirement:

Large packagings intended to contain sharp objects such as broken glass and needles shall be resistant to puncture and retain liquids under the performance test conditions in chapter 6.6.

LP622	PACKING INSTRUCTION	LP622

This instruction applies to waste of UN 3549 transported for disposal.

The following large packagings are authorized provided the general provisions of **4.1.1** and **4.1.3** are met:

Inner packagings	Intermediate packagings	Outer packagings
metal plastics	metal plastics	steel (50A) aluminium (50B) metal other than steel or aluminium (50N) plywood (50D) rigid fibreboard (50G) rigid plastics (50H)

The outer packaging shall conform to the packing group I performance level for solids.

Additional requirement:

1. Fragile articles shall be contained in either a rigid inner packaging or a rigid intermediate packaging.
2. Inner packagings containing sharp objects such as broken glass and needles shall be rigid and resistant to puncture.
3. The inner packaging, the intermediate packaging and the outer packaging shall be capable of retaining liquids. Outer packagings that are not capable of retaining liquids by design shall be fitted with a liner or suitable measure of retaining liquids.
4. The inner packaging and/or the intermediate packaging may be flexible. When flexible packagings are used, they shall be capable of passing the impact resistance test of at least 165g according to ISO 7765-1:1988 "Plastics film and sheeting – Determination of impact resistance by the free-falling dart method – Part 1: Staircase methods" and the tear resistance test of at least 480g in both parallel and perpendicular planes with respect to the length of the bag in accordance with ISO 6383-2:1983 "Plastics – Film and sheeting – Determination of tear resistance – Part 2: Elmendorf method". The maximum net mass of each flexible inner packaging shall be 30kg.
5. Each flexible intermediate packaging shall contain only one inner packaging.
6. Inner packagings containing a small amount of free liquid may be included in intermediate packaging provided that there is sufficient absorbent or solidifying material in the inner or intermediate packaging to absorb or solidify all the liquid content present. Suitable absorbent material which withstands the temperatures and vibrations liable to occur under normal conditions of transport shall be used.
7. Intermediate packagings shall be secured in outer packagings with suitable cushioning and/or absorbent material.

LP902	PACKING INSTRUCTION	LP902
This instruction applies to UN 3268.		

(1) Packaged articles:

The following large packagings are authorized, provided that the general provisions of **4.1.1** and **4.1.3** are met:

Rigid large packagings conforming to the packing group III performance level, made of:

    steel (50A);

    aluminium (50B);

    metal other than steel or aluminium (50N);

    rigid plastics (50H);

    natural wood (50C);

    plywood (50D);

    reconstituted wood (50F);

    rigid fibreboard (50G).

The packagings shall be designed and constructed to prevent movement of the articles and inadvertent operation during normal conditions of transport.

(2) Unpackaged articles:

The articles may also be transported unpackaged in dedicated handling devices, vehicles, containers or wagons when moved to, from, or between where they are manufactured and an assembly plant including intermediate handling locations.

Additional requirement:

Any pressure receptacle shall be in accordance with the requirements of the competent authority for the substance(s) contained in the pressure receptacle(s).

LP903	PACKING INSTRUCTION	LP903

This instruction applies to large cells with a gross mass of more than 500 g, large batteries with a gross mass of more than 12 kg, and equipment containing large cells or large batteries of UN Nos. 3090, 3091, 3480, 3481, 3551 and 3552.

The following large packagings are authorized for a single battery and for cells, batteries and equipment containing cells or batteries, provided that the general provisions of **4.1.1** and **4.1.3** are met:

Rigid large packagings conforming to the packing group II performance level, made of:

    steel (50A);

    aluminium (50B);

    metal other than steel or aluminium (50N);

    rigid plastics (50H);

    natural wood (50C);

    plywood (50D);

    reconstituted wood (50F);

    rigid fibreboard (50G).

Cells, batteries or equipment shall be placed in inner packagings or separated by other suitable means, such as placement in trays or by dividers, to ensure protection against damage that may be caused under normal conditions of transport by:

(a) its movement or placement within the large packaging;

(b) contact with other cells, batteries or equipment within the large packaging; and

(c) any loads arising from the superimposed weight of cells, batteries, equipment and packaging components above the cell, battery or equipment within the large packaging.

When multiple cells, batteries or items of equipment, are packed in the large packaging, bags (e.g., plastics) alone shall not be used to satisfy these requirements.

Additional requirement:

Batteries shall be protected against short circuit.

LP904	PACKING INSTRUCTION	LP904

This instruction applies to single damaged or defective batteries and to single items of equipment containing damaged or defective cells and batteries of UN Nos. 3090, 3091, 3480, 3481, 3551 and 3552.

The following large packagings are authorized for a single damaged or defective battery and for a single item of equipment containing damaged or defective cells and batteries, provided the general provisions of **4.1.1** and **4.1.3** are met.

For batteries and equipment containing cells and batteries:

Rigid large packagings conforming to the packing group II performance level, made of:

    steel (50A);

    aluminium (50B);

    metal other than steel or aluminium (50N);

    rigid plastics (50H);

    plywood (50D).

Large packagings shall also meet the following requirements:

(a) The damaged or defective battery or equipment containing such cells or batteries shall be individually packed in an inner packaging and placed inside of an outer packaging. The inner packaging or outer packaging shall be leak-proof to prevent the potential release of electrolyte.

(b) The inner packaging shall be surrounded by sufficient non-combustible and electrically non-conductive thermal insulation material to protect against a dangerous evolution of heat.

(c) Sealed packagings shall be fitted with a venting device when appropriate.

(d) Appropriate measures shall be taken to minimize the effects of vibrations and shocks, prevent movement of the battery or the equipment within the package that may lead to further damage and a dangerous condition during transport. Cushioning material that is non-combustible and electrically non-conductive may also be used to meet this requirement.

(e) The non combustibility of the thermal insulation material and the cushioning material shall be assessed according to a standard recognized in the country where the packaging is designed or manufactured.

For leaking batteries and cells, sufficient inert absorbent material shall be added to the inner or outer packaging to absorb any release of electrolyte.

Additional requirements:

    Batteries and cells shall be protected against short circuit.

| LP905 | PACKING INSTRUCTION | LP905 |

This instruction applies to UN Nos. 3090, 3091, 3480, 3481, 3551 and 3552 production runs consisting of not more than 100 cells or batteries and to pre-production prototypes of cells or batteries when these prototypes are transported for testing.

The following large packagings are authorized for a single battery and for a single item of equipment containing cells and batteries, provided that the general provisions of **4.1.1** and **4.1.3** are met:

(1) For a single battery:

Rigid large packagings conforming to the packing group II performance level, made of:

    steel (50A);

    aluminium (50B);

    metal other than steel or aluminium (50N);

    rigid plastics (50H);

    natural wood (50C);

    plywood (50D);

    reconstituted wood (50F);

    rigid fibreboard (50G).

Large packagings shall also meet the following requirements:

(a) A battery of different size, shape or mass may be packed in an outer packaging of a tested design type listed above provided the total gross mass of the package does not exceed the gross mass for which the design type has been tested;

(b) The battery shall be packed in an inner packaging and placed inside the outer packaging;

(c) The inner packaging shall be completely surrounded by sufficient non-combustible and electrically non-conductive thermal insulation material to protect against a dangerous evolution of heat;

(d) Appropriate measures shall be taken to minimize the effects of vibration and shocks and prevent movement of the battery within the package that may lead to damage and a dangerous condition during transport. When cushioning material is used to meet this requirement it shall be non-combustible and electrically non-conductive; and

(e) The non-combustibility of the thermal insulation material and the cushioning material shall be assessed according to a standard recognized in the country where the large packaging is designed or manufactured.

(2) For a single item of equipment containing cells or batteries:

Rigid large packagings conforming to the packing group II performance level, made of:

    Steel (50A);

    Aluminium (50B);

    Metal other than steel or aluminium (50N);

    Rigid plastics (50H);

    Natural wood (50C);

    Plywood (50D);

    Reconstituted wood (50F);

    Rigid fibreboard (50G).

Cont'd on next page

LP905	**PACKING INSTRUCTION** *(cont'd)*	LP905

Large packagings shall also meet the following requirements:

(a) A single item of equipment of different size, shape or mass may be packed in an outer packaging of a tested design type listed above provided the total gross mass of the package does not exceed the gross mass for which the design type has been tested;

(b) The equipment shall be constructed or packed in such a manner as to prevent accidental operation during transport;

(c) Appropriate measures shall be taken to minimize the effects of vibration and shocks and prevent movement of the equipment within the package that may lead to damage and a dangerous condition during transport. When cushioning material is used to meet this requirement, it shall be non-combustible and electrically non-conductive; and

(d) The non-combustibility of the cushioning material shall be assessed according to a standard recognized in the country where the large packaging is designed or manufactured.

Additional requirement:

Cells and batteries shall be protected against short circuit.

LP906	**PACKING INSTRUCTION**	LP906

This instruction applies to damaged or defective batteries of UN Nos. 3090, 3091, 3480, 3481, 3551 and 3552 liable to rapidly disassemble, dangerously react, produce a flame or a dangerous evolution of heat or a dangerous emission of toxic, corrosive or flammable gases or vapours under normal conditions of transport.

The following large packagings are authorized, provided that the general provisions of **4.1.1** and **4.1.3** are met:

For batteries and items of equipment containing batteries:

Rigid large packagings conforming to the packing group I performance level, made of:

    steel (50A);

    aluminium (50B);

    metal other than steel or aluminium (50N);

    rigid plastics (50H);

    plywood (50D);

    rigid fibreboard (50G)

(1) The large packaging shall be capable of meeting the following additional performance requirements in case of rapid disassembly, dangerous reaction, production of a flame or a dangerous evolution of heat or a dangerous emission of toxic, corrosive or flammable gases or vapours of the battery:

    (a) The outside surface temperature of the completed package shall not have a temperature of more than 100 °C. A momentary spike in temperature up to 200 °C is acceptable;

    (b) No flame shall occur outside the package;

    (c) No projectiles shall exit the package;

    (d) The structural integrity of the package shall be maintained; and

    (e) The large packagings shall have a gas management system (e.g. filter system, air circulation, containment for gas, gas tight packaging etc.), as appropriate.

(2) The additional large packaging performance requirements shall be verified by a test as specified by the competent authority [a].

A verification report shall be available on request. As a minimum requirement, the name of the batteries, their type as defined in section 38.3.2.3 of the *Manual of Tests and Criteria*, the maximum number of batteries, the total mass of batteries, the total energy content of the batteries, the large packaging identification and the test data according to the verification method as specified by the competent authority shall be listed in the verification report. A set of specific instructions describing the way to use the package shall also be part of the verification report.

[a] *(see next page)*

Cont'd on next page

LP906	PACKING INSTRUCTION *(cont'd)*	LP906

(3) When dry ice or liquid nitrogen is used as a coolant, the requirements of section 5.5.3 shall apply. The inner packaging and outer packaging shall maintain their integrity at the temperature of the refrigerant used as well as the temperatures and the pressures which could result if refrigeration were lost.

(4) The specific instructions for use of the package shall be made available by the packaging manufacturers and subsequent distributors to the consignor. They shall include at least the identification of the batteries and items of equipment that may be contained inside the packaging, the maximum number of batteries contained in the package and the maximum total of the batteries' energy content, as well as the configuration inside the package, including the separations and protections used during the performance verification test.

Additional requirement:

Batteries shall be protected against short circuit.

---

[a] *The following criteria, as relevant, may be considered to assess the performance of the large packaging:*

(a) *The assessment shall be done under a quality management system (as described e.g. in section 2.9.4 (e)) allowing for the traceability of tests results, reference data and characterization models used;*

(b) *The list of hazards expected in case of thermal runaway for the battery type, in the condition it is transported (e.g. usage of an inner packaging, state of charge (SOC), use of sufficient non-combustible, electrically non-conductive and absorbent cushioning material etc.), shall be clearly identified and quantified; the reference list of possible hazards for batteries (e.g. rapidly disassemble, dangerously react, produce a flame or a dangerous evolution of heat or a dangerous emission of toxic, corrosive or flammable gases or vapours) can be used for this purpose. The quantification of these hazards shall rely on available scientific literature;*

(c) *The mitigating effects of the large packaging shall be identified and characterized, based on the nature of the protections provided and the construction material properties. A list of technical characteristics and drawings shall be used to support this assessment (density [$kg \cdot m^{-3}$], specific heat capacity [$J \cdot kg^{-1} \cdot K^{-1}$], heating value [$kJ \cdot kg^{-1}$], thermal conductivity [$W \cdot m^{-1} \cdot K^{-1}$], melting temperature and flammability temperature [K], heat transfer coefficient of the outer packaging [$W \cdot m^{-2} \cdot K^{-1}$], ...);*

(d) *The test and any supporting calculations shall assess the result of a thermal run-away of the battery inside the large packaging in the normal conditions of transport;*

(e) *In case the SOC of the battery is not known, the assessment used, shall be done with the highest possible SOC corresponding to the battery use conditions;*

(f) *The surrounding conditions in which the large packaging may be used and transported shall be described (including for possible consequences of gas or smoke emissions on the environment, such as ventilation or other methods) according to the gas management system of the large packaging;*

(g) *The tests or the model calculation shall consider the worst case scenario for the thermal runaway triggering and propagation inside the battery: this scenario includes the worst possible failure in the normal transport condition, the maximum heat and flame emissions for the possible propagation of the reaction;*

(h) *These scenarios shall be assessed over a period long enough to allow all the possible consequences to occur (e.g. 24 hours).*

(i) *In the case of multiple batteries and multiple items of equipment containing batteries, additional requirements such as the maximum number of batteries and items of equipment, the total maximum energy content of the batteries, and the configuration inside the package, including separations and protections of the parts, shall be considered.*

4.1.5   **Special packing provisions for goods of Class 1**

4.1.5.1   The general provisions of section 4.1.1 shall be met.

4.1.5.2   All packagings for Class 1 goods shall be so designed and constructed that:

      (a)   They will protect the explosives, prevent them escaping and cause no increase in the risk of unintended ignition or initiation when subjected to normal conditions of transport including foreseeable changes in temperature, humidity and pressure;

      (b)   The complete package can be handled safely in normal conditions of transport; and

      (c)   The packages will withstand any loading imposed on them by foreseeable stacking to which they will be subject during transport so that they do not add to the risk presented by the explosives, the containment function of the packagings is not harmed, and they are not distorted in a way or to an extent which will reduce their strength or cause instability of a stack.

4.1.5.3   All explosive substances and articles, as prepared for transport, shall have been classified in accordance with the procedures detailed in 2.1.3.

4.1.5.4   Class 1 goods shall be packed in accordance with the appropriate packing instruction shown in Column 8 of the Dangerous Goods List, as detailed in 4.1.4.

4.1.5.5   Unless otherwise specified in these Regulations, packagings, including IBCs and large packagings, shall conform to the requirements of chapters 6.1, 6.5 or 6.6, as appropriate, and shall meet their test requirements for packing group II.

4.1.5.6   The closure device of packagings containing liquid explosives shall ensure a double protection against leakage.

4.1.5.7   The closure device of metal drums shall include a suitable gasket; if a closure device includes a screw-thread, the ingress of explosive substances into the screw-thread shall be prevented.

4.1.5.8   Packagings for water soluble substances shall be water-resistant. Packagings for desensitized or phlegmatized substances shall be closed to prevent changes in concentration during transport.

4.1.5.9   When the packaging includes a double envelope filled with water which may freeze during transport, a sufficient quantity of an anti-freeze agent shall be added to the water to prevent freezing. Anti-freeze that could create a fire hazard because of its inherent flammability shall not be used.

4.1.5.10   Nails, staples and other closure devices made of metal without protective covering shall not penetrate to the inside of the outer packaging unless the inner packaging adequately protects the explosives against contact with the metal.

4.1.5.11   Inner packagings, fittings and cushioning materials and the placing of explosive substances or articles in packages shall be accomplished in a manner which prevents the explosive substances or articles from becoming loose in the outer packaging under normal conditions of transport. Metallic components of articles shall be prevented from making contact with metal packagings. Articles containing explosive substances not enclosed in an outer casing shall be separated from each other in order to prevent friction and impact. Padding, trays, partitioning in the inner or outer packaging, mouldings or receptacles may be used for this purpose.

4.1.5.12   Packagings shall be made of materials compatible with, and impermeable to, the explosives contained in the package, so that neither interaction between the explosives and the packaging materials, nor leakage, causes the explosive to become unsafe to transport, or the hazard division or compatibility group to change.

4.1.5.13   The ingress of explosive substances into the recesses of seamed metal packagings shall be prevented.

4.1.5.14   Plastics packagings shall not be liable to generate or accumulate sufficient static electricity so that a discharge could cause the packaged explosive substances or articles to initiate, ignite or function.

4.1.5.15   Large and robust explosives articles, normally intended for military use, without their means of initiation or with their means of initiation containing at least two effective protective features, may be carried unpackaged. When such articles have propelling charges or are self-propelled, their ignition systems shall be protected against stimuli encountered during normal conditions of transport. A negative result in test series 4 on an unpackaged article indicates that the article can be considered for transport unpackaged. Such unpackaged articles may be fixed to cradles or contained in crates or other suitable handling, storage or launching devices in such a way that they will not become loose during normal conditions of transport.

Where such large explosive articles are as part of their operational safety and suitability tests subjected to test regimes that meet the intentions of these Regulations and such tests have been successfully undertaken, the competent authority may approve such articles to be transported under these Regulations.

4.1.5.16   Explosive substances shall not be packed in inner or outer packagings where the differences in internal and external pressures, due to thermal or other effects, could cause an explosion or rupture of the package.

4.1.5.17   Whenever loose explosive substances or the explosive substance of an uncased or partly cased article may come into contact with the inner surface of metal packagings (1A1, 1A2, 1B1, 1B2, 4A, 4B and metal receptacles), the metal packaging shall be provided with an inner liner or coating (see 4.1.1.2).

4.1.5.18   Packing instruction P101 may be used for any explosive provided the package has been approved by a competent authority regardless of whether the packaging complies with the packing instruction assignment in the Dangerous Goods List.

4.1.6   Special packing provisions for goods of Class 2

4.1.6.1   *General requirements*

4.1.6.1.1   This section provides general requirements applicable to the use of pressure receptacles for the transport of Class 2 gases and other dangerous goods in pressure receptacles (e.g. UN 1051 hydrogen cyanide, stabilized). Pressure receptacles shall be constructed and closed so as to prevent any loss of contents which might be caused under normal conditions of transport, including by vibration, or by changes in temperature, humidity or pressure (resulting from change in altitude, for example).

4.1.6.1.2   Parts of pressure receptacles which are in direct contact with dangerous goods shall not be affected or weakened by those dangerous goods and shall not cause a dangerous effect (e.g. catalysing a reaction or reacting with the dangerous goods). The provisions of ISO 11114-1:2020 and ISO 11114-2:2021 shall be met as applicable.

4.1.6.1.3   Pressure receptacles, including their closures, shall be selected to contain a gas or a mixture of gases according to the requirements of 6.2.1.2 and the requirements of the specific packing instructions of 4.1.4.1. This section also applies to pressure receptacles which are elements of MEGCs.

4.1.6.1.4   Refillable pressure receptacles shall not be filled with a gas or gas mixture different from that previously contained unless the necessary operations for change of gas service have been performed. The change of service for compressed and liquefied gases shall be in accordance with ISO 11621:1997, as applicable. In addition, a pressure receptacle that previously contained a Class 8 corrosive substance or a substance of another class with a corrosive subsidiary hazard shall not be authorized for the transport of a Class 2 substance unless the necessary inspection and testing as specified in 6.2.1.6 have been performed.

4.1.6.1.5   Prior to filling, the filler shall perform an inspection of the pressure receptacle and ensure that the pressure receptacle is authorized for the gas and, in case of a chemical under pressure, for the propellant to be transported and that the provisions of these Regulations have been met. Shut-off valves shall be closed after filling and remain closed during transport. The consignor shall verify that the closures and equipment are not leaking.

4.1.6.1.6　Pressure receptacles shall be filled according to the working pressures, filling ratios and provisions specified in the appropriate packing instruction for the specific substance being filled and taking into account the lowest pressure rating of any component. Service equipment having a pressure rating lower than other components shall nevertheless comply with 6.2.1.3.1. Reactive gases and gas mixtures shall be filled to a pressure such that if complete decomposition of the gas occurs, the working pressure of the pressure receptacle shall not be exceeded.

4.1.6.1.7　Pressure receptacles, including their closures, shall conform to the design, construction, inspection and testing requirements detailed in chapter 6.2. When outer packagings are prescribed, the pressure receptacles shall be firmly secured therein. Unless otherwise specified in the detailed packing instructions, one or more inner packagings may be enclosed in an outer packaging.

4.1.6.1.8　Valves shall be designed and constructed in such a way that they are inherently able to withstand damage without release of the contents or shall be protected from damage which could cause inadvertent release of the contents of the pressure receptacle, by one of the following methods:

(a) Valves are placed inside the neck of the pressure receptacle and protected by a threaded plug or cap;

(b) Valves are protected by caps or guards. Caps shall possess vent-holes of sufficient cross-sectional area to evacuate the gas if leakage occurs at the valves;

(c) Valves are protected by shrouds or permanent protective attachments;

(d) Pressure receptacles are transported in frames, (e.g. bundles); or

(e) Pressure receptacles are transported in an outer packaging. The packaging as prepared for transport shall be capable of meeting the drop test specified in 6.1.5.3 at the packing group I performance level.

For pressure receptacles with valves as described in (b), the requirements of ISO 11117:1998, ISO 11117:2008 + Cor 1:2009 or ISO 11117:2019 shall be met. Requirements for shrouds and permanent protective attachments used as valve protection under (c), are given in the relevant pressure receptacle shell design standards, see 6.2.2.1. Valves with inherent protection used for refillable pressure receptacles shall meet the requirements of clause 4.6.2 of ISO 10297:2006 or clause 5.5.2 of ISO 10297:2014 or clause 5.5.2 of ISO 10297:2014 + Amd 1:2017, or in case of self-closing valves, of clause 5.4.2 of ISO 17879:2017. For valves with inherent protection used for non-refillable cylinders, the requirements of clause 9.2.5 of ISO 11118:2015 or of clause 9.2.5 of ISO 11118:2015 + Amd 1:2019 shall be met.

For metal hydride storage systems, the valve protection requirements specified in ISO 16111:2008 or ISO 16111:2018 shall be met.

4.1.6.1.9　Non-refillable pressure receptacles shall:

(a) Be transported in an outer packaging, such as a box, or crate, or in shrink-wrapped trays or stretch-wrapped trays;

(b) Be of a water capacity less than or equal to 1.25 litres when filled with flammable or toxic gas;

(c) Not be used for toxic gases with an LC50 less than or equal to 200 ml/m^3; and

(d) Not be repaired after being put into service.

4.1.6.1.10 Refillable pressure receptacles, other than closed cryogenic receptacles, shall be periodically inspected according to the provisions of 6.2.1.6 and packing instruction P200, P205, P206 or P208, as applicable. Pressure relief valves for closed cryogenic receptacles shall be subject to periodic inspections and tests according to the provisions of 6.2.1.6.3 and packing instruction P203. Pressure receptacles shall not be filled after they become due for periodic inspection but may be transported after the expiry of the time limit.

4.1.6.1.11 Repairs shall be consistent with the fabrication and testing requirements of the applicable design and construction standards and are only permitted as indicated in the relevant periodic inspection standards specified in 6.2.2.4. Pressure receptacles, other than the jacket of closed cryogenic receptacles, shall not be subjected to repairs of any of the following:

    (a) Weld cracks or other weld defects;

    (b) Cracks in walls;

    (c) Leaks or defects in the material of the wall, head or bottom.

4.1.6.1.12 Pressure receptacles shall not be offered for filling:

    (a) When damaged to such an extent that the integrity of the pressure receptacle or its service equipment may be affected;

    (b) Unless the pressure receptacle and its service equipment has been examined and found to be in good working order; or

    (c) Unless the required certification, retest, and filling marks are legible.

4.1.6.1.13 Filled pressure receptacles shall not be offered for transport;

    (a) When leaking;

    (b) When damaged to such an extent that the integrity of the pressure receptacle or its service equipment may be affected;

    (c) Unless the pressure receptacle and its service equipment has been examined and found to be in good working order; or

    (d) Unless the required certification, retest, and filling marks are legible.

4.1.7 Special packing provisions for organic peroxides (Division 5.2) and self-reactive substances of Division 4.1

4.1.7.0.1 For organic peroxides, all receptacles shall be "effectively closed". Where significant internal pressure may develop in a package by the evolution of a gas, a vent may be fitted, provided the gas emitted will not cause danger, otherwise the degree of filling shall be limited. Any venting device shall be so constructed that liquid will not escape when the package is in an upright position and it shall be able to prevent ingress of impurities. The outer packaging, if any, shall be so designed as not to interfere with the operation of the venting device.

4.1.7.1 *Use of packagings (except IBCs)*

4.1.7.1.1 Packagings for organic peroxides and self-reactive substances shall conform to the requirements of chapter 6.1 and shall meet its test requirements for packing group II.

4.1.7.1.2 The packing methods for organic peroxides and self-reactive substances are listed in packing instruction P520 and are designated OP1 to OP8. The quantities specified for each packing method are the maximum quantities authorized per package.

4.1.7.1.3 The packing methods appropriate for the individual currently assigned organic peroxides and self-reactive substances are listed in 2.4.2.3.2.3 and 2.5.3.2.4.

4.1.7.1.4   For new organic peroxides, new self-reactive substances or new formulations of currently assigned organic peroxides or self-reactive substances, the following procedure shall be used to assign the appropriate packing method:

(a) ORGANIC PEROXIDE, TYPE B or SELF-REACTIVE SUBSTANCE, TYPE B:

Packing method OP5 shall be assigned, provided that the organic peroxide (or self-reactive substance) satisfies the criteria of 2.5.3.3.2 (b) (resp. 2.4.2.3.3.2 (b)) in a packaging authorized by the packing method. If the organic peroxide (or self-reactive substance) can only satisfy these criteria in a smaller packaging than those authorized by packing method OP5 (viz. one of the packagings listed for OP1 to OP4), then the corresponding packing method with the lower OP number is assigned;

(b) ORGANIC PEROXIDE, TYPE C or SELF-REACTIVE SUBSTANCE, TYPE C:

Packing method OP6 shall be assigned, provided that the organic peroxide (or self-reactive substance) satisfies the criteria of 2.5.3.3.2 (c) (resp. 2.4.2.3.3.2 (c)) in packaging authorized by the packing method. If the organic peroxide (or self-reactive substance) can only satisfy these criteria in a smaller packaging than those authorized by packing method OP6 then the corresponding packing method with the lower OP number is assigned;

(c) ORGANIC PEROXIDE, TYPE D or SELF-REACTIVE SUBSTANCE, TYPE D:

Packing method OP7 shall be assigned to this type of organic peroxide or self-reactive substance;

(d) ORGANIC PEROXIDE, TYPE E or SELF-REACTIVE SUBSTANCE, TYPE E:

Packing method OP8 shall be assigned to this type of organic peroxide or self-reactive substance;

(e) ORGANIC PEROXIDE, TYPE F or SELF-REACTIVE SUBSTANCE, TYPE F:

Packing method OP8 shall be assigned to this type of organic peroxide or self-reactive substance.

4.1.7.2   *Use of intermediate bulk containers*

4.1.7.2.1   The currently assigned organic peroxides specifically listed in packing instruction IBC520 may be transported in IBCs in accordance with this packing instruction. IBCs shall conform to the requirements of chapter 6.5 and shall meet its test requirements for packing group II.

4.1.7.2.2   Other organic peroxides and self-reactive substances of type F may be transported in IBCs under conditions established by the competent authority of the country of origin when, on the basis of the appropriate tests, that competent authority is satisfied that such transport may be safely conducted. The tests undertaken shall include those necessary:

(a) To prove that the organic peroxide (or self-reactive substance) complies with the principles for classification given in 2.5.3.3.2 (f), exit box F of figure 2.5.1; (resp. 2.4.2.3.3.2 (f), exit box F of figure 2.4.1);

(b) To prove the compatibility of all materials normally in contact with the substance during the transport;

(c) To determine, when applicable, the control and emergency temperatures associated with the transport of the product in the IBC concerned as derived from the SADT;

(d) To design, when applicable, pressure and emergency relief devices; and

(e) To determine if any special provisions are necessary for safe transport of the substance.

4.1.7.2.3　　For self-reactive substances temperature control is required according to 2.4.2.3.4. For organic peroxides temperature control is required according to 2.5.3.4.1. Temperature control provisions are given in 7.1.5.3.

4.1.7.2.4　　Emergencies to be taken into account are self-accelerating decomposition and fire engulfment. To prevent explosive rupture of metal IBCs with a complete metal casing, the emergency-relief devices shall be designed to vent all the decomposition products and vapours evolved during self-accelerating decomposition or during a period of not less than one hour of complete fire engulfment calculated by the equations given in 4.2.1.13.8.

4.1.8　　Special packing provisions for infectious substances of Category A (Division 6.2, UN Nos. 2814 and 2900)

4.1.8.1　　Consignors of infectious substances shall ensure that packages are prepared in such a manner that they arrive at their destination in good condition and present no hazard to persons or animals during transport.

4.1.8.2　　The definitions in 1.2.1 and the general packing provisions of 4.1.1.1 to 4.1.1.14, except 4.1.1.10 to 4.1.1.12, apply to infectious substances packages. However, liquids shall only be filled into packagings which have an appropriate resistance to the internal pressure that may develop under normal conditions of transport.

4.1.8.3　　An itemized list of contents shall be enclosed between the secondary packaging and the outer packaging. When the infectious substances to be transported are unknown, but suspected of meeting the criteria for inclusion in category A, the words "suspected category A infectious substance" shall be shown, in parentheses, following the proper shipping name on the document inside the outer packaging.

4.1.8.4　　Before an empty packaging is returned to the consignor, or sent elsewhere, it shall be disinfected or sterilized to nullify any hazard and any label or mark indicating that it had contained an infectious substance shall be removed or obliterated.

4.1.8.5　　Provided an equivalent level of performance is maintained, the following variations in the primary receptacles placed within a secondary packaging are allowed without further testing of the completed package:

(a) Primary receptacles of equivalent or smaller size as compared to the tested primary receptacles may be used provided:

(i) The primary receptacles are of similar design to the tested primary receptacle (e.g. shape: round, rectangular, etc.);

(ii) The material of construction of the primary receptacle (glass, plastics, metal, etc.) offers resistance to impact and stacking forces equal to or greater than that of the originally tested primary receptacle;

(iii) The primary receptacles have the same or smaller openings and the closure is of similar design (e.g. screw cap, friction lid, etc.);

(iv) Sufficient additional cushioning material is used to take up void spaces and to prevent significant movement of the primary receptacles; and

(v) Primary receptacles are oriented within the secondary packaging in the same manner as in the tested package;

(b) A lesser number of the tested primary receptacles, or of the alternative types of primary receptacles identified in (a) above, may be used provided sufficient cushioning is added to fill the void space(s) and to prevent significant movement of the primary receptacles.

4.1.9 Special packing provisions for radioactive material

4.1.9.1 *General*

4.1.9.1.1 Radioactive material, packagings and packages shall meet the requirements of chapter 6.4. The quantity of radioactive material in a package shall not exceed the limits specified in 2.7.2.2, 2.7.2.4.1, 2.7.2.4.4, 2.7.2.4.5, 2.7.2.4.6, SP336 of chapter 3.3 and 4.1.9.3.

The types of packages for radioactive materials covered by these Regulations, are:

(a) Excepted package (see 1.5.1.5);

(b) Industrial package Type 1 (Type IP-1 package);

(c) Industrial package Type 2 (Type IP-2 package);

(d) Industrial package Type 3 (Type IP-3 package);

(e) Type A package;

(f) Type B(U) package;

(g) Type B(M) package;

(h) Type C package.

Packages containing fissile material or uranium hexafluoride are subject to additional requirements.

4.1.9.1.2 The non-fixed contamination on the external surfaces of any package shall be kept as low as practicable and, under routine conditions of transport, shall not exceed the following limits:

(a) 4 Bq/cm^2 for beta and gamma emitters and low toxicity alpha emitters; and

(b) 0.4 Bq/cm^2 for all other alpha emitters.

These limits are applicable when averaged over any area of 300 cm^2 of any part of the surface.

4.1.9.1.3 A package shall not contain any items other than those that are necessary for the use of the radioactive material. The interaction between these items and the package under the conditions of transport applicable to the design, shall not reduce the safety of the package.

4.1.9.1.4 Except as provided in 7.1.8.5.5, the level of non-fixed contamination on the external and internal surfaces of overpacks, freight containers and conveyances shall not exceed the limits specified in 4.1.9.1.2. This requirement does not apply to the internal surfaces of freight containers being used as packagings, either loaded or empty.

4.1.9.1.5 For radioactive material having other dangerous properties the package design shall take into account those properties. Radioactive material with a subsidiary hazard, packaged in packages that do not require competent authority approval, shall be transported in packagings, IBCs, tanks or bulk containers fully complying with the requirements of the relevant chapters of part 6 as appropriate, as well as applicable requirements of chapters 4.1, 4.2 or 4.3 for that subsidiary hazard.

4.1.9.1.6 Before a packaging is first used to transport radioactive material, it shall be confirmed that it has been manufactured in conformity with the design specifications to ensure compliance with the relevant provisions of these Regulations and any applicable certificate of approval. The following requirements shall also be fulfilled, if applicable:

(a) If the design pressure of the containment system exceeds 35 kPa (gauge), it shall be ensured that the containment system of each packaging conforms to the approved design requirements relating to the capability of that system to maintain its integrity under that pressure;

(b) For each packaging intended for use as a Type B(U), Type B(M) or Type C package and for each packaging intended to contain fissile material, it shall be ensured that the effectiveness of its shielding and containment and, where necessary, the heat transfer characteristics and the effectiveness of the confinement system, are within the limits applicable to or specified for the approved design;

(c) For each packaging intended to contain fissile material, it shall be ensured that the effectiveness of the criticality safety features is within the limits applicable to or specified for the design and in particular where, in order to comply with the requirements of 6.4.11.1 neutron poisons are specifically included, checks shall be performed to confirm the presence and distribution of those neutron poisons.

4.1.9.1.7 Before each shipment of any package, it shall be ensured that the package contains neither:

(a) Radionuclides different from those specified for the package design; nor

(b) Contents in a form, or physical or chemical state different from those specified for the package design.

4.1.9.1.8 Before each shipment of any package, it shall be ensured that all the requirements specified in the relevant provisions of these Regulations and in the applicable certificates of approval have been fulfilled. The following requirements shall also be fulfilled, if applicable:

(a) It shall be ensured that lifting attachments which do not meet the requirements of 6.4.2.2 have been removed or otherwise rendered incapable of being used for lifting the package, in accordance with 6.4.2.3;

(b) Each Type B(U), Type B(M) and Type C package shall be held until equilibrium conditions have been approached closely enough to demonstrate compliance with the requirements for temperature and pressure unless an exemption from these requirements has received unilateral approval;

(c) For each Type B(U), Type B(M) and Type C package, it shall be ensured by inspection and/or appropriate tests that all closures, valves and other openings of the containment system through which the radioactive contents might escape are properly closed and, where appropriate, sealed in the manner for which the demonstrations of compliance with the requirements of 6.4.8.8 and 6.4.10.3 were made;

(d) For packages containing fissile material the measurement specified in 6.4.11.5 (b) and the tests to demonstrate closure of each package as specified in 6.4.11.8 shall be performed;

(e) For packages intended to be used for shipment after storage, it shall be ensured that all packaging components and radioactive contents have been maintained during storage in a manner such that all the requirements specified in the relevant provisions of these Regulations and in the applicable certificates of approval have been fulfilled.

4.1.9.1.9 The consignor shall also have a copy of any instructions with regard to the proper closing of the package and any preparation for shipment before making any shipment under the terms of the certificates.

4.1.9.1.10 Except for consignments under exclusive use, the transport index of any package or overpack shall not exceed 10, nor shall the criticality safety index of any package or overpack exceed 50.

4.1.9.1.11 Except for packages or overpacks transported under exclusive use by rail or by road under the conditions specified in 7.2.3.1.2 (a), or under exclusive use and special arrangement by vessel or by air under the conditions specified in 7.2.3.2.1 or 7.2.3.3.3 respectively, the maximum dose rate at any point on any external surface of a package or overpack shall not exceed 2 mSv/h.

4.1.9.1.12 The maximum dose rate at any point on any external surface of a package or overpack under exclusive use shall not exceed 10 mSv/h.

4.1.9.2 *Requirements and controls for transport of LSA material and SCO*

4.1.9.2.1 The quantity of LSA material or SCO in a single Type IP-1 package, Type IP-2 package, Type IP-3 package, or object or collection of objects, whichever is appropriate, shall be so restricted that the external dose rate at 3 m from the unshielded material or object or collection of objects does not exceed 10 mSv/h.

4.1.9.2.2 For LSA material and SCO which are or contain fissile material, which is not excepted under 2.7.2.3.5, the applicable requirements of 7.1.8.4.1 and 7.1.8.4.2 shall be met.

4.1.9.2.3 For LSA material and SCO which are or contain fissile material, the applicable requirements of 6.4.11.1 shall be met.

4.1.9.2.4 LSA material and SCO in groups LSA-I, SCO-I and SCO-III may be transported unpackaged under the following conditions:

(a) All unpackaged material other than ores containing only naturally occurring radionuclides shall be transported in such a manner that under routine conditions of transport there will be no escape of the radioactive contents from the conveyance nor will there be any loss of shielding;

(b) Each conveyance shall be under exclusive use, except when only transporting SCO-I on which the contamination on the accessible and the inaccessible surfaces is not greater than ten times the applicable level specified in 2.7.1.2;

(c) For SCO-I where it is suspected that non-fixed contamination exists on inaccessible surfaces in excess of the values specified in 2.7.2.3.2 (a)(i), measures shall be taken to ensure that the radioactive material is not released into the conveyance;

(d) Unpackaged fissile material shall meet the requirements of 2.7.2.3.5 (e);

(e) For SCO-III:

(i) Transport shall be under exclusive use by road, rail, inland waterway or sea.

(ii) Stacking shall not be permitted.

(iii) All activities associated with the shipment, including radiation protection, emergency response and any special precautions or special administrative or operational controls that are to be employed during transport shall be described in a transport plan. The transport plan shall demonstrate that the overall level of safety in transport is at least equivalent to that which would be provided if the requirements of 6.4.7.14 (only for the test specified in 6.4.15.6, preceded by the tests specified in 6.4.15.2 and 6.4.15.3 had been met.

(iv) The requirements of 6.4.5.1 and 6.4.5.2 for a Type IP-2 package shall be satisfied, except that the maximum damage referred to in 6.4.15.4 may be determined based on provisions in the transport plan, and the requirements of 6.4.15.5 are not applicable.

(v) The object and any shielding are secured to the conveyance in accordance with 6.4.2.1.

(vi) The shipment shall be subject to multilateral approval.

4.1.9.2.5   LSA material and SCO, except as otherwise specified in 4.1.9.2.4, shall be packaged in accordance with table 4.1.9.2.5.

Table 4.1.9.2.5: Industrial package requirements for LSA material and SCO

Radioactive contents	Industrial package type	
	Exclusive use	Not under exclusive use
LSA-I		
Solid[a]	Type IP-1	Type IP-1
Liquid	Type IP-1	Type IP-2
LSA-II		
Solid	Type IP-2	Type IP-2
Liquid and gas	Type IP-2	Type IP-3
LSA-III	Type IP-2	Type IP-3
SCO-I[a]	Type IP-1	Type IP-1
SCO-II	Type IP-2	Type IP-2

[a] *Under the conditions specified in 4.1.9.2.4, LSA-I material and SCO-I may be transported unpackaged.*

4.1.9.3   *Packages containing fissile material*

4.1.9.3.1   The contents of packages containing fissile material shall be as specified for the package design either directly in these Regulations or in the certificate of approval.

CHAPTER 4.2

USE OF PORTABLE TANKS AND MULTIPLE-ELEMENT GAS CONTAINERS (MEGCs)

4.2.1 General provisions for the use of portable tanks for the transport of substances of Class 1 and Classes 3 to 9

4.2.1.1　　This section provides general requirements applicable to the use of portable tanks for the transport of substances of Classes 1, 3, 4, 5, 6, 7, 8 and 9. In addition to these general requirements, portable tanks shall conform to the design, construction, inspection and testing requirements detailed in 6.7.2. Substances shall be transported in portable tanks conforming to the applicable portable tank instruction identified in Column 10 of the Dangerous Goods List and described in 4.2.5.2.6 (T1 to T23) and the portable tank special provisions assigned to each substance in Column 11 of the Dangerous Goods List and described in 4.2.5.3.

4.2.1.2　　During transport, portable tanks shall be adequately protected against damage to the shell and service equipment resulting from lateral and longitudinal impact and overturning. If the shell and service equipment are so constructed as to withstand impact or overturning it need not be protected in this way. Examples of such protection are given in 6.7.2.17.5.

4.2.1.3　　Certain substances are chemically unstable. They are accepted for transport only when the necessary steps have been taken to prevent their dangerous decomposition, transformation or polymerization during transport. To this end, care shall in particular be taken to ensure that shells do not contain any substances liable to promote these reactions.

4.2.1.4　　The temperature of the outer surface of the shell excluding openings and their closures or of the thermal insulation shall not exceed 70 °C during transport. When necessary, the shell shall be thermally insulated.

4.2.1.5　　Empty portable tanks not cleaned and not gas-free shall comply with the same requirements as portable tanks filled with the previous substance.

4.2.1.6　　Substances shall not be transported in the same or adjoining compartments of shells when they may react dangerously with each other and cause:

　　　　(a)　Combustion and/or evolution of considerable heat;

　　　　(b)　Evolution of flammable, toxic or asphyxiant gases;

　　　　(c)　The formation of corrosive substances;

　　　　(d)　The formation of unstable substances;

　　　　(e)　Dangerous rise in pressure.

4.2.1.7　　The design approval certificate, the test report and the certificate showing the results of the initial inspection and test for each portable tank issued by the competent authority or its authorized body shall be retained by the authority or body and the owner. Owners shall be able to provide this documentation upon the request of any competent authority.

4.2.1.8　　Unless the name of the substance(s) being transported appears on the metal plate described in 6.7.2.20.2, a copy of the certificate specified in 6.7.2.18.1 shall be made available upon the request of a competent authority or its authorized body and readily provided by the consignor, consignee or agent, as appropriate.

4.2.1.9 *Degree of filling*

4.2.1.9.1 Prior to filling, the consignor shall ensure that the appropriate portable tank is used and that the portable tank is not loaded with substances which in contact with the materials of the shell, gaskets, service equipment and any protective linings, are likely to react dangerously with them to form dangerous products or appreciably weaken these materials. The consignor may need to consult the manufacturer of the substance in conjunction with the competent authority for guidance on the compatibility of the substance with the portable tank materials.

4.2.1.9.1.1 Portable tanks shall not be filled above the extent provided in 4.2.1.9.2 to 4.2.1.9.6. The applicability of 4.2.1.9.2, 4.2.1.9.3 or 4.2.1.9.5.1 to individual substances is specified in the applicable portable tank instructions or special provisions in 4.2.5.2.6 or 4.2.5.3 and Columns 10 or 11 of the Dangerous Goods List.

4.2.1.9.2 The maximum degree of filling (in %) for general use is determined by the formula:

$$\text{Degree of filling} = \frac{97}{1 + \alpha (t_r - t_f)}$$

4.2.1.9.3 The maximum degree of filling (in %) for liquids of Division 6.1 and Class 8, in packing groups I and II, and liquids with an absolute vapour pressure of more than 175 kPa (1.75 bar) at 65 °C, is determined by the formula:

$$\text{Degree of filling} = \frac{95}{1 + \alpha (t_r - t_f)}$$

4.2.1.9.4 In these formulae, α is the mean coefficient of cubical expansion of the liquid between the mean temperature of the liquid during filling (t_f) and the maximum mean bulk temperature during transport (t_r) (both in °C). For liquids transported under ambient conditions α could be calculated by the formula:

$$\alpha = \frac{d_{15} - d_{50}}{35 d_{50}}$$

in which d_{15} and d_{50} are the densities of the liquid at 15 °C and 50 °C, respectively.

4.2.1.9.4.1 The maximum mean bulk temperature (t_r) shall be taken as 50 °C except that, for journeys under temperate or extreme climatic conditions, the competent authorities concerned may agree to a lower or require a higher temperature, as appropriate.

4.2.1.9.5 The requirements of 4.2.1.9.2 to 4.2.1.9.4.1 do not apply to portable tanks which contain substances maintained at a temperature above 50 °C during transport (e.g. by means of a heating device). For portable tanks equipped with a heating device, a temperature regulator shall be used to ensure the maximum degree of filling is not more than 95 % full at any time during transport.

4.2.1.9.5.1 The maximum degree of filling (in %) for solids transported above their melting points and for elevated temperature liquids shall be determined by the following formula:

$$\text{Degree of filling} = 95 \frac{d_r}{d_f}$$

in which d_f and d_r are the densities of the liquid at the mean temperature of the liquid during filling and the maximum mean bulk temperature during transport respectively.

4.2.1.9.6 Portable tanks shall not be offered for transport:

(a) With a degree of filling, for liquids having a viscosity less than 2 680 mm²/s at 20 °C or maximum temperature of the substance during transport in the case of the heated substance, of more than 20 % but less than 80 % unless the shells of portable tanks are divided, by partitions or surge plates, into sections of not more than 7 500 litres capacity;

(b)   With residue of substances previously transported adhering to the outside of the shell or service equipment;

(c)   When leaking or damaged to such an extent that the integrity of the portable tank or its lifting or securing arrangements may be affected; and

(d)   Unless the service equipment has been examined and found to be in good working order.

4.2.1.9.7   Forklift pockets of portable tanks shall be closed off when the tank is filled. This provision does not apply to portable tanks which according to 6.7.2.17.4 need not be provided with a means of closing off the forklift pockets.

4.2.1.10 *Additional provisions applicable to the transport of Class 3 substances in portable tanks*

4.2.1.10.1   All portable tanks intended for the transport of flammable liquids shall be closed and be fitted with relief devices in accordance with 6.7.2.8 to 6.7.2.15.

4.2.1.10.1.1   For portable tanks intended for use only on land, the pertinent regulations governing transport by land may allow open venting systems.

4.2.1.11 *Additional provisions applicable to the transport of Class 4 substances (other than Division 4.1 self-reactive substances) in portable tanks*

   Reserved.

NOTE: *For Division 4.1 self-reactive substances, see 4.2.1.13.1.*

4.2.1.12 *Additional provisions applicable to the transport of Division 5.1 substances in portable tanks*

   Reserved.

4.2.1.13 *Additional provisions applicable to the transport of Division 5.2 substances and Division 4.1 self-reactive substances in portable tanks*

4.2.1.13.1   Each substance shall have been tested and a report submitted to the competent authority of the country of origin for approval. Notification thereof shall be sent to the competent authority of the country of destination. The notification shall contain relevant transport information and the report with test results. The tests undertaken shall include those necessary:

(a)   To prove the compatibility of all materials normally in contact with the substance during transport;

(b)   To provide data for the design of the pressure and emergency relief devices taking into account the design characteristics of the portable tank.

   Any additional provision necessary for safe transport of the substance shall be clearly described in the report.

4.2.1.13.2   The following provisions apply to portable tanks intended for the transport of Type F organic peroxides or Type F self-reactive substances with a Self-Accelerating Decomposition Temperature (SADT) of 55 °C or more. In case of conflict these provisions prevail over those specified in section 6.7.2. Emergencies to be taken into account are self-accelerating decomposition of the substance and fire-engulfment as described in 4.2.1.13.8.

4.2.1.13.3   The additional provisions for transport of organic peroxides or self-reactive substances with an SADT less than 55 °C in portable tanks shall be specified by the competent authority of the country of origin. Notification thereof shall be sent to the competent authority of the country of destination.

4.2.1.13.4   The portable tank shall be designed for a test pressure of at least 0.4 MPa (4 bar).

4.2.1.13.5   Portable tanks shall be fitted with temperature sensing devices.

4.2.1.13.6   Portable tanks shall be fitted with pressure-relief devices and emergency-relief devices. Vacuum-relief devices may also be used. Pressure-relief devices shall operate at pressures determined according to both the properties of the substance and the construction characteristics of the portable tank. Fusible elements are not allowed in the shell.

4.2.1.13.7   The pressure-relief devices shall consist of spring-loaded valves fitted to prevent significant build-up within the portable tank of the decomposition products and vapours released at a temperature of 50 °C. The capacity and start-to-discharge pressure of the relief valves shall be based on the results of the tests specified in 4.2.1.13.1. The start-to-discharge pressure shall, however, in no case be such that liquid would escape from the valve(s) if the portable tank were overturned.

4.2.1.13.8   The emergency-relief devices may be of the spring-loaded or frangible types, or a combination of the two, designed to vent all the decomposition products and vapours evolved during a period of not less than one hour of complete fire-engulfment as calculated by the following formula:

$$q = 70961 \times F \times A^{0.82}$$

where:

q = heat absorption [W]
A = wetted area [m^2]
F = insulation factor
F = 1 for non-insulated shells, or

$$F = \frac{U(923 - T)}{47032} \text{ for insulated shells}$$

where:

K = heat conductivity of insulation layer [W·m^{-1}·K^{-1}]
L = thickness of insulation layer [m]
U = K/L = heat transfer coefficient of the insulation [W·m^{-2}·K^{-1}]
T = temperature of substance at relieving conditions [K]

The start-to-discharge pressure of the emergency-relief device(s) shall be higher than that specified in 4.2.1.13.7 and based on the results of the tests referred to in 4.2.1.13.1. The emergency-relief devices shall be dimensioned in such a way that the maximum pressure in the portable tank never exceeds the test pressure of the tank.

NOTE: *An example of a method to determine the size of emergency-relief devices is given in appendix 5 of the "Manual of Tests and Criteria".*

4.2.1.13.9   For insulated portable tanks the capacity and setting of emergency-relief device(s) shall be determined assuming a loss of insulation from 1 % of the surface area.

4.2.1.13.10   Vacuum-relief devices and spring-loaded valves shall be provided with flame arresters. Due attention shall be paid to the reduction of the relief capacity caused by the flame arrester.

4.2.1.13.11   Service equipment such as valves and external piping shall be so arranged that no substance remains in them after filling the portable tank.

4.2.1.13.12   Portable tanks may be either insulated or protected by a sun-shield. If the SADT of the substance in the portable tank is 55 °C or less, or the portable tank is constructed of aluminium, the portable tank shall be completely insulated. The outer surface shall be finished in white or bright metal.

4.2.1.13.13   The degree of filling shall not exceed 90 % at 15 °C.

4.2.1.13.14   The mark as required in 6.7.2.20.2 shall include the UN number and the technical name with the approved concentration of the substance concerned.

4.2.1.13.15   Organic peroxides and self-reactive substances specifically listed in portable tank instruction T23 in 4.2.5.2.6 may be transported in portable tanks.

4.2.1.14   *Additional provisions applicable to the transport of Division 6.1 substances in portable tanks*

Reserved.

4.2.1.15   *Additional provisions applicable to the transport of Division 6.2 substances in portable tanks*

Reserved.

4.2.1.16   *Additional provisions applicable to the transport of Class 7 substances in portable tanks*

4.2.1.16.1   Portable tanks used for the transport of radioactive material shall not be used for the transport of other goods.

4.2.1.16.2   The degree of filling for portable tanks shall not exceed 90 % or, alternatively, any other value approved by the competent authority.

4.2.1.17   *Additional provisions applicable to the transport of Class 8 substances in portable tanks*

4.2.1.17.1   Pressure-relief devices of portable tanks used for the transport of Class 8 substances shall be inspected at intervals not exceeding one year.

4.2.1.18   *Additional provisions applicable to the transport of Class 9 substances in portable tanks*

Reserved.

4.2.1.19   *Additional provisions applicable to the transport of solid substances transported above their melting point*

4.2.1.19.1   Solid substances transported or offered for transport above their melting point which are not assigned a portable tank instruction in Column 10 of the Dangerous Goods List or when the assigned portable tank instruction does not apply to transport at temperatures above their melting point may be transported in portable tanks provided that the solid substances are classified in Divisions 4.1, 4.2, 4.3, 5.1 or 6.1 or Classes 8 or 9 and have no subsidiary hazard other than that of Division 6.1 or Class 8 and are in packing group II or III.

4.2.1.19.2   Unless otherwise indicated in the Dangerous Goods List of chapter 3.2, portable tanks used for the transport of these solid substances above their melting point shall conform to the provisions of portable tank instruction T4 for solid substances of packing group III or T7 for solid substances of packing group II. A portable tank that affords an equivalent or greater level of safety may be selected according to 4.2.5.2.5. The maximum degree of filling (in %) shall be determined according to 4.2.1.9.5 (TP3).

4.2.2   **General provisions for the use of portable tanks for the transport of non-refrigerated liquefied gases and chemicals under pressure**

4.2.2.1   This section provides general requirements applicable to the use of portable tanks for the transport of non-refrigerated liquefied gases and chemicals under pressure.

4.2.2.2		Portable tanks shall conform to the design, construction, inspection and testing requirements detailed in 6.7.3. Non-refrigerated liquefied gases and chemicals under pressure shall be transported in portable tanks conforming to portable tank instruction T50 as described in 4.2.5.2.6 and any portable tank special provisions assigned to specific non-refrigerated liquefied gases in Column 11 of the Dangerous Goods List and described in 4.2.5.3.

4.2.2.3		During transport, portable tanks shall be adequately protected against damage to the shell and service equipment resulting from lateral and longitudinal impact and overturning. If the shell and service equipment are so constructed as to withstand impact or overturning it need not be protected in this way. Examples of such protection are given in 6.7.3.13.5.

4.2.2.4		Certain non-refrigerated liquefied gases are chemically unstable. They are accepted for transport only when the necessary steps have been taken to prevent their dangerous decomposition, transformation or polymerization during transport. To this end, care shall in particular be taken to ensure that portable tanks do not contain any non-refrigerated liquefied gases liable to promote these reactions.

4.2.2.5		Unless the name of the gas(es) being transported appears on the metal plate described in 6.7.3.16.2, a copy of the certificate specified in 6.7.3.14.1 shall be made available upon a competent authority request and readily provided by the consignor, consignee or agent, as appropriate.

4.2.2.6		Empty portable tanks not cleaned and not gas-free shall comply with the same requirements as portable tanks filled with the previous non-refrigerated liquefied gas.

## 4.2.2.7	*Filling*

4.2.2.7.1		Prior to filling the consignor shall ensure that the portable tank is approved for the non-refrigerated liquefied gas or the propellant of the chemical under pressure to be transported and that the portable tank is not loaded with non-refrigerated liquefied gases, or with chemicals under pressure which in contact with the materials of the shell, gaskets and service equipment, are likely to react dangerously with them to form dangerous products or appreciably weaken these materials. During filling, the temperature of the non-refrigerated liquefied gas or propellant of chemicals under pressure shall fall within the limits of the design temperature range.

4.2.2.7.2		The maximum mass of non-refrigerated liquefied gas per litre of shell capacity (kg/l) shall not exceed the density of the non-refrigerated liquefied gas at 50 °C multiplied by 0.95. Furthermore, the shell shall not be liquid-full at 60 °C.

4.2.2.7.3		Portable tanks shall not be filled above their maximum permissible gross mass and the maximum permissible load mass specified for each gas to be transported.

4.2.2.8		Portable tanks shall not be offered for transport:

  (a)	In an ullage condition liable to produce an unacceptable hydraulic force due to surge within the portable tank;

  (b)	When leaking;

  (c)	When damaged to such an extent that the integrity of the tank or its lifting or securing arrangements may be affected; and

  (d)	Unless the service equipment has been examined and found to be in good working order.

4.2.2.9		Forklift pockets of portable tanks shall be closed off when the tank is filled. This provision does not apply to portable tanks which according to 6.7.3.13.4 need not be provided with a means of closing off the forklift pockets.

4.2.3 General provisions for the use of portable tanks for the transport of refrigerated liquefied gases

4.2.3.1 This section provides general requirements applicable to the use of portable tanks for the transport of refrigerated liquefied gases.

4.2.3.2 Portable tanks shall conform to the design, construction, inspection and testing requirements detailed in 6.7.4. Refrigerated liquefied gases shall be transported in portable tanks conforming to portable tank instruction T75 as described in 4.2.5.2.6 and the portable tank special provisions assigned to each substance in Column 11 of the Dangerous Goods List and described in 4.2.5.3.

4.2.3.3 During transport, portable tanks shall be adequately protected against damage to the shell and service equipment resulting from lateral and longitudinal impact and overturning. If the shell and service equipment are so constructed as to withstand impact or overturning it need not be protected in this way. Examples of such protection are provided in 6.7.4.12.5.

4.2.3.4 Unless the name of the gas(es) being transported appears on the metal plate described in 6.7.4.15.2, a copy of the certificate specified in 6.7.4.13.1 shall be made available upon a competent authority request and readily provided by the consignor, consignee or agent, as appropriate.

4.2.3.5 Empty portable tanks not cleaned and not gas-free shall comply with the same requirements as portable tanks filled with the previous substance.

4.2.3.6 *Filling*

4.2.3.6.1 Prior to filling the consignor shall ensure that the portable tank is approved for the refrigerated liquefied gas to be transported and that the portable tank is not loaded with refrigerated liquefied gases which in contact with the materials of the shell, gaskets and service equipment, are likely to react dangerously with them to form dangerous products or appreciably weaken these materials. During filling, the temperature of the refrigerated liquefied gas shall be within the limits of the design temperature range.

4.2.3.6.2 In estimating the initial quantity of gas filled into the shell, the necessary holding time for the intended journey including any delays which might be encountered shall be taken into consideration. The initial quantity of gas filled into the shell, except as provided for in 4.2.3.6.3 and 4.2.3.6.4, shall be such that if the contents, except helium, were to be raised to a temperature at which the vapour pressure is equal to the maximum allowable working pressure (MAWP) the volume occupied by liquid would not exceed 98 %.

4.2.3.6.3 Shells intended for the transport of helium can be filled up to but not above the inlet of the pressure-relief device.

4.2.3.6.4 A higher initial quantity of gas filled into the shell may be allowed, subject to approval by the competent authority, when the intended duration of transport is considerably shorter than the holding time.

4.2.3.7 *Actual holding time*

4.2.3.7.1 The actual holding time shall be calculated for each journey in accordance with a procedure recognized by the competent authority, on the basis of the following:

(a) The reference holding time for the refrigerated liquefied gas to be transported (see 6.7.4.2.8.1) (as indicated on the plate referred to in 6.7.4.15.1);

(b) The actual filling density;

(c) The actual filling pressure;

(d) The lowest set pressure of the pressure limiting device(s).

4.2.3.7.2 The actual holding time shall be marked either on the portable tank itself or on a metal plate firmly secured to the portable tank, in accordance with 6.7.4.15.2.

4.2.3.7.3   The date at which the actual holding time ends shall be entered in the transport document (see 5.4.1.5.13).

4.2.3.8   Portable tanks shall not be offered for transport:

(a) In an ullage condition liable to produce an unacceptable hydraulic force due to surge within the shell;

(b) When leaking;

(c) When damaged to such an extent that the integrity of the portable tank or its lifting or securing arrangements may be affected;

(d) Unless the service equipment has been examined and found to be in good working order;

(e) Unless the actual holding time for the refrigerated liquefied gas being transported has been determined in accordance with 4.2.3.7 and the portable tank is marked in accordance with 6.7.4.15.2; and

(f) Unless the duration of transport, after taking into consideration any delays which might be encountered, does not exceed the actual holding time.

4.2.3.9   Forklift pockets of portable tanks shall be closed off when the tank is filled. This provision does not apply to portable tanks which according to 6.7.4.12.4 need not be provided with a means of closing off the forklift pockets.

4.2.4   General provisions for the use of multiple-element gas containers (MEGCs)

4.2.4.1   This section provides general requirements applicable to the use of multiple-element gas containers (MEGCs) for the transport of non-refrigerated gases.

4.2.4.2   MEGCs shall conform to the design, construction, inspection and testing requirements detailed in 6.7.5. The elements of MEGCs shall be periodically inspected according to the provisions set out in P200 and in 6.2.1.6.

4.2.4.3   During transport, MEGCs shall be protected against damage to the elements and service equipment resulting from lateral and longitudinal impact and overturning. If the elements and service equipment are so constructed as to withstand impact or overturning, they need not be protected in this way. Examples of such protection are given in 6.7.5.10.4.

4.2.4.4   The periodic testing and inspection requirements for MEGCs are specified in 6.7.5.12. MEGCs or their elements shall not be charged or filled after they become due for periodic inspection but may be transported after the expiry of the time limit.

4.2.4.5   *Filling*

4.2.4.5.1   Prior to filling, the MEGC shall be inspected to ensure that it is authorized for the gas to be transported and that the applicable provisions of these Regulations have been met.

4.2.4.5.2   Elements of MEGCs shall be filled according to the working pressures, filling ratios and filling provisions specified in packing instruction P200 for the specific gas being filled into each element. In no case shall a MEGC or group of elements be filled as a unit in excess of the lowest working pressure of any given element.

4.2.4.5.3   MEGCs shall not be filled above their maximum permissible gross mass.

4.2.4.5.4   Isolation valves shall be closed after filling and remain closed during transport. Toxic gases of division 2.3 shall only be transported in MEGCs where each element is equipped with an isolation valve.

4.2.4.5.5   The opening(s) for filling shall be closed by caps or plugs. The leakproofness of the closures and equipment shall be verified by the consignor after filling.

4.2.4.5.6   MEGCs shall not be offered for filling:

    (a)   when damaged to such an extent that the integrity of the pressure receptacles or its structural or service equipment may be affected;

    (b)   unless the pressure receptacles and its structural and service equipment has been examined and found to be in good working order; and

    (c)   unless the required certification, retest, and filling marks are legible.

4.2.4.6   Charged MEGCs shall not be offered for transport:

    (a)   when leaking;

    (b)   when damaged to such an extent that the integrity of the pressure receptacles or its structural or service equipment may be affected;

    (c)   unless the pressure receptacles and its structural and service equipment have been examined and found to be in good working order; and

    (d)   unless the required certification, retest, and filling marks are legible.

4.2.4.7   Empty MEGCs that have not been cleaned and purged shall comply with the same requirements as MEGCs filled with the previous substance.

4.2.5   Portable tank instructions and special provisions

4.2.5.1   *General*

4.2.5.1.1   This section includes the portable tank instructions and special provisions applicable to dangerous goods authorized to be transported in portable tanks. Each portable tank instruction is identified by an alpha-numeric designation (e.g. T1). Column 10 of the Dangerous Goods List in chapter 3.2 indicates the portable tank instruction that shall be used for each substance permitted for transport in a portable tank. When no portable tank instruction appears in Column 10 for a specific dangerous goods entry then transport of the substance in portable tanks is not permitted unless a competent authority approval is granted as detailed in 6.7.1.3. Portable tank special provisions are assigned to specific dangerous goods in Column 11 of the Dangerous Goods List in chapter 3.2. Each portable tank special provision is identified by an alpha-numeric designation (e.g. TP1). A listing of the portable tank special provisions is provided in 4.2.5.3.

NOTE: The gases authorized for transport in MEGCs are indicated in the column "MEGC" in tables 1 and 2 of packing instruction P200 in 4.1.4.1.

4.2.5.2   *Portable tank instructions*

4.2.5.2.1   Portable tank instructions apply to dangerous goods of Classes 1 to 9. Portable tank instructions provide specific information relevant to portable tanks provisions applicable to specific substances. These provisions shall be met in addition to the general provisions of this chapter and the general requirements of chapter 6.7 or chapter 6.9.

4.2.5.2.2   For substances of Class 1 and Classes 3 to 9, the portable tank instructions indicate the applicable minimum test pressure, the minimum shell thickness (in reference steel or the minimum shell thickness of fibre-reinforced plastics), bottom opening requirements and pressure relief requirements. In T23, self-reactive substances of Division 4.1 and Division 5.2 organic peroxides permitted to be transported in portable tanks are listed along with the applicable control and emergency temperatures.

4.2.5.2.3   Non-refrigerated liquefied gases are assigned to portable tank instruction T50. T50 provides the maximum allowable working pressures, bottom opening requirements, pressure relief requirements and filling ratio requirements for non-refrigerated liquefied gases permitted for transport in portable tanks.

4.2.5.2.4   Refrigerated liquefied gases are assigned to portable tank instruction T75.

4.2.5.2.5   *Determination of the appropriate portable tank instructions*

When a specific portable tank instruction is specified in Column 10 for a specific dangerous goods entry, additional portable tanks which possess higher test pressures, greater shell thicknesses, more stringent bottom opening and pressure-relief device arrangements may be used. The following guidelines apply to determining the appropriate portable tanks which may be used for transport of particular substances:

Portable tank instruction specified	Portable tank instructions also permitted
T1	T2, T3, T4, T5, T6, T7, T8, T9, T10, T11, T12, T13, T14, T15, T16, T17, T18, T19, T20, T21, T22
T2	T4, T5, T7, T8, T9, T10, T11, T12, T13, T14, T15, T16, T17, T18, T19, T20, T21, T22
T3	T4, T5, T6, T7, T8, T9, T10, T11, T12, T13, T14, T15, T16, T17, T18, T19, T20, T21, T22
T4	T5, T7, T8, T9, T10, T11, T12, T13, T14, T15, T16, T17, T18, T19, T20, T21, T22
T5	T10, T14, T19, T20, T22
T6	T7, T8, T9, T10, T11, T12, T13, T14, T15, T16, T17, T18, T19, T20, T21, T22
T7	T8, T9, T10, T11, T12, T13, T14, T15, T16, T17, T18, T19, T20, T21, T22
T8	T9, T10, T13, T14, T19, T20, T21, T22
T9	T10, T13, T14, T19, T20, T21, T22
T10	T14, T19, T20, T22
T11	T12, T13, T14, T15, T16, T17, T18, T19, T20, T21, T22
T12	T14, T16, T18, T19, T20, T22
T13	T14, T19, T20, T21, T22
T14	T19, T20, T22
T15	T16, T17, T18, T19, T20, T21, T22
T16	T18, T19, T20, T22
T17	T18, T19, T20, T21, T22
T18	T19, T20, T22
T19	T20, T22
T20	T22
T21	T22
T22	None
T23	None

4.2.5.2.6   *Portable tank instructions*

Portable tank instructions specify the requirements applicable to a portable tank when used for the transport of specific substances. Portable tank instructions T1 to T22 specify the applicable minimum test pressure, the minimum shell thickness (in mm reference steel) or the minimum shell thickness for fibre reinforced plastics (FRP) portable tanks, and the pressure-relief and bottom-opening requirements.

T1 - T22	PORTABLE TANK INSTRUCTIONS			T1 - T22
These portable tank instructions apply to liquid and solid substances of Class 1 and Classes 3 to 9. The general provisions of section 4.2.1 and the requirements of section 6.7.2 shall be met. The instructions for portable tanks with FRP shells apply to substances of Classes or Divisions 1, 3, 5.1, 6.1, 6.2, 8 and 9. Additionally, the requirements of chapter 6.9 apply to the portable tanks with FRP shells.				
Portable tank instruction	Minimum test pressure (bar)	Minimum shell thickness (in mm-reference steel) (see 6.7.2.4)	Pressure-relief requirements[a] (see 6.7.2.8)	Bottom opening requirements[b] (see 6.7.2.6)
T1	1.5	See 6.7.2.4.2	Normal	See 6.7.2.6.2
T2	1.5	See 6.7.2.4.2	Normal	See 6.7.2.6.3
T3	2.65	See 6.7.2.4.2	Normal	See 6.7.2.6.2
T4	2.65	See 6.7.2.4.2	Normal	See 6.7.2.6.3
T5	2.65	See 6.7.2.4.2	See 6.7.2.8.3	Not Allowed
T6	4	See 6.7.2.4.2	Normal	See 6.7.2.6.2
T7	4	See 6.7.2.4.2	Normal	See 6.7.2.6.3
T8	4	See 6.7.2.4.2	Normal	Not allowed
T9	4	6 mm	Normal	Not allowed
T10	4	6 mm	See 6.7.2.8.3	Not allowed
T11	6	See 6.7.2.4.2	Normal	See 6.7.2.6.3
T12	6	See 6.7.2.4.2	See 6.7.2.8.3	See 6.7.2.6.3
T13	6	6 mm	Normal	Not allowed
T14	6	6 mm	See 6.7.2.8.3	Not allowed
T15	10	See 6.7.2.4.2	Normal	See 6.7.2.6.3
T16	10	See 6.7.2.4.2	See 6.7.2.8.3	See 6.7.2.6.3
T17	10	6 mm	Normal	See 6.7.2.6.3
T18	10	6 mm	See 6.7.2.8.3	See 6.7.2.6.3
T19	10	6 mm	See 6.7.2.8.3	Not allowed
T20	10	8 mm	See 6.7.2.8.3	Not allowed
T21	10	10 mm	Normal	Not allowed
T22	10	10 mm	See 6.7.2.8.3	Not allowed

[a]   When the word "Normal" is indicated, all the requirements of 6.7.2.8 apply except for 6.7.2.8.3.

[b]   When this column indicates "not allowed", bottom openings are not permitted when the substance to be transported is a liquid (see 6.7.2.6.1). When the substance to be transported is a solid at all temperatures encountered under normal conditions of transport, bottom openings conforming to the requirements of 6.7.2.6.2 are authorized.

| T23 | PORTABLE TANK INSTRUCTION | | | | | | | T23 |

This portable tank instruction applies to self-reactive substances of Division 4.1 and organic peroxides of Division 5.2. The general provisions of section 4.2.1 and the requirements of section 6.7.2 shall be met. The provisions specific to self-reactive substances of Division 4.1 and organic peroxides of Division 5.2 in 4.2.1.13 shall also be met. The formulations not listed in 2.4.2.3.2.3 or 2.5.3.2.4 but listed below may also be transported packed in accordance with packing method OP8 of packing instruction P520 of 4.1.4.1, with the same control and emergency temperatures, if applicable.

UN No	Substance	Min. test pressure (bar)	Min. shell thickness (mm-reference steel)	Bottom opening requirements	Pressure-relief requirements	Degree of filling	Control temp.	Emergency temp.
3109	ORGANIC PEROXIDE, TYPE F, LIQUID	4	See 6.7.2.4.2	See 6.7.2.6.3	See 6.7.2.8.2 4.2.1.13.6 4.2.1.13.7 4.2.1.13.8	See 4.2.1.13.13		
	tert-Butyl hydroperoxide[a], not more than 72 % with water							
	tert-Butyl hydroperoxide, not more than 56 % in diluent type B[b]							
	Cumyl hydroperoxide, not more than 90 % in diluent type A							
	Di-tert-butyl peroxide, not more than 32 % in diluent type A							
	Isopropyl cumyl hydroperoxide, not more than 72 % in diluent type A							
	p-Menthyl hydroperoxide, not more than 72 % in diluent type A							
	Pinanyl hydroperoxide, not more than 56 % in diluent type A							
3110	ORGANIC PEROXIDE TYPE F, SOLID Dicumyl peroxide[c]	4	See 6.7.2.4.2	See 6.7.2.6.3	See 6.7.2.8.2 4.2.1.13.6 4.2.1.13.7 4.2.1.13.8	See 4.2.1.13.13		
3119	ORGANIC PEROXIDE, TYPE F, LIQUID, TEMPERATURE CONTROLLED	4	See 6.7.2.4.2	See 6.7.2.6.3	See 6.7.2.8.2 4.2.1.13.6 4.2.1.13.7 4.2.1.13.8	See 4.2.1.13.13	[d]	[d]
	tert-Amyl peroxyneodecanoate, not more than 47 % in diluent type A						-10 °C	-5 °C

[a]   *Provided that steps have been taken to achieve the safety equivalence of 65 % tert-Butyl hydroperoxide and 35 % water.*

[b]   *Diluent type B is tert-Butyl alcohol*

[c]   *Maximum quantity per portable tank 2 000 kg.*

[d]   *As approved by the competent authority.*

Cont'd on next page

T23	PORTABLE TANK INSTRUCTION *(cont'd)*							T23
UN No	Substance	Min. test pressure (bar)	Min. shell thickness (mm-reference steel)	Bottom opening requirements	Pressure-relief requirements	Degree of filling	Control temp.	Emergency temp.
3119 *(cont'd)*	tert-Butyl peroxyacetate, not more than 32 % in diluent type B						+30 °C	+35 °C
	tert-Butyl peroxy-2-ethylhexanoate, not more than 32 % in diluent type B						+15 °C	+20 °C
	tert-Butyl peroxypivalate, not more than 27 % in diluent type B						+5 °C	+10 °C
	tert-Butyl peroxy-3,5,5-trimethyl-hexanoate, not more than 32 % in diluent type B						+35 °C	+40 °C
	Di-(3,5,5-trimethyl-hexanoyl) peroxide, not more than 38 % in diluent type A or type B						0 °C	+5 °C
	Peroxyacetic acid, distilled, type F, stabilized[e]						+30 °C	+35 °C
3120	ORGANIC PEROXIDE, TYPE F, SOLID, TEMPERATURE CONTROLLED	4	See 6.7.2.4.2	See 6.7.2.6.3	See 6.7.2.8.2 4.2.1.13.6 4.2.1.13.7 4.2.1.13.8	See 4.2.1.13.13	[d]	[d]
3229	SELF-REACTIVE LIQUID TYPE F	4	See 6.7.2.4.2	See 6.7.2.6.3	See 6.7.2.8.2 4.2.1.13.6 4.2.1.13.7 4.2.1.13.8	See 4.2.1.13.13		
3230	SELF-REACTIVE SOLID TYPE F	4	See 6.7.2.4.2	See 6.7.2.6.3	See 6.7.2.8.2 4.2.1.13.6 4.2.1.13.7 4.2.1.13.8	See 4.2.1.13.13		
3239	SELF-REACTIVE LIQUID TYPE F, TEMPERATURE CONTROLLED	4	See 6.7.2.4.2	See 6.7.2.6.3	See 6.7.2.8.2 4.2.1.13.6 4.2.1.13.7 4.2.1.13.8	See 4.2.1.13.13	[d]	[d]
3240	SELF-REACTIVE SOLID TYPE F, TEMPERATURE CONTROLLED	4	See 6.7.2.4.2	See 6.7.2.6.3	See 6.7.2.8.2 4.2.1.13.6 4.2.1.13.7 4.2.1.13.8	See 4.2.1.13.13	[d]	[d]

[d] As approved by the competent authority.

[e] *Formulation derived from distillation of peroxyacetic acid originating from peroxyacetic acid in concentration of not more than 41 % with water, total active oxygen (peroxyacetic acid+H_2O_2) ≤ 9.5 %, which fulfils the criteria of 2.5.3.3.2 (f). "CORROSIVE" subsidiary hazard placard required (Model No 8, see 5.2.2.2.2).*

T50	PORTABLE TANK INSTRUCTION				T50

This portable tank instruction applies to non-refrigerated liquefied gases and chemicals under pressure (UN Nos. 3500, 3501, 3502, 3503, 3504 and 3505). The general provisions of section 4.2.2 and the requirements of section 6.7.3 shall be met.

UN No	Non-refrigerated liquefied gases	Max. allowable working pressure (bar) Small; Bare; Sunshield; Insulated; respectively[a]	Openings below liquid level	Pressure-relief requirements[b] (see 6.7.3.7)	Maximum filling ratio
1005	Ammonia, anhydrous	29.0 25.7 22.0 19.7	Allowed	See 6.7.3.7.3	0.53
1009	Bromotrifluoromethane (Refrigerant gas R 13B1)	38.0 34.0 30.0 27.5	Allowed	Normal	1.13
1010	Butadienes, stabilized	7.5 7.0 7.0 7.0	Allowed	Normal	0.55
1010	Butadienes and hydrocarbon mixture, stabilized	See MAWP definition in 6.7.3.1	Allowed	Normal	See 4.2.2.7
1011	Butane	7.0 7.0 7.0 7.0	Allowed	Normal	0.51
1012	Butylene	8.0 7.0 7.0 7.0	Allowed	Normal	0.53
1017	Chlorine	19.0 17.0 15.0 13.5	Not allowed	See 6.7.3.7.3	1.25
1018	Chlorodifluoromethane (Refrigerant gas R 22)	26.0 24.0 21.0 19.0	Allowed	Normal	1.03
1020	Chloropentafluoroethane (Refrigerant gas R 115)	23.0 20.0 18.0 16.0	Allowed	Normal	1.06
1021	1-Chloro-1,2,2,2-tetrafluoroethane (Refrigerant gas R 124)	10.3 9.8 7.9 7.0	Allowed	Normal	1.20

[a] "Small" means tanks having a shell with a diameter of 1.5 metres or less; "Bare" means tanks having a shell with a diameter of more than 1.5 metres without insulation or sun shield (see 6.7.3.2.12); "Sunshield" means tanks having a shell with a diameter of more than 1.5 metres with sun shield (see 6.7.3.2.12); "Insulated" means tanks having a shell with a diameter of more than 1.5 metres with insulation (see 6.7.3.2.12); (see definition of "Design reference temperature" in 6.7.3.1).

[b] The word "Normal" in the pressure relief requirements column indicates that a frangible disc as specified in 6.7.3.7.3 is not required.

Cont'd on next page

T50		PORTABLE TANK INSTRUCTION *(cont'd)*			T50
UN No	Non-refrigerated liquefied gases	Max. allowable working pressure (bar) Small; Bare; Sunshield; Insulated; respectively[a]	Openings below liquid level	Pressure-relief requirements[b] (see 6.7.3.7)	Maximum filling ratio
1027	Cyclopropane	18.0 16.0 14.5 13.0	Allowed	Normal	0.53
1028	Dichlorodifluoromethane (Refrigerant gas R 12)	16.0 15.0 13.0 11.5	Allowed	Normal	1.15
1029	Dichlorofluoromethane (Refrigerant gas R 21)	7.0 7.0 7.0 7.0	Allowed	Normal	1.23
1030	1,1-Difluoroethane (Refrigerant gas R 152a)	16.0 14.0 12.4 11.0	Allowed	Normal	0.79
1032	Dimethylamine, anhydrous	7.0 7.0 7.0 7.0	Allowed	Normal	0.59
1033	Dimethyl ether	15.5 13.8 12.0 10.6	Allowed	Normal	0.58
1036	Ethylamine	7.0 7.0 7.0 7.0	Allowed	Normal	0.61
1037	Ethyl chloride	7.0 7.0 7.0 7.0	Allowed	Normal	0.80
1040	Ethylene oxide with nitrogen up to a total pressure of 1MPa (10 bar) at 50 °C	- - - 10.0	Not allowed	See 6.7.3.7.3	0.78
1041	Ethylene oxide and carbon dioxide mixture with more than 9 % but not more than 87 % ethylene oxide	See MAWP definition in 6.7.3.1	Allowed	Normal	See 4.2.2.7

[a] "Small" means tanks having a shell with a diameter of 1.5 metres or less; "Bare" means tanks having a shell with a diameter of more than 1.5 metres without insulation or sun shield (see 6.7.3.2.12); "Sunshield" means tanks having a shell with a diameter of more than 1.5 metres with sun shield (see 6.7.3.2.12); "Insulated" means tanks having a shell with a diameter of more than 1.5 metres with insulation (see 6.7.3.2.12); (see definition of "Design reference temperature" in 6.7.3.1).

[b] The word "Normal" in the pressure relief requirements column indicates that a frangible disc as specified in 6.7.3.7.3 is not required.

Cont'd on next page

T50	PORTABLE TANK INSTRUCTION *(cont'd)*				T50
UN No	Non-refrigerated liquefied gases	Max. allowable working pressure (bar) Small; Bare; Sunshield; Insulated; respectively[a]	Openings below liquid level	Pressure-relief requirements[b] (see 6.7.3.7)	Maximum filling ratio
1055	Isobutylene	8.1 7.0 7.0 7.0	Allowed	Normal	0.52
1060	Methylacetylene and propadiene mixture, stabilized	28.0 24.5 22.0 20.0	Allowed	Normal	0.43
1061	Methylamine, anhydrous	10.8 9.6 7.8 7.0	Allowed	Normal	0.58
1062	Methyl bromide with not more than 2 % chloropicrin	7.0 7.0 7.0 7.0	Not allowed	See 6.7.3.7.3	1.51
1063	Methyl chloride (Refrigerant gas R 40)	14.5 12.7 11.3 10.0	Allowed	Normal	0.81
1064	Methyl mercaptan	7.0 7.0 7.0 7.0	Not allowed	See 6.7.3.7.3	0.78
1067	Dinitrogen tetroxide	7.0 7.0 7.0 7.0	Not allowed	See 6.7.3.7.3	1.30
1075	Petroleum gas, liquefied	See MAWP definition in 6.7.3.1	Allowed	Normal	See 4.2.2.7
1077	Propylene	28.0 24.5 22.0 20.0	Allowed	Normal	0.43
1078	Refrigerant gas, n.o.s.	See MAWP definition in 6.7.3.1	Allowed	Normal	See 4.2.2.7
1079	Sulphur dioxide	11.6 10.3 8.5 7.6	Not allowed	See 6.7.3.7.3	1.23

[a] *"Small" means tanks having a shell with a diameter of 1.5 metres or less; "Bare" means tanks having a shell with a diameter of more than 1.5 metres without insulation or sun shield (see 6.7.3.2.12); "Sunshield" means tanks having a shell with a diameter of more than 1.5 metres with sun shield (see 6.7.3.2.12); "Insulated" means tanks having a shell with a diameter of more than 1.5 metres with insulation (see 6.7.3.2.12); (see definition of "Design reference temperature" in 6.7.3.1).*

[b] *The word "Normal" in the pressure relief requirements column indicates that a frangible disc as specified in 6.7.3.7.3 is not required.*

Cont'd on next page

T50	PORTABLE TANK INSTRUCTION *(cont'd)*				T50
UN No	Non-refrigerated liquefied gases	Max. allowable working pressure (bar) Small; Bare; Sunshield; Insulated; respectively[a]	Openings below liquid level	Pressure-relief requirements[b] (see 6.7.3.7)	Maximum filling ratio
1082	Trifluorochloroethylene, stabilized (Refrigerant gas R 1113)	17.0 15.0 13.1 11.6	Not allowed	See 6.7.3.7.3	1.13
1083	Trimethylamine, anhydrous	7.0 7.0 7.0 7.0	Allowed	Normal	0.56
1085	Vinyl bromide, stabilized	7.0 7.0 7.0 7.0	Allowed	Normal	1.37
1086	Vinyl chloride, stabilized	10.6 9.3 8.0 7.0	Allowed	Normal	0.81
1087	Vinyl methyl ether, stabilized	7.0 7.0 7.0 7.0	Allowed	Normal	0.67
1581	Chloropicrin and methyl bromide mixture with more than 2 % chloropicrin	7.0 7.0 7.0 7.0	Not allowed	See 6.7.3.7.3	1.51
1582	Chloropicrin and methyl chloride mixture	19.2 16.9 15.1 13.1	Not allowed	See 6.7.3.7.3	0.81
1858	Hexafluoropropylene (Refrigerant gas R 1216)	19.2 16.9 15.1 13.1	Allowed	Normal	1.11
1912	Methyl chloride and methylene chloride mixture	15.2 13.0 11.6 10.1	Allowed	Normal	0.81
1958	1,2-Dichloro-1,1,2,2-tetrafluoroethane (Refrigerant gas R 114)	7.0 7.0 7.0 7.0	Allowed	Normal	1.30
1965	Hydrocarbon gas, mixture liquefied, n.o.s.	See MAWP definition in 6.7.3.1	Allowed	Normal	See 4.2.2.7

[a] "Small" means tanks having a shell with a diameter of 1.5 metres or less; "Bare" means tanks having a shell with a diameter of more than 1.5 metres without insulation or sun shield (see 6.7.3.2.12); "Sunshield" means tanks having a shell with a diameter of more than 1.5 metres with sun shield (see 6.7.3.2.12); "Insulated" means tanks having a shell with a diameter of more than 1.5 metres with insulation (see 6.7.3.2.12); (see definition of "Design reference temperature" in 6.7.3.1).

[b] The word "Normal" in the pressure relief requirements column indicates that a frangible disc as specified in 6.7.3.7.3 is not required.

Cont'd on next page

T50	PORTABLE TANK INSTRUCTION *(cont'd)*				T50
UN No	Non-refrigerated liquefied gases	Max. allowable working pressure (bar) Small; Bare; Sunshield; Insulated; respectively[a]	Openings below liquid level	Pressure-relief requirements[b] (see 6.7.3.7)	Maximum filling ratio
1969	Isobutane	8.5 7.5 7.0 7.0	Allowed	Normal	0.49
1973	Chlorodifluoromethane and chloropentafluoroethane mixture with fixed boiling point, with approximately 49 % chlorodifluoromethane (Refrigerant gas R 502)	28.3 25.3 22.8 20.3	Allowed	Normal	1.05
1974	Chlorodifluorobromomethane (Refrigerant gas R 12B1)	7.4 7.0 7.0 7.0	Allowed	Normal	1.61
1976	Octafluorocyclobutane (Refrigerant gas RC 318)	8.8 7.8 7.0 7.0	Allowed	Normal	1.34
1978	Propane	22.5 20.4 18.0 16.5	Allowed	Normal	0.42
1983	1-Chloro-2,2,2-trifluoroethane (Refrigerant gas R 133a)	7.0 7.0 7.0 7.0	Allowed	Normal	1.18
2035	1,1,1-Trifluoroethane (Refrigerant gas R 143a)	31.0 27.5 24.2 21.8	Allowed	Normal	0.76
2424	Octafluoropropane (Refrigerant gas R 218)	23.1 20.8 18.6 16.6	Allowed	Normal	1.07
2517	1-Chloro-1,1-difluoroethane (Refrigerant gas R 142b)	8.9 7.8 7.0 7.0	Allowed	Normal	0.99
2602	Dichlorodifluoromethane and difluoroethane azeotropic mixture with approximately 74 % dichlorodifluoromethane (Refrigerant gas R 500)	20.0 18.0 16.0 14.5	Allowed	Normal	1.01

[a] "Small" means tanks having a shell with a diameter of 1.5 metres or less; "Bare" means tanks having a shell with a diameter of more than 1.5 metres without insulation or sun shield (see 6.7.3.2.12); "Sunshield" means tanks having a shell with a diameter of more than 1.5 metres with sun shield (see 6.7.3.2.12); "Insulated" means tanks having a shell with a diameter of more than 1.5 metres with insulation (see 6.7.3.2.12); (see definition of "Design reference temperature" in 6.7.3.1).

[b] The word "Normal" in the pressure relief requirements column indicates that a frangible disc as specified in 6.7.3.7.3 is not required.

Cont'd on next page

T50	PORTABLE TANK INSTRUCTION *(cont'd)*				T50
UN No	Non-refrigerated liquefied gases	Max. allowable working pressure (bar) Small; Bare; Sunshield; Insulated; respectively[a]	Openings below liquid level	Pressure-relief requirements[b] (see 6.7.3.7)	Maximum filling ratio
3057	Trifluoroacetyl chloride	14.6 12.9 11.3 9.9	Not allowed	6.7.3.7.3	1.17
3070	Ethylene oxide and dichlorodifluoromethane mixture with not more than 12.5 % ethylene oxide	14.0 12.0 11.0 9.0	Allowed	6.7.3.7.3	1.09
3153	Perfluoro (methyl vinyl ether)	14.3 13.4 11.2 10.2	Allowed	Normal	1.14
3159	1,1,1,2-Tetrafluoroethane (Refrigerant gas R 134a)	17.7 15.7 13.8 12.1	Allowed	Normal	1.04
3161	Liquefied gas, flammable, n.o.s.	See MAWP definition in 6.7.3.1	Allowed	Normal	See 4.2.2.7
3163	Liquefied gas, n.o.s.	See MAWP definition in 6.7.3.1	Allowed	Normal	See 4.2.2.7
3220	Pentafluoroethane (Refrigerant gas R 125)	34.4 30.8 27.5 24.5	Allowed	Normal	0.87
3252	Difluoromethane (Refrigerant gas R 32)	43.0 39.0 34.4 30.5	Allowed	Normal	0.78
3296	Heptafluoropropane (Refrigerant gas R 227)	16.0 14.0 12.5 11.0	Allowed	Normal	1.20
3297	Ethylene oxide and chlorotetrafluoroethane mixture, with not more than 8.8 % ethylene oxide	8.1 7.0 7.0 7.0	Allowed	Normal	1.16
3298	Ethylene oxide and pentafluoroethane mixture, with not more than 7.9 % ethylene oxide	25.9 23.4 20.9 18.6	Allowed	Normal	1.02

[a] "Small" means tanks having a shell with a diameter of 1.5 metres or less; "Bare" means tanks having a shell with a diameter of more than 1.5 metres without insulation or sun shield (see 6.7.3.2.12); "Sunshield" means tanks having a shell with a diameter of more than 1.5 metres with sun shield (see 6.7.3.2.12); "Insulated" means tanks having a shell with a diameter of more than 1.5 metres with insulation (see 6.7.3.2.12); (see definition of "Design reference temperature" in 6.7.3.1).

[b] The word "Normal" in the pressure relief requirements column indicates that a frangible disc as specified in 6.7.3.7.3 is not required.

Cont'd on next page

T50	PORTABLE TANK INSTRUCTION *(cont'd)*				T50
UN No	Non-refrigerated liquefied gases	Max. allowable working pressure (bar) Small; Bare; Sunshield; Insulated; respectively[a]	Openings below liquid level	Pressure-relief requirements[b] (see 6.7.3.7)	Maximum filling ratio
3299	Ethylene oxide and tetrafluoroethane mixture, with not more than 5.6 % ethylene oxide	16.7 14.7 12.9 11.2	Allowed	Normal	1.03
3318	Ammonia solution, relative density less than 0.880 at 15 °C in water, with more than 50 % ammonia	See MAWP definition in 6.7.3.1	Allowed	See 6.7.3.7.3	See 4.2.2.7
3337	Refrigerant gas R 404A	31.6 28.3 25.3 22.5	Allowed	Normal	0.82
3338	Refrigerant gas R 407A	31.3 28.1 25.1 22.4	Allowed	Normal	0.94
3339	Refrigerant gas R 407B	33.0 29.6 26.5 23.6	Allowed	Normal	0.93
3340	Refrigerant gas R 407C	29.9 26.8 23.9 21.3	Allowed	Normal	0.95
3500	Chemical under pressure, n.o.s.	See MAWP definition in 6.7.3.1	Allowed	See 6.7.3.7.3	TP4[c]
3501	Chemical under pressure, flammable, n.o.s.	See MAWP definition in 6.7.3.1	Allowed	See 6.7.3.7.3	TP4[c]
3502	Chemical under pressure, toxic, n.o.s.	See MAWP definition in 6.7.3.1	Allowed	See 6.7.3.7.3	TP4[c]
3503	Chemical under pressure, corrosive, n.o.s.	See MAWP definition in 6.7.3.1	Allowed	See 6.7.3.7.3	TP4[c]
3504	Chemical under pressure, flammable, toxic, n.o.s.	See MAWP definition in 6.7.3.1	Allowed	See 6.7.3.7.3	TP4[c]
3505	Chemical under pressure, flammable, corrosive, n.o.s.	See MAWP definition in 6.7.3.1	Allowed	See 6.7.3.7.3	TP4[c]

[a] *"Small" means tanks having a shell with a diameter of 1.5 metres or less; "Bare" means tanks having a shell with a diameter of more than 1.5 metres without insulation or sun shield (see 6.7.3.2.12); "Sunshield" means tanks having a shell with a diameter of more than 1.5 metres with sun shield (see 6.7.3.2.12); "Insulated" means tanks having a shell with a diameter of more than 1.5 metres with insulation (see 6.7.3.2.12); (see definition of "Design reference temperature" in 6.7.3.1).*

[b] *The word "Normal" in the pressure relief requirements column indicates that a frangible disc as specified in 6.7.3.7.3 is not required.*

[c] *For UN Nos. 3500, 3501, 3502, 3503, 3504 and 3505, the degree of filling shall be considered instead of the maximum filling ratio.*

T75	PORTABLE TANK INSTRUCTION	T75
This portable tank instruction applies to refrigerated liquefied gases. The general provisions of section 4.2.3 and the requirements of section 6.7.4 shall be met.		

4.2.5.3 *Portable tank special provisions*

Portable tank special provisions are assigned to certain substances to indicate provisions which are in addition to or in lieu of those provided by the portable tank instructions or the requirements in chapter 6.7. Portable tank special provisions are identified by an alphanumeric designation beginning with the letters "TP" (tank provision) and are assigned to specific substances in Column 11 of the Dangerous Goods List in chapter 3.2. The following is a list of the portable tank special provisions:

TP1　　　　　The degree of filling prescribed in 4.2.1.9.2 shall not be exceeded

$$\text{Degree of filling} = \frac{97}{1 + \alpha(t_r - t_f)}$$

TP2　　　　　The degree of filling prescribed in 4.2.1.9.3 shall not be exceeded

$$\text{Degree of filling} = \frac{95}{1 + \alpha(t_r - t_f)}$$

TP3　　　　　The maximum degree of filling (in %) for solids transported above their melting points and for elevated temperature liquids shall be determined in accordance with 4.2.1.9.5.

$$\text{Degree of filling} = 95 \frac{d_r}{d_f}$$

TP4　　　　　The degree of filling shall not exceed 90 % or, alternatively, any other value approved by the competent authority (see 4.2.1.16.2).

TP5　　　　　The restrictions on filling prescribed in 4.2.3.6 shall be met.

TP6　　　　　To prevent the tank bursting in any event, including fire engulfment, it shall be provided with pressure-relief devices which are adequate in relation to the capacity of the tank and to the nature of the substance transported. The device shall also be compatible with the substance.

TP7　　　　　Air shall be eliminated from the vapour space by nitrogen or other means.

TP8　　　　　The test pressure for the portable tank may be reduced to 1.5 bar when the flash point of the substances transported is greater than 0 °C.

TP9　　　　　A substance under this description shall only be transported in a portable tank under an approval granted by the competent authority.

TP10　　　　A lead lining, not less than 5 mm thick, which shall be tested annually, or another suitable lining material approved by the competent authority is required. A portable tank may be offered for transport after the date of expiry of the last lining inspection for a period not to exceed three months beyond that date, after emptying but before cleaning, for purposes of performing the next required test or inspection prior to refilling.

TP12　　　　*Deleted.*

TP13　　　　Self-contained breathing apparatus shall be provided when this substance is transported.

TP16　　　　The tank shall be fitted with a special device to prevent under-pressure and excess pressure during normal transport conditions. This device shall be approved by the competent authority. Pressure-relief requirements are as indicated in 6.7.2.8.3 to prevent crystallization of the product in the pressure-relief valve.

TP17　　　　Only inorganic non-combustible materials shall be used for thermal insulation of the tank.

TP18	Temperature shall be maintained between 18 °C and 40 °C. Portable tanks containing solidified methacrylic acid shall not be reheated during transport.
TP19	At the time of construction, the minimum shell thickness determined according to 6.7.3.4 shall be increased by 3 mm as a corrosion allowance. Shell thickness shall be verified ultrasonically at intervals midway between periodic hydraulic tests and shall never be lower than the minimum shell thickness determined according to 6.7.3.4.
TP20	This substance shall only be transported in insulated tanks under a nitrogen blanket.
TP21	The shell thickness shall be not less than 8 mm. Tanks shall be hydraulically tested and internally inspected at intervals not exceeding 2.5 years.
TP22	Lubricant for joints or other devices shall be oxygen compatible.
TP23	*Deleted.*
TP24	The portable tank may be fitted with a device located under maximum filling conditions in the vapour space of the shell to prevent the build up of excess pressure due to the slow decomposition of the substance transported. This device shall also prevent an unacceptable amount of leakage of liquid in the case of overturning or entry of foreign matter into the tank. This device shall be approved by the competent authority or its authorized body.
TP25	Sulphur trioxide 99.95 % pure and above may be transported in tanks without an inhibitor provided that it is maintained at a temperature equal to or above 32.5 °C.
TP26	When transported under heated conditions, the heating device shall be fitted outside the shell. For UN 3176 this requirement only applies when the substance reacts dangerously with water.
TP27	A portable tank having a minimum test pressure of 4 bar may be used if it is shown that a test pressure of 4 bar or less is acceptable according to the test pressure definition in 6.7.2.1.
TP28	A portable tank having a minimum test pressure of 2.65 bar may be used if it is shown that a test pressure of 2.65 bar or less is acceptable according to the test pressure definition in 6.7.2.1.
TP29	A portable tank having a minimum test pressure of 1.5 bar may be used if it is shown that a test pressure of 1.5 bar or less is acceptable according to the test pressure definition in 6.7.2.1.
TP30	This substance shall be transported in insulated tanks.
TP31	This substance may only be transported in tanks in the solid state.
TP32	For UN Nos. 0331, 0332 and 3375, portable tanks may be used subject to the following conditions:

    (a) To avoid unnecessary confinement, each portable tank constructed of metal or fibre-reinforced plastics shall be fitted with a pressure-relief device that may be of the reclosing spring-loaded type, a frangible disc or a fusible element. The set to discharge or burst pressure, as applicable, shall not be greater than 2.65 bar for portable tanks with minimum test pressures greater than 4 bar;

    (b) For UN 3375 only, the suitability for transport in tanks shall be demonstrated. One method to evaluate this suitability is test 8 (d) in test series 8 (see *Manual of Tests and Criteria*, part 1, sub-section 18.7);

    (c) Substances shall not be allowed to remain in the portable tank for any period that could result in caking. Appropriate measures shall be taken to avoid accumulation and packing of substances in the tank (e.g. cleaning, etc).

TP33	The portable tank instruction assigned for this substance applies for granular and powdered solids and for solids which are filled and discharged at temperatures above their melting point which are cooled and transported as a solid mass. For solids which are transported above their melting point see 4.2.1.19.
TP34	Portable tanks need not be subjected to the impact test in 6.7.4.14.1 if the portable tank is marked "NOT FOR RAIL TRANSPORT" on the plate specified in 6.7.4.15.1 and also in letters of at least 10 cm high on both sides of the outer jacket.
TP35	*Deleted.*
TP36	Fusible elements in the vapour space may be used on portable tanks.
TP37	*Deleted.*
TP38	*Deleted.*
TP39	*Deleted.*
TP40	Portable tanks shall not be transported when connected with spray application equipment.
TP41	The 2.5 year internal examination may be waived or substituted by other test methods or inspection procedures specified by the competent authority or its authorized body, provided that the portable tank is dedicated to the transport of the organometallic substances to which this tank special provision is assigned. However, this examination is required when the conditions of 6.7.2.19.7 are met.
TP42	Portable tanks are not authorized for the transport of caesium or rubidium dispersions.

4.2.6 **Transitional measures**

Portable tanks and MEGCs manufactured before 1 January 2012, that conform to the marking requirements of 6.7.2.20.1, 6.7.3.16.1, 6.7.4.15.1 or 6.7.5.13.1 of the Model Regulations on the Transport of Dangerous Goods annexed to the 15th revised edition of the Recommendations on the Transport of Dangerous Goods, as relevant, may continue to be used if they comply with all other relevant requirements of the current edition of the Model Regulations including, when applicable, the requirement of 6.7.2.20.1 (g) for marking the symbol "S" on the plate when the shell or the compartment is divided by surge plates into sections of not more than 7 500 litres capacity. When the shell, or the compartment, was already divided by surge plates into sections of not more than 7 500 litres capacity before 1 January 2012, the capacity of the shell, or respectively of the compartment, need not be supplemented with the symbol "S" until the next periodic inspection or test according to 6.7.2.19.5 is performed.

Portable tanks manufactured before 1 January 2014 need not be marked with the portable tank instruction as required in 6.7.2.20.2, 6.7.3.16.2 and 6.7.4.15.2 until the next periodic inspection and test.

Portable tanks and MECGs manufactured before 1 January 2014 need not comply with the requirements of 6.7.2.13.1 (f), 6.7.3.9.1 (e), 6.7.4.8.1 (e) and 6.7.5.6.1 (d) concerning the marking of the pressure relief devices.

CHAPTER 4.3

USE OF BULK CONTAINERS

4.3.1   **General provisions**

4.3.1.1   This section provides general requirements applicable to the use of containers for the transport of solid substances in bulk. Substances shall be transported in bulk containers conforming to the applicable bulk container instruction identified by the letters BK in Column 10 of the Dangerous Goods List, with the following meaning:

BK1: the transport in sheeted bulk containers is permitted
BK2: the transport in closed bulk containers is permitted
BK3: the transport in flexible bulk containers is permitted

The bulk container used shall conform to the requirements of chapter 6.8.

4.3.1.2   Except as provided in 4.3.1.3, bulk containers shall only be used when a substance is assigned to a bulk container code in Column 10 of the Dangerous Goods List in chapter 3.2.

4.3.1.3   When a substance is not assigned a bulk container code in Column 10 of the Dangerous Goods List in chapter 3.2, interim approval for transport may be issued by the competent authority of the country of origin. The approval shall be included in the documentation of the consignment and contain, as a minimum, the information normally provided in the bulk container instruction and the conditions under which the substance shall be transported. Appropriate measures should be initiated by the competent authority to include the assignment in the Dangerous Goods List.

4.3.1.4   Substances which may become liquid at temperatures likely to be encountered during transport, are not permitted in bulk containers.

4.3.1.5   Bulk containers shall be siftproof and shall be so closed that none of the contents can escape under normal conditions of transport including the effect of vibration, or by changes of temperature, humidity or pressure.

4.3.1.6   Bulk solids shall be loaded into bulk containers and evenly distributed in a manner that minimises movement that could result in damage to the container or leakage of the dangerous goods.

4.3.1.7   Where venting devices are fitted they shall be kept clear and operable.

4.3.1.8   Bulk solids shall not react dangerously with the material of the bulk container, gaskets, equipment including lids and tarpaulins and with protective coatings which are in contact with the contents or significantly weaken them. Bulk containers shall be so constructed or adapted that the goods can not penetrate between wooden floor coverings or come into contact with those parts of the bulk containers that may be affected by the materials or residues thereof.

4.3.1.9   Before being filled and offered for transport each bulk container shall be inspected and cleaned to ensure that it does not contain any residue on the interior or exterior of the bulk container that could:

(a)   cause a dangerous reaction with the substance intended for transport;

(b)   detrimentally affect the structural integrity of the bulk container; or

(c)   affect the dangerous goods retention capabilities of the bulk container.

4.3.1.10   During transport, no dangerous residues shall adhere to the outer surfaces of bulk containers.

4.3.1.11   If several closure systems are fitted in series, the system which is located nearest to the substance to be transported shall be closed first before filling.

4.3.1.12   Empty bulk containers that have contained a dangerous substance shall be treated in the same manner as is required by these Regulations for a filled bulk container, unless adequate measures have been taken to nullify any hazard.

4.3.1.13   If bulk containers are used for the transport of bulk goods liable to cause a dust explosion, or evolve flammable vapours (e. g. for certain wastes) measures shall be taken to exclude sources of ignition and prevent dangerous electrostatic discharge during transport filling or discharge of the substance.

4.3.1.14   Substances, for example wastes, which may react dangerously with one another and substances of different classes and goods not subject to these Regulations, which are liable to react dangerously with one another shall not be mixed together in the same bulk container. Dangerous reactions are:

(a) combustion and/or evolution of considerable heat;

(b) emission of flammable and/or toxic gases;

(c) formation of corrosive liquids; or

(d) formation of unstable substances.

4.3.1.15   Before a bulk container is filled it shall be visually examined to ensure it is structurally serviceable, its interior walls, ceiling and floors are free from protrusions or damage and that any inner liners or substance retaining equipment are free from rips, tears or any damage that would compromise its cargo retention capabilities. Structurally serviceable means the bulk container does not have major defects in its structural components, such as top and bottom side rails, top and bottom end rails, door sill and header, floor cross members, corner posts, and corner fittings in a freight container. Major defects include:

(a) Bends, cracks or breaks in structural or supporting members, or any damage to service or operational equipment that affect the integrity of the container;

(b) Any distortion of the overall configuration or any damage to lifting attachments or handling equipment interface features great enough to prevent proper alignment of handling equipment, mounting and securing chassis or vehicle, or insertion into ships' cells; and, where applicable

(c) Door hinges, door seals and hardware that are seized, twisted, broken, missing, or otherwise inoperative;

4.3.1.16   Before a flexible bulk container is filled it shall be visually examined to ensure it is structurally serviceable, its textile slings, load-bearing structure straps, body fabric, lock device parts including metal and textile parts are free from protrusions or damage and that inner liners are free from rips, tears or any damage.

4.3.1.16.1   For flexible bulk containers, the period of use permitted for the transport of dangerous goods shall be two years from the date of manufacture of the flexible bulk container.

4.3.1.16.2   A venting device shall be fitted if a dangerous accumulation of gases may develop within the flexible bulk container. The vent shall be so designed that the penetration of foreign substances or the ingress of water is prevented under normal conditions of transport.

4.3.2   Additional provisions applicable to bulk goods of Divisions 4.2, 4.3, 5.1, 6.2 and Classes 7 and 8

4.3.2.1   *Bulk goods of Division 4.2*

Only closed bulk containers (code BK2) may be used. The total mass carried in a bulk container shall be such that its spontaneous ignition temperature is greater than 55 °C.

4.3.2.2   *Bulk goods of Division 4.3*

Only closed bulk containers (code BK2) and flexible bulk containers (code BK3) may be used. These goods shall be transported in bulk containers which are waterproof.

4.3.2.3   *Bulk goods of Division 5.1*

Bulk containers shall be so constructed or adapted that the goods cannot come into contact with wood or any other incompatible material.

4.3.2.4   *Bulk goods of Division 6.2*

4.3.2.4.1   *Bulk transport of animal material of Division 6.2*

Animal material containing infectious substances (UN Nos. 2814, 2900 and 3373) is authorized for transport in bulk containers provided the following conditions are met:

(a) Sheeted bulk containers BK1 are permitted provided that they are not filled to maximum capacity to avoid substances coming into contact with the sheeting. Closed bulk containers BK2 are also permitted;

(b) Closed and sheeted bulk containers, and their openings, shall be leak-proof by design or by the fitting of a suitable liner;

(c) The animal material shall be thoroughly treated with an appropriate disinfectant before loading prior to transport;

(d) Sheeted bulk containers shall be covered by an additional top liner weighted down by absorbent material treated with an appropriate disinfectant;

(e) Closed or sheeted bulk containers shall not be re-used until after they have been thoroughly cleaned and disinfected.

NOTE: Additional provisions may be required by appropriate national health authorities.

4.3.2.4.2   *Bulk wastes of Division 6.2 (UN 3291)*

(a) Only closed bulk containers (BK2) shall be permitted;

(b) Closed bulk containers and their openings shall be leakproof by design. These bulk containers shall have non porous interior surfaces and shall be free from cracks or other features which could damage packagings inside, impede disinfection or permit inadvertent release;

(c) Wastes of UN 3291 shall be contained within the closed bulk container in UN type tested and approved sealed leakproof plastics bags tested for solids of packing group II and marked in accordance with 6.1.3.1. Such plastics bags shall be capable of passing the tests for tear and impact resistance according to ISO 7765-1:1988 "Plastics film and sheeting – Determination of impact resistance by the free-falling dart method – Part 1: Staircase methods" and ISO 6383-2:1983 "Plastics – Film and sheeting – Determination of tear resistance – Part 2: Elmendorf method". Each bag shall have an impact resistance of at least 165 g and a tear resistance of at least 480 g in both parallel and perpendicular planes with respect to the length of the bag. The maximum net mass of each plastics bag shall be 30 kg;

(d) Single articles exceeding 30 kg such as soiled mattresses may be transported without the need for a plastics bag when authorized by the competent authority;

(e) Wastes of UN 3291 which contain liquids shall only be transported in plastics bags containing sufficient absorbent material to absorb the entire amount of liquid without it spilling in the bulk container;

(f) Wastes of UN 3291 containing sharp objects shall only be transported in UN type tested and approved rigid packagings meeting the provisions of packing instructions P621, IBC620 or LP621;

(g) Rigid packagings specified in packing instructions P621, IBC620 or LP621 may also be used. They shall be properly secured to prevent damage during normal conditions of transport. Wastes transported in rigid packagings and plastics bags together in the same closed bulk container shall be adequately segregated from each other, e.g. by suitable rigid barriers or dividers, mesh nets or otherwise securing, such that they prevent damage to the packagings during normal conditions of transport;

(h) Wastes of UN 3291 in plastics bags shall not be compressed in a closed bulk container in such a way that bags may be rendered no longer leakproof;

(i) The closed bulk container shall be inspected for leakage or spillage after each journey. If any wastes of UN 3291 have leaked or been spilled in the closed bulk container, it shall not be re-used until after it has been thoroughly cleaned and, if necessary, disinfected or decontaminated with an appropriate agent. No other goods shall be transported together with UN 3291 other than medical or veterinary wastes. Any such other wastes transported in the same closed bulk container shall be inspected for possible contamination.

4.3.2.5 *Bulk material of Class 7*

For the transport of unpackaged radioactive material, see 4.1.9.2.4.

4.3.2.6 *Bulk goods of Class 8*

Only closed bulk containers (code BK2) may be used. These goods shall be transported in bulk containers which are watertight.

PART 5

CONSIGNMENT PROCEDURES

CHAPTER 5.1

GENERAL PROVISIONS

5.1.1 Application and general provisions

5.1.1.1 This part sets forth the provisions for dangerous goods consignments relative to authorization of consignments and advance notifications, marking, labelling, documentation (by manual, electronic data processing (EDP) or electronic data interchange (EDI) techniques) and placarding.

5.1.1.2 Except as otherwise provided in these Regulations, no person may offer dangerous goods for transport unless those goods are properly marked, labelled, placarded, described and certified on a transport document, and otherwise in a condition for transport as required by this part.

NOTE: In accordance with the GHS, a GHS pictogram not required by these Regulations should only appear in transport as part of a complete GHS label and not independently (see GHS 1.4.10.4.4).

5.1.2 Use of overpacks

5.1.2.1 Unless marks and labels representative of all dangerous goods in the overpack are visible, the overpack shall be:

(a) marked with the word "OVERPACK". The lettering of the "OVERPACK" mark shall be at least 12 mm high; and

(b) labelled and marked with the proper shipping name, UN number and other marks, as required for packages by chapter 5.2, for each item of dangerous goods contained in the overpack.

Labelling of overpacks containing radioactive material shall be in accordance with 5.2.2.1.12.

NOTE: The size requirement for the "OVERPACK" mark shall apply as from 1 January 2016.

5.1.2.2 Each package of dangerous goods contained in the overpack shall comply with all applicable provisions of these Regulations. The "overpack" mark is an indication of compliance with this requirement. The intended function of each package shall not be impaired by the overpack.

5.1.2.3 Each package bearing package orientation marks as prescribed in 5.2.1.7 of these Regulations and which is overpacked or placed in a large packaging shall be oriented in accordance with such marks.

5.1.3 Empty packagings

5.1.3.1 Other than for Class 7, a packaging which previously contained dangerous goods shall be identified, marked, labelled and placarded as required for those dangerous goods unless steps such as cleaning, purging of vapours or refilling with a non-dangerous substance are taken to nullify any hazard.

5.1.3.2 Freight containers, tanks, IBCs, as well as other packagings and overpacks, used for the transport of radioactive material shall not be used for the storage or transport of other goods unless decontaminated below the level of 0.4 Bq/cm² for beta and gamma emitters and low toxicity alpha emitters and 0.04 Bq/cm² for all other alpha emitters.

5.1.4 Mixed packing

When two or more dangerous goods are packed within the same outer packaging, the package shall be labelled and marked as required for each substance. Subsidiary hazard labels need not be applied if the hazard is already represented by a primary hazard label.

5.1.5 General provisions for Class 7

5.1.5.1 *Approval of shipments and notification*

5.1.5.1.1 *General*

In addition to the approval of package designs described in chapter 6.4, multilateral shipment approval is also required in certain circumstances (5.1.5.1.2 and 5.1.5.1.3). In some circumstances it is also necessary to notify competent authorities of a shipment (5.1.5.1.4).

5.1.5.1.2 *Shipment approvals*

Multilateral approval shall be required for:

(a) The shipment of Type B(M) packages not conforming to the requirements of 6.4.7.5 or designed to allow controlled intermittent venting;

(b) The shipment of Type B(M) packages containing radioactive material with an activity greater than 3 000 A1 or 3 000 A2, as appropriate, or 1 000 TBq, whichever is the lower;

(c) The shipment of packages containing fissile materials if the sum of the criticality safety indexes of the packages in a single freight container or in a single conveyance exceeds 50. Excluded from this requirement shall be shipments by seagoing vessels, if the sum of the criticality safety indexes does not exceed 50 for any hold, compartment or defined deck area and the distance of 6 m between groups of packages or overpacks as required in table 7.1.8.4.2 is met;

(d) Radiation protection programmes for shipments by special use vessels in accordance with 7.2.3.2.2; and

(e) The shipment of SCO-III.

except that a competent authority may authorize transport into or through its country without shipment approval, by a specific provision in its design approval (see 5.1.5.2.1).

5.1.5.1.3 *Shipment approval by special arrangement*

A competent authority may approve provisions under which consignments that do not satisfy all the applicable requirements of these Regulations may be transported under special arrangement (see 1.5.4).

5.1.5.1.4 *Notifications*

Notification to competent authorities is required as follows:

(a) Before the first shipment of any package requiring competent authority approval, the consignor shall ensure that copies of each applicable competent authority certificate applying to that package design have been submitted to the competent authority of the country of origin of the shipment and to the competent authority of each country through or into which the consignment is to be transported. The consignor is not required to await an acknowledgement from the competent authority, nor is the competent authority required to make such acknowledgement of receipt of the certificate;

(b) For each of the following types of shipments:

(i) Type C packages containing radioactive material with an activity greater than 3 000 A1 or 3 000 A2, as appropriate, or 1 000 TBq, whichever is the lower;

(ii) Type B(U) packages containing radioactive material with an activity greater than 3 000 A1 or 3 000 A2, as appropriate, or 1 000 TBq, whichever is the lower;

(iii) Type B(M) packages;

(iv) Shipment under special arrangement,

the consignor shall notify the competent authority of the country of origin of the shipment and the competent authority of each country through or into which the consignment is to be transported. This notification shall be in the possession of each competent authority prior to the commencement of the shipment, and preferably at least 7 days in advance;

(c) The consignor is not required to send a separate notification if the required information has been included in the application for approval of shipment (see 6.4.23.2);

(d) The consignment notification shall include:

(i) sufficient information to enable the identification of the package or packages including all applicable certificate numbers and identification marks;

(ii) information on the date of shipment, the expected date of arrival and proposed routeing;

(iii) the names of the radioactive material or nuclides;

(iv) descriptions of the physical and chemical forms of the radioactive material, or whether it is special form radioactive material or low dispersible radioactive material; and

(v) the maximum activity of the radioactive contents during transport expressed in units of becquerels (Bq) with an appropriate SI prefix symbol (see 1.2.2.1). For fissile material, the mass of fissile material (or of each fissile nuclide for mixtures when appropriate) in units of grams (g), or multiples thereof, may be used in place of activity.

5.1.5.2   *Certificates issued by Competent Authority*

5.1.5.2.1   Certificates issued by the competent authority are required for the following:

(a) Designs for

(i) special form radioactive material;

(ii) low dispersible radioactive material;

(iii) fissile material excepted under 2.7.2.3.5 (f);

(iv) packages containing 0.1 kg or more of uranium hexafluoride;

(v) packages containing fissile material unless excepted by 2.7.2.3.5, 6.4.11.2 or 6.4.11.3;

(vi) Type B(U) packages and Type B(M) packages;

(vii) Type C packages;

(b) Special arrangements;

(c) Certain shipments (see 5.1.5.1.2);

(d) Determination of the basic radionuclide values referred to in 2.7.2.2.1 for individual radionuclides which are not listed in table 2.7.2.2.1 (see 2.7.2.2.2 (a));

(e) Alternative activity limits for an exempt consignment of instruments or articles (see 2.7.2.2.2 (b));

The certificates shall confirm that the applicable requirements are met, and for design approvals shall attribute to the design an identification mark.

The certificates of approval for the package design and the shipment may be combined into a single certificate.

Certificates and applications for these certificates shall be in accordance with the requirements in 6.4.23.

5.1.5.2.2 The consignor shall be in possession of a copy of each applicable certificate.

5.1.5.2.3 For package designs where it is not required that a competent authority issue a certificate of approval, the consignor shall, on request, make available for inspection by the relevant competent authority, documentary evidence of the compliance of the package design with all the applicable requirements.

5.1.5.3 *Determination of transport index (TI) and criticality safety index (CSI)*

5.1.5.3.1 The transport index (TI) for a package, overpack or freight container, or for unpackaged LSA-I, SCO-I or SCO-III, shall be the number derived in accordance with the following procedure:

(a) Determine the maximum dose rate in units of millisieverts per hour (mSv/h) at a distance of 1 m from the external surfaces of the package, overpack, freight container, or unpackaged LSA-I, SCO-I or SCO-III. The value determined shall be multiplied by 100. For uranium and thorium ores and their concentrates, the maximum dose rate at any point 1 m from the external surface of the load may be taken as:

0.4 mSv/h   for ores and physical concentrates of uranium and thorium;
0.3 mSv/h   for chemical concentrates of thorium;
0.02 mSv/h   for chemical concentrates of uranium, other than uranium hexafluoride;

(b) For tanks, freight containers and unpackaged LSA-I, SCO-I and SCO-III, the value determined in step (a) above shall be multiplied by the appropriate factor from table 5.1.5.3.1;

(c) The value obtained in steps (a) and (b) above shall be rounded up to the first decimal place (e.g. 1.13 becomes 1.2), except that a value of 0.05 or less may be considered as zero and the resulting number is the *TI* value.

Table 5.1.5.3.1: Multiplication factors for tanks, freight containers and unpackaged LSA-I, SCO-I and SCO-III

Size of load [a]	Multiplication factor
size of load ≤ 1 m^2	1
1 m^2 < size of load ≤ 5 m^2	2
5 m^2 < size of load ≤ 20 m^2	3
20 m^2 < size of load	10

[a] *Largest cross-sectional area of the load being measured.*

5.1.5.3.2 The TI for each rigid overpack, freight container or conveyance shall be determined as the sum of the TIs of all the packages contained therein. For a shipment from a single consignor, the consignor may determine the TI by direct measurement of dose rate.

The TI for a non-rigid overpack shall be determined only as the sum of the TIs of all the packages within the overpack.

5.1.5.3.3 The criticality safety index for each overpack or freight container shall be determined as the sum of the CSIs of all the packages contained. The same procedure shall be followed for determining the total sum of the CSIs in a consignment or aboard a conveyance.

5.1.5.3.4 Packages, overpacks and freight containers shall be assigned to either category I-WHITE, II-YELLOW or III-YELLOW in accordance with the conditions specified in table 5.1.5.3.4 and with the following requirements:

- (a) For a package, overpack or freight container, both the transport index and the surface dose rate conditions shall be taken into account in determining which is the appropriate category. Where the transport index satisfies the condition for one category but the surface dose rate satisfies the condition for a different category, the package, overpack or freight container shall be assigned to the higher category. For this purpose, category I-WHITE shall be regarded as the lowest category;

- (b) The TI shall be determined following the procedures specified in 5.1.5.3.1 and 5.1.5.3.2;

- (c) If the surface dose rate is greater than 2 mSv/h, the package or overpack shall be transported under exclusive use and under the provisions of 7.2.3.1.3, 7.2.3.2.1, or 7.2.3.3.3, as appropriate;

- (d) A package transported under a special arrangement shall be assigned to category III-YELLOW except under the provisions of 5.1.5.3.5;

- (e) An overpack or freight container which contains packages transported under special arrangement shall be assigned to category III-YELLOW except under the provisions of 5.1.5.3.5.

Table 5.1.5.3.4: Categories of packages, overpacks and freight containers

Conditions		Category
Transport index	**Maximum dose rate at any point on external surface**	
0^a	Not more than 0.005 mSv/h	I-WHITE
More than 0 but not more than 1^a	More than 0.005 mSv/h but not more than 0.5 mSv/h	II-YELLOW
More than 1 but not more than 10	More than 0.5 mSv/h but not more than 2 mSv/h	III-YELLOW
More than 10	More than 2 mSv/h but not more than 10 mSv/h	III-YELLOW [b]

[a] *If the measured TI is not greater than 0.05, the value quoted may be zero in accordance with 5.1.5.3.1(c).*

[b] *Shall also be transported under exclusive use except for freight containers (see table 7.1.8.3.3).*

5.1.5.3.5 In all cases of international transport of packages requiring competent authority approval of design or shipment, for which different approval types apply in the different countries concerned by the shipment, the categorization shall be in accordance with the certificate of the country of origin of design.

5.1.5.4 *Specific provisions for excepted packages of radioactive material of Class 7*

5.1.5.4.1 Excepted packages of radioactive material of Class 7 shall be legibly and durably marked on the outside of the packaging with:

- (a) The UN number preceded by the letters "UN";

- (b) An identification of either the consignor or consignee, or both; and

(c) The permissible gross mass if this exceeds 50 kg.

5.1.5.4.2 The documentation requirements of chapter 5.4 do not apply to excepted packages of radioactive material of Class 7, except that:

(a) The UN number preceded by the letters "UN" and the name and address of the consignor and the consignee and, if relevant, the identification mark for each competent authority certificate of approval (see 5.4.1.5.7.1 (g)) shall be shown on a transport document such as a bill of lading, air waybill or other similar document complying with the requirements of 5.4.1.2.1 to 5.4.1.2.4;

(b) The requirements of 5.4.1.6.2 and, if relevant, those of 5.4.1.5.7.1 (g), 5.4.1.5.7.3 and 5.4.1.5.7.4 shall apply;

(c) The requirements of 5.4.2 and 5.4.4 shall apply.

5.1.5.4.3 The requirements of 5.2.1.5.8 and 5.2.2.1.12.5 shall apply if relevant.

CHAPTER 5.2

MARKING AND LABELLING

5.2.1 Marking

5.2.1.1 Unless provided otherwise in these Regulations, the proper shipping name for the dangerous goods as determined in accordance with 3.1.2 and the corresponding UN number preceded by the letters "UN", shall be displayed on each package. The UN number and the letters "UN" shall be at least 12 mm high, except for packages of 30 litres capacity or less or of 30 kg maximum net mass and for cylinders of 60 l water capacity or less when they shall be at least 6 mm in height and except for packages of 5 l capacity or less or of 5 kg maximum net mass when they shall be of an appropriate size. In the case of unpackaged articles the mark shall be displayed on the article, on its cradle or on its handling, storage or launching device. For goods of Division 1.4, Compatibility Group S, the division and compatibility group letter shall also be marked unless the label for 1.4S is displayed. A typical package mark is:

Corrosive liquid, acidic, organic, n.o.s. (Caprylyl chloride) UN 3265

5.2.1.2 All package marks required by 5.2.1.1:

(a) Shall be readily visible and legible;

(b) Shall be able to withstand open weather exposure without a substantial reduction in effectiveness;

(c) Shall be displayed on a background of contrasting colour on the external surface of the package; and

(d) Shall not be located with other package marks that could substantially reduce their effectiveness.

5.2.1.3 Salvage packagings including large salvage packagings and salvage pressure receptacles shall additionally be marked with the word "SALVAGE". The lettering of the "SALVAGE" mark shall be at least 12 mm high.

NOTE: *The size requirement for the "SALVAGE" mark shall apply as from 1 January 2016.*

5.2.1.4 Intermediate bulk containers of more than 450 litres capacity and large packagings shall be marked on two opposing sides.

5.2.1.5 *Special marking provisions for radioactive material*

5.2.1.5.1 Each package shall be legibly and durably marked on the outside of the packaging with an identification of either the consignor or consignee, or both. Each overpack shall be legibly and durably marked on the outside of the overpack with an identification of either the consignor or consignee, or both unless these marks of all packages within the overpack are clearly visible.

5.2.1.5.2 The marking of excepted packages of radioactive material of Class 7 shall be as required by 5.1.5.4.1.

5.2.1.5.3 Each package of gross mass exceeding 50 kg shall have its permissible gross mass legibly and durably marked on the outside of the packaging.

5.2.1.5.4 Each package which conforms to:

(a) a Type IP-1 package, a Type IP-2 package or a Type IP-3 package design shall be legibly and durably marked on the outside of the packaging with "TYPE IP-1", "TYPE IP-2" or "TYPE IP-3" as appropriate;

(b) a Type A package design shall be legibly and durably marked on the outside of the packaging with "TYPE A";

(c) a Type IP-2 package, a Type IP-3 or a Type A package design shall be legibly and durably marked on the outside of the packaging with the international vehicle registration code (VRI Code) of the country of origin of design and either the name of the manufacturer or other identification of the packaging specified by the competent authority of the country of origin of design.

5.2.1.5.5 Each package which conforms to a design approved under one or more of paragraphs 5.1.5.2.1, 6.4.22.1 to 6.4.22.4, 6.4.23.4 to 6.4.23.7 and 6.4.24.2 shall be legibly and durably marked on the outside of the package with the following information:

(a) the identification mark allocated to that design by the competent authority;

(b) a serial number to uniquely identify each packaging which conforms to that design;

(c) Type B(U)", "Type B(M)" or "Type C", in the case of a Type B(U), Type B(M) or Type C package design.

5.2.1.5.6 Each package which conforms to a Type B(U), Type B(M) or Type C package design shall have the outside of the outermost receptacle which is resistant to the effects of fire and water plainly marked by embossing, stamping or other means resistant to the effects of fire and water with the trefoil symbol shown in the figure below:

Figure 5.2.1: Basic trefoil symbol

Proportions based on a central circle of radius X.
The minimum allowable size of X shall be 4 mm.

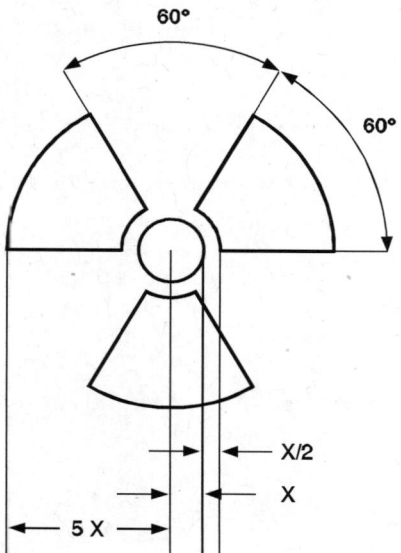

Any mark on the package made in accordance with the requirements of 5.2.1.5.4 (a) and (b) and 5.2.1.5.5 (c) relating to the package type that does not relate to the UN number and proper shipping name assigned to the consignment shall be removed or covered.

5.2.1.5.7　　　Where LSA-I or SCO-I material is contained in receptacles or wrapping materials and is transported under exclusive use as permitted by 4.1.9.2.4, the outer surface of these receptacles or wrapping materials may bear the mark "RADIOACTIVE LSA-I" or "RADIOACTIVE SCO-I", as appropriate.

5.2.1.5.8　　　In all cases of international transport of packages requiring competent authority approval of design or shipment, for which different approval types apply in the different countries concerned by the shipment, marking shall be in accordance with the certificate of the country of origin of the design.

5.2.1.6　*Special marking provisions for environmentally hazardous substances*

5.2.1.6.1　　　Unless otherwise specified in these Regulations, packages containing environmentally hazardous substances meeting the criteria of 2.9.3 (UN Nos. 3077 and 3082) shall be durably marked with the environmentally hazardous substance mark.

5.2.1.6.2　　　The environmentally hazardous substance mark shall be located adjacent to the marks required by 5.2.1.1. The requirements of 5.2.1.2 and 5.2.1.4 shall be met.

5.2.1.6.3　　　The environmentally hazardous substance mark shall be as shown in figure 5.2.2.

Figure 5.2.2: Environmentally hazardous substance mark

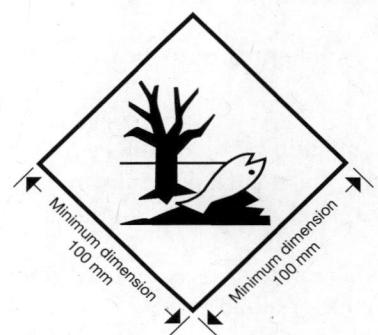

The mark shall be in the form of a square set at an angle of 45 degrees (diamond-shaped). The symbol (fish and tree) shall be black on white or suitable contrasting background. The minimum dimensions shall be 100 mm × 100 mm and the minimum width of line forming the diamond shall be 2 mm. If the size of the package so requires, the dimensions/line thickness may be reduced, provided the mark remains clearly visible. Where dimensions are not specified, all features shall be in approximate proportion to those shown.

NOTE:　　*The labelling provisions of 5.2.2 apply in addition to any requirement for packages to bear the environmentally hazardous substance mark.*

5.2.1.7　*Orientation arrows*

5.2.1.7.1　　　Except as provided in 5.2.1.7.2:

(a) Combination packagings having inner packagings containing liquid dangerous goods;

(b) Single packagings fitted with vents;

(c) Closed or open cryogenic receptacles intended for the transport of refrigerated liquefied gases; and

(d) Machinery or apparatus containing liquid dangerous goods when it is required to ensure the liquid dangerous goods remain in their intended orientation (see special provision 301 of chapter 3.3),

shall be legibly marked with package orientation arrows which are similar to the illustration shown below or with those meeting the specifications of ISO 780:1997. The orientation arrows shall appear on two opposite vertical sides of the package with the arrows pointing in the correct upright direction. They shall be rectangular and of a size that is clearly visible commensurate with the size of the package. Depicting a rectangular border around the arrows is optional.

Figure 5.2.3	Figure 5.2.4

Two black or red arrows on white or suitable contrasting background.
The rectangular border is optional

All features shall be in approximate proportion to those shown.

5.2.1.7.2　　Orientation arrows are not required on:

(a) Outer packagings containing pressure receptacles except closed or open cryogenic receptacles;

(b) Outer packagings containing dangerous goods in inner packagings each containing not more than 120 ml, with sufficient absorbent material between the inner and outer packagings to completely absorb the liquid contents;

(c) Outer packagings containing division 6.2 infectious substances in primary receptacles each containing not more than 50 ml;

(d) Type IP-2, type IP-3, type A, type B(U), type B(M) or type C packages containing Class 7 radioactive material;

(e) Outer packagings containing articles which are leak-tight in all orientations (e.g. alcohol or mercury in thermometers, aerosols, etc.); or

(f) Outer packagings containing dangerous goods in hermetically sealed inner packagings each containing not more than 500 ml.

5.2.1.7.3　　Arrows for purposes other than indicating proper package orientation shall not be displayed on a package marked in accordance with this sub-section.

5.2.1.8　　*Excepted quantities mark*

Packages containing excepted quantities of dangerous goods shall be marked according to 3.5.4.

5.2.1.9　　*Lithium or sodium ion battery mark*

5.2.1.9.1　　Packages containing lithium or sodium ion cells or batteries prepared in accordance with special provision 188 shall be marked as shown in figure 5.2.5.

5.2.1.9.2　　The mark shall indicate the UN number, preceded by the letters "UN", i.e. "UN 3090" for lithium metal cells or batteries, "UN 3480" for lithium ion cells or batteries, or "UN 3551" for sodium ion cells or batteries. Where the cells or batteries are contained in, or packed with, equipment, the UN number, preceded by the letters "UN", i.e. "UN 3091", "UN 3481" or "UN 3552" as appropriate shall be indicated. Where a package contains cells or batteries assigned to different UN numbers, all applicable UN numbers shall be indicated on one or more marks.

Figure 5.2.5: Lithium or sodium ion battery mark

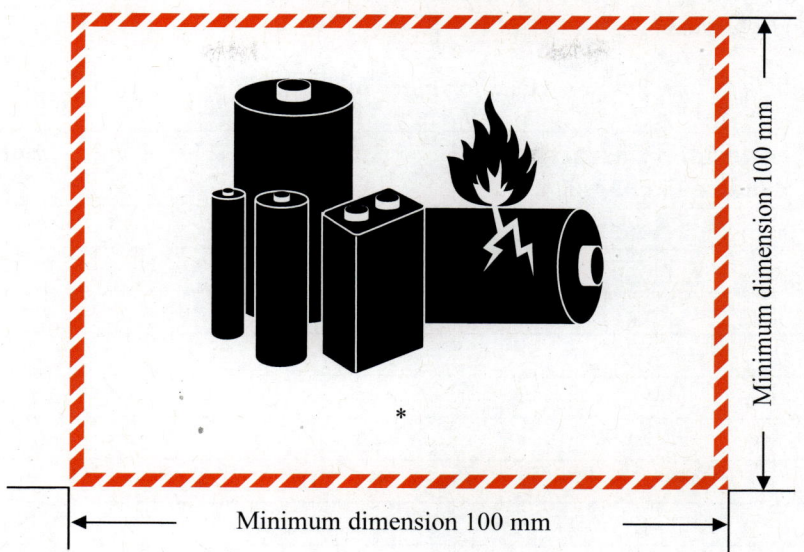

*   *Place for UN number(s)*

The mark shall be in the form of a rectangle or a square with hatched edging. The dimensions shall be a minimum of 100 mm wide × 100 mm high and the minimum width of the hatching shall be 5 mm. The symbol (group of batteries, one damaged and emitting flame, above the UN number(s)) shall be black on white or suitable contrasting background. The hatching shall be red. If the size of the package so requires, the dimensions may be reduced to not less than 100 mm wide × 70 mm high. Where dimensions are not specified, all features shall be in approximate proportion to those shown.

NOTE: *The mark shown in figure 5.2.5 in 5.2.1.9 of the twenty-first revised edition of the Recommendations on the Transport of Dangerous Goods, Model Regulations, may continue to be applied until 31 December 2026.*

5.2.2   Labelling

5.2.2.1   *Labelling provisions*

NOTE: *These provisions relate essentially to danger labels. However, additional marks or symbols indicating precautions to be taken in handling or storing a package (e.g. a symbol representing an umbrella indicating that a package shall be kept dry) may be displayed on a package if appropriate.*

5.2.2.1.1   Labels identifying primary and subsidiary hazards shall conform to models Nos. 1 to 9 illustrated in 5.2.2.2.2. The "EXPLOSIVE" subsidiary hazard label is model No. 1.

5.2.2.1.2   Where articles or substances are specifically listed in the Dangerous Goods List, a danger class label shall be affixed for the hazard shown in Column 3. A subsidiary hazard label shall also be affixed for any hazard indicated by a class or division number in the Column 4 of the Dangerous Goods List. However, special provisions indicated in Column 6 may also require a subsidiary hazard label where no subsidiary hazard is indicated in Column 4 or may exempt from the requirement for a subsidiary hazard label where such a hazard is indicated in the Dangerous Goods List.

5.2.2.1.3   Except as provided in 5.2.2.1.3.1, if a substance which meets the definition of more than one class is not specifically listed by name in the Dangerous Goods List in chapter 3.2, the provisions in chapter 2.0 shall be used to determine the primary hazard class of the goods. In addition to the label required for that primary hazard class, subsidiary hazard labels shall also be applied as specified in the Dangerous Goods List.

5.2.2.1.3.1 Packages containing substances of Class 8 need not bear subsidiary hazard label model No. 6.1 if the toxicity arises solely from the destructive effect on tissue. Packages containing substances of Division 4.2 need not bear subsidiary hazard label model No. 4.1.

5.2.2.1.4 *Labels for Class 2 gases with subsidiary hazard(s)*

Division	Subsidiary hazard(s) shown in chapter 2.2	Primary hazard label	Subsidiary hazard label(s)
2.1	None	2.1	None
2.2	None	2.2	None
	5.1	2.2	5.1
2.3	None	2.3	None
	2.1	2.3	2.1
	5.1	2.3	5.1
	5.1, 8	2.3	5.1, 8
	8	2.3	8
	2.1, 8	2.3	2.1, 8

5.2.2.1.5 Three separate labels have been provided for Class 2, one for flammable gases of Division 2.1 (red), one for non-flammable, non-toxic gases of Division 2.2 (green) and one for toxic gases of Division 2.3 (white). Where the Dangerous Goods List indicates that a Class 2 gas possesses single or multiple subsidiary hazards, labels shall be used in accordance with the table in 5.2.2.1.4.

5.2.2.1.6 Except as provided in 5.2.2.2.1.2, each label shall:

(a) Be located on the same surface of the package near the proper shipping name mark, if the package dimensions are adequate;

(b) Be so placed on the packaging that they are not covered or obscured by any part or attachment to the packaging or any other label or mark; and

(c) When primary and subsidiary hazard labels are required, be displayed next to each other.

Where a package is of such an irregular shape or small size that a label cannot be satisfactorily affixed, the label may be attached to the package by a securely affixed tag or other suitable means.

5.2.2.1.7 Intermediate bulk containers of more than 450 litres capacity and large packagings shall be labelled on two opposing sides.

5.2.2.1.8 Labels shall be affixed on a surface of contrasting colour.

5.2.2.1.9 *Special provisions for the labelling of self-reactive substances*

An "EXPLOSIVE" subsidiary hazard label (Model No. 1) shall be applied for type B self-reactive substances, unless the competent authority has permitted this label to be dispensed with for a specific packaging because test data have proved that the self-reactive substance in such a packaging does not exhibit explosive behaviour.

5.2.2.1.10 *Special provisions for the labelling of organic peroxides*

The Division 5.2 label (model No. 5.2) shall be affixed to packages containing organic peroxides classified as types B, C, D, E or F. This label also implies that the product may be flammable and hence no "FLAMMABLE LIQUID", subsidiary hazard label (model No. 3) is required. In addition, the following subsidiary hazard labels shall be applied:

(a) An "EXPLOSIVE" subsidiary hazard label (model No. 1) for organic peroxides type B, unless the competent authority has permitted this label to be dispensed with for a specific packaging because test data have proved that the organic peroxide in such a packaging does not exhibit explosive behaviour;

(b) A "CORROSIVE" subsidiary hazard label (model No. 8) is required when packing group I or II criteria of Class 8 are met.

5.2.2.1.11 *Special provisions for the labelling of infectious substances packages*

In addition to the primary hazard label (model No. 6.2), infectious substances packages shall bear any other label required by the nature of the contents.

5.2.2.1.12 *Special provisions for the labelling of radioactive material*

5.2.2.1.12.1 Except when enlarged labels are used in accordance with 5.3.1.1.5.1, each package, overpack and freight container containing radioactive material shall bear the labels conforming to the applicable models Nos. 7A, 7B or 7C, according to the appropriate category. Labels shall be affixed to two opposite sides on the outside of the package or overpack or on the outside of all four sides of a freight container or tank. In addition, each package, overpack and freight container containing fissile material, other than fissile material excepted under the provisions of 2.7.2.3.5 shall bear labels conforming to model No. 7E; such labels, where applicable shall be affixed adjacent to the labels conforming to the applicable model Nos. 7A, 7B or 7C. Labels shall not cover the marks specified in 5.2.1. Any labels which do not relate to the contents shall be removed or covered.

5.2.2.1.12.2 Each label conforming to the applicable model No. 7A, 7B or 7C shall be completed with the following information:

(a) Contents:

(i) except for LSA-I material, the name(s) of the radionuclide(s) as taken from table 2.7.2.2.1, using the symbols prescribed therein. For mixtures of radionuclides, the most restrictive nuclides shall be listed to the extent the space on the line permits. The group of LSA or SCO shall be shown following the name(s) of the radionuclide(s). The terms "LSA-II", "LSA-III", "SCO-I" and "SCO-II" shall be used for this purpose;

(ii) for LSA-I material, the term "LSA-I" is all that is necessary; the name of the radionuclide is not necessary;

(b) Activity: The maximum activity of the radioactive contents during transport expressed in units of becquerels (Bq) with the appropriate SI prefix symbol (see 1.2.2.1). For fissile material, the total mass of fissile nuclides in units of grams (g), or multiples thereof, may be used in place of activity;

(c) For overpacks and freight containers the "contents" and "activity" entries on the label shall bear the information required in 5.2.2.1.12.2 (a) and 5.2.2.1.12.2 (b), respectively, totalled together for the entire contents of the overpack or freight container except that on labels for overpacks or freight containers containing mixed loads of packages containing different radionuclides, such entries may read "See Transport Documents";

(d) Transport index: The number determined in accordance with 5.1.5.3.1 and 5.1.5.3.2 (except for category I-WHITE).

5.2.2.1.12.3 Each label conforming to the model No. 7E shall be completed with the criticality safety index (CSI) as stated in the certificate of approval applicable in the countries through or into which the consignment is transported and issued by the competent authority or as specified in 6.4.11.2 or 6.4.11.3.

5.2.2.1.12.4 For overpacks and freight containers, the label conforming to model No. 7E shall bear the sum of the criticality safety indexes of all the packages contained therein.

5.2.2.1.12.5   In all cases of international transport of packages requiring competent authority approval of design or shipment, for which different approval types apply in the different countries concerned by the shipment, labelling shall be in accordance with the certificate of the country of origin of design.

5.2.2.1.13   *Labels for articles containing dangerous goods transported as UN Nos. 3537, 3538, 3539, 3540, 3541, 3542, 3543, 3544, 3545, 3546, 3547 and 3548*

5.2.2.1.13.1   Packages containing articles or articles transported unpackaged shall bear labels according to 5.2.2.1.2 reflecting the hazards established according to 2.0.5. If the article contains one or more lithium or sodium ion batteries with, for lithium metal batteries, an aggregate lithium content of 2 g or less, and for lithium ion or sodium ion batteries, a watt-hour rating of 100 Wh or less, the lithium or sodium ion battery mark (figure 5.2.5) shall be affixed to the package or unpackaged article. If the article contains one or more lithium or sodium ion batteries with, for lithium metal batteries, an aggregate lithium content of more than 2 g and for lithium ion or sodium ion batteries, a watt-hour rating of more than 100 Wh, the battery label (5.2.2.2.2 No. 9A) shall be affixed to the package or unpackaged article.

5.2.2.1.13.2   When it is required to ensure articles containing liquid dangerous goods remain in their intended orientation, orientation marks meeting 5.2.1.7.1 shall be affixed and visible on at least two opposite vertical sides of the package or of the unpackaged article where possible, with the arrows pointing in the correct upright direction.

5.2.2.2   *Provisions for labels*

5.2.2.2.1   Labels shall satisfy the provisions of this section and conform, in terms of colour, symbols and general format, to the specimen labels shown in 5.2.2.2.2.

NOTE: *Where appropriate, labels in 5.2.2.2.2 are shown with a dotted outer boundary as provided for in 5.2.2.2.1.1. This is not required when the label is applied on a background of contrasting colour.*

5.2.2.2.1.1   Labels shall be configured as shown in figure 5.2.6.

Figure 5.2.6: Class/division label

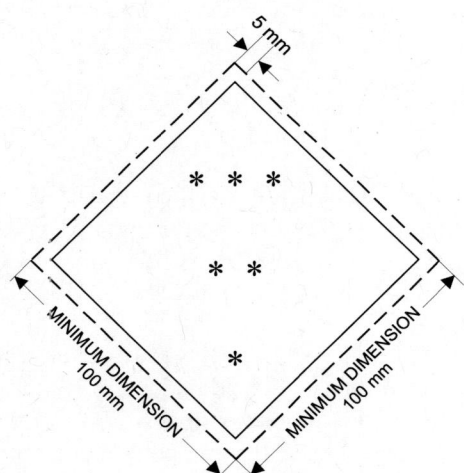

*   The class or, for divisions 5.1 and 5.2, the Division number shall be shown in the bottom corner.

**   Additional text/numbers/symbol/letters shall (if mandatory) or may (if optional) be shown in this bottom half.

***   The class or division symbol or, for divisions 1.4, 1.5 and 1.6, the division number and for Model No 7E the word "FISSILE" shall be shown in this top half.

5.2.2.2.1.1.1   Labels shall be displayed on a background of contrasting colour, or shall have either a dotted or solid outer boundary line.

5.2.2.2.1.1.2   The label shall be in the form of a square set at an angle of 45 degrees (diamond-shaped). The minimum dimensions shall be 100 mm × 100 mm. There shall be a line inside the edge forming the diamond which shall be parallel and approximately 5 mm from the outside of that line to the edge of the label.

5.2.2.2.1.1.3   If the size of the package so requires the dimensions may be reduced proportionally, provided the symbols and other elements of the label remain clearly visible. Dimensions for cylinders shall comply with 5.2.2.2.1.2.

5.2.2.2.1.2   Cylinders for Class 2 may, on account of their shape, orientation and securing mechanisms for transport, bear labels representative of those specified in this section, which have been reduced in size, according to ISO 7225:2005 "Gas cylinders – Precautionary labels", for display on the non-cylindrical part (shoulder) of such cylinders. Labels may overlap to the extent provided for by ISO 7225:2005, however, in all cases, the labels representing the primary hazard and the numbers appearing on any label shall remain fully visible and the symbols recognisable.

NOTE: *When the diameter of the cylinder is too small to permit the display of the reduced size labels on the non-cylindrical upper part of the cylinder, the reduced sized labels may be displayed on the cylindrical part.*

5.2.2.2.1.3   With the exception of labels for divisions 1.4, 1.5 and 1.6 of Class 1, the upper half of the label shall contain the pictorial symbol and the lower half shall contain the class or division number 1, 2, 3, 4, 5.1, 5.2, 6, 7, 8 or 9 as appropriate. However, for label model No. 9A, the upper half of the label shall only contain the seven vertical stripes of the symbol and the lower half shall contain the group of batteries of the symbol and the class number. Except for label model No. 9A, the label may include such text as the UN number, or words describing the hazard class (e.g. "flammable") in accordance with 5.2.2.2.1.5 provided that the text does not obscure or detract from the other required label elements.

5.2.2.2.1.4   In addition, except for divisions 1.4, 1.5 and 1.6, labels for Class 1 shall show in the lower half, above the class number, the division number and the compatibility group letter for the substance or article. Labels for divisions 1.4, 1.5 and 1.6 shall show in the upper half the division number, and in the lower half the class number and the compatibility group letter. For Division 1.4, Compatibility Group S, no label is generally required. However, in cases where a label is considered necessary for such goods, it shall be based on model No. 1.4.

5.2.2.2.1.5   On labels other than those for material of Class 7, the insertion of any text (other than the class or division number) in the space below the symbol shall be confined to particulars indicating the nature of the hazard and precautions to be taken in handling. For label 9A, no text other than the class mark shall be included in the bottom part of the label.

5.2.2.2.1.6   The symbols, text and numbers shall be shown in black on all labels except for:

  (a)   The Class 8 label, where the text (if any) and class number shall appear in white;

  (b)   Labels with entirely green, red or blue backgrounds where they may be shown in white;

  (c)   The Division 5.2 label, where the symbol may be shown in white; and

  (d)   The Division 2.1 label displayed on cylinders and gas cartridges for liquefied petroleum gases, where they may be shown in the background colour of the receptacle if adequate contrast is provided.

5.2.2.2.1.7   All labels shall be able to withstand open weather exposure without a substantial reduction in effectiveness.

5.2.2.2.2   *Specimen labels*

Label model No.	Division or Category	Symbol and symbol colour	Background	Figure in bottom corner (and figure colour)	Specimen labels	Note
		Class 1: Explosive substances or articles				
1	Divisions 1.1, 1.2, 1.3	Exploding bomb: black	Orange	1 (black)		** Place for division – to be left blank if explosive is the subsidiary hazard * Place for compatibility group – to be left blank if explosive is the subsidiary hazard
1.4	Division 1.4	1.4: black Numerals shall be about 30 mm in height and be about 5 mm thick (for a label measuring 100 mm × 100 mm)	Orange	1 (black)		* Place for compatibility group
1.5	Division 1.5	1.5: black Numerals shall be about 30 mm in height and be about 5 mm thick (for a label measuring 100 mm × 100 mm)	Orange	1 (black)		* Place for compatibility group
1.6	Division 1.6	1.6: black Numerals shall be about 30 mm in height and be about 5 mm thick (for a label measuring 100 mm × 100 mm)	Orange	1 (black)		* Place for compatibility group

Label model No.	Division or Category	Symbol and symbol colour	Background	Figure in bottom corner (and figure colour)	Specimen labels		Note
			Class 2: Gases				
2.1	Division 2.1: Flammable gases	Flame: black or white (except as provided for in 5.2.2.2.1.6 d))	Red	2 (black or white) (except as provided for in 5.2.2.2.1.6 (d))			-
2.2	Division 2.2: Non-flammable, non-toxic gases	Gas cylinder: black or white	Green	2 (black or white)			-
2.3	Division 2.3: Toxic gases	Skull and crossbones: black	White	2 (black)			-

- 173 -

Label model No.	Division or Category	Symbol and symbol colour	Background	Figure in bottom corner (and figure colour)	Specimen labels	Note
3	-	Flame: black or white	Red	3 (black or white)		-
Class 3: Flammable liquids						
Class 4: Flammable solids; substances liable to spontaneous combustion; substances which, in contact with water, emit flammable gases						
4.1	Division 4.1: Flammable solids, self-reactive substances, polymerizing substances and solid desensitized explosives	Flame: black	White with 7 vertical red stripes	4 (black)		-
4.2	Division 4.2: Substances liable to spontaneous combustion	Flame: black	Upper half white, lower half red	4 (black)		-
4.3	Division 4.3: Substances which, in contact with water emit flammable gases	Flame: black or white	Blue	4 (black or white)		-

Label model No.	Division or Category	Symbol and symbol colour	Background	Figure in bottom corner (and figure colour)	Specimen labels	Note
\multicolumn{7}{c}{**Class 5: Oxidizing substances and organic peroxides**}					
5.1	Division 5.1: Oxidizing substances	Flame over circle: black	Yellow	5.1 (black)		-
5.2	Division 5.2: Organic peroxides	Flame: black or white	Upper half red, lower half yellow	5.2 (black)		-
\multicolumn{7}{c}{**Class 6: Toxic substances and infectious substances**}					
6.1	Division 6.1: Toxic substances	Skull and crossbones: black	White	6 (black)		-
6.2	Division 6.2: Infectious substances	Three crescents superimposed on a circle: black	White	6 (black)		The lower half of the label may bear the inscriptions: "INFECTIOUS SUBSTANCE" and "In the case of damage or leakage immediately notify Public Health Authority" in black colour

Label model No.	Division or Category	Symbol and symbol colour	Background	Figure in bottom corner (and figure colour)	Specimen labels	Note
Class 7: Radioactive material						
7A	Category I - WHITE	Trefoil: black	White	7 (black)		Text (mandatory), black in lower half of label: "RADIOACTIVE" "CONTENTS ..." "ACTIVITY ..." One red vertical bar shall follow the word: "RADIOACTIVE"
7B	Category II - YELLOW	Trefoil: black	Upper half yellow with white border, lower half white	7 (black)		Text (mandatory), black in lower half of label: "RADIOACTIVE" "CONTENTS ..." "ACTIVITY ..." In a black outlined box: "TRANSPORT INDEX"; Two red vertical bars shall follow the word: "RADIOACTIVE"
7C	Category III - YELLOW	Trefoil: black	Upper half yellow with white border, lower half white	7 (black)		Text (mandatory), black in lower half of label: "RADIOACTIVE" "CONTENTS ..." "ACTIVITY ..." In a black outlined box: "TRANSPORT INDEX". Three red vertical bars shall follow the word: "RADIOACTIVE"
7E	Fissile material	-	White	7 (black)		Text (mandatory): black in upper half of label: "FISSILE"; In a black outlined box in the lower half of label: "CRITICALITY SAFETY INDEX"

Label model No.	Division or Category	Symbol and symbol colour	Background	Figure in bottom corner (and figure colour)	Specimen labels	Note
Class 8: Corrosive substances						
8	-	Liquids, spilling from two glass vessels and attacking a hand and a metal: black	Upper half white, lower half black with white border	8 (white)		-
Class 9: Miscellaneous dangerous substances and articles, including environmentally hazardous substances						
9	-	7 vertical stripes in upper half: black	White	9 underlined (black)		-
9A	-	7 vertical stripes in upper half: black; battery group, one broken and emitting flame in lower half: black	White	9 underlined (black)		-

CHAPTER 5.3

PLACARDING AND MARKING OF CARGO TRANSPORT UNITS AND BULK CONTAINERS

5.3.1 **Placarding**

5.3.1.1 *Placarding provisions*

5.3.1.1.1 *Deleted.*

5.3.1.1.2 Placards shall be affixed to the exterior surface of cargo transport units and bulk containers to provide a warning that the contents of the unit are dangerous goods and present hazards. Placards shall correspond to the primary hazard of the goods contained in the cargo transport unit and bulk container except that:

(a) Placards are not required on cargo transport units carrying any quantity of explosives of Division 1.4, Compatibility Group S; and

(b) Placards indicating the highest hazard only need be affixed on cargo transport units carrying substances and articles of more than one division in Class 1.

Placards shall be displayed on a background of contrasting colour, or shall have either a dotted or solid outer boundary line.

5.3.1.1.3 Placards shall also be displayed for those subsidiary hazards for which a subsidiary hazard label is required according to 5.2.2.1.2. However, cargo transport units containing goods of more than one class need not bear a subsidiary hazard placard if the hazard represented by that placard is already indicated by a primary hazard placard.

5.3.1.1.4 Cargo transport units carrying dangerous goods or the residue of dangerous goods in unpurged tanks or empty uncleaned bulk containers shall display placards clearly visible on at least two opposing sides of the units and in any case in such a position as may be seen by all those involved in the loading or unloading process. Where the cargo transport unit has a multiple compartment tank which is carrying two or more dangerous goods and/or the residues of dangerous goods, appropriate placards shall be displayed along each side at the position of the relevant compartments. If all compartments have to bear the same placards, these placards need to be displayed only once along each side of the cargo transport unit. For portable tanks with a capacity of not more than 3 000 litres and with an available surface area insufficient to affix the prescribed placards, placards may be replaced by labels conforming to 5.2.2.2 to be affixed on two opposite sides of the portable tank.

5.3.1.1.5 *Special provisions for Class 7*

5.3.1.1.5.1 Large freight containers carrying unpackaged LSA-I material or SCO-I or SCO-III or packages other than excepted packages, and tanks shall bear four placards which conform to the model No.7D given in figure 5.3.1. The placards shall be affixed in a vertical orientation to each side wall and each end wall of the large freight container or tank. Any placards which do not relate to the contents shall be removed. Instead of using both labels and placards, it is permitted as an alternative to use enlarged labels only, as shown in label models Nos. 7A, 7B and 7C, except having the minimum size shown in figure 5.3.1.

5.3.1.1.5.2 Rail and road vehicles carrying packages, overpacks or freight containers labelled with any of the labels shown in 5.2.2.2.2 as models Nos. 7A, 7B, 7C and 7E, or carrying consignments under exclusive use, shall display the placard shown in figure 5.3.1 (model No.7D) on each of:

(a) the two external lateral walls in the case of a rail vehicle;

(b) the two external lateral walls and the external rear wall in the case of a road vehicle.

In the case of a vehicle without sides the placards may be affixed directly on the cargo-carrying unit provided that they are readily visible; in the case of physically large tanks or freight containers, the placards on the tanks or freight containers shall suffice. In the case of vehicles which have insufficient area to allow the fixing of larger placards, the dimensions of the placard as described in figure 5.3.1 may be reduced to 100 mm. Any placards which do not relate to the contents shall be removed.

5.3.1.2 *Specifications for placards*

5.3.1.2.1 Except as provided in 5.3.1.2.2 for the Class 7 placard, and in 5.3.2.3.2 for the environmentally hazardous substance mark, a placard shall be configured as shown in figure 5.3.0.

Figure 5.3.0: Placard (except for class 7)

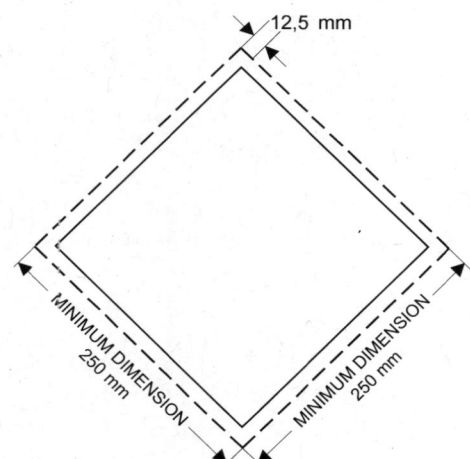

The placard shall be in the form of a square set at an angle of 45 degrees (diamond-shaped). The minimum dimensions shall be 250 mm × 250 mm (to the edge of the placard). The line inside the edge shall be parallel and 12.5 mm from the outside of that line to the edge of the placard. The symbol and line inside the edge shall correspond in colour to the label for the class or division of the dangerous goods in question. The class or division symbol/numeral shall be positioned and sized in proportion to those prescribed in 5.2.2.2 for the corresponding class or division of the dangerous goods in question. The placard shall display the number of the class or division (and for goods in Class 1, the compatibility group letter) of the dangerous goods in question in the manner prescribed in 5.2.2.2 for the corresponding label, in digits not less than 25 mm high. Where dimensions are not specified, all features shall be in approximate proportion to those shown.

5.3.1.2.2 For Class 7, the placard shall have minimum overall dimensions of 250 mm by 250 mm (except as permitted by 5.3.1.1.5.2) with a black line running 5 mm inside the edge and parallel with it, and shall be otherwise as shown in figure 5.3.1 below. When different dimensions are used, the relative proportions shall be maintained. The number "7" shall not be less than 25 mm high. The background colour of the upper half of the placard shall be yellow and of the lower half white, the colour of the trefoil and the printing shall be black. The use of the word "RADIOACTIVE" in the bottom half is optional to allow the use of this placard to display the appropriate United Nations number for the consignment.

Figure 5.3.1: Placard for radioactive material of Class 7

(No. 7D)

Symbol (trefoil): black; Background: upper half yellow with white border, lower half white; The lower half shall show the word RADIOACTIVE or alternatively, when required (see 5.3.2.1), the appropriate UN number; and the figure "7" in the bottom corner

5.3.2   Marking

5.3.2.1   *Display of UN numbers*

5.3.2.1.1   Except for goods of Class 1, the UN number shall be displayed as required by this section on consignments of:

(a) Solids, liquids or gases transported in tank cargo transport units including on each component of a multicompartment tank cargo transport unit;

(b) Solids in bulk containers;

(c) Packaged dangerous goods of a single commodity which constitute a full load for the cargo transport unit;

(d) Unpackaged LSA-I material, SCO-I or SCO-III of Class 7 in or on a vehicle, or in a freight container, or in a tank; and

(e) Packaged radioactive material with a single UN number in or on a vehicle, or in a freight container, when required to be transported under exclusive use.

5.3.2.1.2   The UN number for the goods shall be displayed in black digits not less than 65 mm high, either:

(a) Against a white background in the area below the pictorial symbol and above the class or division number and the compatibility group letter in a manner that does not obscure or detract from the other required label elements (see figures 5.3.1 and 5.3.2); or

(b) On an orange rectangular panel not less than 120 mm high and 300 mm wide, with a 10 mm black border, to be placed immediately adjacent to each placard (see figure 5.3.3). For portable tanks with a capacity of not more than 3 000 litres and with an available surface area insufficient to affix the prescribed placards, the UN number may be displayed on an orange rectangular panel of appropriately reduced size on the external surface of the tank in characters not less than 25 mm high.

5.3.2.1.3   *Examples of display of UN numbers*

Figure 5.3.2   **Figure 5.3.3**

*   location of class or division number
**   location of UN number

5.3.2.2   *Elevated temperature substance mark*

Cargo transport units containing a substance that is transported or offered for transport in a liquid state at a temperature equal to or exceeding 100 °C or in a solid state at a temperature equal to or exceeding 240 °C shall bear on each side and on each end the mark shown in figure 5.3.4.

Figure 5.3.4: Mark for carriage at elevated temperature

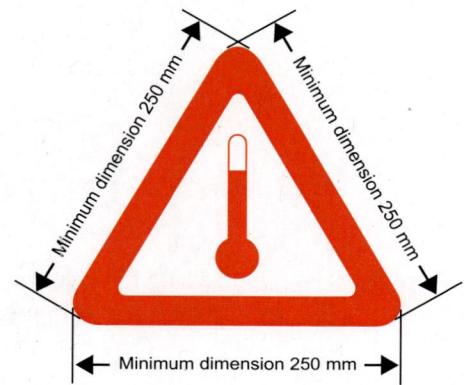

The mark shall be an equilateral triangle. The colour of the mark shall be red. The minimum dimension of the sides shall be 250 mm. For portable tanks with a capacity of not more than 3 000 litres and with an available surface area insufficient to affix the prescribed marks, the minimum dimensions of the sides may be reduced to 100 mm. Where dimensions are not specified, all features shall be in approximate proportion to those shown.

5.3.2.3   *Environmentally hazardous substance mark*

5.3.2.3.1   A cargo transport unit or bulk container containing environmentally hazardous substances meeting the criteria of 2.9.3 (UN Nos. 3077 and 3082) shall be marked on at least two opposing sides of the unit or bulk container and in any case in such a position as may be seen by all those involved in the loading or unloading processes, with the environmentally hazardous substance mark to be affixed in accordance with the provisions of 5.3.1.1.4 for placards.

5.3.2.3.2   The environmentally hazardous substance mark for cargo transport units and bulk containers shall be as described in 5.2.1.6.3 and figure 5.2.2, except that the minimum dimensions shall be 250 mm × 250 mm. For portable tanks with a capacity of not more than 3 000 litres and with an available surface area insufficient to affix the prescribed marks, the minimum dimensions may be reduced to 100 mm × 100 mm.

NOTE: *The requirements of 5.3.2.3.2 shall apply as from 1st January 2017.*

CHAPTER 5.4

DOCUMENTATION

Introductory note

NOTE: *These Regulations do not preclude the use of electronic data processing (EDP) and electronic data interchange (EDI) transmission techniques as an alternative to paper documentation. All references to "dangerous goods transport document" in this chapter also include provision of the required information by use of EDP and EDI transmission techniques.*

5.4.1 Dangerous goods transport information

5.4.1.1 *General*

5.4.1.1.1 Except as otherwise provided, the consignor who offers dangerous goods for transport shall give to the carrier the information applicable to those dangerous goods, including any additional information and documentation as specified in these Regulations. This information may be provided on a dangerous goods transport document or, with the agreement of the carrier, by EDP or EDI techniques.

5.4.1.1.2 When a paper document is used, the consignor shall give the initial carrier a copy of the dangerous goods transport document, completed and signed as required in this chapter.

5.4.1.1.3 When the dangerous goods transport information is given to the carrier by EDP or EDI techniques, the consignor shall be able to produce the information without delay as a paper document, with the information in the sequence required by this chapter.

5.4.1.2 *Form of the transport document*

5.4.1.2.1 A dangerous goods transport document may be in any form, provided it contains all of the information required by these Regulations.

5.4.1.2.2 If both dangerous and non-dangerous goods are listed in one document, the dangerous goods shall be listed first, or otherwise be emphasised.

5.4.1.2.3 *Continuation page*

A dangerous goods transport document may consist of more than one page, provided pages are consecutively numbered.

5.4.1.2.4 The information on a dangerous goods transport document shall be easy to identify, legible and durable.

5.4.1.2.5 *Example of a dangerous goods transport document*

The form shown in figure 5.4.1 at the end of this chapter is an example of a dangerous goods transport document[1].

---

[1] *For standardized formats, see also the relevant recommendations of the UNECE United Nations Centre for Trade Facilitation and Electronic Business (UN/CEFACT), in particular Recommendation No. 1 (United Nations Lay-out Key for Trade Documents) (ECE/TRADE/137, edition 81.3), UN Layout Key for Trade Documents - Guidelines for Applications (ECE/TRADE/270, edition 2002), Revised Recommendation No. 11 (Documentary Aspects of the International Transport of Dangerous Goods) (ECE/TRADE/C/CEFACT/2008/8) and Recommendation No. 22 (Lay-out Key for standard Consignment Instructions) (ECE/TRADE/168, edition 1989). Refer also to the UN/CEFACT Summary of Trade Facilitation Recommendations (ECE/TRADE/346, edition 2006) and the United Nations Trade Data Elements Directory (UNTDED) (ECE/TRADE/362, edition 2005).*

5.4.1.3 *Consignor, consignee and date*

The name and address of the consignor and the consignee of the dangerous goods shall be included on the dangerous goods transport document. The date the dangerous goods transport document or an electronic copy of it was prepared or given to the initial carrier shall be included.

5.4.1.4 *Information required on the dangerous goods transport document*

5.4.1.4.1 *Dangerous goods description*

The dangerous goods transport document shall contain the following information for each dangerous substance, material or article offered for transport:

(a) The UN number preceded by the letters "UN";

(b) The proper shipping name, as determined according to 3.1.2, including the technical name enclosed in parenthesis, as applicable (see 3.1.2.8);

(c) The primary hazard class or, when assigned, the division of the goods, including for Class 1, the compatibility group letter. The words "Class" or "Division" may be included preceding the primary hazard class or division numbers;

(d) Subsidiary hazard class or division number(s) corresponding to the subsidiary hazard label(s) required to be applied, when assigned, shall be entered following the primary hazard class or division and shall be enclosed in parenthesis. The words "Class" or "Division" may be included preceding the subsidiary hazard class or division numbers;

(e) Where assigned, the packing group for the substance or article which may be preceded by "PG" (e.g. "PG II").

5.4.1.4.2 *Sequence of the dangerous goods description*

The five elements of the dangerous goods description specified in 5.4.1.4.1 shall be shown in the order listed above (i.e. (a), (b), (c), (d), (e)) with no information interspersed, except as provided in these Regulations. Examples of a dangerous goods description are:

UN1098 ALLYL ALCOHOL 6.1 (3) I
UN1098, ALLYL ALCOHOL, Division 6.1, (Class 3), PG I

NOTE: *In addition to the requirements of these Regulations, other elements of information may be required by the competent authority or for certain modes of transport (e.g. flash point for sea transport). Unless permitted or required by these Regulations, additional information shall be placed after the dangerous goods description.*

5.4.1.4.3 *Information which supplements the proper shipping name in the dangerous goods description*

The proper shipping name in the dangerous goods description shall be supplemented as follows:

(a) Technical names for "n.o.s." and other generic descriptions: Proper shipping names that are assigned special provision 274 or 318 in Column 6 of the Dangerous Goods List shall be supplemented with their technical or chemical group names as described in 3.1.2.8;

(b) Empty uncleaned packagings, bulk containers and tanks: Empty means of containment (including packagings, IBCs, bulk containers, portable tanks, tank-vehicles and tank-wagons) which contain the residue of dangerous goods of classes other than Class 7 shall be described as such by, for example, placing the words "EMPTY

UNCLEANED" or "RESIDUE LAST CONTAINED" before or after the dangerous goods description specified in 5.4.1.4.1 (a) to (e);

(c) Wastes: For waste dangerous goods (other than radioactive wastes) which are being transported for disposal, or for processing for disposal, the proper shipping name shall be preceded by the word "WASTE", unless this is already a part of the proper shipping name;

(d) Molten substances: When a substance, which is solid in accordance with the definition in 1.2.1, is offered for transport in the molten state, the qualifying word "MOLTEN" shall be added as part of the proper shipping name, unless it is already part of the proper shipping name (see 3.1.2.5);

(e) Elevated temperature substances: If the proper shipping name of a substance which is transported or offered for transport in a liquid state at a temperature equal to or exceeding 100 °C, or in a solid state at a temperature equal to or exceeding 240 °C, does not convey the elevated temperature condition (for example, by using the term "MOLTEN" or "ELEVATED TEMPERATURE" as part of the shipping name), the word "HOT" shall immediately precede the proper shipping name.

(f) Stabilized and temperature controlled substances: Unless already part of the proper shipping name the word "STABILIZED" shall be added to the proper shipping name if stabilization is used and the words "TEMPERATURE CONTROLLED" shall be added to the proper shipping name if stabilization is by temperature control or a combination of chemical stabilization and temperature control (see 3.1.2.6).

5.4.1.5 *Information required in addition to the dangerous goods description*

In addition to the dangerous goods description the following information shall be included after the dangerous goods description on the dangerous goods transport document.

5.4.1.5.1 *Total quantity of dangerous goods*

Except for empty uncleaned packagings, the total quantity of dangerous goods covered by the description (by volume or mass as appropriate) of each item of dangerous goods bearing a different proper shipping name, UN number or packing group shall be included. For Class 1 dangerous goods, the quantity shall be the net explosive mass. For dangerous goods transported in salvage packagings, an estimate of the quantity of dangerous goods shall be given. The number and kind (e.g. drum, box, etc.) of packages shall also be indicated. UN packaging codes may only be used to supplement the description of the kind of package (e.g. one box (4G)). Abbreviations may be used to specify the unit of measurement for the total quantity.

NOTE: *The number, type and capacity of each inner packaging within the outer packaging of a combination packaging is not required to be indicated.*

5.4.1.5.2 *Limited quantities*

When dangerous goods are transported according to the exceptions for dangerous goods packed in limited quantities provided for in Column 7a of the Dangerous Goods List and chapter 3.4, the words "limited quantity" or "LTD QTY" shall be included.

5.4.1.5.3 *Salvage packagings including large salvage packagings and salvage pressure receptacles*

For dangerous goods transported in salvage packagings in accordance with 4.1.1.18, including large salvage packagings, larger size packagings or large packagings of appropriate type and performance level to be used as a salvage packaging, the words "SALVAGE PACKAGING" shall be included.

For dangerous goods transported in salvage pressure receptacles in accordance with 4.1.1.19, the words "SALVAGE PRESSURE RECEPTACLE" shall be included.

5.4.1.5.4   *Substances stabilized by temperature control*

If the words "TEMPERATURE CONTROLLED" are part of the proper shipping name (see also 3.1.2.6), the control and emergency temperatures (see 7.1.5.3) shall be indicated in the transport document, as follows:

"Control temperature: .... °C Emergency temperature: .... °C"

5.4.1.5.5   *Self-reactive substances, polymerizing substances and organic peroxides*

For self-reactive substances, organic peroxides and polymerizing substances which require temperature control during transport, the control and emergency temperatures (see 7.1.5.3) shall be indicated on the dangerous goods transport document, as follows:

"Control temperature: .... ° C Emergency temperature: .... °C"

5.4.1.5.5.1   When for certain self-reactive substances of Division 4.1 and organic peroxides of Division 5.2 the competent authority has permitted the "EXPLOSIVE" subsidiary hazard label (model No. 1) to be dispensed with for the specific package, a statement to this effect shall be included.

5.4.1.5.5.2   When organic peroxides and self-reactive substances are transported under conditions where approval is required (for organic peroxides, see 2.5.3.2.5, 4.1.7.2.2, 4.2.1.13.1 and 4.2.1.13.3; for self-reactive substances, see 2.4.2.3.2.4 and 4.1.7.2.2), a statement to this effect shall be included in the dangerous goods transport document. A copy of the classification approval and conditions of transport for non-listed organic peroxides and self-reactive substances shall be attached to the dangerous goods transport document.

5.4.1.5.5.3   When a sample of an organic peroxide (see 2.5.3.2.5.1) or a self-reactive substance (see 2.4.2.3.2.4(b)) is transported, a statement to this effect shall be included in the dangerous goods transport document.

5.4.1.5.6   *Infectious substances*

The full address of the consignee shall be shown on the document, together with the name of a responsible person and his telephone number.

5.4.1.5.7   *Radioactive material*

5.4.1.5.7.1   The following information shall be included for each consignment of Class 7 material, as applicable, in the order given:

(a)   The name or symbol of each radionuclide or, for mixtures of radionuclides, an appropriate general description or a list of the most restrictive nuclides;

(b)   A description of the physical and chemical form of the material, or a notation that the material is special form radioactive material or low dispersible radioactive material. A generic chemical description is acceptable for chemical form;

(c)   The maximum activity of the radioactive contents during transport expressed in units of becquerels (Bq) with an appropriate SI prefix symbol (see 1.2.2.1). For fissile material, the mass of fissile material (or mass of each fissile nuclide for mixtures when appropriate) in units of grams (g), or appropriate multiples thereof, may be used in place of activity;

(d)   The category of the package, overpack or freight container, as assigned per 5.1.5.3.4, i.e. I-WHITE, II-YELLOW, III-YELLOW;

(e)   The TI as determined per 5.1.5.3.1 and 5.1.5.3.2 (except for category I-WHITE);

(f)   For fissile material:

(i) Shipped under one exception of 2.7.2.3.5 (a) to (f), reference to that paragraph;

(ii) Shipped under 2.7.2.3.5 (c) to (e), the total mass of fissile nuclides;

(iii) Contained in a package for which one of 6.4.11.2 (a) to (c) or 6.4.11.3 is applied, reference to that paragraph;

(iv) The criticality safety index, where applicable.;

(g) The identification mark for each competent authority certificate of approval (special form radioactive material, low dispersible radioactive material, fissile material excepted under 2.7.2.3.5 (f), special arrangement, package design, or shipment) applicable to the consignment;

(h) For consignments of more than one package, the information contained in 5.4.1.4.1 (a) to (c) and 5.4.1.5.7.1 (a) to (g) shall be given for each package. For packages in an overpack, freight container, or conveyance, a detailed statement of the contents of each package within the overpack, freight container, or conveyance and, where appropriate, of each overpack, freight container, or conveyance shall be included. If packages are to be removed from the overpack, freight container, or conveyance at a point of intermediate unloading, appropriate transport documents shall be made available;

(i) Where a consignment is required to be shipped under exclusive use, the statement "EXCLUSIVE USE SHIPMENT"; and

(j) For LSA-II, LSA-III, SCO-I, SCO-II and SCO-III, the total activity of the consignment as a multiple of A_2. For radioactive material for which the A_2 value is unlimited, the multiple of A_2 shall be zero.

5.4.1.5.7.2 The transport document shall include a statement regarding actions, if any, that are required to be taken by the carrier. The statement shall be in the languages deemed necessary by the carrier or the authorities concerned, and shall include at least the following points:

(a) Supplementary requirements for loading, stowage, transport, handling and unloading of the package, overpack or freight container including any special stowage provisions for the safe dissipation of heat (see 7.1.8.3.2), or a statement that no such requirements are necessary;

(b) Restrictions on the mode of transport or conveyance and any necessary routeing instructions;

(c) Emergency arrangements appropriate to the consignment.

5.4.1.5.7.3 In all cases of international transport of packages requiring competent authority approval of design or shipment, for which different approval types apply in the different countries concerned by the shipment, the UN number and proper shipping name required in 5.4.1.4.1 shall be in accordance with the certificate of the country of origin of design.

5.4.1.5.7.4 The applicable competent authority certificates need not necessarily accompany the consignment. The consignor shall make them available to the carrier(s) before loading and unloading.

5.4.1.5.8 *Transport of solids in bulk containers*

For bulk containers other than freight containers, the following statement shall be shown on the transport document (see 6.8.4.6):

"Bulk container BK(x)^2 approved by the competent authority of…"

5.4.1.5.9   *Transport of IBCs or portable tanks after the date of expiry of the last periodic test or inspection*

For transport in accordance with 4.1.2.2 (b), 6.7.2.19.6 (b), 6.7.3.15.6 (b) or 6.7.4.14.6 (b), a statement to this effect shall be included in the transport document, as follows: "Transport in accordance with 4.1.2.2 (b)", "Transport in accordance with 6.7.2.19.6 (b)", "Transport in accordance with 6.7.3.15.6 (b)" or "Transport in accordance with 6.7.4.14.6 (b)" as appropriate.

5.4.1.5.10   *Firework classification reference*

When fireworks of UN Nos. 0333, 0334, 0335, 0336 and 0337 are transported, the dangerous goods transport document shall include a classification reference(s) issued by the competent authority.

The classification reference(s) shall consist of the competent authority's state, indicated by the distinguishing sign used on vehicles in international road traffic^3, the competent authority identification and a unique serial reference. Examples of such classification references are:

GB/HSE123456
D/BAM1234
USA EX20091234.

5.4.1.5.11   *Classification where new data is available (see 2.0.0.2)*

For transport in accordance with 2.0.0.2, a statement to this effect shall be included in the transport document, as follows "Classified in accordance with 2.0.0.2".

5.4.1.5.12   *Additional information in the case of the application of special provisions*

Where, in accordance with a special provision in chapter 3.3, additional information is necessary, this additional information shall be included in the dangerous goods transport document.

5.4.1.5.13   *Actual holding time*

In the case of portable tanks carrying refrigerated liquefied gases the consignor shall enter in the transport document the date at which the actual holding time ends, in the following format:

"END OF HOLDING TIME: ………….. (DD/MM/YYYY)".

5.4.1.6   Certification

5.4.1.6.1   The dangerous goods transport document shall include a certification or declaration that the consignment is acceptable for transport and that the goods are properly packaged, marked and labelled, and in proper condition for transport in accordance with the applicable regulations. The text for this certification is:

"I hereby declare that the contents of this consignment are fully and accurately described above^4 by the proper shipping name, and are classified, packaged, marked and labelled/placarded, and are in all respects in proper condition for transport according to applicable international and national governmental regulations."

The certification shall be signed and dated by the consignor. Facsimile signatures are acceptable where applicable laws and regulations recognize the legal validity of facsimile signatures.

---

^{2} *x shall be replaced with "1" or "2" as appropriate.*
^{3} *Distinguishing sign of the State of registration used on motor vehicles and trailers in international road traffic, e.g. in accordance with the Geneva Convention on Road Traffic of 1949 or the Vienna Convention on Road Traffic of 1968.*
^{4} *or below*

5.4.1.6.2   If the dangerous goods documentation is presented to the carrier by means of EDP or EDI transmission techniques, the signature(s) may be electronic signature(s) or may be replaced by the name(s) (in capitals) of the person authorized to sign.

5.4.1.6.3   When the dangerous goods transport information is given to a carrier by EDP or EDI techniques and subsequently the dangerous goods are transferred to a carrier that requires a paper dangerous goods transport document, the carrier shall ensure that the paper document indicates "Original received electronically" and the name of the signatory shall be shown in capital letters.

5.4.2   Container/vehicle packing certificate

5.4.2.1   When dangerous goods are packed or loaded into any container[5] or vehicle which will be transported by sea, those responsible for packing of the container or vehicle shall provide a "container/vehicle packing certificate" specifying the container/vehicle identification number(s) and certifying that the operation has been carried out in accordance with the following conditions:

(a) The container/vehicle was clean, dry and apparently fit to receive the goods;

(b) Packages, which need to be segregated in accordance with applicable segregation requirements, have not been packed together onto or in the container/vehicle;

(c) All packages have been externally inspected for damage, and only sound packages have been loaded;

(d) All goods have been properly loaded and, where necessary, adequately braced with securing material to suit the mode(s) of transport for the intended journey;

(e) Goods loaded in bulk have been evenly distributed within the container/vehicle;

(f) For consignments including goods of Class 1 other than Division 1.4, the container/vehicle is structurally serviceable in accordance with 7.1.3.2.1;

(g) The container/vehicle and packages are properly marked, labelled and placarded, as appropriate;

(h) When substances presenting a risk of asphyxiation are used for cooling or conditioning purposes (such as dry ice (UN 1845) or nitrogen, refrigerated liquid (UN 1977) or argon, refrigerated liquid (UN 1951)), the container/vehicle is externally marked in accordance with 5.5.3.6; and

(i) A dangerous goods transport document, as indicated in 5.4.1.1, has been received for each dangerous goods consignment loaded in the container/vehicle.

NOTE: *The container/vehicle packing certificate is not required for tanks.*

5.4.2.2   The information required in the dangerous goods transport document and the container/vehicle packing certificate may be incorporated into a single document, if not, these documents shall be attached. If the information is incorporated into a single document, the document shall include a signed declaration such as "It is declared that the packing of the goods into the container/vehicle has been carried out in accordance with the applicable provisions". This declaration shall be dated and the person signing this declaration shall be

---

[5]   *Container means an article of transport equipment that is of a permanent character and accordingly strong enough to be suitable for repeated use; specially designed to facilitate the transport of goods, by one or more modes of transport, without intermediate reloading; designed to be secured and/or readily handled, having fittings for these purposes, and approved in accordance with the International Convention for Safe Containers (CSC), 1972, as amended. The term "container" includes neither vehicle nor packaging. However, a container that is transported on a chassis is included.*

identified on the document. Facsimile signatures are acceptable where applicable laws and regulations recognize the legal validity of facsimile signatures.

5.4.2.3   If the container/vehicle packing certificate is presented to the carrier by means of EDP or EDI transmission techniques, the signature(s) may be electronic signature(s) or may be replaced by the name(s) (in capitals) of the person authorized to sign.

5.4.2.4   When the container/vehicle packing certificate is given to a carrier by EDP or EDI techniques and subsequently the dangerous goods are transferred to a carrier that requires a paper dangerous goods transport document, the carrier shall ensure that the paper document indicates "Original received electronically" and the name of the signatory shall be shown in capital letters.

5.4.3 Emergency response information

For consignments for which a dangerous goods transport document is required by these Regulations, appropriate information shall be immediately available at all times for use in emergency response to accidents and incidents involving dangerous goods in transport. The information shall be available away from the packages containing the dangerous goods and immediately accessible in the event of an accident or incident. Methods of compliance include:

(a)   Appropriate entries in the transport document; or

(b)   Provision of a separate document such as a safety data sheet; or

(c)   Provision of a separate document, such as the International Civil Aviation Organization (ICAO) "Emergency Response Guidance for Aircraft Incidents Involving Dangerous Goods" or the International Maritime Organization (IMO) "Emergency Procedures for Ships Carrying Dangerous Goods" and "Medical First Aid Guide in Accidents Involving Dangerous Goods", for use in conjunction with the transport document.

5.4.4 Retention of dangerous goods transport information

5.4.4.1   The consignor shall retain a copy of the dangerous goods transport document and additional information and documentation as specified in these Regulations, for a minimum period of three months.

5.4.4.2   When the documents are kept electronically or in a computer system, the consignor shall be able to reproduce them in a printed form.

Figure 5.4.1: Multimodal Dangerous Goods Form (next page)

MULTIMODAL DANGEROUS GOODS FORM

1. Shipper / Consignor / Sender	2. Transport document number	
	3. Page 1 of pages	4. Shipper's reference
		5. Freight Forwarder's reference
6. Consignee	7. Carrier (to be completed by the carrier)	

SHIPPER'S DECLARATION

I hereby declare that the contents of this consignment are fully and accurately described below by the proper shipping name, and are classified, packaged, marked and labelled /placarded and are in all respects in proper condition for transport according to the applicable international and national governmental regulations.

8. This shipment is within the limitations prescribed for: (Delete non-applicable)		9. Additional handling information
PASSENGER AND CARGO AIRCRAFT	CARGO AIRCRAFT ONLY	
10. Vessel / flight no. and date	11. Port / place of loading	
12. Port / place of discharge	13. Destination	

14. Shipping marks	* Number and kind of packages; description of goods	Gross mass (kg)	Net mass	Cube (m³)

* FOR DANGEROUS GOODS: you must specify: UN No., proper shipping name, hazard class, packing group (where assigned) and any other element of information required under applicable national and international regulations

15. Container identification No./ vehicle registration No.	16. Seal number (s)	17. Container/vehicle size & type	18. Tare (kg)	19. Total gross mass (including tare) (kg)

CONTAINER/VEHICLE PACKING CERTIFICATE	**21. RECEIVING ORGANISATION RECEIPT**	
I hereby declare that the goods described above have been packed/loaded into the container/vehicle identified above in accordance with the applicable provisions ** MUST BE COMPLETED AND SIGNED FOR ALL CONTAINER/VEHICLE LOADS BY PERSON RESPONSIBLE FOR PACKING/LOADING	Received the above number of packages/containers/trailers in apparent good order and condition unless stated hereon: RECEIVING ORGANISATION REMARKS:	
20. Name of company	Haulier's name	22. Name of company (OF SHIPPER PREPARING THIS NOTE)
Name / Status of declarant	Vehicle reg. no.	Name / Status of declarant
Place and date	Signature and date	Place and date
Signature of declarant	DRIVER'S SIGNATURE	Signature of declarant

** For the purposes of these Model Regulations, see 5.4.2.1

MULTIMODAL DANGEROUS GOODS FORM

Continuation Sheet

1. Shipper / Consignor /Sender	2. Transport document number	
	3. Page 1 of Pages	4. Shipper's reference
		5. Freight Forwarder's reference

14. Shipping marks	* Number and kind of packages; description of goods	Gross mass (kg)	Net mass	Cube (m³)

* FOR DANGEROUS GOODS: you must specify: UN No., proper shipping name, hazard class, packing group (where assigned) and any other element of information required under applicable national and international regulations

CHAPTER 5.5

SPECIAL PROVISIONS

5.5.1   *Deleted.*

5.5.2   **Special provisions applicable to fumigated cargo transport units (UN 3359)**

5.5.2.1   *General*

5.5.2.1.1   Fumigated cargo transport units (UN 3359) containing no other dangerous goods are not subject to any provisions of these Regulations other than those of this section.

5.5.2.1.2   When the fumigated cargo transport unit is loaded with dangerous goods in addition to the fumigant, any provision of these Regulations relevant to these goods (including placarding, marking and documentation) applies in addition to the provisions of this section.

5.5.2.1.3   Only cargo transport units that can be closed in such a way that the escape of gas is reduced to a minimum shall be used for the transport of cargo under fumigation.

5.5.2.2   *Training*

Persons engaged in the handling of fumigated cargo transport units shall be trained commensurate with their responsibilities.

5.5.2.3   *Marking and placarding*

5.5.2.3.1   A fumigated cargo transport unit shall be marked with a warning mark, as specified in 5.5.2.3.2, affixed at each access point in a location where it will be easily seen by persons opening or entering the cargo transport unit. This mark shall remain on the cargo transport unit until the following provisions are met:

(a)   The fumigated cargo transport unit has been ventilated to remove harmful concentrations of fumigant gas; and

(b)   The fumigated goods or materials have been unloaded.

5.5.2.3.2   The fumigation warning mark shall be as shown in figure 5.5.1.

Figure 5.5.1: Fumigation warning mark

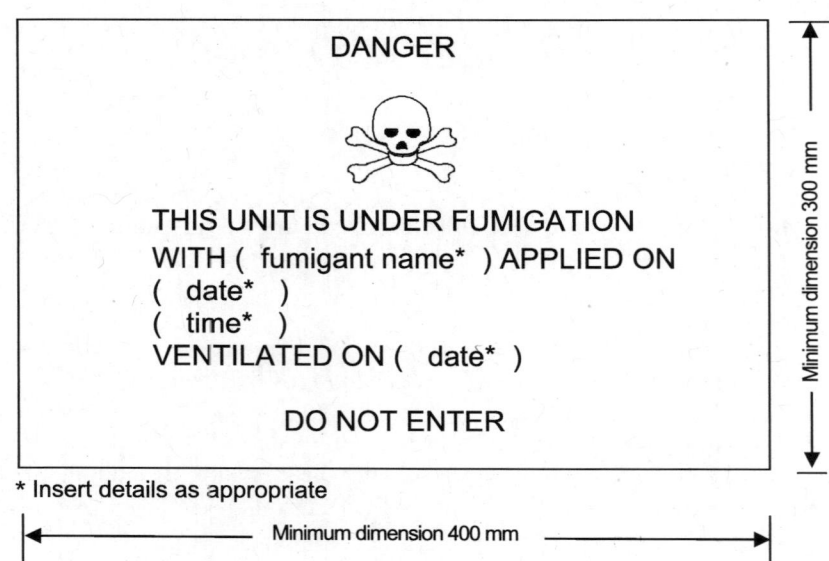

The mark shall be a rectangle. The minimum dimensions shall be 400 mm wide × 300 mm high and the minimum width of the outer line shall be 2 mm. The mark shall be in black print on a white background with lettering not less than 25 mm high. Where dimensions are not specified, all features shall be in approximate proportion to those shown.

5.5.2.3.3   If the fumigated cargo transport unit has been completely ventilated either by opening the doors of the unit or by mechanical ventilation after fumigation, the date of ventilation shall be marked on the fumigation warning mark.

5.5.2.3.4   When the fumigated cargo transport unit has been ventilated and unloaded, the fumigation warning mark shall be removed.

5.5.2.3.5   Class 9 placards (Model No. 9, see 5.2.2.2.2) shall not be affixed to a fumigated cargo transport unit except as required for other Class 9 substances or articles packed therein.

5.5.2.4   *Documentation*

5.5.2.4.1   Documents associated with the transport of cargo transport units that have been fumigated and have not been completely ventilated before transport shall include the following information:

   (a)   UN 3359, fumigated cargo transport unit, 9, or UN 3359, fumigated cargo transport unit, class 9;

   (b)   The date and time of fumigation; and

   (c)   The type and amount of the fumigant used.

5.5.2.4.2   The transport document may be in any form, provided it contains the information required in 5.5.2.4.1. This information shall be easy to identify, legible and durable.

5.5.2.4.3   Instructions for disposal of any residual fumigant including fumigation devices (if used) shall be provided.

5.5.2.4.4   A document is not required when the fumigated cargo transport unit has been completely ventilated and the date of ventilation has been marked on the warning mark (see 5.5.2.3.3 and 5.5.2.3.4).

5.5.3 **Special provisions applicable to packages and cargo transport units containing substances presenting a risk of asphyxiation when used for cooling or conditioning purposes (such as dry ice (UN 1845) or nitrogen, refrigerated liquid (UN 1977) or argon, refrigerated liquid (UN 1951) or nitrogen)**

NOTE: *In the context of this section the term "conditioning" may be used in a broader scope and includes protection.*

5.5.3.1 *Scope*

5.5.3.1.1 This section is not applicable to substances which may be used for cooling or conditioning purposes when transported as a consignment of dangerous goods. When they are transported as a consignment, these substances shall be transported under the relevant entry of the Dangerous Goods List in chapter 3.2 in accordance with the associated conditions of transport.

5.5.3.1.2 This section is not applicable to gases in cooling cycles.

5.5.3.1.3 Dangerous goods used for cooling or conditioning portable tanks or MEGCs during transport are not subject to this section.

5.5.3.1.4 Cargo transport units containing substances used for cooling or conditioning purposes include cargo transport units containing substances used for cooling or conditioning purposes inside packages as well as cargo transport units with unpackaged substances used for cooling or conditioning purposes.

5.5.3.2 *General*

5.5.3.2.1 Cargo transport units containing substances used for cooling or conditioning purposes (other than fumigation) during transport are not subject to any provisions of these Regulations other than those of this section.

5.5.3.2.2 When dangerous goods are loaded in cargo transport units containing substances used for cooling or conditioning purposes any provisions of these Regulations relevant to these dangerous goods apply in addition to the provisions of this section.

5.5.3.2.3 For air transport, arrangements between consignor and operator shall be made for each consignment, to ensure that ventilation safety procedures are followed.

5.5.3.2.4 Persons engaged in the handling or transport of cargo transport units containing substances used for cooling or conditioning purposes shall be trained commensurate with their responsibilities.

5.5.3.3 *Packages containing a coolant or conditioner*

5.5.3.3.1 Packaged dangerous goods requiring cooling or conditioning assigned to packing instructions P203, P620, P650 or P800 of 4.1.4.1 shall meet the appropriate requirements of that packing instruction.

5.5.3.3.2 For packaged dangerous goods requiring cooling or conditioning assigned to other packing instructions, the packages shall be capable of withstanding very low temperatures and shall not be affected or significantly weakened by the coolant or conditioner. Packages shall be designed and constructed to permit the release of gas to prevent a build-up of pressure that could rupture the packaging. The dangerous goods shall be packed in such a way as to prevent movement after the dissipation of any coolant or conditioner.

5.5.3.3.3 Packages containing a coolant or conditioner shall be transported in well ventilated cargo transport units.

5.5.3.4 *Marking of packages containing a coolant or conditioner*

5.5.3.4.1 Packages containing dangerous goods used for cooling or conditioning shall be marked with the proper shipping name of these dangerous goods followed by the words "AS COOLANT" or "AS CONDITIONER" as appropriate.

5.5.3.4.2 The marks shall be durable, legible and placed in such a location and of such a size relative to the package as to be readily visible.

5.5.3.5 *Cargo transport units containing unpackaged dry ice*

5.5.3.5.1 If dry ice in unpackaged form is used, it shall not come into direct contact with the metal structure of a cargo transport unit to avoid embrittlement of the metal. Measures shall be taken to provide adequate insulation between the dry ice and the cargo transport unit by providing a minimum of 30 mm separation (e.g. by using suitable low heat conducting materials such as timber planks, pallets etc).

5.5.3.5.2 Where dry ice is placed around packages, measures shall be taken to ensure that packages remain in the original position during transport after the dry ice has dissipated.

5.5.3.6 *Marking of cargo transport units*

5.5.3.6.1 Cargo transport units containing dangerous goods used for cooling or conditioning purposes shall be marked with a warning mark, as specified in 5.5.3.6.2 affixed at each access point in a location where it will be easily seen by persons opening or entering the cargo transport unit. This mark shall remain on the cargo transport unit until the following provisions are met:

    (a) The cargo transport unit has been ventilated to remove harmful concentrations of coolant or conditioner; and

    (b) The cooled or conditioned goods have been unloaded.

5.5.3.6.2 The warning mark shall be as shown in figure 5.5.2

Figure 5.5.2: Asphyxiation warning mark for cargo transport units

*

    * Insert proper shipping name or the name of the asphyxiant gas used as the coolant/conditioner. The lettering shall be in capitals, all be on one line and shall be at least 25 mm high. If the length of the proper shipping name is too long to fit in the space provided, the lettering may be reduced to the maximum size possible to fit. For example: CARBON DIOXIDE, SOLID. Additional information such as "AS COOLANT" or "AS CONDITIONER" may be added.

    The mark shall be a rectangle. The minimum dimensions shall be 150 mm wide × 250 mm high. The word "WARNING" shall be in red or white and be at least 25 mm high. Where dimensions are not specified, all features shall be in approximate proportion to those shown.

5.5.3.7 *Documentation*

5.5.3.7.1   Documents (such as a bill of lading or cargo manifest) associated with the transport of cargo transport units containing or have contained substances used for cooling or conditioning purposes and have not been completely ventilated before transport shall include the following information:

    (a)   The UN number preceded by the letters "UN"; and

    (b)   The proper shipping name followed by the words "AS COOLANT" or "AS CONDITIONER" as appropriate.

    For example: UN 1845, CARBON DIOXIDE, SOLID, AS COOLANT.

5.5.3.7.2   The transport document may be in any form, provided it contains the information required in 5.5.3.7.1. This information shall be easy to identify, legible and durable.

5.5.4 Dangerous goods in equipment in use or intended for use during transport

5.5.4.1　　Dangerous goods (e.g. lithium batteries, fuel cell cartridges) contained in equipment such as data loggers and cargo tracking devices, attached to or placed in packages, overpacks, containers or load compartments are not subject to any provisions of these Regulations other than the following:

(a) the equipment shall be in use or intended for use during transport;

(b) the contained dangerous goods (e.g. lithium batteries, fuel cell cartridges) shall meet the applicable construction and test requirements specified in these Regulations; and

(c) the equipment shall be capable of withstanding the shocks and loadings normally encountered during transport.

5.5.4.2　　When such equipment containing dangerous goods is transported as a consignment, the relevant entry of the Dangerous Goods List in chapter 3.2 shall be used and all applicable provisions of these Regulations shall apply.

PART 6

REQUIREMENTS FOR THE CONSTRUCTION AND TESTING OF PACKAGINGS, INTERMEDIATE BULK CONTAINERS (IBCs), LARGE PACKAGINGS, PORTABLE TANKS, MULTIPLE-ELEMENT GAS CONTAINERS (MEGCs) AND BULK CONTAINERS

CHAPTER 6.1

REQUIREMENTS FOR THE CONSTRUCTION AND TESTING OF PACKAGINGS

6.1.1   **General**

6.1.1.1   The requirements of this chapter do not apply to:

    (a)   Packages containing radioactive material, which shall comply with the Regulations of the International Atomic Energy Agency (IAEA), except that:

        (i)   Radioactive material possessing other dangerous properties (subsidiary hazards) shall also comply with special provision 172; and

        (ii)   Low specific activity (LSA) material and surface contaminated objects (SCO) may be carried in certain packagings defined in these Regulations provided that the supplementary provisions set out in the IAEA Regulations are also met;

    (b)   Pressure receptacles;

    (c)   Packages whose net mass exceeds 400 kg;

    (d)   Packagings for liquids, other than combination packagings, with a capacity exceeding 450 litres;

    (e)   Packagings for Division 6.2 infectious substances of Category A except for UN 3549.

6.1.1.2   The requirements for packagings in 6.1.4 are based on packagings currently used. In order to take into account progress in science and technology, there is no objection to the use of packagings having specifications different from those in 6.1.4, provided that they are equally effective, acceptable to the competent authority and able to successfully fulfil the requirements described in 6.1.1.3 and 6.1.5. Methods of testing other than those described in these Regulations are acceptable, provided they are equivalent.

6.1.1.3   Every packaging intended to contain liquids shall successfully undergo a suitable leakproofness test. This test is part of a quality assurance programme as stipulated in 6.1.1.4 which shows the capability of meeting the appropriate test level indicated in 6.1.5.4.3:

    (a)   Before it is first used for transport;

    (b)   After remanufacturing or reconditioning, before it is re-used for transport.

For this test, packagings need not have their own closures fitted.

The inner receptacle of composite packagings may be tested without the outer packaging provided the test results are not affected. This test is not necessary for inner packagings of combination packagings.

6.1.1.4   Packagings shall be manufactured, reconditioned and tested under a quality assurance programme which satisfies the competent authority in order to ensure that each packaging meets the requirements of this chapter.

NOTE: *ISO 16106:2020 "Transport packages for dangerous goods – Dangerous goods packagings, intermediate bulk containers (IBCs) and large packagings – Guidelines for the application of ISO 9001" provides acceptable guidance on procedures which may be followed.*

6.1.1.5   Manufacturers and subsequent distributors of packagings shall provide information regarding procedures to be followed and a description of the types and dimensions of closures (including required gaskets) and any other components needed to ensure that packages as presented for transport are capable of passing the applicable performance tests of this chapter.

6.1.2   Code for designating types of packagings

6.1.2.1   The code consists of:

    (a)   An Arabic numeral indicating the kind of packaging, e.g. drum, jerrican, etc., followed by;

    (b)   A capital letter(s) in Latin characters indicating the nature of the material, e.g. steel, wood, etc., followed where necessary by;

    (c)   An Arabic numeral indicating the category of packaging within the kind to which the packaging belongs.

6.1.2.2   In the case of composite packagings, two capital letters in Latin characters are used in sequence in the second position of the code. The first indicates the material of the inner receptacle and the second that of the outer packaging.

6.1.2.3   In the case of combination packagings, only the code number for the outer packaging is used.

6.1.2.4   The letters "T" or "V" or "W" may follow the packaging code. The letter "T" signifies a salvage packaging conforming to the requirements of 6.1.5.1.11. The letter "V" signifies a special packaging conforming to the requirements of 6.1.5.1.7. The letter "W" signifies that the packaging, although of the same type indicated by the code, is manufactured to a specification different from that in 6.1.4 and is considered equivalent under the requirements of 6.1.1.2.

6.1.2.5   The following numerals shall be used for the kinds of packaging:

1. Drum
2. *(Reserved)*
3. Jerrican
4. Box
5. Bag
6. Composite packaging

6.1.2.6   The following capital letters shall be used for the types of material:

A. Steel (all types and surface treatments)
B. Aluminium
C. Natural wood
D. Plywood
F. Reconstituted wood
G. Fibreboard
H. Plastics material
L. Textile
M. Paper, multiwall
N. Metal (other than steel or aluminium)
P. Glass, porcelain or stoneware

NOTE: *"Plastics materials" is taken to include other polymeric materials such as rubber.*

6.1.2.7   The following table indicates the codes to be used for designating types of packagings depending on the kind of packagings, the material used for their construction and their category; it also refers to the paragraphs to be consulted for the appropriate requirements:

Kind	Material	Category	Code	Paragraph
1. Drums	A. Steel	non-removable head	1A1	6.1.4.1
		removable head	1A2	
	B. Aluminium	non-removable head	1B1	6.1.4.2
		removable head	1B2	
	D. Plywood		1D	6.1.4.5
	G. Fibre		1G	6.1.4.7
	H. Plastics	non-removable head	1H1	6.1.4.8
		removable head	1H2	
	N. Metal, other than steel or aluminium	non-removable head	1N1	6.1.4.3
		removable head	1N2	
2. (Reserved)				
3. Jerricans	A. Steel	non-removable head	3A1	6.1.4.4
		removable head	3A2	
	B. Aluminium	non-removable head	3B1	6.1.4.4
		removable head	3B2	
	H. Plastics	non-removable head	3H1	6.1.4.8
		removable head	3H2	
4. Boxes	A. Steel		4A	6.1.4.14
	B. Aluminium		4B	6.1.4.14
	C. Natural wood	ordinary	4C1	6.1.4.9
		with sift-proof walls	4C2	
	D. Plywood		4D	6.1.4.10
	F. Reconstituted wood		4F	6.1.4.11
	G. Fibreboard		4G	6.1.4.12
	H. Plastics	expanded	4H1	6.1.4.13
		solid	4H2	
	N. Metal, other than steel or aluminium		4N	6.1.4.14
5. Bags	H. Woven plastics	without inner liner or coating	5H1	6.1.4.16
		sift-proof	5H2	
		water-resistant	5H3	
	H. Plastics film		5H4	6.1.4.17
	L. Textile	without inner liner or coating	5L1	6.1.4.15
		sift proof	5L2	
		water-resistant	5L3	
	M. Paper	multiwall	5M1	6.1.4.18
		multiwall, water-resistant	5M2	

Kind	Material	Category	Code	Paragraph
6. Composite packagings	H. Plastics receptacle	in steel drum	6HA1	6.1.4.19
		in steel crate or box	6HA2	6.1.4.19
		in aluminium drum	6HB1	6.1.4.19
		in aluminium crate or box	6HB2	6.1.4.19
		in wooden box	6HC	6.1.4.19
		in plywood drum	6HD1	6.1.4.19
		in plywood box	6HD2	6.1.4.19
		in fibre drum	6HG1	6.1.4.19
		in fibreboard box	6HG2	6.1.4.19
		in plastics drum	6HH1	6.1.4.19
		in solid plastics box	6HH2	6.1.4.19
	P. Glass, porcelain or stoneware receptacle	in steel drum	6PA1	6.1.4.20
		in steel crate or box	6PA2	6.1.4.20
		in aluminium drum	6PB1	6.1.4.20
		in aluminium crate or box	6PB2	6.1.4.20
		in wooden box	6PC	6.1.4.20
		in plywood drum	6PD1	6.1.4.20
		in wickerwork hamper	6PD2	6.1.4.20
		in fibre drum	6PG1	6.1.4.20
		in fibreboard box	6PG2	6.1.4.20
		in expanded plastics packaging	6PH1	6.1.4.20
		in solid plastics packaging	6PH2	6.1.4.20

6.1.3 Marking

NOTE 1: *The marks indicate that the packaging which bears them correspond to a successfully tested design type and that it complies with the requirements of this chapter which are related to the manufacture, but not to the use, of the packaging. In itself, therefore, the marks do not necessarily confirm that the packaging may be used for any substance: generally the type of packaging (e.g. steel drum), its maximum capacity and/or mass, and any special requirements are specified for each substance in part 3 of these Regulations.*

NOTE 2: *The marks are intended to be of assistance to packaging manufacturers, reconditioners, packaging users, carriers and regulatory authorities. In relation to the use of a new packaging, the original marks are a means for its manufacturer(s) to identify the type and to indicate those performance test regulations that have been met.*

NOTE 3: *The marks do not always provide full details of the test levels, etc., and these may need to be taken further into account, e.g. by reference to a test certificate, to test reports or to a register of successfully tested packagings. For example, a packaging having an X or Y mark may be used for substances to which a packing group having a lesser degree of danger has been assigned with the relevant maximum permissible value of the relative density[1] determined by taking into account the factor 1.5 or 2.25 indicated in the test requirements for packagings in 6.1.5 as appropriate, i.e. packing group I packaging tested for products of relative density 1.2 could be used as a packing group II packaging for products of relative density 1.8 or a packing group III packaging of relative density 2.7, provided of course that all the performance criteria can still be met with the higher relative density product.*

6.1.3.1 Each packaging intended for use according to these Regulations shall bear marks on a non-removable component which are durable, legible and placed in a location and of such a size relative to the

---

[1] *Relative density (d) is considered to be synonymous with Specific Gravity (SG) and is used throughout this text.*

packaging as to be readily visible. For packages with a gross mass of more than 30 kg, the marks or a duplicate thereof shall appear on the top or on a side of the packaging. Letters, numerals and symbols shall be at least 12 mm high, except for packagings of 30 *l* capacity or less or of 30 kg maximum net mass, when they shall be at least 6 mm in height and except for packagings of 5 *l* capacity or less or of 5 kg maximum net mass when they shall be of an appropriate size.

NOTE: *The provisions of 6.1.3.1 of the twenty-second revised edition of the Recommendations on the Transport of Dangerous Goods, Model Regulations may continue to be applied until 31 December 2026. Packagings manufactured before 1 January 2027 according to the provisions applicable at the date of manufacture may continue to be used.*

The marks shall show:

(a) The United Nations packaging symbol $\binom{u}{n}$.

This symbol shall not be used for any purpose other than certifying that a packaging, a flexible bulk container, a portable tank or a MEGC complies with the relevant requirements in chapter 6.1, 6.2, 6.3, 6.5, 6.6, 6.7 or 6.8.

For embossed metal packagings the capital letters "UN" may be applied as the symbol;

(b) The code designating the type of packaging according to 6.1.2;

(c) A code in two parts:

(i) a letter designating the packing group(s) for which the design type has been successfully tested:

X for packing groups I, II and III
Y for packing groups II and III
Z for packing group III only;

(ii) the relative density, rounded off to the first decimal, for which the design type has been tested for packagings without inner packagings intended to contain liquids; this may be omitted when the relative density does not exceed 1.2. For packagings intended to contain solids or inner packagings, the maximum gross mass in kilograms;

(d) Either the letter "S" denoting that the packaging is intended for the transport of solids or inner packagings or, for packagings (other than combination packagings) intended to contain liquids, the hydraulic test pressure which the packaging was shown to withstand in kPa rounded down to the nearest 10 kPa;

(e) The last two digits of the year during which the packaging was manufactured. Packagings of types 1H and 3H shall also be appropriately marked with the month of manufacture; this may be marked on the packaging in a different place from the remainder of the marks. An appropriate method is:

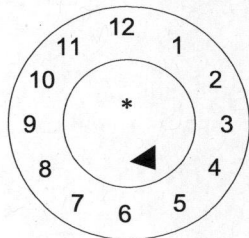

* The last two digits of the year of manufacture may be displayed at that place. In such a case and when the clock is placed adjacent to the UN design type mark, the indication of the year in the mark may be waived. However, when the clock is not placed adjacent to the UN design type mark, the two digits of the year in the mark and in the clock shall be identical.

NOTE: *Other methods that provide the minimum required information in a durable, visible and legible form are also acceptable.*

(f) The State authorizing the allocation of the mark, indicated by the distinguishing sign used on vehicles in international road traffic[2];

(g) The name of the manufacturer or other identification of the packaging specified by the competent authority.

6.1.3.2 In addition to the durable marks prescribed in 6.1.3.1, every new metal drum of a capacity greater than 100 litres shall bear the marks described in 6.1.3.1 (a) to (e) on the bottom, with an indication of the nominal thickness of at least the metal used in the body (in mm, to 0.1 mm), in permanent form (e.g. embossed). When the nominal thickness of either head of a metal drum is thinner than that of the body, the nominal thicknesses of the top head, body, and bottom head shall be marked on the bottom in permanent form (e.g. embossed), for example "1.0-1.2-1.0" or "0.9-1.0-1.0". Nominal thicknesses of metal shall be determined according to the appropriate ISO standard, for example ISO 3574:1999 for steel. The marks indicated in 6.1.3.1 (f) and (g) shall not be applied in a permanent form (e.g. embossed) except as provided in 6.1.3.5.

6.1.3.3 Every packaging other than those referred to in 6.1.3.2 liable to undergo a reconditioning process shall bear the marks indicated in 6.1.3.1 (a) to (e) in a permanent form. Marks are permanent if they are able to withstand the reconditioning process (e.g. embossed). For packagings other than metal drums of a capacity greater than 100 litres, these permanent marks may replace the corresponding durable marks prescribed in 6.1.3.1.

6.1.3.4 For remanufactured metal drums, if there is no change to the packaging type and no replacement or removal of integral structural components, the required marks need not be permanent (e.g. embossed). Every other remanufactured metal drum shall bear the marks in 6.1.3.1 (a) to (e) in a permanent form (e.g. embossed) on the top head or side.

6.1.3.5 Metal drums made from materials (e.g. stainless steel) designed to be reused repeatedly may bear the marks indicated in 6.1.3.1 (f) and (g) in a permanent form (e.g. embossed).

6.1.3.6 Packagings manufactured with recycled plastics material as defined in 1.2.1 shall be marked "REC". This mark shall be placed near the marks prescribed in 6.1.3.1.

6.1.3.7 Marks shall be applied in the sequence shown in 6.1.3.1; each mark required in these sub-paragraphs and when appropriate, (h) to (j) of 6.1.3.8, shall be clearly separated, e.g. by a slash or space, so as to be easily identifiable. For examples, see 6.1.3.10.

Any additional marks authorized by a competent authority shall still enable the other marks required in 6.1.3.1 to be correctly identified.

6.1.3.8 After reconditioning a packaging, the reconditioner shall apply to it, in sequence, durable marks showing:

(h) The State in which the reconditioning was carried out, indicated by the distinguishing sign used on vehicles in international road traffic[2];

---

[2] *Distinguishing sign of the State of registration used on motor vehicles and trailers in international road traffic, e.g. in accordance with the Geneva Convention on Road Traffic of 1949 or the Vienna Convention on Road Traffic of 1968.*

(i) The name of the reconditioner or other identification of the packaging specified by the competent authority;

(j) The year of reconditioning; the letter "R"; and, for every packaging successfully passing the leakproofness test in 6.1.1.3, the additional letter "L".

6.1.3.9 When, after reconditioning, the marks required by 6.1.3.1 (a) to (d) no longer appear on the top head or the side of a metal drum, the reconditioner also shall apply them in a durable form followed by 6.1.3.8 (h), (i) and (j). These marks shall not identify a greater performance capability than that for which the original design type had been tested and marked.

6.1.3.10 *Examples for marking NEW packagings*

ⓤⓝ	4G/Y145/S/02 NL/VL823	as in 6.1.3.1 (a), (b), (c), (d) and (e) as in 6.1.3.1 (f) and (g)	For a new fibreboard box
ⓤⓝ	1A1/Y1.4/150/98 NL/VL824	as in 6.1.3.1 (a), (b), (c), (d) and (e) as in 6.1.3.1 (f) and (g)	For a new steel drum to contain liquids
ⓤⓝ	1A2/Y150/S/01 NL/VL825	as in 6.1.3.1 (a), (b), (c), (d) and (e) as in 6.1.3.1 (f) and (g)	For a new steel drum to contain solids, or inner packagings
ⓤⓝ	4HW/Y136/S/98 NL/VL826	as in 6.1.3.1 (a), (b), (c), (d) and (e) as in 6.1.3.1 (f) and (g)	For a new plastics box of equivalent specification
ⓤⓝ	1A2/Y/100/01 USA/MM5	as in 6.1.3.1 (a), (b), (c), (d) and (e) as in 6.1.3.1 (f) and (g)	For a remanufactured steel drum to contain liquids

6.1.3.11 *Examples for marking RECONDITIONED packagings*

ⓤⓝ	1A1/Y1.4/150/97 NL/RB/01 RL	as in 6.1.3.1 (a), (b), (c), (d) and (e) as in 6.1.3.8 (h), (i) and (j)
ⓤⓝ	1A2/Y150/S/99 USA/RB/00 R	as in 6.1.3.1 (a), (b), (c), (d), and (e) as in 6.1.3.8 (h), (i) and (j)

6.1.3.12 *Example for marking SALVAGE packagings*

ⓤⓝ	1A2T/Y300/S/01 USA/abc	as in 6.1.3.1 (a), (b), (c), (d) and (e) as in 6.1.3.1 (f) and (g)

NOTE: *The marking, for which examples are given in 6.1.3.10, 6.1.3.11 and 6.1.3.12, may be applied in a single line or in multiple lines provided the correct sequence is respected.*

6.1.3.13 Where a packaging conforms to one or more than one tested packaging design type, including one or more than one tested IBC or large packaging design type, the packaging may bear more than one mark to indicate the relevant performance test requirements that have been met. Where more than one mark appears on a packaging, the marks shall appear in close proximity to one another and each mark shall appear in its entirety.

6.1.4 Requirements for packagings

6.1.4.0 *General requirements*

Any permeation of the substance contained in the packaging shall not constitute a danger under normal conditions of transport.

6.1.4.1 *Steel drums*

    1A1   non-removable head
    1A2   removable head

6.1.4.1.1   Body and heads shall be constructed of steel sheet of a suitable type and of adequate thickness in relation to the capacity of the drum and to its intended use.

NOTE: *In the case of carbon steel drums, "suitable" steels are identified in ISO 3573:1999 "Hot rolled carbon steel sheet of commercial and drawing qualities" and ISO 3574:1999 "Cold-reduced carbon steel sheet of commercial and drawing qualities". For carbon steel drums below 100 litres "suitable" steels in addition to the above standards are also identified in ISO 11949:1995 "Cold-reduced electrolytic tinplate", ISO 11950:1995 "Cold-reduced electrolytic chromium/chromium oxide-coated steel" and ISO 11951:1995 "Cold-reduced blackplate in coil form for the production of tinplate or electrolytic chromium/chromium oxide-coated steel".*

6.1.4.1.2   Body seams shall be welded on drums intended to contain more than 40 litres of liquid. Body seams shall be mechanically seamed or welded on drums intended to contain solids or 40 litres or less of liquids.

6.1.4.1.3   Chimes shall be mechanically seamed or welded. Separate reinforcing rings may be applied.

6.1.4.1.4   Drums may have rolling hoops, either expanded or separate. If there are separate rolling hoops they shall be fitted tightly on the body and so secured that they cannot shift. Rolling hoops shall not be spot welded.

6.1.4.1.5   Openings for filling, emptying and venting in the bodies or heads of non-removable head (1A1) drums shall not exceed 7 cm in diameter. Drums with larger openings are considered to be of the removable head type (1A2). Closures for openings in the bodies and heads of drums shall be so designed and applied that they will remain secure and leakproof under normal conditions of transport. Closure flanges may be mechanically seamed or welded in place. Gaskets or other sealing elements shall be used with closures, unless the closure is inherently leakproof.

6.1.4.1.6   Closure devices for removable head drums shall be so designed and applied that they will remain secure and drums will remain leakproof under normal conditions of transport. Gaskets or other sealing elements shall be used with all removable heads.

6.1.4.1.7   If materials used for body, heads, closures and fittings are not in themselves compatible with the contents to be transported, suitable internal protective coatings or treatments shall be applied. These coatings or treatments shall retain their protective properties under normal conditions of transport.

6.1.4.1.8   Maximum capacity of drum: 450 litres

6.1.4.1.9   Maximum net mass: 400 kg

6.1.4.2 *Aluminium drums*

    1B1   non-removable head
    1B2   removable head

6.1.4.2.1   Body and heads shall be constructed of aluminium at least 99 % pure or of an aluminium base alloy. Material shall be of a suitable type and of adequate thickness in relation to the capacity of the drum and to its intended use.

6.1.4.2.2   All seams shall be welded. Chime seams, if any, shall be reinforced by the application of separate reinforcing rings.

6.1.4.2.3   Drums may have rolling hoops, either expanded or separate. If there are separate rolling hoops they shall be fitted tightly on the body and so secured that they cannot shift. Rolling hoops shall not be spot welded.

6.1.4.2.4   Openings for filling, emptying and venting in the bodies or heads of non-removable head (1B1) drums shall not exceed 7 cm in diameter. Drums with larger openings are considered to be of the removable head type (1B2). Closures for openings in the bodies and heads of drums shall be so designed and applied that they will remain secure and leakproof under normal conditions of transport. Closure flanges shall be welded in place so that the weld provides a leakproof seam. Gaskets or other sealing elements shall be used with closures, unless the closure is inherently leakproof.

6.1.4.2.5   Closure devices for removable head drums shall be so designed and applied that they will remain secure and drums will remain leakproof under normal conditions of transport. Gaskets or other sealing elements shall be used with all removable heads.

6.1.4.2.6   If materials used for body, heads, closures and fittings are not in themselves compatible with the contents to be transported, suitable internal protective coatings or treatments shall be applied. These coatings or treatments shall retain their protective properties under normal conditions of transport.

6.1.4.2.7   Maximum capacity of drum: 450 litres

6.1.4.2.8   Maximum net mass: 400 kg

6.1.4.3   *Drums of metal other than steel or aluminium*

   1N1   non-removable head
   1N2   removable head

6.1.4.3.1   The body and heads shall be constructed of a metal or of a metal alloy other than steel or aluminium. Material shall be of a suitable type and of adequate thickness in relation to the capacity of the drum and to its intended use.

6.1.4.3.2   Chime seams, if any, shall be reinforced by the application of separate reinforcing rings. All seams, if any, shall be joined (welded, soldered, etc.) in accordance with the technical state of the art for the used metal or metal alloy.

6.1.4.3.3   Drums may have rolling hoops, either expanded or separate. If there are separate rolling hoops they shall be fitted tightly on the body and so secured that they cannot shift. Rolling hoops shall not be spot welded.

6.1.4.3.4   Openings for filling, emptying and venting in the bodies or heads of non-removable head (1N1) drums shall not exceed 7 cm in diameter. Drums with larger openings are considered to be of the removable head type (1N2). Closures for openings in the bodies and heads of drums shall be so designed and applied that they will remain secure and leakproof under normal conditions of transport. Closure flanges shall be joined in place (welded, solded, etc.) in accordance with the technical state of the art for the used metal or metal alloy so that the seam join is leakproof. Gaskets or other sealing elements shall be used with closures, unless the closure is inherently leakproof.

6.1.4.3.5   Closure devices for removable head drums shall be so designed and applied that they will remain secure and drums will remain leakproof under normal conditions of transport. Gaskets or other sealing elements shall be used with all removable heads.

6.1.4.3.6   If materials used for body, heads, closures and fittings are not in themselves compatible with the contents to be transported, suitable internal protective coatings or treatments shall be applied. These coatings or treatments shall retain their protective properties under normal conditions of transport.

6.1.4.3.7   Maximum capacity of drum: 450 litres

6.1.4.3.8   Maximum net mass: 400 kg

6.1.4.4   *Steel or aluminium jerricans*

    3A1   steel, non-removable head
    3A2   steel, removable head
    3B1   aluminium, non-removable head
    3B2   aluminium, removable head

6.1.4.4.1   Body and heads shall be constructed of steel sheet, of aluminium at least 99 % pure or of an aluminium base alloy. Material shall be of a suitable type and of adequate thickness in relation to the capacity of the jerrican and to its intended use.

6.1.4.4.2   Chimes of steel jerricans shall be mechanically seamed or welded. Body seams of steel jerricans intended to contain more than 40 litres of liquid shall be welded. Body seams of steel jerricans intended to contain 40 litres or less shall be mechanically seamed or welded. For aluminium jerricans, all seams shall be welded. Chime seams, if any, shall be reinforced by the application of a separate reinforcing ring.

6.1.4.4.3   Openings in jerricans (3A1 and 3B1) shall not exceed 7 cm in diameter. Jerricans with larger openings are considered to be of the removable head type (3A2 and 3B2). Closures shall be so designed that they will remain secure and leakproof under normal conditions of transport. Gaskets or other sealing elements shall be used with closures, unless the closure is inherently leakproof.

6.1.4.4.4   If materials used for body, heads, closures and fittings are not in themselves compatible with the contents to be transported, suitable internal protective coatings or treatments shall be applied. These coatings or treatments shall retain their protective properties under normal conditions of transport.

6.1.4.4.5   Maximum capacity of jerrican: 60 litres

6.1.4.4.6   Maximum net mass: 120 kg

6.1.4.5   *Plywood drums*

    1D

6.1.4.5.1   The wood used shall be well-seasoned, commercially dry and free from any defect likely to lessen the effectiveness of the drum for the purpose intended. If a material other than plywood is used for the manufacture of the heads, it shall be of a quality equivalent to the plywood.

6.1.4.5.2   At least two-ply plywood shall be used for the body and at least three-ply plywood for the heads; the plies shall be firmly glued together by a water-resistant adhesive with their grain crosswise.

6.1.4.5.3   The body and heads of the drum and their joins shall be of a design appropriate to the capacity of the drum and to its intended use.

6.1.4.5.4   In order to prevent sifting of the contents, lids shall be lined with kraft paper or some other equivalent material which shall be securely fastened to the lid and extend to the outside along its full circumference.

6.1.4.5.5   Maximum capacity of drum: 250 litres

6.1.4.5.6   Maximum net mass: 400 kg

6.1.4.6   *Deleted.*

6.1.4.7 *Fibre drums*

1G

6.1.4.7.1 The body of the drum shall consist of multiple plies of heavy paper or fibreboard (without corrugations) firmly glued or laminated together and may include one or more protective layers of bitumen, waxed kraft paper, metal foil, plastics material, etc.

6.1.4.7.2 Heads shall be of natural wood, fibreboard, metal, plywood, plastics or other suitable material and may include one or more protective layers of bitumen, waxed kraft paper, metal foil, plastics material, etc.

6.1.4.7.3 The body and heads of the drum and their joins shall be of a design appropriate to the capacity of the drum and to its intended use.

6.1.4.7.4 The assembled packaging shall be sufficiently water-resistant so as not to delaminate under normal conditions of transport.

6.1.4.7.5 Maximum capacity of drum: 450 litres

6.1.4.7.6 Maximum net mass: 400 kg

6.1.4.8 *Plastics drums and jerricans*

1H1	drums, non-removable head
1H2	drums, removable head
3H1	jerricans, non-removable head
3H2	jerricans, removable head

6.1.4.8.1 The packaging shall be manufactured from suitable plastics material and be of adequate strength in relation to its capacity and intended use. Except for recycled plastics material as defined in 1.2.1, no used material other than production residues or regrind from the same manufacturing process may be used. The packaging shall be adequately resistant to ageing and to degradation caused either by the substance contained or by ultra-violet radiation.

6.1.4.8.2 If protection against ultra-violet radiation is required, it shall be provided by the addition of carbon black or other suitable pigments or inhibitors. These additives shall be compatible with the contents and remain effective throughout the life of the packaging. Where use is made of carbon black, pigments or inhibitors other than those used in the manufacture of the tested design type, retesting may be waived if the carbon black content does not exceed 2 % by mass or if the pigment content does not exceed 3 % by mass; the content of inhibitors of ultra-violet radiation is not limited.

6.1.4.8.3 Additives serving purposes other than protection against ultra-violet radiation may be included in the composition of the plastics material provided that they do not adversely affect the chemical and physical properties of the material of the packaging. In such circumstances, retesting may be waived.

6.1.4.8.4 The wall thickness at every point of the packaging shall be appropriate to its capacity and intended use, taking into account the stresses to which each point is liable to be exposed.

6.1.4.8.5 Openings for filling, emptying and venting in the bodies or heads of non-removable head drums (1H1) and jerricans (3H1) shall not exceed 7 cm in diameter. Drums and jerricans with larger openings are considered to be of the removable head type (1H2 and 3H2). Closures for openings in the bodies or heads of drums and jerricans shall be so designed and applied that they will remain secure and leakproof under normal conditions of transport. Gaskets or other sealing elements shall be used with closures unless the closure is inherently leakproof.

6.1.4.8.6 Closure devices for removable head drums and jerricans shall be so designed and applied that they will remain secure and leakproof under normal conditions of transport. Gaskets shall be used with all removable heads unless the drum or jerrican design is such that, where the removable head is properly secured, the drum or jerrican is inherently leakproof.

6.1.4.8.7   Maximum capacity of drums and jerricans:

   1H1, 1H2: 450 litres
   3H1, 3H2: 60 litres

6.1.4.8.8   Maximum net mass:

   1H1, 1H2: 400 kg
   3H1, 3H2: 120 kg

6.1.4.9   ***Boxes of natural wood***

   4C1   ordinary
   4C2   with sift-proof walls

6.1.4.9.1   The wood used shall be well-seasoned, commercially dry and free from defects that would materially lessen the strength of any part of the box. The strength of the material used and the method of construction shall be appropriate to the capacity and intended use of the box. The tops and bottoms may be made of water-resistant reconstituted wood such as hardboard, particle board or other suitable type.

6.1.4.9.2   Fastenings shall be resistant to vibration experienced under normal conditions of transport. End grain nailing shall be avoided whenever practicable. Joins which are likely to be highly stressed shall be made using clenched or annular ring nails or equivalent fastenings.

6.1.4.9.3   Box 4C2: each part shall consist of one piece or be equivalent thereto. Parts are considered equivalent to one piece when one of the following methods of glued assembly is used: Lindermann joint, tongue and groove joint, ship lap or rabbet joint or butt joint with at least two corrugated metal fasteners at each joint.

6.1.4.9.4   Maximum net mass: 400 kg

6.1.4.10   ***Plywood boxes***

   4D

6.1.4.10.1   Plywood used shall be at least 3-ply. It shall be made from well-seasoned rotary cut, sliced or sawn veneer, commercially dry and free from defects that would materially lessen the strength of the box. The strength of the material used and the method of construction shall be appropriate to the capacity and intended use of the box. All adjacent plies shall be glued with water-resistant adhesive. Other suitable materials may be used together with plywood in the construction of boxes. Boxes shall be firmly nailed or secured to corner posts or ends or be assembled by equally suitable devices.

6.1.4.10.2   Maximum net mass: 400 kg

6.1.4.11   ***Reconstituted wood boxes***

   4F

6.1.4.11.1   The walls of boxes shall be made of water-resistant reconstituted wood such as hardboard, particle board or other suitable type. The strength of the material used and the method of construction shall be appropriate to the capacity of the boxes and to their intended use.

6.1.4.11.2   Other parts of the boxes may be made of other suitable material.

6.1.4.11.3   Boxes shall be securely assembled by means of suitable devices.

6.1.4.11.4   Maximum net mass: 400 kg

6.1.4.12 *Fibreboard boxes (including corrugated fibreboard boxes)*

        4G

6.1.4.12.1 Strong and good quality solid or double-faced corrugated fibreboard (single or multiwall) shall be used, appropriate to the capacity of the box and to its intended use. The water resistance of the outer surface shall be such that the increase in mass, as determined in a test carried out over a period of 30 minutes by the Cobb method of determining water absorption, is not greater than 155 g/m^2 - see ISO 535:2014. It shall have proper bending qualities. Fibreboard shall be cut, creased without scoring, and slotted so as to permit assembly without cracking, surface breaks or undue bending. The fluting of corrugated fibreboard shall be firmly glued to the facings.

6.1.4.12.2 The ends of boxes may have a wooden frame or be entirely of wood or other suitable material. Reinforcements of wooden battens or other suitable material may be used.

6.1.4.12.3 Manufacturing joins in the body of boxes shall be taped, lapped and glued, or lapped and stitched with metal staples. Lapped joins shall have an appropriate overlap.

6.1.4.12.4 Where closing is effected by gluing or taping, a water-resistant adhesive shall be used.

6.1.4.12.5 Boxes shall be designed so as to provide a good fit to the contents.

6.1.4.12.6 Maximum net mass: 400 kg

6.1.4.13 *Plastics boxes*

        4H1   expanded plastics boxes
        4H2   solid plastics boxes

6.1.4.13.1 The box shall be manufactured from suitable plastics material and be of adequate strength in relation to its capacity and intended use. The box shall be adequately resistant to ageing and to degradation caused either by the substance contained or by ultra-violet radiation.

6.1.4.13.2 An expanded plastics box shall comprise two parts made of a moulded expanded plastics material, a bottom section containing cavities for the inner packagings and a top section covering and interlocking with the bottom section. The top and bottom sections shall be designed so that the inner packagings fit snugly. The closure cap for any inner packaging shall not be in contact with the inside of the top section of this box.

6.1.4.13.3 For dispatch, an expanded plastics box shall be closed with a self-adhesive tape having sufficient tensile strength to prevent the box from opening. The adhesive tape shall be weather resistant and its adhesive compatible with the expanded plastics material of the box. Other closing devices at least equally effective may be used.

6.1.4.13.4 For solid plastics boxes, protection against ultra-violet radiation, if required, shall be provided by the addition of carbon black or other suitable pigments or inhibitors. These additives shall be compatible with the contents and remain effective throughout the life of the box. Where use is made of carbon black, pigments or inhibitors other than those used in the manufacture of the tested design type, retesting may be waived if the carbon black content does not exceed 2 % by mass or if the pigment content does not exceed 3 % by mass; the content of inhibitors of ultra-violet radiation is not limited.

6.1.4.13.5 Additives serving purposes other than protection against ultra-violet radiation may be included in the composition of the plastics material provided that they do not adversely affect the chemical or physical properties of the material of the box. In such circumstances, retesting may be waived.

6.1.4.13.6 Solid plastics boxes shall have closure devices made of a suitable material of adequate strength and so designed as to prevent the box from unintentional opening.

6.1.4.13.7　　　　Maximum net mass:

     4H1: 60 kg
     4H2: 400 kg

6.1.4.14　　　　***Steel, aluminium or other metal boxes***

     4A steel boxes
     4B aluminium boxes
     4N metal, other than steel or aluminium, boxes

6.1.4.14.1　　　　The strength of the metal and the construction of the box shall be appropriate to the capacity of the box and to its intended use.

6.1.4.14.2　　　　Boxes shall be lined with fibreboard or felt packing pieces or shall have an inner liner or coating of suitable material, as required. If a double seamed metal liner is used, steps shall be taken to prevent the ingress of substances, particularly explosives, into the recesses of the seams.

6.1.4.14.3　　　　Closures may be of any suitable type; they shall remain secured under normal conditions of transport.

6.1.4.14.4　　　　Maximum net mass: 400 kg

6.1.4.15　　　　***Textile bags***

     5L1 without inner liner or coating
     5L2 sift-proof
     5L3 water-resistant

6.1.4.15.1　　　　The textiles used shall be of good quality. The strength of the fabric and the construction of the bag shall be appropriate to the capacity of the bag and to its intended use.

6.1.4.15.2　　　　Bags, sift-proof, 5L2: the bag shall be made sift-proof, for example by the use of:

    (a) Paper bonded to the inner surface of the bag by a water-resistant adhesive such as bitumen; or

    (b) Plastics film bonded to the inner surface of the bag; or

    (c) One or more inner liners made of paper or plastics material.

6.1.4.15.3　　　　Bags, water-resistant, 5L3: to prevent the entry of moisture the bag shall be made waterproof, for example by the use of:

    (a) Separate inner liners of water-resistant paper (e.g. waxed kraft paper, tarred paper or plastics-coated kraft paper); or

    (b) Plastics film bonded to the inner surface of the bag; or

    (c) One or more inner liners made of plastics material.

6.1.4.15.4　　　　Maximum net mass: 50 kg

6.1.4.16 *Woven plastics bags*

        5H1   without inner liner or coating
        5H2   sift-proof
        5H3   water-resistant

6.1.4.16.1   Bags shall be made from stretched tapes or monofilaments of a suitable plastics material. The strength of the material used and the construction of the bag shall be appropriate to the capacity of the bag and to its intended use.

6.1.4.16.2   If the fabric is woven flat, the bags shall be made by sewing or some other method ensuring closure of the bottom and one side. If the fabric is tubular, the bag shall be closed by sewing, weaving or some other equally strong method of closure.

6.1.4.16.3   Bags, sift-proof, 5H2: the bag shall be made sift-proof, for example by means of:

    (a)   Paper or a plastics film bonded to the inner surface of the bag; or

    (b)   One or more separate inner liners made of paper or plastics material.

6.1.4.16.4   Bags, water-resistant, 5H3: to prevent the entry of moisture, the bag shall be made waterproof, for example by means of:

    (a)   Separate inner liners of water-resistant paper (e.g. waxed kraft paper, double-tarred kraft paper or plastics-coated kraft paper); or

    (b)   Plastics film bonded to the inner or outer surface of the bag; or

    (c)   One or more inner plastics liners.

6.1.4.16.5   Maximum net mass: 50 kg

6.1.4.17 *Plastics film bags*

        5H4

6.1.4.17.1   Bags shall be made of a suitable plastics material. The strength of the material used and the construction of the bag shall be appropriate to the capacity of the bag and to its intended use. Joins and closures shall withstand pressures and impacts liable to occur under normal conditions of transport.

6.1.4.17.2   Maximum net mass: 50 kg

6.1.4.18 *Paper bags*

        5M1   multiwall
        5M2   multiwall, water-resistant

6.1.4.18.1   Bags shall be made of a suitable kraft paper or of an equivalent paper with at least three plies, the middle ply of which may be net-cloth with adhesive bonding to the outer ply. The strength of the paper and the construction of the bags shall be appropriate to the capacity of the bag and to its intended use. Joins and closures shall be sift-proof.

6.1.4.18.2   Bags 5M2: to prevent the entry of moisture, a bag of four plies or more shall be made waterproof by the use of either a water-resistant ply as one of the two outermost plies or a water-resistant barrier made of a suitable protective material between the two outermost plies; a bag of three plies shall be made waterproof by the use of a water-resistant ply as the outermost ply. Where there is a danger of the substance contained reacting with moisture or where it is packed damp, a waterproof ply or barrier, such as double-tarred kraft paper, plastics-coated kraft paper, plastics film bonded to the inner surface of the bag, or one or more inner plastics liners, shall also be placed next to the substance. Joins and closures shall be waterproof.

6.1.4.18.3   Maximum net mass: 50 kg

6.1.4.19   *Composite packagings (plastics material)*

        6HA1   plastics receptacle with outer steel drum
        6HA2   plastics receptacle with outer steel crate or box
        6HB1   plastics receptacle with outer aluminium drum
        6HB2   plastics receptacle with outer aluminium crate or box
        6HC   plastics receptacle with outer wooden box
        6HD1   plastics receptacle with outer plywood drum
        6HD2   plastics receptacle with outer plywood box
        6HG1   plastics receptacle with outer fibre drum
        6HG2   plastics receptacle with outer fibreboard box
        6HH1   plastics receptacle with outer plastics drum
        6HH2   plastics receptacle with outer solid plastics box

6.1.4.19.1   *Inner receptacle*

6.1.4.19.1.1   The requirements of 6.1.4.8.1 and 6.1.4.8.3 to 6.1.4.8.6 apply to inner plastics receptacles.

6.1.4.19.1.2   The inner plastics receptacle shall fit snugly inside the outer packaging, which shall be free of any projection that might abrade the plastics material.

6.1.4.19.1.3   Maximum capacity of inner receptacle:

      6HA1, 6HB1, 6HD1, 6HG1, 6HH1: 250 litres
      6HA2, 6HB2, 6HC, 6HD2, 6HG2, 6HH2: 60 litres

6.1.4.19.1.4   Maximum net mass:

      6HA1, 6HB1, 6HD1, 6HG1, 6HH1: 400 kg
      6HA2, 6HB2, 6HC, 6HD2, 6HG2, 6HH2: 75 kg

6.1.4.19.2   *Outer packaging*

6.1.4.19.2.1   Plastics receptacle with outer steel or aluminium drum 6HA1 or 6HB1; the relevant requirements of 6.1.4.1 or 6.1.4.2, as appropriate, apply to the construction of the outer packaging.

6.1.4.19.2.2   Plastics receptacle with outer steel or aluminium crate or box 6HA2 or 6HB2; the relevant requirements of 6.1.4.14 apply to the construction of the outer packaging.

6.1.4.19.2.3   Plastics receptacle with outer wooden box 6HC; the relevant requirements of 6.1.4.9 apply to the construction of the outer packaging.

6.1.4.19.2.4   Plastics receptacle with outer plywood drum 6HD1; the relevant requirements of 6.1.4.5 apply to the construction of the outer packaging.

6.1.4.19.2.5   Plastics receptacle with outer plywood box 6HD2; the relevant requirements of 6.1.4.10 apply to the construction of the outer packaging.

6.1.4.19.2.6   Plastics receptacle with outer fibre drum 6HG1; the requirements of 6.1.4.7.1 to 6.1.4.7.4 apply to the construction of the outer packaging.

6.1.4.19.2.7   Plastics receptacle with outer fibreboard box 6HG2; the relevant requirements of 6.1.4.12 apply to the construction of the outer packaging.

6.1.4.19.2.8   Plastics receptacle with outer plastics drum 6HH1; the requirements of 6.1.4.8.1 and 6.1.4.8.2 to 6.1.4.8.6 apply to the construction of the outer packaging.

6.1.4.19.2.9   Plastics receptacles with outer solid plastics box (including corrugated plastics material) 6HH2; the requirements of 6.1.4.13.1 and 6.1.4.13.4 to 6.1.4.13.6 apply to the construction of the outer packaging.

6.1.4.20   *Composite packagings (glass, porcelain or stoneware)*

	6PA1	receptacle with outer steel drum
	6PA2	receptacle with outer steel crate or box
	6PB1	receptacle with outer aluminium drum
	6PB2	receptacle with outer aluminium crate or box
	6PC	receptacle with outer wooden box
	6PD1	receptacle with outer plywood drum
	6PD2	receptacle with outer wickerwork hamper
	6PG1	receptacle with outer fibre drum
	6PG2	receptacle with outer fibreboard box
	6PH1	receptacle with outer expanded plastics packaging
	6PH2	receptacle with outer solid plastics packaging

6.1.4.20.1   *Inner receptacle*

6.1.4.20.1.1   Receptacles shall be of a suitable form (cylindrical or pear-shaped) and be made of good quality material free from any defect that could impair their strength. The walls shall be sufficiently thick at every point.

6.1.4.20.1.2   Screw-threaded plastics closures, ground glass stoppers or closures at least equally effective shall be used as closures for receptacles. Any part of the closure likely to come into contact with the contents of the receptacle shall be resistant to those contents. Care shall be taken to ensure that the closures are so fitted as to be leakproof and are suitably secured to prevent any loosening during transport. If vented closures are necessary, they shall comply with 4.1.1.8.

6.1.4.20.1.3   The receptacle shall be firmly secured in the outer packaging by means of cushioning and/or absorbent materials.

6.1.4.20.1.4   Maximum capacity of receptacle: 60 litres

6.1.4.20.1.5   Maximum net mass: 75 kg

6.1.4.20.2   *Outer packaging*

6.1.4.20.2.1   Receptacle with outer steel drum 6PA1; the relevant requirements of 6.1.4.1 apply to the construction of the outer packaging. The removable lid required for this type of packaging may nevertheless be in the form of a cap.

6.1.4.20.2.2   Receptacle with outer steel crate or box 6PA2; the relevant requirements of 6.1.4.14 apply to the construction of the outer packaging. For cylindrical receptacles the outer packaging shall, when upright, rise above the receptacle and its closure. If the crate surrounds a pear-shaped receptacle and is of matching shape, the outer packaging shall be fitted with a protective cover (cap).

6.1.4.20.2.3   Receptacle with outer aluminium drum 6PB1; the relevant requirements of 6.1.4.2 apply to the construction of the outer packaging.

6.1.4.20.2.4   Receptacle with outer aluminium crate or box 6PB2; the relevant requirements of 6.1.4.14 apply to the construction of the outer packaging.

6.1.4.20.2.5   Receptacle with outer wooden box 6PC; the relevant requirements of 6.1.4.9 apply to the construction of the outer packaging.

6.1.4.20.2.6   Receptacle with outer plywood drum 6PD1; the relevant requirements of 6.1.4.5 apply to the construction of the outer packaging.

6.1.4.20.2.7 Receptacle with outer wickerwork hamper 6PD2; the wickerwork hamper shall be properly made with material of good quality. It shall be fitted with a protective cover (cap) so as to prevent damage to the receptacle.

6.1.4.20.2.8 Receptacle with outer fibre drum 6PG1; the relevant requirements of 6.1.4.7.1 to 6.1.4.7.4 apply to the construction of the outer packaging.

6.1.4.20.2.9 Receptacle with outer fibreboard box 6PG2; the relevant requirements of 6.1.4.12 apply to the construction of the outer packaging.

6.1.4.20.2.10 Receptacle with outer expanded plastics or solid plastics packaging (6PH1 or 6PH2); the materials of both outer packagings shall meet the relevant requirements of 6.1.4.13. Solid plastics packaging shall be manufactured from high density polyethylene or some other comparable plastics material. The removable lid for this type of packaging may nevertheless be in the form of a cap.

6.1.5 Test requirements for packagings

6.1.5.1 *Performance and frequency of tests*

6.1.5.1.1 The design type of each packaging shall be tested as provided in 6.1.5 in accordance with procedures established by the competent authority.

6.1.5.1.2 Each packaging design type shall successfully pass the tests prescribed in this chapter before being used. A packaging design type is defined by the design, size, material and thickness, manner of construction and packing, but may include various surface treatments. It also includes packagings which differ from the design type only in their lesser design height.

6.1.5.1.3 Tests shall be repeated on production samples at intervals established by the competent authority. For such tests on paper or fibreboard packagings, preparation at ambient conditions is considered equivalent to the requirements of 6.1.5.2.3.

6.1.5.1.4 Tests shall also be repeated after each modification which alters the design, material or manner of construction of a packaging.

6.1.5.1.5 The competent authority may permit the selective testing of packagings that differ only in minor respects from a tested type, e.g. smaller sizes of inner packagings or inner packagings of lower net mass; and packagings such as drums, bags and boxes which are produced with small reductions in external dimension(s).

6.1.5.1.6 *Reserved.*

NOTE: *For the conditions for using different inner packagings in an outer packaging and permissible variations in inner packagings, see 4.1.1.5.1. These conditions do not limit the use of inner packagings when applying 6.1.5.1.7.*

6.1.5.1.7 Articles or inner packagings of any type for solids or liquids may be assembled and transported without testing in an outer packaging under the following conditions:

    (a) The outer packaging shall have been successfully tested in accordance with 6.1.5.3 with fragile (e.g. glass) inner packagings containing liquids using the packing group I drop height;

    (b) The total combined gross mass of inner packagings shall not exceed one half the gross mass of inner packagings used for the drop test in (a) above;

    (c) The thickness of cushioning material between inner packagings and between inner packagings and the outside of the packaging shall not be reduced below the corresponding thicknesses in the originally tested packaging; and if a single inner packaging was used in the original test, the thicknesses of cushioning between inner packagings shall not be less than the thickness of cushioning between the outside of the packaging and the inner packaging in the original test. If either fewer or smaller inner packagings are used (as compared to the inner packagings used in the drop test), sufficient additional cushioning material shall be used to take up void spaces;

(d) The outer packaging shall have passed successfully the stacking test in 6.1.5.6 while empty. The total mass of identical packages shall be based on the combined mass of inner packagings used for the drop test in (a) above;

(e) Inner packagings containing liquids shall be completely surrounded with a sufficient quantity of absorbent material to absorb the entire liquid contents of the inner packagings;

(f) If the outer packaging is intended to contain inner packagings for liquids and is not leakproof, or is intended to contain inner packagings for solids and is not siftproof, a means of containing any liquid or solid contents in the event of leakage shall be provided in the form of a leakproof liner, plastics bag or other equally efficient means of containment. For packagings containing liquids, the absorbent material required in (e) above shall be placed inside the means of containing the liquid contents;

(g) For air transport, packagings shall comply with 4.1.1.4.1;

(h) Packagings shall be marked in accordance with 6.1.3 as having been tested to packing group I performance for combination packagings. The marked gross mass in kilograms shall be the sum of the mass of the outer packaging plus one half of the mass of the inner packaging(s) as used for the drop test referred to in (a) above. Such a packaging mark shall also contain a letter "V" as described in 6.1.2.4.

6.1.5.1.8 The competent authority may at any time require proof, by tests in accordance with this section, that serially-produced packagings meet the requirements of the design type tests.

6.1.5.1.9 If an inner treatment or coating is required for safety reasons, it shall retain its protective properties even after the tests.

6.1.5.1.10 Provided the validity of the test results is not affected and with the approval of the competent authority, several tests may be made on one sample.

6.1.5.1.11 *Salvage packagings*

Salvage packagings (see 1.2.1) shall be tested and marked in accordance with the provisions applicable to packing group II packagings intended for the transport of solids or inner packagings, except as follows:

(a) The test substance used in performing the tests shall be water, and the packagings shall be filled to not less than 98 % of their maximum capacity. It is permissible to use additives, such as bags of lead shot, to achieve the requisite total package mass so long as they are placed so that the test results are not affected. Alternatively, in performing the drop test, the drop height may be varied in accordance with 6.1.5.3.5 (b);

(b) Packagings shall, in addition, have been successfully subjected to the leakproofness test at 30 kPa, with the results of this test reflected in the test report required by 6.1.5.7; and

(c) Packagings shall be marked with the letter "T" as described in 6.1.2.4.

6.1.5.2 *Preparation of packagings for testing*

6.1.5.2.1 Tests shall be carried out on packagings prepared as for transport including, with respect to combination packagings, the inner packagings used. Inner or single receptacles or packagings other than bags shall be filled to not less than 98 % of their maximum capacity for liquids or 95 % for solids. Bags shall be filled to the maximum mass at which they may be used. For combination packagings where the inner packaging is designed to carry liquids and solids, separate testing is required for both liquid and solid contents. The substances or articles to be transported in the packagings may be replaced by other substances or articles except where this would invalidate the results of the tests. For solids, when another substance is used it shall have the same physical characteristics (mass, grain size, etc.) as the substance to be carried. It is permissible to use additives, such as bags of lead shot, to achieve the requisite total package mass, so long as they are placed so that the test results are not affected.

6.1.5.2.2 In the drop tests for liquids, when another substance is used, it shall be of similar relative density and viscosity to those of the substance being transported. Water may also be used for the liquid drop test under the conditions in 6.1.5.3.5.

6.1.5.2.3 Paper or fibreboard packagings shall be conditioned for at least 24 hours in an atmosphere having a controlled temperature and relative humidity (r.h.). There are three options, one of which shall be chosen. The preferred atmosphere is 23 ± 2 °C and 50 % ± 2 % r.h. The two other options are 20 ± 2 °C and 65 % ± 2 % r.h. or 27 ± 2 °C and 65 % ± 2 % r.h.

NOTE: *Average values shall fall within these limits. Short-term fluctuations and measurement limitations may cause individual measurements to vary by up to ± 5 % relative humidity without significant impairment of test reproducibility.*

6.1.5.2.4 Additional steps shall be taken to ascertain that the plastics material used in the manufacture of plastics drums, plastics jerricans and composite packagings (plastics material) intended to contain liquids complies with the requirements in 6.1.1.2, 6.1.4.8.1 and 6.1.4.8.3. This may be done, for example, by submitting sample receptacles or packagings to a preliminary test extending over a long period, for example six months, during which the samples would remain filled with the substances they are intended to contain, and after which the samples shall be submitted to the applicable tests listed in 6.1.5.3, 6.1.5.4, 6.1.5.5 and 6.1.5.6. For substances which may cause stress-cracking or weakening in plastics drums or jerricans, the sample, filled with the substance or another substance that is known to have at least as severe a stress-cracking influence on the plastics material in question, shall be subjected to a superimposed load equivalent to the total mass of identical packages which might be stacked on it during transport. The minimum height of the stack including the test sample shall be 3 metres.

6.1.5.3 *Drop test*

6.1.5.3.1 *Number of test samples (per design type and manufacturer) and drop orientation*

For other than flat drops the centre of gravity shall be vertically over the point of impact.

Where more than one orientation is possible for a given drop test, the orientation most likely to result in failure of the packaging shall be used.

Packaging	No. of test samples	Drop orientation
Steel drums Aluminum drums Metal drums, other than steel or aluminum drums Steel jerricans Aluminum jerricans Plywood drums Fibre drums Plastics drums and jerricans Composite packagings which are in the shape of a drum	Six (three for each drop)	*First drop* (using three samples): the packaging shall strike the target diagonally on the chime or, if the packaging has no chime, on a circumferential seam or an edge. *Second drop* (using the other three samples): the packaging shall strike the target on the weakest part not tested by the first drop, for example a closure or, for some cylindrical drums, the welded longitudinal seam of the drum body.
Boxes of natural wood Plywood boxes Reconstituted wood boxes Fibreboard boxes Plastics boxes Steel or aluminum boxes Composite packagings which are in the shape of a box	Five (one for each drop)	*First drop*: flat on the bottom *Second drop*: flat on the top *Third drop*: flat on the long side *Fourth drop*: flat on the short side *Fifth drop*: on a corner
Bags – single-ply with a side seam	Three (three drops per bag)	*First drop*: flat on a wide face *Second drop*: flat on a narrow face *Third drop*: on an end of the bag
Bags – single-ply without a side seam, or multi-ply	Three (two drops per bag)	*First drop*: flat on a wide face *Second drop*: on an end of the bag

6.1.5.3.2   *Special preparation of test samples for the drop test*

The temperature of the test sample and its contents shall be reduced to -18 °C or lower for the following packagings:

(a) Plastics drums (see 6.1.4.8);

(b) Plastics jerricans (see 6.1.4.8);

(c) Plastics boxes other than expanded plastics boxes (see 6.1.4.13);

(d) Composite packagings (plastics material) (see 6.1.4.19); and

(e) Combination packagings with plastics inner packagings, other than plastics bags intended to contain solids or articles.

Where test samples are prepared in this way, the conditioning in 6.1.5.2.3 may be waived. Test liquids shall be kept in the liquid state by the addition of anti-freeze if necessary.

6.1.5.3.3   Removable head packagings for liquids shall not be dropped until at least 24 hours after filling and closing to allow for any possible gasket relaxation.

6.1.5.3.4   *Target*

The target shall be a non-resilient and horizontal surface and shall be:

(a) Integral and massive enough to be immovable;

(b) Flat with a surface kept free from local defects capable of influencing the test results;

(c) Rigid enough to be non-deformable under test conditions and not liable to become damaged by the tests; and

(d) Sufficiently large to ensure that the test package falls entirely upon the surface.

6.1.5.3.5 *Drop height*

For solids and liquids, if the test is performed with the solid or liquid to be carried or with another substance having essentially the same physical characteristics:

Packing group I	Packing group II	Packing group III
1.8 m	1.2 m	0.8 m

For liquids in single packagings and for inner packagings of combination packagings, if the test is performed with water:

NOTE: *The term water includes water/antifreeze solutions with a minimum specific gravity of 0.95 for testing at - 18 °C.*

(a) Where the substances to be transported have a relative density not exceeding 1.2:

Packing group I	Packing group II	Packing group III
1.8 m	1.2 m	0.8 m

(b) Where the substances to be transported have a relative density exceeding 1.2, the drop height shall be calculated on the basis of the relative density (d) of the substance to be carried, rounded up to the first decimal, as follows:

Packing group I	Packing group II	Packing group III
$d \times 1.5$ (m)	$d \times 1.0$ (m)	$d \times 0.67$ (m)

6.1.5.3.6 *Criteria for passing the test*

6.1.5.3.6.1 Each packaging containing liquid shall be leakproof when equilibrium has been reached between the internal and external pressures, except for inner packagings of combination packagings when it is not necessary that the pressures be equalized.

6.1.5.3.6.2 Where a packaging for solids undergoes a drop test and its upper face strikes the target, the test sample passes the test if the entire contents are retained by an inner packaging or inner receptacle (e.g. a plastics bag), even if the closure while retaining its containment function, is no longer sift-proof.

6.1.5.3.6.3 The packaging or outer packaging of a composite or combination packaging shall not exhibit any damage liable to affect safety during transport. Inner receptacles, inner packagings, or articles shall remain completely within the outer packaging and there shall be no leakage of the filling substance from the inner receptacle(s) or inner packaging(s).

6.1.5.3.6.4 Neither the outermost ply of a bag nor an outer packaging may exhibit any damage liable to affect safety during transport.

6.1.5.3.6.5 A slight discharge from the closure(s) upon impact is not considered to be a failure of the packaging provided that no further leakage occurs.

6.1.5.3.6.6 No rupture is permitted in packagings for goods of Class 1 which would permit the spillage of loose explosive substances or articles from the outer packaging.

6.1.5.4 **Leakproofness test**

The leakproofness test shall be performed on all design types of packagings intended to contain liquids; however, this test is not required for the inner packagings of combination packagings.

6.1.5.4.1 *Number of test samples:* three test samples per design type and manufacturer.

6.1.5.4.2	*Special preparation of test samples for the test:* either vented closures shall be replaced by similar non-vented closures or the vent shall be sealed.

6.1.5.4.3	*Test method and pressure to be applied:* the packagings including their closures shall be restrained under water for 5 minutes while an internal air pressure is applied, the method of restraint shall not affect the results of the test.

The air pressure (gauge) to be applied shall be:

Packing group I	Packing group II	Packing group III
Not less than 30 kPa (0.3 bar)	Not less than 20 kPa (0.2 bar)	Not less than 20 kPa (0.2 bar)

Other methods at least equally effective may be used.

6.1.5.4.4	*Criterion for passing the test:* there shall be no leakage.

### 6.1.5.5	*Internal pressure (hydraulic) test*

6.1.5.5.1	*Packagings to be tested:* the internal pressure (hydraulic) test shall be carried out on all design types of metal, plastics and composite packagings intended to contain liquids. This test is not required for inner packagings of combination packagings.

6.1.5.5.2	*Number of test samples:* three test samples per design type and manufacturer.

6.1.5.5.3	*Special preparation of packagings for testing:* either vented closures shall be replaced by similar non-vented closures or the vent shall be sealed.

6.1.5.5.4	*Test method and pressure to be applied:* metal packagings and composite packagings (glass, porcelain or stoneware) including their closures shall be subjected to the test pressure for 5 minutes. Plastics packagings and composite packagings (plastics material) including their closures shall be subjected to the test pressure for 30 minutes. This pressure is the one to be included in the mark required by 6.1.3.1 (d). The manner in which the packagings are supported shall not invalidate the test. The test pressure shall be applied continuously and evenly; it shall be kept constant throughout the test period. The hydraulic pressure (gauge) applied, as determined by any one of the following methods, shall be:

(a)	Not less than the total gauge pressure measured in the packaging (i.e. the vapour pressure of the filling liquid and the partial pressure of the air or other inert gases, minus 100 kPa) at 55 °C, multiplied by a safety factor of 1.5; this total gauge pressure shall be determined on the basis of a maximum degree of filling in accordance with 4.1.1.4 and a filling temperature of 15 °C;

(b)	Not less than 1.75 times the vapour pressure at 50 °C of the liquid to be transported, minus 100 kPa but with a minimum test pressure of 100 kPa;

(c)	Not less than 1.5 times the vapour pressure at 55 °C of the liquid to be transported, minus 100 kPa but with a minimum test pressure of 100 kPa.

6.1.5.5.5	In addition, packagings intended to contain liquids of packing group I shall be tested to a minimum test pressure of 250 kPa (gauge) for a test period of 5 or 30 minutes depending upon the material of construction of the packaging.

6.1.5.5.6	The special requirements for air transport, including minimum test pressures, may not be covered in 6.1.5.5.4.

6.1.5.5.7	*Criterion for passing the test:* no packaging may leak.

6.1.5.6   *Stacking test*

All design types of packagings other than bags are subject to a stacking test.

6.1.5.6.1   *Number of test samples*: three test samples per design type and manufacturer.

6.1.5.6.2   *Test method*: the test sample shall be subjected to a force applied to the top surface of the test sample equivalent to the total weight of identical packages which might be stacked on it during transport; where the contents of the test sample are liquids with relative density different from that of the liquid to be transported, the force shall be calculated in relation to the latter. The minimum height of the stack including the test sample shall be 3 metres. The duration of the test shall be 24 hours except that plastics drums, jerricans, and composite packagings 6HH1 and 6HH2 intended for liquids shall be subjected to the stacking test for a period of 28 days at a temperature of not less than 40 °C.

6.1.5.6.3   *Criterion for passing the test*: no test sample may leak. In composite packagings or combination packagings, there shall be no leakage of the filling substance from the inner receptacle or inner packaging. No test sample may show any deterioration which could adversely affect transport safety or any distortion liable to reduce its strength or cause instability in stacks of packages. Plastics packagings shall be cooled to ambient temperature before the assessment.

6.1.5.7   **Test Report**

6.1.5.7.1   A test report containing at least the following particulars shall be drawn up and shall be available to the users of the packaging:

1. Name and address of the test facility;

2. Name and address of applicant (where appropriate);

3. A unique test report identification;

4. Date of the test report;

5. Manufacturer of the packaging;

6. Description of the packaging design type (e.g. dimensions, materials, closures, thickness, etc.), including method of manufacture (e.g. blow moulding) and which may include drawing(s) and/or photograph(s);

7. Maximum capacity;

8. Characteristics of test contents, e.g. viscosity and relative density for liquids and particle size for solids. For plastics packagings subject to the internal pressure test in 6.1.5.5, the temperature of the water used;

9. Test descriptions and results;

10. The test report shall be signed with the name and status of the signatory.

6.1.5.7.2   The test report shall contain statements that the packaging prepared as for transport was tested in accordance with the appropriate requirements of this chapter and that the use of other packaging methods or components may render it invalid. A copy of the test report shall be available to the competent authority.

CHAPTER 6.2

REQUIREMENTS FOR THE CONSTRUCTION AND TESTING OF PRESSURE RECEPTACLES, AEROSOL DISPENSERS, SMALL RECEPTACLES CONTAINING GAS (GAS CARTRIDGES) AND FUEL CELL CARTRIDGES CONTAINING LIQUEFIED FLAMMABLE GAS

NOTE: *Aerosol dispensers, small receptacles containing gas (gas cartridges) and fuel cell cartridges containing liquefied flammable gas are not subject to the requirements of 6.2.1 to 6.2.3.*

6.2.1   General requirements

6.2.1.1   *Design and construction*

6.2.1.1.1   Pressure receptacles shall be designed, manufactured, tested and equipped in such a way as to withstand all conditions, including fatigue, to which they will be subjected during normal conditions of transport and intended use.

6.2.1.1.2   In recognition of scientific and technological advances, and recognizing that pressure receptacles other than those that bear "UN" certification marks may be used on a national or regional basis, pressure receptacles conforming to requirements other than those specified in these Regulations may be used if approved by the competent authorities in the countries of transport and use.

6.2.1.1.3   In no case shall the minimum wall thickness be less than that specified in the design and construction technical standards.

6.2.1.1.4   For welded pressure receptacles, only metals of weldable quality shall be welded.

6.2.1.1.5   The test pressure of pressure receptacle shells and bundles of cylinders shall be in accordance with packing instruction P200, or, for a chemical under pressure, with packing instruction P206. The test pressure for closed cryogenic receptacles shall be in accordance with packing instruction P203. The test pressure of a metal hydride storage system shall be in accordance with packing instruction P205. The test pressure of a cylinder shell for an adsorbed gas shall be in accordance with packing instruction P208.

6.2.1.1.6   Cylinders or cylinder shells assembled in bundles shall be structurally supported and held together as a unit. Cylinders or cylinder shells shall be secured in a manner that prevents movement in relation to the structural assembly and movement that would result in the concentration of harmful local stresses. Manifold assemblies (e.g. manifold, valves, and pressure gauges) shall be designed and constructed such that they are protected from impact damage and forces normally encountered in transport. Manifolds shall have at least the same test pressure as the cylinders. For toxic liquefied gases, each cylinder shell shall have an isolation valve to ensure that each cylinder can be filled separately and that no interchange of cylinder contents can occur during transport.

6.2.1.1.7   Contact between dissimilar metals which could result in damage by galvanic action shall be avoided.

6.2.1.1.8   *Additional requirements for the construction of closed cryogenic receptacles for refrigerated liquefied gases*

6.2.1.1.8.1   The mechanical properties of the metal used shall be established for each pressure receptacle, including the impact strength and the bending coefficient.

6.2.1.1.8.2   The pressure receptacles shall be thermally insulated. The thermal insulation shall be protected against impact by means of a jacket. If the space between the inner vessel and the jacket is evacuated of air (vacuum-insulation), the jacket shall be designed to withstand without permanent deformation an external pressure of at least 100 kPa (1 bar) calculated in accordance with a recognised technical code or a calculated critical collapsing pressure of not less than 200 kPa (2 bar) gauge pressure. If the jacket is so closed as to be gas-tight (e.g. in the case of vacuum-insulation), a device shall be provided to prevent any dangerous pressure from developing in the insulating layer in the event of inadequate gas-tightness of the inner vessel or its service equipment. The device shall prevent moisture from penetrating into the insulation.

6.2.1.1.8.3   Closed cryogenic receptacles intended for the transport of refrigerated liquefied gases having a boiling point below -182 °C at atmospheric pressure shall not include materials which may react with oxygen or oxygen enriched atmospheres in a dangerous manner, when located in parts of the thermal insulation where there is a risk of contact with oxygen or with oxygen enriched liquid.

6.2.1.1.8.4   Closed cryogenic receptacles shall be designed and constructed with suitable lifting and securing arrangements.

6.2.1.1.9   *Additional requirements for the construction of acetylene cylinders*

Cylinder shells for UN 1001 acetylene, dissolved, and UN 3374 acetylene, solvent free, shall be filled with a porous material, uniformly distributed, of a type that conforms to the requirements and testing specified by a standard or technical code recognised by the competent authority and which:

(a)   Is compatible with the cylinder shell and does not form harmful or dangerous compounds either with the acetylene or with the solvent in the case of UN 1001; and

(b)   Is capable of preventing the spread of decomposition of the acetylene in the porous material.

In the case of UN 1001, the solvent shall be compatible with those parts of the cylinder that are in contact with it.

6.2.1.2   *Materials*

6.2.1.2.1   Construction materials of pressure receptacles which are in direct contact with dangerous goods shall not be affected or weakened by the dangerous goods intended to be transported and shall not cause a dangerous effect e.g. catalysing a reaction or reacting with the dangerous goods.

6.2.1.2.2   Pressure receptacles shall be made of the materials specified in the design and construction technical standards and the applicable packing instruction for the substances intended for transport in the pressure receptacle. The materials shall be resistant to brittle fracture and to stress corrosion cracking as indicated in the design and construction technical standards.

6.2.1.3   *Service equipment*

6.2.1.3.1   Service equipment subjected to pressure, excluding porous, absorbent or adsorbent material, pressure relief devices, pressure gauges or indicators, shall be designed and constructed so that the burst pressure is at least 1.5 times the test pressure of the pressure receptacle.

6.2.1.3.2   Service equipment shall be configured or designed to prevent damage and unintended opening that could result in the release of the pressure receptacle contents during normal conditions of handling and transport. All closures shall be protected in the same manner as is required for valves in 4.1.6.1.8. Manifold piping leading to shut-off valves shall be sufficiently flexible to protect the shut-off valves and the piping from shearing or releasing the pressure receptacle contents.

6.2.1.3.3   Pressure receptacles which are not capable of being handled manually or rolled, shall be fitted with handling devices (skids, rings, straps) ensuring that they can be safely handled by mechanical means and so arranged as not to impair the strength of, nor cause undue stresses, in the pressure receptacle.

6.2.1.3.4   Individual pressure receptacles shall be equipped with pressure relief devices as specified in P200 (1), P205 or 6.2.1.3.6.4 and 6.2.1.3.6.5. Pressure-relief devices shall be designed to prevent the entry of foreign matter, the leakage of gas and the development of any dangerous excess pressure. When fitted, pressure relief devices on manifolded horizontal pressure receptacles filled with flammable gas shall be arranged to discharge freely to the open air in such a manner as to prevent any impingement of escaping gas upon the pressure receptacle itself under normal conditions of transport.

6.2.1.3.5　　Pressure receptacles whose filling is measured by volume shall be provided with a level indicator.

6.2.1.3.6　　*Additional requirements for closed cryogenic receptacles*

6.2.1.3.6.1　　Each filling and discharge opening in a closed cryogenic receptacle used for the transport of flammable refrigerated liquefied gases shall be fitted with at least two mutually independent shut-off devices in series, the first being a stop-valve, the second being a cap or equivalent device.

6.2.1.3.6.2　　For sections of piping which can be closed at both ends and where liquid product can be trapped, a method of automatic pressure-relief shall be provided to prevent excess pressure build-up within the piping.

6.2.1.3.6.3　　Each connection on a closed cryogenic receptacle shall be clearly marked to indicate its function (e.g. vapour or liquid phase).

6.2.1.3.6.4　　Pressure-relief devices

6.2.1.3.6.4.1　　Every closed cryogenic receptacle shall be provided with at least one pressure-relief device. The pressure-relief device shall be of the type that will resist dynamic forces including surge.

6.2.1.3.6.4.2　　Closed cryogenic receptacles may, in addition, have a frangible disc in parallel with the spring loaded device(s) in order to meet the requirements of 6.2.1.3.6.5.

6.2.1.3.6.4.3　　Connections to pressure-relief devices shall be of sufficient size to enable the required discharge to pass unrestricted to the pressure-relief device.

6.2.1.3.6.4.4　　All pressure-relief device inlets shall under maximum filling conditions be situated in the vapour space of the closed cryogenic receptacle and the devices shall be so arranged as to ensure that the escaping vapour is discharged unrestrictedly.

6.2.1.3.6.5　　Capacity and setting of pressure-relief devices

NOTE:　　*In relation to pressure-relief devices of closed cryogenic receptacles, MAWP means the maximum effective gauge pressure permissible at the top of a loaded closed cryogenic receptacle in its operating position including the highest effective pressure during filling and discharge.*

6.2.1.3.6.5.1　　The pressure-relief device shall open automatically at a pressure not less than the MAWP and be fully open at a pressure equal to 110 % of the MAWP. It shall, after discharge, close at a pressure not lower than 10 % below the pressure at which discharge starts and shall remain closed at all lower pressures.

6.2.1.3.6.5.2　　Frangible discs shall be set to rupture at a nominal pressure which is the lower of either the test pressure or 150 % of the MAWP.

6.2.1.3.6.5.3　　In the case of the loss of vacuum in a vacuum-insulated closed cryogenic receptacle the combined capacity of all pressure-relief devices installed shall be sufficient so that the pressure (including accumulation) inside the closed cryogenic receptacle does not exceed 120 % of the MAWP.

6.2.1.3.6.5.4　　The required capacity of the pressure-relief devices shall be calculated in accordance with an established technical code recognized by the competent authority[1].

---

[1]　　*See for example CGA Publications S-1.2-2003 "Pressure Relief Device Standards-Part 2-Cargo and Portable Tanks for Compressed Gases" and S-1.1-2003 "Pressure Relief Device Standards-Part 1-Cylinders for Compressed Gases".*

6.2.1.4 *Approval of pressure receptacles*

6.2.1.4.1　　The conformity of pressure receptacles shall be assessed at time of manufacture as required by the competent authority. The technical documentation shall include full specifications on design and construction, and full documentation on the manufacturing and testing.

6.2.1.4.2　　Quality assurance systems shall conform to the requirements of the competent authority.

6.2.1.4.3　　Pressure receptacle shells and the inner vessels of closed cryogenic receptacles shall be inspected tested and approved by an inspection body.

6.2.1.4.4　　For refillable cylinders, pressure drums and tubes the conformity assessment of the shell and the closure(s) may be carried out separately. In these cases, an additional assessment of the final assembly is not required.

For bundles of cylinders, the cylinder shells and the valve(s) may be assessed separately, but an additional assessment of the complete assembly is required.

For closed cryogenic receptacles, the inner vessels and the closures may be assessed separately, but an additional assessment of the complete assembly is required.

For acetylene cylinders, conformity assessment shall comprise either:

(a) One assessment of conformity covering both the cylinder shell and the contained porous material; or

(b) A separate assessment of conformity for the empty cylinder shell and an additional assessment of conformity covering the cylinder shell with the contained porous material.

6.2.1.5　　*Initial inspection and test*

6.2.1.5.1　　New pressure receptacles, other than closed cryogenic receptacles, metal hydride storage systems and bundles of cylinders, shall be subjected to testing and inspection during and after manufacture in accordance with the applicable design standards or recognised technical codes including the following:

On an adequate sample of pressure receptacle shells:

(a) Testing of the mechanical characteristics of the material of construction;

(b) Verification of the minimum wall thickness;

(c) Verification of the homogeneity of the material for each manufacturing batch;

(d) Inspection of the external and internal conditions;

(e) Inspection of the threads used to fit closures;

(f) Verification of the conformance with the design standard;

For all pressure receptacle shells:

(g) A hydraulic pressure test. Pressure receptacle shells shall meet the acceptance criteria specified in the design and construction technical standard or technical code;

NOTE: *With the agreement of the competent authority, the hydraulic pressure test may be replaced by a test using a gas, where such an operation does not entail any danger.*

(h) Inspection and assessment of manufacturing defects and either repairing them or rendering the pressure receptacle shells unserviceable. In the case of welded pressure receptacle shells, particular attention shall be paid to the quality of the welds;

(i) An inspection of the marks on the pressure receptacle shells;

(j) In addition, cylinder shells intended for the transport of UN 1001 acetylene, dissolved, and UN 3374 acetylene, solvent free, shall be inspected to ensure proper installation and condition of the porous material and, if applicable, the quantity of solvent.

On an adequate sample of closures:

(k) Verification of materials;

(l) Verification of dimensions;

(m) Verification of cleanliness;

(n) Inspection of completed assembly;

(o) Verification of the presence of marks.

For all closures:

(p) Testing for leakproofness

6.2.1.5.2 Closed cryogenic receptacles shall be subjected to testing and inspection during and after manufacture in accordance with the applicable design standards or recognized technical codes including the following:

On an adequate sample of inner vessels:

(a) Testing of the mechanical characteristics of the material of construction;

(b) Verification of the minimum wall thickness;

(c) Inspection of the external and internal conditions;

(d) Verification of the conformance with the design standard or technical code;

(e) Inspection of welds by radiographic, ultrasonic or other suitable non-destructive test method according to the applicable design and construction standard or technical code.

For all inner vessels:

(f) A hydraulic pressure test. The inner vessel shall meet the acceptance criteria specified in the design and construction technical standard or technical code;

NOTE: *With the agreement of the competent authority, the hydraulic pressure test may be replaced by a test using a gas, where such an operation does not entail any danger.*

(g) Inspection and assessment of manufacturing defects and either repairing them or rendering the inner vessel unserviceable;

(h) An inspection of the marks.

On an adequate sample of closures:

(i) Verification of materials;

(j) Verification of dimensions;

(k) Verification of cleanliness;

(l) Inspection of completed assembly;

(m) Verification of the presence of marks.

For all closures:

(n) Testing for leakproofness.

On an adequate sample of completed closed cryogenic receptacles:

(o) Testing the satisfactory operation of service equipment;

(p) Verification of the conformance with the design standard or code.

For all completed closed cryogenic receptacles:

(q) Testing for leakproofness.

NOTE: *Closed cryogenic receptacles which were constructed in accordance with the initial inspection and test requirements of 6.2.1.5.2 applicable in the twenty-first revised edition of the Model Regulations but which do not however conform to the requirements of 6.2.1.5.2 relating to the initial inspection and test applicable in the twenty-second revised edition of the Model Regulations, may continue to be used.*

6.2.1.5.3   For metal hydride storage systems, it shall be verified that the inspections and tests specified in 6.2.1.5.1 (a), (b), (c), (d), (e) if applicable, (f), (g), (h) and (i) have been performed on an adequate sample of the pressure receptacle shells used in the metal hydride storage system. In addition, on an adequate sample of metal hydride storage systems, the inspections and tests specified in 6.2.1.5.1 (c) and (f) shall be performed, as well as 6.2.1.5.1 (e), if applicable, and inspection of the external conditions of the metal hydride storage system.

Additionally, all metal hydride storage systems shall undergo the initial inspections and tests specified in 6.2.1.5.1 (h) and (i), as well as a leakproofness test and a test of the satisfactory operation of the service equipment.

6.2.1.5.4   For bundles of cylinders the cylinder shells and closures shall be subjected to initial inspection and tests specified in 6.2.1.5.1. An adequate sample of frames shall be proof load tested to two times the maximum gross weight of the bundles of cylinders.

Additionally, all manifolds of bundle of cylinders shall undergo a hydraulic pressure test and all the completed bundles of cylinders shall undergo a leakproofness test.

NOTE: *With the agreement of the competent authority, the hydraulic pressure test may be replaced by a test using a gas, where such an operation does not entail any danger.*

6.2.1.6   *Periodic inspection and test*

6.2.1.6.1   Refillable pressure receptacles, other than cryogenic receptacles, shall be subjected to periodic inspections and tests by a body authorized by the competent authority, in accordance with the following:

(a) Check of the external conditions of the pressure receptacle and verification of the equipment and the external marks;

(b) Check of the internal conditions of the pressure receptacle (e.g. internal inspection, verification of minimum wall thickness);

(c) Checking of the threads either:

(i) if there is evidence of corrosion; or

(ii) if the closures or other service equipment are removed;

(d) A hydraulic pressure test of the pressure receptacle shell and, if necessary, verification of the characteristics of the material by suitable tests;

NOTE 1: *With the agreement of the competent authority, the hydraulic pressure test may be replaced by a test using a gas, where such an operation does not entail any danger.*

NOTE 2: *For seamless steel cylinder shells and tube shells the check of 6.2.1.6.1 (b) and hydraulic pressure test of 6.2.1.6.1 (d) may be replaced by a procedure conforming to ISO 16148:2016 + Amd 1:2020 "Gas cylinders – Refillable seamless steel gas cylinders and tubes – Acoustic emission examination (AT) and follow-up ultrasonic examination (UT) for periodic inspection and testing".*

NOTE 3: *The check of internal conditions of 6.2.1.6.1 (b) and the hydraulic pressure test of 6.2.1.6.1 (d) may be replaced by ultrasonic examination carried out in accordance with ISO 18119:2018 + Amd 1:2021 for seamless steel and seamless aluminium alloy cylinder shells. For a transitional period until 31 December 2026 the standard ISO 18119:2018 may be used for this same purpose. For a transitional period until 31 December 2024 the standard ISO 10461:2005 + Amd 1:2006 may be used for seamless aluminium alloy cylinder shells and ISO 6406:2005 may be used for seamless steel cylinder shells for this same purpose.*

NOTE 4: *For bundles of cylinders the hydraulic test specified in (d) above shall be carried out on the cylinder shells and on the manifolds.*

(e) Check of service equipment, if to be reintroduced into service. This check may be carried out separately from the inspection of the pressure receptacle shell; and

(f) A leakproofness test of bundles of cylinders after reassembly.

NOTE: *For the periodic inspection and test frequencies, see packing instruction P200 or, for a chemical under pressure, packing instruction P206 of 4.1.4.1.*

6.2.1.6.2 Cylinders intended for the transport of UN 1001 acetylene, dissolved and UN 3374 acetylene, solvent free, shall be examined only as specified in 6.2.1.6.1 (a), (c) and (e). In addition, the condition of the porous material (e.g. cracks, top clearance, loosening, settlement) shall be examined.

6.2.1.6.3 Pressure relief valves for closed cryogenic receptacles shall be subject to periodic inspections and tests.

6.2.1.7 *Requirements for manufacturers*

6.2.1.7.1 The manufacturer shall be technically able and shall possess all resources required for the satisfactory manufacture of pressure receptacles; this relates in particular to qualified personnel:

(a) to supervise the entire manufacturing process;

(b) to carry out joining of materials; and

(c) to carry out the relevant tests.

6.2.1.7.2 A proficiency test of the manufacturers of pressure receptacle shells and the inner vessels of closed cryogenic receptacle shall in all instances be carried out by an inspection body approved by the competent authority of the country of approval. Proficiency testing of manufacturers of closures shall be carried out if the competent authority requires it. This test shall be carried out either during design type approval or during production inspection and certification.

6.2.1.8 *Requirements for inspection bodies*

6.2.1.8.1 Inspection bodies shall be independent from manufacturing enterprises and competent to perform the tests, inspections and approvals required.

6.2.2 **Requirements for UN pressure receptacles**

In addition to the general requirements of section 6.2.1, UN pressure receptacles shall comply with the requirements of this section, including the standards, as applicable. Manufacture of new pressure receptacles or service equipment according to any particular standard in 6.2.2.1 and 6.2.2.3 is not permitted after the date shown in the right hand column of the tables.

NOTE 1: *With the agreement of the competent authority, more recently published versions of the standards, if available, may be used.*

NOTE 2: *UN pressure receptacles constructed according to standards applicable at the date of manufacture may continue in use subject to the periodic inspection provisions of these Regulations.*

6.2.2.1 *Design, construction and initial inspection and test*

6.2.2.1.1 The following standards apply for the design, construction, and initial inspection and test of refillable UN cylinder shells, except that inspection requirements related to the conformity assessment system and approval shall be in accordance with 6.2.2.5:

Reference	Title	Applicable for manufacture
ISO 9809-1:1999	Gas cylinders – Refillable seamless steel gas cylinders - Design, construction and testing - Part 1: Quenched and tempered steel cylinders with tensile strength less than 1 100 MPa *NOTE: The note concerning the F factor in section 7.3 of this standard shall not be applied for UN cylinders.*	Until 31 December 2018
ISO 9809-1:2010	Gas cylinders -- Refillable seamless steel gas cylinders -- Design, construction and testing -- Part 1: Quenched and tempered steel cylinders with tensile strength less than 1 100 MPa	Until 31 December 2026
ISO 9809-1:2019	Gas cylinders — Design, construction and testing of refillable seamless steel gas cylinders and tubes — Part 1: Quenched and tempered steel cylinders and tubes with tensile strength less than 1 100 MPa	Until further notice
ISO 9809-2:2000	Gas cylinders – Refillable seamless steel gas cylinders - Design, construction and testing - Part 2: Quenched and tempered steel cylinders with tensile strength greater than or equal to 1 100 MPa	Until 31 December 2018
ISO 9809-2:2010	Gas cylinders – Refillable seamless steel gas cylinders – Design, construction and testing – Part 2: Quenched and tempered steel cylinders with tensile strength greater than or equal to 1 100 MPa	Until 31 December 2026
ISO 9809-2:2019	Gas cylinders – Design, construction and testing of refillable seamless steel gas cylinders and tubes – Part 2: Quenched and tempered steel cylinders and tubes with tensile strength greater than or equal to 1 100 MPa	Until further notice

Reference	Title	Applicable for manufacture
ISO 9809-3:2000	Gas cylinders – Refillable seamless steel gas cylinders - Design, construction and testing - Part 3: Normalized steel cylinders	Until 31 December 2018
ISO 9809-3:2010	Gas cylinders -- Refillable seamless steel gas cylinders -- Design, construction and testing -- Part 3: Normalized steel cylinders	Until 31 December 2026
ISO 9809-3:2019	Gas cylinders — Design, construction and testing of refillable seamless steel gas cylinders and tubes — Part 3: Normalized steel cylinders and tubes	Until further notice
ISO 9809-4:2014	Gas cylinders – Refillable seamless steel gas cylinders – Design, construction and testing – Part 4: Stainless steel cylinders with an Rm value of less than 1 100 MPa	Until 31 December 2028
ISO 9809-4:2021	Gas cylinders – Design, construction and testing of refillable seamless steel gas cylinders and tubes – Part 4: Stainless steel cylinders with an Rm value of less than 1 100 MPa *NOTE: Small quantities are a batch of cylinders not exceeding 200.*	Until further notice
ISO 7866:1999	Gas cylinders – Refillable seamless aluminium alloy gas cylinders – Design, construction and testing *NOTE: The note concerning the F factor in section 7.2 of this standard shall not be applied for UN cylinders. Aluminium alloy 6351A – T6 or equivalent shall not be authorized.*	Until 31 December 2020
ISO 7866: 2012+ Cor 1:2014	Gas cylinders – Refillable seamless aluminium alloy gas cylinders – Design, construction and testing *NOTE: Aluminium alloy 6351A or equivalent shall not be used.*	Until further notice
ISO 4706:2008	Gas cylinders – Refillable welded steel cylinders – Test pressure 60 bar and below	Until further notice
ISO 18172-1:2007	Gas cylinders – Refillable welded stainless steel cylinders – Part 1: Test pressure 6 MPa and below	Until further notice
ISO 20703:2006	Gas cylinders – Refillable welded aluminium-alloy cylinders – Design, construction and testing	Until further notice
ISO 11119-1:2002	Gas cylinders of composite construction – Specification and test methods – Part 1: Hoop wrapped composite gas cylinders	Until 31 December 2020
ISO 11119-1:2012	Gas cylinders – Refillable composite gas cylinders and tubes – Design, construction and testing – Part 1: Hoop wrapped fibre reinforced composite gas cylinders and tubes up to 450 *l*	Until 31 December 2028
ISO 11119-1:2020	Gas cylinders — Design, construction and testing of refillable composite gas cylinders and tubes — Part 1: Hoop wrapped fibre reinforced composite gas cylinders and tubes up to 450 *l*	Until further notice
ISO 11119-2:2002	Gas cylinders of composite construction – Specification and test methods – Part 2: Fully wrapped fibre reinforced composite gas cylinders with load-sharing metal liners	Until 31 December 2020
ISO 11119-2:2012 + Amd 1:2014	Gas cylinders – Refillable composite gas cylinders and tubes – Design, construction and testing – Part 2: Fully wrapped fibre reinforced composite gas cylinders and tubes up to 450 *l* with load-sharing metal liners	Until 31 December 2028

Reference	Title	Applicable for manufacture
ISO 11119-2:2020	Gas cylinders — Design, construction and testing of refillable composite gas cylinders and tubes — Part 2: Fully wrapped fibre reinforced composite gas cylinders and tubes up to 450 *l* with load-sharing metal liners	Until further notice
ISO 11119-3:2002	Gas cylinders of composite construction – Specification and test methods – Part 3: Fully wrapped fibre reinforced composite gas cylinders with non-load-sharing metallic or non-metallic liners *NOTE: This standard shall not be used for linerless cylinders manufactured from two parts joined together.*	Until 31 December 2020
ISO 11119-3:2013	Gas cylinders – Refillable composite gas cylinders and tubes – Design, construction and testing – Part 3: Fully wrapped fibre reinforced composite gas cylinders and tubes up to 450 *l* with non-load-sharing metallic or non-metallic liners *NOTE: This standard shall not be used for linerless cylinders manufactured from two parts joined together.*	Until 31 December 2028
ISO 11119-3:2020	Gas cylinders — Design, construction and testing of refillable composite gas cylinders and tubes — Part 3: Fully wrapped fibre reinforced composite gas cylinders and tubes up to 450 *l* with non-load-sharing metallic or non-metallic liners or without liners	Until further notice
ISO 11119-4:2016	Gas cylinders – Refillable composite gas cylinders – Design, construction and testing – Part 4: Fully wrapped fibre reinforced composite gas cylinders up to 150 *l* with load-sharing welded metallic liners	Until further notice

NOTE 1: *In the above referenced standards composite cylinder shells shall be designed for a design life of not less than 15 years.*

NOTE 2: *Composite cylinder shells with a design life longer than 15 years shall not be filled after 15 years from the date of manufacture, unless the design has successfully passed a service life test programme. The programme shall be part of the initial design type approval and shall specify inspections and tests to demonstrate that composite cylinder shells manufactured accordingly remain safe to the end of their design life. The service life test programme and the results shall be approved by the competent authority of the country of approval that is responsible for the initial approval of the cylinder design. The service life of a composite cylinder shell shall not be extended beyond its initial approved design life.*

6.2.2.1.2 The following standards apply for the design, construction, and initial inspection and test of UN tube shells, except that inspection requirements related to the conformity assessment system and approval shall be in accordance with 6.2.2.5:

Reference	Title	Applicable for manufacture
ISO 11120:1999	Gas cylinders – Refillable seamless steel tubes for compressed gas transport, of water capacity between 150 l and 3 000 *l* – Design, construction and testing *NOTE: The note concerning the F factor in section 7.1 of this standard shall not be applied for UN tubes*	Until 31 December 2022
ISO 11120:2015	Gas cylinders – Refillable seamless steel tubes of water capacity between 150 *l* and 3 000 *l* – Design, construction and testing	Until further notice

Reference	Title	Applicable for manufacture
ISO 11119-1:2012	Gas cylinders – Refillable composite gas cylinders and tubes – Design, construction and testing – Part 1: Hoop wrapped fibre reinforced composite gas cylinders and tubes up to 450 *l*	Until 31 December 2028
ISO 11119-1:2020	Gas cylinders — Design, construction and testing of refillable composite gas cylinders and tubes — Part 1: Hoop wrapped fibre reinforced composite gas cylinders and tubes up to 450 *l*	Until further notice
ISO 11119-2:2012 + Amd 1:2014	Gas cylinders – Refillable composite gas cylinders and tubes – Design, construction and testing – Part 2: Fully wrapped fibre reinforced composite gas cylinders and tubes up to 450 *l* with load-sharing metal liners	Until 31 December 2028
ISO 11119-2:2020	Gas cylinders — Design, construction and testing of refillable composite gas cylinders and tubes — Part 2: Fully wrapped fibre reinforced composite gas cylinders and tubes up to 450 *l* with load-sharing metal liners	Until further notice
ISO 11119-3:2013	Gas cylinders – Refillable composite gas cylinders and tubes – Design, construction and testing – Part 3: Fully wrapped fibre reinforced composite gas cylinders and tubes up to 450 L with non-load-sharing metallic or non-metallic liners ***NOTE:*** *This standard shall not be used for linerless cylinders manufactured from two parts joined together.*	Until 31 December 2028
ISO 11119-3:2020	Gas cylinders — Design, construction and testing of refillable composite gas cylinders and tubes — Part 3: Fully wrapped fibre reinforced composite gas cylinders and tubes up to 450 *l* with non-load-sharing metallic or non-metallic liners or without liners	Until further notice
ISO 11515:2013	Gas cylinders – Refillable composite reinforced tubes of water capacity between 450 L and 3 000 L – Design, construction and testing	Until 31 December 2026
ISO 11515:2013 + Amd 1:2018	Gas cylinders – Refillable composite reinforced tubes of water capacity between 450 L and 3000 L – Design, construction and testing	Until further notice
ISO 9809-1:2019	Gas cylinders — Design, construction and testing of refillable seamless steel gas cylinders and tubes — Part 1: Quenched and tempered steel cylinders and tubes with tensile strength less than 1 100 MPa	Until further notice
ISO 9809-2:2019	Gas cylinders – Design, construction and testing of refillable seamless steel gas cylinders and tubes – Part 2: Quenched and tempered steel cylinders and tubes with tensile strength greater than or equal to 1 100 MPa	Until further notice
ISO 9809-3:2019	Gas cylinders — Design, construction and testing of refillable seamless steel gas cylinders and tubes — Part 3: Normalized steel cylinders and tubes	Until further notice

NOTE 1: *In the above referenced standards composite tube shells shall be designed for a design life of not less than 15 years.*

NOTE 2: *Composite tube shells with a design life longer than 15 years shall not be filled after 15 years from the date of manufacture, unless the design has successfully passed a service life test programme. The programme shall be part of the initial design type approval and shall specify inspections and tests to demonstrate that composite tube shells manufactured accordingly remain safe to the end of their design life.*

The service life test programme and the results shall be approved by the competent authority of the country of approval that is responsible for the initial approval of the tube design. The service life of a composite tube shell shall not be extended beyond its initial approved design life.

6.2.2.1.3   The following standards apply for the design, construction and initial inspection and test of UN acetylene cylinders, except that inspection requirements related to the conformity assessment system and approval shall be in accordance with 6.2.2.5:

For the cylinder shell:

Reference	Title	Applicable for manufacture
ISO 9809-1:1999	Gas cylinders – Refillable seamless steel gas cylinders – Design, construction and testing – Part 1: Quenched and tempered steel cylinders with tensile strength less than 1 100 MPa **NOTE:** *The note concerning the F factor in section 7.3 of this standard shall not be applied for UN cylinders.*	Until 31 December 2018
ISO 9809-1:2010	Gas cylinders – Refillable seamless steel gas cylinders – Design, construction and testing – Part 1: Quenched and tempered steel cylinders with tensile strength less than 1 100 MPa	Until 31 December 2026
ISO 9809-1:2019	Gas cylinders — Design, construction and testing of refillable seamless steel gas cylinders and tubes — Part 1: Quenched and tempered steel cylinders and tubes with tensile strength less than 1 100 MPa	Until further notice
ISO 9809-3:2000	Gas cylinders – Refillable seamless steel gas cylinders – Design, construction and testing – Part 3: Normalized steel cylinders	Until 31 December 2018
ISO 9809-3:2010	Gas cylinders – Refillable seamless steel gas cylinders – Design, construction and testing – Part 3: Normalized steel cylinders	Until 31 December 2026
ISO 9809-3:2019	Gas cylinders — Design, construction and testing of refillable seamless steel gas cylinders and tubes — Part 3: Normalized steel cylinders and tubes	Until further notice
ISO 4706:2008	Gas cylinders – Refillable welded steel cylinders – Test pressure 60 bar and below	Until further notice
ISO 7866:2012 + Cor 1:2014	Gas cylinders – Refillable seamless aluminum alloy gas cylinders – Design, construction and testing **NOTE:** *Aluminum alloy 6351A or equivalent shall not be used*	Until further notice

For acetylene cylinder including the porous material:

Reference	Title	Applicable for manufacture
ISO 3807-1:2000	Cylinders for acetylene – Basic requirements - Part 1: Cylinders without fusible plugs	Until 31 December 2020
ISO 3807-2:2000	Cylinders for acetylene – Basic requirements - Part 2: Cylinders with fusible plugs	Until 31 December 2020
ISO 3807: 2013	Gas cylinders – Acetylene cylinders – Basic requirements and type testing	Until further notice

6.2.2.1.4　　The following standards apply for the design, construction, and initial inspection and test of UN closed cryogenic receptacles, except that inspection requirements related to the conformity assessment system and approval shall be in accordance with 6.2.2.5:

Reference	Title	Applicable for manufacture
ISO 21029-1:2004	Cryogenic vessels – Transportable vacuum insulated vessels of not more than 1 000 litres volume – Part 1: Design, fabrication, inspection and tests	Until 31 December 2026
ISO 21029-1:2018 + Amd 1:2019	Cryogenic vessels – Transportable vacuum insulated vessels of not more than 1 000 litres volume – Part 1: Design, fabrication, inspection and tests	Until further notice

6.2.2.1.5　　The following standards apply for the design, construction, and initial inspection and test of UN metal hydride storage systems, except that inspection requirements related to the conformity assessment system and approval shall be in accordance with 6.2.2.5:

Reference	Title	Applicable for manufacture
ISO 16111:2008	Transportable gas storage devices – Hydrogen absorbed in reversible metal hydride	Until 31 December 2026
ISO 16111:2018	Transportable gas storage devices – Hydrogen absorbed in reversible metal hydride	Until further notice

6.2.2.1.6　　The following standards apply for the design, construction and initial inspection and test of UN bundles of cylinders. Each cylinder in a UN bundle of cylinders shall be a UN cylinder or UN cylinder shell complying with the requirements of 6.2.2. The inspection requirements related to the conformity assessment system and approval for UN bundles of cylinders shall be in accordance with 6.2.2.5.

Reference	Title	Applicable for manufacture
ISO 10961:2010	Gas cylinders – Cylinder bundles – Design, manufacture, testing and inspection	Until 31 December 2026
ISO 10961:2019	Gas cylinders – Cylinder bundles – Design, manufacture, testing and inspection	Until further notice

NOTE:　　*Changing one or more cylinders or cylinder shells of the same design type, including the same test pressure, in an existing UN bundle of cylinders does not require a new conformity assessment of the existing bundle. Service equipment of the bundle of cylinders can also be replaced without requiring a new conformity assessment if it complies with the design type approval.*

6.2.2.1.7　　The following standards apply for the design, construction and initial inspection and test of UN cylinders for adsorbed gases except that the inspection requirements related to the conformity assessment system and approval shall be in accordance with 6.2.2.5.

Reference	Title	Applicable for manufacture
ISO 11513:2011	Gas cylinders – Refillable welded steel cylinders containing materials for sub-atmospheric gas packaging (excluding acetylene) – Design, construction, testing, use and periodic inspection	Until 31 December 2026

Reference	Title	Applicable for manufacture
ISO 11513:2019	Gas cylinders – Refillable welded steel cylinders containing materials for sub-atmospheric gas packaging (excluding acetylene) – Design, construction, testing, use and periodic inspection	Until further notice
ISO 9809-1:2010	Gas cylinders – Refillable seamless steel gas cylinders – Design, construction and testing – Part 1: Quenched and tempered steel cylinders with tensile strength less than 1 100 MPa	Until 31 December 2026
ISO 9809-1:2019	Gas cylinders — Design, construction and testing of refillable seamless steel gas cylinders and tubes — Part 1: Quenched and tempered steel cylinders and tubes with tensile strength less than 1 100 MPa	Until further notice

6.2.2.1.8 The following standards apply for the design, construction and initial inspection and test of UN pressure drums, except that inspection requirements related to the conformity assessment system and approval shall be in accordance with 6.2.2.5:

Reference	Title	Applicable for manufacture
ISO 21172-1:2015	Gas cylinders – Welded steel pressure drums up to 3 000 litres capacity for the transport of gases – Design and construction – Part 1: Capacities up to 1 000 litres *NOTE: Irrespective of section 6.3.3.4 of this standard, welded steel gas pressure drums with dished ends convex to pressure may be used for the transport of corrosive substances provided all applicable requirements of these Regulations are met.*	Until 31 December 2026
ISO 21172-1:2015 + Amd 1:2018	Gas cylinders – Welded steel pressure drums up to 3 000 litres capacity for the transport of gases – Design and construction – Part 1: Capacities up to 1 000 litres;	Until further notice
ISO 4706: 2008	Gas cylinders – Refillable welded steel cylinders – Test pressure 60 bar and below;	Until further notice
ISO 18172-1:2007	Gas cylinders – Refillable welded stainless steel cylinders – Part 1: Test pressure 6 MPa and below	Until further notice

6.2.2.1.9 The following standards apply to the design, construction and initial inspection and test of non-refillable UN cylinders except that the inspection requirements related to the conformity assessment system and approval shall be in accordance with 6.2.2.5.

Reference	Title	Applicable for manufacture
ISO 11118:1999	Gas cylinders – Non-refillable metallic gas cylinders – Specification and test methods	Until 31 December 2020
ISO 13340:2001	Transportable gas cylinders – Cylinder valves for non-refillable cylinders – Specification and prototype testing	Until 31 December 2020
ISO 11118:2015	Gas cylinders – Non-refillable metallic gas cylinders – Specification and test methods	Until 31 December 2026
ISO 11118:2015 + Amd 1:2019	Gas cylinders - Non-refillable metallic gas cylinders - Specification and test methods	Until further notice

6.2.2.2 *Materials*

In addition to the material requirements specified in the design and construction standards, and any restrictions specified in the applicable packing instruction for the gas(es) to be transported (e.g. packing instruction P200 or P205), the following standards apply to material compatibility:

Reference	Title
ISO 11114-1:2020	Gas cylinders – Compatibility of cylinder and valve materials with gas contents – Part 1: Metallic materials
ISO 11114-2:2021	Gas cylinders – Compatibility of cylinder and valve materials with gas contents – Part 2: Non-metallic materials

6.2.2.3 *Closures and their protection*

The following standards apply to the design, construction, and initial inspection and test of closures and their protection:

Reference	Title	Applicable for manufacture
ISO 11117:1998	Gas cylinders – Valve protection caps and valve guards for industrial and medical gas cylinders – Design, construction and tests	Until 31 December 2014
ISO 11117:2008 + Cor 1:2009	Gas cylinders – Valve protection caps and valve guards – Design, construction and tests	Until 31 December 2026
ISO 11117:2019	Gas cylinders – Valve protection caps and guards – Design, construction and tests	Until further notice
ISO 10297:1999	Gas cylinders – Refillable gas cylinder valves – Specification and type testing	Until 31 December 2008
ISO 10297:2006	Gas cylinders – Refillable gas cylinder valves – Specification and type testing	Until 31 December 2020
ISO 10297:2014	Gas cylinders – Cylinder valves – Specification and type testing	Until 31 December 2022
ISO 10297:2014 + Amd 1:2017	Gas cylinders – Cylinder valves – Specification and type testing;	Until further notice
ISO 14246:2014	Gas cylinders – Cylinder valves – Manufacturing tests and examination	Until 31 December 2024
ISO 14246:2014 + Amd 1:2017	Gas cylinders – Cylinder valves – Manufacturing tests and examinations	Until further notice
ISO 17871:2015	Gas cylinders – Quick-release cylinders valves- Specification and type testing **NOTE:** *This standard shall not be used for flammable gases.*	Until 31 December 2026
ISO 17871:2020	Gas cylinders – Quick-release cylinder valves – Specification and type testing.	Until further notice
ISO 17879:2017	Gas cylinders – Self-closing cylinder valves – Specification and type testing **NOTE:** *This standard shall not be applied to self-closing valves in acetylene cylinders.*	Until further notice
ISO 23826:2021	Gas cylinders – Ball valves – Specification and testing	Until further notice

For UN metal hydride storage systems, the requirements specified in the following standard apply to closures and their protection:

Reference	Title	Applicable for manufacture
ISO 16111:2008	Transportable gas storage devices – Hydrogen absorbed in reversible metal hydride	Until 31 December 2026
ISO 16111:2018	Transportable gas storage devices – Hydrogen absorbed in reversible metal hydride	Until further notice

6.2.2.4 *Periodic inspection and test*

The following standards apply to the periodic inspection and testing of UN pressure receptacles:

Reference	Title	Applicable
ISO 6406:2005	Seamless steel gas cylinders – Periodic inspection and testing	Until 31 December 2024
ISO 18119:2018	Gas cylinders – Seamless steel and seamless aluminium-alloy gas cylinders and tubes – Periodic inspection and testing	Until 31 December 2026
ISO 18119:2018 +Amd 1:2021	Gas cylinders – Seamless steel and seamless aluminium-alloy gas cylinders and tubes — Periodic inspection and testing	Until further notice
ISO 10460:2005	Gas cylinders – Welded carbon-steel gas cylinders – Periodic inspection and testing **NOTE:** *The repair of welds described in clause 12.1 of this standard shall not be permitted. Repairs described in clause 12.2 require the approval of the competent authority which approved the periodic inspection and test body in accordance with 6.2.2.6.*	Until 31 December 2024
ISO 10460:2018	Gas cylinders – Welded aluminium-alloy, carbon and stainless steel gas cylinders – Periodic inspection and testing.	Until further notice
ISO 10461:2005 + Amd 1:2006	Seamless aluminium-alloy gas cylinders – Periodic inspection and testing	Until 31 December 2024
ISO 10462:2013	Gas cylinders – Acetylene cylinders – Periodic inspection and maintenance.	Until 31 December 2024
ISO 10462:2013 + Amd1:2019	Gas cylinders – Acetylene cylinders – Periodic inspection and maintenance	Until further notice
ISO 11513:2011	Gas cylinders – Refillable welded steel cylinders containing materials for sub-atmospheric gas packaging (excluding acetylene) – Design, construction, testing, use and periodic inspection	Until 31 December 2024
ISO 11513:2019	Gas cylinders – Refillable welded steel cylinders containing materials for sub-atmospheric gas packaging (excluding acetylene) – Design, construction, testing, use and periodic inspection	Until further notice
ISO 11623:2015	Gas cylinders – Composite construction – Periodic inspection and testing	Until further notice
ISO 22434:2006	Transportable gas cylinders – Inspection and maintenance of cylinder valves **NOTE:** *These requirements may be met at times other than at the periodic inspection and test of UN cylinders*	Until further notice
ISO 20475:2018	Gas cylinders – Cylinder bundles – Periodic inspection and testing	Until further notice

Reference	Title	Applicable
ISO 23088:2020	Gas cylinders – Periodic inspection and testing of welded steel pressure drums — Capacities up to 1 000 *l*	Until further notice

The following standards apply to the periodic inspection and testing of UN metal hydride storage systems:

Reference	Title	Applicable
ISO 16111:2008	Transportable gas storage devices – Hydrogen absorbed in reversible metal hydride	Until 31 December 2024
ISO 16111:2018	Transportable gas storage devices – Hydrogen absorbed in reversible metal hydride	Until further notice

6.2.2.5 *Conformity assessment system and approval for manufacture of pressure receptacles*

6.2.2.5.0 *Definitions*

For the purposes of this section:

Conformity assessment system means a system for competent authority approval of a manufacturer, by pressure receptacle design type approval, approval of manufacturer's quality system and approval of inspection bodies;

Design type means a pressure receptacle design as specified by a particular pressure receptacle standard;

Verify means confirm by examination or provision of objective evidence that specified requirements have been fulfilled;

NOTE: *In this subsection when separate assessment is used the term pressure receptacle shall refer to pressure receptacle, pressure receptacle shell, inner vessel of the closed cryogenic receptacle or closure, as appropriate.*

6.2.2.5.1 The requirements of 6.2.2.5 shall be used for the conformity assessments of pressure receptacles. Paragraph 6.2.1.4.4 gives details of which parts of pressure receptacles may be conformity assessed separately. However, the requirements of 6.2.2.5 may be replaced by requirements specified by the competent authority in the following cases:

(a) conformity assessment of closures;

(b) conformity assessment of the complete assembly of bundles of cylinders provided the cylinder shells have been conformity assessed in accordance with the requirements of 6.2.2.5; and

(c) conformity assessment of the complete assembly of closed cryogenic receptacles provided the inner vessel has been conformity assessed in accordance with the requirements of 6.2.2.5.

6.2.2.5.2 *General requirements*

Competent Authority

6.2.2.5.2.1 The competent authority that approves the pressure receptacle shall approve the conformity assessment system for the purpose of ensuring that pressure receptacles conform to the requirements of these Regulations. In instances where the competent authority that approves a pressure receptacle is not the competent authority in the country of manufacture, the marks of the approval country and the country of manufacture shall be indicated in the pressure receptacle marks (see 6.2.2.7 and 6.2.2.8).

The competent authority of the country of approval shall supply, upon request, evidence demonstrating compliance to this conformity assessment system to its counterpart in a country of use.

6.2.2.5.2.2　　The competent authority may delegate its functions in this conformity assessment system in whole or in part.

6.2.2.5.2.3　　The competent authority shall ensure that a current list of approved inspection bodies and their identity marks and approved manufacturers and their identity marks is available.

Inspection body

6.2.2.5.2.4　　The inspection body shall be approved by the competent authority for the inspection of pressure receptacles and shall:

    (a)　Have a staff with an organisational structure, capable, trained, competent, and skilled, to satisfactorily perform its technical functions;

    (b)　Have access to suitable and adequate facilities and equipment;

    (c)　Operate in an impartial manner and be free from any influence which could prevent it from doing so;

    (d)　Ensure commercial confidentiality of the commercial and proprietary activities of the manufacturer and other bodies;

    (e)　Maintain clear demarcation between actual inspection body functions and unrelated functions;

    (f)　Operate a documented quality system;

    (g)　Ensure that the tests and inspections specified in the relevant pressure receptacle standard and these Regulations are performed; and

    (h)　Maintain an effective and appropriate report and record system in accordance with 6.2.2.5.6.

6.2.2.5.2.5　　The inspection body shall perform design type approval, pressure receptacle production testing and inspection, and certification to verify conformity with the relevant pressure receptacle standard (see 6.2.2.5.4 and 6.2.2.5.5).

Manufacturer

6.2.2.5.2.6　　The manufacturer shall:

    (a)　Operate a documented quality system in accordance with 6.2.2.5.3;

    (b)　Apply for design type approvals in accordance with 6.2.2.5.4;

    (c)　Select an inspection body from the list of approved inspection bodies maintained by the competent authority in the country of approval; and

    (d)　Maintain records in accordance with 6.2.2.5.6.

Testing laboratory

6.2.2.5.2.7　　The testing laboratory shall have:

    (a)　Staff with an organisational structure, sufficient in number, competence, and skill; and

(b) Suitable and adequate facilities and equipment to perform the tests required by the manufacturing standard to the satisfaction of the inspection body.

6.2.2.5.3 *Manufacturer's quality system*

6.2.2.5.3.1 The quality system shall contain all the elements, requirements, and provisions adopted by the manufacturer. It shall be documented in a systematic and orderly manner in the form of written policies, procedures and instructions.

The contents shall in particular include adequate descriptions of:

(a) The organisational structure and responsibilities of personnel with regard to design and product quality;

(b) The design control and design verification techniques, processes, and procedures that will be used when designing the pressure receptacles;

(c) the relevant pressure receptacle manufacturing, quality control, quality assurance and process operation instructions that will be used;

(d) Quality records, such as inspection reports, test data and calibration data;

(e) Management reviews to ensure the effective operation of the quality system arising from the audits in accordance with 6.2.2.5.3.2;

(f) The process describing how customer requirements are met;

(g) The process for control of documents and their revision;

(h) The means for control of non-conforming pressure receptacles, purchased components, in - process and final materials; and

(i) Training programmes and qualification procedures for relevant personnel.

6.2.2.5.3.2 Audit of the quality system

The quality system shall be initially assessed to determine whether it meets the requirements in 6.2.2.5.3.1 to the satisfaction of the competent authority.

The manufacturer shall be notified of the results of the audit. The notification shall contain the conclusions of the audit and any corrective actions required.

Periodic audits shall be carried out, to the satisfaction of the competent authority, to ensure that the manufacturer maintains and applies the quality system. Reports of the periodic audits shall be provided to the manufacturer.

6.2.2.5.3.3 Maintenance of the quality system

The manufacturer shall maintain the quality system as approved in order that it remains adequate and efficient. The manufacturer shall notify the competent authority that approved the quality system, of any intended changes. The proposed changes shall be evaluated in order to determine whether the amended quality system will still satisfy the requirements in 6.2.2.5.3.1.

6.2.2.5.4 *Approval process*

Initial design type approval

6.2.2.5.4.1 The initial design type approval shall consist of approval of the manufacturer's quality system and approval of the pressure receptacle design to be produced. An application for an initial design type approval shall meet the requirements of 6.2.2.5.4.2 to 6.2.2.5.4.6 and 6.2.2.5.4.9.

6.2.2.5.4.2   A manufacturer desiring to produce pressure receptacles in accordance with a pressure receptacle standard and these Regulations shall apply for, obtain, and retain a design type approval certificate issued by the competent authority in the country of approval for at least one pressure receptacle design type in accordance with the procedure given in 6.2.2.5.4.9. This certificate shall, on request, be submitted to the competent authority of the country of use.

6.2.2.5.4.3   An application shall be made for each manufacturing facility and shall include:

(a) The name and registered address of the manufacturer and in addition, if the application is submitted by an authorised representative, its name and address;

(b) The address of the manufacturing facility (if different from the above);

(c) The name and title of the person(s) responsible for the quality system;

(d) The designation of the pressure receptacle and the relevant pressure receptacle standard;

(e) Details of any refusal of approval of a similar application by any other competent authority;

(f) The identity of the inspection body for design type approval;

(g) Documentation on the manufacturing facility as specified under 6.2.2.5.3.1; and

(h) The technical documentation required for design type approval, which shall enable verification of the conformity of the pressure receptacles with the requirements of the relevant pressure receptacle design standard. The technical documentation shall cover the design and method of manufacture and shall contain, as far as is relevant for assessment, at least the following:

(i) pressure receptacle design standard, design and manufacturing drawings, showing components and subassemblies, if any;

(ii) descriptions and explanations necessary for the understanding of the drawings and intended use of the pressure receptacles;

(iii) a list of the standards necessary to fully define the manufacturing process;

(iv) design calculations and material specifications; and

(v) design type approval test reports, describing the results of examinations and tests carried out in accordance with 6.2.2.5.4.9.

6.2.2.5.4.4   An initial audit in accordance with 6.2.2.5.3.2 shall be performed to the satisfaction of the competent authority.

6.2.2.5.4.5   If the manufacturer is denied approval, the competent authority shall provide written detailed reasons for such denial.

6.2.2.5.4.6   Following approval, changes to the information submitted under 6.2.2.5.4.3 relating to the initial approval shall be provided to the competent authority.

Subsequent design type approvals

6.2.2.5.4.7   An application for a subsequent design type approval shall encompass the requirements of 6.2.2.5.4.8 and 6.2.2.5.4.9, provided a manufacturer is in the possession of an initial design type approval. In such a case, the manufacturer's quality system according to 6.2.2.5.3 shall have been approved during the initial design type approval and shall be applicable for the new design.

6.2.2.5.4.8   The application shall include:

(a) The name and address of the manufacturer and in addition, if the application is submitted by an authorised representative, its name and address;

(b) Details of any refusal of approval of a similar application by any other competent authority;

(c) Evidence that initial design type approval has been granted; and

(d) The technical documentation, as described in 6.2.2.5.4.3 (h).

Procedure for design type approval

6.2.2.5.4.9   The inspection body shall:

(a) Examine the technical documentation to verify that:

(i) the design is in accordance with the relevant provisions of the standard, and

(ii) the prototype lot has been manufactured in conformity with the technical documentation and is representative of the design;

(b) Verify that the production inspections have been carried out as required in accordance with 6.2.2.5.5;

(c) As required by the pressure receptacle standard or technical code, carry out or supervise the tests of pressure receptacles as required for design type approval;

(d) Perform or have performed the examinations and tests specified in the pressure receptacle standard to determine that:

(i) the standard has been applied and fulfilled, and

(ii) the procedures adopted by the manufacturer meet the requirements of the standard; and

(e) Ensure that the various type approval examinations and tests are correctly and competently carried out.

After prototype testing has been carried out with satisfactory results and all applicable requirements of 6.2.2.5.4 have been satisfied, a design type approval certificate shall be issued, which shall include the name and address of the manufacturer, results and conclusions of the examination, and the necessary data for identification of the design type. If it was not possible to evaluate exhaustively the compatibility of the materials of construction with the contents of the pressure receptacle when the certificate was issued, a statement that compatibility assessment was not completed shall be included in the design type approval certificate.

If the manufacturer is denied a design type approval, the competent authority shall provide written detailed reasons for such denial.

6.2.2.5.4.10   Modifications to approved design types

The manufacturer shall either:

(a) Inform the issuing competent authority of modifications to the approved design type, where such modifications do not constitute a new design, as specified in the pressure receptacle standard; or

(b) Request a subsequent design type approval where such modifications constitute a new design according to the relevant pressure receptacle standard. This additional approval shall be given in the form of an amendment to the original design type approval certificate.

6.2.2.5.4.11   Upon request, the competent authority shall communicate to any other competent authority, information concerning design type approval, modifications of approvals and withdrawn approvals.

6.2.2.5.5   *Production inspection and certification*

General requirements

An inspection body, or its delegate, shall carry out the inspection and certification of each pressure receptacle. The inspection body selected by the manufacturer for inspection and testing during production may be different from the inspection body used for the design type approval testing.

Where it can be demonstrated to the satisfaction of the inspection body that the manufacturer has trained competent inspectors, independent of the manufacturing operations, inspection may be performed by those inspectors. In such a case, the manufacturer shall maintain training records of the inspectors.

The inspection body shall verify that the inspections by the manufacturer, and tests performed on those pressure receptacles, fully conform to the standard and the requirements of these Regulations. Should non-conformance in conjunction with this inspection and testing be determined, the permission to have inspection performed by the manufacturer's inspectors may be withdrawn.

The manufacturer shall, after approval by the inspection body, make a declaration of conformity with the certified design type. The application of the pressure receptacle certification marks shall be considered a declaration that the pressure receptacle complies with the applicable pressure receptacle standards and the requirements of this conformity assessment system and these Regulations. The inspection body shall affix or delegate the manufacturer to affix the pressure receptacle certification marks and the registered mark of the inspection body to each approved pressure receptacle.

A certificate of compliance, signed by the inspection body and the manufacturer, shall be issued before the pressure receptacles are filled.

6.2.2.5.6   *Records*

Design type approval and certificate of compliance records shall be retained by the manufacturer and the inspection body for not less than 20 years.

6.2.2.6   ***Approval system for periodic inspection and test of pressure receptacles***

6.2.2.6.1   *Definition*

For the purposes of this section:

Approval system means a system for competent authority approval of a body performing periodic inspection and test of pressure receptacles (hereinafter referred to as "periodic inspection and test body"), including approval of that body's quality system.

6.2.2.6.2   *General requirements*

Competent authority

6.2.2.6.2.1   The competent authority shall establish an approval system for the purpose of ensuring that the periodic inspection and test of pressure receptacles conform to the requirements of these Regulations. In instances where the competent authority that approves a body performing periodic inspection and test of a pressure receptacle is not the competent authority of the country approving the manufacture of the pressure receptacle, the marks of the approval country of periodic inspection and test shall be indicated in the pressure receptacle marks (see 6.2.2.7).

The competent authority of the country of approval for the periodic inspection and test shall supply, upon request, evidence demonstrating compliance to this approval system including the records of the periodic inspection and test to its counterpart in a country of use.

The competent authority of the country of approval may terminate the approval certificate referred to in 6.2.2.6.4.1, upon evidence demonstrating non-compliance with the approval system.

6.2.2.6.2.2   The competent authority may delegate its functions in this approval system, in whole or in part.

6.2.2.6.2.3   The competent authority shall ensure that a current list of approved periodic inspection and test bodies and their identity marks is available.

Periodic inspection and test body

6.2.2.6.2.4   The periodic inspection and test body shall be approved by the competent authority and shall:

(a)   Have a staff with an organisational structure, capable, trained, competent, and skilled, to satisfactorily perform its technical functions;

(b)   Have access to suitable and adequate facilities and equipment;

(c)   Operate in an impartial manner and be free from any influence which could prevent it from doing so;

(d)   Ensure commercial confidentiality;

(e)   Maintain clear demarcation between actual periodic inspection and test body functions and unrelated functions;

(f)   Operate a documented quality system accordance with 6.2.2.6.3;

(g)   Apply for approval in accordance with 6.2.2.6.4;

(h)   Ensure that the periodic inspections and tests are performed in accordance with 6.2.2.6.5; and

(i)   Maintain an effective and appropriate report and record system in accordance with 6.2.2.6.6.

6.2.2.6.3   *Quality system and audit of the periodic inspection and test body*

6.2.2.6.3.1   Quality system

The quality system shall contain all the elements, requirements, and provisions adopted by the periodic inspection and test body. It shall be documented in a systematic and orderly manner in the form of written policies, procedures, and instructions.

The quality system shall include:

(a)   A description of the organisational structure and responsibilities;

(b)   The relevant inspection and test, quality control, quality assurance, and process operation instructions that will be used;

(c)   Quality records, such as inspection reports, test data, calibration data and certificates;

(d) Management reviews to ensure the effective operation of the quality system arising from the audits performed in accordance with 6.2.2.6.3.2;

(e) A process for control of documents and their revision;

(f) A means for control of non-conforming pressure receptacles; and

(g) Training programmes and qualification procedures for relevant personnel.

6.2.2.6.3.2 Audit

The periodic inspection and test body and its quality system shall be audited in order to determine whether it meets the requirements of these Regulations to the satisfaction of the competent authority.

An audit shall be conducted as part of the initial approval process (see 6.2.2.6.4.3). An audit may be required as part of the process to modify an approval (see 6.2.2.6.4.6).

Periodic audits shall be conducted, to the satisfaction of the competent authority, to ensure that the periodic inspection and test body continues to meet the requirements of these Regulations.

The periodic inspection and test body shall be notified of the results of any audit. The notification shall contain the conclusions of the audit and any corrective actions required.

6.2.2.6.3.3 Maintenance of the quality system

The periodic inspection and test body shall maintain the quality system as approved in order that it remains adequate and efficient.

The periodic inspection and test body shall notify the competent authority that approved the quality system, of any intended changes, in accordance with the process for modification of an approval in 6.2.2.6.4.6.

6.2.2.6.4 *Approval process for periodic inspection and test bodies*

Initial approval

6.2.2.6.4.1 A body desiring to perform periodic inspection and test of pressure receptacles in accordance with a pressure receptacle standard and these Regulations shall apply for, obtain, and retain an approval certificate issued by the competent authority.

This written approval shall, on request, be submitted to the competent authority of a country of use.

6.2.2.6.4.2 An application shall be made for each periodic inspection and test body and shall include:

(a) The name and address of the periodic inspection and test body and, if the application is submitted by an authorised representative, its name and address;

(b) The address of each facility performing periodic inspection and test;

(c) The name and title of the person(s) responsible for the quality system;

(d) The designation of the pressure receptacles, the periodic inspection and test methods, and the relevant pressure receptacle standards met by the quality system;

(e) Documentation on each facility, the equipment, and the quality system as specified under 6.2.2.6.3.1;

(f) The qualifications and training records of the periodic inspection and test personnel; and

(g) Details of any refusal of approval of a similar application by any other competent authority.

6.2.2.6.4.3 The competent authority shall:

(a) Examine the documentation to verify that the procedures are in accordance with the requirements of the relevant pressure receptacle standards and these Regulations; and

(b) Conduct an audit in accordance with 6.2.2.6.3.2 to verify that the inspections and tests are carried out as required by the relevant pressure receptacle standards and these Regulations, to the satisfaction of the competent authority.

6.2.2.6.4.4 After the audit has been carried out with satisfactory results and all applicable requirements of 6.2.2.6.4 have been satisfied, an approval certificate shall be issued. It shall include the name of the periodic inspection and test body, the registered mark, the address of each facility, and the necessary data for identification of its approved activities (e.g. designation of pressure receptacles, periodic inspection and test method and pressure receptacle standards).

6.2.2.6.4.5 If the periodic inspection and test body is denied approval, the competent authority shall provide written detailed reasons for such denial.

Modifications to periodic inspection and test body approvals

6.2.2.6.4.6 Following approval, the periodic inspection and test body shall notify the issuing competent authority of any modifications to the information submitted under 6.2.2.6.4.2 relating to the initial approval.

The modifications shall be evaluated in order to determine whether the requirements of the relevant pressure receptacle standards and these Regulations will be satisfied. An audit in accordance with 6.2.2.6.3.2 may be required. The competent authority shall accept or reject these modifications in writing, and an amended approval certificate shall be issued as necessary.

6.2.2.6.4.7 Upon request, the competent authority shall communicate to any other competent authority, information concerning initial approvals, modifications of approvals, and withdrawn approvals.

6.2.2.6.5 *Periodic inspection and test and certification*

The application of the periodic inspection and test marks to a pressure receptacle shall be considered a declaration that the pressure receptacle complies with the applicable pressure receptacle standards and the requirements of these Regulations. The periodic inspection and test body shall affix the periodic inspection and test marks, including its registered mark, to each approved pressure receptacle (see 6.2.2.7.7).

A record certifying that a pressure receptacle has passed the periodic inspection and test shall be issued by the periodic inspection and test body, before the pressure receptacle is filled.

6.2.2.6.6 *Records*

The periodic inspection and test body shall retain records of pressure receptacle periodic inspection and tests (both passed and failed) including the location of the test facility, for not less than 15 years.

The owner of the pressure receptacle shall retain an identical record until the next periodic inspection and test unless the pressure receptacle is permanently removed from service.

6.2.2.7 *Marking of refillable UN pressure receptacles*

NOTE: *Marking requirements for UN metal hydride storage systems are given in 6.2.2.9, marking requirements for UN bundles of cylinders are given in 6.2.2.10 and marking requirements for closures are given in 6.2.2.11.*

6.2.2.7.1 Refillable UN pressure receptacle shells and closed cryogenic receptacles shall be marked clearly and legibly with certification, operational and manufacturing marks. These marks shall be permanently affixed (e.g. stamped, engraved, or etched). The marks shall be on the shoulder, top end or neck of the pressure receptacle shell or on a permanently affixed component of the pressure receptacle (e.g. welded collar or corrosion resistant plate welded on the outer jacket of a closed cryogenic receptacle). Except for the UN packaging symbol, the minimum size of the marks shall be 5 mm for pressure receptacles with a diameter greater than or equal to 140 mm and 2.5 mm for pressure receptacles with a diameter less than 140 mm. The minimum size of the UN packaging symbol shall be 10 mm for pressure receptacles with a diameter greater than or equal to 140 mm and 5 mm for pressure receptacles with a diameter less than 140 mm.

6.2.2.7.2 The following certification marks shall be applied:

(a) The United Nations packaging symbol $\overset{u}{\underset{n}{\bigcirc}}$.

This symbol shall not be used for any purpose other than certifying that a packaging, a flexible bulk container, a portable tank or a MEGC complies with the relevant requirements in chapter 6.1, 6.2, 6.3, 6.5, 6.6, 6.7 or 6.8;

(b) The technical standard (e.g. ISO 9809-1) used for design, manufacture and testing;

NOTE: *For acetylene cylinders the standard ISO 3807 shall also be marked.*

(c) The character(s) identifying the country of approval as indicated by the distinguishing sign used on vehicles in international road traffic[2];

NOTE: *For the purpose of this mark the country of approval means the country of the competent authority that authorized the initial inspection and test of the individual receptacle at the time of manufacture.*

(d) The identity mark or stamp of the inspection body that is registered with the competent authority of the country authorizing the marking;

(e) The date of the initial inspection, the year (four digits) followed by the month (two digits) separated by a slash (i.e. "/");

NOTE: *When an acetylene cylinder is conformity assessed in accordance with 6.2.1.4.4 (b) and the inspection bodies for the cylinder shell and the acetylene cylinder are different, their respective marks (d) are required. Only the initial inspection date (e) of the completed acetylene cylinder is required. If the country of approval of the inspection body responsible for the initial inspection and test is different a second mark (c) shall be applied.*

6.2.2.7.3 The following operational marks shall be applied:

(f) The test pressure in bar, preceded by the letters "PH" and followed by the letters "BAR";

(g) The mass of the empty pressure receptacle including all permanently attached integral parts (e.g. neck ring, foot ring, etc.) in kilograms, followed by the letters "KG". This mass shall not include the mass of closure(s), valve protection cap or valve guard, any

---

[2] *Distinguishing sign of the State of registration used on motor vehicles and trailers in international road traffic, e.g. in accordance with the Geneva Convention on Road Traffic of 1949 or the Vienna Convention on Road Traffic of 1968.*

coating, or porous material for acetylene. The mass shall be expressed to three significant figures rounded up to the last digit. For cylinders of less than 1 kg, the mass shall be expressed to two significant figures rounded up to the last digit. In the case of pressure receptacles for UN 1001 acetylene, dissolved and UN 3374 acetylene, solvent free, at least one decimal shall be shown after the decimal point and two digits for pressure receptacles of less than 1 kg;

(h) The minimum guaranteed wall thickness of the pressure receptacle in millimetres followed by the letters "MM". This mark is not required for pressure receptacles with a water capacity less than or equal to 1 litre or for composite cylinders or for closed cryogenic receptacles;

(i) In the case of pressure receptacles for compressed gases, UN 1001 acetylene, dissolved, and UN 3374 acetylene, solvent free, the working pressure in bar, preceded by the letters "PW". In the case of closed cryogenic receptacles, the maximum allowable working pressure preceded by the letters "MAWP";

NOTE: When a cylinder shell is intended for use as an acetylene cylinder (including the porous material), the working pressure mark is not required until the acetylene cylinder is completed.

(j) In the case of pressure receptacles for liquefied gases, refrigerated liquefied gases and dissolved gases, the water capacity in litres expressed to three significant digits rounded down to the last digit, followed by the letter "L". If the value of the minimum or nominal water capacity is an integer, the figures after the decimal point may be neglected;

(k) In the case of cylinders for UN 1001 acetylene, dissolved:

   (i) the tare in kilograms consisting of the total of the mass of the empty cylinder shell, the service equipment (including porous material) not removed during filling, any coating, the solvent and the saturation gas expressed to three significant figures rounded down to the last digit followed by the letters "KG". At least one decimal shall be shown after the decimal point. For pressure receptacles of less than 1 kg, the mass shall be expressed to two significant figures rounded down to the last digit;

   (ii) the identity of the porous material (e.g.: name or trademark); and

   (iii) the total mass of the filled acetylene cylinder in kilograms followed by the letters "KG";

(l) In the case of cylinders for UN 3374 acetylene, solvent free:

   (i) the tare in kilograms consisting of the total of the mass of the empty cylinder shell, the service equipment (including porous material) not removed during filling and any coating expressed to three significant figures rounded down to the last digit followed by the letters "KG". At least one decimal shall be shown after the decimal point. For pressure receptacles of less than 1 kg, the mass shall be expressed to two significant figures rounded down to the last digit;

   (ii) the identity of the porous material (e.g.: name or trademark); and

   (iii) the total mass of the filled acetylene cylinder in kilograms followed by the letters "KG";

NOTE: Acetylene cylinders constructed in accordance with the twenty-first revised edition of the Model Regulations which are not marked in accordance with 6.2.2.7.3 (k) or (l) applicable in the twenty-second revised edition of the Model Regulations, may continue to be used until the next periodic inspection and test two years after the coming into force of the twenty-third revised edition of the Model Regulation where they have to be marked according to the twenty-third revised edition of the Model Regulations or be taken out of operation.

6.2.2.7.4   The following manufacturing marks shall be applied:

(m)   Identification of the cylinder thread (e.g. 25E). This mark is not required for closed cryogenic receptacles;

NOTE: *Information on marks that may be used for identifying threads for cylinders is given in ISO/TR 11364, "Gas cylinders – Compilation of national and international valve stem/gas cylinder neck threads and their identification and marking system".*

(n)   The manufacturer's mark registered by the competent authority. When the country of manufacture is not the same as the country of approval, then the manufacturer's mark shall be preceded by the character(s) identifying the country of manufacture as indicated by the distinguishing sign used on vehicles in international road traffic[2]. The country mark and the manufacturer's mark shall be separated by a space or slash;

NOTE: *For acetylene cylinders, if the manufacturer of the acetylene cylinder and the manufacturer of the cylinder shell are different, only the mark of the manufacturer of the completed acetylene cylinder is required.*

(o)   The serial number assigned by the manufacturer;

(p)   In the case of steel pressure receptacles and composite pressure receptacles with steel liner intended for the transport of gases with a risk of hydrogen embrittlement, the letter "H" showing compatibility of the steel (see ISO 11114-1:2020);

(q)   For composite cylinders and tubes having a limited design life, the letters "FINAL" followed by the design life shown as the year (four digits) followed by the month (two digits) separated by a slash (i.e. "/").

(r)   For composite cylinders and tubes having a limited design life greater than 15 years and for composite cylinders and tubes having non-limited design life, the letters "SERVICE" followed by the date 15 years from the date of manufacture (initial inspection) shown as the year (four digits) followed by the month (two digits) separated by a slash (i.e. "/").

NOTE: *Once the initial design type has passed the service life test programme requirements in accordance with 6.2.2.1.1 NOTE 2 or 6.2.2.1.2 NOTE 2, future production no longer requires this initial service life mark. The initial service life mark shall be made unreadable on cylinders and tubes of a design type that has met the service life test programme requirements.*

6.2.2.7.5   The above marks shall be placed in three groups:

- Manufacturing marks shall be the top grouping and shall appear consecutively in the sequence given in 6.2.2.7.4 except for the marks described in 6.2.2.7.4 (q) and (r) which shall be adjacent to the periodic inspection and test marks of 6.2.2.7.7.

- The operational marks in 6.2.2.7.3 shall be the middle grouping and the test pressure (f) shall be immediately preceded by the working pressure (i) when the latter is required.

---

[2] *Distinguishing sign of the State of registration used on motor vehicles and trailers in international road traffic, e.g. in accordance with the Geneva Convention on Road Traffic of 1949 or the Vienna Convention on Road Traffic of 1968.*

- Certification marks shall be the bottom grouping and shall appear in the sequence given in 6.2.2.7.2.

The following is an example of marking a cylinder.

```
     (m)       (n)        (o)        (p)
     25E    D   MF      765432       H
    ─────────────────────────────────────
     (i)       (f)        (g)        (j)       (h)
    PW200   PH300BAR    62.1 KG     50 L     5.8 MM
    ─────────────────────────────────────
     (a)       (b)        (c)        (d)       (e)
     (UN)    ISO 9809-1    F         IB      2000/12
```

6.2.2.7.6 Other marks are allowed in areas other than the side wall, provided they are made in low stress areas and are not of a size and depth that will create harmful stress concentrations. In the case of closed cryogenic receptacles, such marks may be on a separate plate attached to the outer jacket. Such marks shall not conflict with required marks.

6.2.2.7.7 In addition to the preceding marks, each refillable pressure receptacle that meets the periodic inspection and test requirements of 6.2.2.4 shall be marked indicating:

(a) The character(s) identifying the country authorizing the body performing the periodic inspection and test as indicated by the distinguishing sign used on vehicles in international road traffic[2]. This mark is not required if this body is approved by the competent authority of the country approving manufacture;

(b) The registered mark of the body authorised by the competent authority for performing periodic inspection and test;

(c) The date of the periodic inspection and test, the year (two digits) followed by the month (two digits) separated by a slash (i.e. "/"). Four digits may be used to indicate the year.

The above marks shall appear consecutively in the sequence given.

6.2.2.7.8 The marks in accordance with 6.2.2.7.7 may be engraved on a metallic ring affixed to the cylinder or pressure drum when the valve is installed, and which is removable only by disconnecting the valve from the cylinder or pressure drum.

6.2.2.7.9 *Deleted.*

6.2.2.8 *Marking of non-refillable UN cylinders*

6.2.2.8.1 Non-refillable UN cylinders shall be marked clearly and legibly with certification and gas or cylinder specific marks. These marks shall be permanently affixed (e.g. stencilled, stamped, engraved, or etched) on the cylinder. Except when stencilled, the marks shall be on the shoulder, top end or neck of the cylinder shell or on a permanently affixed component of the cylinder (e.g. welded collar). Except for the UN

---

[2] *Distinguishing sign of the State of registration used on motor vehicles and trailers in international road traffic, e.g. in accordance with the Geneva Convention on Road Traffic of 1949 or the Vienna Convention on Road Traffic of 1968.*

packaging symbol and the "DO NOT REFILL" mark, the minimum size of the marks shall be 5 mm for cylinders with a diameter greater than or equal to 140 mm and 2.5 mm for cylinders with a diameter less than 140 mm. The minimum size of the UN packaging symbol shall be 10 mm for cylinders with a diameter greater than or equal to 140 mm and 5 mm for cylinders with a diameter less than 140 mm. The minimum size of the "DO NOT REFILL" mark shall be 5 mm.

6.2.2.8.2   The marks listed in 6.2.2.7.2 to 6.2.2.7.4 shall be applied with the exception of (g), (h), and (m). The serial number (o) may be replaced by the batch number. In addition, the words "DO NOT REFILL" in letters of at least 5 mm in height are required.

6.2.2.8.3   The requirements of 6.2.2.7.5 shall apply.

NOTE: *Non-refillable cylinders may, on account of their size, substitute a label for these permanent marks.*

6.2.2.8.4   Other marks are allowed provided they are made in low stress areas other than the side wall and are not of a size and depth that will create harmful stress concentrations. Such marks shall not conflict with required marks.

6.2.2.9   *Marking of UN metal hydride storage systems*

6.2.2.9.1   UN metal hydride storage systems shall be marked clearly and legibly with the marks listed below. These marks shall be permanently affixed (e.g. stamped, engraved, or etched) on the metal hydride storage system. The marks shall be on the shoulder, top end or neck of the metal hydride storage system or on a permanently affixed component of the metal hydride storage system. Except for the United Nations packaging symbol, the minimum size of the marks shall be 5 mm for metal hydride storage systems with a smallest overall dimension greater than or equal to 140 mm and 2.5 mm for metal hydride storage systems with a smallest overall dimension less than 140 mm. The minimum size of the United Nations packaging symbol shall be 10 mm for metal hydride storage systems with a smallest overall dimension greater than or equal to 140 mm and 5 mm for metal hydride storage systems with a smallest overall dimension less than 140 mm.

6.2.2.9.2   The following marks shall be applied:

(a)   The United Nations packaging symbol $\overset{u}{\underset{n}{\bigcirc}}$.

This symbol shall not be used for any purpose other than certifying that a packaging, a flexible bulk container, a portable tank or a MEGC complies with the relevant requirements in chapter 6.1, 6.2, 6.3, 6.5, 6.6, 6.7 or 6.8;

(b)   "ISO 16111" (the technical standard used for design, manufacture and testing);

(c)   The character(s) identifying the country of approval as indicated by the distinguishing sign used on vehicles in international road traffic[2];

NOTE: *For the purpose of this mark the country of approval means the country of the competent authority that authorized the initial inspection and test of the individual system at the time of manufacture.*

(d)   The identity mark or stamp of the inspection body that is registered with the competent authority of the country authorizing the marking;

---

[2]   *Distinguishing sign of the State of registration used on motor vehicles and trailers in international road traffic, e.g. in accordance with the Geneva Convention on Road Traffic of 1949 or the Vienna Convention on Road Traffic of 1968.*

(e) The date of the initial inspection, the year (four digits) followed by the month (two digits) separated by a slash (i.e. "/");

(f) The test pressure of the receptacle in bar, preceded by the letters "PH" and followed by the letters "BAR";

(g) The rated charging pressure of the metal hydride storage system in bar, preceded by the letters "RCP" and followed by the letters "BAR";

(h) The manufacturer's mark registered by the competent authority. When the country of manufacture is not the same as the country of approval, then the manufacturer's mark shall be preceded by the character(s) identifying the country of manufacture as indicated by the distinguishing sign used on vehicles in international road traffic[2]. The country mark and the manufacturer's mark shall be separated by a space or slash;

(i) The serial number assigned by the manufacturer;

(j) In the case of steel receptacles and composite receptacles with steel liner, the letter "H" showing compatibility of the steel (see ISO 11114-1:2020); and,

(k) In the case of metal hydride storage systems having limited life, the date of expiry, denoted by the letters "FINAL" followed by the year (four digits) followed by the month (two digits) separated by a slash (i.e. "/").

The certification marks specified in (a) to (e) above shall appear consecutively in the sequence given. The test pressure (f) shall be immediately preceded by the rated charging pressure (g). The manufacturing marks specified in (h) to (k) above shall appear consecutively in the sequence given.

6.2.2.9.3 Other marks are allowed in areas other than the side wall, provided they are made in low stress areas and are not of a size and depth that will create harmful stress concentrations. Such marks shall not conflict with required marks.

6.2.2.9.4 In addition to the preceding marks, each metal hydride storage system that meets the periodic inspection and test requirements of 6.2.2.4 shall be marked indicating:

(a) The character(s) identifying the country authorizing the body performing the periodic inspection and test, as indicated by the distinguishing sign used on vehicles in international road traffic[2]. This mark is not required if this body is approved by the competent authority of the country approving manufacture;

(b) The registered mark of the body authorised by the competent authority for performing periodic inspection and test;

(c) The date of the periodic inspection and test, the year (two digits) followed by the month (two digits) separated by a slash (i.e. "/"). Four digits may be used to indicate the year.

The above marks shall appear consecutively in the sequence given.

6.2.2.10 *Marking of bundles of cylinders*

6.2.2.10.1 Individual cylinder shells in a bundle of cylinders shall be marked in accordance with 6.2.2.7. Individual closures in a bundle of cylinders shall be marked in accordance with 6.2.2.11.

6.2.2.10.2 Refillable UN bundles of cylinders shall be marked clearly and legibly with certification, operational, and manufacturing marks. These marks shall be permanently affixed (e.g. stamped, engraved, or

---

[2] *Distinguishing sign of the State of registration used on motor vehicles and trailers in international road traffic, e.g. in accordance with the Geneva Convention on Road Traffic of 1949 or the Vienna Convention on Road Traffic of 1968.*

etched) on a plate permanently attached to the frame of the bundle of cylinders. Except for the UN packaging symbol, the minimum size of the marks shall be 5 mm. The minimum size of the UN packaging symbol shall be 10 mm.

6.2.2.10.3   The following marks shall be applied:

(a) The certification marks specified in 6.2.2.7.2 (a), (b), (c), (d) and (e);

(b) The operational marks specified in 6.2.2.7.3 (f), (i), (j) and the total of the mass of the frame of the bundle and all permanently attached parts (cylinder shells and service equipment). Bundles intended for the carriage of UN 1001 acetylene, dissolved and UN 3374 acetylene, solvent free shall bear the tare as specified in clause B.4.2 of ISO 10961:2010; and

(c) The manufacturing marks specified in 6.2.2.7.4 (n), (o) and, where applicable, (p).

6.2.2.10.4   The marks shall be placed in three groups:

(a) The manufacturing marks shall be the top grouping and shall appear consecutively in the sequence given in 6.2.2.10.3 (c);

(b) The operational marks in 6.2.2.10.3 (b) shall be the middle grouping and the operational mark specified in 6.2.2.7.3 (f) shall be immediately preceded by the operational mark specified in 6.2.2.7.3 (i) when the latter is required;

(c) Certification marks shall be the bottom grouping and shall appear in the sequence given in 6.2.2.10.3 (a).

6.2.2.11   *Marking of closures for refillable UN pressure receptacles*

For closures the following permanent marks shall be applied clearly and legibly, (e.g. stamped, engraved or etched):

(a) Manufacturer's identification mark;

(b) Design standard or design standard designation;

(c) Date of manufacture (year and month or year and week) and

(d) The identity mark of the inspection body responsible for the initial inspection and test, if applicable.

The valve test pressure shall be marked when it is less than the test pressure which is indicated by the rating of the valve filling connection.

NOTE: *Closures of refillable pressure receptacles manufactured before 1 January 2027 in accordance with the requirements applicable in the twenty-first revised edition of the Model Regulations which are not marked in accordance with the requirements of 6.2.2.11 applicable in the twenty second revised edition may continue to be used.*

6.2.3   **Requirements for non-UN pressure receptacles**

6.2.3.1   Pressure receptacles not designed, constructed, inspected, tested and approved according to the requirements of 6.2.2 shall be designed, constructed, inspected, tested and approved in accordance with the provisions of a technical code recognised by the competent authority and the general requirements of 6.2.1.

6.2.3.2   Pressure receptacles designed, constructed, inspected, tested and approved under the provisions of this section shall not be marked with the UN packaging symbol.

6.2.3.3 For metallic cylinders, tubes, pressure drums, bundles of cylinders and salvage pressure receptacles, the construction shall be such that the minimum burst ratio (burst pressure divided by test pressure) is:

      1.50   for refillable pressure receptacles,

      2.00   for non-refillable pressure receptacles.

6.2.3.4 Marking shall be in accordance with the requirements of the competent authority of the country of use.

6.2.3.5 *Salvage pressure receptacles*

To permit the safe handling and disposal of the pressure receptacles transported within the salvage pressure receptacle, the design may include equipment not otherwise used for cylinders or pressure drums such as flat heads, quick opening devices and openings in the cylindrical part.

Instructions on the safe handling and use of the salvage pressure receptacle shall be clearly shown in the documentation for the application to the competent authority and shall form part of the approval certificate. In the approval certificate, the pressure receptacles authorized to be transported in a salvage pressure receptacle shall be indicated. A list of the materials of construction of all parts likely to be in contact with the dangerous goods shall also be included.

A copy of the approval certificate shall be delivered by the manufacturer to the owner of a salvage pressure receptacle.

The marking of salvage pressure receptacles according to 6.2.3 shall be determined by the competent authority taking into account suitable marking provisions of 6.2.2.7 as appropriate. The marking shall include the water capacity and test pressure of the salvage pressure receptacle.

NOTE: *These provisions for salvage pressure receptacles may be applied for new salvage pressure receptacles as from 1 January 2013, unless otherwise authorized, and shall be applied for all new salvage pressure receptacles as from 1 January 2014. Salvage pressure receptacles approved in accordance with national regulations may be used with the approval of the competent authorities of the countries of use.*

6.2.4 Requirements for aerosol dispensers, small receptacles containing gas (gas cartridges) and fuel cell cartridges containing liquefied flammable gas

6.2.4.1 The internal pressure of aerosol dispensers at 50 °C shall not exceed 1.2 MPa (12 bar) when using flammable liquefied gases, 1.32 MPa (13.2 bar) when using non-flammable liquefied gases, and 1.5 MPa (15 bar) when using non-flammable compressed or dissolved gases. In case of a mixture of several gases, the stricter limit shall apply.

6.2.4.2 Each filled aerosol dispenser or gas cartridge or fuel cell cartridge shall be subjected to a test in a hot water bath in accordance with 6.2.4.2.1 or an approved water bath alternative in accordance with 6.2.4.2.2.

6.2.4.2.1 *Hot water bath test*

6.2.4.2.1.1 The temperature of the water bath and the duration of the test shall be such that the internal pressure reaches that which would be reached at 55 °C (50 °C if the liquid phase does not exceed 95 % of the capacity of the aerosol dispenser, gas cartridge or the fuel cell cartridge at 50 °C). If the contents are sensitive to heat or if the aerosol dispensers, gas cartridges or the fuel cell cartridges are made of plastics material which softens at this test temperature, the temperature of the bath shall be set at between 20 °C and 30 °C but, in addition, one aerosol dispenser, gas cartridge or the fuel cell cartridge in 2 000 shall be tested at the higher temperature.

6.2.4.2.1.2 No leakage or permanent deformation of an aerosol dispenser, gas cartridge or the fuel cell cartridge may occur, except that a plastic aerosol dispenser, gas cartridge or the fuel cell cartridge may be deformed through softening provided that it does not leak.

6.2.4.2.2 *Alternative methods*

With the approval of the competent authority alternative methods that provide an equivalent level of safety may be used provided that the requirements of 6.2.4.2.2.1 and, as appropriate, 6.2.4.2.2.2 or 6.2.4.2.3 are met.

6.2.4.2.2.1 Quality system

Aerosol dispenser, gas cartridge or the fuel cell cartridge fillers and component manufacturers shall have a quality system. The quality system shall implement procedures to ensure that all aerosol dispensers, gas cartridges or the fuel cell cartridges that leak or that are deformed are rejected and not offered for transport.

The quality system shall include:

(a) A description of the organizational structure and responsibilities;

(b) The relevant inspection and test, quality control, quality assurance, and process operation instructions that will be used;

(c) Quality records, such as inspection reports, test data, calibration data and certificates;

(d) Management reviews to ensure the effective operation of the quality system;

(e) A process for control of documents and their revision;

(f) A means for control of non-conforming aerosol dispensers, gas cartridges or the fuel cell cartridges;

(g) Training programmes and qualification procedures for relevant personnel; and

(h) Procedures to ensure that there is no damage to the final product.

An initial audit and periodic audits shall be conducted to the satisfaction of the competent authority. These audits shall ensure the approved system is and remains adequate and efficient. Any proposed changes to the approved system shall be notified to the competent authority in advance.

6.2.4.2.2.2 Aerosol dispensers

6.2.4.2.2.2.1 Pressure and leak testing of aerosol dispensers before filling

Each empty aerosol dispenser shall be subjected to a pressure equal to or in excess of the maximum expected in the filled aerosol dispensers at 55 °C (50 °C if the liquid phase does not exceed 95 % of the capacity of the receptacle at 50 °C). This shall be at least two-thirds of the design pressure of the aerosol dispenser. If any aerosol dispenser shows evidence of leakage at a rate equal to or greater than 3.3×10^{-2} mbar·l·s^{-1} at the test pressure, distortion or other defect, it shall be rejected.

6.2.4.2.2.2.2 Testing of the aerosol dispensers after filling

Prior to filling the filler shall ensure that the crimping equipment is set appropriately and the specified propellant is used.

Each filled aerosol dispenser shall be weighed and leak tested. The leak detection equipment shall be sufficiently sensitive to detect at least a leak rate of 2.0×10^{-3} mbar·l·s^{-1} at 20 °C.

Any filled aerosol dispenser that shows evidence of leakage, deformation or excessive mass shall be rejected.

6.2.4.2.2.3 Gas cartridges and fuel cell cartridges

6.2.4.2.2.3.1 Pressure testing of gas cartridges and fuel cell cartridges

Each gas cartridge or fuel cell cartridge shall be subjected to a test pressure equal to or in excess of the maximum expected in the filled receptacle at 55 °C (50 °C if the liquid phase does not exceed 95 % of the capacity of the receptacle at 50 °C). This test pressure shall be that specified for the gas cartridge or fuel cell cartridge and shall not be less than two thirds the design pressure of the gas cartridge or fuel cell cartridge. If any gas cartridge or fuel cell cartridge shows evidence of leakage at a rate equal to or greater than 3.3×10^{-2} mbar·l·s^{-1} at the test pressure or distortion or any other defect, it shall be rejected.

6.2.4.2.2.3.2 Leak testing gas cartridges and fuel cell cartridges

Prior to filling and sealing, the filler shall ensure that the closures (if any), and the associated sealing equipment are closed appropriately and the specified gas is used.

Each filled gas cartridge or fuel cell cartridge shall be checked for the correct mass of gas and shall be leak tested. The leak detection equipment shall be sufficiently sensitive to detect at least a leak rate of 2.0×10^{-3} mbar·l·s^{-1} at 20 °C.

Any gas cartridge or fuel cell cartridge that has gas masses not in conformity with the declared mass limits or shows evidence of leakage or deformation, shall be rejected.

6.2.4.2.3 With the approval of the competent authority, aerosols and receptacles, small, are not subject to 6.2.4.2.1 and 6.2.4.2.2, if they are required to be sterile but may be adversely affected by water bath testing, provided:

- (a) They contain a non-flammable gas and either

  - (i) contain other substances that are constituent parts of pharmaceutical products for medical, veterinary or similar purposes;

  - (ii) contain other substances used in the production process for pharmaceutical products; or

  - (iii) are used in medical, veterinary or similar applications;

- (b) An equivalent level of safety is achieved by the manufacturer's use of alternative methods for leak detection and pressure resistance, such as helium detection and water bathing a statistical sample of at least 1 in 2000 from each production batch; and

- (c) For pharmaceutical products according to (a) (i) and (iii) above, they are manufactured under the authority of a national health administration. If required by the competent authority, the principles of Good Manufacturing Practice (GMP) established by the World Health Organization (WHO)[3] shall be followed.

---

[3] *WHO Publication: "Quality assurance of pharmaceuticals. A compendium of guidelines and related materials. Volume 2: Good manufacturing practices and inspection".*

CHAPTER 6.3

REQUIREMENTS FOR THE CONSTRUCTION AND TESTING OF PACKAGINGS FOR DIVISION 6.2 INFECTIOUS SUBSTANCES OF CATEGORY A (UN Nos. 2814 AND 2900)

6.3.1 General

6.3.1.1 The requirements of this chapter apply to packagings intended for the transport of infectious substances of Category A, UN Nos. 2814 and 2900.

6.3.2 Requirements for packagings

6.3.2.1 The requirements for packagings in this section are based on packagings, as specified in 6.1.4, currently used. In order to take into account progress in science and technology, there is no objection to the use of packagings having specifications different from those in this chapter provided that they are equally effective, acceptable to the competent authority and able to successfully fulfil the requirements described in 6.3.5. Methods of testing other than those described in these Regulations are acceptable provided they are equivalent.

6.3.2.2 Packagings shall be manufactured and tested under a quality assurance programme which satisfies the competent authority in order to ensure that each packaging meets the requirements of this chapter.

NOTE: *ISO 16106:2020 "Transport packages for dangerous goods – Dangerous goods packagings, intermediate bulk containers (IBCs) and large packagings – Guidelines for the application of ISO 9001" provides acceptable guidance on procedures which may be followed.*

6.3.2.3 Manufacturers and subsequent distributors of packagings shall provide information regarding procedures to be followed and a description of the types and dimensions of closures (including required gaskets) and any other components needed to ensure that packages as presented for transport are capable of passing the applicable performance tests of this chapter.

6.3.3 Code for designating types of packagings

6.3.3.1 The codes for designating types of packagings are set out in 6.1.2.7.

6.3.3.2 The letters "U" or "W" may follow the packaging code. The letter "U" signifies a special packaging conforming to the requirements of 6.3.5.1.6. The letter "W" signifies that the packaging, although, of the same type indicated by the code is manufactured to a specification different from that in 6.1.4 and is considered equivalent under the requirements of 6.3.2.1.

6.3.4 Marking

NOTE 1: *The marks indicate that the packaging which bears them corresponds to a successfully tested design type and that it complies with the requirements of this chapter which are related to the manufacture, but not to the use, of the packaging.*

NOTE 2: *The marks are intended to be of assistance to packaging manufacturers, reconditioners, packaging users, carriers and regulatory authorities.*

NOTE 3: *The marks do not always provide full details of the test levels, etc., and these may need to be taken further into account, e.g. by reference to a test certificate, to test reports or to a register of successfully tested packagings.*

6.3.4.1 Each packaging intended for use according to these Regulations shall bear marks which are durable, legible and placed in a location and of such a size relative to the packaging as to be readily visible. For packages with a gross mass of more than 30 kg, the marks or a duplicate thereof shall appear on the top or on a side of the packaging. Letters, numerals and symbols shall be at least 12 mm high, except for packagings of 30 *l* capacity or less or 30 kg maximum net mass, when they shall be at least 6 mm in height and for packagings of 5 *l* capacity or less or 5 kg maximum net mass when they shall be of an appropriate size.

6.3.4.2 A packaging that meets the requirements of this section and of 6.3.5 shall be marked with:

(a) The United Nations packaging symbol ⓤ/ⓝ .

This symbol shall not be used for any purpose other than certifying that a packaging, a flexible bulk container, a portable tank or a MEGC complies with the relevant requirements in chapter 6.1, 6.2, 6.3, 6.5, 6.6, 6.7 or 6.8.;

(b) The code designating the type of packaging according to the requirements of 6.1.2;

(c) The text "CLASS 6.2";

(d) The last two digits of the year of manufacture of the packaging;

(e) The state authorizing the allocation of the mark, indicated by the distinguishing sign used on vehicles in international road traffic[1];

(f) The name of the manufacturer or other identification of the packaging specified by the competent authority;

(g) For packagings meeting the requirements of 6.3.5.1.6, the letter "U", inserted immediately following the mark required in (b) above.

6.3.4.3 Marks shall be applied in the sequence shown in 6.3.4.2 (a) to (g); each mark required in these sub-paragraphs shall be clearly separated, e.g. by a slash or space, so as to be easily identifiable. For example, see 6.3.4.4.

Any additional marks authorized by a competent authority shall still enable the marks required in 6.3.4.1 to be correctly identified.

6.3.4.4 *Example of marking*

ⓤ/ⓝ	4G/CLASS 6.2/06	as in 6.3.4.2 (a), (b), (c) and (d)
	S/SP-9989-ERIKSSON	as in 6.3.4.2 (e) and (f)

6.3.5 Test requirements for packagings

6.3.5.1 *Performance and frequency of tests*

6.3.5.1.1 The design type of each packaging shall be tested as provided in this section in accordance with procedures established by the competent authority.

6.3.5.1.2 Each packaging design type shall successfully pass the tests prescribed in this chapter before being used. A packaging design type is defined by the design, size, material and thickness, manner of construction and packing, but may include various surface treatments. It also includes packagings which differ from the design type only in their lesser design height.

6.3.5.1.3 Tests shall be repeated on production samples at intervals established by the competent authority.

---

[1] *Distinguishing sign of the State of registration used on motor vehicles and trailers in international road traffic, e.g. in accordance with the Geneva Convention on Road Traffic of 1949 or the Vienna Convention on Road Traffic of 1968.*

6.3.5.1.4　　Tests shall also be repeated after each modification which alters the design, material or manner of construction of a packaging.

6.3.5.1.5　　The competent authority may permit the selective testing of packagings that differ only in minor respects from a tested type, e.g. smaller sizes or lower net mass of primary receptacles; and packagings such as drums and boxes which are produced with small reductions in external dimension(s).

6.3.5.1.6　　Primary receptacles of any type may be assembled within a secondary packaging and transported without testing in the rigid outer packaging under the following conditions:

(a) The rigid outer packaging shall have been successfully tested in accordance with 6.3.5.2.2 with fragile (e.g., glass) primary receptacles;

(b) The total combined gross mass of primary receptacles shall not exceed one half the gross mass of primary receptacles used for the drop test in (a) above;

(c) The thickness of cushioning between primary receptacles and between primary receptacles and the outside of the secondary packaging shall not be reduced below the corresponding thicknesses in the originally tested packaging; and if a single primary receptacle was used in the original test, the thickness of cushioning between primary receptacles shall not be less than the thickness of cushioning between the outside of the secondary packaging and the primary receptacle in the original test. When either fewer or smaller primary receptacles are used (as compared to the primary receptacles used in the drop test), sufficient additional cushioning material shall be used to take up the void spaces;

(d) The rigid outer packaging shall have successfully passed the stacking test in 6.1.5.6 while empty. The total mass of identical packages shall be based on the combined mass of the packagings used in the drop test in (a) above;

(e) For primary receptacles containing liquids, an adequate quantity of absorbent material to absorb the entire liquid content of the primary receptacles shall be present;

(f) If the rigid outer packaging is intended to contain primary receptacles for liquids and is not leakproof, or is intended to contain primary receptacles for solids and is not siftproof, a means of containing any liquid or solid contents in the event of leakage shall be provided in the form of a leakproof liner, plastics bag or other equally effective means of containment;

(g) In addition to the marks prescribed in 6.3.4.2 (a) to (f), packagings shall be marked in accordance with 6.3.4.2 (g).

6.3.5.1.7　　The competent authority may at any time require proof, by tests in accordance with this section, that serially-produced packagings meet the requirements of the design type tests.

6.3.5.1.8　　Provided the validity of the test results is not affected and with the approval of the competent authority, several tests may be made on one sample.

6.3.5.2　　*Preparation of packagings for testing*

6.3.5.2.1　　Samples of each packaging shall be prepared as for transport except that a liquid or solid infectious substance shall be replaced by water or, where conditioning at $-18\ °C$ is specified, by water/antifreeze. Each primary receptacle shall be filled to not less than 98 % of its capacity.

NOTE:　　*The term water includes water/antifreeze solution with a minimum specific gravity of 0.95 for testing at $-18\ °C$.*

6.3.5.2.2   *Tests and number of samples required*

Tests required for packaging types

Type of packaging [a]			Tests required					
Rigid outer packaging	Primary receptacle		Water spray 6.3.5.3.5.1	Cold conditioning 6.3.5.3.5.2	Drop 6.3.5.3	Additional drop 6.3.5.3.5.3	Puncture 6.3.5.4	Stack 6.1.5.6
	Plastics	Other	No. of samples	No. of samples	No. of samples	No. of samples	No. of samples	
Fibreboard box	x		5	5	10	Required on one sample when the packaging is intended to contain dry ice.	2	Required on three samples when testing a "U"-marked packaging as defined in 6.3.5.1.6 for specific provisions.
		x	5	0	5		2	
Fibreboard drum	x		3	3	6		2	
		x	3	0	3		2	
Plastics box	x		0	5	5		2	
		x	0	5	5		2	
Plastics drum/ jerrican	x		0	3	3		2	
		x	0	3	3		2	
Boxes of other material	x		0	5	5		2	
		x	0	0	5		2	
Drums/ jerricans of other material	x		0	3	3		2	
		x	0	0	3		2	

[a] "Type of packaging" categorizes packagings for test purposes according to the kind of packaging and its material characteristics.

NOTE 1:   In instances where a primary receptacle is made of two or more materials, the material most liable to damage determines the appropriate test.

NOTE 2:   The material of the secondary packagings are not taken into consideration when selecting the test or conditioning for the test.

Explanation for use of the table:

If the packaging to be tested consists of a fibreboard outer box with a plastics primary receptacle, five samples must undergo the water spray test (see 6.3.5.3.5.1) prior to dropping and another five must be conditioned to – 18 °C (see 6.3.5.3.5.2) prior to dropping. If the packaging is to contain dry ice then one further single sample shall be dropped in accordance with 6.3.5.3.5.3.

Packagings prepared as for transport shall be subjected to the tests in 6.3.5.3 and 6.3.5.4. For outer packagings, the headings in the table relate to fibreboard or similar materials whose performance may be rapidly affected by moisture; plastics which may embrittle at low temperature; and other materials such as metal whose performance is not affected by moisture or temperature.

6.3.5.3   Drop test

6.3.5.3.1   *Drop height and target*

Samples shall be subjected to free-fall drops from a height of 9 m onto a non-resilient, horizontal, flat, massive and rigid surface in conformity with 6.1.5.3.4.

6.3.5.3.2   *Number of test samples and drop orientation*

6.3.5.3.2.1   Where the samples are in the shape of a box; five shall be dropped one in each of the following orientations:

   (a)   flat on the base;

(b) flat on the top;

(c) flat on the longest side;

(d) flat on the shortest side;

(e) on a corner.

6.3.5.3.2.2 Where the samples are in the shape of a drum or a jerrican, three shall be dropped one in each of the following orientations:

(a) diagonally on the top edge, with the centre of gravity directly above the point of impact;

(b) diagonally on the base edge;

(c) flat on the body or side.

6.3.5.3.3 While the sample shall be released in the required orientation, it is accepted that for aerodynamic reasons the impact may not take place in that orientation.

6.3.5.3.4 Following the appropriate drop sequence, there shall be no leakage from the primary receptacle(s) which shall remain protected by cushioning/absorbent material in the secondary packaging.

6.3.5.3.5 *Special preparation of test sample for the drop test*

6.3.5.3.5.1 Fibreboard - Water spray test

Fibreboard outer packagings: The sample shall be subjected to a water spray that simulates exposure to rainfall of approximately 5 cm per hour for at least one hour. It shall then be subjected to the test described in 6.3.5.3.1.

6.3.5.3.5.2 Plastics material – Cold conditioning

Plastics primary receptacles or outer packagings: The temperature of the test sample and its contents shall be reduced to -18 °C or lower for a period of at least 24 hours and within 15 minutes of removal from that atmosphere the test sample shall be subjected to the test described in 6.3.5.3.1. Where the sample contains dry ice, the conditioning period shall be reduced to 4 hours.

6.3.5.3.5.3 Packagings intended to contain dry ice – Additional drop test

Where the packaging is intended to contain dry ice, a test additional to that specified in 6.3.5.3.1 and, when appropriate, in 6.3.5.3.5.1 or 6.3.5.3.5.2 shall be carried out. One sample shall be stored so that all the dry ice dissipates and then that sample shall be dropped in one of the orientations described in 6.3.5.3.2.1 or in 6.3.5.3.2.2, as appropriate; which shall be that most likely to result in failure of the packaging.

6.3.5.4 *Puncture test*

6.3.5.4.1 *Packagings with a gross mass of 7 kg or less*

Samples shall be placed on a level hard surface. A cylindrical steel rod with a mass of at least 7 kg, a diameter of 38 mm and the impact end edges a radius not exceeding 6 mm (see figure 6.3.1), shall be dropped in a vertical free fall from a height of 1 m, measured from the impact end to the impact surface of the sample. One sample shall be placed on its base. A second sample shall be placed in an orientation perpendicular to that used for the first. In each instance the steel rod shall be aimed to impact the primary receptacle. Following each impact, penetration of the secondary packaging is acceptable, provided that there is no leakage from the primary receptacle(s);

6.3.5.4.2   *Packagings with a gross mass exceeding 7 kg*

Samples shall be dropped on to the end of a cylindrical steel rod. The rod shall be set vertically in a level hard surface. It shall have a diameter of 38 mm and the edges of its upper end shall have a radius not exceeding 6 mm (see figure 6.3.1). The rod shall protrude from the surface a distance at least equal to that between the centre of the primary receptacle(s) and the outer surface of the outer packaging with a minimum of 200 mm. One sample shall be dropped with its top face lowermost in a vertical free fall from a height of 1 m, measured from the top of the steel rod. A second sample shall be dropped from the same height in an orientation perpendicular to that used for the first. In each instance the packaging shall be so orientated that the steel rod would be capable of penetrating the primary receptacle(s). Following each impact, penetration of the secondary packaging is acceptable provided that there is no leakage from the primary receptacle(s).

Figure 6.3.1

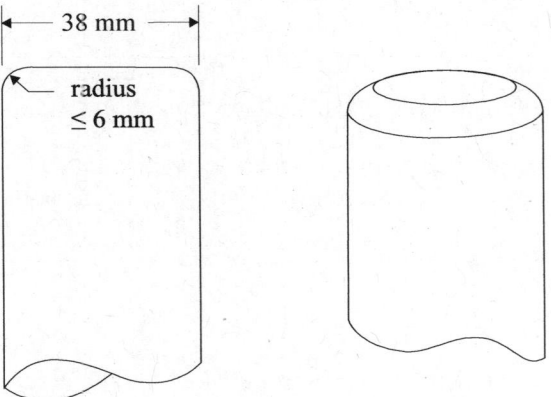

6.3.5.5   *Test report*

6.3.5.5.1   A written test report containing at least the following particulars shall be drawn up and shall be available to the users of the packaging:

1. Name and address of the test facility;

2. Name and address of applicant (where appropriate);

3. A unique test report identification;

4. Date of the test and of the report;

5. Manufacturer of the packaging;

6. Description of the packaging design type (e.g. dimensions, materials, closures, thickness, etc.), including method of manufacture (e.g. blow moulding) and which may include drawing(s) and/or photograph(s);

7. Maximum capacity;

8. Test contents;

9. Test descriptions and results;

10. The test report shall be signed with the name and status of the signatory.

6.3.5.5.2   The test report shall contain statements that the packaging prepared as for transport was tested in accordance with the appropriate requirements of this chapter and that the use of other packaging methods or components may render it invalid. A copy of the test report shall be available to the competent authority.

CHAPTER 6.4

REQUIREMENTS FOR THE CONSTRUCTION, TESTING AND APPROVAL OF PACKAGES FOR RADIOACTIVE MATERIAL AND FOR THE APPROVAL OF SUCH MATERIAL

6.4.1 *Reserved.*

6.4.2 **General requirements**

6.4.2.1 The package shall be so designed in relation to its mass, volume and shape that it can be easily and safely transported. In addition, the package shall be so designed that it can be properly secured in or on the conveyance during transport.

6.4.2.2 The design shall be such that any lifting attachments on the package will not fail when used in the intended manner and that, if failure of the attachments should occur, the ability of the package to meet other requirements of these Regulations would not be impaired. The design shall take account of appropriate safety factors to cover snatch lifting.

6.4.2.3 Attachments and any other features on the outer surface of the package which could be used to lift it shall be designed either to support its mass in accordance with the requirements of 6.4.2.2 or shall be removable or otherwise rendered incapable of being used during transport.

6.4.2.4 As far as practicable, the packaging shall be so designed that the external surfaces are free from protruding features and can be easily decontaminated.

6.4.2.5 As far as practicable, the outer layer of the package shall be so designed as to prevent the collection and the retention of water.

6.4.2.6 Any features added to the package at the time of transport which are not part of the package shall not reduce its safety.

6.4.2.7 The package shall be capable of withstanding the effects of any acceleration, vibration or vibration resonance which may arise under routine conditions of transport without any deterioration in the effectiveness of the closing devices on the various receptacles or in the integrity of the package as a whole. In particular, nuts, bolts and other securing devices shall be so designed as to prevent them from becoming loose or being released unintentionally, even after repeated use.

6.4.2.8 The design of the package shall take into account ageing mechanisms.

6.4.2.9 The materials of the packaging and any components or structures shall be physically and chemically compatible with each other and with the radioactive contents. Account shall be taken of their behaviour under irradiation.

6.4.2.10 All valves through which the radioactive contents could escape shall be protected against unauthorized operation.

6.4.2.11 The design of the package shall take into account ambient temperatures and pressures that are likely to be encountered in routine conditions of transport.

6.4.2.12 A package shall be so designed that it provides sufficient shielding to ensure that, under routine conditions of transport and with the maximum radioactive contents that the package is designed to contain, the dose rate at any point on the external surface of the package would not exceed the values specified in 2.7.2.4.1.2, 4.1.9.1.11 and 4.1.9.1.12, as applicable, with account taken of 7.1.8.3.3 (b) and 7.2.3.1.2.

6.4.2.13   For radioactive material having other dangerous properties the package design shall take into account those properties; see 2.0.3.1, 2.0.3.2 and 4.1.9.1.5.

6.4.2.14   Manufacturers and subsequent distributors of packagings shall provide information regarding procedures to be followed and a description of the types and dimensions of closures (including required gaskets) and any other components needed to ensure that packages as presented for transport are capable of passing the applicable performance tests of this chapter.

6.4.3   Additional requirements for packages transported by air

6.4.3.1   For packages to be transported by air, the temperature of the accessible surfaces shall not exceed 50 °C at an ambient temperature of 38 °C with no account taken for insolation.

6.4.3.2   Packages to be transported by air shall be so designed that, if they were exposed to ambient temperatures ranging from -40 °C to +55 °C, the integrity of containment would not be impaired.

6.4.3.3   Packages containing radioactive material, to be transported by air, shall be capable of withstanding, without loss or dispersal of radioactive contents from the containment system, an internal pressure which produces a pressure differential of not less than maximum normal operating pressure plus 95 kPa.

6.4.4   Requirements for excepted packages

An excepted package shall be designed to meet the requirements specified in 6.4.2.1-6.4.2.13 and in addition, the requirements of 6.4.7.2 if it contains fissile material allowed by one of the provisions of 2.7.2.3.5 (a) to (f), and the requirements of 6.4.3 if carried by air.

6.4.5   Requirements for industrial packages

6.4.5.1   Type IP-1, IP-2, and IP-3 packages shall meet the requirements specified in 6.4.2 and 6.4.7.2, and, if appropriate, the additional requirements for packages transported by air specified in 6.4.3.

6.4.5.2   A Type IP-2 package shall, if it were subjected to the tests specified in 6.4.15.4 and 6.4.15.5, prevent:

(a) Loss or dispersal of the radioactive contents; and

(b) More than a 20 % increase in the maximum dose rate at any external surface of the package.

6.4.5.3   A Type IP-3 package shall meet all the requirements specified in 6.4.7.2 to 6.4.7.15.

6.4.5.4   *Alternative requirements for Type IP-2 and IP-3 packages*

6.4.5.4.1   Packages may be used as Type IP-2 package provided that:

(a) They satisfy the requirements of 6.4.5.1;

(b) They are designed to satisfy the requirements prescribed for packing group I or II in chapter 6.1 of these Regulations; and

(c) When subjected to the tests required for packing group I or II in chapter 6.1, they would prevent:

  (i) loss or dispersal of the radioactive contents; and

  (ii) more than a 20 % increase in the maximum dose rate at any external surface of the package.

6.4.5.4.2   Portable tanks may also be used as Type IP-2 or IP-3 packages, provided that:

(a)   They satisfy the requirements of 6.4.5.1;

(b)   They are designed to satisfy the requirements prescribed in chapter 6.7 of these Regulations and are capable of withstanding a test pressure of 265 kPa; and

(c)   They are designed so that any additional shielding which is provided shall be capable of withstanding the static and dynamic stresses resulting from handling and routine conditions of transport and of preventing more than a 20 % increase in the maximum dose rate at any external surface of the portable tanks.

6.4.5.4.3   Tanks, other than portable tanks, may also be used as Type IP-2 or IP-3 package for transporting LSA-I and LSA-II as prescribed in table 4.1.9.2.5, provided that:

(a)   They satisfy the requirements of 6.4.5.1;

(b)   They are designed to satisfy the requirements prescribed in regional or national regulations for the transport of dangerous goods and are capable of withstanding a test pressure of 265 kPa; and

(c)   They are designed so that any additional shielding which is provided shall be capable of withstanding the static and dynamic stresses resulting from handling and routine conditions of transport and of preventing more than a 20 % increase in the maximum dose rate at any external surface of the tanks.

6.4.5.4.4   Freight containers with the characteristics of a permanent enclosure may also be used as Type IP-2 or IP-3 package, provided that:

(a)   The radioactive contents are restricted to solid materials;

(b)   They satisfy the requirements of 6.4.5.1; and

(c)   They are designed to conform to ISO 1496-1:1990 "Series 1 Freight Containers – Specifications and Testing – Part 1: General Cargo Containers" and subsequent amendments 1:1993, 2:1998, 3:2005, 4:2006 and 5:2006, excluding dimensions and ratings. They shall be designed such that if subjected to the tests prescribed in that document and the accelerations occurring during routine conditions of transport they would prevent:

(i)   loss or dispersal of the radioactive contents; and

(ii) more than a 20 % increase in the maximum dose rate at any external surface of the freight containers.

6.4.5.4.5   Metal intermediate bulk containers may also be used as Type IP-2 or IP-3 package provided that:

(a)   They satisfy the requirements of 6.4.5.1; and

(b)   They are designed to satisfy the requirements prescribed in chapter 6.5 of these Regulations for packing group I or II, and if they were subjected to the tests prescribed in that chapter, but with the drop test conducted in the most damaging orientation, they would prevent:

(i)   loss or dispersal of the radioactive contents; and

(ii) more than a 20 % increase in the maximum dose rate at any external surface of the intermediate bulk container.

6.4.6 Requirements for packages containing uranium hexafluoride

6.4.6.1   Packages designed to contain uranium hexafluoride shall meet the requirements which pertain to the radioactive and fissile properties of the material prescribed elsewhere in these Regulations. Except as allowed in 6.4.6.4, uranium hexafluoride in quantities of 0.1 kg or more shall also be packaged and transported in accordance with the provisions of ISO 7195:2005 "Nuclear Energy – Packaging of uranium hexafluoride (UF_6) for transport", and the requirements of 6.4.6.2 and 6.4.6.3.

6.4.6.2   Each package designed to contain 0.1 kg or more of uranium hexafluoride shall be designed so that the package would meet the following requirements:

(a) Withstand without leakage and without unacceptable stress, as specified in ISO 7195:2005, the structural test as specified in 6.4.21 except as allowed in 6.4.6.4;

(b) Withstand without loss or dispersal of the uranium hexafluoride the free drop test specified in 6.4.15.4; and

(c) Withstand without rupture of the containment system the thermal test specified in 6.4.17.3 except as allowed in 6.4.6.4.

6.4.6.3   Packages designed to contain 0.1 kg or more of uranium hexafluoride shall not be provided with pressure relief devices.

6.4.6.4   Subject to multilateral approval, packages designed to contain 0.1 kg or more of uranium hexafluoride may be transported if the packages are designed:

(a) to international or national standards other than ISO 7195:2005 provided an equivalent level of safety is maintained;

(b) to withstand without leakage and without unacceptable stress a test pressure of less than 2.76 MPa as specified in 6.4.21; and/or

(c) to contain 9 000 kg or more of uranium hexafluoride and the packages do not meet the requirement of 6.4.6.2 (c).

In all other respects the requirements specified in 6.4.6.1 to 6.4.6.3 shall be satisfied.

6.4.7 Requirements for Type A packages

6.4.7.1   Type A packages shall be designed to meet the general requirements of 6.4.2, the requirements of 6.4.3 if transported by air, and of 6.4.7.2 to 6.4.7.17.

6.4.7.2   The smallest overall external dimension of the package shall not be less than 10 cm.

6.4.7.3   The outside of the package shall incorporate a feature such as a seal, which is not readily breakable and which, while intact, will be evidence that it has not been opened.

6.4.7.4   Any tie-down attachments on the package shall be so designed that, under normal and accident conditions of transport, the forces in those attachments shall not impair the ability of the package to meet the requirements of these Regulations.

6.4.7.5   The design of the package shall take into account temperatures ranging from -40 °C to +70 °C for the components of the packaging. Attention shall be given to freezing temperatures for liquids and to the potential degradation of packaging materials within the given temperature range.

6.4.7.6   The design and manufacturing techniques shall be in accordance with national or international standards, or other requirements, acceptable to the competent authority.

6.4.7.7   The design shall include a containment system securely closed by a positive fastening device which cannot be opened unintentionally or by a pressure which may arise within the package.

6.4.7.8   Special form radioactive material may be considered as a component of the containment system.

6.4.7.9   If the containment system forms a separate unit of the package, the containment system shall be capable of being securely closed by a positive fastening device which is independent of any other part of the packaging.

6.4.7.10   The design of any component of the containment system shall take into account, where applicable, the radiolytic decomposition of liquids and other vulnerable materials and the generation of gas by chemical reaction and radiolysis.

6.4.7.11   The containment system shall retain its radioactive contents under a reduction of ambient pressure to 60 kPa.

6.4.7.12   All valves, other than pressure relief valves, shall be provided with an enclosure to retain any leakage from the valve.

6.4.7.13   A radiation shield which encloses a component of the package specified as a part of the containment system shall be so designed as to prevent the unintentional release of that component from the shield. Where the radiation shield and such component within it form a separate unit, the radiation shield shall be capable of being securely closed by a positive fastening device which is independent of any other packaging structure.

6.4.7.14   A package shall be so designed that if it were subjected to the tests specified in 6.4.15, it would prevent:

(a) Loss or dispersal of the radioactive contents; and

(b) More than a 20 % increase in the maximum dose rate at any external surface of the package.

6.4.7.15   The design of a package intended for liquid radioactive material shall make provision for ullage to accommodate variations in the temperature of the contents, dynamic effects and filling dynamics.

Type A packages to contain liquids

6.4.7.16   A Type A package designed to contain liquid radioactive material shall, in addition:

(a) Be adequate to meet the conditions specified in 6.4.7.14 (a) above if the package is subjected to the tests specified in 6.4.16; and

(b) Either

(i) be provided with sufficient absorbent material to absorb twice the volume of the liquid contents. Such absorbent material shall be suitably positioned so as to contact the liquid in the event of leakage; or

(ii) be provided with a containment system composed of primary inner and secondary outer containment components designed to enclose the liquid contents completely and ensure their retention, within the secondary outer containment components, even if the primary inner components leak.

Type A packages to contain gas

6.4.7.17   A Type A package designed for gases shall prevent loss or dispersal of the radioactive contents if the package were subjected to the tests specified in 6.4.16, except for a Type A package designed for tritium gas or for noble gases.

6.4.8 Requirements for Type B(U) packages

6.4.8.1 Type B(U) packages shall be designed to meet the requirements specified in 6.4.2, the requirements specified in 6.4.3 if carried by air, and of 6.4.7.2 to 6.4.7.15, except as specified in 6.4.7.14 (a), and, in addition, the requirements specified in 6.4.8.2 to 6.4.8.15.

6.4.8.2 A package shall be so designed that, under the ambient conditions specified in 6.4.8.5 and 6.4.8.6 heat generated within the package by the radioactive contents shall not, under normal conditions of transport, as demonstrated by the tests in 6.4.15, adversely affect the package in such a way that it would fail to meet the applicable requirements for containment and shielding if left unattended for a period of one week. Particular attention shall be paid to the effects of heat, which may cause one or more of the following:

(a) Alter the arrangement, the geometrical form or the physical state of the radioactive contents or, if the radioactive material is enclosed in a can or receptacle (for example, clad fuel elements), cause the can, receptacle or radioactive material to deform or melt;

(b) Lessening of the efficiency of the packaging through differential thermal expansion or cracking or melting of the radiation shielding material;

(c) In combination with moisture, accelerate corrosion.

6.4.8.3 A package shall be so designed that, under the ambient condition specified in 6.4.8.5 and in the absence of insolation, the temperature of the accessible surfaces of a package shall not exceed 50 °C, unless the package is transported under exclusive use.

6.4.8.4 Except as required in 6.4.3.1 for a package transported by air, the maximum temperature of any surface readily accessible during transport of a package under exclusive use shall not exceed 85 °C in the absence of insolation under the ambient conditions specified in 6.4.8.5. Account may be taken of barriers or screens intended to give protection to persons without the need for the barriers or screens being subject to any test.

6.4.8.5 The ambient temperature shall be assumed to be 38 °C.

6.4.8.6 The solar insolation conditions shall be assumed to be as specified in table 6.4.8.6.

Table 6.4.8.6: Insolation data

Case	Form and location of surface	Insolation for 12 hours per day (W/m^2)
1	Flat surfaces transported horizontally-downward facing	0
2	Flat surfaces transported horizontally-upward facing	800
3	Surfaces transported vertically	200[a]
4	Other downward facing (not horizontal) surfaces	200[a]
5	All other surfaces	400[a]

[a] *Alternatively, a sine function may be used, with an absorption coefficient adopted and the effects of possible reflection from neighbouring objects neglected.*

6.4.8.7 A package which includes thermal protection for the purpose of satisfying the requirements of the thermal test specified in 6.4.17.3 shall be so designed that such protection will remain effective if the package is subjected to the tests specified in 6.4.15 and 6.4.17.2 (a) and (b) or 6.4.17.2 (b) and (c), as appropriate. Any such protection on the exterior of the package shall not be rendered ineffective by ripping, cutting, skidding, abrasion or rough handling.

6.4.8.8 A package shall be so designed that, if it were subjected to:

(a) The tests specified in 6.4.15, it would restrict the loss of radioactive contents to not more than 10^{-6} A_2 per hour; and

(b) The tests specified in 6.4.17.1, 6.4.17.2 (b), 6.4.17.3, and 6.4.17.4 and either the test in:

    (i) 6.4.17.2 (c), when the package has a mass not greater than 500 kg, an overall density not greater than 1 000 kg/m^3 based on the external dimensions, and radioactive contents greater than 1 000 A_2 not as special form radioactive material; or

    (ii) 6.4.17.2 (a), for all other packages;

it would meet the following requirements:

- Retain sufficient shielding to ensure that the dose rate at 1 m from the surface of the package would not exceed 10 mSv/h with the maximum radioactive contents which the package is designed to contain; and

- Restrict the accumulated loss of radioactive contents in a period of one week to not more than 10 A_2 for krypton-85 and not more than A_2 for all other radionuclides.

Where mixtures of different radionuclides are present, the provisions of 2.7.2.2.4 to 2.7.2.2.6 shall apply except that for krypton-85 an effective $A_2(i)$ value equal to 10 A_2 may be used. For case (a) above, the assessment shall take into account the external non-fixed contamination limits of 4.1.9.1.2.

6.4.8.9 A package for radioactive contents with activity greater than 10^5 A_2 shall be so designed that if it were subjected to the enhanced water immersion test specified in 6.4.18, there would be no rupture of the containment system.

6.4.8.10 Compliance with the permitted activity release limits shall depend neither upon filters nor upon a mechanical cooling system.

6.4.8.11 A package shall not include a pressure relief system from the containment system which would allow the release of radioactive material to the environment under the conditions of the tests specified in 6.4.15 and 6.4.17.

6.4.8.12 A package shall be so designed that if it were at the maximum normal operating pressure and it were subjected to the tests specified in 6.4.15 and 6.4.17, the level of strains in the containment system would not attain values which would adversely affect the package in such a way that it would fail to meet the applicable requirements.

6.4.8.13 A package shall not have a maximum normal operating pressure in excess of a gauge pressure of 700 kPa.

6.4.8.14 A package containing low dispersible radioactive material shall be so designed that any features added to the low dispersible radioactive material that are not part of it, or any internal components of the packaging shall not adversely affect the performance of the low dispersible radioactive material.

6.4.8.15 A package shall be designed for an ambient temperature range from -40 °C to +38 °C.

6.4.9 Requirements for Type B(M) packages

6.4.9.1 Type B(M) packages shall meet the requirements for Type B(U) packages specified in 6.4.8.1, except that for packages to be transported solely within a specified country or solely between specified countries, conditions other than those given in 6.4.7.5, 6.4.8.4 to 6.4.8.6, and 6.4.8.9 to 6.4.8.15 above may be assumed with the approval of the competent authorities of these countries. The requirements for Type B(U) packages specified in 6.4.8.4, 6.4.8.9 to 6.4.8.15 shall be met as far as practicable.

6.4.9.2　　　　Intermittent venting of Type B(M) packages may be permitted during transport, provided that the operational controls for venting are acceptable to the relevant competent authorities.

6.4.10　　Requirements for Type C packages

6.4.10.1　　　Type C packages shall be designed to meet the requirements specified in 6.4.2 and 6.4.3, and of 6.4.7.2 to 6.4.7.15, except as specified in 6.4.7.14 (a), and of the requirements specified in 6.4.8.2 to 6.4.8.6, 6.4.8.10 to 6.4.8.15, and, in addition, of 6.4.10.2 to 6.4.10.4.

6.4.10.2　　　A package shall be capable of meeting the assessment criteria prescribed for tests in 6.4.8.8 (b) and 6.4.8.12 after burial in an environment defined by a thermal conductivity of 0.33 W/(m·K) and a temperature of 38 °C in the steady state. Initial conditions for the assessment shall assume that any thermal insulation of the package remains intact, the package is at the maximum normal operating pressure and the ambient temperature is 38 °C.

6.4.10.3　　　A package shall be so designed that, if it were at the maximum normal operating pressure and subjected to:

(a) The tests specified in 6.4.15, it would restrict the loss of radioactive contents to not more than 10^{-6} A_2 per hour; and

(b) The test sequences in 6.4.20.1,

(i) it would retain sufficient shielding to ensure that the dose rate at 1 m from the surface of the package would not exceed 10 mSv/h with the maximum radioactive contents which the package is designed to contain; and

(ii) it would restrict the accumulated loss of radioactive contents in a period of 1 week to not more than 10 A_2 for krypton-85 and not more than A_2 for all other radionuclides.

Where mixtures of different radionuclides are present, the provisions of 2.7.2.2.4 to 2.7.2.2.6 shall apply except that for krypton-85 an effective $A_2(i)$ value equal to 10 A_2 may be used. For case (a) above, the assessment shall take into account the external contamination limits of 4.1.9.1.2.

6.4.10.4　　　A package shall be so designed that there will be no rupture of the containment system following performance of the enhanced water immersion test specified in 6.4.18.

6.4.11　　Requirements for packages containing fissile material

6.4.11.1　　　Fissile material shall be transported so as to;

(a) Maintain subcriticality during routine, normal and accident conditions of transport; in particular, the following contingencies shall be considered:

(i) water leaking into or out of packages;

(ii) the loss of efficiency of built-in neutron absorbers or moderators;

(iii) rearrangement of the contents either within the package or as a result of loss from the package;

(iv) reduction of spaces within or between packages;

(v) packages becoming immersed in water or buried in snow; and

(vi) temperature changes; and

(b) Meet the requirements:

(i) of 6.4.7.2 except for unpackaged material when specifically allowed by 2.7.2.3.5 (e);

(ii) prescribed elsewhere in these Regulations which pertain to the radioactive properties of the material;

(iii) of 6.4.7.3 unless the material is excepted by 2.7.2.3.5;

(iv) of 6.4.11.4 to 6.4.11.14, unless the material is excepted by 2.7.2.3.5, 6.4.11.2 or 6.4.11.3.

6.4.11.2 Packages containing fissile material that meet the provisions of subparagraph (d) and one of the provisions of (a) to (c) below are excepted from the requirements of 6.4.11.4 to 6.4.11.14.

(a) Packages containing fissile material in any form provided that:

(i) The smallest external dimension of the package is not less than 10 cm;

(ii) The criticality safety index of the package is calculated using the following formula:

$$CSI = 50 \times 5 \times \left(\frac{\text{Mass of U-235 in package (g)}}{Z} + \frac{\text{Mass of other fissile nuclides* in package (g)}}{280} \right)$$

* Plutonium may be of any isotopic composition provided that the amount of Pu-241 is less than that of Pu-240 in the package

where the values of Z are taken from table 6.4.11.2.

(iii) The CSI of any package does not exceed 10;

(b) Packages containing fissile material in any form provided that:

(i) The smallest external dimension of the package is not less than 30 cm;

(ii) The package, after being subjected to the tests specified in 6.4.15.1 to 6.4.15.6;

- Retains its fissile material contents;

- Preserves the minimum overall outside dimensions of the package to at least 30 cm;

- Prevents the entry of a 10 cm cube.

(iii) The criticality safety index of the package is calculated using the following formula:

$$CSI = 50 \times 2 \times \left(\frac{\text{Mass of U-235 in package (g)}}{Z} + \frac{\text{Mass of other fissile nuclides* in package (g)}}{280} \right)$$

* Plutonium may be of any isotopic composition provided that the amount of Pu-241 is less than that of Pu-240 in the package

where the values of Z are taken from table 6.4.11.2.

(iv) The criticality safety index of any package does not exceed 10;

(c) Packages containing fissile material in any form provided that:

(i) The smallest external dimension of the package is not less than 10 cm;

(ii) The package, after being subjected to the tests specified in 6.4.15.1 to 6.4.15.6;

- Retains its fissile material contents;

- Preserves the minimum overall outside dimensions of the package to at least 10 cm;

- Prevents the entry of a 10 cm cube.

(iii) The CSI of the package is calculated using the following formula:

$$CSI = 50 \times 2 \times \left(\frac{\text{Mass of U-235 in package (g)}}{450} + \frac{\text{Mass of other fissile nuclides* in package (g)}}{280} \right)$$

* Plutonium may be of any isotopic composition provided that the amount of Pu-241 is less than that of Pu-240 in the package

(iv) The total mass of fissile nuclides in any package does not exceed 15 g;

(d) The total mass of beryllium, hydrogenous material enriched in deuterium, graphite and other allotropic forms of carbon in an individual package shall not be greater than the mass of fissile nuclides in the package except where the total concentration of these materials does not exceed 1 g in any 1 000 g of material. Beryllium incorporated in copper alloys up to 4 % in weight of the alloy does not need to be considered.

Table 6.4.11.2: Values of Z for calculation of criticality safety index in accordance with 6.4.11.2

Enrichement[a]	Z
Uranium enriched up to 1.5 %	2200
Uranium enriched up to 5 %	850
Uranium enriched up to 10 %	660
Uranium enriched up to 20 %	580
Uranium enriched up to 100 %	450

[a] *If a package contains uranium with varying enrichments of U-235, then the value corresponding to the highest enrichment shall be used for Z.*

6.4.11.3 Packages containing not more than 1 000 g of plutonium are excepted from the application of 6.4.11.4 to 6.4.11.14 provided that:

(a) Not more than 20 % of the plutonium by mass is fissile nuclides;

(b) The criticality safety index of the package is calculated using the following formula:

$$CSI = 50 \times 2 \times \frac{\text{mass of plutonium (g)}}{1000}$$

(c) If uranium is present with the plutonium, the mass of uranium shall be no more than 1 % of the mass of the plutonium.

6.4.11.4 Where the chemical or physical form, isotopic composition, mass or concentration, moderation ratio or density, or geometric configuration is not known, the assessments of 6.4.11.8 to 6.4.11.13 shall be performed assuming that each parameter that is not known has the value which gives the maximum neutron multiplication consistent with the known conditions and parameters in these assessments.

6.4.11.5 For irradiated nuclear fuel the assessments of 6.4.11.8 to 6.4.11.13 shall be based on an isotopic composition demonstrated to provide either:

(a) The maximum neutron multiplication during the irradiation history; or

(b) A conservative estimate of the neutron multiplication for the package assessments. After irradiation but prior to shipment, a measurement shall be performed to confirm the conservatism of the isotopic composition.

6.4.11.6 The package, after being subjected to the tests specified in 6.4.15, shall:

(a) Preserve the minimum overall outside dimensions of the package to at least 10 cm; and

(b) Prevent the entry of a 10 cm cube.

6.4.11.7 The package shall be designed for an ambient temperature range of -40 °C to +38 °C unless the competent authority specifies otherwise in the certificate of approval for the package design.

6.4.11.8 For a package in isolation, it shall be assumed that water can leak into or out of all void spaces of the package, including those within the containment system. However, if the design incorporates special features to prevent such leakage of water into or out of certain void spaces, even as a result of error, absence of leakage may be assumed in respect of those void spaces. Special features shall include either of the following:

(a) Multiple high standard water barriers, not less than two of which would remain watertight if the package were subject to the tests prescribed in 6.4.11.13 (b), a high degree of quality control in the manufacture, maintenance and repair of packagings and tests to demonstrate the closure of each package before each shipment; or

(b) For packages containing uranium hexafluoride only, with maximum enrichment of 5 mass percent uranium-235:

(i) packages where, following the tests prescribed in 6.4.11.13 (b), there is no physical contact between the valve or the plug and any other component of the packaging other than at its original point of attachment and where, in addition, following the test prescribed in 6.4.17.3 the valves and the plug remain leaktight; and

(ii) a high degree of quality control in the manufacture, maintenance and repair of packagings coupled with tests to demonstrate closure of each package before each shipment.

6.4.11.9 It shall be assumed that the confinement system is closely reflected by at least 20 cm of water or such greater reflection as may additionally be provided by the surrounding material of the packaging. However, when it can be demonstrated that the confinement system remains within the packaging following the tests prescribed in 6.4.11.13 (b), close reflection of the package by at least 20 cm of water may be assumed in 6.4.11.10 (c).

6.4.11.10 The package shall be subcritical under the conditions of 6.4.11.8 and 6.4.11.9 with the package conditions that result in the maximum neutron multiplication consistent with:

(a) Routine conditions of transport (incident free);

(b) The tests specified in 6.4.11.12 (b);

(c) The tests specified in 6.4.11.13 (b).

6.4.11.11 For packages to be transported by air:

(a) The package shall be subcritical under conditions consistent with the Type C package tests specified in 6.4.20.1 assuming reflection by at least 20 cm of water but no water inleakage; and

(b) In the assessment of 6.4.11.10, use of special features as specified in 6.4.11.8 is allowed provided that leakage of water into or out of the void spaces is prevented when the package is submitted to the Type C package tests specified in 6.4.20.1 followed by the water leakage test specified in 6.4.19.3.

6.4.11.12 A number "N" shall be derived, such that five times "N" packages shall be subcritical for the arrangement and package conditions that provide the maximum neutron multiplication consistent with the following:

(a) There shall not be anything between the packages, and the package arrangement shall be reflected on all sides by at least 20 cm of water; and

(b) The state of the packages shall be their assessed or demonstrated condition if they had been subjected to the tests specified in 6.4.15.

6.4.11.13 A number "N" shall be derived, such that two times "N" packages shall be subcritical for the arrangement and package conditions that provide the maximum neutron multiplication consistent with the following:

(a) Hydrogenous moderation between packages, and the package arrangement reflected on all sides by at least 20 cm of water; and

(b) The tests specified in 6.4.15 followed by whichever of the following is the more limiting:

(i) the tests specified in 6.4.17.2 (b) and, either 6.4.17.2 (c) for packages having a mass not greater than 500 kg and an overall density not greater than 1 000 kg/m^3 based on the external dimensions, or 6.4.17.2 (a) for all other packages; followed by the test specified in 6.4.17.3 and completed by the tests specified in 6.4.19.1 to 6.4.19.3; or

(ii) the test specified in 6.4.17.4; and

(c) Where any part of the fissile material escapes from the containment system following the tests specified in 6.4.11.13 (b), it shall be assumed that fissile material escapes from each package in the array and all of the fissile material shall be arranged in the configuration and moderation that results in the maximum neutron multiplication with close reflection by at least 20 cm of water.

6.4.11.14 The criticality safety index (CSI) for packages containing fissile material shall be obtained by dividing the number 50 by the smaller of the two values of N derived in 6.4.11.12 and 6.4.11.13 (i.e. CSI = 50/N). The value of the criticality safety index may be zero, provided that an unlimited number of packages is subcritical (i.e. N is effectively equal to infinity in both cases).

6.4.12 Test procedures and demonstration of compliance

6.4.12.1 Demonstration of compliance with the performance standards required in 2.7.2.3.3.1, 2.7.2.3.3.2, 2.7.2.3.4.1, 2.7.2.3.4.2, 2.7.2.3.4.3 and 6.4.2 to 6.4.11 must be accomplished by any of the methods listed below or by a combination thereof.

(a) Performance of tests with specimens representing special form radioactive material, or low dispersible radioactive material or with prototypes or samples of the packaging, where the contents of the specimen or the packaging for the tests shall simulate as closely as practicable the expected range of radioactive contents and the specimen or packaging to be tested shall be prepared as presented for transport;

(b) Reference to previous satisfactory demonstrations of a sufficiently similar nature;

(c) Performance of tests with models of appropriate scale incorporating those features which are significant with respect to the item under investigation when engineering experience has shown results of such tests to be suitable for design purposes. When a scale model is used, the need for adjusting certain test parameters, such as penetrator diameter or compressive load, shall be taken into account;

(d) Calculation, or reasoned argument, when the calculation procedures and parameters are generally agreed to be reliable or conservative.

6.4.12.2   After the specimen, prototype or sample has been subjected to the tests, appropriate methods of assessment shall be used to assure that the requirements for the test procedures have been fulfilled in compliance with the performance and acceptance standards prescribed in 2.7.2.3.3.1, 2.7.2.3.3.2, 2.7.2.3.4.1, 2.7.2.3.4.2, 2.7.2.3.4.3 and 6.4.2 to 6.4.11.

6.4.12.3   All specimens shall be inspected before testing in order to identify and record faults or damage including the following:

(a) Divergence from the design;

(b) Defects in manufacture;

(c) Corrosion or other deterioration; and

(d) Distortion of features.

The containment system of the package shall be clearly specified. The external features of the specimen shall be clearly identified so that reference may be made simply and clearly to any part of such specimen.

6.4.13   Testing the integrity of the containment system and shielding and evaluating criticality safety

After each test or group of tests or sequence of the applicable tests, as appropriate, specified in 6.4.15 to 6.4.21:

(a) Faults and damage shall be identified and recorded;

(b) It shall be determined whether the integrity of the containment system and shielding has been retained to the extent required in 6.4.2 to 6.4.11 for the package under test; and

(c) For packages containing fissile material, it shall be determined whether the assumptions and conditions used in the assessments required by 6.4.11.1 to 6.4.11.14 for one or more packages are valid.

6.4.14   Target for drop tests

The target for the drop tests specified in 2.7.2.3.3.5 (a), 6.4.15.4, 6.4.16 (a), 6.4.17.2 and 6.4.20.2 shall be a flat, horizontal surface of such a character that any increase in its resistance to displacement or deformation upon impact by the specimen would not significantly increase the damage to the specimen.

6.4.15   Test for demonstrating ability to withstand normal conditions of transport

6.4.15.1   The tests are: the water spray test, the free drop test, the stacking test and the penetration test. Specimens of the package shall be subjected to the free drop test, the stacking test and the penetration test, preceded in each case by the water spray test. One specimen may be used for all the tests, provided that the requirements of 6.4.15.2 are fulfilled.

6.4.15.2 The time interval between the conclusion of the water spray test and the succeeding test shall be such that the water has soaked in to the maximum extent, without appreciable drying of the exterior of the specimen. In the absence of any evidence to the contrary, this interval shall be taken to be two hours if the water spray is applied from four directions simultaneously. No time interval shall elapse, however, if the water spray is applied from each of the four directions consecutively.

6.4.15.3 Water spray test: The specimen shall be subjected to a water spray test that simulates exposure to rainfall of approximately 5 cm per hour for at least one hour.

6.4.15.4 Free drop test: The specimen shall drop onto the target so as to suffer maximum damage in respect of the safety features to be tested.

(a) The height of the drop measured from the lowest point of the specimen to the upper surface of the target, shall be not less than the distance specified in table 6.4.15.4 for the applicable mass. The target shall be as defined in 6.4.14;

(b) For rectangular fibreboard or wood packages not exceeding a mass of 50 kg, a separate specimen shall be subjected to a free drop onto each corner from a height of 0.3 m;

(c) For cylindrical fibreboard packages not exceeding a mass of 100 kg, a separate specimen shall be subjected to a free drop onto each of the quarters of each rim from a height of 0.3 m.

Table 6.4.15.4: Free drop distance for testing packages to normal conditions of transport

Package Mass (kg)	Free drop distance (m)
Package mass < 5 000	1.2
5 000 ≤ Package mass < 10 000	0.9
10 000 ≤ Package mass < 15 000	0.6
15 000 ≤ Package mass	0.3

6.4.15.5 Stacking test: Unless the shape of the packaging effectively prevents stacking, the specimen shall be subjected, for a period of 24 h, to a compressive load equal to the greater of the following:

(a) The equivalent of 5 times the maximum weight of the package;

(b) The equivalent of 13 kPa multiplied by the vertically projected area of the package.

The load shall be applied uniformly to two opposite sides of the specimen, one of which shall be the base on which the package would typically rest.

6.4.15.6 Penetration test: The specimen shall be placed on a rigid, flat, horizontal surface which will not move significantly while the test is being carried out.

(a) A bar of 3.2 cm in diameter with a hemispherical end and a mass of 6 kg shall be dropped and directed to fall, with its longitudinal axis vertical, onto the centre of the weakest part of the specimen, so that, if it penetrates sufficiently far, it will hit the containment system. The bar shall not be significantly deformed by the test performance;

(b) The height of the drop of the bar, measured from its lower end to the intended point of impact on the upper surface of the specimen, shall be 1 m.

6.4.16 **Additional tests for Type A packages designed for liquids and gases**

A specimen or separate specimens shall be subjected to each of the following tests unless it can be demonstrated that one test is more severe for the specimen in question than the other, in which case one specimen shall be subjected to the more severe test.

(a) Free drop test: The specimen shall drop onto the target so as to suffer the maximum damage in respect of containment. The height of the drop measured from the lowest part of the specimen to the upper surface of the target shall be 9 m. The target shall be as defined in 6.4.14;

(b) Penetration test: The specimen shall be subjected to the test specified in 6.4.15.6 except that the height of drop shall be increased to 1.7 m from the 1 m specified in 6.4.15.6 (b).

6.4.17 **Tests for demonstrating ability to withstand accident conditions in transport**

6.4.17.1 The specimen shall be subjected to the cumulative effects of the tests specified in 6.4.17.2 and 6.4.17.3, in that order. Following these tests, either this specimen or a separate specimen shall be subjected to the effect(s) of the water immersion test(s) as specified in 6.4.17.4 and, if applicable, 6.4.18.

6.4.17.2 *Mechanical test:* The mechanical test consists of three different drop tests. Each specimen shall be subjected to the applicable drops as specified in 6.4.8.8 or 6.4.11.13. The order in which the specimen is subjected to the drops shall be such that, on completion of the mechanical test, the specimen shall have suffered such damage as will lead to the maximum damage in the thermal test which follows.

(a) For drop I, the specimen shall drop onto the target so as to suffer the maximum damage, and the height of the drop measured from the lowest point of the specimen to the upper surface of the target shall be 9 m. The target shall be as defined in 6.4.14;

(b) For drop II, the specimen shall drop onto a bar rigidly mounted perpendicularly on the target so as to suffer the maximum damage. The height of the drop measured from the intended point of impact of the specimen to the upper surface of the bar shall be 1 m. The bar shall be of solid mild steel of circular cross-section, (15.0 ± 0.5) cm in diameter and 20 cm long unless a longer bar would cause greater damage, in which case a bar of sufficient length to cause maximum damage shall be used. The upper end of the bar shall be flat and horizontal with its edge rounded off to a radius of not more than 6 mm. The target on which the bar is mounted shall be as described in 6.4.14;

(c) For drop III, the specimen shall be subjected to a dynamic crush test by positioning the specimen on the target so as to suffer maximum damage by the drop of a 500 kg mass from 9 m onto the specimen. The mass shall consist of a solid mild steel plate 1 m by 1 m and shall fall in a horizontal attitude. The height of the drop shall be measured from the underside of the plate to the highest point of the specimen. The target on which the specimen rests shall be as defined in 6.4.14. The lower face of the steel plate shall have its edges and corners rounded off to a radius of not more than 6 mm.

6.4.17.3 *Thermal test:* The specimen shall be in thermal equilibrium under conditions of an ambient temperature of 38 °C, subject to the solar insolation conditions specified in table 6.4.8.6 and subject to the design maximum rate of internal heat generation within the package from the radioactive contents. Alternatively, any of these parameters are allowed to have different values prior to and during the test, providing due account is taken of them in the subsequent assessment of package response.

The thermal test shall then consist of:

(a) Exposure of a specimen for a period of 30 minutes to a thermal environment which provides a heat flux at least equivalent to that of a hydrocarbon fuel/air fire in sufficiently quiescent ambient conditions to give a minimum average flame emissivity coefficient of 0.9 and an average temperature of at least 800 °C, fully engulfing the specimen, with a surface absorbtivity coefficient of 0.8 or that value which the package may be demonstrated to possess if exposed to the fire specified, followed by;

(b) Exposure of the specimen to an ambient temperature of 38 °C, subject to the solar insolation conditions specified in table 6.4.8.6 and subject to the design maximum rate of internal heat generation within the package by the radioactive contents for a sufficient period to ensure that temperatures in the specimen are decreasing in all parts of the specimen and/or are approaching initial steady state conditions. Alternatively, any of these parameters are allowed to have different values following cessation of heating, providing due account is taken of them in the subsequent assessment of package response.

During and following the test the specimen shall not be artificially cooled and any combustion of materials of the specimen shall be permitted to proceed naturally.

6.4.17.4   *Water immersion test:* The specimen shall be immersed under a head of water of at least 15 m for a period of not less than eight hours in the attitude which will lead to maximum damage. For demonstration purposes, an external gauge pressure of at least 150 kPa shall be considered to meet these conditions.

6.4.18   Enhanced water immersion test for Type B(U) and Type B(M) packages containing more than 10^5 A_2 and Type C packages

Enhanced water immersion test: The specimen shall be immersed under a head of water of at least 200 m for a period of not less than one hour. For demonstration purposes, an external gauge pressure of at least 2 MPa shall be considered to meet these conditions.

6.4.19   Water leakage test for packages containing fissile material

6.4.19.1   Packages for which water in-leakage or out-leakage to the extent which results in greatest reactivity has been assumed for purposes of assessment under 6.4.11.8 to 6.4.11.13 shall be excepted from the test.

6.4.19.2   Before the specimen is subjected to the water leakage test specified below, it shall be subjected to the tests in 6.4.17.2 (b), and either 6.4.17.2 (a) or (c) as required by 6.4.11.13, and the test specified in 6.4.17.3.

6.4.19.3   The specimen shall be immersed under a head of water of at least 0.9 m for a period of not less than eight hours and in the attitude for which maximum leakage is expected.

6.4.20   Tests for Type C packages

6.4.20.1   Specimens shall be subjected to the effects of each of the following test sequences in the orders specified:

(a) The tests specified in 6.4.17.2 (a), 6.4.17.2 (c), 6.4.20.2 and 6.4.20.3; and

(b) The test specified in 6.4.20.4.

Separate specimens are allowed to be used for each of the sequences (a) and (b).

6.4.20.2   *Puncture/tearing test:* The specimen shall be subjected to the damaging effects of a vertical solid probe made of mild steel. The orientation of the package specimen and the impact point on the package surface shall be such as to cause maximum damage at the conclusion of the test sequence specified in 6.4.20.1 (a).

(a) The specimen, representing a package having a mass less than 250 kg, shall be placed on a target and subjected to a probe having a mass of 250 kg falling from a height of 3 m above the intended impact point. For this test the probe shall be a 20 cm diameter cylindrical bar with the striking end forming a frustum of a right circular cone with the following dimensions: 30 cm height and 2.5 cm in diameter at the top with its edge rounded off to a radius of not more than 6 mm. The target on which the specimen is placed shall be as specified in 6.4.14;

(b) For packages having a mass of 250 kg or more, the base of the probe shall be placed on a target and the specimen dropped onto the probe. The height of the drop, measured from the point of impact with the specimen to the upper surface of the probe shall be 3 m. For this test the probe shall have the same properties and dimensions as specified in (a) above, except that the length and mass of the probe shall be such as to incur maximum damage to the specimen. The target on which the base of the probe is placed shall be as specified in 6.4.14.

6.4.20.3 *Enhanced thermal test:* The conditions for this test shall be as specified in 6.4.17.3, except that the exposure to the thermal environment shall be for a period of 60 minutes.

6.4.20.4 *Impact test:* The specimen shall be subject to an impact on a target at a velocity of not less than 90 m/s, at such an orientation as to suffer maximum damage. The target shall be as defined in 6.4.14, except that the target surface may be at any orientation as long as the surface is normal to the specimen path.

6.4.21 Tests for packagings designed to contain uranium hexafluoride

Specimens that comprise or simulate packagings designed to contain 0.1 kg or more of uranium hexafluoride shall be tested hydraulically at an internal pressure of at least 1.38 MPa but, when the test pressure is less than 2.76 MPa, the design shall require multilateral approval. For retesting packagings, any other equivalent non-destructive testing may be applied subject to multilateral approval.

6.4.22 Approvals of package designs and materials

6.4.22.1 The approval of designs for packages containing 0.1 kg or more of uranium hexafluoride requires that:

(a) Each design that meets the requirements of 6.4.6.4 shall require multilateral approval;

(b) Each design that meets the requirements of 6.4.6.1 to 6.4.6.3 shall require unilateral approval by the competent authority of the country of origin of the design, unless multilateral approval is otherwise required by these Regulations.

6.4.22.2 Each Type B(U) and Type C package design shall require unilateral approval, except that:

(a) A package design for fissile material, which is also subject to 6.4.22.4, 6.4.23.7, and 5.1.5.2.1 shall require multilateral approval; and

(b) A Type B(U) package design for low dispersible radioactive material shall require multilateral approval.

6.4.22.3 Each Type B(M) package design, including those for fissile material which are also subject to 6.4.22.4, 6.4.23.7 and 5.1.5.2.1 and those for low dispersible radioactive material, shall require multilateral approval.

6.4.22.4 Each package design for fissile material which is not excepted by any of the paragraphs 2.7.2.3.5 (a) to (f), 6.4.11.2 and 6.4.11.3 shall require multilateral approval.

6.4.22.5 The design for special form radioactive material shall require unilateral approval. The design for low dispersible radioactive material shall require multilateral approval (see also 6.4.23.8).

6.4.22.6 The design for a fissile material excepted from "FISSILE" classification in accordance with 2.7.2.3.5 (f) shall require multilateral approval.

6.4.22.7　　Alternative activity limits for an exempt consignment of instruments or articles in accordance with 2.7.2.2.2 (b) shall require multilateral approval.

6.4.23　　Applications and approvals for radioactive material transport

6.4.23.1　　*Reserved.*

6.4.23.2　　An application for approval of shipment shall include:

(a) The period of time, related to the shipment, for which the approval is sought;

(b) The actual radioactive contents, the expected modes of transport, the type of conveyance, and the probable or proposed route; and

(c) The details of how the precautions and administrative or operational controls, referred to in the certificate of approval for the package design, if applicable, issued under 5.1.5.2.1 (a) (v), (vi) or (vii), are to be put into effect.

6.4.23.2.1　　An application for approval of SCO-III shipments shall include:

(a) A statement of the respects in which, and of the reasons why, the consignment is considered SCO-III;

(b) Justification for choosing SCO-III by demonstrating that:

　(i) No suitable packaging currently exists;

　(ii) Designing and/or constructing a packaging or segmenting the object is not practically, technically or economically feasible;

　(iii) No other viable alternative exists;

(c) A detailed description of the proposed radioactive contents with reference to their physical and chemical states and the nature of the radiation emitted;

(d) A detailed statement of the design of the SCO-III, including complete engineering drawings and schedules of materials and methods of manufacture;

(e) All information necessary to satisfy the competent authority that the requirements of 4.1.9.2.4 (e) and the requirements of 7.1.8.2, if applicable, are satisfied;

(f) A transport plan;

(g) A specification of the applicable management system as required in 1.5.3.1.

6.4.23.3　　An application for approval of shipments under special arrangement shall include all the information necessary to satisfy the competent authority that the overall level of safety in transport is at least equivalent to that which would be provided if all the applicable requirements of these Regulations had been met.

　　The application shall also include:

(a) A statement of the respects in which, and of the reasons why, the shipment cannot be made in full accordance with the applicable requirements; and

(b) A statement of any special precautions or special administrative or operational controls which are to be employed during transport to compensate for the failure to meet the applicable requirements.

6.4.23.4 An application for approval of Type B(U) or Type C package design shall include:

(a) A detailed description of the proposed radioactive contents with reference to their physical and chemical states and the nature of the radiation emitted;

(b) A detailed statement of the design, including complete engineering drawings and schedules of materials and methods of manufacture;

(c) A statement of the tests which have been done and their results, or evidence based on calculative methods or other evidence that the design is adequate to meet the applicable requirements;

(d) The proposed operating and maintenance instructions for the use of the packaging;

(e) If the package is designed to have a maximum normal operating pressure in excess of 100 kPa gauge, a specification of the materials of manufacture of the containment system, the samples to be taken, and the tests to be made;

(f) If the package is to be used for shipment after storage, a justification of considerations to ageing mechanisms in the safety analysis and within the proposed operating and maintenance instructions;

(g) Where the proposed radioactive contents are irradiated nuclear fuel, a statement and a justification of any assumption in the safety analysis relating to the characteristics of the fuel and a description of any pre-shipment measurement as required by 6.4.11.5 (b);

(h) Any special stowage provisions necessary to ensure the safe dissipation of heat from the package considering the various modes of transport to be used and type of conveyance or freight container;

(i) A reproducible illustration, not larger than 21 cm by 30 cm, showing the make-up of the package;

(j) A specification of the applicable management system as required by 1.5.3.1; and

(k) For packages which are to be used for shipment after storage, a gap analysis programme describing a systematic procedure for a periodic evaluation of changes of Regulations, changes in technical knowledge and changes of the state of the package design during storage.

6.4.23.5 An application for approval of a Type B(M) package design shall include, in addition to the general information required in 6.4.23.4 for Type B(U) packages:

(a) A list of the requirements specified in 6.4.7.5, 6.4.8.4 to 6.4.8.6 and 6.4.8.9 to 6.4.8.15 with which the package does not conform;

(b) Any proposed supplementary operational controls to be applied during transport not regularly provided for in these Regulations, but which are necessary to ensure the safety of the package or to compensate for the deficiencies listed in (a) above;

(c) A statement relative to any restrictions on the mode of transport and to any special loading, carriage, unloading or handling procedures; and

(d) A statement of the range of ambient conditions (temperature, solar radiation) which are expected to be encountered during transport and which have been taken into account in the design.

6.4.23.6 The application for approval of designs for packages containing 0.1 kg or more of uranium hexafluoride shall include all information necessary to satisfy the competent authority that the design meets the applicable requirements 6.4.6.1, and a specification of the applicable management system as required in 1.5.3.1.

6.4.23.7   An application for a fissile package approval shall include all information necessary to satisfy the competent authority that the design meets the applicable requirements of 6.4.11.1, and a specification of the applicable management system as required by 1.5.3.1.

6.4.23.8   An application for approval of design for special form radioactive material and design for low dispersible radioactive material shall include:

    (a) A detailed description of the radioactive material or, if a capsule, the contents; particular reference shall be made to both physical and chemical states;

    (b) A detailed statement of the design of any capsule to be used;

    (c) A statement of the tests which have been done and their results, or evidence based on calculations to show that the radioactive material is capable of meeting the performance standards, or other evidence that the special form radioactive material or low dispersible radioactive material meets the applicable requirements of these Regulations;

    (d) A specification of the applicable management system as required in 1.5.3.1; and

    (e) Any proposed pre-shipment actions for use in the consignment of special form radioactive material or low dispersible radioactive material.

6.4.23.9   An application for approval of design for fissile material excepted from "FISSILE" classification in accordance with table 2.7.2.1.1, under 2.7.2.3.5 (f) shall include:

    (a) A detailed description of the material; particular reference shall be made to both physical and chemical states;

    (b) A statement of the tests that have been carried out and their results, or evidence based on calculation methods to show that the material is capable of meeting the requirements specified in 2.7.2.3.6;

    (c) A specification of the applicable management system as required in 1.5.3.1;

    (d) A statement of specific actions to be taken prior to shipment.

6.4.23.10   An application for approval of alternative activity limits for an exempt consignment of instruments or articles shall include:

    (a) An identification and detailed description of the instrument or article, its intended uses and the radionuclide(s) incorporated;

    (b) The maximum activity of the radionuclide(s) in the instrument or article;

    (c) Maximum external dose rates arising from the instrument or article;

    (d) The chemical and physical forms of the radionuclide(s) contained in the instrument or article;

    (e) Details of the construction and design of the instrument or article, particularly as related to the containment and shielding of the radionuclide in routine, normal and accident conditions of transport;

    (f) The applicable management system, including the quality testing and verification procedures to be applied to radioactive sources, components and finished products to ensure that the maximum specified activity of radioactive material or the maximum dose rates specified for the instrument or article are not exceeded, and that the instruments or articles are constructed according to the design specifications;

(g) The maximum number of instruments or articles expected to be shipped per consignment and annually;

(h) Dose assessments in accordance with the principles and methodologies set out in the Radiation Protection and Safety of Radiation Sources: International Basic Safety Standards, IAEA Safety Standards Series No. GSR Part 3, IAEA, Vienna (2014), including individual doses to transport workers and members of the public and, if appropriate, collective doses arising from routine, normal and accident conditions of transport, based on representative transport scenarios the consignments are subject to.

6.4.23.11 Each certificate of approval issued by a competent authority shall be assigned an identification mark. The mark shall be of the following generalized type:

VRI/Number/Type Code

(a) Except as provided in 6.4.23.12 (b), VRI represents the distinguishing sign used on vehicles in international road traffic[1];

(b) The number shall be assigned by the competent authority, and shall be unique and specific with regard to the particular design or shipment or alternative activity limit for exempt consignment. The identification mark of the approval of shipment shall be clearly related to the identification mark of the approval of design;

(c) The following type codes shall be used in the order listed to indicate the types of certificate of approval issued:

AF   Type A package design for fissile material
B(U) Type B(U) package design (B(U)F if for fissile material)
B(M) Type B(M) package design (B(M)F if for fissile material)
C   Type C package design (CF if for fissile material)
IF   Industrial package design for fissile material
S   Special form radioactive material
LD   Low dispersible radioactive material
FE   Fissile material complying with the requirements of 2.7.2.3.6
T   Shipment
X   Special arrangement
AL   Alternative activity limits for an exempt consignment of instruments or articles

In the case of package designs for non-fissile or fissile excepted uranium hexafluoride, where none of the above codes apply, then the following type codes shall be used:

H(U) Unilateral approval
H(M) Multilateral approval;

6.4.23.12 These identification marks shall be applied as follows:

(a) Each certificate and each package shall bear the appropriate identification mark, comprising the symbols prescribed in 6.4.23.11 (a), (b) and (c) above, except that, for packages, only the applicable design type codes shall appear following the second stroke, that is, the "T" or "X" shall not appear in the identification mark on the package.

---

[1] *Distinguishing sign of the State of registration used on motor vehicles and trailers in international road traffic, e.g. in accordance with the Geneva Convention on Road Traffic of 1949 or the Vienna Convention on Road Traffic of 1968.*

Where the approval of design and the approval of shipment are combined, the applicable type codes do not need to be repeated. For example:

A/132/B(M)F: A Type B(M) package design approved for fissile material, requiring multilateral approval, for which the competent authority of Austria has assigned the design number 132 (to be marked on both the package and on the certificate of approval for the package design);

A/132/B(M)FT: The approval of shipment issued for a package bearing the identification mark elaborated above (to be marked on the certificate only);

A/137/X: An approval of special arrangement approval issued by the competent authority of Austria, to which the number 137 has been assigned (to be marked on the certificate only);

A/139/IF: An Industrial package design for fissile material approved by the competent authority of Austria, to which package design number 139 has been assigned (to be marked on both the package and on the certificate of approval for the package design); and

A/145/H(U): A package design for fissile excepted uranium hexafluoride approved by the competent authority of Austria, to which package design number 145 has been assigned (to be marked on both the package and on the certificate of approval for the package design);

(b) Where multilateral approval is effected by validation in accordance with 6.4.23.20, only the identification mark issued by the country of origin of the design or shipment shall be used. Where multilateral approval is effected by issue of certificates by successive countries, each certificate shall bear the appropriate identification mark and the package whose design was so approved shall bear all appropriate identification marks.

For example:

A/132/B(M)F
CH/28/B(M)F

would be the identification mark of a package which was originally approved by Austria and was subsequently approved, by separate certificate, by Switzerland. Additional identification marks would be tabulated in a similar manner on the package;

(c) The revision of a certificate shall be indicated by a parenthetical expression following the identification mark on the certificate. For example, A/132/B(M)F (Rev.2) would indicate revision 2 of the Austrian certificate of approval for the package design; or A/132/B(M)F (Rev.0) would indicate the original issuance of the Austrian certificate of approval for the package design. For original issuances, the parenthetical entry is optional and other words such as "original issuance" may also be used in place of "Rev.0". Certificate revision numbers may only be issued by the country issuing the original certificate of approval;

(d) Additional symbols (as may be necessitated by national requirements) may be added in brackets to the end of the identification mark; for example, A/132/B(M)F (SP503);

(e) It is not necessary to alter the identification mark on the packaging each time that a revision to the design certificate is made. Such re-marking shall be required only in those cases where the revision to the package design certificate involves a change in the letter type codes for the package design following the second stroke.

6.4.23.13   Each certificate of approval issued by a competent authority for special form radioactive material or low dispersible radioactive material shall include the following information:

    (a)   Type of certificate;

    (b)   The competent authority identification mark;

    (c)   The issue date and an expiry date;

    (d)   List of applicable national and international regulations, including the edition of the IAEA Regulations for the Safe Transport of Radioactive Material under which the special form radioactive material or low dispersible radioactive material is approved;

    (e)   The identification of the special form radioactive material or low dispersible radioactive material;

    (f)   A description of the special form radioactive material or low dispersible radioactive material;

    (g)   Design specifications for the special form radioactive material or low dispersible radioactive material which may include references to drawings;

    (h)   A specification of the radioactive contents which includes the activities involved and which may include the physical and chemical form;

    (i)   A specification of the applicable management system as required in 1.5.3.1;

    (j)   Reference to information provided by the applicant relating to specific actions to be taken prior to shipment;

    (k)   If deemed appropriate by the competent authority, reference to the identity of the applicant;

    (l)   Signature and identification of the certifying official.

6.4.23.14   Each certificate of approval issued by a competent authority for material excepted from classification as "FISSILE" shall include the following information:

    (a)   Type of certificate;

    (b)   The competent authority identification mark;

    (c)   The issue date and an expiry date;

    (d)   List of applicable national and international regulations, including the edition of the IAEA Regulations for the Safe Transport of Radioactive Material under which the exception is approved;

    (e)   A description of the excepted material;

    (f)   Limiting specifications for the excepted material;

    (g)   A specification of the applicable management system as required in 1.5.3.1;

    (h)   Reference to information provided by the applicant relating to specific actions to be taken prior to shipment;

    (i)   If deemed appropriate by the competent authority, reference to the identity of the applicant;

(j) Signature and identification of the certifying official;

(k) Reference to documentation that demonstrates compliance with 2.7.2.3.6.

6.4.23.15 Each certificate of approval issued by a competent authority for a special arrangement shall include the following information:

(a) Type of certificate;

(b) The competent authority identification mark;

(c) The issue date and an expiry date;

(d) Mode(s) of transport;

(e) Any restrictions on the modes of transport, type of conveyance, freight container, and any necessary routeing instructions;

(f) List of applicable national and international regulations, including the edition of the IAEA Regulations for the Safe Transport of Radioactive Material under which the special arrangement is approved;

(g) The following statement: "This certificate does not relieve the consignor from compliance with any requirement of the government of any country through or into which the package will be transported.";

(h) References to certificates for alternative radioactive contents, other competent authority validation, or additional technical data or information, as deemed appropriate by the competent authority;

(i) Description of the packaging by a reference to the drawings or a specification of the design. If deemed appropriate by the competent authority, a reproducible illustration, not larger than 21 cm by 30 cm, showing the make-up of the package shall also be provided, accompanied by a brief description of the packaging, including materials of manufacture, gross mass, general outside dimensions and appearance;

(j) A specification of the authorized radioactive contents, including any restrictions on the radioactive contents which might not be obvious from the nature of the packaging. This shall include the physical and chemical forms, the activities involved (including those of the various isotopes, if appropriate), mass in grams (for fissile material or for each fissile nuclide when appropriate), and whether special form radioactive material, low dispersible radioactive material or fissile material excepted under 2.7.2.3.5 (f) if applicable;

(k) Additionally, for packages containing fissile material:

   (i) a detailed description of the authorized radioactive contents;

   (ii) the value of the criticality safety index;

   (iii) reference to the documentation that demonstrates the criticality safety of the package;

   (iv) any special features, on the basis of which the absence of water from certain void spaces has been assumed in the criticality assessment;

   (v) any allowance (based on 6.4.11.5 (b)) for a change in neutron multiplication assumed in the criticality assessment as a result of actual irradiation experience; and

(vi) the ambient temperature range for which the special arrangement has been approved;

(l) A detailed listing of any supplementary operational controls required for preparation, loading, carriage, unloading and handling of the consignment, including any special stowage provisions for the safe dissipation of heat;

(m) If deemed appropriate by the competent authority, reasons for the special arrangement;

(n) Description of the compensatory measures to be applied as a result of the shipment being under special arrangement;

(o) Reference to information provided by the applicant relating to the use of the packaging or specific actions to be taken prior to the shipment;

(p) A statement regarding the ambient conditions assumed for purposes of design if these are not in accordance with those specified in 6.4.8.5, 6.4.8.6, and 6.4.8.15, as applicable;

(q) Any emergency arrangements deemed necessary by the competent authority;

(r) A specification of the applicable management system as required in 1.5.3.1;

(s) If deemed appropriate by the competent authority, reference to the identity of the applicant and to the identity of the carrier;

(t) Signature and identification of the certifying official.

6.4.23.16　Each certificate of approval for a shipment issued by a competent authority shall include the following information:

(a) Type of certificate;

(b) The competent authority identification mark(s);

(c) The issue date and an expiry date;

(d) List of applicable national and international regulations, including the edition of the IAEA Regulations for the Safe Transport of Radioactive Material under which the shipment is approved;

(e) Any restrictions on the modes of transport, type of conveyance, freight container, and any necessary routeing instructions;

(f) The following statement: "This certificate does not relieve the consignor from compliance with any requirement of the government of any country through or into which the package will be transported.";

(g) A detailed listing of any supplementary operational controls required for preparation, loading, carriage, unloading and handling of the consignment, including any special stowage provisions for the safe dissipation of heat or maintenance of criticality safety;

(h) Reference to information provided by the applicant relating to specific actions to be taken prior to the shipment;

(i) Reference to the applicable certificate(s) of approval of design;

(j) A specification of the actual radioactive contents, including any restrictions on the radioactive contents which might not be obvious from the nature of the packaging. This shall include the physical and chemical forms, the total activities involved (including those of the various isotopes, if appropriate), mass in grams (for fissile material or for each fissile nuclide when appropriate), and whether special form radioactive material, low dispersible radioactive material or fissile material excepted under 2.7.2.3.5 (f) if applicable;

(k) Any emergency arrangements deemed necessary by the competent authority;

(l) A specification of the applicable management system as required in 1.5.3.1;

(m) If deemed appropriate by the competent authority, reference to the identity of the applicant;

(n) Signature and identification of the certifying official.

6.4.23.17 Each certificate of approval of the design of a package issued by a competent authority shall include the following information:

(a) Type of certificate;

(b) The competent authority identification mark;

(c) The issue date and an expiry date;

(d) Any restriction on the modes of transport, if appropriate;

(e) List of applicable national and international regulations, including the edition of the IAEA Regulations for the Safe Transport of Radioactive Material under which the design is approved;

(f) The following statement: "This certificate does not relieve the consignor from compliance with any requirement of the government of any country through or into which the package will be transported.";

(g) References to certificates for alternative radioactive contents, other competent authority validation, or additional technical data or information, as deemed appropriate by the competent authority;

(h) A statement authorizing shipment where approval of shipment is required under 5.1.5.1.2, if deemed appropriate;

(i) Identification of the packaging;

(j) Description of the packaging by a reference to the drawings or specification of the design. If deemed appropriate by the competent authority, a reproducible illustration, not larger than 21 cm by 30 cm, showing the make-up of the package shall also be provided, accompanied by a brief description of the packaging, including materials of manufacture, gross mass, general outside dimensions and appearance;

(k) Specification of the design by reference to the drawings;

(l) A specification of the authorized radioactive content, including any restrictions on the radioactive contents which might not be obvious from the nature of the packaging. This shall include the physical and chemical forms, the activities involved (including those of the various isotopes, if appropriate), mass in grams (for fissile material the total mass of fissile nuclides or the mass for each fissile nuclide, when appropriate) and whether special form radioactive material, low dispersible radioactive material or fissile material excepted under 2.7.2.3.5 (f), if applicable;

(m) A description of the containment system;

(n) For package designs containing fissile material which require multilateral approval of the package design in accordance with 6.4.22.4:

    (i) a detailed description of the authorized radioactive contents;

    (ii) a description of the confinement system;

    (iii) the value of the criticality safety index;

    (iv) reference to the documentation that demonstrates the criticality safety of the package;

    (v) any special features, on the basis of which the absence of water from certain void spaces has been assumed in the criticality assessment;

    (vi) any allowance (based on 6.4.11.5 (b)) for a change in neutron multiplication assumed in the criticality assessment as a result of actual irradiation experience; and

    (vii) the ambient temperature range for which the package design has been approved;

(o) For Type B(M) packages, a statement specifying those prescriptions of 6.4.7.5, 6.4.8.4, 6.4.8.5, 6.4.8.6 and 6.4.8.9 to 6.4.8.15 with which the package does not conform and any amplifying information which may be useful to other competent authorities;

(p) For package designs subject to 6.4.24.2, a statement specifying those requirements of the current regulations with which the package does not conform;

(q) For packages containing more than 0.1 kg of uranium hexafluoride, a statement specifying those prescriptions of 6.4.6.4 which apply if any and any amplifying information which may be useful to other competent authorities;

(r) A detailed listing of any supplementary operational controls required for preparation, loading, carriage, unloading and handling of the consignment, including any special stowage provisions for the safe dissipation of heat;

(s) Reference to information provided by the applicant relating to the use of the packaging or specific actions to be taken prior to shipment;

(t) A statement regarding the ambient conditions assumed for purposes of design if these are not in accordance with those specified in 6.4.8.5, 6.4.8.6 and 6.4.8.15, as applicable;

(u) A specification of the applicable management system as required in 1.5.3.1;

(v) Any emergency arrangements deemed necessary by the competent authority;

(w) If deemed appropriate by the competent authority, reference to the identity of the applicant;

(x) Signature and identification of the certifying official.

6.4.23.18 Each certificate issued by a competent authority for alternative activity limits for an exempt consignment of instruments or articles according to 5.1.5.2.1 (d) shall include the following information:

    (a) Type of certificate;

    (b) The competent authority identification mark;

    (c) The issue date and an expiry date;

(d) List of applicable national and international regulations, including the edition of the IAEA Regulations for the Safe Transport of Radioactive Material under which the exemption is approved;

(e) The identification of the instrument or article;

(f) A description of the instrument or article;

(g) Design specifications for the instrument or article;

(h) A specification of the radionuclide(s), the approved alternative activity limit(s) for the exempt consignment(s) of the instrument(s) or article(s);

(i) Reference to documentation that demonstrates compliance with 2.7.2.2.2 (b);

(j) If deemed appropriate by the competent authority, reference to the identity of the applicant;

(k) Signature and identification of the certifying official.

6.4.23.19 The competent authority shall be informed of the serial number of each packaging manufactured to a design approved by them under 6.4.22.2, 6.4.22.3, 6.4.22.4 and 6.4.24.2.

6.4.23.20 Multilateral approval may be by validation of the original certificate issued by the competent authority of the country of origin of the design or shipment. Such validation may take the form of an endorsement on the original certificate or the issuance of a separate endorsement, annex, supplement, etc., by the competent authority of the country through or into which the shipment is made.

6.4.24 Transitional measures for Class 7

Packages not requiring competent authority approval of design under the 1985, 1985 (as amended 1990), 1996, 1996 (revised), 1996 (as amended 2003), 2005, 2009 and 2012 editions of the IAEA Regulations for the Safe Transport of Radioactive Material

6.4.24.1 Packages not requiring competent authority approval of design (excepted packages, Type IP-1, Type IP-2, Type IP-3 and Type A packages) shall meet these Regulations in full, except that:

(a) Packages that meet the requirements of the 1985 or 1985 (as amended 1990) editions of the IAEA Regulations for the Safe Transport of Radioactive Material:

(i) May continue in transport provided that they were prepared for transport prior to 31 December 2003 and subject to the requirements of 6.4.24.5, if applicable; or

(ii) May continue to be used, provided that all the following conditions are met:

- They were not designed to contain uranium hexafluoride;

- The applicable requirements of 1.5.3.1 of these Regulations are applied;

- The activity limits and classification in chapter 2.7 of these Regulations are applied;

- The requirements and controls for transport in parts 1, 3, 4, 5 and 7 of these Regulations are applied; and

- The packaging was not manufactured or modified after 31 December 2003;

(b) Packages that meet the requirements of the 1996, 1996 (revised), 1996 (as amended 2003), 2005, 2009 or 2012 editions of the IAEA Regulations for the Safe Transport of Radioactive Material:

(i) May continue in transport provided that they were prepared for transport prior to 31 December 2025 and are subject to the requirements of 6.4.24.5, if applicable; or

(ii) May continue to be used, provided that all the following conditions are met:

- The applicable requirements of 1.5.3.1 of these Regulations are applied;

- The activity limits and classification in chapter 2.7 of these Regulations are applied;

- The requirements and controls for transport in parts 1, 3, 4, 5 and 7 of these Regulations are applied; and

- The packaging was not manufactured or modified after 31 December 2025.

Package designs approved under the 1985, 1985 (as amended 1990), 1996, 1996 (revised), 1996 (as amended 2003), 2005, 2009 and 2012 editions of the IAEA Regulations for the Safe Transport of Radioactive Material

6.4.24.2 Packages requiring competent authority approval of the design shall meet these Regulations in full except that:

(a) Packagings that were manufactured to a package design approved by the competent authority under the provisions of the 1985 or 1985 (as amended 1990) editions of the IAEA Regulations for the Safe Transport of Radioactive Material may continue to be used provided that all of the following conditions are met:

(i) The package design is subject to multilateral approval;

(ii) The applicable requirements of 1.5.3.1 of these Regulations are applied;

(iii) The activity limits and classification in chapter 2.7 of these Regulations are applied;

(iv) The requirements and controls for transport in parts 1, 3, 4, 5 and 7 of these Regulations are applied;

(v) For a package containing fissile material and transported by air, the requirement of 6.4.11.11 is met;

(b) Packagings that were manufactured to a package design approved by the competent authority under the provisions of the 1996, 1996 (revised), 1996 (as amended 2003), 2005, 2009 or 2012 editions of the IAEA Regulations for the Safe Transport of Radioactive Material may continue to be used provided that all of the following conditions are met:

(i) The package design is subject to multilateral approval after 31 December 2025;

(ii) The applicable requirements of 1.5.3.1 of these Regulations are applied;

(iii) The activity limits and material restrictions of chapter 2.7 of these Regulations are applied;

(iv) The requirements and controls for transport in parts 1, 3, 4, 5 and 7 of these Regulations are applied.

6.4.24.3 No new manufacture of packagings to a package design meeting the provisions of the 1985, and 1985 (as amended 1990) editions of the IAEA Regulations for the Safe Transport of Radioactive Material shall be permitted to commence.

6.4.24.4   No new manufacture of packagings of a package design meeting the provisions of the 1996, 1996 (revised), 1996 (as amended 2003), 2005, 2009 or 2012 editions of the IAEA Regulations for the Safe Transport of Radioactive Material shall be permitted to commence after 31 December 2028.

Packages excepted from the requirements for fissile materials under the Regulations annexed to the 16th revised edition or the seventeenth revised edition of the United Nations Recommendations on the Transport of Dangerous Goods (2009 edition of the IAEA Regulations for the Safe Transport of Radioactive Material)

6.4.24.5   Packages containing fissile material that is excepted from classification as "FISSILE" according to 2.7.2.3.5 (a)(i) or (iii) of the Regulations annexed to the sixteenth revised edition or the seventeenth revised edition of the United Nations Recommendations on the Transport of Dangerous Goods (paras. 417 (a) (i) or (iii) of the 2009 edition of the IAEA Regulations for the Safe Transport of Radioactive Material) prepared for transport before 31 December 2014 may continue in transport and may continue to be classified as non-fissile or fissile-excepted except that the consignment limits in table 2.7.2.3.5 of these editions shall apply to the conveyance. The consignment shall be transported under exclusive use.

Special form radioactive material approved under the 1985, 1985 (as amended 1990), 1996, 1996 (revised), 1996 (as amended 2003), 2005, 2009 and 2012 editions of the IAEA Regulations for the Safe Transport of Radioactive Material

6.4.24.6   Special form radioactive material manufactured to a design which had received unilateral approval by the competent authority under the 1985, 1985 (as amended 1990) , 1996, 1996 (revised), 1996 (as amended 2003), 2005, 2009 or 2012 editions of the IAEA Regulations for the Safe Transport of Radioactive Material may continue to be used when in compliance with the mandatory management system in accordance with the applicable requirements of 1.5.3.1. There shall be no new manufacture of special form radioactive material to a design that had received unilateral approval by the competent authority under the 1985 or 1985 (as amended 1990) editions of the IAEA Regulations for the Safe Transport of Radioactive Material. No new manufacture of special form radioactive material to a design that had received unilateral approval by the competent authority under the 1996, 1996 (revised), 1996 (as amended 2003), 2005, 2009 or 2012 editions of the IAEA Regulations for the Safe Transport of Radioactive Material shall be permitted to commence after 31 December 2025.

CHAPTER 6.5

REQUIREMENTS FOR THE CONSTRUCTION AND TESTING OF INTERMEDIATE BULK CONTAINERS

6.5.1 **General requirements**

6.5.1.1 *Scope*

6.5.1.1.1   The requirements of this chapter apply to IBCs intended for the transport of certain dangerous goods. The provisions set out general requirements for multimodal transport and do not establish special requirements that may be required for a particular mode.

6.5.1.1.2   The requirements for IBCs in 6.5.3 are based on IBCs currently in use. In order to take into account progress in science and technology, there is no objection to the use of IBCs having specifications different from those in 6.5.3 and 6.5.5, provided that they are equally effective, acceptable to the competent authority and able to successfully fulfil the requirements described in 6.5.4 and 6.5.6. Methods of inspection and testing other than those described in these Regulations are acceptable, provided they are equivalent.

6.5.1.1.3   The construction, equipment, testing, marking and operation of IBCs shall be subject to acceptance by the competent authority of the country in which the IBCs are approved.

6.5.1.1.4   Manufacturers and subsequent distributors of IBCs shall provide information regarding procedures to be followed and a description of the types and dimensions of closures (including required gaskets) and any other components needed to ensure that IBCs as presented for transport are capable of passing the applicable performance tests of this chapter.

6.5.1.2 *Definitions*

Body (for all categories of IBCs other than composite IBCs) means the receptacle proper, including openings and their closures, but does not include service equipment;

Handling device (for flexible IBCs) means any sling, loop, eye or frame attached to the body of the IBC or formed from a continuation of the IBC body material;

Maximum permissible gross mass means the mass of the IBC and any service or structural equipment together with the maximum net mass;

Plastics material, when used in connection with inner receptacles for composite IBCs, is taken to include other polymeric materials such as rubber;

Protected (for metal IBCs) means being provided with additional protection against impact, the protection taking the form of, for example, a multi-layer (sandwich) or double wall construction or a frame with a metal lattice-work casing;

Service equipment means filling and discharge devices and, according to the category of IBC, pressure-relief or venting, safety, heating and heat-insulating devices and measuring instruments;

Structural equipment (for all categories of IBCs other than flexible IBCs) means the reinforcing, fastening, handling, protective or stabilizing members of the body, including the base pallet for composite IBCs with plastics inner receptacle, fibreboard and wooden IBCs;

Woven plastics (for flexible IBCs) means a material made from stretched tapes or monofilaments of a suitable plastics material.

6.5.1.3 *Categories of IBCs*

6.5.1.3.1 *Metal IBCs* consist of a metal body together with appropriate service and structural equipment.

6.5.1.3.2 *Flexible IBCs* consist of a body constituted of film, woven fabric or any other flexible material or combinations thereof, and if necessary an inner coating or liner, together with any appropriate service equipment and handling devices.

6.5.1.3.3 *Rigid plastics IBCs* consist of a rigid plastics body, which may have structural equipment together with appropriate service equipment.

6.5.1.3.4 *Composite IBCs* consist of structural equipment in the form of a rigid outer casing enclosing a plastics inner receptacle together with any service or other structural equipment. They are so constructed that the inner receptacle and outer casing once assembled, form and are used as, an integrated single unit to be filled, stored, transported or emptied as such.

6.5.1.3.5 *Fibreboard IBCs* consist of a fibreboard body with or without separate top and bottom caps, if necessary an inner liner (but no inner packagings), appropriate service and structural equipment.

6.5.1.3.6 *Wooden IBCs* consist of a rigid or collapsible wooden body together with an inner liner (but no inner packagings) and appropriate service and structural equipment.

6.5.1.4 *Designatory code system for IBCs*

6.5.1.4.1 The code shall consist of two Arabic numerals as specified in (a); followed by a capital letter(s) specified in (b); followed, when specified in an individual section, by an Arabic numeral indicating the category of IBC.

(a)

Type	For solids filled or discharged		For liquids
	by gravity	under pressure of more than 10 kPa (0.1 bar)	
Rigid	11	21	31
Flexible	13	-	-

(b) Materials

    A. Steel (all types and surface treatments)
    B. Aluminium
    C. Natural wood
    D. Plywood
    F. Reconstituted wood
    G. Fibreboard
    H. Plastics material
    L. Textile
    M. Paper, multiwall
    N. Metal (other than steel or aluminium).

6.5.1.4.2 For composite IBCs, two capital letters in Latin characters shall be used in sequence in the second position of the code. The first shall indicate the material of the inner receptacle of the IBC and the second that of the outer packaging of the IBC.

6.5.1.4.3 The following types and codes of IBC are assigned:

Material	Category	Code	Paragraph
Metal			6.5.5.1
A. Steel	for solids, filled or discharged by gravity	11A	
	for solids, filled or discharged under pressure	21A	
	for liquids	31A	
B. Aluminium	for solids, filled or discharged by gravity	11B	
	for solids, filled or discharged under pressure	21B	
	for liquids	31B	
N. Other than steel or aluminium	for solids, filled or discharged by gravity	11N	
	for solids, filled or discharged under pressure	21N	
	for liquids	31N	
Flexible			6.5.5.2
H. Plastics	woven plastics without coating or liner	13H1	
	woven plastics, coated	13H2	
	woven plastics with liner	13H3	
	woven plastics, coated and with liner	13H4	
	plastics film	13H5	
L. Textile	without coating or liner	13L1	
	coated	13L2	
	with liner	13L3	
	coated and with liner	13L4	
M. Paper	multiwall	13M1	
	multiwall, water-resistant	13M2	
H. Rigid Plastics	for solids, filled or discharged by gravity, fitted with structural equipment	11H1	6.5.5.3
	for solids, filled or discharged by gravity, freestanding	11H2	
	for solids, filled or discharged under pressure, fitted with structural equipment	21H1	
	for solids, filled or discharged under pressure, freestanding	21H2	
	for liquids, fitted with structural equipment	31H1	
	for liquids, freestanding	31H2	
HZ. Composite with plastic inner receptacle[a]	for solids, filled or discharged by gravity, with rigid plastics inner receptacle	11HZ1	6.5.5.4
	for solids, filled or discharged by gravity, with flexible plastics inner receptacle	11HZ2	
	for solids, filled or discharged under pressure, with rigid plastics inner receptacle	21HZ1	
	for solids, filled or discharged under pressure, with flexible plastics inner receptacle	21HZ2	
	for liquids, with rigid plastics inner receptacle	31HZ1	
	for liquids, with flexible plastics inner receptacle	31HZ2	
G. Fibreboard	for solids, filled or discharged by gravity	11G	6.5.5.5
Wooden			6.5.5.6
C. Natural wood	for solids, filled or discharged by gravity with inner liner	11C	
D. Plywood	for solids, filled or discharged by gravity, with inner liner	11D	
F. Reconstituted wood	for solids, filled or discharged by gravity, with inner liner	11F	

[a] *The code shall be completed by replacing the letter Z with a capital letter in accordance with 6.5.1.4.1 (b) to indicate the nature of the material used for the outer casing.*

6.5.1.4.4   The letter "W" may follow the IBC code. The letter "W" signifies that the IBC, although of the same type indicated by the code, is manufactured to a specification different from those in section 6.5.5 and is considered equivalent in accordance with the requirements in 6.5.1.1.2.

6.5.2 Marking

6.5.2.1 *Primary marking*

6.5.2.1.1 Each IBC manufactured and intended for use according to these Regulations shall bear marks which are durable, legible and placed in a location so as to be readily visible. Letters, numerals and symbols shall be at least 12 mm high and shall show:

(a) The United Nations packaging symbol .

This symbol shall not be used for any purpose other than certifying that a packaging, a flexible bulk container, a portable tank or a MEGC complies with the relevant requirements in chapter 6.1, 6.2, 6.3, 6.5, 6.6, 6.7 or 6.8.

For metal IBCs on which the marks are stamped or embossed, the capital letters "UN" may be applied instead of the symbol;

(b) The code designating the type of IBC according to 6.5.1.4;

(c) A capital letter designating the packing group(s) for which the design type has been approved:

   (i) X for packing groups I, II and III (IBCs for solids only);

   (ii) Y for packing groups II and III;

   (iii) Z for packing group III only;

(d) The month and year (last two digits) of manufacture;

(e) The State authorizing the allocation of the mark; indicated by the distinguishing sign used on vehicles in international road traffic[1];

(f) The name or symbol of the manufacturer and other identification of the IBC as specified by the competent authority;

(g) The stacking test load in kg. For IBCs not designed for stacking, the figure "0" shall be shown;

(h) The maximum permissible gross mass in kg.

The primary marks required above shall be applied in the sequence of the subparagraphs above. The marks required by 6.5.2.2 and any further mark authorized by a competent authority shall still enable the primary marks to be correctly identified.

Each mark applied in accordance with (a) to (h) and with 6.5.2.2 shall be clearly separated, e.g. by a slash or space, so as to be easily identifiable.

6.5.2.1.2 IBCs manufactured from recycled plastics material as defined in 1.2.1 shall be marked "REC". For rigid IBCs this mark shall be placed near the marks prescribed in 6.5.2.1.1. For the inner receptacle of composite IBCs, this mark shall be placed near the marks prescribed in 6.5.2.2.4.

---

[1] *Distinguishing sign of the State of registration used on motor vehicles and trailers in international road traffic, e.g. in accordance with the Geneva Convention on Road Traffic of 1949 or the Vienna Convention on Road Traffic of 1968.*

6.5.2.1.3   *Examples of marking for various types of IBC in accordance with (a) to (h) above*

(un)	11A/Y/02 99 NL/Mulder 007 5500/1500	For a metal IBC for solids discharged by gravity and made from steel/for packing groups II and III/ manufactured in February 1999/authorized by the Netherlands/manufactured by Mulder and of a design type to which the competent authority has allocated serial number 007/the stacking test load in kg/the maximum permissible gross mass in kg.
(un)	13H3/Z/03 01 F/Meunier 1713 0/1500	For a flexible IBC for solids discharged for instance by gravity and made from woven plastics with a liner/not designed to be stacked.
(un)	31H1/Y/04 99 GB/9099 10800/1200	For a rigid plastics IBC for liquids made from plastics with structural equipment withstanding the stack load.
(un)	31HA1/Y/05 01 D/Muller 1683 10800/1200	For a composite IBC for liquids with a rigid plastics inner receptacle and a steel outer casing.
(un)	11C/X/01 02 S/Aurigny 9876 3000/910	For a wooden IBC for solids with an inner liner and authorized for packing groups I, II and III solids.

6.5.2.1.4   Where an IBC conforms to one or more than one tested IBC design type, including one or more than one tested packaging or large packaging design type, the IBC may bear more than one mark to indicate the relevant performance test requirements that have been met. Where more than one mark appears on an IBC, the marks shall appear in close proximity to one another and each mark shall appear in its entirety.

6.5.2.2   *Additional marking*

6.5.2.2.1   Each IBC shall bear the marks required in 6.5.2.1 and, in addition, the following information which may appear on a corrosion-resistant plate permanently attached in a place readily accessible for inspection:

Additional marks	Category of IBC				
	Metal	Rigid Plastics	Composite	Fibreboard	Wooden
Capacity in litres[a] at 20 °C	X	X	X		
Tare mass in kg[a]	X	X	X	X	X
Test (gauge) pressure, in kPa or bar[a], if applicable		X	X		
Maximum filling/discharge pressure in kPa or bar[a], if applicable	X	X	X		
Body material and its minimum thickness in mm	X				
Date of last leakproofness test, if applicable (month and year)	X	X	X		
Date of last inspection (month and year)	X	X	X		
Serial number of the manufacturer	X				

[a]   The unit used shall be indicated.

6.5.2.2.2   The maximum permitted stacking load applicable shall be displayed on a symbol as shown in figure 6.5.1 or figure 6.5.2. The symbol shall be durable and clearly visible.

Figure 6.5.1

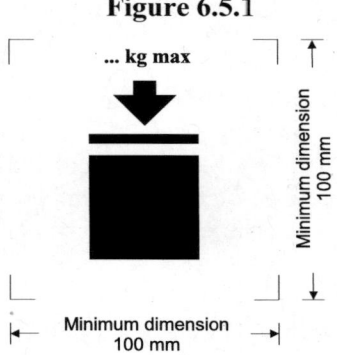

IBCs capable of being stacked

Figure 6.5.2

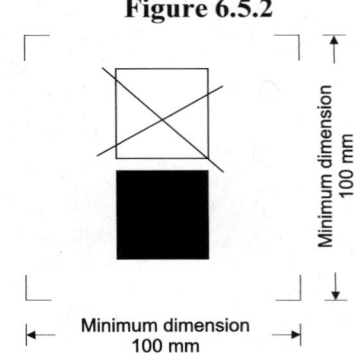

IBCs NOT capable of being stacked

The minimum dimensions shall be 100 mm × 100 mm. The letters and numbers indicating the mass shall be at least 12 mm high. The area within the printer's marks indicated by the dimensional arrows shall be square. Where dimensions are not specified, all features shall be in approximate proportion to those shown. The mass marked above the symbol shall not exceed the load imposed during the design type test (see 6.5.6.6.4) divided by 1.8.

NOTE: *The provisions of 6.5.2.2.2 shall apply to all IBCs manufactured, repaired or remanufactured as from 1 January 2011. The provisions of 6.5.2.2.2 of the seventeenth revised edition of the Recommendations on the Transport of Dangerous Goods, Model Regulations may continue to be applied to all IBCs manufactured, repaired or remanufactured between 1 January 2011 and 31 December 2016.*

6.5.2.2.3　　In addition to the marks required in 6.5.2.1, flexible IBCs may bear a pictogram indicating recommended lifting methods.

6.5.2.2.4　　Inner receptacles that are of composite IBC design type shall be identified by the application of the marks indicated in 6.5.2.1.1 (b), (c), (d) where this date is that of the manufacture of the plastics inner receptacle, (e) and (f). The UN packaging symbol shall not be applied. The marks shall be applied in the sequence shown in 6.5.2.1.1. They shall be durable, legible and placed in a location so as to be readily accessible for inspection after assembling the inner receptacle in the outer casing. When the marks on the inner receptacle are not readily accessible for inspection due to the design of the outer casing, a duplicate of the required marks on the inner receptacle shall be placed on the outer casing preceded by the wording "Inner receptacle". This duplicate shall be durable, legible and placed in a location so as to be readily accessible for inspection.

The date of the manufacture of the plastics inner receptacle may alternatively be marked on the inner receptacle adjacent to the remainder of the marks. In such a case, the date may be waived from the remainder of the marks. An example of an appropriate marking method is:

NOTE 1: *Other methods that provide the minimum required information in a durable, visible and legible form are also acceptable.*

NOTE 2: *The date of manufacture of the inner receptacle may be different from the marked date of manufacture (see 6.5.2.1), repair (see 6.5.4.5.3) or remanufacture (see 6.5.2.4) of the composite IBC.*

6.5.2.2.5   Where a composite IBC is designed in such a manner that the outer casing is intended to be dismantled for transport when empty (such as for return of the IBC for reuse to the original consignor), each of the parts intended to be detached when so dismantled shall be marked with the month and year of manufacture and the name or symbol of the manufacturer and other identification of the IBC as specified by the competent authority (6.5.2.1.1(f)).

6.5.2.3   *Conformity to design type:* The marks indicate that IBCs correspond to a successfully tested design type and that the requirements referred to in the certificate have been met.

6.5.2.4   *Marking of remanufactured composite IBCs (31HZ1)*

The marks specified in 6.5.2.1.1 and 6.5.2.2 shall be removed from the original IBC or made permanently illegible and new marks shall be applied to an IBC remanufactured in accordance with these Regulations.

6.5.3   Construction requirements

6.5.3.1   *General requirements*

6.5.3.1.1   IBCs shall be resistant to or adequately protected from deterioration due to the external environment.

6.5.3.1.2   IBCs shall be so constructed and closed that none of the contents can escape under normal conditions of transport including the effect of vibration, or by changes in temperature, humidity or pressure.

6.5.3.1.3   IBCs and their closures shall be constructed of materials compatible with their contents, or be protected internally, so that they are not liable:

    (a)   To be attacked by the contents so as to make their use dangerous;

    (b)   To cause the contents to react or decompose, or form harmful or dangerous compounds with the IBCs.

6.5.3.1.4   Gaskets, where used, shall be made of materials not subject to attack by the contents of the IBCs.

6.5.3.1.5   All service equipment shall be so positioned or protected as to minimize the risk of escape of the contents owing to damage during handling and transport.

6.5.3.1.6   IBCs, their attachments and their service and structural equipment shall be designed to withstand, without loss of contents, the internal pressure of the contents and the stresses of normal handling and transport. IBCs intended for stacking shall be designed for stacking. Any lifting or securing features of IBCs shall be of sufficient strength to withstand the normal conditions of handling and transport without gross distortion or failure and shall be so positioned that no undue stress is caused in any part of the IBC.

6.5.3.1.7   Where an IBC consists of a body within a framework it shall be so constructed that:

    (a)   The body does not chafe or rub against the framework so as to cause material damage to the body;

    (b)   The body is retained within the framework at all times;

    (c)   The items of equipment are fixed in such a way that they cannot be damaged if the connections between body and frame allow relative expansion or movement.

6.5.3.1.8   Where a bottom discharge valve is fitted, it shall be capable of being made secure in the closed position and the whole discharge system shall be suitably protected from damage. Valves having lever closures shall be able to be secured against accidental opening and the open or closed position shall be readily apparent.

For IBCs containing liquids, a secondary means of sealing the discharge aperture shall also be provided, e.g. by a blank flange or equivalent device.

6.5.4 Testing, certification and inspection

6.5.4.1 *Quality assurance*: the IBCs shall be manufactured, remanufactured, repaired and tested under a quality assurance programme which satisfies the competent authority, in order to ensure that each manufactured, remanufactured or repaired IBC meets the requirements of this chapter.

NOTE: *ISO 16106:2020 "Transport packages for dangerous goods – Dangerous goods packagings, intermediate bulk containers (IBCs) and large packagings – Guidelines for the application of ISO 9001" provides acceptable guidance on procedures which may be followed.*

6.5.4.2 *Test requirements*: IBCs shall be subject to design type tests and, if applicable, to initial and periodic inspections and tests in accordance with 6.5.4.4.

6.5.4.3 *Certification*: in respect of each design type of IBC a certificate and mark (as in 6.5.2) shall be issued attesting that the design type including its equipment meets the test requirements.

6.5.4.4 *Inspection and testing*

NOTE: *See also 6.5.4.5 for tests and inspections on repaired IBCs.*

6.5.4.4.1 Every metal, rigid plastics and composite IBC shall be inspected to the satisfaction of the competent authority:

(a) Before it is put into service (including after remanufacture), and thereafter at intervals not exceeding five years, with regard to:

   (i) conformity to design type including marks;

   (ii) internal and external condition;

   (iii) proper functioning of service equipment;

   Thermal insulation, if any, need be removed only to the extent necessary for a proper examination of the body of the IBC;

(b) At intervals of not more than two and a half years, with regard to:

   (i) external condition;

   (ii) proper functioning of service equipment;

   Thermal insulation, if any, need be removed only to the extent necessary for a proper examination of the body of the IBC.

Each IBC shall correspond in all respects to its design type.

6.5.4.4.2 Every metal, rigid plastics and composite IBC for liquids, or for solids which are filled or discharged under pressure, shall undergo a suitable leakproofness test. This test is part of a quality assurance programme as stipulated in 6.5.4.1 which shows the capability of meeting the appropriate test level indicated in 6.5.6.7.3:

(a) Before it is first used for transport;

(b) At intervals of not more than two and a half years.

For this test the IBC shall be fitted with the primary bottom closure. The inner receptacle of a composite IBC may be tested without the outer casing, provided that the test results are not affected.

6.5.4.4.3   A report of each inspection and test shall be kept by the owner of the IBC at least until the next inspection or test. The report shall include the results of the inspection and test and shall identify the party performing the inspection and test (see also the marking requirements in 6.5.2.2.1).

6.5.4.4.4   The competent authority may at any time require proof, by tests in accordance with this chapter, that IBCs meet the requirements of the design type tests.

6.5.4.5   *Repaired IBCs*

6.5.4.5.1   When an IBC is impaired as a result of impact (e.g. accident) or any other cause, it shall be repaired or otherwise maintained (see definition of *"Routine maintenance of IBCs"* in 1.2.1), so as to conform to the design type. The bodies of rigid plastics IBCs and the inner receptacles of composite IBCs that are impaired shall be replaced.

6.5.4.5.2   In addition to any other testing and inspection requirements in these Regulations, an IBC shall be subjected to the full testing and inspection requirements set out in 6.5.4.4, and the required reports shall be prepared, whenever it is repaired.

6.5.4.5.3   The Party performing the tests and inspections after the repair shall durably mark the IBC near the manufacturer's UN design type marks to show:

(a)   The State in which the tests and inspections were carried out;

(b)   The name or authorized symbol of the party performing the tests and inspections; and

(c)   The date (month and year) of the tests and inspections.

6.5.4.5.4   Test and inspections performed in accordance with 6.5.4.5.2 may be considered to satisfy the requirements for the two and a half and five-year periodic tests and inspections.

6.5.5   **Specific requirements for IBCs**

6.5.5.1   *Specific requirements for metal IBCs*

6.5.5.1.1   These requirements apply to metal IBCs intended for the transport of solids and liquids. There are three categories of metal IBCs:

(a)   Those for solids which are filled or discharged by gravity (11A, 11B, 11N);

(b)   Those for solids which are filled or discharged at a gauge pressure greater than 10 kPa (0.1 bar) (21A, 21B, 21N); and

(c)   Those for liquids (31A, 31B, 31N).

6.5.5.1.2   Bodies shall be made of suitable ductile metal in which the weldability has been fully demonstrated. Welds shall be skilfully made and afford complete safety. Low-temperature performance shall be taken into account when appropriate.

6.5.5.1.3   Care shall be taken to avoid damage by galvanic action due to the juxtaposition of dissimilar metals.

6.5.5.1.4   Aluminium IBCs intended for the carriage of flammable liquids shall have no movable parts, such as covers, closures, etc., made of unprotected steel liable to rust, which might cause a dangerous reaction by coming into frictional or percussive contact with the aluminium.

6.5.5.1.5　　Metal IBCs shall be made of metals which meet the following requirements:

(a) For steel the elongation at fracture, in %, shall not be less than $\dfrac{10000}{Rm}$ with an absolute minimum of 20 %, where Rm = guaranteed minimum tensile strength of the steel to be used, in N/mm^2;

(b) For aluminium the elongation at fracture, in %, shall not be less than $\dfrac{10000}{6Rm}$ with an absolute minimum of 8 % where Rm = guaranteed minimum tensile strength of the aluminium to be used, in N/mm^2.

Specimens used to determine the elongation at fracture shall be taken transversely to the direction of rolling and be so secured that:

$$L_0 = 5d \quad \text{or}$$

$$L_0 = 5.65\sqrt{A}$$

where: L_0 = gauge length of the specimen before the test

　　　　d = diameter

　　　　A = cross-sectional area of test specimen.

6.5.5.1.6　　*Minimum wall thickness*

Metal IBCs with a capacity of more than 1500 *l* shall comply with the following minimum wall thickness requirement:

(a) For a reference steel having a product of Rm × A$_o$ = 10 000, the wall thickness shall not be less than:

Wall thickness (T) in mm			
Types 11A, 11B, 11N		Types 21A, 21B, 21N, 31A, 31B, 31N	
Unprotected	Protected	Unprotected	Protected
T = C/2 000 + 1.5	T = C/2 000 + 1.0	T = C/1 000 + 1.0	T = C/2 000 + 1.5

where: A_0 = minimum elongation (as a percentage) of the reference steel to be used on fracture under tensile stress (see 6.5.5.1.5);

　　　　C = capacity in litres;

(b) For metals other than the reference steel described in (a), the minimum wall thickness is given by the following equivalence formula:

$$e_1 = \dfrac{21.4 \times e_0}{\sqrt[3]{Rm_1\, A_1}}$$

where: e_1 = required equivalent wall thickness of the metal to be used (in mm);

　　　　e_0 = required minimum wall thickness for the reference steel (in mm);

　　　　Rm_1 = guaranteed minimum tensile strength of the metal to be used (in N/mm^2) (see (c));

　　　　A_1 = minimum elongation (as a percentage) of the metal to be used on fracture under tensile stress (see 6.5.5.1.5);

However, in no case shall the wall thickness be less than 1.5 mm;

(c) For purposes of the calculation described in (b), the guaranteed minimum tensile strength of the metal to be used (Rm_1) shall be the minimum value according to national or international material standards. However, for austenitic steels, the specified minimum value for Rm according to the material standards may be increased by up to 15 % when a greater value is attested in the material inspection certificate. When no material standard exists for the material in question, the value of Rm shall be the minimum value attested in the material inspection certificate.

6.5.5.1.7   Pressure relief requirements: IBCs for liquids shall be capable of releasing a sufficient amount of vapour in the event of fire engulfment to ensure that no rupture of the body will occur. This can be achieved by conventional pressure-relief devices or by other constructional means. The start-to-discharge pressure shall not be higher than 65 kPa (0.65 bar) and no lower than the total gauge pressure experienced in the IBC (i.e. the vapour pressure of the filling substance plus the partial pressure of the air or other inert gases, minus 100 kPa (1 bar)) at 55 °C, determined on the basis of a maximum degree of filling as defined in 4.1.1.4. The required relief devices shall be fitted in the vapour space.

6.5.5.2   *Specific requirements for flexible IBCs*

6.5.5.2.1   These requirements apply to flexible IBCs of the following types:

13H1	woven plastics without coating or liner
13H2	woven plastics, coated
13H3	woven plastics with liner
13H4	woven plastics, coated and with liner
13H5	plastics film
13L1	textile without coating or liner
13L2	textile, coated
13L3	textile with liner
13L4	textile, coated and with liner
13M1	paper, multiwall
13M2	paper, multiwall, water-resistant

Flexible IBCs are intended for the transport of solids only.

6.5.5.2.2   Bodies shall be manufactured from suitable materials. The strength of the material and the construction of the flexible IBC shall be appropriate to its capacity and its intended use.

6.5.5.2.3   All materials used in the construction of flexible IBCs of types 13M1 and 13M2 shall, after complete immersion in water for not less than 24 hours, retain at least 85 % of the tensile strength as measured originally on the material conditioned to equilibrium at 67 % relative humidity or less.

6.5.5.2.4   Seams shall be formed by stitching, heat sealing, gluing or any equivalent method. All stitched seam-ends shall be secured.

6.5.5.2.5   Flexible IBCs shall provide adequate resistance to ageing and to degradation caused by ultraviolet radiation or the climatic conditions, or by the substance contained, thereby rendering them appropriate to their intended use.

6.5.5.2.6   For flexible plastics IBCs where protection against ultraviolet radiation is required, it shall be provided by the addition of carbon black or other suitable pigments or inhibitors. These additives shall be compatible with the contents and remain effective throughout the life of the body. Where use is made of carbon black, pigments or inhibitors other than those used in the manufacture of the tested design type, re-testing may be waived if changes in the carbon black content, the pigment content or the inhibitor content do not adversely affect the physical properties of the material of construction.

6.5.5.2.7   Additives may be incorporated into the material of the body to improve the resistance to ageing or to serve other purposes, provided that these do not adversely affect the physical or chemical properties of the material.

6.5.5.2.8   No material recovered from used receptacles shall be used in the manufacture of IBC bodies. Production residues or scrap from the same manufacturing process may, however, be used. Component parts such as fittings and pallet bases may also be used provided such components have not in any way been damaged in previous use.

6.5.5.2.9   When filled, the ratio of height to width shall be not more than 2:1.

6.5.5.2.10   The liner shall be made of a suitable material. The strength of the material used and the construction of the liner shall be appropriate to the capacity of the IBC and the intended use. Joins and closures shall be sift proof and capable of withstanding pressures and impacts liable to occur under normal conditions of handling and transport.

6.5.5.3   *Specific requirements for rigid plastics IBCs*

6.5.5.3.1   These requirements apply to rigid plastics IBCs for the transport of solids or liquids. Rigid plastics IBCs are of the following types:

- 11H1   fitted with structural equipment designed to withstand the whole load when IBCs are stacked, for solids which are filled or discharged by gravity
- 11H2   freestanding, for solids which are filled or discharged by gravity
- 21H1   fitted with structural equipment designed to withstand the whole load when IBCs are stacked, for solids which are filled or discharged under pressure
- 21H2   freestanding, for solids which are filled or discharged under pressure
- 31H1   fitted with structural equipment designed to withstand the whole load when IBCs are stacked, for liquids
- 31H2   freestanding, for liquids.

6.5.5.3.2   The body shall be manufactured from suitable plastics material of known specifications and be of adequate strength in relation to its capacity and its intended use. Except for recycled plastics material as defined in 1.2.1, no used material other than production residues or regrind from the same manufacturing process may be used. The material shall be adequately resistant to ageing and to degradation caused by the substance contained or, where relevant, by ultraviolet radiation. Low temperature performance shall be taken into account when appropriate. Any permeation of the substance contained shall not constitute a danger under normal conditions of transport.

6.5.5.3.3   Where protection against ultraviolet radiation is required, it shall be provided by the addition of carbon black or other suitable pigments or inhibitors. These additives shall be compatible with the contents and remain effective throughout the life of the body. Where use is made of carbon black, pigments or inhibitors other than those used in the manufacture of the tested design type, re-testing may be waived if changes in the carbon black content, the pigment content or the inhibitor content do not adversely affect the physical properties of the material of construction.

6.5.5.3.4   Additives may be incorporated in the material of the body to improve the resistance to ageing or to serve other purposes, provided that these do not adversely affect the physical or chemical properties of the material.

6.5.5.4   *Specific requirements for composite IBCs with plastics inner receptacles*

6.5.5.4.1   These requirements apply to composite IBCs for the transport of solids and liquids of the following types:

- 11HZ1   composite IBCs with a rigid plastics inner receptacle, for solids filled or discharged by gravity
- 11HZ2   composite IBCs with a flexible plastics inner receptacle, for solids filled or discharged by gravity
- 21HZ1   composite IBCs with a rigid plastics inner receptacle, for solids filled or discharged under pressure
- 21HZ2   composite IBCs with a flexible plastics inner receptacle, for solids filled or discharged under pressure

31HZ1 composite IBCs with a rigid plastics inner receptacle, for liquids
31HZ2 composite IBCs with a flexible plastics inner receptacle, for liquids.

This code shall be completed by replacing the letter Z by a capital letter in accordance with 6.5.1.4.1 (b) to indicate the nature of the material used for the outer casing.

6.5.5.4.2 The inner receptacle is not intended to perform a containment function without its outer casing. A "rigid" inner receptacle is a receptacle which retains its general shape when empty without closures in place and without benefit of the outer casing. Any inner receptacle that is not "rigid" is considered to be "flexible".

6.5.5.4.3 The outer casing normally consists of rigid material formed so as to protect the inner receptacle from physical damage during handling and transport but is not intended to perform the containment function. It includes the base pallet where appropriate.

6.5.5.4.4 A composite IBC with a fully enclosing outer casing shall be so designed that the integrity of the inner container may be readily assessed following the leakproofness and hydraulic tests.

6.5.5.4.5 IBCs of type 31HZ2 shall be limited to a capacity of not more than 1250 litres.

6.5.5.4.6 The inner receptacle shall be manufactured from suitable plastics material of known specifications and be of adequate strength in relation to its capacity and its intended use. Except for recycled plastics material as defined in 1.2.1, no used material other than production residues or regrind from the same manufacturing process may be used. The material shall be adequately resistant to ageing and to degradation caused by the substance contained or, where relevant, by ultraviolet radiation. Low temperature performance shall be taken into account when appropriate. Any permeation of the substance contained shall not constitute a danger under normal conditions of transport.

6.5.5.4.7 Where protection against ultraviolet radiation is required, it shall be provided by the addition of carbon black or other suitable pigments or inhibitors. These additives shall be compatible with the contents and remain effective throughout the life of the inner receptacle. Where use is made of carbon black, pigments or inhibitors, other than those used in the manufacture of the tested design type, retesting may be waived if changes in carbon black content, the pigment content or the inhibitor content do not adversely affect the physical properties of the material of construction.

6.5.5.4.8 Additives may be incorporated in the material of the inner receptacle to improve the resistance to ageing or to serve other purposes, provided that these do not adversely affect the physical or chemical properties of the material.

6.5.5.4.9 The inner receptacle of IBCs type 31HZ2 shall consist of at least three plies of film.

6.5.5.4.10 The strength of the material and the construction of the outer casing shall be appropriate to the capacity of the composite IBC and its intended use.

6.5.5.4.11 The outer casing shall be free of any projection that might damage the inner receptacle.

6.5.5.4.12 Outer casings of steel or aluminium shall be constructed of a suitable metal of adequate thickness.

6.5.5.4.13 Outer casings of natural wood shall be of well-seasoned wood, commercially dry and free from defects that would materially lessen the strength of any part of the casing. The tops and bottoms may be made of water-resistant reconstituted wood such as hardboard, particle board or other suitable type.

6.5.5.4.14 Outer casings of plywood shall be made of well-seasoned rotary cut, sliced or sawn veneer, commercially dry and free from defects that would materially lessen the strength of the casing. All adjacent plies shall be glued with water-resistant adhesive. Other suitable materials may be used with plywood for the construction of casings. Casings shall be firmly nailed or secured to corner posts or ends or be assembled by equally suitable devices.

6.5.5.4.15   The walls of outer casings of reconstituted wood shall be made of water-resistant reconstituted wood such as hardboard, particle board or other suitable type. Other parts of the casings may be made of other suitable material.

6.5.5.4.16   For fibreboard outer casings, strong and good quality solid or double-faced corrugated fibreboard (single or multiwall) shall be used appropriate to the capacity of the casing and to its intended use. The water resistance of the outer surface shall be such that the increase in mass, as determined in a test carried out over 30 minutes by the Cobb method of determining water absorption, is not greater than 155 g/m² - see ISO 535:2014. It shall have proper bending qualities. Fibreboard shall be cut, creased without scoring, and slotted so as to permit assembly without cracking, surface breaks or undue bending. The fluting of corrugated fibreboard shall be firmly glued to the facings.

6.5.5.4.17   The ends of fibreboard outer casings may have a wooden frame or be entirely of wood. Reinforcements of wooden battens may be used.

6.5.5.4.18   Manufacturing joins in the fibreboard outer casing shall be taped, lapped and glued, or lapped and stitched with metal staples. Lapped joins shall have an appropriate overlap. Where closing is effected by gluing or taping, a water-resistant adhesive shall be used.

6.5.5.4.19   Where the outer casing is of plastics material, the relevant requirements of 6.5.5.4.6 to 6.5.5.4.8 apply.

6.5.5.4.20   The outer casing of a 31HZ2 shall enclose the inner receptacle on all sides.

6.5.5.4.21   Any integral pallet base forming part of an IBC or any detachable pallet shall be suitable for mechanical handling with the IBC filled to its maximum permissible gross mass.

6.5.5.4.22   The pallet or integral base shall be designed so as to avoid any protrusion of the base of the IBC that might be liable to damage in handling.

6.5.5.4.23   The outer casing shall be secured to any detachable pallet to ensure stability in handling and transport. Where a detachable pallet is used, its top surface shall be free from sharp protrusions that might damage the IBC.

6.5.5.4.24   Strengthening devices such as timber supports to increase stacking performance may be used but shall be external to the inner receptacle.

6.5.5.4.25   Where IBCs are intended for stacking, the bearing surface shall be such as to distribute the load in a safe manner. Such IBCs shall be designed so that the load is not supported by the inner receptacle.

6.5.5.5   *Specific requirements for fibreboard IBCs*

6.5.5.5.1   These requirements apply to fibreboard IBCs for the transport of solids which are filled or discharged by gravity. Fibreboard IBCs are of the following type: 11G.

6.5.5.5.2   Fibreboard IBCs shall not incorporate top lifting devices.

6.5.5.5.3   The body shall be made of strong and good quality solid or double-faced corrugated fibreboard (single or multiwall), appropriate to the capacity of the IBC and to its intended use. The water resistance of the outer surface shall be such that the increase in mass, as determined in a test carried out over a period of 30 minutes by the Cobb method of determining water absorption, is not greater than 155 g/m² - see ISO 535:2014. It shall have proper bending qualities. Fibreboard shall be cut, creased without scoring, and slotted so as to permit assembly without cracking, surface breaks or undue bending. The fluting or corrugated fibreboard shall be firmly glued to the facings.

6.5.5.5.4   The walls, including top and bottom, shall have a minimum puncture resistance of 15 J measured according to ISO 3036:1975.

6.5.5.5.5   Manufacturing joins in the body of IBCs shall be made with an appropriate overlap and shall be taped, glued, stitched with metal staples or fastened by other means at least equally effective. Where joins are effected by gluing or taping, a water-resistant adhesive shall be used. Metal staples shall pass completely through all pieces to be fastened and be formed or protected so that any inner liner cannot be abraded or punctured by them.

6.5.5.5.6   The liner shall be made of a suitable material. The strength of the material used and the construction of the liner shall be appropriate to the capacity of the IBC and the intended use. Joins and closures shall be sift-proof and capable of withstanding pressures and impacts liable to occur under normal conditions of handling and transport.

6.5.5.5.7   Any integral pallet base forming part of an IBC or any detachable pallet shall be suitable for mechanical handling with the IBC filled to its maximum permissible gross mass.

6.5.5.5.8   The pallet or integral base shall be designed so as to avoid any protrusion of the base of the IBC that might be liable to damage in handling.

6.5.5.5.9   The body shall be secured to any detachable pallet to ensure stability in handling and transport. Where a detachable pallet is used, its top surface shall be free from sharp protrusions that might damage the IBC.

6.5.5.5.10   Strengthening devices such as timber supports to increase stacking performance may be used but shall be external to the liner.

6.5.5.5.11   Where IBCs are intended for stacking, the bearing surface shall be such as to distribute the load in a safe manner.

6.5.5.6   *Specific requirements for wooden IBCs*

6.5.5.6.1   These requirements apply to wooden IBCs for the transport of solids which are filled or discharged by gravity. Wooden IBCs are of the following types:

        11C   natural wood with inner liner
        11D   plywood with inner liner
        11F   reconstituted wood with inner liner.

6.5.5.6.2   Wooden IBCs shall not incorporate top lifting devices.

6.5.5.6.3   The strength of the materials used and the method of construction of the body shall be appropriate to the capacity and intended use of the IBC.

6.5.5.6.4   Natural wood shall be well-seasoned, commercially dry and free from defects that would materially lessen the strength of any part of the IBC. Each part of the IBC shall consist of one piece or be equivalent thereto. Parts are considered equivalent to one piece when a suitable method of glued assembly is used as for instance Lindermann joint, tongue and groove joint, ship lap or rabbet joint; or butt joint with at least two corrugated metal fasteners at each joint, or when other methods at least equally effective are used.

6.5.5.6.5   Bodies of plywood shall be at least 3-ply. It shall be made of well-seasoned rotary cut, sliced or sawn veneer, commercially dry and free from defects that would materially lessen the strength of the body. All adjacent plies shall be glued with water-resistant adhesive. Other suitable materials may be used with plywood for the construction of the body.

6.5.5.6.6   Bodies of reconstituted wood shall be made of water-resistant reconstituted wood such as hardboard, particle board or other suitable type.

6.5.5.6.7   IBCs shall be firmly nailed or secured to corner posts or ends or be assembled by equally suitable devices.

6.5.5.6.8   The liner shall be made of a suitable material. The strength of the material used and the construction of the liner shall be appropriate to the capacity of the IBC and the intended use. Joins and closures shall be sift-proof and capable of withstanding pressures and impacts liable to occur under normal conditions of handling and transport.

6.5.5.6.9   Any integral pallet base forming part of an IBC or any detachable pallet shall be suitable for mechanical handling with the IBC filled to its maximum permissible gross mass.

6.5.5.6.10   The pallet or integral base shall be designed so as to avoid any protrusion of the base of the IBC that might be liable to damage in handling.

6.5.5.6.11   The body shall be secured to any detachable pallet to ensure stability in handling and transport. Where a detachable pallet is used, its top surface shall be free from sharp protrusions that might damage the IBC.

6.5.5.6.12   Strengthening devices such as timber supports to increase stacking performance may be used but shall be external to the liner.

6.5.5.6.13   Where IBCs are intended for stacking, the bearing surface shall be such as to distribute the load in a safe manner.

6.5.6   Test requirements for IBCs

6.5.6.1   *Performance and frequency of tests*

6.5.6.1.1   Each IBC design type shall successfully pass the tests prescribed in this chapter before being used. An IBC design type is defined by the design, size, material and thickness, manner of construction and means of filling and discharging but may include various surface treatments. It also includes IBCs which differ from the design type only in their lesser external dimensions.

6.5.6.1.2   Tests shall be carried out on IBCs prepared for transport. IBCs shall be filled as indicated in the relevant sections. The substances to be transported in the IBCs may be replaced by other substances except where this would invalidate the results of the tests. For solids, when another substance is used it shall have the same physical characteristics (mass, grain size, etc.) as the substance to be carried. It is permissible to use additives, such as bags of lead shot, to achieve the requisite total package mass, so long as they are placed so that the test results are not affected.

6.5.6.2   *Design type tests*

6.5.6.2.1   One IBC of each design type, size, wall thickness and manner of construction shall be submitted to the tests listed in the order shown in 6.5.6.3.5 and as set out in 6.5.6.4 to 6.5.6.13. These design type tests shall be carried out as required by the competent authority.

6.5.6.2.2   The competent authority may permit the selective testing of IBCs which differ only in minor respects from a tested type, e.g. with small reductions in external dimensions.

6.5.6.2.3   If detachable pallets are used in the tests, the test report issued in accordance with 6.5.6.14 shall include a technical description of the pallets used.

6.5.6.3   *Preparation of IBCs for testing*

6.5.6.3.1   Paper and fibreboard IBCs and composite IBCs with fibreboard outer casings shall be conditioned for at least 24 hours in an atmosphere having a controlled temperature and relative humidity (r.h.). There are three options, one of which shall be chosen. The preferred atmosphere is 23 ± 2 °C and $50\% \pm 2\%$ r.h. The two other options are 20 ± 2 °C and $65\% \pm 2\%$ r.h.; or 27 ± 2 °C and $65\% \pm 2\%$ r.h.

NOTE: *Average values shall fall within these limits. Short-term fluctuations and measurement limitations may cause individual measurements to vary by up to ±5 % relative humidity without significant impairment of test reproducibility.*

6.5.6.3.2　Additional steps shall be taken to ascertain that the plastics material used in the manufacture of rigid plastics IBCs (Types 31H1 and 31H2) and composite IBCs (Types 31HZ1 and 31HZ2) complies respectively with the requirements in 6.5.5.3.2 to 6.5.5.3.4 and 6.5.5.4.6 to 6.5.5.4.8.

6.5.6.3.3　This may be done, for example, by submitting sample IBCs to a preliminary test extending over a long period, for example six months, during which the samples would remain filled with the substances they are intended to contain or with substances which are known to have at least as severe a stress-cracking, weakening or molecular degradation influence on the plastics materials in question, and after which the samples shall be submitted to the applicable tests listed on the table in 6.5.6.3.5.

6.5.6.3.4　Where the behaviour of the plastics material has been established by other means, the above compatibility test may be dispensed with.

6.5.6.3.5　*Design type tests required and sequential order*

Type of IBC	Vibration [f]	Bottom lift	Top lift [a]	Stacking [b]	Leak-proofness	Hydraulic pressure	Drop	Tear	Topple	Righting [e]
Metal:										
11A, 11B, 11N	-	1st [a]	2nd	3rd	-	-	4th [e]	-	-	-
21A, 21B, 21N	-	1st [a]	2nd	3rd	4th	5th	6th [e]	-	-	-
31A, 31B, 31N	1st	2nd [a]	3rd	4th	5th	6th	7th [e]	-	-	-
Flexible [d]	-	-	x [c]	x	-	-	x	x	x	x
Rigid plastics:										
11H1, 11H2	-	1st [a]	2nd	3rd	-	-	4th	-	-	-
21H1, 21H2	-	1st [a]	2nd	3rd	4th	5th	6th	-	-	-
31H1, 31H2	1st	2nd [a]	3rd	4th	5th	6th	7th	-	-	-
Composite:										
11HZ1, 11HZ2	-	1st [a]	2nd	3rd	-	-	4th [e]	-	-	-
21HZ1, 21HZ2	-	1st [a]	2nd	3rd	4th	5th	6th [e]	-	-	-
31HZ1, 31HZ2	1st	2nd [a]	3rd	4th	5th	6th	7th [e]	-	-	-
Fibreboard	-	1st	-	2nd	-	-	3rd	-	-	-
Wooden	-	1st	-	2nd	-	-	3rd	-	-	-

[a]　*When IBCs are designed for this method of handling.*
[b]　*When IBCs are designed to be stacked.*
[c]　*When IBCs are designated to be lifted from the top or the side.*
[d]　*Required test indicated by x; an IBC which has passed one test may be used for other tests, in any order.*
[e]　*Another IBC of the same design may be used for the drop test.*
[f]　*Another IBC of the same design may be used for the vibration test.*

6.5.6.4　**Bottom lift test**

6.5.6.4.1　*Applicability*

For all fibreboard and wooden IBCs, and for all types of IBC which are fitted with means of lifting from the base, as a design type test.

6.5.6.4.2　*Preparation of the IBC for test*

The IBC shall be filled. A load shall be added and evenly distributed. The mass of the filled IBC and the load shall be 1.25 times the maximum permissible gross mass.

6.5.6.4.3　*Method of testing*

The IBC shall be raised and lowered twice by a lift truck with the forks centrally positioned and spaced at three quarters of the dimension of the side of entry (unless the points of entry are fixed). The forks shall penetrate to three quarters of the direction of entry. The test shall be repeated from each possible direction of entry.

6.5.6.4.4 *Criteria for passing the test*

No permanent deformation which renders the IBC, including the base pallet, if any, unsafe for transport and no loss of contents.

6.5.6.5 **Top lift test**

6.5.6.5.1 *Applicability*

For all types of IBC which are designed to be lifted from the top and for flexible IBCs designed to be lifted from the top or the side, as a design type test.

6.5.6.5.2 *Preparation of the IBC for test*

Metal, rigid plastics and composite IBCs shall be filled. A load shall be added and evenly distributed. The mass of the filled IBC and the load shall be twice the maximum permissible gross mass.

Flexible IBCs shall be filled with a representative material and then shall be loaded to six times their maximum permissible gross mass, the load being evenly distributed.

6.5.6.5.3 *Methods of testing*

Metal and flexible IBCs shall be lifted in the manner for which they are designed until clear of the floor and maintained in that position for a period of five minutes.

Rigid plastics and composite IBCs shall be lifted:

(a) By each pair of diagonally opposite lifting devices, so that the hoisting forces are applied vertically, for a period of five minutes; and

(b) By each pair of diagonally opposite lifting devices, so that the hoisting forces are applied toward the centre at 45° to the vertical, for a period of five minutes.

6.5.6.5.4 Other methods of top lift testing and preparation at least equally effective may be used for flexible IBCs.

6.5.6.5.5 *Criteria for passing the test*

(a) Metal, rigid plastics and composite IBCs: the IBC remains safe for normal conditions of transport, there is no observable permanent deformation of the IBC, including the base pallet, if any, and no loss of contents;

(b) Flexible IBCs: no damage to the IBC or its lifting devices which renders the IBC unsafe for transport or handling and no loss of contents;

6.5.6.6 **Stacking test**

6.5.6.6.1 *Applicability*

For all types of IBC which are designed to be stacked on each other, as a design type test.

6.5.6.6.2 *Preparation of the IBC for test*

The IBC shall be filled to its maximum permissible gross mass. If the specific gravity of the product being used for testing makes this impracticable, the IBC shall be additionally loaded so that it is tested at its maximum permissible gross mass, the load being evenly distributed.

6.5.6.6.3 *Methods of testing*

(a) The IBC shall be placed on its base on level hard ground and subjected to a uniformly distributed superimposed test load (see 6.5.6.6.4). IBCs shall be subjected to the test load for a period of at least:

(i) 5 minutes, for metal IBCs;

(ii) 28 days at 40 °C, for rigid plastics IBCs of types 11H2, 21H2 and 31H2 and for composite IBCs with outer casings of plastics material which bear the stacking load (i.e., types 11HH1, 11HH2, 21HH1, 21HH2, 31HH1 and 31HH2);

(iii) 24 hours, for all other types of IBCs;

(b) The load shall be applied by one of the following methods:

(i) one or more IBCs of the same type filled to the maximum permissible gross mass stacked on the test IBC;

(ii) appropriate masses loaded onto either a flat plate or a reproduction of the base of the IBC, which is stacked on the test IBC.

6.5.6.6.4 *Calculation of superimposed test load*

The load to be placed on the IBC shall be 1.8 times the combined maximum permissible gross mass of the number of similar IBCs that may be stacked on top of the IBC during transport.

6.5.6.6.5 *Criteria for passing the test*

(a) All types of IBCs other than flexible IBCs: no permanent deformation which renders the IBC including the base pallet, if any, unsafe for transport and no loss of contents;

(b) Flexible IBCs: no deterioration of the body which renders the IBC unsafe for transport and no loss of contents.

6.5.6.7 *Leakproofness test*

6.5.6.7.1 *Applicability*

For those types of IBCs used for liquids or for solids filled or discharged under pressure, as a design type test and periodic test.

6.5.6.7.2 *Preparation of the IBC for test*

The test shall be carried out before the fitting of any thermal insulation equipment. Vented closures shall either be replaced by similar non-vented closures or the vent shall be sealed.

6.5.6.7.3 *Method of testing and pressure to be applied*

The test shall be carried out for a period of at least 10 minutes using air at a gauge pressure of not less than 20 kPa (0.2 bar). The air tightness of the IBC shall be determined by a suitable method such as by air-pressure differential test or by immersing the IBC in water or, for metal IBCs, by coating the seams and joints with a soap solution. In the latter case a correction factor shall be applied for the hydrostatic pressure.

6.5.6.7.4 *Criterion for passing the test*

No leakage of air.

6.5.6.8 *Hydraulic pressure test*

6.5.6.8.1 *Applicability*

For those types of IBCs used for liquids or for solids filled or discharged under pressure, as a design type test.

6.5.6.8.2 *Preparation of the IBC for test*

The test shall be carried out before the fitting of any thermal insulation equipment. Pressure-relief devices shall be removed and their apertures plugged, or shall be rendered inoperative.

6.5.6.8.3 *Method of testing*

The test shall be carried out for a period of at least 10 minutes applying a hydraulic pressure not less than that indicated in 6.5.6.8.4. The IBCs shall not be mechanically restrained during the test.

6.5.6.8.4 *Pressures to be applied*

6.5.6.8.4.1 Metal IBCs

(a) For IBCs of types 21A, 21B and 21N, for packing group I solids, a 250 kPa (2.5 bar) gauge pressure;

(b) For IBCs of types 21A, 21B, 21N, 31A, 31B and 31N, for packing groups II or III substances, a 200 kPa (2 bar) gauge pressure;

(c) In addition, for IBCs of types 31A, 31B and 31N, a 65 kPa (0.65 bar) gauge pressure. This test shall be performed before the 200 kPa test.

6.5.6.8.4.2 Rigid plastics and composite IBCs

(a) For IBCs of types 21H1, 21H2, 21HZ1 and 21HZ2: 75 kPa (0.75 bar) (gauge);

(b) For IBCs of types 31H1, 31H2, 31HZ1 and 31HZ2: whichever is the greater of two values, the first as determined by one of the following methods:

    (i) the total gauge pressure measured in the IBC (i.e. the vapour pressure of the filling substance and the partial pressure of the air or other inert gases, minus 100 kPa) at 55 °C multiplied by a safety factor of 1.5; this total gauge pressure shall be determined on the basis of a maximum degree of filling in accordance with 4.1.1.4 and a filling temperature of 15 °C;

    (ii) 1.75 times the vapour pressure at 50 °C of the substance to be transported minus 100 kPa, but with a minimum test pressure of 100 kPa;

    (iii) 1.5 times the vapour pressure at 55 °C of the substance to be transported minus 100 kPa, but with a minimum test pressure of 100 kPa;

and the second as determined by the following method:

    (iv) twice the static pressure of the substance to be transported, with a minimum of twice the static pressure of water.

6.5.6.8.5 *Criteria for passing the test(s)*

(a) For IBCs of types 21A, 21B, 21N, 31A, 31B and 31N, when subjected to the test pressure specified in 6.5.6.8.4.1 (a) or (b): no leakage;

(b) For IBCs of types 31A, 31B and 31N, when subjected to the test pressure specified in 6.5.6.8.4.1 (c): neither permanent deformation which would render the IBC unsafe for transport, nor leakage;

(c) For rigid plastics and composite IBCs: no permanent deformation which would render the IBC unsafe for transport and no leakage.

6.5.6.9 *Drop test*

6.5.6.9.1 *Applicability*

For all types of IBCs, as a design type test.

6.5.6.9.2 *Preparation of the IBC for test*

(a) Metal IBCs: the IBC shall be filled to not less than 95 % of its maximum capacity for solids or 98 % of its maximum capacity for liquids. Pressure-relief devices shall be removed and their apertures plugged, or shall be rendered inoperative;

(b) Flexible IBCs: the IBC shall be filled to the maximum permissible gross mass, the contents being evenly distributed;

(c) Rigid plastics and composite IBCs: the IBC shall be filled to not less than 95 % of its maximum capacity for solids or 98 % of its maximum capacity for liquids. Arrangements provided for pressure-relief may be removed and plugged or rendered inoperative. Testing of IBCs shall be carried out when the temperature of the test sample and its contents has been reduced to minus 18 °C or lower. Where test samples of composite IBCs are prepared in this way the conditioning specified in 6.5.6.3.1 may be waived. Test liquids shall be kept in the liquid state, if necessary by the addition of anti-freeze. This conditioning may be disregarded if the materials in question are of sufficient ductility and tensile strength at low temperatures;

(d) Fibreboard and wooden IBCs: The IBC shall be filled to not less than 95 % of its maximum capacity.

6.5.6.9.3 *Method of testing*

The IBC shall be dropped on its base onto a non-resilient, horizontal, flat, massive and rigid surface in conformity with the requirements of 6.1.5.3.4, in such a manner as to ensure that the point of impact is that part of the base of the IBC considered to be the most vulnerable. IBCs of 0.45 m^3 or less capacity shall also be dropped:

(a) Metal IBCs: on the most vulnerable part other than the part of the base tested in the first drop;

(b) Flexible IBCs: on the most vulnerable side;

(c) Rigid plastics, composite, fibreboard and wooden IBCs: flat on a side, flat on the top and on a corner.

The same IBC or a different IBC of the same design may be used for each drop.

6.5.6.9.4 *Drop height*

For solids and liquids, if the test is performed with the solid or liquid to be transported or with another substance having essentially the same physical characteristics:

Packing group I	Packing group II	Packing group III
1.8 m	1.2 m	0.8 m

For liquids if the test is performed with water:

(a) Where the substances to be transported have a relative density not exceeding 1.2:

Packing group II	Packing group III
1.2 m	0.8 m

(b) Where the substances to be transported have a relative density exceeding 1.2, the drop heights shall be calculated on the basis of the relative density (d) of the substance to be transported rounded up to the first decimal as follows:

Packing group II	Packing group III
d × 1.0 m	d × 0.67 m

6.5.6.9.5 *Criteria for passing the test(s)*

(a) Metal IBCs: no loss of contents;

(b) Flexible IBCs: no loss of contents. A slight discharge, e.g. from closures or stitch holes, upon impact shall not be considered to be a failure of the IBC provided that no further leakage occurs after the IBC has been raised clear of the ground;

(c) Rigid plastics, composite, fibreboard and wooden IBCs: no loss of contents. A slight discharge from a closure upon impact shall not be considered to be a failure of the IBC provided that no further leakage occurs;

(d) All IBCs: no damage which renders the IBC unsafe to be transported for salvage or for disposal, and no loss of contents. In addition, the IBC shall be capable of being lifted by an appropriate means until clear of the floor for five minutes.

NOTE: *The criteria in (d) apply to design types for IBCs manufactured as from 1 January 2011.*

6.5.6.10 **Tear test**

6.5.6.10.1 *Applicability*

For all types of flexible IBCs, as a design type test.

6.5.6.10.2 *Preparation of the IBC for test*

The IBC shall be filled to not less than 95 % of its capacity and to its maximum permissible gross mass, the contents being evenly distributed.

6.5.6.10.3 *Method of testing*

Once the IBC is placed on the ground, a 100 mm knife score, completely penetrating the wall of a wide face, is made at a 45° angle to the principal axis of the IBC, halfway between the bottom surface and the top level of the contents. The IBC shall then be subjected to a uniformly distributed superimposed load equivalent to twice the maximum permissible gross mass. The load shall be applied for at least five minutes. An IBC which is designed to be lifted from the top or the side shall then, after removal of the superimposed load, be lifted clear of the floor and maintained in that position for a period of five minutes.

6.5.6.10.4 *Criterion for passing the test*

The cut shall not propagate more than 25 % of its original length.

6.5.6.11 *Topple test*

6.5.6.11.1 *Applicability*

For all types of flexible IBCs, as a design type test.

6.5.6.11.2 *Preparation of the IBC for test*

The IBC shall be filled to not less than 95 % of its capacity and to its maximum permissible gross mass, the contents being evenly distributed.

6.5.6.11.3 *Method of testing*

The IBC shall be caused to topple on to any part of its top on to a rigid, non-resilient, smooth, flat and horizontal surface.

6.5.6.11.4 *Topple height*

Packing group I	Packing group II	Packing group III
1.8 m	1.2 m	0.8 m

6.5.6.11.5 *Criterion for passing the test*

No loss of contents. A slight discharge, e.g. from closures or stitch holes, upon impact shall not be considered to be a failure of the IBC provided that no further leakage occurs.

6.5.6.12 *Righting test*

6.5.6.12.1 *Applicability*

For all flexible IBCs designed to be lifted from the top or side, as a design type test.

6.5.6.12.2 *Preparation of the IBC for test*

The IBC shall be filled to not less than 95 % of its capacity and to its maximum permissible gross mass, the contents being evenly distributed.

6.5.6.12.3 *Method of testing*

The IBC, lying on its side, shall be lifted at a speed of at least 0.1 m/s to upright position, clear of the floor, by one lifting device or by two lifting devices when four are provided.

6.5.6.12.4 *Criterion for passing the test*

No damage to the IBC or its lifting devices which renders the IBC unsafe for transport or handling.

6.5.6.13 *Vibration test*

6.5.6.13.1 *Applicability*

For all IBCs used for liquids, as a design type test.

NOTE: *This test applies to design types for IBCs manufactured as from 1 January 2011.*

6.5.6.13.2 *Preparation of the IBC for test*

A sample IBC shall be selected at random and shall be fitted and closed as for transport. The IBC shall be filled with water to not less than 98 % of its maximum capacity.

6.5.6.13.3   *Test method and duration*

6.5.6.13.3.1   The IBC shall be placed in the center of the test machine platform with a vertical sinusoidal, double amplitude (peak-to peak displacement) of 25 mm ± 5 %. If necessary, restraining devices shall be attached to the platform to prevent the specimen from moving horizontally off the platform without restricting vertical movement.

6.5.6.13.3.2   The test shall be conducted for one hour at a frequency that causes part of the base of the IBC to be momentarily raised from the vibrating platform for part of each cycle to such a degree that a metal shim can be completely inserted intermittently at, at least, one point between the base of the IBC and the test platform. The frequency may need to be adjusted after the initial set point to prevent the packaging from going into resonance. Nevertheless, the test frequency shall continue to allow placement of the metal shim under the IBC as described in this paragraph. The continuing ability to insert the metal shim is essential to passing the test. The metal shim used for this test shall be at least 1.6 mm thick, 50 mm wide, and be of sufficient length to be inserted between the IBC and the test platform a minimum of 100 mm to perform the test.

6.5.6.13.4   *Criteria for passing the test*

No leakage or rupture shall be observed. In addition, no breakage or failure of structural components, such as broken welds or failed fastenings, shall be observed.

6.5.6.14   Test report

6.5.6.14.1   A test report containing at least the following particulars shall be drawn up and shall be available to the users of the IBC:

1. Name and address of the test facility

2. Name and address of applicant (where appropriate)

3. A unique test report identification

4. Date of the test report

5. Manufacturer of the IBC

6. Description of the IBC design type (e.g. dimensions, materials, closures, thickness, etc.) including method of manufacture (e.g. blow moulding) and which may include drawing(s) and/or photograph(s)

7. Maximum capacity

8. Characteristics of test contents, e.g. viscosity and relative density for liquids and particle size for solids. For rigid plastics and composite IBCs subject to the hydraulic pressure test in 6.5.6.8, the temperature of the water used.

9. Test descriptions and results

10. The test report shall be signed with the name and status of the signatory

6.5.6.14.2   The test report shall contain statements that the IBC prepared as for transport was tested in accordance with the appropriate requirements of this chapter and that the use of other packaging methods or components may render it invalid. A copy of the test report shall be available to the competent authority.

CHAPTER 6.6

REQUIREMENTS FOR THE CONSTRUCTION AND TESTING OF LARGE PACKAGINGS

6.6.1 **General**

6.6.1.1 The requirements of this chapter do not apply to:

(a) Class 2, except articles including aerosols;

(b) Class 6.2, except clinical waste of UN 3291;

(c) Class 7 packages containing radioactive material.

6.6.1.2 Large packagings shall be manufactured, tested and remanufactured under a quality assurance programme which satisfies the competent authority in order to ensure that each manufactured or remanufactured large packaging meets the requirements of this chapter.

NOTE: *ISO 16106:2020 "Transport packages for dangerous goods – Dangerous goods packagings, intermediate bulk containers (IBCs) and large packagings – Guidelines for the application of ISO 9001" provides acceptable guidance on procedures which may be followed.*

6.6.1.3 The specific requirements for large packagings in 6.6.4 are based on large packagings currently used. In order to take into account progress in science and technology, there is no objection to the use of large packagings having specifications different from those in 6.6.4 provided they are equally effective, acceptable to the competent authority and able to successfully fulfil the requirements described in 6.6.5. Methods of testing other than those described in these Regulations are acceptable provided they are equivalent.

6.6.1.4 Manufacturers and subsequent distributors of packagings shall provide information regarding procedures to be followed and a description of the types and dimensions of closures (including required gaskets) and any other components needed to ensure that packages as presented for transport are capable of passing the applicable performance tests of this chapter.

6.6.2 **Code for designating types of large packagings**

6.6.2.1 The code used for large packagings consists of:

(a) Two Arabic numerals:

50 for rigid large packagings; or
51 for flexible large packagings; and

(b) Capital letters in Latin characters indicating the nature of the material, e.g. wood, steel, etc. The capital letters used shall be those shown in 6.1.2.6.

6.6.2.2 The letters "T" or "W" may follow the large packaging code. The letter "T" signifies a large salvage packaging conforming to the requirements of 6.6.5.1.9. The letter "W" signifies that the large packaging, although of the same type indicated by the code, is manufactured to a specification different from those in 6.6.4 and is considered equivalent in accordance with the requirements in 6.6.1.3.

6.6.3 Marking

6.6.3.1 *Primary marking*

Each large packaging manufactured and intended for the use according to these Regulations shall bear marks which are durable, legible and placed in a location so as to be readily visible. Letters, numerals and symbols shall be at least 12 mm high and shall show:

(a) The United Nations packaging symbol .

This symbol shall not be used for any purpose other than certifying that a packaging, a flexible bulk container, a portable tank or a MEGC complies with the relevant requirements in chapter 6.1, 6.2, 6.3, 6.5, 6.6, 6.7 or 6.8.

For metal large packagings on which the marks are stamped or embossed, the capital letters "UN" may be applied instead of the symbol;

(b) The code "50" designating a large rigid packaging or "51" for flexible large packagings, followed by the material type in accordance with 6.5.1.4.1 (b);

(c) A capital letter designating the packing group(s) for which the design type has been approved:

X for packing groups I, II and III
Y for packing groups II and III
Z for packing group III only;

(d) The month and year (last two digits) of manufacture;

(e) The State authorising the allocation of the mark; indicated by the distinguishing sign used on vehicles in international road traffic[1];

(f) The name or symbol of the manufacturer and other identification of the large packagings as specified by the competent authority;

(g) The stacking test load in kg. For large packagings not designed for stacking the figure "0" shall be shown;

(h) The maximum permissible gross mass in kilograms.

The primary mark required above shall be applied in the sequence of the sub-paragraphs.

Each mark applied in accordance with (a) to (h) shall be clearly separated, e.g. by a slash or space, so as to be easily identifiable.

---

[1] *Distinguishing sign of the State of registration used on motor vehicles and trailers in international road traffic, e.g. in accordance with the Geneva Convention on Road Traffic of 1949 or the Vienna Convention on Road Traffic of 1968.*

6.6.3.2 *Examples of marking*

ⓤⓝ	50 A/X/05/01/N/PQRS 2500/1000	For a large steel packaging suitable for stacking; stacking load: 2 500 kg; maximum gross mass: 1 000 kg.
ⓤⓝ	50AT/Y/05/01/B/PQRS 2500/1000	For a large steel salvage packaging suitable for stacking; stacking load: 2 500 kg; maximum gross mass: 1 000 kg.
ⓤⓝ	50 H/Y04/02/D/ABCD 9870/800	For a large plastics packaging not suitable for stacking; maximum gross mass: 800 kg.
ⓤⓝ	51H/Z/06/01/S/19990/500	For a large flexible packaging not suitable for stacking; maximum gross mass: 500 kg.

6.6.3.3 The maximum permitted stacking load applicable shall be displayed on a symbol as shown in figure 6.6.1 or figure 6.6.2. The symbol shall be durable and clearly visible.

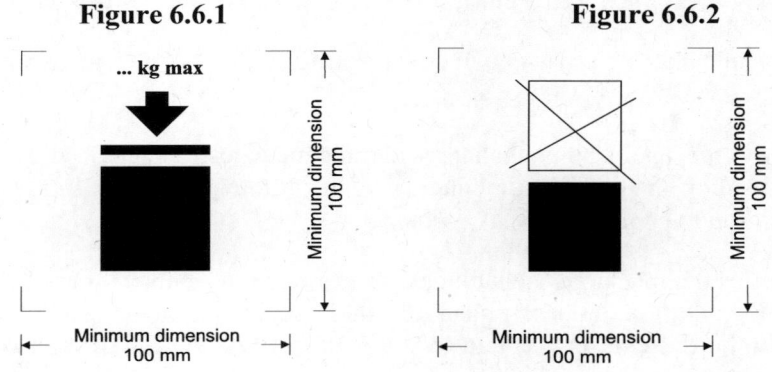

Figure 6.6.1 — Large packagings capable of being stacked

Figure 6.6.2 — Large packagings NOT capable of being stacked

The minimum dimensions shall be 100 mm × 100 mm. The letters and numbers indicating the mass shall be at least 12 mm high. The area within the printer's marks indicated by the dimensional arrows shall be square. Where dimensions are not specified, all features shall be in approximate proportion to those shown. The mass marked above the symbol shall not exceed the load imposed during the design type test (see 6.6.5.3.3.4) divided by 1.8.

NOTE: *The provisions of 6.6.3.3 shall apply to all large packagings manufactured, repaired or remanufactured as from 1 January 2015. The provisions of 6.6.3.3 from the seventeenth revised edition of the Recommendations on the Transport of Dangerous Goods, Model Regulations may continue to be applied to all large packagings manufactured, repaired or remanufactured between 1 January 2015 and 31 December 2016.*

6.6.3.4 Where a large packaging conforms to one or more than one tested large packaging design type, including one or more than one tested packaging or IBC design type, the large packaging may bear more than one mark to indicate the relevant performance test requirements that have been met. Where more than one mark appears on a large packaging, the marks shall appear in close proximity to one another and each mark shall appear in its entirety.

6.6.4 **Specific requirements for large packagings**

6.6.4.1 *Specific requirements for metal large packagings*

        50A   steel
        50B   aluminium
        50N   metal (other than steel or aluminium)

6.6.4.1.1   The large packaging shall be made of suitable ductile metal in which the weldability has been fully demonstrated. Welds shall be skilfully made and afford complete safety. Low-temperature performance shall be taken into account when appropriate.

6.6.4.1.2   Care shall be taken to avoid damage by galvanic action due to the juxtaposition of dissimilar metals.

6.6.4.2   *Specific requirements for flexible material large packagings*

        51H   flexible plastics
        51M   flexible paper

6.6.4.2.1   The large packaging shall be manufactured from suitable materials. The strength of the material and the construction of the flexible large packagings shall be appropriate to its capacity and its intended use.

6.6.4.2.2   All materials used in the construction of flexible large packagings of types 51M shall, after complete immersion in water for not less than 24 hours, retain at least 85 % of the tensile strength as measured originally on the material conditioned to equilibrium at 67 % relative humidity or less.

6.6.4.2.3   Seams shall be formed by stitching, heat sealing, gluing or any equivalent method. All stitched seam-ends shall be secured.

6.6.4.2.4   Flexible large packagings shall provide adequate resistance to ageing and to degradation caused by ultraviolet radiation or the climatic conditions, or by the substance contained, thereby rendering them appropriate to their intended use.

6.6.4.2.5   For plastics flexible large packagings where protection against ultraviolet radiation is required, it shall be provided by the addition of carbon black or other suitable pigments or inhibitors. These additives shall be compatible with the contents and remain effective throughout the life of the large packaging. Where use is made of carbon black, pigments or inhibitors other than those used in the manufacture of the tested design type, re-testing may be waived if changes in the carbon black content, the pigment content or the inhibitor content do not adversely affect the physical properties of the material of construction.

6.6.4.2.6   Additives may be incorporated into the material of the large packaging to improve the resistance to ageing or to serve other purposes, provided that these do not adversely affect the physical or chemical properties of the material.

6.6.4.2.7   When filled, the ratio of height to width shall be not more than 2:1.

6.6.4.3   *Specific requirements for plastics large packagings*

        50H   rigid plastics

6.6.4.3.1   The large packaging shall be manufactured from suitable plastics material of known specifications and be of adequate strength in relation to its capacity and its intended use. The material shall be adequately resistant to ageing and to degradation caused by the substance contained or, where relevant, by ultraviolet radiation. Low temperature performance shall be taken into account when appropriate. Any permeation of the substance contained shall not constitute a danger under normal conditions of transport.

6.6.4.3.2   Where protection against ultraviolet radiation is required, it shall be provided by the addition of carbon black or other suitable pigments or inhibitors. These additives shall be compatible with the contents and remain effective throughout the life of the outer packaging. Where use is made of carbon black, pigments or inhibitors other than those used in the manufacture of the tested design type, re-testing may be waived if changes in the carbon black content, the pigment content or the inhibitor content do not adversely affect the physical properties of the material of construction.

6.6.4.3.3　　Additives may be incorporated in the material of the large packaging to improve the resistance to ageing or to serve other purposes, provided that these do not adversely affect the physical or chemical properties of the material.

6.6.4.4　　Specific requirements for fibreboard large packagings

　　　　50G　　rigid fibreboard

6.6.4.4.1　　Strong and good quality solid or double-faced corrugated fibreboard (single or multiwall) shall be used, appropriate to the capacity of the large packagings and to their intended use. The water resistance of the outer surface shall be such that the increase in mass, as determined in a test carried out over a period of 30 minutes by the Cobb method of determining water absorption, is not greater than 155 g/m^2 – see ISO 535:2014. It shall have proper bending qualities. Fibreboard shall be cut, creased without scoring, and slotted so as to permit assembly without cracking, surface breaks or undue bending. The fluting or corrugated fibreboard shall be firmly glued to the facings.

6.6.4.4.2　　The walls, including top and bottom, shall have a minimum puncture resistance of 15 J measured according to ISO 3036:1975.

6.6.4.4.3　　Manufacturing joins in the outer packaging of large packagings shall be made with an appropriate overlap and shall be taped, glued, stitched with metal staples or fastened by other means at least equally effective. Where joins are effected by gluing or taping, a water-resistant adhesive shall be used. Metal staples shall pass completely through all pieces to be fastened and be formed or protected so that any inner liner cannot be abraded or punctured by them.

6.6.4.4.4　　Any integral pallet base forming part of a large packaging or any detachable pallet shall be suitable for mechanical handling with the large packaging filled to its maximum permissible gross mass.

6.6.4.4.5　　The pallet or integral base shall be designed so as to avoid any protrusion of the base of the large packaging that might be liable to damage in handling.

6.6.4.4.6　　The body shall be secured to any detachable pallet to ensure stability in handling and transport. Where a detachable pallet is used, its top surface shall be free from sharp protrusions that might damage the large packaging.

6.6.4.4.7　　Strengthening devices such as timber supports to increase stacking performance may be used but shall be external to the liner.

6.6.4.4.8　　Where large packagings are intended for stacking, the bearing surface shall be such as to distribute the load in a safe manner.

6.6.4.5　　*Specific requirements for wooden large packagings*

　　　　50C　　natural wood
　　　　50D　　plywood
　　　　50F　　reconstituted wood

6.6.4.5.1　　The strength of the materials used and the method of construction shall be appropriate to the capacity and intended use of the large packagings.

6.6.4.5.2　　Natural wood shall be well-seasoned, commercially dry and free from defects that would materially lessen the strength of any part of the large packagings. Each part of the large packagings shall consist of one piece or be equivalent thereto. Parts are considered equivalent to one piece when a suitable method of glued assembly is used as for instance Lindermann joint, tongue and groove joint, ship lap or rabbet joint; or butt joint with at least two corrugated metal fasteners at each joint, or when other methods at least equally effective are used.

6.6.4.5.3　　Large packagings of plywood shall be at least 3-ply. They shall be made of well-seasoned rotary cut, sliced or sawn veneer, commercially dry and free from defects that would materially lessen the strength of the large packaging. All adjacent plies shall be glued with water-resistant adhesive. Other suitable materials may be used with plywood for the construction of the large packaging.

6.6.4.5.4   Large packagings of reconstituted wood shall be made of water-resistant reconstituted wood such as hardboard, particle board or other suitable type.

6.6.4.5.5   Large packagings shall be firmly nailed or secured to corner posts or ends or be assembled by equally suitable devices.

6.6.4.5.6   Any integral pallet base forming part of a large packaging or any detachable pallet shall be suitable for mechanical handling with the large packaging filled to its maximum permissible gross mass.

6.6.4.5.7   The pallet or integral base shall be designed so as to avoid any protrusion of the base of the large packaging that might be liable to damage in handling.

6.6.4.5.8   The body shall be secured to any detachable pallet to ensure stability in handling and transport. Where a detachable pallet is used, its top surface shall be free from sharp protrusions that might damage the large packaging.

6.6.4.5.9   Strengthening devices such as timber supports to increase stacking performance may be used but shall be external to the liner.

6.6.4.5.10   Where large packagings are intended for stacking, the bearing surface shall be such as to distribute the load in a safe manner.

6.6.5   Test requirements for large packagings

6.6.5.1   *Performance and frequency of test*

6.6.5.1.1   The design type of each large packaging shall be tested as provided in 6.6.5.3 in accordance with procedures established by the competent authority.

6.6.5.1.2   Each large packaging design type shall successfully pass the tests prescribed in this chapter before being used. A large packaging design type is defined by the design, size, material and thickness, manner of construction and packing, but may include various surface treatments. It also includes large packagings which differ from the design type only in their lesser design height.

6.6.5.1.3   Tests shall be repeated on production samples at intervals established by the competent authority. For such tests on fibreboard large packagings, preparation at ambient conditions is considered equivalent to the provisions of 6.6.5.2.4.

6.6.5.1.4   Tests shall also be repeated after each modification which alters the design, material or manner of construction of large packagings.

6.6.5.1.5   The competent authority may permit the selective testing of large packagings that differ only in minor respects from a tested type, e.g. smaller sizes of inner packagings or inner packagings of lower net mass; and large packagings which are produced with small reductions in external dimension(s).

6.6.5.1.6   *Reserved.*

NOTE: *For the conditions for assembling different inner packagings in a large packaging and permissible variations in inner packagings, see 4.1.1.5.1.*

6.6.5.1.7   The competent authority may at any time require proof, by tests in accordance with this section, that serially-produced large packagings meet the requirements of the design type tests.

6.6.5.1.8   Provided the validity of the test results is not affected and with the approval of the competent authority, several tests may be made on one sample.

6.6.5.1.9 *Large salvage packagings*

Large salvage packagings shall be tested and marked in accordance with the provisions applicable to packing group II large packagings intended for the transport of solids or inner packagings, except as follows:

(a) The test substance used in performing the tests shall be water, and the large salvage packagings shall be filled to not less than 98 % of their maximum capacity. It is permissible to use additives, such as bags of lead shot, to achieve the requisite total package mass so long as they are placed so that the test results are not affected. Alternatively, in performing the drop test, the drop height may be varied in accordance with 6.6.5.3.4.4.2 (b);

(b) Large salvage packagings shall, in addition, have been successfully subjected to the leakproofness test at 30 kPa, with the results of this test reflected in the test report required by 6.6.5.4; and

(c) Large salvage packagings shall be marked with the letter "T" as described in 6.6.2.2.

6.6.5.2 *Preparation for testing*

6.6.5.2.1 Tests shall be carried out on large packagings prepared as for transport including the inner packagings or articles used. Inner packagings shall be filled to not less than 98 % of their maximum capacity for liquids or 95 % for solids. For large packagings where the inner packagings are designed to carry liquids and solids, separate testing is required for both liquid and solid contents. The substances in the inner packagings or the articles to be transported in the large packagings may be replaced by other material or articles except where this would invalidate the results of the tests. When other inner packagings or articles are used they shall have the same physical characteristics (mass, etc) as the inner packagings or articles to be carried. It is permissible to use additives, such as bags of lead shot, to achieve the requisite total package mass, so long as they are placed so that the test results are not affected.

6.6.5.2.2 In the drop tests for liquids, when another substance is used, it shall be of similar relative density and viscosity to those of the substance being transported. Water may also be used for the liquid drop test under the conditions in 6.6.5.3.4.4.

6.6.5.2.3 Large packagings made of plastics materials and large packagings containing inner packagings of plastic materials - other than bags intended to contain solids or articles - shall be drop tested when the temperature of the test sample and its contents has been reduced to -18 °C or lower. This conditioning may be disregarded if the materials in question are of sufficient ductility and tensile strength at low temperatures. Where test sample are prepared in this way, the conditioning in 6.6.5.2.4 may be waived. Test liquids shall be kept in the liquid state by the addition of anti-freeze if necessary.

6.6.5.2.4 Large packagings of fibreboard shall be conditioned for at least 24 hours in an atmosphere having a controlled temperature and relative humidity (r.h). There are three options, one of which shall be chosen.

The preferred atmosphere is 23 ± 2 °C and 50 % ± 2 % r.h. The two other options are: 20 ± 2 °C and 65 % ± 2 % r.h.; or 27 ± 2 °C and 65 % ± 2 % r.h.

NOTE: *Average values shall fall within these limits. Short-term fluctuations and measurement limitations may cause individual measurements to vary by up to ± 5 % relative humidity without significant impairment of test reproducibility.*

6.6.5.3 *Test requirements*

6.6.5.3.1 *Bottom lift test*

6.6.5.3.1.1 Applicability

For all types of large packagings which are fitted with means of lifting from the base, as a design type test.

6.6.5.3.1.2 Preparation of large packaging for test

The large packaging shall be loaded to 1.25 times its maximum permissible gross mass, the load being evenly distributed.

6.6.5.3.1.3 Method of testing

The large packaging shall be raised and lowered twice by a lift truck with the forks centrally positioned and spaced at three quarters of the dimension of the side of entry (unless the points of entry are fixed). The forks shall penetrate to three quarters of the direction of entry. The test shall be repeated from each possible direction of entry.

6.6.5.3.1.4 Criteria for passing the test

No permanent deformation which renders the large packaging unsafe for transport and no loss of contents.

6.6.5.3.2 *Top lift test*

6.6.5.3.2.1 Applicability

For types of large packagings which are intended to be lifted from the top and fitted with means of lifting, as a design type test.

6.6.5.3.2.2 Preparation of large packaging for test

The large packaging shall be loaded to twice its maximum permissible gross mass. A flexible large packaging shall be loaded to six times its maximum permissible gross mass, the load being evenly distributed.

6.6.5.3.2.3 Method of testing

The large packaging shall be lifted in the manner for which it is designed until clear of the floor and maintained in that position for a period of five minutes.

6.6.5.3.2.4 Criteria for passing the test

(a) All types of large packagings other than flexible large packagings: no permanent deformation which renders the large packaging, including the base pallet, if any, unsafe for transport and no loss of contents;

(b) Flexible large packagings: no damage to the large packaging or its lifting devices which renders the large packaging unsafe for transport or handling and no loss of contents.

6.6.5.3.3 *Stacking test*

6.6.5.3.3.1 Applicability

For all types of large packagings which are designed to be stacked on each other, as a design type test.

6.6.5.3.3.2   Preparation of large packaging for test

The large packaging shall be filled to its maximum permissible gross mass.

6.6.5.3.3.3   Method of testing

The large packaging shall be placed on its base on level hard ground and subjected to a uniformly distributed superimposed test load (see 6.6.5.3.3.4) for a period of at least five minutes: for large packagings of wood, fibreboard and plastics materials the period shall be 24 h.

6.6.5.3.3.4   Calculation of superimposed test load

The load to be placed on the large packaging shall be 1.8 times the combined maximum permissible gross mass of the number of similar large packaging that may be stacked on top of the large packaging during transport.

6.6.5.3.3.5   Criteria for passing the test

(a) All types of large packagings other than flexible large packagings: no permanent deformation which renders the large packaging including the base pallet, if any, unsafe for transport and no loss of contents;

(b) Flexible large packagings: no deterioration of the body which renders the large packaging unsafe for transport and no loss of contents.

6.6.5.3.4   *Drop test*

6.6.5.3.4.1   Applicability

For all types of large packagings as a design type test.

6.6.5.3.4.2   Preparation of large packaging for testing

The large packaging shall be filled in accordance with 6.6.5.2.1.

6.6.5.3.4.3   Method of testing

The large packaging shall be dropped onto a non resilient, horizontal, flat, massive and rigid surface in conformity with the requirements of 6.1.5.3.4, in such a manner as to ensure that the point of impact is that part of the base of the large packaging considered to be the most vulnerable.

6.6.5.3.4.4   Drop height

NOTE: *Large packagings for substances and articles of Class 1 shall be tested at the packing group II performance level.*

6.6.5.3.4.4.1   For inner packagings containing solid or liquid substances or articles, if the test is performed with the solid, liquid or articles to be transported, or with another substance or article having essentially the same characteristics:

Packing group I	Packing group II	Packing group III
1.8 m	1.2 m	0.8 m

6.6.5.3.4.4.2   For inner packagings containing liquids if the test is performed with water:

(a) Where the substances to be transported have a relative density not exceeding 1.2:

Packing group I	Packing group II	Packing group III
1.8 m	1.2 m	0.8 m

(b) Where the substances to be transported have a relative density exceeding 1.2, the drop height shall be calculated on the basis of the relative density (d) of the substance to be carried, rounded up to the first decimal, as follows:

Packing group I	Packing group II	Packing group III
$d \times 1.5$ (m)	$d \times 1.0$ (m)	$d \times 0.67$ (m)

6.6.5.3.4.5   Criteria for passing the test

6.6.5.3.4.5.1   The large packaging shall not exhibit any damage liable to affect safety during transport. There shall be no leakage of the filling substance from inner packaging(s) or article(s).

6.6.5.3.4.5.2   No rupture is permitted in large packagings for articles of Class 1 which would permit the spillage of loose explosive substances or articles from the large packaging.

6.6.5.3.4.5.3   Where a large packaging undergoes a drop test, the sample passes the test if the entire contents are retained even if the closure is no longer sift-proof.

6.6.5.4   *Certification and test report*

6.6.5.4.1   In respect of each design type of large packaging a certificate and mark (as in 6.6.3) shall be issued attesting that the design type including its equipment meets the test requirements.

6.6.5.4.2   A test report containing at least the following particulars shall be drawn up and shall be available to the users of the large packaging:

1. Name and address of the test facility;

2. Name and address of applicant (where appropriate);

3. A unique test report identification;

4. Date of the test report;

5. Manufacturer of the large packaging;

6. Description of the large packaging design type (e.g. dimensions, materials, closures, thickness, etc) and/or photograph(s);

7. Maximum capacity/maximum permissible gross mass;

8. Characteristics of test contents, e.g. types and descriptions of inner packagings or articles used;

9. Test descriptions and results;

10. The test report shall be signed with the name and status of the signatory.

6.6.5.4.3   The test report shall contain statements that the large packaging prepared as for transport was tested in accordance with the appropriate provisions of this chapter and that the use of other packaging methods or components may render it invalid. A copy of the test report shall be available to the competent authority.

CHAPTER 6.7

REQUIREMENTS FOR THE DESIGN, CONSTRUCTION, INSPECTION AND TESTING OF PORTABLE TANKS AND MULTIPLE-ELEMENT GAS CONTAINERS (MEGCs)

NOTE: *The requirements of this chapter also apply to portable tanks with shells made of fibre-reinforced plastics (FRP) to the extent indicated in chapter 6.9.*

6.7.1 **Application and general requirements**

6.7.1.1 The requirements of this chapter apply to portable tanks intended for the transport of dangerous goods, and to MEGCs intended for the transport of non-refrigerated gases of Class 2, by all modes of transport. In addition to the requirements of this chapter, unless otherwise specified, the applicable requirements of the International Convention for Safe Containers (CSC) 1972, as amended, shall be fulfilled by any multimodal portable tank or MEGC which meets the definition of a "container" within the terms of that Convention. Additional requirements may apply to offshore portable tanks or MEGCs that are handled in open seas.

6.7.1.2 In recognition of scientific and technological advances, the technical requirements of this chapter may be varied by alternative arrangements. These alternative arrangements shall offer a level of safety not less than that given by the requirements of this chapter with respect to the compatibility with substances transported and the ability of the portable tank or MEGC to withstand impact, loading and fire conditions. For international transport, alternative arrangement portable tanks or MEGCs shall be approved by the applicable competent authorities.

6.7.1.3 When a substance is not assigned a portable tank instruction (T1 to T23, T50 or T75) in Column 10 of the Dangerous Goods List in chapter 3.2, interim approval for transport may be issued by the competent authority of the country of origin. The approval shall be included in the documentation of the consignment and contain as a minimum the information normally provided in the portable tank instructions and the conditions under which the substance shall be transported. Appropriate measures shall be initiated by the competent authority to include the assignment in the Dangerous Goods List.

6.7.2 **Requirements for the design, construction, inspection and testing of portable tanks intended for the transport of substances of Class 1 and Classes 3 to 9**

6.7.2.1 ***Definitions***

For the purposes of this section:

Design pressure means the pressure to be used in calculations required by a recognized pressure vessel code. The design pressure shall be not less than the highest of the following pressures:

(a) The maximum effective gauge pressure allowed in the shell during filling or discharge; or

(b) The sum of:

(i) the absolute vapour pressure (in bar) of the substance at 65 °C (at highest temperature during filling, discharge or transport for substances transported above 65 °C), minus 1 bar; and

(ii) the partial pressure (in bar) of air or other gases in the ullage space being determined by a maximum ullage temperature of 65 °C and a liquid expansion due to an increase in mean bulk temperature of $t_r - t_f$ (t_f = filling temperature usually 15 °C; t_r = 50 °C maximum mean bulk temperature); and

(iii) a head pressure determined on the basis of the static forces specified in 6.7.2.2.12, but not less than 0.35 bar; or

(c) Two thirds of the minimum test pressure specified in the applicable portable tank instruction in 4.2.5.2.6;

Design temperature range for the shell shall be -40 °C to 50 °C for substances transported under ambient conditions. For the other substances handled under elevated temperature conditions the design temperature shall be not less than the maximum temperature of the substance during filling, discharge or transport. More severe design temperatures shall be considered for portable tanks subjected to severe climatic conditions;

Fine grain steel means steel which has a ferritic grain size of 6 or finer when determined in accordance with ASTM E 112-96 or as defined in EN 10028-3, Part 3;

Fusible element means a non-reclosable pressure relief device that is thermally actuated;

Leakproofness test means a test using gas subjecting the shell and its service equipment to an effective internal pressure of not less than 25 % of the MAWP;

Maximum allowable working pressure (MAWP) means a pressure that shall be not less than the highest of the following pressures measured at the top of the shell while in operating position:

(a) The maximum effective gauge pressure allowed in the shell during filling or discharge; or

(b) The maximum effective gauge pressure to which the shell is designed which shall be not less than the sum of:

(i) the absolute vapour pressure (in bar) of the substance at 65 °C (at the highest temperature during filling, discharge or transport for substances transported above 65 °C), minus 1 bar; and

(ii) the partial pressure (in bar) of air or other gases in the ullage space being determined by a maximum ullage temperature of 65 °C and a liquid expansion due to an increase in mean bulk temperature of $t_r - t_f$ (t_f = filling temperature, usually 15 °C; t_r = 50 °C, maximum mean bulk temperature);

Maximum permissible gross mass (MPGM) means the sum of the tare mass of the portable tank and the heaviest load authorized for transport;

Mild steel means a steel with a guaranteed minimum tensile strength of 360 N/mm^2 to 440 N/mm^2 and a guaranteed minimum elongation at fracture conforming to 6.7.2.3.3.3;

Offshore portable tank means a portable tank specially designed for repeated use for transport of dangerous goods to, from and between offshore facilities. An offshore portable tank is designed and constructed in accordance with the Guidelines for the Approval of Containers Handled in Open Seas specified by the International Maritime Organization in document MSC/Circ.860.

Portable tank means a multimodal tank used for the transport of substances of Class 1 and Classes 3 to 9. The portable tank includes a shell fitted with service equipment and structural equipment necessary for the transport of dangerous substances. The portable tank shall be capable of being filled and discharged without the removal of its structural equipment. It shall possess stabilizing members external to the shell, and shall be capable of being lifted when full. It shall be designed primarily to be loaded onto a transport vehicle or ship and shall be equipped with skids, mountings or accessories to facilitate mechanical handling. Road tank-vehicles, rail tank-wagons, non-metallic tanks and intermediate bulk containers (IBCs) are not considered to fall within the definition for portable tanks;

Reference steel means a steel with a tensile strength of 370 N/mm^2 and an elongation at fracture of 27 %;

Service equipment means measuring instruments and filling, discharge, venting, safety, heating, cooling and insulating devices;

Shell means the part of the portable tank which retains the substance intended for transport (tank proper), including openings and their closures, but does not include service equipment or external structural equipment;

Structural equipment means the reinforcing, fastening, protective and stabilizing members external to the shell;

Test pressure means the maximum gauge pressure at the top of the shell during the hydraulic pressure test equal to not less than 1.5 times the design pressure. The minimum test pressure for portable tanks intended for specific substances is specified in the applicable portable tank instruction in 4.2.5.2.6.

6.7.2.2 *General design and construction requirements*

6.7.2.2.1 Shells shall be designed and constructed in accordance with the requirements of a pressure vessel code recognized by the competent authority. Shells shall be made of metallic materials suitable for forming. The materials shall in principle conform to national or international material standards. For welded shells only a material whose weldability has been fully demonstrated shall be used. Welds shall be skilfully made and afford complete safety. When the manufacturing process or the materials make it necessary, the shells shall be suitably heat-treated to guarantee adequate toughness in the weld and in the heat affected zones. In choosing the material, the design temperature range shall be taken into account with respect to risk of brittle fracture, to stress corrosion cracking and to resistance to impact. When fine grain steel is used, the guaranteed value of the yield strength shall be not more than 460 N/mm^2 and the guaranteed value of the upper limit of the tensile strength shall be not more than 725 N/mm^2 according to the material specification. Aluminium may only be used as a construction material when indicated in a portable tank special provision assigned to a specific substance in Column 11 of the Dangerous Goods List or when approved by the competent authority. When aluminium is authorized, it shall be insulated to prevent significant loss of physical properties when subjected to a heat load of 110 kW/m^2 for a period of not less than 30 minutes. The insulation shall remain effective at all temperatures less than 649 °C and shall be jacketed with a material with a melting point of not less than 700 °C. Portable tank materials shall be suitable for the external environment in which they may be transported.

6.7.2.2.2 Portable tank shells, fittings, and pipework shall be constructed from materials which are:

(a) Substantially immune to attack by the substance(s) intended to be transported; or

(b) Properly passivated or neutralized by chemical reaction; or

(c) Lined with corrosion-resistant material directly bonded to the shell or attached by equivalent means.

6.7.2.2.3 Gaskets shall be made of materials not subject to attack by the substance(s) intended to be transported.

6.7.2.2.4 When shells are lined, the lining shall be substantially immune to attack by the substance(s) intended to be transported, homogeneous, non porous, free from perforations, sufficiently elastic and compatible with the thermal expansion characteristics of the shell. The lining of every shell, shell fittings and piping shall be continuous, and shall extend around the face of any flange. Where external fittings are welded to the tank, the lining shall be continuous through the fitting and around the face of external flanges.

6.7.2.2.5 Joints and seams in the lining shall be made by fusing the material together or by other equally effective means.

6.7.2.2.6 Contact between dissimilar metals which could result in damage by galvanic action shall be avoided.

6.7.2.2.7 The materials of the portable tank, including any devices, gaskets, linings and accessories, shall not adversely affect the substance(s) intended to be transported in the portable tank.

6.7.2.2.8   Portable tanks shall be designed and constructed with supports to provide a secure base during transport and with suitable lifting and tie-down attachments.

6.7.2.2.9   Portable tanks shall be designed to withstand, without loss of contents, at least the internal pressure due to the contents, and the static, dynamic and thermal loads during normal conditions of handling and transport. The design shall demonstrate that the effects of fatigue, caused by repeated application of these loads through the expected life of the portable tank, have been taken into account.

6.7.2.2.9.1   For portable tanks that are intended for use offshore, the dynamic stresses imposed by handling in open seas shall be taken into account.

6.7.2.2.10   A shell which is to be equipped with a vacuum-relief device shall be designed to withstand, without permanent deformation, an external pressure of not less than 0.21 bar above the internal pressure. The vacuum-relief device shall be set to relieve at a vacuum setting not greater than minus 0.21 bar unless the shell is designed for a higher external over pressure, in which case the vacuum-relief pressure of the device to be fitted shall be not greater than the tank design vacuum pressure. A shell used for the transport of solid substances of packing groups II or III only, which do not liquefy during transport, may be designed for a lower external pressure, subject to competent authority approval. In this case, the vacuum-relief device shall be set to relieve at this lower pressure. A shell that is not to be fitted with a vacuum-relief device shall be designed to withstand, without permanent deformation, an external pressure of not less than 0.4 bar above the internal pressure.

6.7.2.2.11   Vacuum-relief devices used on portable tanks intended for the transport of substances meeting the flash point criteria of Class 3, including elevated temperature substances transported at or above their flash point, shall prevent the immediate passage of flame into the shell, or the portable tank shall have a shell capable of withstanding, without leakage an internal explosion resulting from the passage of flame into the shell.

6.7.2.2.12   Portable tanks and their fastenings shall, under the maximum permissible load, be capable of absorbing the following separately applied static forces:

(a) In the direction of travel: twice the MPGM multiplied by the acceleration due to gravity $(g)^1$;

(b) Horizontally at right angles to the direction of travel: the MPGM (when the direction of travel is not clearly determined, the forces shall be equal to twice the MPGM) multiplied by the acceleration due to gravity $(g)^1$;

(c) Vertically upwards: the MPGM multiplied by the acceleration due to gravity $(g)^1$; and

(d) Vertically downwards: twice the MPGM (total loading including the effect of gravity) multiplied by the acceleration due to gravity $(g)^1$.

6.7.2.2.13   Under each of the forces in 6.7.2.2.12, the safety factor to be observed shall be as follows:

(a) For metals having a clearly defined yield point, a safety factor of 1.5 in relation to the guaranteed yield strength; or

(b) For metals with no clearly defined yield point, a safety factor of 1.5 in relation to the guaranteed 0.2 % proof strength and, for austenitic steels, the 1 % proof strength.

6.7.2.2.14   The values of yield strength or proof strength shall be the values according to national or international material standards. When austenitic steels are used, the specified minimum values of yield strength or proof strength according to the material standards may be increased by up to 15 % when these greater values are attested in the material inspection certificate. When no material standard exists for the metal in question, the value of yield strength or proof strength used shall be approved by the competent authority.

---

[1] *For calculation purposes $g = 9.81$ m/s^2.*

6.7.2.2.15   Portable tanks shall be capable of being electrically earthed when intended for the transport of substances meeting the flash point criteria of Class 3 including elevated temperature substances transported at or above their flash point. Measures shall be taken to prevent dangerous electrostatic discharge.

6.7.2.2.16   When required for certain substances by the applicable portable tank instruction indicated in Column 10 of the Dangerous Goods List and described in 4.2.5.2.6, or by a portable tank special provision indicated in Column 11 of the Dangerous Goods List and described in 4.2.5.3, portable tanks shall be provided with additional protection, which may take the form of additional shell thickness or a higher test pressure, the additional shell thickness or higher test pressure being determined in the light of the inherent risks associated with the transport of the substances concerned.

6.7.2.2.17   Thermal insulation directly in contact with the shell intended for substances transported at elevated temperature shall have an ignition temperature at least 50 °C higher than the maximum design temperature of the tank.

6.7.2.3   *Design criteria*

6.7.2.3.1   Shells shall be of a design capable of being stress-analysed mathematically or experimentally by resistance strain gauges, or by other methods approved by the competent authority.

6.7.2.3.2   Shells shall be designed and constructed to withstand a hydraulic test pressure not less than 1.5 times the design pressure. Specific requirements are laid down for certain substances in the applicable portable tank instruction indicated in Column 10 of the Dangerous Goods List and described in 4.2.5.2.6 or by a portable tank special provision indicated in Column 11 of the Dangerous Goods List and described in 4.2.5.3. Attention is drawn to the minimum shell thickness requirements for these tanks specified in 6.7.2.4.1 to 6.7.2.4.10.

6.7.2.3.3   For metals exhibiting a clearly defined yield point or characterized by a guaranteed proof strength (0.2 % proof strength, generally, or 1 % proof strength for austenitic steels) the primary membrane stress σ (sigma) in the shell shall not exceed 0.75 Re or 0.50 Rm, whichever is lower, at the test pressure, where:

Re = yield strength in N/mm^2, or 0.2 % proof strength or, for austenitic steels, 1 % proof strength;
Rm = minimum tensile strength in N/mm^2.

6.7.2.3.3.1   The values of Re and Rm to be used shall be the specified minimum values according to national or international material standards. When austenitic steels are used, the specified minimum values for Re and Rm according to the material standards may be increased by up to 15 % when greater values are attested in the material inspection certificate. When no material standard exists for the metal in question, the values of Re and Rm used shall be approved by the competent authority or its authorized body.

6.7.2.3.3.2   Steels which have a Re/Rm ratio of more than 0.85 are not allowed for the construction of welded shells. The values of Re and Rm to be used in determining this ratio shall be the values specified in the material inspection certificate.

6.7.2.3.3.3   Steels used in the construction of shells shall have an elongation at fracture, in %, of not less than 10 000/Rm with an absolute minimum of 16 % for fine grain steels and 20 % for other steels. Aluminium and aluminium alloys used in the construction of shells shall have an elongation at fracture, in %, of not less than 10 000/6Rm with an absolute minimum of 12 %.

6.7.2.3.3.4   For the purpose of determining actual values for materials, it shall be noted that for sheet metal, the axis of the tensile test specimen shall be at right angles (transversely) to the direction of rolling. The permanent elongation at fracture shall be measured on test specimens of rectangular cross sections in accordance with ISO 6892:1998 using a 50 mm gauge length.

6.7.2.4   *Minimum shell thickness*

6.7.2.4.1   The minimum shell thickness shall be the greater thickness based on:

(a) The minimum thickness determined in accordance with the requirements of 6.7.2.4.2 to 6.7.2.4.10;

(b) The minimum thickness determined in accordance with the recognized pressure vessel code including the requirements in 6.7.2.3; and

(c) The minimum thickness specified in the applicable portable tank instruction indicated in Column 10 of the Dangerous Goods List and described in 4.2.5.2.6, or by a portable tank special provision indicated in Column 11 of the Dangerous Goods List and described in 4.2.5.3.

6.7.2.4.2 The cylindrical portions, ends (heads) and manhole covers of shells not more than 1.80 m in diameter shall be not less than 5 mm thick in the reference steel or of equivalent thickness in the metal to be used. Shells more than 1.80 m in diameter shall be not less than 6 mm thick in the reference steel or of equivalent thickness in the metal to be used, except that for powdered or granular solid substances of Packing Group II or III the minimum thickness requirement may be reduced to not less than 5 mm thick in the reference steel or of equivalent thickness in the metal to be used.

6.7.2.4.3 When additional protection against shell damage is provided, portable tanks with test pressures less than 2.65 bar, may have the minimum shell thickness reduced, in proportion to the protection provided, as approved by the competent authority. However, shells not more than 1.80 m in diameter shall be not less than 3 mm thick in the reference steel or of equivalent thickness in the metal to be used. Shells more than 1.80 m in diameter shall be not less than 4 mm thick in the reference steel or of equivalent thickness in the metal to be used.

6.7.2.4.4 The cylindrical portions, ends (heads) and manhole covers of all shells shall be not less than 3 mm thick regardless of the material of construction.

6.7.2.4.5 The additional protection referred to in 6.7.2.4.3 may be provided by overall external structural protection, such as suitable "sandwich" construction with the outer sheathing (jacket) secured to the shell, double wall construction or by enclosing the shell in a complete framework with longitudinal and transverse structural members.

6.7.2.4.6 The equivalent thickness of a metal other than the thickness prescribed for the reference steel in 6.7.2.4.3 shall be determined using the following formula:

$$e_1 = \frac{21.4 e_0}{\sqrt[3]{Rm_1 \times A_1}}$$

where:

e_1 = required equivalent thickness (in mm) of the metal to be used;

e_0 = minimum thickness (in mm) of the reference steel specified in the applicable portable tank instruction indicated in Column 10 of the Dangerous Goods List and described in 4.2.5.2.6 or by a portable tank special provision indicated in Column 11 of the Dangerous Goods List and described in 4.2.5.3;

Rm_1 = guaranteed minimum tensile strength (in N/mm^2) of the metal to be used (see 6.7.2.3.3);

A_1 = guaranteed minimum elongation at fracture (in %) of the metal to be used according to national or international standards.

6.7.2.4.7 When in the applicable portable tank instruction in 4.2.5.2.6, a minimum thickness of 8 mm or 10 mm is specified, it shall be noted that these thicknesses are based on the properties of the reference steel and a shell diameter of 1.80 m. When a metal other than mild steel (see 6.7.2.1) is used or the shell has a diameter of more than 1.80 m, the thickness shall be determined using the following formula:

$$e_1 = \frac{21.4 e_0 d_1}{1.8 \sqrt[3]{Rm_1 \times A_1}}$$

where:

e_1 = required equivalent thickness (in mm) of the metal to be used;

e_0 = minimum thickness (in mm) of the reference steel specified in the applicable portable tank instruction indicated in Column 10 of the Dangerous Goods List and described in 4.2.5.2.6 or by a portable tank special provision indicated in Column 11 of the Dangerous Goods List and described in 4.2.5.3;

d_1 = diameter of the shell (in m), but not less than 1.80 m;

Rm_1 = guaranteed minimum tensile strength (in N/mm^2) of the metal to be used (see 6.7.2.3.3);

A_1 = guaranteed minimum elongation at fracture (in %) of the metal to be used according to national or international standards.

6.7.2.4.8　　In no case shall the wall thickness be less than that prescribed in 6.7.2.4.2, 6.7.2.4.3 and 6.7.2.4.4. All parts of the shell shall have a minimum thickness as determined by 6.7.2.4.2 to 6.7.2.4.4. This thickness shall be exclusive of any corrosion allowance.

6.7.2.4.9　　When mild steel is used (see 6.7.2.1), calculation using the formula in 6.7.2.4.6 is not required.

6.7.2.4.10　　There shall be no sudden change of plate thickness at the attachment of the ends (heads) to the cylindrical portion of the shell.

6.7.2.5　*Service equipment*

6.7.2.5.1　　Service equipment shall be so arranged as to be protected against the risk of being wrenched off or damaged during handling and transport. When the connection between the frame and the shell allows relative movement between the sub-assemblies, the equipment shall be so fastened as to permit such movement without risk of damage to working parts. The external discharge fittings (pipe sockets, shut-off devices), the internal stop-valve and its seating shall be protected against the danger of being wrenched off by external forces (for example using shear sections). The filling and discharge devices (including flanges or threaded plugs) and any protective caps shall be capable of being secured against unintended opening.

6.7.2.5.2　　All openings in the shell, intended for filling or discharging the portable tank shall be fitted with a manually operated stop-valve located as close to the shell as reasonably practicable. Other openings, except for openings leading to venting or pressure-relief devices, shall be equipped with either a stop-valve or another suitable means of closure located as close to the shell as reasonably practicable.

6.7.2.5.3　　All portable tanks shall be fitted with a manhole or other inspection openings of a suitable size to allow for internal inspection and adequate access for maintenance and repair of the interior. Compartmented portable tanks shall have a manhole or other inspection openings for each compartment.

6.7.2.5.4　　As far as reasonably practicable, external fittings shall be grouped together. For insulated portable tanks, top fittings shall be surrounded by a spill collection reservoir with suitable drains.

6.7.2.5.5　　Each connection to a portable tank shall be clearly marked to indicate its function.

6.7.2.5.6　　Each stop-valve or other means of closure shall be designed and constructed to a rated pressure not less than the MAWP of the shell taking into account the temperatures expected during transport. All stop-valves with screwed spindles shall close by a clockwise motion of the handwheel. For other stop-valves the position (open and closed) and direction of closure shall be clearly indicated. All stop-valves shall be designed to prevent unintentional opening.

6.7.2.5.7　　No moving parts, such as covers, components of closures, etc., shall be made of unprotected corrodible steel when they are liable to come into frictional or percussive contact with aluminium portable tanks intended for the transport of substances meeting the flash point criteria of Class 3 including elevated temperature substances transported at or above their flash point.

6.7.2.5.8   Piping shall be designed, constructed and installed so as to avoid the risk of damage due to thermal expansion and contraction, mechanical shock and vibration. All piping shall be of a suitable metallic material. Welded pipe joints shall be used wherever possible.

6.7.2.5.9   Joints in copper tubing shall be brazed or have an equally strong metal union. The melting point of brazing materials shall be no lower than 525 °C. The joints shall not decrease the strength of the tubing as may happen when cutting threads.

6.7.2.5.10   The burst pressure of all piping and pipe fittings shall be not less than the highest of four times the MAWP of the shell or four times the pressure to which it may be subjected in service by the action of a pump or other device (except pressure-relief devices).

6.7.2.5.11   Ductile metals shall be used in the construction of valves and accessories.

6.7.2.5.12   The heating system shall be designed or controlled so that a substance cannot reach a temperature at which the pressure in the tank exceeds its MAWP or causes other hazards (e.g. dangerous thermal decomposition).

6.7.2.5.13   The heating system shall be designed or controlled so that power for internal heating elements shall not be available unless the heating elements are completely submerged. The temperature at the surface of the heating elements for internal heating equipment, or the temperature at the shell for external heating equipment shall, in no case, exceed 80 % of the autoignition temperature (in °C) of the substance transported.

6.7.2.5.14   If an electrical heating system is installed inside the tank, it shall be equipped with an earth leakage circuit breaker with a releasing current of less than 100 mA.

6.7.2.5.15   Electrical switch cabinets mounted to tanks shall not have a direct connection to the tank interior and shall provide protection of at least the equivalent of type IP56 according to IEC 144 or IEC 529.

6.7.2.6   *Bottom openings*

6.7.2.6.1   Certain substances shall not be transported in portable tanks with bottom openings. When the applicable portable tank instruction identified in Column 10 of the Dangerous Goods List and described in 4.2.5.2.6 indicates that bottom openings are prohibited there shall be no openings below the liquid level of the shell when it is filled to its maximum permissible filling limit. When an existing opening is closed it shall be accomplished by internally and externally welding one plate to the shell.

6.7.2.6.2   Bottom discharge outlets for portable tanks carrying certain solid, crystallizable or highly viscous substances shall be equipped with not less than two serially fitted and mutually independent shut-off devices. The design of the equipment shall be to the satisfaction of the competent authority or its authorized body and shall include:

> (a) An external stop-valve, fitted as close to the shell as reasonably practicable, and so designed as to prevent any unintended opening through impact or other inadvertent act; and
>
> (b) A liquid tight closure at the end of the discharge pipe, which may be a bolted blank flange or a screw cap.

6.7.2.6.3   Every bottom discharge outlet, except as provided in 6.7.2.6.2, shall be equipped with three serially fitted and mutually independent shut-off devices. The design of the equipment shall be to the satisfaction of the competent authority or its authorized body and include:

> (a) A self-closing internal stop-valve, that is a stop-valve within the shell or within a welded flange or its companion flange, such that:
>
> > (i) The control devices for the operation of the valve are designed so as to prevent any unintended opening through impact or other inadvertent act;

(ii) The valve may be operable from above or below;

(iii) If possible, the setting of the valve (open or closed) shall be capable of being verified from the ground;

(iv) Except for portable tanks having a capacity of not more than 1 000 litres, it shall be possible to close the valve from an accessible position of the portable tank that is remote from the valve itself; and

(v) The valve shall continue to be effective in the event of damage to the external device for controlling the operation of the valve;

(b) An external stop-valve fitted as close to the shell as reasonably practicable; and

(c) A liquid tight closure at the end of the discharge pipe, which may be a bolted blank flange or a screw cap.

6.7.2.6.4 For a lined shell, the internal stop-valve required by 6.7.2.6.3 (a) may be replaced by an additional external stop-valve. The manufacturer shall satisfy the requirements of the competent authority or its authorized body.

6.7.2.7 *Safety relief devices*

6.7.2.7.1 All portable tanks shall be fitted with at least one pressure-relief device. All relief devices shall be designed, constructed and marked to the satisfaction of the competent authority or its authorized body.

6.7.2.8 *Pressure-relief devices*

6.7.2.8.1 Every portable tank with a capacity not less than 1 900 litres and every independent compartment of a portable tank with a similar capacity, shall be provided with one or more pressure-relief devices of the spring-loaded type and may in addition have a frangible disc or fusible element in parallel with the spring-loaded devices except when prohibited by reference to 6.7.2.8.3 in the applicable portable tank instruction in 4.2.5.2.6. The pressure-relief devices shall have sufficient capacity to prevent rupture of the shell due to over pressurization or vacuum resulting from filling, discharging, or from heating of the contents.

6.7.2.8.2 Pressure-relief devices shall be designed to prevent the entry of foreign matter, the leakage of liquid and the development of any dangerous excess pressure.

6.7.2.8.3 When required for certain substances by the applicable portable tank instruction identified in Column 10 of the Dangerous Goods List and described in 4.2.5.2.6, portable tanks shall have a pressure-relief device approved by the competent authority. Unless a portable tank in dedicated service is fitted with an approved relief device constructed of materials compatible with the load, the relief device shall comprise a frangible disc preceding a spring-loaded pressure-relief device. When a frangible disc is inserted in series with the required pressure-relief device, the space between the frangible disc and the pressure-relief device shall be provided with a pressure gauge or suitable tell-tale indicator for the detection of disc rupture, pinholing, or leakage which could cause a malfunction of the pressure-relief system. The frangible disc shall rupture at a nominal pressure 10 % above the start to discharge pressure of the relief device.

6.7.2.8.4 Every portable tank with a capacity less than 1 900 litres shall be fitted with a pressure-relief device which may be a frangible disc when this disc complies with the requirements of 6.7.2.11.1. When no spring-loaded pressure-relief device is used, the frangible disc shall be set to rupture at a nominal pressure equal to the test pressure. In addition, fusible elements conforming to 6.7.2.10.1 may also be used.

6.7.2.8.5 When the shell is fitted for pressure discharge, the inlet line shall be provided with a suitable pressure-relief device set to operate at a pressure not higher than the MAWP of the shell, and a stop-valve shall be fitted as close to the shell as reasonably practicable.

6.7.2.9 *Setting of pressure-relief devices*

6.7.2.9.1   It shall be noted that the pressure-relief devices shall operate only in conditions of excessive rise in temperature, since the shell shall not be subject to undue fluctuations of pressure during normal conditions of transport (see 6.7.2.12.2).

6.7.2.9.2   The required pressure-relief device shall be set to start-to-discharge at a nominal pressure of five-sixths of the test pressure for shells having a test pressure of not more than 4.5 bar and 110 % of two-thirds of the test pressure for shells having a test pressure of more than 4.5 bar. After discharge the device shall close at a pressure not more than 10 % below the pressure at which the discharge starts. The device shall remain closed at all lower pressures. This requirement does not prevent the use of vacuum-relief or combination pressure-relief and vacuum-relief devices.

6.7.2.10   *Fusible elements*

6.7.2.10.1   Fusible elements shall operate at a temperature between 100 °C and 149 °C on condition that the pressure in the shell at the fusing temperature will be not more than the test pressure. They shall be placed at the top of the shell with their inlets in the vapour space and when used for transport safety purposes, they shall not be shielded from external heat. Fusible elements shall not be used on portable tanks with a test pressure which exceeds 2.65 bar unless specified by special provision TP36 in Column 11 of the Dangerous Goods List of chapter 3.2. Fusible elements used on portable tanks intended for the transport of elevated temperature substances shall be designed to operate at a temperature higher than the maximum temperature that will be experienced during transport and shall be to the satisfaction of the competent authority or its authorized body.

6.7.2.11   *Frangible discs*

6.7.2.11.1   Except as specified in 6.7.2.8.3, frangible discs shall be set to rupture at a nominal pressure equal to the test pressure throughout the design temperature range. Particular attention shall be given to the requirements of 6.7.2.5.1 and 6.7.2.8.3 if frangible discs are used.

6.7.2.11.2   Frangible discs shall be appropriate for the vacuum pressures which may be produced in the portable tank.

6.7.2.12   *Capacity of pressure-relief devices*

6.7.2.12.1   The spring-loaded pressure-relief device required by 6.7.2.8.1 shall have a minimum cross sectional flow area equivalent to an orifice of 31.75 mm diameter. Vacuum-relief devices, when used, shall have a cross sectional flow area not less than 284 mm2.

6.7.2.12.2   The combined delivery capacity of the pressure relief system (taking into account the reduction of the flow when the portable tank is fitted with frangible-discs preceding spring-loaded pressure-relief devices or when the spring-loaded pressure-relief devices are provided with a device to prevent the passage of the flame), in condition of complete fire engulfment of the portable tank shall be sufficient to limit the pressure in the shell to 20 % above the start-to-discharge pressure of the pressure limiting device. Emergency pressure-relief devices may be used to achieve the full relief capacity prescribed. These devices may be fusible, spring loaded or frangible disc components, or a combination of spring-loaded and frangible disc devices. The total required capacity of the relief devices may be determined using the formula in 6.7.2.12.2.1 or the table in 6.7.2.12.2.3.

6.7.2.12.2.1   To determine the total required capacity of the relief devices, which shall be regarded as being the sum of the individual capacities of all the contributing devices, the following formula shall be used:

$$Q = 12.4 \frac{FA^{0.82}}{LC} \sqrt{\frac{ZT}{M}}$$

where:

Q = minimum required rate of discharge in cubic metres of air per second (m³/s) at standard conditions: 1 bar and 0 °C (273 K);

F = is a coefficient with the following value:

 for uninsulated shells   F = 1;

 for insulated shells   F = U(649 - t)/13.6

but in no case is less than 0.25, where:

 U = heat transfer coefficient of the insulation, in $kW \cdot m^{-2} \cdot K^{-1}$, at 38 °C

 t = actual temperature of the substance during filling (in °C);

 when this temperature is unknown, let t = 15 °C:

The value of F given above for insulated shells may be taken provided that the insulation is in conformance with 6.7.2.12.2.4;

A = total external surface area of shell in square metres;

Z = the gas compressibility factor in the accumulating condition (when this factor is unknown, let Z equal 1.0);

T = absolute temperature in Kelvin (°C + 273) above the pressure-relief devices in the accumulating condition;

L = the latent heat of vaporization of the liquid, in kJ/kg, in the accumulating condition;

M = molecular mass of the discharged gas;

C = a constant which is derived from one of the following formulae as a function of the ratio k of specific heats:

$$k = \frac{c_p}{c_v}$$

where:

c_p is the specific heat at constant pressure; and
c_v is the specific heat at constant volume.

When k > 1:

$$C = \sqrt{k \left(\frac{2}{k+1} \right)^{\frac{k+1}{k-1}}}$$

When $k = 1$ or   k is unknown:

$$C = \frac{1}{\sqrt{e}} = 0.607$$

where e is the mathematical constant 2.7183

C may also be taken from the following table:

k	C	k	C	k	C
1.00	0.607	1.26	0.660	1.52	0.704
1.02	0.611	1.28	0.664	1.54	0.707
1.04	0.615	1.30	0.667	1.56	0.710
1.06	0.620	1.32	0.671	1.58	0.713
1.08	0.624	1.34	0.674	1.60	0.716
1.10	0.628	1.36	0.678	1.62	0.719
1.12	0.633	1.38	0.681	1.64	0.722
1.14	0.637	1.40	0.685	1.66	0.725
1.16	0.641	1.42	0.688	1.68	0.728
1.18	0.645	1.44	0.691	1.70	0.731
1.20	0.649	1.46	0.695	2.00	0.770
1.22	0.652	1.48	0.698	2.20	0.793
1.24	0.656	1.50	0.701		

6.7.2.12.2.2 As an alternative to the formula above, shells designed for the transport of liquids may have their relief devices sized in accordance with the table in 6.7.2.12.2.3. This table assumes an insulation value of F = 1 and shall be adjusted accordingly when the shell is insulated. Other values used in determining this table are:

$$M = 86.7 \qquad T = 394 \text{ K}$$
$$L = 334.94 \text{ kJ/kg} \qquad C = 0.607$$
$$Z = 1$$

6.7.2.12.2.3 Minimum required rate of discharge, Q, in cubic metres of air per second at 1 bar and 0 °C (273 K)

A Exposed area (square metres)	Q (Cubic metres of air per second)	A Exposed area (square metres)	Q (Cubic metres of air per second)
2	0.230	37.5	2.539
3	0.320	40	2.677
4	0.405	42.5	2.814
5	0.487	45	2.949
6	0.565	47.5	3.082
7	0.641	50	3.215
8	0.715	52.5	3.346
9	0.788	55	3.476
10	0.859	57.5	3.605
12	0.998	60	3.733
14	1.132	62.5	3.860
16	1.263	65	3.987
18	1.391	67.5	4.112
20	1.517	70	4.236
22.5	1.670	75	4.483
25	1.821	80	4.726
27.5	1.969	85	4.967
30	2.115	90	5.206
32.5	2.258	95	5.442
35	2.400	100	5.676

6.7.2.12.2.4   Insulation systems, used for the purpose of reducing venting capacity, shall be approved by the competent authority or its authorized body. In all cases, insulation systems approved for this purpose shall:

    (a)   Remain effective at all temperatures up to 649 °C; and

    (b)   Be jacketed with a material having a melting point of 700 °C or greater.

6.7.2.13   *Marking of pressure-relief devices*

6.7.2.13.1   Every pressure-relief device shall be clearly and permanently marked with the following:

    (a)   The pressure (in bar or kPa) or temperature (in °C) at which it is set to discharge;

    (b)   The allowable tolerance at the discharge pressure for spring-loaded devices;

    (c)   The reference temperature corresponding to the rated pressure for frangible discs;

    (d)   The allowable temperature tolerance for fusible elements; and

    (e)   The rated flow capacity of the spring-loaded pressure relief devices, frangible discs or fusible elements in standard cubic metres of air per second (m^3/s);

    (f)   The cross sectional flow areas of the spring loaded pressure-relief devices, frangible discs and fusible elements in mm^2.

When practicable, the following information shall also be shown:

    (g)   The manufacturer's name and relevant catalogue number.

6.7.2.13.2   The rated flow capacity marked on the spring-loaded pressure-relief devices shall be determined according to ISO 4126-1:2004 and ISO 4126-7:2004.

6.7.2.14   *Connections to pressure-relief devices*

6.7.2.14.1   Connections to pressure-relief devices shall be of sufficient size to enable the required discharge to pass unrestricted to the safety device. No stop-valve shall be installed between the shell and the pressure-relief devices except where duplicate devices are provided for maintenance or other reasons and the stop-valves serving the devices actually in use are locked open or the stop-valves are interlocked so that at least one of the duplicate devices is always in use. There shall be no obstruction in an opening leading to a vent or pressure-relief device which might restrict or cut-off the flow from the shell to that device. Vents or pipes from the pressure-relief device outlets, when used, shall deliver the relieved vapour or liquid to the atmosphere in conditions of minimum back-pressure on the relieving devices.

6.7.2.15   *Siting of pressure-relief devices*

6.7.2.15.1   Each pressure-relief device inlet shall be situated on top of the shell in a position as near the longitudinal and transverse centre of the shell as reasonably practicable. All pressure-relief device inlets shall under maximum filling conditions be situated in the vapour space of the shell and the devices shall be so arranged as to ensure the escaping vapour is discharged unrestrictedly. For flammable substances, the escaping vapour shall be directed away from the shell in such a manner that it cannot impinge upon the shell. Protective devices which deflect the flow of vapour are permissible provided the required relief-device capacity is not reduced.

6.7.2.15.2   Arrangements shall be made to prevent access to the pressure-relief devices by unauthorized persons and to protect the devices from damage caused by the portable tank overturning.

6.7.2.16   *Gauging devices*

6.7.2.16.1   Glass level-gauges and gauges made of other fragile material, which are in direct communication with the contents of the tank shall not be used.

6.7.2.17 *Portable tank supports, frameworks, lifting and tie-down attachments*

6.7.2.17.1 Portable tanks shall be designed and constructed with a support structure to provide a secure base during transport. The forces specified in 6.7.2.2.12 and the safety factor specified in 6.7.2.2.13 shall be considered in this aspect of the design. Skids, frameworks, cradles or other similar structures are acceptable.

6.7.2.17.2 The combined stresses caused by portable tank mountings (e.g. cradles, framework, etc.) and portable tank lifting and tie-down attachments shall not cause excessive stress in any portion of the shell. Permanent lifting and tie-down attachments shall be fitted to all portable tanks. Preferably they shall be fitted to the portable tank supports but may be secured to reinforcing plates located on the shell at the points of support.

6.7.2.17.3 In the design of supports and frameworks the effects of environmental corrosion shall be taken into account.

6.7.2.17.4 Forklift pockets shall be capable of being closed off. The means of closing forklift pockets shall be a permanent part of the framework or permanently attached to the framework. Single compartment portable tanks with a length less than 3.65 m need not have closed off forklift pockets provided that:

(a) The shell including all the fittings are well protected from being hit by the forklift blades; and

(b) The distance between the centres of the forklift pockets is at least half of the maximum length of the portable tank.

6.7.2.17.5 When portable tanks are not protected during transport, according to 4.2.1.2, the shells and service equipment shall be protected against damage to the shell and service equipment resulting from lateral or longitudinal impact or overturning. External fittings shall be protected so as to preclude the release of the shell contents upon impact or overturning of the portable tank on its fittings. Examples of protection include:

(a) Protection against lateral impact which may consist of longitudinal bars protecting the shell on both sides at the level of the median line;

(b) Protection of the portable tank against overturning which may consist of reinforcement rings or bars fixed across the frame;

(c) Protection against rear impact which may consist of a bumper or frame;

(d) Protection of the shell against damage from impact or overturning by use of an ISO frame in accordance with ISO 1496-3:1995.

6.7.2.18 *Design approval*

6.7.2.18.1 The competent authority or its authorized body shall issue a design approval certificate for any new design of a portable tank. This certificate shall attest that a portable tank has been surveyed by that authority, is suitable for its intended purpose and meets the requirements of this chapter and where appropriate, the provisions for substances provided in chapter 4.2 and in the Dangerous Goods List in chapter 3.2. When a series of portable tanks are manufactured without change in the design, the certificate shall be valid for the entire series. The certificate shall refer to the prototype test report, the substances or group of substances allowed to be transported, the materials of construction of the shell and lining (when applicable) and an approval number. The approval number shall consist of the distinguishing sign or mark of the State in whose territory the approval was granted, indicated by the distinguishing sign used on vehicles in international road traffic[2], and a registration number. Any alternative arrangements according to 6.7.1.2 shall be indicated on the certificate. A design approval may serve for the approval of smaller portable tanks made of materials of the

---

[2] *Distinguishing sign of the State of registration used on motor vehicles and trailers in international road traffic, e.g. in accordance with the Geneva Convention on Road Traffic of 1949 or the Vienna Convention on Road Traffic of 1968.*

same kind and thickness, by the same fabrication techniques and with identical supports, equivalent closures and other appurtenances.

6.7.2.18.2   The prototype test report for the design approval shall include at least the following:

(a)   The results of the applicable framework test specified in ISO 1496-3:1995;

(b)   The results of the initial inspection and test in 6.7.2.19.3; and

(c)   The results of the impact test in 6.7.2.19.1, when applicable.

6.7.2.19   *Inspection and testing*

6.7.2.19.1   Portable tanks meeting the definition of container in the International Convention for Safe Containers (CSC), 1972, as amended, shall not be used unless they are successfully qualified by subjecting a representative prototype of each design to the Dynamic Longitudinal Impact Test prescribed in the *Manual of Tests and Criteria*, part IV, section 41.

6.7.2.19.2   The shell and items of equipment of each portable tank shall be inspected and tested before being put into service for the first time (initial inspection and test) and thereafter at not more than five-year intervals (5 year periodic inspection and test) with an intermediate periodic inspection and test (2.5 year periodic inspection and test) midway between the 5 year periodic inspections and tests. The 2.5 year inspection and test may be performed within 3 months of the specified date. An exceptional inspection and test shall be performed regardless of the date of the last periodic inspection and test when necessary according to 6.7.2.19.7.

6.7.2.19.3   The initial inspection and test of a portable tank shall include a check of the design characteristics, an internal and external examination of the portable tank and its fittings with due regard to the substances to be transported, and a pressure test. Before the portable tank is placed into service, a leakproofness test and a test of the satisfactory operation of all service equipment shall also be performed. When the shell and its fittings have been pressure-tested separately, they shall be subjected together after assembly to a leakproofness test.

6.7.2.19.4   The 5-year periodic inspection and test shall include an internal and external examination and, as a general rule, a hydraulic pressure test. For tanks only used for the transport of solid substances, other than toxic or corrosive substances that do not liquefy during transport, the hydraulic pressure test may be replaced by a suitable pressure test at 1.5 times the MAWP, subject to competent authority approval. Sheathing, thermal insulation and the like shall be removed only to the extent required for reliable appraisal of the condition of the portable tank. When the shell and equipment have been pressure-tested separately, they shall also be subjected to a leakproofness test together after assembly.

6.7.2.19.5   The intermediate 2.5 year periodic inspection and test shall at least include an internal and external examination of the portable tank and its fittings with due regard to the substances intended to be transported, a leakproofness test and a test of the satisfactory operation of all service equipment. Sheathing, thermal insulation and the like shall be removed only to the extent required for reliable appraisal of the condition of the portable tank. For portable tanks dedicated to the transport of a single substance, the 2.5 year internal examination may be waived or substituted by other test methods or inspection procedures specified by the competent authority or its authorized body.

6.7.2.19.6   A portable tank may not be filled and offered for transport after the date of expiry of the last 5 year or 2.5 year periodic inspection and test as required by 6.7.2.19.2. However a portable tank filled prior to the date of expiry of the last periodic inspection and test may be transported for a period not to exceed three months beyond the date of expiry of the last periodic test or inspection. In addition, a portable tank may be transported after the date of expiry of the last periodic test and inspection:

(a)   After emptying but before cleaning, for purposes of performing the next required test or inspection prior to refilling; and

(b)   Unless otherwise approved by the competent authority, for a period not to exceed six months beyond the date of expiry of the last periodic test or inspection, in order to allow the return of dangerous goods for proper disposal or recycling. Reference to this exemption shall be mentioned in the transport document.

6.7.2.19.6.1 Except as provided for in 6.7.2.19.6, portable tanks which have missed the timeframe for their scheduled 5 year or 2.5 year periodic inspection and test may only be filled and offered for transport if a new 5 year periodic inspection and test is performed according to 6.7.2.19.4.

6.7.2.19.7 The exceptional inspection and test is necessary when the portable tank shows evidence of damaged or corroded areas, or leakage, or other conditions that indicate a deficiency that could affect the integrity of the portable tank. The extent of the exceptional inspection and test shall depend on the amount of damage or deterioration of the portable tank. It shall include at least the 2.5 year inspection and test according to 6.7.2.19.5.

6.7.2.19.8 The internal and external examinations shall ensure that:

(a) The shell is inspected for pitting, corrosion, or abrasions, dents, distortions, defects in welds or any other conditions, including leakage, that might render the portable tank unsafe for transport. The wall thickness shall be verified by appropriate measurement if this inspection indicates a reduction of wall thickness;

(b) The piping, valves, heating/cooling system, and gaskets are inspected for corroded areas, defects, or any other conditions, including leakage, that might render the portable tank unsafe for filling, discharge or transport;

(c) Devices for tightening manhole covers are operative and there is no leakage at manhole covers or gaskets;

(d) Missing or loose bolts or nuts on any flanged connection or blank flange are replaced or tightened;

(e) All emergency devices and valves are free from corrosion, distortion and any damage or defect that could prevent their normal operation. Remote closure devices and self-closing stop-valves shall be operated to demonstrate proper operation;

(f) Linings, if any, are inspected in accordance with criteria outlined by the lining manufacturer;

(g) Required marks on the portable tank are legible and in accordance with the applicable requirements; and

(h) The framework, supports and arrangements for lifting the portable tank are in a satisfactory condition.

6.7.2.19.9 The inspections and tests in 6.7.2.19.1, 6.7.2.19.3, 6.7.2.19.4, 6.7.2.19.5 and 6.7.2.19.7 shall be performed or witnessed by an expert approved by the competent authority or its authorized body. When the pressure test is a part of the inspection and test, the test pressure shall be the one indicated on the data plate of the portable tank. While under pressure, the portable tank shall be inspected for any leaks in the shell, piping or equipment.

6.7.2.19.10 In all cases when cutting, burning or welding operations on the shell have been effected, that work shall be to the approval of the competent authority or its authorized body taking into account the pressure vessel code used for the construction of the shell. A pressure test to the original test pressure shall be performed after the work is completed.

6.7.2.19.11 When evidence of any unsafe condition is discovered, the portable tank shall not be returned to service until it has been corrected and the test is repeated and passed.

6.7.2.20 *Marking*

6.7.2.20.1 Every portable tank shall be fitted with a corrosion resistant metal plate permanently attached to the portable tank in a conspicuous place readily accessible for inspection. When for reasons of portable tank arrangements the plate cannot be permanently attached to the shell, the shell shall be marked with at least the information required by the pressure vessel code. As a minimum, at least the following information shall be marked on the plate by stamping or by any other similar method:

(a) Owner information

　(i) Owner's registration number;

(b) Manufacturing information

　(i) Country of manufacture;

　(ii) Year of manufacture;

　(iii) Manufacturer's name or mark;

　(iv) Manufacturer's serial number;

(c) Approval information

　(i) The United Nations packaging symbol $\left(\begin{smallmatrix}u\\n\end{smallmatrix}\right)$.

　This symbol shall not be used for any purpose other than certifying that a packaging, a flexible bulk container, a portable tank or a MEGC complies with the relevant requirements in chapter 6.1, 6.2, 6.3, 6.5, 6.6, 6.7 or 6.8;

　(ii) Approval country;

　(iii) Authorized body for the design approval;

　(iv) Design approval number;

　(v) Letters 'AA', if the design was approved under alternative arrangements (see 6.7.1.2);

　(vi) Pressure vessel code to which the shell is designed;

(d) Pressures

　(i) MAWP (in bar gauge or kPa gauge)[3];

　(ii) Test pressure (in bar gauge or kPa gauge)[3];

　(iii) Initial pressure test date (month and year);

　(iv) Identification mark of the initial pressure test witness;

　(v) External design pressure[4] (in bar gauge or kPa gauge)[3];

　(vi) MAWP for heating/cooling system (in bar gauge or kPa gauge)[3] (when applicable);

---

[3] *The unit used shall be indicated.*
[4] *See 6.7.2.2.10.*

(e) Temperatures

    (i) Design temperature range (in °C)[3];

(f) Materials

    (i) Shell material(s) and material standard reference(s);

    (ii) Equivalent thickness in reference steel (in mm)[3];

    (iii) Lining material (when applicable);

(g) Capacity

    (i) Tank water capacity at 20 °C (in litres)[3];

    This indication is to be followed by the symbol "S" when the shell is divided by surge plates into sections of not more than 7 500 litres capacity;

    (ii) Water capacity of each compartment at 20 °C (in litres)[3] (when applicable, for multi-compartment tanks).

    This indication is to be followed by the symbol "S" when the compartment is divided by surge plates into sections of not more than 7 500 litres capacity;

(h) Periodic inspections and tests

    (i) Type of the most recent periodic test (2.5-year, 5-year or exceptional);

    (ii) Date of the most recent periodic test (month and year);

    (iii) Test pressure (in bar gauge or kPa gauge)[3] of the most recent periodic test (if applicable);

    (iv) Identification mark of the authorized body who performed or witnessed the most recent test.

---

[3] *The unit used shall be indicated.*

Figure 6.7.2.20.1: Example of a plate for marking

Owner's registration number			
MANUFACTURING INFORMATION			
Country of manufacture			
Year of manufacture			
Manufacturer			
Manufacturer's serial number			
APPROVAL INFORMATION			
ⓤⓝ Approval country			
Authorized body for design approval			
Design approval number		'AA' *(if applicable)*	
Shell design code (pressure vessel code)			
PRESSURES			
MAWP			bar *or* kPa
Test pressure			bar *or* kPa
Initial pressure test date: *(mm/yyyy)*	Witness stamp:		
External design pressure			bar *or* kPa
MAWP for heating/cooling system *(when applicable)*			bar *or* kPa
TEMPERATURES			
Design temperature range	°C to		°C
MATERIALS			
Shell material(s) and material standard reference(s)			
Equivalent thickness in reference steel			mm
Lining material *(when applicable)*			
CAPACITY			
Tank water capacity at 20 °C		litres	'S' *(if applicable)*
Water capacity of compartment ___ at 20 °C *(when applicable, for multi-compartment tanks)*		litres	'S' *(if applicable)*

PERIODIC INSPECTIONS / TESTS

Test type	Test date	Witness stamp and test pressure[a]	Test type	Test date	Witness stamp and test pressure[a]
	(mm/yyyy)	bar *or* kPa		*(mm/yyyy)*	bar *or* kPa

[a] *Test pressure if applicable.*

6.7.2.20.2 The following information shall be durably marked either on the portable tank itself or on a metal plate firmly secured to the portable tank:

> Name of the operator
> Maximum permissible gross mass (MPGM) _____ kg
> Unladen (tare) mass _____ kg
> Portable tank instruction in accordance with 4.2.5.2.6

NOTE: *For the identification of the substances being transported, see also part 5.*

6.7.2.20.3 If a portable tank is designed and approved for handling in open seas, the words "OFFSHORE PORTABLE TANK" shall be marked on the identification plate.

6.7.3 **Requirements for the design, construction, inspection and testing of portable tanks intended for the transport of non-refrigerated liquefied gases**

NOTE: *These requirements also apply to portable tanks intended for the transport of chemicals under pressure (UN Nos. 3500, 3501, 3502, 3503, 3504 and 3505).*

6.7.3.1 *Definitions*

For the purposes of this section:

Design pressure means the pressure to be used in calculations required by a recognized pressure vessel code. The design pressure shall be not less than the highest of the following pressures:

(a) The maximum effective gauge pressure allowed in the shell during filling or discharge; or

(b) The sum of:

(i) the maximum effective gauge pressure to which the shell is designed as defined in (b) of the MAWP definition (see above); and

(ii) a head pressure determined on the basis of the static forces specified in 6.7.3.2.9, but not less than 0.35 bar;

Design reference temperature means the temperature at which the vapour pressure of the contents is determined for the purpose of calculating the MAWP. The design reference temperature shall be less than the critical temperature of the non-refrigerated liquefied gas or liquefied gas propellants of chemicals under pressure intended to be transported to ensure that the gas at all times is liquefied. This value for each portable tank type is as follows:

(a) Shell with a diameter of 1.5 metres or less: 65 °C;

(b) Shell with a diameter of more than 1.5 metres:

(i) without insulation or sun shield: 60 °C;

(ii) with sun shield (see 6.7.3.2.12): 55 °C; and

(iii) with insulation (see 6.7.3.2.12): 50 °C;

Design temperature range for the shell shall be -40 °C to 50 °C for non-refrigerated liquefied gases transported under ambient conditions. More severe design temperatures shall be considered for portable tanks subjected to severe climatic conditions;

Filling density means the average mass of non-refrigerated liquefied gas per litre of shell capacity (kg/l). The filling density is given in portable tank instruction T50 in 4.2.5.2.6;

Leakproofness test means a test using gas subjecting the shell and its service equipment to an effective internal pressure of not less than 25 % of the MAWP;

Maximum allowable working pressure (MAWP) means a pressure that shall be not less than the highest of the following pressures measured at the top of the shell while in operating position, but in no case less than 7 bar:

(a) The maximum effective gauge pressure allowed in the shell during filling or discharge; or

(b) The maximum effective gauge pressure to which the shell is designed, which shall be:

(i) for a non-refrigerated liquefied gas listed in the portable tank instruction T50 in 4.2.5.2.6, the MAWP (in bar) given in T50 portable tank instruction for that gas;

(ii) for other non-refrigerated liquefied gases, not less than the sum of:

- the absolute vapour pressure (in bar) of the non-refrigerated liquefied gas at the design reference temperature minus 1 bar; and

- the partial pressure (in bar) of air or other gases in the ullage space being determined by the design reference temperature and the liquid phase expansion due to an increase of the mean bulk temperature of t_r-t_f (t_f = filling temperature, usually 15 °C, t_r = 50 °C maximum mean bulk temperature);

(iii) for chemicals under pressure, the MAWP (in bar) given in T50 portable tank instruction for the liquefied gas portion of the propellants listed in T50 in 4.2.5.2.6;

Maximum permissible gross mass (MPGM) means the sum of the tare mass of the portable tank and the heaviest load authorized for transport;

Mild steel means a steel with a guaranteed minimum tensile strength of 360 N/mm^2 to 440 N/mm^2 and a guaranteed minimum elongation at fracture conforming to 6.7.3.3.3.3;

Portable tank means a multimodal tank having a capacity of more than 450 litres used for the transport of non-refrigerated liquefied gases of Class 2. The portable tank includes a shell fitted with service equipment and structural equipment necessary for the transport of gases. The portable tank shall be capable of being filled and discharged without the removal of its structural equipment. It shall possess stabilizing members external to the shell, and shall be capable of being lifted when full. It shall be designed primarily to be loaded onto a transport vehicle or ship and shall be equipped with skids, mountings or accessories to facilitate mechanical handling. Road tank-vehicles, rail tank-wagons, non-metallic tanks, intermediate bulk containers (IBCs), gas cylinders and large receptacles are not considered to fall within the definition for portable tanks;

Reference steel means a steel with a tensile strength of 370 N/mm^2 and an elongation at fracture of 27 %;

Service equipment means measuring instruments and filling, discharge, venting, safety and insulating devices;

Shell means the part of the portable tank which retains the non-refrigerated liquefied gas intended for transport (tank proper), including openings and their closures, but does not include service equipment or external structural equipment;

Structural equipment means the reinforcing, fastening, protective and stabilizing members external to the shell;

Test pressure means the maximum gauge pressure at the top of the shell during the pressure test.

6.7.3.2 *General design and construction requirements*

6.7.3.2.1 Shells shall be designed and constructed in accordance with the requirements of a pressure vessel code recognized by the competent authority. Shells shall be made of steel suitable for forming. The materials shall in principle conform to national or international material standards. For welded shells, only a material whose weldability has been fully demonstrated shall be used. Welds shall be skilfully made and afford complete safety. When the manufacturing process or the materials make it necessary, the shells shall be suitability heat-treated to guarantee adequate toughness in the weld and in the heat affected zones. In choosing the material the design temperature range shall be taken into account with respect to risk of brittle fracture, to stress corrosion cracking and to resistance to impact. When fine grain steel is used, the guaranteed value of the yield strength shall be not more than 460 N/mm^2 and the guaranteed value of the upper limit of the tensile strength shall be not more than 725 N/mm^2 according to the material specification. Portable tank materials shall be suitable for the external environment in which they may be transported.

6.7.3.2.2 Portable tank shells, fittings and pipework shall be constructed of materials which are:

    (a) Substantially immune to attack by the non-refrigerated liquefied gas(es) intended to be transported; or

    (b) Properly passivated or neutralized by chemical reaction.

6.7.3.2.3 Gaskets shall be made of materials compatible with the non-refrigerated liquefied gas(es) intended to be transported.

6.7.3.2.4 Contact between dissimilar metals which could result in damage by galvanic action shall be avoided.

6.7.3.2.5 The materials of the portable tank, including any devices, gaskets, and accessories, shall not adversely affect the non-refrigerated liquefied gas(es) intended for transport in the portable tank.

6.7.3.2.6 Portable tanks shall be designed and constructed with supports to provide a secure base during transport and with suitable lifting and tie-down attachments.

6.7.3.2.7 Portable tanks shall be designed to withstand, without loss of contents, at least the internal pressure due to the contents, and the static, dynamic and thermal loads during normal conditions of handling and transport. The design shall demonstrate that the effects of fatigue, caused by repeated application of these loads through the expected life of the portable tank, have been taken into account.

6.7.3.2.8 Shells shall be designed to withstand an external pressure of at least 0.4 bar gauge above the internal pressure without permanent deformation. When the shell is to be subjected to a significant vacuum before filling or during discharge it shall be designed to withstand an external pressure of at least 0.9 bar gauge above the internal pressure and shall be proven at that pressure.

6.7.3.2.9 Portable tanks and their fastenings shall, under the maximum permissible load, be capable of absorbing the following separately applied static forces:

    (a) In the direction of travel: twice the MPGM multiplied by the acceleration due to gravity $(g)^1$;

    (b) Horizontally at right angles to the direction of travel: the MPGM (when the direction of travel is not clearly determined, the forces shall be equal to twice the MPGM) multiplied by the acceleration due to gravity $(g)^1$;

    (c) Vertically upwards: the MPGM multiplied by the acceleration due to gravity $(g)^1$; and

    (d) Vertically downwards: twice the MPGM (total loading including the effect of gravity) multiplied by the acceleration due to gravity $(g)^1$.

6.7.3.2.10 Under each of the forces in 6.7.3.2.9, the safety factor to be observed shall be as follows:

    (a) For steels having a clearly defined yield point, a safety factor of 1.5 in relation to the guaranteed yield strength; or

    (b) For steels with no clearly defined yield point, a safety factor of 1.5 in relation to the guaranteed 0.2 % proof strength and, for austenitic steels, the 1 % proof strength.

6.7.3.2.11 The values of yield strength or proof strength shall be the values according to national or international material standards. When austenitic steels are used, the specified minimum values of yield strength and proof strength according to the material standards may be increased by up to 15 % when these

---

[1] *For calculation purposes $g = 9.81\ m/s^2$.*

greater values are attested in the material inspection certificate. When no material standard exists for the steel in question, the value of yield strength or proof strength used shall be approved by the competent authority.

6.7.3.2.12 When the shells intended for the transport of non-refrigerated liquefied gases are equipped with thermal insulation, the thermal insulation systems shall satisfy the following requirements:

(a) It shall consist of a shield covering not less than the upper third but not more than the upper half of the surface of the shell and separated from the shell by an air space about 40 mm across; or

(b) It shall consist of a complete cladding of adequate thickness of insulating materials protected so as to prevent the ingress of moisture and damage under normal conditions of transport and so as to provide a thermal conductance of not more than 0.67 ($W \cdot m^{-2} \cdot K^{-1}$);

(c) When the protective covering is so closed as to be gas-tight, a device shall be provided to prevent any dangerous pressure from developing in the insulating layer in the event of inadequate gas tightness of the shell or of its items of equipment;

(d) The thermal insulation shall not inhibit access to the fittings and discharge devices.

6.7.3.2.13 Portable tanks intended for the transport of flammable non-refrigerated liquefied gases shall be capable of being electrically earthed.

6.7.3.3 *Design criteria*

6.7.3.3.1 Shells shall be of a circular cross-section.

6.7.3.3.2 Shells shall be designed and constructed to withstand a test pressure not less than 1.3 times the design pressure. The shell design shall take into account the minimum MAWP values provided in portable tank instruction T50 in 4.2.5.2.6 for each non-refrigerated liquefied gas intended for transport. Attention is drawn to the minimum shell thickness requirements for these shells specified in 6.7.3.4.

6.7.3.3.3 For steels exhibiting a clearly defined yield point or characterized by a guaranteed proof strength (0.2 % proof strength, generally, or 1 % proof strength for austenitic steels) the primary membrane stress σ (sigma) in the shell shall not exceed 0.75 Re or 0.50 Rm, whichever is lower, at the test pressure, where:

Re = yield strength in N/mm^2, or 0.2 % proof strength or, for austenitic steels, 1 % proof strength;
Rm = minimum tensile strength in N/mm^2.

6.7.3.3.3.1 The values of Re and Rm to be used shall be the specified minimum values according to national or international material standards. When austenitic steels are used, the specified minimum values for Re and Rm according to the material standards may be increased by up to 15 % when these greater values are attested in the material inspection certificate. When no material standard exists for the steel in question, the values of Re and Rm used shall be approved by the competent authority or its authorized body.

6.7.3.3.3.2 Steels which have an Re/Rm ratio of more than 0.85 are not allowed for the construction of welded shells. The values of Re and Rm to be used in determining this ratio shall be the values specified in the material inspection certificate.

6.7.3.3.3.3 Steels used in the construction of shells shall have an elongation at fracture, in %, of not less than 10 000/Rm with an absolute minimum of 16 % for fine grain steels and 20 % for other steels.

6.7.3.3.3.4 For the purpose of determining actual values for materials, it shall be noted that for sheet metal, the axis of the tensile test specimen shall be at right angles (transversely) to the direction of rolling. The permanent elongation at fracture shall be measured on test specimens of rectangular cross sections in accordance with ISO 6892:1998 using a 50 mm gauge length.

6.7.3.4 *Minimum shell thickness*

6.7.3.4.1 The minimum shell thickness shall be the greater thickness based on:

(a) The minimum thickness determined in accordance with the requirements in 6.7.3.4; and

(b) The minimum thickness determined in accordance with the recognized pressure vessel code including the requirements in 6.7.3.3.

In addition, any relevant portable tank special provision indicated in Column 11 of the Dangerous Goods List and described in 4.2.5.3 shall be taken into account.

6.7.3.4.2 The cylindrical portions, ends (heads) and manhole covers of shells of not more than 1.80 m in diameter shall be not less than 5 mm thick in the reference steel or of equivalent thickness in the steel to be used. Shells of more than 1.80 m in diameter shall be not less than 6 mm thick in the reference steel or of equivalent thickness in the steel to be used.

6.7.3.4.3 The cylindrical portions, ends (heads) and manhole covers of all shells shall be not less than 4 mm thick regardless of the material of construction.

6.7.3.4.4 The equivalent thickness of a steel other than the thickness prescribed for the reference steel in 6.7.3.4.2 shall be determined using the following formula:

$$e_1 = \frac{21.4e_0}{\sqrt[3]{Rm_1 \times A_1}}$$

where:

e_1 = required equivalent thickness (in mm) of the steel to be used;

e_0 = minimum thickness (in mm) for the reference steel specified in 6.7.3.4.2;

Rm_1 = guaranteed minimum tensile strength (in N/mm^2) of the steel to be used (see 6.7.3.3.3);

A_1 = guaranteed minimum elongation at fracture (in %) of the steel to be used according to national or international standards.

6.7.3.4.5 In no case shall the wall thickness be less than that prescribed in 6.7.3.4.1 to 6.7.3.4.3. All parts of the shell shall have a minimum thickness as determined by 6.7.3.4.1 to 6.7.3.4.3. This thickness shall be exclusive of any corrosion allowance.

6.7.3.4.6 When mild steel is used (see 6.7.3.1), calculation using the formula in 6.7.3.4.4 is not required.

6.7.3.4.7 There shall be no sudden change of plate thickness at the attachment of the ends (heads) to the cylindrical portion of the shell.

6.7.3.5 *Service equipment*

6.7.3.5.1 Service equipment shall be so arranged as to be protected against the risk of being wrenched off or damaged during handling and transport. When the connection between the frame and the shell allows relative movement between the sub-assemblies, the equipment shall be so fastened as to permit such movement without risk of damage to working parts. The external discharge fittings (pipe sockets, shut-off devices), the internal stop-valve and its seating shall be protected against the danger of being wrenched off by external forces (for example using shear sections). The filling and discharge devices (including flanges or threaded plugs) and any protective caps shall be capable of being secured against unintended opening.

6.7.3.5.2 All openings with a diameter of more than 1.5 mm in shells of portable tanks, except openings for pressure-relief devices, inspection openings and closed bleed holes, shall be fitted with at least three mutually independent shut-off devices in series, the first being an internal stop-valve, excess flow valve or equivalent device, the second being an external stop-valve and the third being a blank flange or equivalent device.

6.7.3.5.2.1 When a portable tank is fitted with an excess flow valve the excess flow valve shall be so fitted that its seating is inside the shell or inside a welded flange or, when fitted externally, its mountings shall be designed so that in the event of impact its effectiveness shall be maintained. The excess flow valves shall be selected and fitted so as to close automatically when the rated flow specified by the manufacturer is reached. Connections and accessories leading to or from such a valve shall have a capacity for a flow more than the rated flow of the excess flow valve.

6.7.3.5.3 For filling and discharge openings the first shut-off device shall be an internal stop-valve and the second shall be a stop-valve placed in an accessible position on each discharge and filling pipe.

6.7.3.5.4 For filling and discharge bottom openings of portable tanks intended for the transport of flammable and/or toxic non-refrigerated liquefied gases or chemicals under pressure the internal stop-valve shall be a quick closing safety device which closes automatically in the event of unintended movement of the portable tank during filling or discharge or fire engulfment. Except for portable tanks having a capacity of not more than 1 000 litres, it shall be possible to operate this device by remote control.

6.7.3.5.5 In addition to filling, discharge and gas pressure equalizing orifices, shells may have openings in which gauges, thermometers and manometers can be fitted. Connections for such instruments shall be made by suitable welded nozzles or pockets and not be screwed connections through the shell.

6.7.3.5.6 All portable tanks shall be fitted with manholes or other inspection openings of suitable size to allow for internal inspection and adequate access for maintenance and repair of the interior.

6.7.3.5.7 External fittings shall be grouped together so far as reasonably practicable.

6.7.3.5.8 Each connection on a portable tank shall be clearly marked to indicate its function.

6.7.3.5.9 Each stop-valve or other means of closure shall be designed and constructed to a rated pressure not less than the MAWP of the shell taking into account the temperatures expected during transport. All stop-valves with a screwed spindle shall close by a clockwise motion of the handwheel. For other stop-valves the position (open and closed) and direction of closure shall be clearly indicated. All stop-valves shall be designed to prevent unintentional opening.

6.7.3.5.10 Piping shall be designed, constructed and installed so as to avoid the risk of damage due to thermal expansion and contraction, mechanical shock and vibration. All piping shall be of suitable metallic material. Welded pipe joints shall be used wherever possible.

6.7.3.5.11 Joints in copper tubing shall be brazed or have an equally strong metal union. The melting point of brazing materials shall be no lower than 525 °C. The joints shall not decrease the strength of tubing as may happen when cutting threads.

6.7.3.5.12 The burst pressure of all piping and pipe fittings shall be not less than the highest of four times the MAWP of the shell or four times the pressure to which it may be subjected in service by the action of a pump or other device (except pressure-relief devices).

6.7.3.5.13 Ductile metals shall be used in the construction of valves and accessories.

6.7.3.6 *Bottom openings*

6.7.3.6.1 Certain non-refrigerated liquefied gases shall not be transported in portable tanks with bottom openings. When portable tank instruction T50 in 4.2.5.2.6 indicates that bottom openings are not allowed, there shall be no openings below the liquid level of the shell when it is filled to its maximum permissible filling limit.

6.7.3.7 *Pressure-relief devices*

6.7.3.7.1 Portable tanks shall be provided with one or more spring-loaded pressure-relief devices. The pressure-relief devices shall open automatically at a pressure not less than the MAWP and be fully open at a pressure equal to 110 % of the MAWP. These devices shall, after discharge, close at a pressure not lower than 10 % below the pressure at which discharge starts and shall remain closed at all lower pressures. The pressure-relief devices shall be of a type that will resist dynamic forces including liquid surge. Frangible discs not in series with a spring-loaded pressure-relief device are not permitted.

6.7.3.7.2 Pressure-relief devices shall be designed to prevent the entry of foreign matter, the leakage of gas and the development of any dangerous excess pressure.

6.7.3.7.3 Portable tanks intended for the transport of certain non-refrigerated liquefied gases identified in portable tank instruction T50 in 4.2.5.2.6 shall have a pressure-relief device approved by the competent authority. Unless a portable tank in dedicated service is fitted with an approved relief device constructed of materials compatible with the load, such device shall comprise a frangible disc preceding a spring-loaded device. The space between the frangible disc and the device shall be provided with a pressure gauge or a suitable tell-tale indicator. This arrangement permits the detection of disc rupture, pinholing or leakage which could cause a malfunction of the pressure-relief device. The frangible discs shall rupture at a nominal pressure 10 % above the start-to-discharge pressure of the relief device.

6.7.3.7.4 In the case of multi-purpose portable tanks, the pressure-relief devices shall open at a pressure indicated in 6.7.3.7.1 for the gas having the highest maximum allowable pressure of the gases allowed to be transported in the portable tank.

6.7.3.8 *Capacity of relief devices*

6.7.3.8.1 The combined delivery capacity of the relief devices shall be sufficient that, in the event of total fire engulfment, the pressure (including accumulation) inside the shell does not exceed 120 % of the MAWP. Spring-loaded relief devices shall be used to achieve the full relief capacity prescribed. In the case of multi-purpose tanks, the combined delivery capacity of the pressure-relief devices shall be taken for the gas which requires the highest delivery capacity of the gases allowed to be transported in portable tanks.

6.7.3.8.1.1 To determine the total required capacity of the relief devices, which shall be regarded as being the sum of the individual capacities of the several devices, the following formula shall be used:

$$Q = 12.4 \frac{FA^{0.82}}{LC} \sqrt{\frac{ZT}{M}}$$

where:

Q = minimum required rate of discharge in cubic metres of air per second (m³/s) at standard conditions: 1 bar and 0 °C (273 K);

F = is a coefficient with the following value:

for uninsulated shells $F = 1$;

for insulated shells $F = U(649-t)/13.6$

but in no case is less than 0.25 where:

U = heat transfer coefficient of the insulation, in $kW \cdot m^{-2} \cdot K^{-1}$, at 38 °C,

t = actual temperature of the non-refrigerated liquefied gas during filling (°C); when this temperature is unknown, let $t = 15$ °C:

The value of F given above for insulated shells may be taken provided that the insulation is in conformance with 6.7.3.8.1.2;

A = total external surface area of shell in square metres;

Z = the gas compressibility factor in the accumulating condition (when this factor is unknown, let Z equal 1.0);

T = absolute temperature in Kelvin (°C + 273) above the pressure-relief devices in the accumulating condition;

L = the latent heat of vaporization of the liquid, in kJ/kg, in the accumulating condition;

M = molecular mass of the discharged gas;

C = a constant which is derived from one of the following formulae as a function of the ratio k of specific heats:

$$k = \frac{C_p}{C_v}$$

where

c_p is the specific heat at constant pressure; and
c_v is the specific heat at constant volume.

when k > 1:

$$C = \sqrt{k\left(\frac{2}{k+1}\right)^{\frac{k+1}{k-1}}}$$

when k = 1 or k is unknown

$$C = \frac{1}{\sqrt{e}} = 0.607$$

where e is the mathematical constant 2.7183
C may also be taken from the following table:

k	C	k	C	k	C
1.00	0.607	1.26	0.660	1.52	0.704
1.02	0.611	1.28	0.664	1.54	0.707
1.04	0.615	1.30	0.667	1.56	0.710
1.06	0.620	1.32	0.671	1.58	0.713
1.08	0.624	1.34	0.674	1.60	0.716
1.10	0.628	1.36	0.678	1.62	0.719
1.12	0.633	1.38	0.681	1.64	0.722
1.14	0.637	1.40	0.685	1.66	0.725
1.16	0.641	1.42	0.688	1.68	0.728
1.18	0.645	1.44	0.691	1.70	0.731
1.20	0.649	1.46	0.695	2.00	0.770
1.22	0.652	1.48	0.698	2.20	0.793
1.24	0.656	1.50	0.701		

NOTE: *This formula applies only to non-refrigerated liquefied gases which have critical temperatures well above the temperature at the accumulating condition. For gases which have critical temperatures near or below the temperature at the accumulating condition, the calculation of the pressure-relief device delivery capacity shall consider further thermodynamic properties of the gas (see, e.g. CGA S-1.2-2003 Pressure Relief Device Standards – Part 2 – Cargo and Portable Tanks for Compressed Gases).*

6.7.3.8.1.2   Insulation systems, used for the purpose of reducing the venting capacity, shall be approved by the competent authority or its authorized body. In all cases, insulation systems approved for this purpose shall:

    (a)   Remain effective at all temperatures up to 649 °C; and

    (b)   Be jacketed with a material having a melting point of 700 °C or greater.

6.7.3.9   *Marking of pressure-relief devices*

6.7.3.9.1   Every pressure-relief device shall be plainly and permanently marked with the following:

    (a)   The pressure (in bar or kPa) at which it is set to discharge;

    (b)   The allowable tolerance at the discharge pressure for spring-loaded devices;

    (c)   The reference temperature corresponding to the rated pressure for frangible discs; and

    (d)   The rated flow capacity of the device in standard cubic metres of air per second (m^3/s);

    (e)   The cross sectional flow areas of the spring loaded pressure-relief devices and frangible discs in mm^2.

When practicable, the following information shall also be shown:

    (f)   The manufacturer's name and relevant catalogue number.

6.7.3.9.2   The rated flow capacity marked on the pressure-relief devices shall be determined according to ISO 4126-1:2004 and ISO 4126-7:2004.

6.7.3.10   *Connections to pressure-relief devices*

6.7.3.10.1   Connections to pressure-relief devices shall be of sufficient size to enable the required discharge to pass unrestricted to the safety device. No stop-valve shall be installed between the shell and the pressure-relief devices except when duplicate devices are provided for maintenance or other reasons and the stop-valves serving the devices actually in use are locked open or the stop-valves are interlocked so that at least one of the duplicate devices is always operable and capable of meeting the requirements of 6.7.3.8. There shall be no obstruction in an opening leading to a vent or pressure-relief device which might restrict or cut-off the flow from the shell to that device. Vents from the pressure-relief devices, when used, shall deliver the relieved vapour or liquid to the atmosphere in conditions of minimum back-pressure on the relieving device.

6.7.3.11   *Siting of pressure-relief devices*

6.7.3.11.1   Each pressure-relief device inlet shall be situated on top of the shell in a position as near the longitudinal and transverse centre of the shell as reasonably practicable. All pressure relief device inlets shall under maximum filling conditions be situated in the vapour space of the shell and the devices shall be so arranged as to ensure that the escaping vapour is discharged unrestrictedly. For flammable non-refrigerated liquefied gases, the escaping vapour shall be directed away from the shell in such a manner that it cannot impinge upon the shell. Protective devices which deflect the flow of vapour are permissible provided the required relief-device capacity is not reduced.

6.7.3.11.2   Arrangements shall be made to prevent access to the pressure-relief devices by unauthorized persons and to protect the devices from damage caused by the portable tank overturning.

6.7.3.12   *Gauging devices*

6.7.3.12.1   Unless a portable tank is intended to be filled by mass it shall be equipped with one or more gauging devices. Glass level-gauges and gauges made of other fragile material, which are in direct communication with the contents of the shell shall not be used.

6.7.3.13 *Portable tank supports, frameworks, lifting and tie-down attachments*

6.7.3.13.1   Portable tanks shall be designed and constructed with a support structure to provide a secure base during transport. The forces specified in 6.7.3.2.9 and the safety factor specified in 6.7.3.2.10 shall be considered in this aspect of the design. Skids, frameworks, cradles or other similar structures are acceptable.

6.7.3.13.2   The combined stresses caused by portable tank mountings (e.g. cradles, frameworks, etc.) and portable tank lifting and tie-down attachments shall not cause excessive stress in any portion of the shell. Permanent lifting and tie-down attachments shall be fitted to all portable tanks. Preferably they shall be fitted to the portable tank supports but may be secured to reinforcing plates located on the shell at the points of support.

6.7.3.13.3   In the design of supports and frameworks the effects of environmental corrosion shall be taken into account.

6.7.3.13.4   Forklift pockets shall be capable of being closed off. The means of closing forklift pockets shall be a permanent part of the framework or permanently attached to the framework. Single compartment portable tanks with a length less than 3.65 m need not have closed off forklift pockets provided that:

 (a) The shell and all the fittings are well protected from being hit by the forklift blades; and

 (b) The distance between the centres of the forklift pockets is at least half of the maximum length of the portable tank.

6.7.3.13.5   When portable tanks are not protected during transport, according to 4.2.2.3, the shells and service equipment shall be protected against damage to the shell and service equipment resulting from lateral or longitudinal impact or overturning. External fittings shall be protected so as to preclude the release of the shell contents upon impact or overturning of the portable tank on its fittings. Examples of protection include:

 (a) Protection against lateral impact which may consist of longitudinal bars protecting the shell on both sides at the level of the median line;

 (b) Protection of the portable tank against overturning which may consist of reinforcement rings or bars fixed across the frame;

 (c) Protection against rear impact which may consist of a bumper or frame;

 (d) Protection of the shell against damage from impact or overturning by use of an ISO frame in accordance with ISO 1496-3:1995.

6.7.3.14   *Design approval*

6.7.3.14.1   The competent authority or its authorized body shall issue a design approval certificate for any new design of a portable tank. This certificate shall attest that a portable tank has been surveyed by that authority, is suitable for its intended purpose and meets the requirements of this chapter and where appropriate the provisions for gases provided in portable tank instruction T50 in 4.2.5.2.6. When a series of portable tanks are manufactured without change in the design, the certificate shall be valid for the entire series. The certificate shall refer to the prototype test report, the gases allowed to be transported, the materials of construction of the shell and an approval number. The approval number shall consist of the distinguishing sign or mark of the State in whose territory the approval was granted, indicated by the distinguishing sign used on vehicles in international road traffic[2], and a registration number. Any alternative arrangements according to 6.7.1.2 shall be indicated on the certificate. A design approval may serve for the approval of smaller portable tanks made of materials of the same kind and thickness, by the same fabrication techniques and with identical supports, equivalent closures and other appurtenances.

---

[2] *Distinguishing sign of the State of registration used on motor vehicles and trailers in international road traffic, e.g. in accordance with the Geneva Convention on Road Traffic of 1949 or the Vienna Convention on Road Traffic of 1968.*

6.7.3.14.2   The prototype test report for the design approval shall include at least the following:

    (a)   The results of the applicable framework test specified in ISO 1496-3:1995;

    (b)   The results of the initial inspection and test in 6.7.3.15.3; and

    (c)   The results of the impact test in 6.7.3.15.1, when applicable.

6.7.3.15   *Inspection and testing*

6.7.3.15.1   Portable tanks meeting the definition of container in the International Convention for Safe Containers (CSC), 1972, as amended, shall not be used unless they are successfully qualified by subjecting a representative prototype of each design to the Dynamic, Longitudinal Impact Test prescribed in the *Manual of Tests and Criteria*, part IV, section 41.

6.7.3.15.2   The shell and items of equipment of each portable tank shall be inspected and tested before being put into service for the first time (initial inspection and test) and thereafter at not more than five-year intervals (5 year periodic inspection and test) with an intermediate periodic inspection and test (2.5 year periodic inspection and test) midway between the 5 year periodic inspections and tests. The 2.5 year inspection and test may be performed within 3 months of the specified date. An exceptional inspection and test shall be performed regardless of the last periodic inspection and test when necessary according to 6.7.3.15.7.

6.7.3.15.3   The initial inspection and test of a portable tank shall include a check of the design characteristics, an internal and external examination of the portable tank and its fittings with due regard to the non-refrigerated liquefied gases to be transported, and a pressure test referring to the test pressures according to 6.7.3.3.2. The pressure test may be performed as a hydraulic test or by using another liquid or gas with the agreement of the competent authority or its authorized body. Before the portable tank is placed into service, a leakproofness test and a test of the satisfactory operation of all service equipment shall also be performed. When the shell and its fittings have been pressure-tested separately, they shall be subjected together after assembly to a leakproofness test. All welds subject to full stress level in the shell shall be inspected during the initial test by radiographic, ultrasonic, or another suitable non-destructive test method. This does not apply to the jacket.

6.7.3.15.4   The 5 year periodic inspection and test shall include an internal and external examination and, as a general rule, a hydraulic pressure test. Sheathing, thermal insulation and the like shall be removed only to the extent required for reliable appraisal of the condition of the portable tank. When the shell and equipment have been pressure-tested separately, they shall be subjected together after assembly to a leakproofness test.

6.7.3.15.5   The intermediate 2.5 year periodic inspection and test shall at least include an internal and external examination of the portable tank and its fittings with due regard to the non-refrigerated liquefied gases intended to be transported, a leakproofness test and a test of the satisfactory operation of all service equipment. Sheathing thermal insulation and the like shall be removed only to the extent required for reliable appraisal of the condition of the portable tank. For portable tanks intended for the transport of a single non-refrigerated liquefied gas, the 2.5 year internal examination may be waived or substituted by other test methods or inspection procedures specified by the competent authority or its authorized body.

6.7.3.15.6   A portable tank may not be filled and offered for transport after the date of expiry of the last 5 year or 2.5 year periodic inspection and test as required by 6.7.3.15.2. However a portable tank filled prior to the date of expiry of the last periodic inspection and test may be transported for a period not to exceed three months beyond the date of expiry of the last periodic test or inspection. In addition, a portable tank may be transported after the date of expiry of the last periodic test and inspection:

    (a)   After emptying but before cleaning, for purposes of performing the next required test or inspection prior to refilling; and

    (b)   Unless otherwise approved by the competent authority, for a period not to exceed six months beyond the date of expiry of the last periodic test or inspection, in order to allow the return of dangerous goods for proper disposal or recycling. Reference to this exemption shall be mentioned in the transport document.

6.7.3.15.6.1　Except as provided for in 6.7.3.15.6, portable tanks which have missed the timeframe for their scheduled 5 year or 2.5 year periodic inspection and test may only be filled and offered for transport if a new 5 year periodic inspection and test is performed according to 6.7.3.15.4.

6.7.3.15.7　The exceptional inspection and test is necessary when the portable tank shows evidence of damaged or corroded areas, or leakage, or other conditions that indicate a deficiency that could affect the integrity of the portable tank. The extent of the exceptional inspection and test shall depend on the amount of damage or deterioration of the portable tank. It shall include at least the 2.5 year inspection and test according to 6.7.3.15.5.

6.7.3.15.8　The internal and external examinations shall ensure that:

(a) The shell is inspected for pitting, corrosion, or abrasions, dents, distortions, defects in welds or any other conditions, including leakage, that might render the portable tank unsafe for transport. The wall thickness shall be verified by appropriate measurement if this inspection indicates a reduction of wall thickness;

(b) The piping, valves, and gaskets are inspected for corroded areas, defects, or any other conditions, including leakage, that might render the portable tank unsafe for filling, discharge or transport;

(c) Devices for tightening manhole covers are operative and there is no leakage at manhole covers or gaskets;

(d) Missing or loose bolts or nuts on any flanged connection or blank flange are replaced or tightened;

(e) All emergency devices and valves are free from corrosion, distortion and any damage or defect that could prevent their normal operation. Remote closure devices and self-closing stop-valves shall be operated to demonstrate proper operation;

(f) Required marks on the portable tank are legible and in accordance with the applicable requirements; and

(g) The framework, the supports and the arrangements for lifting the portable tank are in satisfactory condition.

6.7.3.15.9　The inspections and tests in 6.7.3.15.1, 6.7.3.15.3, 6.7.3.15.4, 6.7.3.15.5 and 6.7.3.15.7 shall be performed or witnessed by an expert approved by the competent authority or its authorized body. When the pressure test is a part of the inspection and test, the test pressure shall be the one indicated on the data plate of the portable tank. While under pressure, the portable tank shall be inspected for any leaks in the shell, piping or equipment.

6.7.3.15.10　In all cases when cutting, burning or welding operations on the shell have been effected, that work shall be to the approval of the competent authority or its authorized body taking into account the pressure vessel code used for the construction of the shell. A pressure test to the original test pressure shall be performed after the work is completed.

6.7.3.15.11　When evidence of any unsafe condition is discovered, the portable tank shall not be returned to service until it has been corrected and the pressure test is repeated and passed.

6.7.3.16　*Marking*

6.7.3.16.1　Every portable tank shall be fitted with a corrosion resistant metal plate permanently attached to the portable tank in a conspicuous place readily accessible for inspection. When for reasons of portable tank arrangements the plate cannot be permanently attached to the shell, the shell shall be marked with at least the information required by the pressure vessel code. As a minimum, at least the following information shall be marked on the plate by stamping or by any other similar method:

(a) Owner information

    (i) Owner's registration number;

(b) Manufacturing information

    (i) Country of manufacture;

    (ii) Year of manufacture;

    (iii) Manufacturer's name or mark;

    (iv) Manufacturer's serial number;

(c) Approval information

    (i) The United Nations packaging symbol

    This symbol shall not be used for any purpose other than certifying that a packaging, a flexible bulk container, a portable tank or a MEGC complies with the relevant requirements in chapter 6.1, 6.2, 6.3, 6.5, 6.6, 6.7 or 6.8;

    (ii) Approval country;

    (iii) Authorized body for the design approval;

    (iv) Design approval number;

    (v) Letters 'AA', if the design was approved under alternative arrangements (see 6.7.1.2);

    (vi) Pressure vessel code to which the shell is designed;

(d) Pressures

    (i) MAWP (in bar gauge or kPa gauge)[3];

    (ii) Test pressure (in bar gauge or kPa gauge)[3];

    (iii) Initial pressure test date (month and year);

    (iv) Identification mark of the initial pressure test witness;

    (v) External design pressure[6] (in bar gauge or kPa gauge)[3];

(e) Temperatures

    (i) Design temperature range (in °C)[3];

    (ii) Design reference temperature (in °C)[3];

(f) Materials

    (i) Shell material(s) and material standard reference(s);

    (ii) Equivalent thickness in reference steel (in mm)[3];

---

[3] *The unit used shall be indicated.*
[6] *See 6.7.3.2.8.*

(g) Capacity

   (i) Tank water capacity at 20 °C (in litres)[3];

(h) Periodic inspections and tests

   (i) Type of the most recent periodic test (2.5-year, 5-year or exceptional);

   (ii) Date of the most recent periodic test (month and year);

   (iii) Test pressure (in bar gauge or kPa gauge)[3] of the most recent periodic test (if applicable);

   (iv) Identification mark of the authorized body who performed or witnessed the most recent test.

Figure 6.7.3.16.1: Example of a plate for marking

Owner's registration number					
MANUFACTURING INFORMATION					
Country of manufacture					
Year of manufacture					
Manufacturer					
Manufacturer's serial number					
APPROVAL INFORMATION					
	Approval country				
	Authorized body for design approval				
	Design approval number			*'AA' (if applicable)*	
Shell design code (pressure vessel code)					
PRESSURES					
MAWP					bar *or* kPa
Test pressure					bar *or* kPa
Initial pressure test date:	*(mm/yyyy)*	Witness stamp:			
External design pressure					bar *or* kPa
TEMPERATURES					
Design temperature range			°C to		°C
Design reference temperature					°C
MATERIALS					
Shell material(s) and material standard reference(s)					
Equivalent thickness in reference steel					mm
CAPACITY					
Tank water capacity at 20 °C					litres
PERIODIC INSPECTIONS / TESTS					
Test type	Test date	Witness stamp and test pressure[a]	Test type	Test date	Witness stamp and test pressure[a]
	(mm/yyyy)	bar *or* kPa		*(mm/yyyy)*	bar *or* kPa

[a] *Test pressure if applicable.*

---

[3] *The unit used shall be indicated.*

6.7.3.16.2   The following information shall be durably marked either on the portable tank itself or on a metal plate firmly secured to the portable tank:

>   Name of the operator
>   Name of non-refrigerated liquefied gas(es) permitted for transport
>   Maximum permissible load mass for each non-refrigerated liquefied gas permitted _____ kg
>   Maximum permissible gross mass (MPGM) _____ kg
>   Unladen (tare) mass _____ kg
>   Portable tank instruction in accordance with 4.2.5.2.6

NOTE: *For the identification of the non-refrigerated liquefied gases being transported, see also part 5.*

6.7.3.16.3   If a portable tank is designed and approved for handling in open seas, the words "OFFSHORE PORTABLE TANK" shall be marked on the identification plate.

6.7.4   Requirements for the design, construction, inspection and testing of portable tanks intended for the transport of refrigerated liquefied gases

6.7.4.1   *Definitions*

For the purposes of this section:

Holding time means the time that will elapse from the establishment of the initial filling condition until the pressure has risen due to heat influx to the lowest set pressure of the pressure limiting device(s);

Jacket means the outer insulation cover or cladding which may be part of the insulation system;

Leakproofness test means a test using gas subjecting the shell and its service equipment, to an effective internal pressure not less than 90 % of the MAWP;

Maximum allowable working pressure (MAWP) means the maximum effective gauge pressure permissible at the top of the shell of a loaded portable tank in its operating position including the highest effective pressure during filling and discharge;

Maximum permissible gross mass (MPGM) means the sum of the tare mass of the portable tank and the heaviest load authorized for transport;

Minimum design temperature means the temperature which is used for the design and construction of the shell not higher than the lowest (coldest) temperature (service temperature) of the contents during normal conditions of filling, discharge and transport;

Portable tank means a thermally insulated multimodal tank having a capacity of more than 450 litres fitted with service equipment and structural equipment necessary for the transport of refrigerated liquefied gases. The portable tank shall be capable of being filled and discharged without the removal of its structural equipment. It shall possess stabilizing members external to the tank, and shall be capable of being lifted when full. It shall be designed primarily to be loaded onto a transport vehicle or ship and shall be equipped with skids, mountings or accessories to facilitate mechanical handling. Road tank-vehicles, rail tank-wagons, non-metallic tanks, intermediate bulk containers (IBCs), gas cylinders and large receptacles are not considered to fall within the definition for portable tanks;

Reference steel means a steel with a tensile strength of 370 N/mm^2 and an elongation at fracture of 27 %;

Shell means the part of the portable tank which retains the refrigerated liquefied gas intended for transport, including openings and their closures, but does not include service equipment or external structural equipment;

Service equipment means measuring instruments and filling, discharge, venting, safety, pressurizing, cooling and thermal insulation devices;

Structural equipment means the reinforcing, fastening, protective and stabilizing members external to the shell;

Tank means a construction which normally consists of either:

    (a)   A jacket and one or more inner shells where the space between the shell(s) and the jacket is exhausted of air (vacuum insulation) and may incorporate a thermal insulation system; or

    (b)   A jacket and an inner shell with an intermediate layer of solid thermally insulating material (e.g. solid foam);

Test pressure means the maximum gauge pressure at the top of the shell during the pressure test.

6.7.4.2 *General design and construction requirements*

6.7.4.2.1 Shells shall be designed and constructed in accordance with the requirements of a pressure vessel code recognized by the competent authority. Shells and jackets shall be made of metallic materials suitable for forming. Jackets shall be made of steel. Non-metallic materials may be used for the attachments and supports between the shell and jacket, provided their material properties at the minimum design temperature are proven to be sufficient. The materials shall in principle conform to national or international material standards. For welded shells and jackets only materials whose weldability has been fully demonstrated shall be used. Welds shall be skilfully made and afford complete safety. When the manufacturing process or the materials make it necessary, the shell shall be suitably heat treated to guarantee adequate toughness in the weld and in the heat affected zones. In choosing the material, the minimum design temperature shall be taken into account with respect to risk of brittle fracture, to hydrogen embrittlement, to stress corrosion cracking and to resistance to impact. When fine grain steel is used, the guaranteed value of the yield strength shall be not more than 460 N/mm^2 and the guaranteed value of the upper limit of the tensile strength shall be not more than 725 N/mm^2 in accordance with the material specifications. Portable tank materials shall be suitable for the external environment in which they may be transported.

6.7.4.2.2 Any part of a portable tank, including fittings, gaskets and pipe-work, which can be expected normally to come into contact with the refrigerated liquefied gas transported shall be compatible with that refrigerated liquefied gas.

6.7.4.2.3 Contact between dissimilar metals which could result in damage by galvanic action shall be avoided.

6.7.4.2.4 The thermal insulation system shall include a complete covering of the shell(s) with effective insulating materials. External insulation shall be protected by a jacket so as to prevent the ingress of moisture and other damage under normal transport conditions.

6.7.4.2.5 When a jacket is so closed as to be gas-tight, a device shall be provided to prevent any dangerous pressure from developing in the insulation space.

6.7.4.2.6 Portable tanks intended for the transport of refrigerated liquefied gases having a boiling point below minus 182 °C at atmospheric pressure shall not include materials which may react with oxygen or oxygen enriched atmospheres in a dangerous manner, when located in parts of the thermal insulation when there is a risk of contact with oxygen or with oxygen enriched fluid.

6.7.4.2.7 Insulating materials shall not deteriorate unduly in service.

6.7.4.2.8 A reference holding time shall be determined for each refrigerated liquefied gas intended for transport in a portable tank.

6.7.4.2.8.1 The reference holding time shall be determined by a method recognized by the competent authority on the basis of the following:

    (a)   The effectiveness of the insulation system, determined in accordance with 6.7.4.2.8.2;

(b) The lowest set pressure of the pressure limiting device(s);

(c) The initial filling conditions;

(d) An assumed ambient temperature of 30 °C;

(e) The physical properties of the individual refrigerated liquefied gas intended to be transported.

6.7.4.2.8.2 The effectiveness of the insulation system (heat influx in watts) shall be determined by type testing the portable tank in accordance with a procedure recognized by the competent authority. This test shall consist of either:

(a) A constant pressure test (for example at atmospheric pressure) when the loss of refrigerated liquefied gas is measured over a period of time; or

(b) A closed system test when the rise in pressure in the shell is measured over a period of time.

When performing the constant pressure test, variations in atmospheric pressure shall be taken into account. When performing either tests corrections shall be made for any variation of the ambient temperature from the assumed ambient temperature reference value of 30 °C.

NOTE: *For the determination of the actual holding time before each journey, refer to 4.2.3.7.*

6.7.4.2.9 The jacket of a vacuum-insulated double-wall tank shall have either an external design pressure not less than 100 kPa (1 bar) gauge pressure calculated in accordance with a recognized technical code or a calculated critical collapsing pressure of not less than 200 kPa (2 bar) gauge pressure. Internal and external reinforcements may be included in calculating the ability of the jacket to resist the external pressure.

6.7.4.2.10 Portable tanks shall be designed and constructed with supports to provide a secure base during transport and with suitable lifting and tie-down attachments.

6.7.4.2.11 Portable tanks shall be designed to withstand, without loss of contents, at least the internal pressure due to the contents, and the static, dynamic and thermal loads during normal conditions of handling and transport. The design shall demonstrate that the effects of fatigue, caused by repeated application of these loads through the expected life of the portable tank, have been taken into account.

6.7.4.2.12 Portable tanks and their fastenings under the maximum permissible load shall be capable of absorbing the following separately applied static forces:

(a) In the direction of travel: twice the MPGM multiplied by the acceleration due to gravity (g)[1];

(b) Horizontally at right angles to the direction of travel: the MPGM (when the direction of travel is not clearly determined, the forces shall be equal to twice the MPGM) multiplied by the acceleration due to gravity (g)[1];

(c) Vertically upwards: the MPGM multiplied by the acceleration due to gravity (g)[1]; and

(d) Vertically downwards: twice the MPGM (total loading including the effect of gravity) multiplied by the acceleration due to gravity (g)[1].

6.7.4.2.13 Under each of the forces in 6.7.4.2.12, the safety factor to be observed shall be as follows:

(a) For materials having a clearly defined yield point, a safety factor of 1.5 in relation to the guaranteed yield strength; or

---

[1] *For calculation purposes $g = 9.81 \ m/s^2$.*

(b) For materials with no clearly defined yield point, a safety factor of 1.5 in relation to the guaranteed 0.2 % proof strength or, for austenitic steels, the 1 % proof strength.

6.7.4.2.14 The values of yield strength or proof strength shall be the values according to national or international material standards. When austenitic steels are used, the specified minimum values according to the material standards may be increased by up to 15 % when these greater values are attested in the material inspection certificate. When no material standard exists for the metal in question, or when non-metallic materials are used the values of yield strength or proof strength shall be approved by the competent authority.

6.7.4.2.15 Portable tanks intended for the transport of flammable refrigerated liquefied gases shall be capable of being electrically earthed.

6.7.4.3 *Design criteria*

6.7.4.3.1 Shells shall be of a circular cross section.

6.7.4.3.2 Shells shall be designed and constructed to withstand a test pressure not less than 1.3 times the MAWP. For shells with vacuum insulation the test pressure shall not be less than 1.3 times the sum of the MAWP and 100 kPa (1 bar). In no case shall the test pressure be less than 300 kPa (3 bar) gauge pressure. Attention is drawn to the minimum shell thickness requirements, specified in 6.7.4.4.2 to 6.7.4.4.7.

6.7.4.3.3 For metals exhibiting a clearly defined yield point or characterized by a guaranteed proof strength (0.2 % proof strength, generally, or 1 % proof strength for austenitic steels) the primary membrane stress σ (sigma) in the shell shall not exceed 0.75 Re or 0.50 Rm, whichever is lower, at the test pressure, where:

Re = yield strength in N/mm^2, or 0.2 % proof strength or, for austenitic steels, 1 % proof strength;
Rm = minimum tensile strength in N/mm^2.

6.7.4.3.3.1 The values of Re and Rm to be used shall be the specified minimum values according to national or international material standards. When austenitic steels are used, the specified minimum values for Re and Rm according to the material standards may be increased by up to 15 % when greater values are attested in the material inspection certificate. When no material standard exists for the metal in question, the values of Re and Rm used shall be approved by the competent authority or its authorized body.

6.7.4.3.3.2 Steels which have a Re/Rm ratio of more than 0.85 are not allowed for the construction of welded shells. The values of Re and Rm to be used in determining this ratio shall be the values specified in the material inspection certificate.

6.7.4.3.3.3 Steels used in the construction of shells shall have an elongation at fracture, in %, of not less than 10 000/Rm with an absolute minimum of 16 % for fine grain steels and 20 % for other steels. Aluminium and aluminium alloys used in the construction of shells shall have an elongation at fracture, in %, of not less than 10 000/6Rm with an absolute minimum of 12 %.

6.7.4.3.3.4 For the purpose of determining actual values for materials, it shall be noted that for sheet metal, the axis of the tensile test specimen shall be at right angles (transversely) to the direction of rolling. The permanent elongation at fracture shall be measured on test specimens of rectangular cross sections in accordance with ISO 6892:1998 using a 50 mm gauge length.

6.7.4.4 *Minimum shell thickness*

6.7.4.4.1 The minimum shell thickness shall be the greater thickness based on:

(a) The minimum thickness determined in accordance with the requirements in 6.7.4.4.2 to 6.7.4.4.7; and

(b) The minimum thickness determined in accordance with the recognized pressure vessel code including the requirements in 6.7.4.3.

6.7.4.4.2   Shells of not more than 1.80 m in diameter shall be not less than 5 mm thick in the reference steel or of equivalent thickness in the metal to be used. Shells of more than 1.80 m in diameter shall be not less than 6 mm thick in the reference steel or of equivalent thickness in the metal to be used.

6.7.4.4.3   Shells of vacuum-insulated tanks of not more than 1.80 m in diameter shall be not less than 3 mm thick in the reference steel or of equivalent thickness in the metal to be used. Such shells of more than 1.80 m in diameter shall be not less than 4 mm thick in the reference steel or of equivalent thickness in the metal to be used.

6.7.4.4.4   For vacuum-insulated tanks, the aggregate thickness of the jacket and the shell shall correspond to the minimum thickness prescribed in 6.7.4.4.2, the thickness of the shell itself being not less than the minimum thickness prescribed in 6.7.4.4.3.

6.7.4.4.5   Shells shall be not less than 3 mm thick regardless of the material of construction.

6.7.4.4.6   The equivalent thickness of a metal other than the thickness prescribed for the reference steel in 6.7.4.4.2 and 6.7.4.4.3 shall be determined using the following formula:

$$e_1 = \frac{21.4 \times e_0}{\sqrt[3]{Rm_1 \times A_1}}$$

where:

e_1 = required equivalent thickness (in mm) of the metal to be used;

e_0 = minimum thickness (in mm) of the reference steel specified in 6.7.4.4.2 and 6.7.4.4.3;

Rm_1 = guaranteed minimum tensile strength (in N/mm^2) of the metal to be used (see 6.7.4.3.3);

A_1 = guaranteed minimum elongation at fracture (in %) of the metal to be used according to national or international standards.

6.7.4.4.7   In no case shall the wall thickness be less than that prescribed in 6.7.4.4.1 to 6.7.4.4.5. All parts of the shell shall have a minimum thickness as determined by 6.7.4.4.1 to 6.7.4.4.6. This thickness shall be exclusive of any corrosion allowance.

6.7.4.4.8   There shall be no sudden change of plate thickness at the attachment of the ends (heads) to the cylindrical portion of the shell.

6.7.4.5   *Service equipment*

6.7.4.5.1   Service equipment shall be so arranged as to be protected against the risk of being wrenched off or damaged during handling and transport. When the connection between the frame and the tank or the jacket and the shell allows relative movement, the equipment shall be so fastened as to permit such movement without risk of damage to working parts. The external discharge fittings (pipe sockets, shut-off devices), the stop-valve and its seating shall be protected against the danger of being wrenched off by external forces (for example using shear sections). The filling and discharge devices (including flanges or threaded plugs) and any protective caps shall be capable of being secured against unintended opening.

6.7.4.5.2   Each filling and discharge opening in portable tanks used for the transport of flammable refrigerated liquefied gases shall be fitted with at least three mutually independent shut-off devices in series, the first being a stop-valve situated as close as reasonably practicable to the jacket, the second being a stop-valve and the third being a blank flange or equivalent device. The shut-off device closest to the jacket shall be a quick closing device, which closes automatically in the event of unintended movement of the portable tank during filling or discharge or fire engulfment. This device shall also be possible to operate by remote control.

6.7.4.5.3   Each filling and discharge opening in portable tanks used for the transport of non-flammable refrigerated liquefied gases shall be fitted with at least two mutually independent shut-off devices in series, the first being a stop-valve situated as close as reasonably practicable to the jacket, the second a blank flange or equivalent device.

6.7.4.5.4   For sections of piping which can be closed at both ends and where liquid product can be trapped, a method of automatic pressure relief shall be provided to prevent excess pressure build-up within the piping.

6.7.4.5.5   Vacuum insulated tanks need not have an opening for inspection.

6.7.4.5.6   External fittings shall be grouped together so far as reasonably practicable.

6.7.4.5.7   Each connection on a portable tank shall be clearly marked to indicate its function.

6.7.4.5.8   Each stop-valve or other means of closure shall be designed and constructed to a rated pressure not less than the MAWP of the shell taking into account the temperature expected during transport. All stop-valves with a screwed spindle shall be closed by a clockwise motion of the handwheel. In the case of other stop-valves the position (open and closed) and direction of closure shall be clearly indicated. All stop-valves shall be designed to prevent unintentional opening.

6.7.4.5.9   When pressure-building units are used, the liquid and vapour connections to that unit shall be provided with a valve as close to the jacket as reasonably practicable to prevent the loss of contents in case of damage to the pressure-building unit.

6.7.4.5.10   Piping shall be designed, constructed and installed so as to avoid the risk of damage due to thermal expansion and contraction, mechanical shock and vibration. All piping shall be of a suitable material. To prevent leakage due to fire, only steel piping and welded joints shall be used between the jacket and the connection to the first closure of any outlet. The method of attaching the closure to this connection shall be to the satisfaction of the competent authority or its authorized body. Elsewhere pipe joints shall be welded when necessary.

6.7.4.5.11   Joints in copper tubing shall be brazed or have an equally strong metal union. The melting point of brazing materials shall be no lower than 525 °C. The joints shall not decrease the strength of the tubing as may happen when cutting threads.

6.7.4.5.12   The materials of construction of valves and accessories shall have satisfactory properties at the lowest operating temperature of the portable tank.

6.7.4.5.13   The burst pressure of all piping and pipe fittings shall be not less than the highest of four times the MAWP of the shell or four times the pressure to which it may be subjected in service by the action of a pump or other device (except pressure-relief devices).

6.7.4.6   *Pressure-relief devices*

6.7.4.6.1   Every shell shall be provided with not less than two independent spring-loaded pressure-relief devices. The pressure-relief devices shall open automatically at a pressure not less than the MAWP and be fully open at a pressure equal to 110 % of the MAWP. These devices shall, after discharge, close at a pressure not lower than 10 % below the pressure at which discharge starts and shall remain closed at all lower pressures. The pressure-relief devices shall be of the type that will resist dynamic forces including surge.

6.7.4.6.2   Shells for non-flammable refrigerated liquefied gases and hydrogen may in addition have frangible discs in parallel with the spring-loaded devices as specified in 6.7.4.7.2 and 6.7.4.7.3.

6.7.4.6.3   Pressure-relief devices shall be designed to prevent the entry of foreign matter, the leakage of gas and the development of any dangerous excess pressure.

6.7.4.6.4   Pressure-relief devices shall be approved by the competent authority or its authorized body.

6.7.4.7   *Capacity and setting of pressure-relief devices*

6.7.4.7.1   In the case of the loss of vacuum in a vacuum-insulated tank or of loss of 20 % of the insulation of a tank insulated with solid materials, the combined capacity of all pressure-relief devices installed shall be sufficient so that the pressure (including accumulation) inside the shell does not exceed 120 % of the MAWP.

6.7.4.7.2   For non-flammable refrigerated liquefied gases (except oxygen) and hydrogen, this capacity may be achieved by the use of frangible discs in parallel with the required safety-relief devices. Frangible discs shall rupture at nominal pressure equal to the test pressure of the shell.

6.7.4.7.3   Under the circumstances described in 6.7.4.7.1 and 6.7.4.7.2 together with complete fire engulfment the combined capacity of all pressure-relief devices installed shall be sufficient to limit the pressure in the shell to the test pressure.

6.7.4.7.4   The required capacity of the relief devices shall be calculated in accordance with a well-established technical code recognized by the competent authority[7].

6.7.4.8   *Marking of pressure-relief devices*

6.7.4.8.1   Every pressure-relief device shall be plainly and permanently marked with the following:

(a)   The pressure (in bar or kPa) at which it is set to discharge;

(b)   The allowable tolerance at the discharge pressure for spring-loaded devices;

(c)   The reference temperature corresponding to the rated pressure for frangible discs; and

(d)   The rated flow capacity of the device in standard cubic metres of air per second (m^3/s);

(e)   The cross sectional flow areas of the spring loaded pressure-relief devices and frangible discs in mm^2.

When practicable, the following information shall also be shown:

(f)   The manufacturer's name and relevant catalogue number.

6.7.4.8.2   The rated flow capacity marked on the pressure-relief devices shall be determined according to ISO 4126-1:2004 and ISO 4126-7:2004.

6.7.4.9   *Connections to pressure-relief devices*

6.7.4.9.1   Connections to pressure-relief devices shall be of sufficient size to enable the required discharge to pass unrestricted to the safety device. No stop-valve shall be installed between the shell and the pressure-relief devices except when duplicate devices are provided for maintenance or other reasons and the stop-valves serving the devices actually in use are locked open or the stop-valves are interlocked so that the requirements of 6.7.4.7 are always fulfilled. There shall be no obstruction in an opening leading to a vent or pressure-relief device which might restrict or cut-off the flow from the shell to that device. Pipework to vent the vapour or liquid from the outlet of the pressure-relief devices, when used, shall deliver the relieved vapour or liquid to the atmosphere in conditions of minimum back-pressure on the relieving device.

6.7.4.10   *Siting of pressure-relief devices*

6.7.4.10.1   Each pressure-relief device inlet shall be situated on top of the shell in a position as near the longitudinal and transverse centre of the shell as reasonably practicable. All pressure-relief device inlets shall under maximum filling conditions be situated in the vapour space of the shell and the devices shall be so arranged as to ensure that the escaping vapour is discharged unrestrictedly. For refrigerated liquefied gases,

---

[7]   *See for example CGA S-1.2-2003 "Pressure Relief Device Standards-Part 2-Cargo and Portable Tanks for Compressed Gases".*

the escaping vapour shall be directed away from the tank and in such a manner that it cannot impinge upon the tank. Protective devices which deflect the flow of vapour are permissible provided the required relief-device capacity is not reduced.

6.7.4.10.2　　Arrangements shall be made to prevent access to the devices by unauthorized persons and to protect the devices from damage caused by the portable tank overturning.

6.7.4.11　　*Gauging devices*

6.7.4.11.1　　Unless a portable tank is intended to be filled by mass, it shall be equipped with one or more gauging devices. Glass level-gauges and gauges made of other fragile material, which are in direct communication with the contents of the shell shall not be used.

6.7.4.11.2　　A connection for a vacuum gauge shall be provided in the jacket of a vacuum-insulated portable tank.

6.7.4.12　　*Portable tank supports, frameworks, lifting and tie-down attachments*

6.7.4.12.1　　Portable tanks shall be designed and constructed with a support structure to provide a secure base during transport. The forces specified in 6.7.4.2.12 and the safety factor specified in 6.7.4.2.13 shall be considered in this aspect of the design. Skids, frameworks, cradles or other similar structures are acceptable.

6.7.4.12.2　　The combined stresses caused by portable tank mountings (e.g. cradles, frameworks, etc.) and portable tank lifting and tie-down attachments shall not cause excessive stress in any portion of the tank. Permanent lifting and tie-down attachments shall be fitted to all portable tanks. Preferably they shall be fitted to the portable tank supports but may be secured to reinforcing plates located on the tank at the points of support.

6.7.4.12.3　　In the design of supports and frameworks the effects of environmental corrosion shall be taken into account.

6.7.4.12.4　　Forklift pockets shall be capable of being closed off. The means of closing forklift pockets shall be a permanent part of the framework or permanently attached to the framework. Single compartment portable tanks with a length less than 3.65 m need not have closed off forklift pockets provided that:

    (a)　　The tank and all the fittings are well protected from being hit by the forklift blades; and

    (b)　　The distance between the centres of the forklift pockets is at least half of the maximum length of the portable tank.

6.7.4.12.5　　When portable tanks are not protected during transport, according to 4.2.3.3, the shells and service equipment shall be protected against damage to the shell and service equipment resulting from lateral or longitudinal impact or overturning. External fittings shall be protected so as to preclude the release of the shell contents upon impact or overturning of the portable tank on its fittings. Examples of protection include:

    (a)　　Protection against lateral impact which may consist of longitudinal bars protecting the shell on both sides at the level of the median line;

    (b)　　Protection of the portable tank against overturning which may consist of reinforcement rings or bars fixed across the frame;

    (c)　　Protection against rear impact which may consist of a bumper or frame;

    (d)　　Protection of the shell against damage from impact or overturning by use of an ISO frame in accordance with ISO 1496-3:1995;

    (e)　　Protection of the portable tank from impact or overturning by a vacuum insulation jacket.

6.7.4.13 *Design approval*

6.7.4.13.1 The competent authority or its authorized body shall issue a design approval certificate for any new design of a portable tank. This certificate shall attest that a portable tank has been surveyed by that authority, is suitable for its intended purpose and meets the requirements of this chapter. When a series of portable tanks is manufactured without change in the design, the certificate shall be valid for the entire series. The certificate shall refer to the prototype test report, the refrigerated liquefied gases allowed to be transported, the materials of construction of the shell and jacket and an approval number. The approval number shall consist of the distinguishing sign or mark of the State in whose territory the approval was granted, indicated by the distinguishing sign for use in international road traffic[2], and a registration number. Any alternative arrangements according to 6.7.1.2 shall be indicated on the certificate. A design approval may serve for the approval of smaller portable tanks made of materials of the same kind and thickness, by the same fabrication techniques and with identical supports, equivalent closures and other appurtenances.

6.7.4.13.2 The prototype test report for the design approval shall include at least the following:

(a) The results of the applicable frame-work test specified in ISO 1496-3:1995;

(b) The results of the initial inspection and test in 6.7.4.14.3; and

(c) The results of the impact test in 6.7.4.14.1, when applicable.

6.7.4.14 *Inspection and testing*

6.7.4.14.1 Portable tanks meeting the definition of container in the International Convention for Safe Containers (CSC), 1972, as amended, shall not be used unless they are successfully qualified by subjecting a representative prototype of each design to the Dynamic, Longitudinal Impact Test prescribed in the *Manual of Tests and Criteria*, part IV, section 41.

6.7.4.14.2 The tank and items of equipment of each portable tank shall be inspected and tested before being put into service for the first time (initial inspection and test) and thereafter at not more than five-year intervals (5 year periodic inspection and test) with an intermediate periodic inspection and test (2.5 year periodic inspection and test) midway between the 5 year periodic inspections and tests. The 2.5 year inspection and test may be performed within 3 months of the specified date. An exceptional inspection and test shall be performed regardless of the last periodic inspection and test when necessary according to 6.7.4.14.7.

6.7.4.14.3 The initial inspection and test of a portable tank shall include a check of the design characteristics, an internal and external examination of the portable tank shell and its fittings with due regard to the refrigerated liquefied gases to be transported, and a pressure test referring to the test pressures according to 6.7.4.3.2. The pressure test may be performed as a hydraulic test or by using another liquid or gas with the agreement of the competent authority or its authorized body. Before the portable tank is placed into service, a leakproofness test and a test of the satisfactory operation of all service equipment shall also be performed. When the shell and its fittings have been pressure-tested separately, they shall be subjected together after assembly to a leakproofness test. All welds subject to full stress level shall be inspected during the initial test by radiographic, ultrasonic, or another suitable non-destructive test method. This does not apply to the jacket.

6.7.4.14.4 The 5 and 2.5 year periodic inspections and tests shall include an external examination of the portable tank and its fittings with due regard to the refrigerated liquefied gases transported, a leakproofness test, a test of the satisfactory operation of all service equipment and a vacuum reading, when applicable. In the case of non-vacuum insulated tanks, the jacket and insulation shall be removed during the 2.5 year and the 5 year periodic inspections and tests but only to the extent necessary for a reliable appraisal.

6.7.4.14.5 *Deleted.*

---

[2] *Distinguishing sign of the State of registration used on motor vehicles and trailers in international road traffic, e.g. in accordance with the Geneva Convention on Road Traffic of 1949 or the Vienna Convention on Road Traffic of 1968.*

6.7.4.14.6   A portable tank may not be filled and offered for transport after the date of expiry of the last 5 year or 2.5 year periodic inspection and test as required by 6.7.4.14.2. However a portable tank filled prior to the date of expiry of the last periodic inspection and test may be transported for a period not to exceed three months beyond the date of expiry of the last periodic test or inspection. In addition, a portable tank may be transported after the date of expiry of the last periodic test and inspection:

      (a)   After emptying but before cleaning, for purposes of performing the next required test or inspection prior to refilling; and

      (b)   Unless otherwise approved by the competent authority, for a period not to exceed six months beyond the date of expiry of the last periodic test or inspection, in order to allow the return of dangerous goods for proper disposal or recycling. Reference to this exemption shall be mentioned in the transport document.

6.7.4.14.6.1   Except as provided for in 6.7.4.14.6, portable tanks which have missed the timeframe for their scheduled 5 year or 2.5 year periodic inspection and test may only be filled and offered for transport if a new 5 year periodic inspection and test is performed according to 6.7.4.14.4.

6.7.4.14.7   The exceptional inspection and test is necessary when the portable tank shows evidence of damaged or corroded areas, leakage, or any other conditions that indicate a deficiency that could affect the integrity of the portable tank. The extent of the exceptional inspection and test shall depend on the amount of damage or deterioration of the portable tank. It shall include at least the 2.5 year inspection and test according to 6.7.4.14.4.

6.7.4.14.8   The internal examination during the initial inspection and test shall ensure that the shell is inspected for pitting, corrosion, or abrasions, dents, distortions, defects in welds or any other conditions, that might render the portable tank unsafe for transport.

6.7.4.14.9   The external examination shall ensure that:

      (a)   The external piping, valves, pressurizing/cooling systems when applicable and gaskets are inspected for corroded areas, defects, or any other conditions, including leakage, that might render the portable tank unsafe for filling, discharge or transport;

      (b)   There is no leakage at any manhole covers or gaskets;

      (c)   Missing or loose bolts or nuts on any flanged connection or blank flange are replaced or tightened;

      (d)   All emergency devices and valves are free from corrosion, distortion and any damage or defect that could prevent their normal operation. Remote closure devices and self-closing stop-valves shall be operated to demonstrate proper operation;

      (e)   Required marks on the portable tank are legible and in accordance with the applicable requirements; and

      (f)   The framework, the supports and the arrangements for lifting the portable tank are in satisfactory condition.

6.7.4.14.10   The inspections and tests in 6.7.4.14.1, 6.7.4.14.3, 6.7.4.14.4, 6.7.4.14.5 and 6.7.4.14.7 shall be performed or witnessed by an expert approved by the competent authority or its authorized body. When the pressure test is a part of the inspection and test, the test pressure shall be the one indicated on the data plate of the portable tank. While under pressure, the portable tank shall be inspected for any leaks in the shell, piping or equipment.

6.7.4.14.11   In all cases when cutting, burning or welding operations on the shell of a portable tank have been effected, that work shall be to the approval of the competent authority or its authorized body taking into account the pressure vessel code used for the construction of the shell. A pressure test to the original test pressure shall be performed after the work is completed.

6.7.4.14.12   When evidence of any unsafe condition is discovered, the portable tank shall not be returned to service until it has been corrected and the test is repeated and passed.

6.7.4.15   *Marking*

6.7.4.15.1   Every portable tank shall be fitted with a corrosion resistant metal plate permanently attached to the portable tank in a conspicuous place readily accessible for inspection. When for reasons of portable tank arrangements the plate cannot be permanently attached to the shell, the shell shall be marked with at least the information required by the pressure vessel code. As a minimum, at least the following information shall be marked on the plate by stamping or by any other similar method:

(a) Owner information

    (i) Owner's registration number;

(b) Manufacturing information

    (i) Country of manufacture;

    (ii) Year of manufacture;

    (iii) Manufacturer's name or mark;

    (iv) Manufacturer's serial number;

(c) Approval information

    (i) The United Nations packaging symbol $\left(\begin{smallmatrix}u\\n\end{smallmatrix}\right)$.

This symbol shall not be used for any purpose other than certifying that a packaging, a flexible bulk container, a portable tank or a MEGC complies with the relevant requirements in chapter 6.1, 6.2, 6.3, 6.5, 6.6, 6.7 or 6.8;

    (ii) Approval country;

    (iii) Authorized body for the design approval;

    (iv) Design approval number;

    (v) Letters 'AA', if the design was approved under alternative arrangements (see 6.7.1.2);

    (vi) Pressure vessel code to which the shell is designed;

(d) Pressures

    (i) MAWP (in bar gauge or kPa gauge)[3];

    (ii) Test pressure (in bar gauge or kPa gauge)[3];

    (iii) Initial pressure test date (month and year);

    (iv) Identification mark of the initial pressure test witness;

(e) Temperatures

    (i) Minimum design temperature (in °C)[3];

---

[3]   *The unit used shall be indicated.*

(f) Materials

    (i) Shell material(s) and material standard reference(s);

    (ii) Equivalent thickness in reference steel (in mm)[3];

(g) Capacity

    (i) Tank water capacity at 20 °C (in litres)[3];

(h) Insulation

    (i) Either "Thermally insulated" or "Vacuum insulated" (as applicable);

    (ii) Effectiveness of the insulation system (heat influx) (in watts)[3];

(i) Holding times – For each refrigerated liquefied gas permitted to be transported in the portable tank:

    (i) Name, in full, of the refrigerated liquefied gas;

    (ii) Reference holding time (in days or hours)[3];

    (iii) Initial pressure (in bar gauge or kPa gauge)[3];

    (iv) Maximum allowable mass of gas filled (in kg)[3];

(j) Periodic inspections and tests

    (i) Type of the most recent periodic test (2.5-year, 5-year or exceptional);

    (ii) Date of the most recent periodic test (month and year);

    (iii) Identification mark of the authorized body who performed or witnessed the most recent test.

---

[3] *The unit used shall be indicated.*

Figure 6.7.4.15.1: Example of a plate for marking

Owner's registration number			
MANUFACTURING INFORMATION			
Country of manufacture			
Year of manufacture			
Manufacturer			
Manufacturer's serial number			
APPROVAL INFORMATION			
ⓤⓝ	Approval country		
	Authorized body for design approval		
	Design approval number		'AA' *(if applicable)*
Shell design code (pressure vessel code)			
PRESSURES			
MAWP			bar *or* kPa
Test pressure			bar *or* kPa
Initial pressure test date:	*(mm/yyyy)*	Witness stamp:	
TEMPERATURES			
Minimum design temperature			°C
MATERIALS			
Shell material(s) and material standard reference(s)			
Equivalent thickness in reference steel			mm
CAPACITY			
Tank water capacity at 20 °C			litres
INSULATION			
'Thermally insulated' or 'Vacuum insulated' *(as applicable)*			
Heat influx			watts

HOLDING TIMES

Refrigerated liquefied gas(es) permitted	Reference holding time	Initial pressure	Maximum allowable mass of gas filled
	days *or* hours	bar *or* kPa	kg

PERIODIC INSPECTIONS / TESTS

Test type	Test date	Witness stamp	Test type	Test date	Witness stamp
	(mm/yyyy)			*(mm/yyyy)*	

6.7.4.15.2   The following information shall be durably marked either on the portable tank itself or on a metal plate firmly secured to the portable tank.

        Name of the owner and the operator
        Name of the refrigerated liquefied gas being transported (and minimum mean bulk temperature)
        Maximum permissible gross mass (MPGM) _____ kg
        Unladen (tare) mass _____ kg
        Actual holding time for gas being transported _____ days (or hours)
        Portable tank instruction in accordance with 4.2.5.2.6

NOTE: *For the identification of the refrigerated liquefied gas(es) being transported, see also part 5.*

6.7.4.15.3 If a portable tank is designed and approved for handling in open seas, the words "OFFSHORE PORTABLE TANK" shall be marked on the identification plate.

6.7.5 **Requirements for the design, construction, inspection and testing of multiple-element gas containers (MEGCs) intended for the transport of non-refrigerated gases**

6.7.5.1 *Definitions*

For the purposes of this section:

*Element*s are cylinders, tubes or bundles of cylinders;

Leakproofness test means a test using gas subjecting the elements and the service equipment of the MEGC to an effective internal pressure of not less than 20 % of the test pressure;

Manifold means an assembly of piping and valves connecting the filling and/or discharge openings of the elements;

Maximum permissible gross mass (MPGM) means the sum of the tare mass of the MEGC and the heaviest load authorized for transport;

Service equipment means measuring instruments and filling, discharge, venting and safety devices;

Structural equipment means the reinforcing, fastening, protective and stabilizing members external to the elements.

6.7.5.2 *General design and construction requirements*

6.7.5.2.1 The MEGC shall be capable of being filled and discharged without the removal of its structural equipment. It shall possess stabilizing members external to the elements to provide structural integrity for handling and transport. MEGCs shall be designed and constructed with supports to provide a secure base during transport and with lifting and tie-down attachments which are adequate for lifting the MEGC including when loaded to its maximum permissible gross mass. The MEGC shall be designed to be loaded onto a vehicle or vessel and shall be equipped with skids, mountings or accessories to facilitate mechanical handling.

6.7.5.2.2 MEGCs shall be designed, manufactured and equipped in such a way as to withstand all conditions to which they will be subjected during normal conditions of handling and transport. The design shall take into account the effects of dynamic loading and fatigue.

6.7.5.2.3 Elements of an MEGC shall be made of seamless steel or composite construction and be constructed and tested according to chapter 6.2. All of the elements in an MEGC shall be of the same design type.

6.7.5.2.4 Elements of MEGCs, fittings and pipework shall be:

(a) compatible with the substances intended to be transported (for gases see ISO 11114-1:2020 and ISO 11114-2:2021); or

(b) properly passivated or neutralized by chemical reaction.

6.7.5.2.5 Contact between dissimilar metals which could result in damage by galvanic action shall be avoided.

6.7.5.2.6 The materials of the MEGC, including any devices, gaskets, and accessories, shall not adversely affect the gases intended for transport in the MEGC.

6.7.5.2.7 MEGCs shall be designed to withstand, without loss of contents, at least the internal pressure due to the contents, and the static, dynamic and thermal loads during normal conditions of handling and transport. The design shall demonstrate that the effects of fatigue, caused by repeated application of these loads through the expected life of the multiple-element gas container, have been taken into account.

6.7.5.2.8　　　MEGCs and their fastenings shall, under the maximum permissible load, be capable of withstanding the following separately applied static forces:

  (a) in the direction of travel: twice the MPGM multiplied by the acceleration due to gravity (g)[1]

  (b) horizontally at right angles to the direction of travel: the MPGM (when the direction of travel is not clearly determined, the forces shall be equal to twice the MPGM) multiplied by the acceleration due to gravity (g)[1];

  (c) vertically upwards: the MPGM multiplied by the acceleration due to gravity (g)[1]; and

  (d) vertically downwards: twice the MPGM (total loading including the effect of gravity) multiplied by the acceleration due to gravity (g)[1].

6.7.5.2.9　　　Under the forces defined above, the stress at the most severely stressed point of the elements shall not exceed the values given in either the relevant standards of 6.2.2.1 or, if the elements are not designed, constructed and tested according to those standards, in the technical code or standard recognised or approved by the competent authority of the country of use (see 6.2.3.1).

6.7.5.2.10　　　Under each of the forces in 6.7.5.2.8, the safety factor for the framework and fastenings to be observed shall be as follows:

  (a) for steels having a clearly defined yield point, a safety factor of 1.5 in relation to the guaranteed yield strength; or

  (b) for steels with no clearly defined yield point, a safety factor of 1.5 in relation to the guaranteed 0.2 % proof strength and, for austenitic steels, the 1 % proof strength.

6.7.5.2.11　　　MEGCs intended for the transport of flammable gases shall be capable of being electrically earthed.

6.7.5.2.12　　　The elements shall be secured in a manner that prevents undesired movement in relation to the structure and the concentration of harmful localized stresses.

6.7.5.3　　*Service equipment*

6.7.5.3.1　　　Service equipment shall be configured or designed to prevent damage that could result in the release of the pressure receptacle contents during normal conditions of handling and transport. When the connection between the frame and the elements allows relative movement between the sub-assemblies, the equipment shall be so fastened as to permit such movement without damage to working parts. The manifolds, the discharge fittings (pipe sockets, shut-off devices), and the stop-valves shall be protected from being wrenched off by external forces. Manifold piping leading to shut-off valves shall be sufficiently flexible to protect the valves and the piping from shearing, or releasing the pressure receptacle contents. The filling and discharge devices (including flanges or threaded plugs) and any protective caps shall be capable of being secured against unintended opening.

6.7.5.3.2　　　Each element intended for the transport of gases of Division 2.3 shall be fitted with a valve. The manifold for liquefied gases of Division 2.3 shall be so designed that the elements can be filled separately and be kept isolated by a valve capable of being sealed. For the transport of gases of Division 2.1, the elements shall be divided into groups of not more than 3 000 litres each isolated by a valve.

6.7.5.3.3　　　For filling and discharge openings of the MEGC, two valves in series shall be placed in an accessible position on each discharge and filling pipe. One of the valves may be a non-return valve. The filling and discharge devices may be fitted to a manifold. For sections of piping which can be closed at both ends and where a liquid product can be trapped, a pressure-relief valve shall be provided to prevent excessive pressure build-up. The main isolation valves on an MEGC shall be clearly marked to indicate their directions of closure.

---

[1] *For calculation purposes $g = 9.81$ m/s^2.*

Each stop-valve or other means of closure shall be designed and constructed to withstand a pressure equal to or greater than 1.5 times the test pressure of the MEGC. All stop-valves with screwed spindles shall close by a clockwise motion of the handwheel. For other stop-valves, the position (open or closed) and direction of closure shall be clearly indicated. All stop-valves shall be designed and positioned to prevent unintentional opening. Ductile metals shall be used in the construction of valves or accessories.

6.7.5.3.4   Piping shall be designed, constructed and installed so as to avoid damage due to expansion and contraction, mechanical shock and vibration. Joints in tubing shall be brazed or have an equally strong metal union. The melting point of brazing materials shall be no lower than 525 °C. The rated pressure of the service equipment and of the manifold shall be not less than two thirds of the test pressure of the elements.

6.7.5.4   *Pressure-relief devices*

6.7.5.4.1   The elements of MEGCs used for the transport of UN 1013 carbon dioxide and UN 1070 nitrous oxide shall be divided into groups of not more than 3 000 litres each isolated by a valve. Each group shall be fitted with one or more pressure relief devices. If so required by the competent authority of the country of use, MEGCs for other gases shall be fitted with pressure relief devices as specified by that competent authority.

6.7.5.4.2   When pressure relief devices are fitted, every element or group of elements of an MEGC that can be isolated shall then be fitted with one or more pressure relief devices. Pressure relief devices shall be of a type that will resist dynamic forces including liquid surge and shall be designed to prevent the entry of foreign matter, the leakage of gas and the development of any dangerous excess pressure.

6.7.5.4.3   MEGCs used for the transport of certain non-refrigerated gases identified in instruction T50 in 4.2.5.2.6 may have a pressure-relief device as required by the competent authority of the country of use. Unless an MEGC in dedicated service is fitted with an approved pressure relief device constructed of materials compatible with the load, such a device shall comprise a frangible disc preceding a spring-loaded device. The space between the frangible disc and the spring-loaded device may be equipped with a pressure gauge or a suitable telltale indicator. This arrangement permits the detection of disc rupture, pinholing or leakage which could cause a malfunction of the pressure relief device. The frangible disc shall rupture at a nominal pressure 10 % above the start-to-discharge pressure of the spring-loaded device.

6.7.5.4.4   In the case of multi-purpose MEGCs used for the transport of low-pressure liquefied gases, the pressure-relief devices shall open at a pressure as specified in 6.7.3.7.1 for the gas having the highest maximum allowable working pressure of the gases allowed to be transported in the MEGC.

6.7.5.5   *Capacity of pressure relief devices*

6.7.5.5.1   The combined delivery capacity of the pressure relief devices when fitted shall be sufficient that, in the event of total fire engulfment of the MEGC, the pressure (including accumulation) inside the elements does not exceed 120 % of the set pressure of the pressure relief device. The formula provided in CGA S-1.2-2003 "Pressure Relief Device Standards – Part 2 – Cargo and Portable Tanks for Compressed Gases" shall be used to determine the minimum total flow capacity for the system of pressure relief devices. CGA S-1.1-2003 "Pressure Relief Device Standards – Part 1 – Cylinders for Compressed Gases" may be used to determine the relief capacity of individual elements. Spring-loaded pressure relief devices may be used to achieve the full relief capacity prescribed in the case of low pressure liquefied gases. In the case of multi-purpose MEGCs, the combined delivery capacity of the pressure-relief devices shall be taken for the gas which requires the highest delivery capacity of the gases allowed to be transported in the MEGC.

6.7.5.5.2   To determine the total required capacity of the pressure relief devices installed on the elements for the transport of liquefied gases, the thermodynamic properties of the gas shall be considered (see, for example, CGA S-1.2-2003 "Pressure Relief Device Standards – Part 2 – Cargo and Portable Tanks for Compressed Gases" for low pressure liquefied gases and CGA S-1.1-2003 "Pressure Relief Device Standards, Part 1, Cylinders for Compressed Gases" for high pressure liquefied gases).

6.7.5.6   *Marking of pressure-relief devices*

6.7.5.6.1   Pressure relief devices shall be clearly and permanently marked with the following:

(a) the manufacturer's name and relevant catalogue number;

(b) the set pressure and/or the set temperature;

(c) the date of the last test;

(d) The cross sectional flow areas of the spring loaded pressure-relief devices and frangible discs in mm².

6.7.5.6.2　　The rated flow capacity marked on spring loaded pressure relief devices for low pressure liquefied gases shall be determined according to ISO 4126-1:2004 and ISO 4126-7:2004.

6.7.5.7　　*Connections to pressure-relief devices*

6.7.5.7.1　　Connections to pressure-relief devices shall be of sufficient size to enable the required discharge to pass unrestricted to the pressure relief device. No stop-valve shall be installed between the element and the pressure-relief devices, except when duplicate devices are provided for maintenance or other reasons, and the stop-valves serving the devices actually in use are locked open, or the stop-valves are interlocked so that at least one of the duplicate devices is always operable and capable of meeting the requirements of 6.7.5.5. There shall be no obstruction in an opening leading to or leaving from a vent or pressure-relief device which might restrict or cut-off the flow from the element to that device. The opening through all piping and fittings shall have at least the same flow area as the inlet of the pressure relief device to which it is connected. The nominal size of the discharge piping shall be at least as large as that of the pressure relief device outlet. Vents from the pressure-relief devices, when used, shall deliver the relieved vapour or liquid to the atmosphere in conditions of minimum backpressure on the relieving device.

6.7.5.8　　*Siting of pressure-relief devices*

6.7.5.8.1　　Each pressure relief device shall, under maximum filling conditions, be in communication with the vapour space of the elements for the transport of liquefied gases. The devices, when fitted, shall be so arranged as to ensure that the escaping vapour is discharged upwards and unrestrictedly as to prevent any impingement of escaping gas or liquid upon the MEGC, its elements or personnel. For flammable, pyrophoric and oxidizing gases, the escaping gas shall be directed away from the element in such a manner that it cannot impinge upon the other elements. Heat resistant protective devices which deflect the flow of gas are permissible provided the required pressure relief device capacity is not reduced.

6.7.5.8.2　　Arrangements shall be made to prevent access to the pressure-relief devices by unauthorized persons and to protect the devices from damage caused by the MEGC overturning.

6.7.5.9　　*Gauging devices*

6.7.5.9.1　　When a MEGC is intended to be filled by mass, it shall be equipped with one or more gauging devices. Level-gauges made of glass or other fragile material shall not be used.

6.7.5.10　　*MEGC supports, frameworks, lifting and tie-down attachments*

6.7.5.10.1　　MEGCs shall be designed and constructed with a support structure to provide a secure base during transport. The forces specified in 6.7.5.2.8 and the safety factor specified in 6.7.5.2.10 shall be considered in this aspect of the design. Skids, frameworks, cradles or other similar structures are acceptable.

6.7.5.10.2　　The combined stresses caused by element mountings (e.g. cradles, frameworks, etc.) and MEGC lifting and tie-down attachments shall not cause excessive stress in any element. Permanent lifting and tie-down attachments shall be fitted to all MEGCs. In no case shall mountings or attachments be welded onto the elements.

6.7.5.10.3　　In the design of supports and frameworks, the effects of environmental corrosion shall be taken into account.

6.7.5.10.4　　When MEGCs are not protected during transport, according to 4.2.4.3, the elements and service equipment shall be protected against damage resulting from lateral or longitudinal impact or overturning. External fittings shall be protected so as to preclude the release of the elements' contents upon impact or overturning of the MEGC on its fittings. Particular attention shall be paid to the protection of the manifold. Examples of protection include:

(a) protection against lateral impact which may consist of longitudinal bars;

(b) protection against overturning which may consist of reinforcement rings or bars fixed across the frame;

(c) protection against rear impact which may consist of a bumper or frame;

(d) protection of the elements and service equipment against damage from impact or overturning by use of an ISO frame in accordance with the relevant provisions of ISO 1496-3:1995.

6.7.5.11　　*Design approval*

6.7.5.11.1　　The competent authority or its authorized body shall issue a design approval certificate for any new design of a MEGC. This certificate shall attest that the MEGC has been surveyed by that authority, is suitable for its intended purpose and meets the requirements of this chapter, the applicable provisions for gases of chapter 4.1 and of packing instruction P200. When a series of MEGCs are manufactured without change in the design, the certificate shall be valid for the entire series. The certificate shall refer to the prototype test report, the materials of construction of the manifold, the standards to which the elements are made and an approval number. The approval number shall consist of the distinguishing sign or mark of the country granting the approval, indicated by the distinguishing sign used on vehicles in international road traffic[2], and a registration number. Any alternative arrangements according to 6.7.1.2 shall be indicated on the certificate. A design approval may serve for the approval of smaller MEGCs made of materials of the same type and thickness, by the same fabrication techniques and with identical supports, equivalent closures and other appurtenances.

6.7.5.11.2　　The prototype test report for the design approval shall include at least the following:

(a) the results of the applicable framework test specified in ISO 1496-3:1995;

(b) the results of the initial inspection and test specified in 6.7.5.12.3;

(c) the results of the impact test specified in 6.7.5.12.1; and

(d) certification documents verifying that the cylinders and tubes comply with the applicable standards.

6.7.5.12　　*Inspection and testing*

6.7.5.12.1　　MEGCs meeting the definition of container in the International Convention for Safe Containers (CSC), 1972, as amended, shall not be used unless they are successfully qualified by subjecting a representative prototype of each design to the Dynamic, Longitudinal Impact Test prescribed in the *Manual of Tests and Criteria*, part IV, section 41.

6.7.5.12.2　　The elements and items of equipment of each MEGC shall be inspected and tested before being put into service for the first time (initial inspection and test). Thereafter, MEGCs shall be inspected at no more than five-year intervals (5 year periodic inspection). An exceptional inspection and test shall be performed, regardless of the last periodic inspection and test, when necessary according to 6.7.5.12.5.

---

[2] *Distinguishing sign of the State of registration used on motor vehicles and trailers in international road traffic, e.g. in accordance with the Geneva Convention on Road Traffic of 1949 or the Vienna Convention on Road Traffic of 1968.*

6.7.5.12.3   The initial inspection and test of an MEGC shall include a check of the design characteristics, an external examination of the MEGC and its fittings with due regard to the gases to be transported, and a pressure test performed at the test pressures according to packing instruction P200. The pressure test of the manifold may be performed as a hydraulic test or by using another liquid or gas with the agreement of the competent authority or its authorized body. Before the MEGC is placed into service, a leakproofness test and a test of the satisfactory operation of all service equipment shall also be performed. When the elements and their fittings have been pressure-tested separately, they shall be subjected together after assembly to a leakproofness test.

6.7.5.12.4   The 5-year periodic inspection and test shall include an external examination of the structure, the elements and the service equipment in accordance with 6.7.5.12.6. The elements and the piping shall be tested at the periodicity specified in packing instruction P200 and in accordance with the provisions described in 6.2.1.6. When the elements and equipment have been pressure-tested separately, they shall be subjected together after assembly to a leakproofness test.

6.7.5.12.5   An exceptional inspection and test is necessary when the MEGC shows evidence of damaged or corroded areas, leakage, or other conditions that indicate a deficiency that could affect the integrity of the MEGC. The extent of the exceptional inspection and test shall depend on the amount of damage or deterioration of the MEGC. It shall include at least the examinations required under 6.7.5.12.6.

6.7.5.12.6   The examinations shall ensure that:

    (a)   the elements are inspected externally for pitting, corrosion, abrasions, dents, distortions, defects in welds or any other conditions, including leakage, that might render the MEGC unsafe for transport;

    (b)   the piping, valves, and gaskets are inspected for corroded areas, defects, and other conditions, including leakage, that might render the MEGC unsafe for filling, discharge or transport;

    (c)   missing or loose bolts or nuts on any flanged connection or blank flange are replaced or tightened;

    (d)   all emergency devices and valves are free from corrosion, distortion and any damage or defect that could prevent their normal operation. Remote closure devices and self-closing stop-valves shall be operated to demonstrate proper operation;

    (e)   required marks on the MEGC are legible and in accordance with the applicable requirements; and

    (f)   the framework, the supports and the arrangements for lifting the MEGC are in satisfactory condition.

6.7.5.12.7   The inspections and tests in 6.7.5.12.1, 6.7.5.12.3, 6.7.5.12.4 and 6.7.5.12.5 shall be performed or witnessed by a body authorized by the competent authority. When the pressure test is a part of the inspection and test, the test pressure shall be the one indicated on the data plate of the MEGC. While under pressure, the MEGC shall be inspected for any leaks in the elements, piping or equipment.

6.7.5.12.8   When evidence of any unsafe condition is discovered, the MEGC shall not be returned to service until it has been corrected and the applicable tests and verifications are passed.

6.7.5.13   *Marking*

6.7.5.13.1   Every MEGC shall be fitted with a corrosion resistant metal plate permanently attached to the MEGC in a conspicuous place readily accessible for inspection. The metal plate shall not be affixed to the elements. The elements shall be marked in accordance with chapter 6.2. As a minimum, at least the following information shall be marked on the plate by stamping or by any other similar method:

(a) Owner information

    (i) Owner's registration number;

(b) Manufacturing information

    (i) Country of manufacture;

    (ii) Year of manufacture;

    (iii) Manufacturer's name or mark;

    (iv) Manufacturer's serial number;

(c) Approval information

    (i) The United Nations packaging symbol $\left(\begin{smallmatrix}u\\n\end{smallmatrix}\right)$.

    This symbol shall not be used for any purpose other than certifying that a packaging, a flexible bulk container, a portable tank or a MEGC complies with the relevant requirements in chapter 6.1, 6.2, 6.3, 6.5, 6.6, 6.7 or 6.8;

    (ii) Approval country;

    (iii) Authorized body for the design approval;

    (iv) Design approval number;

    (v) Letters 'AA', if the design was approved under alternative arrangements (see 6.7.1.2);

(d) Pressures

    (i) Test pressure (in bar gauge)[3];

    (ii) Initial pressure test date (month and year);

    (iii) Identification mark of the initial pressure test witness;

(e) Temperatures

    (i) Design temperature range (in °C)[3];

(f) Elements / Capacity

    (i) Number of elements;

    (ii) Total water capacity (in litres)[3];

(g) Periodic inspections and tests

    (i) Type of the most recent periodic test (5-year or exceptional);

    (ii) Date of the most recent periodic test (month and year);

    (iii) Identification mark of the authorized body who performed or witnessed the most recent test.

---

[3] *The unit used shall be indicated.*

Figure 6.7.5.13.1: Example of a plate for marking

Owner's registration number			
MANUFACTURING INFORMATION			
Country of manufacture			
Year of manufacture			
Manufacturer			
Manufacturer's serial number			
APPROVAL INFORMATION			
ⓤⓝ	Approval country		
	Authorized body for design approval		
	Design approval number		'AA' *(if applicable)*
PRESSURES			
Test pressure			bar
Initial pressure test date:	*(mm/yyyy)*	Witness stamp:	
TEMPERATURES			
Design temperature range		°C to	°C
ELEMENTS / CAPACITY			
Number of elements			
Total water capacity			litres
PERIODIC INSPECTIONS / TESTS			

Test type	Test date	Witness stamp	Test type	Test date	Witness stamp
	(mm/yyyy)			*(mm/yyyy)*	

6.7.5.13.2 The following information shall be durably marked on a metal plate firmly secured to the MEGC:

        Name of the operator
        Maximum permissible load mass _____ kg
        Working pressure at 15°C _____ bar gauge
        Maximum permissible gross mass (MPGM) _____ kg
        Unladen (tare) mass _____ kg

CHAPTER 6.8

REQUIREMENTS FOR THE DESIGN, CONSTRUCTION, INSPECTION AND TESTING OF BULK CONTAINERS

6.8.1 **Definitions**

For the purposes of this section:

Closed bulk container means a totally closed bulk container having a rigid roof, sidewalls, end walls and floor (including hopper-type bottoms). The term includes bulk containers with an opening roof, side or end wall that can be closed during transport. Closed bulk containers may be equipped with openings to allow for the exchange of vapours and gases with air and which prevent under normal conditions of transport the release of solid contents as well as the penetration of rain and splash water.

Flexible bulk container means a flexible container with a capacity not exceeding 15 m^3 and includes liners and attached handling devices and service equipment.

Sheeted bulk container means an open top bulk container with rigid bottom (including hopper-type bottom), side and end walls and a non-rigid covering;

6.8.2 **Application and general requirements**

6.8.2.1 Bulk containers and their service and structural equipment shall be designed and constructed to withstand, without loss of contents, the internal pressure of the contents and the stresses of normal handling and transport.

6.8.2.2 Where a discharge valve is fitted, it shall be capable of being made secure in the closed position and the whole discharge system shall be suitably protected from damage. Valves having lever closures shall be able to be secured against unintended opening and the open or closed position shall be readily apparent.

6.8.2.3 *Code for designating types of bulk container*

The following table indicates the codes to be used for designating types of bulk containers:

Types of bulk containers	Code
Sheeted bulk container	BK1
Closed bulk container	BK2
Flexible bulk container	BK3

6.8.2.4 In order to take account of progress in science and technology, the use of alternative arrangements which offer at least equivalent safety as provided by the requirements of this chapter may be considered by the competent authority.

6.8.3 **Requirements for the design, construction, inspection and testing of freight containers used as BK1 or BK2 bulk containers**

6.8.3.1 *Design and construction requirements*

6.8.3.1.1 The general design and construction requirements of this section are deemed to be met if the bulk container complies with the requirements of ISO 1496-4:1991 "Series 1 Freight containers – Specification and testing – Part 4: Non pressurized containers for dry bulk" and the container is siftproof.

6.8.3.1.2 Freight containers designed and tested in accordance with ISO 1496-1:1990 "Series 1 Freight containers – Specification and testing – Part 1: General cargo containers for general purposes" shall be equipped with operational equipment which is, including its connection to the freight container, designed to strengthen the end walls and to improve the longitudinal restraint as necessary to comply with the test requirements of ISO 1496-4:1991 as relevant.

6.8.3.1.3   Bulk containers shall be siftproof. Where a liner is used to make the container siftproof it shall be made of a suitable material. The strength of material used for, and the construction of, the liner shall be appropriate to the capacity of the container and its intended use. Joins and closures of the liner shall withstand pressures and impacts liable to occur under normal conditions of handling and transport. For ventilated bulk containers any liner shall not impair the operation of ventilating devices.

6.8.3.1.4   The operational equipment of bulk containers designed to be emptied by tilting shall be capable of withstanding the total filling mass in the tilted orientation.

6.8.3.1.5   Any movable roof or side or end wall or roof section shall be fitted with locking devices with securing devices designed to show the locked state to an observer at ground level.

6.8.3.2   *Service equipment*

6.8.3.2.1   Filling and discharge devices shall be so constructed and arranged as to be protected against the risk of being wrenched off or damaged during transport and handling. The filling and discharge devices shall be capable of being secured against unintended opening. The open and closed position and direction of closure shall be clearly indicated.

6.8.3.2.2   Seals of openings shall be so arranged as to avoid any damage by the operation, filling and emptying of the bulk container.

6.8.3.2.3   Where ventilation is required bulk containers shall be equipped with means of air exchange, either by natural convection, e.g. by openings, or active elements, e.g. fans. The ventilation shall be designed to prevent negative pressures in the container at all times. Ventilating elements of bulk containers for the transport of flammable substances or substances emitting flammable gases or vapours shall be designed so as not to be a source of ignition.

6.8.3.3   *Inspection and testing*

6.8.3.3.1   Freight containers used maintained and qualified as bulk containers in accordance with the requirements of this section shall be tested and approved in accordance with the International Convention for Safe Containers (CSC), 1972, as amended.

6.8.3.3.2   Freight containers used and qualified as bulk containers shall be inspected periodically according to the International Convention for Safe Containers (CSC), 1972, as amended.

6.8.3.4   *Marking*

6.8.3.4.1   Freight containers used as bulk containers shall be marked with a Safety Approval Plate in accordance with the International Convention for Safe Containers (CSC), 1972, as amended.

6.8.4   Requirements for the design, construction and approval of BK1 and BK2 bulk containers other than freight containers

6.8.4.1   Bulk containers covered in this section include skips, offshore bulk containers, bulk bins, swap bodies, trough shaped containers, roller containers, and load compartments of vehicles.

6.8.4.2   These bulk containers shall be designed and constructed so as to be strong enough to withstand the shocks and loadings normally encountered during transport including, as applicable, transhipment between modes of transport.

6.8.4.3   Vehicles shall comply with the requirements of, and be acceptable to, the competent authority responsible for land transport of the materials to be transported in bulk.

6.8.4.4   These bulk containers shall be approved by the competent authority and the approval shall include the code for designating types of bulk containers in accordance with 6.8.2.3 and the requirements for inspection and testing as appropriate.

6.8.4.5   Where it is necessary to use a liner in order to retain the dangerous goods it shall meet the provisions of 6.8.3.1.3.

6.8.4.6   The following statement shall be shown on the transport document: "Bulk container BK(x)[1] approved by the competent authority of ......".

6.8.5   Requirements for the design, construction, inspection and testing of flexible bulk containers BK3

6.8.5.1   *Design and construction requirements*

6.8.5.1.1   Flexible bulk containers shall be sift-proof.

6.8.5.1.2   Flexible bulk containers shall be completely closed to prevent the release of contents.

6.8.5.1.3   Flexible bulk containers shall be waterproof.

6.8.5.1.4   Parts of the flexible bulk container which are in direct contact with dangerous goods:

    (a)   Shall not be affected or significantly weakened by those dangerous goods;

    (b)   Shall not cause a dangerous effect e.g. catalysing a reaction or reacting with the dangerous goods; and

    (c)   Shall not allow permeation of the dangerous goods that could constitute a danger under normal conditions of transport.

6.8.5.2   *Service equipment and handling devices*

6.8.5.2.1   Filling and discharge devices shall be so constructed as to be protected against damage during transport and handling. The filling and discharge devices shall be capable of being secured against unintended opening.

6.8.5.2.2   Slings of the flexible bulk container, if fitted, shall withstand pressure and dynamic forces which can appear in normal conditions of handling and transport.

6.8.5.2.3   The handling devices shall be strong enough to withstand repeated use.

6.8.5.3   *Inspection and testing*

6.8.5.3.1   Each flexible bulk container design type shall successfully pass the tests prescribed in this chapter before being used.

6.8.5.3.2   Tests shall also be repeated after each modification of design type which alters the design, material or manner of construction of a flexible bulk container.

6.8.5.3.3   Tests shall be carried out on flexible bulk containers prepared as for transport. Flexible bulk containers shall be filled to the maximum mass at which they may be used and the contents shall be evenly distributed. The substances to be transported in the flexible bulk container may be replaced by other substances except where this would invalidate the results of the tests. When another substance is used it shall have the same physical characteristics (mass, grain size, etc.) as the substance to be transported. It is permissible to use additives, such as bags of lead shot, to achieve the requisite total mass of the flexible bulk container, so long as they are placed so that the test results are not affected.

---

[1]   *x shall be replaced with "1" or "2" as appropriate.*

6.8.5.3.4   Flexible bulk containers shall be manufactured and tested under a quality assurance programme which satisfies the competent authority, in order to ensure that each manufactured flexible bulk container meets the requirements of this chapter.

6.8.5.3.5   *Drop test*

6.8.5.3.5.1   Applicability

For all types of flexible bulk containers, as a design type test.

6.8.5.3.5.2   Preparation for testing

The flexible bulk container shall be filled to its maximum permissible gross mass.

6.8.5.3.5.3   The flexible bulk container shall be dropped onto a target surface that is non-resilient and horizontal. The target surface shall be:

(a)   Integral and massive enough to be immovable;

(b)   Flat with a surface kept free from local defects capable of influencing the test results;

(c)   Rigid enough to be non-deformable under test conditions and not liable to become damaged by the tests; and

(d)   Sufficiently large to ensure that the test flexible bulk container falls entirely upon the surface.

Following the drop, the flexible bulk container shall be restored to the upright position for observation.

6.8.5.3.5.4   Drop height shall be:

Packing group III: 0.8 m

6.8.5.3.5.5   Criteria for passing the test:

(a)   There shall be no loss of contents. A slight discharge, e.g. from closures or stitch holes, upon impact shall not be considered to be a failure of the flexible bulk container provided that no further leakage occurs after the container has been restored to the upright position;

(b)   There shall be no damage which renders the flexible bulk container unsafe to be transported for salvage or for disposal.

6.8.5.3.6   *Top lift test*

6.8.5.3.6.1   Applicability

For all types of flexible bulk containers as a design type test.

6.8.5.3.6.2   Preparation for testing

Flexible bulk containers shall be filled to six times the maximum net mass, the load being evenly distributed.

6.8.5.3.6.3   A flexible bulk container shall be lifted in the manner for which it is designed until clear of the floor and maintained in that position for a period of five minutes.

6.8.5.3.6.4   Criteria for passing the test: there shall be no damage to the flexible bulk container or its lifting devices which renders the flexible bulk container unsafe for transport or handling, and no loss of contents.

6.8.5.3.7   *Topple test*

6.8.5.3.7.1   Applicability

For all types of flexible bulk containers as a design type test.

6.8.5.3.7.2   Preparation for testing

The flexible bulk container shall be filled to its maximum permissible gross mass.

6.8.5.3.7.3   Flexible bulk container shall be toppled onto any part of its top by lifting the side furthest from the drop edge upon a target surface that is non-resilient and horizontal. The target surface shall be:

(a)   Integral and massive enough to be immovable;

(b)   Flat with a surface kept free from local defects capable of influencing the test results;

(c)   Rigid enough to be non-deformable under test conditions and not liable to become damaged by the tests; and

(d)   Sufficiently large to ensure that the test flexible bulk container falls entirely upon the surface.

6.8.5.3.7.4   For all flexible bulk containers, the topple height is specified as follows:

Packing group III: 0.8 m

6.8.5.3.7.5   Criterion for passing the test: there shall be no loss of contents. A slight discharge, e.g., from closures or stitch holes, upon impact shall not be considered to be a failure of the flexible bulk container provided that no further leakage occurs.

6.8.5.3.8   *Righting test*

6.8.5.3.8.1   Applicability

For all types of flexible bulk containers designed to be lifted from the top or side, as a design type test.

6.8.5.3.8.2   Preparation for testing

The flexible bulk container shall be filled to not less than 95 % of its capacity and to its maximum permissible gross mass.

6.8.5.3.8.3   The flexible bulk container, lying on its side, shall be lifted at a speed of at least 0.1 m/s to an upright position, clear of the floor, by no more than half of the lifting devices.

6.8.5.3.8.4   Criterion for passing the test: there shall be no damage to the flexible bulk container or its lifting devices which renders the flexible bulk container unsafe for transport or handling.

6.8.5.3.9   *Tear test*

6.8.5.3.9.1   Applicability

For all types of flexible bulk containers as a design type test.

6.8.5.3.9.2   Preparation for testing

The flexible bulk container shall be filled to its maximum permissible gross mass.

6.8.5.3.9.3   With the flexible bulk container placed on the ground, a 300 mm cut shall be made, completely penetrating all layers of the flexible bulk container on a wall of a wide face. The cut shall be made at a 45° angle to the principal axis of the flexible bulk container, halfway between the bottom surface and the top level of the contents. The flexible bulk container shall then be subjected to a uniformly distributed superimposed load equivalent to twice the maximum gross mass. The load must be applied for at least fifteen minutes. A flexible bulk container which is designed to be lifted from the top or the side shall, after removal of the superimposed load, be lifted clear of the floor and maintained in that position for a period of fifteen minutes.

6.8.5.3.9.4   Criterion for passing the test: the cut shall not propagate more than 25 % of its original length.

6.8.5.3.10   *Stacking test*

6.8.5.3.10.1   Applicability

For all types of flexible bulk containers as a design type test.

6.8.5.3.10.2   Preparation for testing

The flexible bulk container shall be filled to its maximum permissible gross mass.

6.8.5.3.10.3   The flexible bulk container shall be subjected to a force applied to its top surface that is four times the design load-carrying capacity for 24 hours.

6.8.5.3.10.4   Criterion for passing the test: there shall be no loss of contents during the test or after removal of the load.

6.8.5.4   ***Test report***

6.8.5.4.1   A test report containing at least the following particulars shall be drawn up and shall be available to the users of the flexible bulk container:

1. Name and address of the test facility;

2. Name and address of applicant (where appropriate);

3. Unique test report identification;

4. Date of the test report;

5. Manufacturer of the flexible bulk container;

6. Description of the flexible bulk container design type (e.g. dimensions, materials, closures, thickness, etc) and/or photograph(s);

7. Maximum capacity/maximum permissible gross mass;

8. Characteristics of test contents, e.g. particle size for solids;

9. Test descriptions and results;

10. The test report shall be signed with the name and status of the signatory.

6.8.5.4.2   The test report shall contain statements that the flexible bulk container prepared as for transport was tested in accordance with the appropriate provisions of this chapter and that the use of other containment methods or components may render it invalid. A copy of the test report shall be available to the competent authority.

6.8.5.5 *Marking*

6.8.5.5.1 Each flexible bulk container manufactured and intended for use according to these Regulations shall bear marks that are durable, legible and placed in a location so as to be readily visible. Letters, numerals and symbols shall be at least 24 mm high and shall show:

(a) The United Nations packaging symbol $\overset{u}{\underset{n}{\bigcirc}}$.

This symbol shall not be used for any purpose other than certifying that a packaging, a flexible bulk container, a portable tank or a MEGC complies with the relevant requirements in chapter 6.1, 6.2, 6.3, 6.5, 6.6, 6.7 or 6.8;

(b) The code BK3;

(c) A capital letter designating the packing group(s) for which the design type has been approved:

Z for packing group III only;

(d) The month and year (last two digits) of manufacture;

(e) The character(s) identifying the country authorizing the allocation of the mark; as indicated by the distinguishing signs used on vehicles in international road traffic[2];

(f) The name or symbol of the manufacturer and other identification of the flexible bulk container as specified by the competent authority;

(g) The stacking test load in kg;

(h) The maximum permissible gross mass in kg.

Marks shall be applied in the sequence shown in (a) to (h); each mark required in these subparagraphs shall be clearly separated, e.g. by a slash or space and presented in a way that ensures that all of the parts of the mark are easily identified.

6.8.5.5.2 *Example of marking*

 BK3/Z/11 09
RUS/NTT/MK-14-10
56000/14000

---

[2] *Distinguishing sign of the State of registration used on motor vehicles and trailers in international road traffic, e.g. in accordance with the Geneva Convention on Road Traffic of 1949 or the Vienna Convention on Road Traffic of 1968.*

CHAPTER 6.9

REQUIREMENTS FOR THE DESIGN, CONSTRUCTION, INSPECTION AND TESTING OF PORTABLE TANKS WITH SHELLS MADE OF FIBRE REINFORCED PLASTICS (FRP) MATERIALS

6.9.1 Application and general requirements

6.9.1.1 The requirements of section 6.9.2 apply to portable tanks with an FRP shell intended for the transport of dangerous goods of Classes or Divisions 1, 3, 5.1, 6.1, 6.2, 8 and 9 by all modes of transport. In addition to the requirements of this chapter, unless otherwise specified, the applicable requirements of the International Convention for Safe Containers (CSC) 1972, as amended, shall be fulfilled by any multimodal portable tank with FRP shell which meets the definition of a "container" within the terms of that Convention.

6.9.1.2 The requirements of this chapter do not apply to offshore portable tanks.

6.9.1.3 The requirements of chapter 4.2, and section 6.7.2 apply to FRP portable tank shells except for those concerning the use of metal materials for the construction of a portable tank shell and additional requirements stated in this chapter.

6.9.1.4 In recognition of scientific and technological advances, the technical requirements of this chapter may be varied by alternative arrangements. These alternative arrangements shall offer a level of safety not less than that given by the requirements of this chapter with respect to compatibility with substances transported and the ability of the FRP portable tank to withstand impact, loading and fire conditions. For international transport, alternative arrangement FRP portable tanks shall be approved by the applicable competent authorities.

6.9.2 Requirements for the design, construction, inspection and testing of FRP portable tanks

6.9.2.1 *Definitions*

For the purposes of this section, the definitions of 6.7.2.1 apply except for definitions related to metal materials ("Fine grain steel", "Mild steel" and "Reference steel") for the construction of the shell of a portable tank.

Additionally, the following definitions apply to portable tanks with an FRP shell:

External layer means the part of the shell which is directly exposed to the atmosphere;

Fibre-Reinforced Plastic (FRP) means material consisting of fibrous and/or particulate reinforcement contained within a thermoset or thermoplastic polymer (matrix);

Filament winding means a process for constructing FRP structures in which continuous reinforcements (filament, tape, or other), either previously impregnated with a matrix material or impregnated during winding, are placed over a rotating mandrel. Generally, the shape is a surface of revolution and may include ends (heads);

FRP shell means a closed part of cylindrical shape with an interior volume intended for transport of chemical substances;

FRP tank means a portable tank constructed with an FRP shell and ends (heads), service equipment, safety relief devices and other installed equipment;

Glass transition temperature (Tg) means a characteristic value of the temperature range over which the glass transition takes place;

Hand layup means a process for moulding reinforced plastics in which reinforcement and resin are placed on a mould;

Liner means a layer on the inner surface of an FRP shell preventing contact with the dangerous goods being transported;

Mat means a fibre reinforcement made of random, chopped or twisted fibres bonded together as sheets of various length and thickness;

Parallel shell-sample means an FRP specimen, which must be representative of the shell, constructed in parallel to the shell construction if it is not possible to use cut-outs from the shell itself. The parallel shell-sample may be flat or curved;

Representative sample means a sample cut out from the shell;

Resin infusion means an FRP construction method by which dry reinforcement is placed into a matched mould, single sided mould with vacuum bag, or otherwise, and liquid resin is supplied to the part through the use of external applied pressure at the inlet and/or application of full or partial vacuum pressure at the vent;

Structural layer means FRP layers of a shell required to sustain the design loads;

Veil means a thin mat with high absorbency used in FRP product plies where polymeric matrix surplus fraction content is required (surface evenness, chemical resistance, leakage-proof, etc.).

6.9.2.2 *General design and construction requirements*

6.9.2.2.1 The requirements of 6.7.1 and 6.7.2.2 apply to FRP portable tanks. For areas of the shell that are made from FRP, the following requirements of chapter 6.7 are exempt: 6.7.2.2.1, 6.7.2.2.9.1, 6.7.2.2.13 and 6.7.2.2.14. Shells shall be designed and constructed in accordance with the requirements of a pressure vessel code, applicable to FRP materials, recognized by the competent authority.

In addition, the following requirements apply.

6.9.2.2.2 *Manufacturer's quality system*

6.9.2.2.2.1 The quality system shall contain all the elements, requirements, and provisions adopted by the manufacturer. It shall be documented in a systematic and orderly manner in the form of written policies, procedures, and instructions.

6.9.2.2.2.2 The contents shall in particular include adequate descriptions of:

(a) The organizational structure and responsibilities of personnel with regard to design and product quality;

(b) The design control and design verification techniques, processes, and procedures that will be used when designing the portable tanks;

(c) The relevant manufacturing, quality control, quality assurance and process operation instructions that will be used;

(d) Quality records, such as inspection reports, test data and calibration data;

(e) Management reviews to ensure the effective operation of the quality system arising from the audits in accordance with 6.9.2.2.2.4;

(f) The process describing how customer requirements are met;

(g) The process for control of documents and their revision;

(h) The means for control of non-conforming portable tanks, purchased components, in-process and final materials; and

(i) Training programmes and qualification procedures for relevant personnel.

6.9.2.2.2.3 Under the quality system, the following minimum requirements shall be met for each FRP portable tank manufactured:

(a) Use of an inspection and test plan (ITP);

(b) Visual inspections;

(c) Verification of fibre orientation and mass fraction by means of documented control process;

(d) Verification of fibre and resin quality and characteristics by means of certificates or other documentation;

(e) Verification of liner quality and characteristics by means of certificates or other documentation;

(f) Verification of whichever is applicable of formed thermoplastic resin characteristic or degree of cure of thermoset resin, by direct or indirect means (e.g. Barcol test or differential scanning calorimetry) to be determined in accordance with 6.9.2.7.1.2 (h), or by creep testing of a representative sample or parallel shell-sample in accordance with 6.9.2.7.1.2 (e) for a period of 100 hours;

(g) Documentation of whichever is applicable of thermoplastic resin forming processes or thermoset resin cure and post-cure processes; and

(h) Retention and archiving of shell samples for future inspection and shell verification (e.g. from manhole cut out) for a period of 5 years.

6.9.2.2.2.4 Audit of the quality system

The quality system shall be initially assessed to determine whether it meets the requirements in 6.9.2.2.2.1 to 6.9.2.2.2.3 to the satisfaction of the competent authority.

The manufacturer shall be notified of the results of the audit. The notification shall contain the conclusions of the audit and any corrective actions required.

Periodic audits shall be carried out, to the satisfaction of the competent authority, to ensure that the manufacturer maintains and applies the quality system. Reports of the periodic audits shall be provided to the manufacturer.

6.9.2.2.2.5 Maintenance of the quality system

The manufacturer shall maintain the quality system as approved in order that it remains adequate and efficient.

The manufacturer shall notify the competent authority that approved the quality system of any intended changes. The proposed changes shall be evaluated to determine whether the amended quality system will still satisfy the requirements in 6.9.2.2.2.1 to 6.9.2.2.2.3.

6.9.2.2.3 *FRP Shells*

6.9.2.2.3.1 FRP shells shall have a secure connection with structural elements of the portable tank frame. FRP shell supports and attachments to the frame shall cause no local stress concentrations exceeding the design allowables of the shell structure in accordance with the provisions stated in this chapter for all operating and test conditions.

6.9.2.2.3.2　　Shells shall be made of suitable materials, capable of operating within a minimum design temperature range of -40 °C to +50 °C, unless temperature ranges are specified for specific more severe climatic or operating conditions (e.g. heating elements), by the competent authority of the country where the transport operation is being performed.

6.9.2.2.3.3　　If a heating system is installed, it shall comply with 6.7.2.5.12 to 6.7.2.5.15 and with the following requirements:

- (a) The maximum operating temperature of the heating elements integrated or connected to the shell shall not exceed the maximum design temperature of the tank;

- (b) The heating elements shall be designed, controlled, and utilized so that the temperature of the carried substance cannot exceed the maximum design temperature of the tank or a value at which the internal pressure exceeds MAWP; and

- (c) Structures of the tank and its heating elements shall allow examination of the shell with respect to possible effects of overheating.

6.9.2.2.3.4　　Shells shall consist of the following elements:

- Liner;

- Structural layer;

- External layer.

NOTE: *The elements may be combined if all applicable functional criteria are met.*

6.9.2.2.3.5　　The liner is the inner element of the shell designed as the primary barrier to provide for the long-term chemical resistance in relation to the substances to be carried, to prevent any dangerous reaction with the contents or the formation of dangerous compounds and any substantial weakening of the structural layer owing to the diffusion of products through the liner. Chemical compatibility shall be verified in accordance with 6.9.2.7.1.3.

The liner may be an FRP liner or a thermoplastic liner.

6.9.2.2.3.6　　FRP liners shall consist of the following two components:

- (a) Surface layer ("gel-coat"): adequate resin rich surface layer, reinforced with a veil, compatible with the resin and contents. This layer shall have a maximum fibre mass content of 30 % and have a minimum thickness of 0.25 and a maximum thickness of 0.60 mm;

- (b) Strengthening layer(s): layer or several layers with a minimum thickness of 2 mm, containing a minimum of 900 g/m² of glass mat or chopped fibres with a mass content in glass of not less than 30 % unless equivalent safety is demonstrated for a lower glass content.

6.9.2.2.3.7　　If the liner consists of thermoplastic sheets, they shall be welded together in the required shape, using a qualified welding procedure and personnel. Welded liners shall have a layer of electrically conductive media placed against the non-liquid contact surface of the welds to facilitate spark testing. Durable bonding between liners and the structural layer shall be achieved by the use of an appropriate method.

6.9.2.2.3.8　　The structural layer shall be designed to withstand the design loads according to 6.7.2.2.12, 6.9.2.2.3.1, 6.9.2.3.2, 6.9.2.3.4 and 6.9.2.3.6.

6.9.2.2.3.9　　The external layer of resin or paint shall provide adequate protection of the structural layers of the tank from environmental and service exposure, including to UV radiation and salt fog, and occasional splash exposure to cargoes.

6.9.2.2.3.10   Resins

The processing of the resin mixture shall be carried out in compliance with the recommendations of the supplier. These resins can be:

- Unsaturated polyester resins;

- Vinyl ester resins;

- Epoxy resins;

- Phenolic resins;

- Thermoplastic resins.

The resin heat distortion temperature (HDT), determined in accordance with 6.9.2.7.1.1 shall be at least 20 °C higher than the maximum design temperature of the shell as defined in 6.9.2.2.3.2, but shall in any case not be lower than 70 °C.

6.9.2.2.3.11   Reinforcement material

The reinforcement material of the structural layers shall be selected such that they meet the requirements of the structural layer.

For the liner glass fibres of at a minimum type C or ECR according to ISO 2078:1993 + Amd 1:2015 shall be used. Thermoplastic veils may only be used for the liner when their compatibility with the intended contents has been demonstrated.

6.9.2.2.3.12   Additives

Additives necessary for the treatment of the resin, such as catalysts, accelerators, hardeners and thixotropic substances as well as materials used to improve the tank, such as fillers, colours, pigments etc. shall not cause weakening of the material, taking into account lifetime and temperature expectancy of the design.

6.9.2.2.3.13 FRP shells, their attachments and their service and structural equipment shall be designed to withstand the loads mentioned in 6.7.2.2.12, 6.9.2.2.3, 6.9.2.3.2, 6.9.2.3.4 and 6.9.2.3.6 without loss of contents (other than quantities of gas escaping through any degassing vents) during the design lifetime.

6.9.2.2.3.14   Special requirements for the carriage of substances with a flash-point of not more than 60 °C

6.9.2.2.3.14.1   FRP tanks used for the carriage of flammable liquids with a flash-point of not more than 60 °C shall be constructed to ensure the elimination of static electricity from the various component parts to avoid the accumulation of dangerous charges.

6.9.2.2.3.14.2   The electrical surface resistance of the inside and outside of the shell as established by measurements shall not be higher than 10^9 Ω. This may be achieved by the use of additives in the resin or interlaminate conducting sheets, such as metal or carbon network.

6.9.2.2.3.14.3   The discharge resistance to earth as established by measurements shall not be higher than 10^7 Ω.

6.9.2.2.3.14.4   All components of the shell shall be electrically connected to each other and to the metal parts of the service and structural equipment of the tank and to the vehicle. The electrical resistance between components and equipment in contact with each other shall not exceed 10 Ω.

6.9.2.2.3.14.5   The electrical surface-resistance and discharge resistance shall be measured initially on each manufactured tank or a specimen of the shell in accordance with the procedure recognized by the competent authority. In the event of damage to the shell, requiring repair, the electrical resistance shall be re-measured.

6.9.2.2.3.15   The tank shall be designed to withstand, without significant leakage, the effects of a full engulfment in fire for 30 minutes as specified by the test requirements in 6.9.2.7.1.5. Testing may be waived with the agreement of the competent authority, where sufficient proof can be provided by tests with comparable tank designs.

6.9.2.2.3.16   Construction process for FRP shells

6.9.2.2.3.16.1   Filament winding, hand layup, resin infusion, or other appropriate composite production processes shall be used for construction of FRP shells.

6.9.2.2.3.16.2   The weight of the fibre reinforcement shall conform to that set forth in the procedure specification with a tolerance of +10 % and −0 %. One or more of the fibre types specified in 6.9.2.2.3.11 and in the procedure specification shall be used for reinforcement of shells.

6.9.2.2.3.16.3   The resin system shall be one of the resin systems specified in 6.9.2.2.3.10. No filler, pigment, or dye additions shall be used which will interfere with the natural colour of the resin except as permitted by the procedure specification.

6.9.2.3   *Design criteria*

6.9.2.3.1   FRP shells shall be of a design capable of being stress-analysed mathematically or experimentally by resistance strain gauges, or by other methods approved by the competent authority.

6.9.2.3.2   FRP shells shall be designed and constructed to withstand the test pressure. Specific provisions are laid down for certain substances in the applicable portable tank instruction indicated in column 10 of the Dangerous Goods List and described in 4.2.5, or by a portable tank special provision indicated in column 11 of the Dangerous Goods List and described in 4.2.5.3. The minimum wall thickness of the FRP shell shall not be less than that specified in 6.9.2.4.

6.9.2.3.3   At the specified test pressure the maximum tensile relative deformation measured in mm/mm in the shell shall not result in the formation of microcracks, and therefore not be greater than the first measured point of elongation based fracture or damage of the resin, measured during tensile tests prescribed under 6.9.2.7.1.2 (c).

6.9.2.3.4   For internal test pressure, external design pressure specified in 6.7.2.2.10, static loads specified in 6.7.2.2.12 and static gravity loads caused by the contents with the maximum density specified for the design and at maximum filling degree, failure criteria (*FC*) in the longitudinal direction, circumferential direction, and any other in-plane direction of the composite layup shall not exceed the following value:

$$FC \leq \frac{1}{K}$$

where:

$$K = K_0 \times K_1 \times K_2 \times K_3 \times K_4 \times K_5$$

where:

- **K**   shall have a minimum value of 4.

- **K_0**   is a strength factor. For the general design the value for K_0 shall be equal to or more than 1.5. The value of K_0 shall be multiplied by a factor of two, unless the shell is provided with protection against damage consisting of a complete metal skeleton including longitudinal and transverse structural members;

- **K_1**   is a factor related to the deterioration in the material properties due to creep and ageing. It shall be determined by the formula:

$$K_1 = \frac{1}{\alpha\beta}$$

where "α" is the creep factor and "β" is the ageing factor determined in accordance with 6.9.2.7.1.2 (e) and (f), respectively. When used in calculation, factors α and β shall be between 0 and 1.

Alternatively, a conservative value of K_1 = 2 may be applied for the purpose of undertaking the numerical validation exercise in 6.9.2.3.4 (this does not remove the need to perform testing to determine α and β);

K_2 is a factor related to the service temperature and the thermal properties of the resin, determined by the following equation, with a minimum value of 1: K_2 = 1.25 - 0.0125 (HDT - 70) where HDT is the heat distortion temperature of the resin, in °C;

K_3 is a factor related to the fatigue of the material; the value of K_3 = 1.75 shall be used unless otherwise agreed with the competent authority. For the dynamic design as outlined in 6.7.2.2.12 the value of K_3 = 1.1 shall be used;

K_4 is a factor related to resin curing and has the following values:

1.0 where curing is carried out in accordance with an approved and documented process, and the quality system described under 6.9.2.2.2 includes verification of degree of cure for each FRP portable tank using a direct measurement approach, such as differential scanning calorimetry (DSC) determined via ISO 11357-2:2016, as per 6.9.2.7.1.2 (h);

1.1 where thermoplastic resin forming or thermoset resin curing is carried out in accordance with an approved and documented process, and the quality system described under 6.9.2.2.2 includes verification of whichever is applicable formed thermoplastic resin characteristics or degree of cure of thermoset resin, for each FRP portable tank using an indirect measurement approach as per 6.9.2.7.1.2 (h), such as Barcol testing via ASTM D2583:2013-03 or EN 59:2016, HDT via ISO 75-1:2013, thermo-mechanical analysis (TMA) via ISO 11359-1:2014, or dynamic thermo-mechanical analysis (DMA) via ISO 6721-11:2019;

1.5 in other cases.

K_5 is a factor related to the portable tank instruction in 4.2.5.2.6:

1.0 for T1 to T19;

1.33 for T20;

1.67 for T21 to T22.

A design validation exercise using numerical analysis and a suitable composite failure criterion is to be undertaken to verify that the stresses in the plies in the shell are below the allowables. Suitable composite failure criteria include, but are not limited to, Tsai-Wu, Tsai-Hill, Hashin, Yamada-Sun, Strain Invariant Failure Theory, Maximum Strain, or Maximum Stress. Other relations for the strength criteria are allowed upon agreement with the competent authority. The method and results of this design validation exercise are to be submitted to the competent authority.

The allowables are to be determined using experiments to derive parameters required by the chosen failure criteria combined with factor of safety K, the strength values measured as per 6.9.2.7.1.2 (c), and the maximum elongation strain criteria prescribed in 6.9.2.3.5. The analysis of joints is to be undertaken in accordance with the allowables determined in 6.9.2.3.7 and the strength values measured as per 6.9.2.7.1.2 (g). Buckling is to be considered in accordance with 6.9.2.3.6. Design of openings and metallic inclusions is to be considered in accordance with 6.9.2.3.8.

6.9.2.3.5 At any of the stresses as defined in 6.7.2.2.12 and 6.9.2.3.4, the resulting elongation in any direction shall not exceed the value indicated in the following table or one tenth of the elongation at fracture of the resin determined by ISO 527-2:2012, whichever is lower.

Examples of known limits are presented in the table below.

Type of resin	Maximum strain in tension (%)
Unsaturated polyester or phenolic	0.2
Vinylester	0.25
Epoxy	0.3
Thermoplastic	See 6.9.2.3.3

6.9.2.3.6 For the external design pressure the minimum safety factor for linear buckling analysis of the shell shall be as defined in the applicable pressure vessel code but not less than three.

6.9.2.3.7 The adhesive bondlines and/or overlay laminates used in the joints, including the end joints, connection between the equipment and shell, the joints of the surge plates and the partitions with the shell shall be capable of withstanding the loads of 6.7.2.2.12, 6.9.2.2.3.1, 6.9.2.3.2, 6.9.2.3.4 and 6.9.2.3.6. In order to avoid concentrations of stresses in the overlay lamination, the applied taper shall not be steeper than 1:6. The shear strength between the overlay laminate and the tank components to which it is bonded shall not be less than:

$$\tau = \gamma \frac{Q}{l} \leq \frac{\tau_R}{K}$$

where:

τ_R is the interlaminar shear strength according to ISO 14130:1997 and Cor 1:2003;

Q is the load per unit width of the interconnection;

K is the safety factor determined as per 6.9.2.3.4;

l is the length of the overlay laminate;

γ is the notch factor relating average joint stress to peak joint stress at failure initiation location.

Other calculation methods for the joints are allowed following approval with the competent authority.

6.9.2.3.8 Metallic flanges and their closures are permitted to be used in FRP shells, under design requirements of 6.7.2. Openings in the FRP shell shall be reinforced to provide at least the same safety factors against the static and dynamic stresses as specified in 6.7.2.2.12, 6.9.2.3.2, 6.9.2.3.4 and 6.9.2.3.6 as that for the shell itself. The number of openings shall be minimized. The axis ratio of oval-shaped openings shall be not more than 2.

If metallic flanges or componentry are integrated into the FRP shell using bonding, then the characterisation method stated in 6.9.2.3.7 shall apply to the joint between the metal and FRP. If the metallic flanges or componentry are fixed in an alternative fashion, e.g. threaded fastener connections, then the appropriate provisions of the relevant pressure vessel standard shall apply.

6.9.2.3.9 Check calculations of the strength of the shell shall be performed by finite element method simulating the shell layups, joints within FRP shell, joints of between the FRP shell and the container frame, and openings. Treatment of singularities shall be undertaken using an appropriate method according to the applicable pressure vessel code.

6.9.2.4 *Minimum wall thickness of the shell*

6.9.2.4.1 Minimum thickness of the FRP shell shall be confirmed by check calculations of the strength of the shell considering strength requirements given in 6.9.2.3.4.

6.9.2.4.2 Minimum thickness of the FRP shell structural layers shall be determined in accordance with 6.9.2.3.4, however, in any case the minimum thickness of the structural layers shall be at least 3 mm.

6.9.2.5 *Equipment components for portable tanks with FRP shell*

Service equipment, bottom openings, pressure relief devices, gauging devices, supports, frameworks, lifting and tie-down attachments of portable tanks shall meet the requirements of 6.7.2.5 to 6.7.2.17. If any other metallic features are required to be integrated into the FRP shell, then the provisions of 6.9.2.3.8 shall apply.

6.9.2.6 *Design approval*

6.9.2.6.1 Design approval of FRP portable tanks shall be as per 6.7.2.18 requirements. The following additional requirements apply to FRP portable tanks.

6.9.2.6.2 The prototype test report for the purpose of the design approval shall additionally include the following:

(a) Results of the material tests used for FRP shell fabrication in accordance with 6.9.2.7.1 requirements;

(b) Results of the ball drop test in accordance with the requirements of 6.9.2.7.1.4.

(c) Results the fire resistance test in accordance with provisions of 6.9.2.7.1.5.

6.9.2.6.3 A service life inspection programme shall be established, which shall be a part of the operation manual, to monitor the condition of the tank at periodic inspections. The inspection programme shall focus on the critical stress locations identified in the design analysis performed under 6.9.2.3.4. The inspection method shall take into account the potential damage mode at the critical stress location (e.g, tensile stress or interlaminate stress). The inspection shall be a combination of visual and non-destructive testing (e.g., acoustic emissions, ultrasonic evaluation, thermographic). For heating elements, the service life inspection programme shall allow an examination of the shell or its representative locations to take into account the effects of overheating.

6.9.2.6.4 A representative prototype tank shall be subjected to tests as specified below. For this purpose, service equipment may be replaced by other items if necessary.

6.9.2.6.4.1 The prototype shall be inspected for compliance with the design type specification. This shall include an internal and external inspection and measurement of the main dimensions.

6.9.2.6.4.2 The prototype, equipped with strain gauges at all locations of high strain, as identified by the design validation exercise in accordance with 6.9.2.3.4, shall be subjected to the following loads and the strain shall be recorded:

(a) Filled with water to the maximum filling degree. The measuring results shall be used to calibrate the design calculations according to 6.9.2.3.4;

(b) Filled with water to the maximum filling degree and subjected to static loads in all three directions mounted by the base corner castings without additional mass applied external to the shell. For comparison with the design calculation according to 6.9.2.3.4 the strains recorded shall be extrapolated in relation to the quotient of the accelerations required in 6.7.2.2.12 and measured;

(c) Filled with water and subjected to the specified test pressure. Under this load, the shell shall exhibit no visual damage or leakage.

The stress corresponding to the measured strain level shall not exceed the minimum factor of safety calculated in 6.9.2.3.4 under any of these loading conditions.

6.9.2.7 *Additional provisions applicable to FRP portable tanks*

6.9.2.7.1 *Material testing*

6.9.2.7.1.1 Resins

Resin tensile elongation shall be determined in accordance with ISO 527-2:2012. The heat distortion temperature (HDT) of the resin shall be determined in accordance with ISO 75-1:2013.

6.9.2.7.1.2 Shell samples

Prior to testing, all coatings shall be removed from the samples. If shell samples are not possible then parallel shell samples may be used. The tests shall cover:

(a) Thickness of the laminates of the central shell wall and the ends;

(b) Mass content and composition of composite reinforcement by ISO 1172:1996 or ISO 14127:2008, as well as orientation and arrangement of reinforcement layers;

(c) Tensile strength, elongation at fracture and modulus of elasticity according to ISO 527-4:1997 or ISO 527-5:2009 for the circumferential and longitudinal directions of the shell. For areas of the FRP shell, tests shall be performed on representative laminates in accordance with ISO 527-4:1997 or ISO 527-5:2009, to permit evaluation of the suitability of safety factor (K). A minimum of six specimens per measure of tensile strength shall be used, and the tensile strength shall be taken as the average minus two standard deviations;

(d) Bending deflection and strength shall be established by the three-point or four-point bending test according to ISO 14125:1998 + Amd 1:2011 using a sample with a minimum width of 50 mm and a support distance of at least 20 times the wall thickness. A minimum of five specimens shall be used.

(e) Creep factor α shall be determined by taking the average result of at least two specimens with the configuration described in (d), subject to creep in three-point or four-point bending, at the maximum design temperature nominated under 6.9.2.2.3.2, for a period of 1 000 hours. The following test is to be undertaken for each specimen:

(i) Place specimen into bending apparatus, unloaded, in oven set to maximum design temperature and allow to acclimatise for a period of not less than 60 minutes;

(ii) Load specimen bending in accordance with ISO 14125:1998 + Amd 1:2011 at flexural stress equal to the strength determined in (d) divided by four. Maintain mechanical load at maximum design temperature without interruption for not less than 1 000 hours;

(iii) Measure the initial deflection six minutes after full load application in (e) (ii). Specimen shall remain loaded in test rig;

(iv) Measure the final deflection 1 000 hours after full load application in (e) (ii); and

(v) Calculate the creep factor α by dividing the initial deflection from (e) (iii) by the final deflection from (e) (iv).

(f) Ageing factor β shall be determined by taking the average result of at least two specimens with the configuration described in (d), subject to loading in static three-point or four-point bending, in conjunction with immersion in water at the maximum design temperature nominated under 6.9.2.2.3.2 for a period of 1 000 hours. The following test is to be undertaken for each specimen:

    (i) Prior to testing or conditioning, specimens shall be dried in an oven at 80 °C for a period of 24 hours;

    (ii) The specimen shall be loaded in three-point or four-point bending at ambient temperature, in accordance with to ISO 14125:1998 + Amd 1:2011, at the flexural stress level equal to the strength determined in (d) divided by four. Measure the initial deflection 6 minutes after full load application. Remove specimen from test rig;

    (iii) Immerse unloaded specimen in water at the maximum design temperature for a period of not less than 1 000 hours without interruption to the water conditioning period. When conditioning period has lapsed, remove specimens, keep damp at ambient temperature, and complete (f) (iv) within three days;

    (iv) The specimen shall be subject to second round of static loading, in a manner identical to (f) (ii). Measure the final deflection six minutes after full load application. Remove specimen from test rig; and

    (v) Calculate the ageing factor β by dividing the initial deflection from (f) (ii) by the final deflection from (f) (iv).

(g) The interlaminar shear strength of the joints shall be measured by testing representative samples in accordance with ISO 14130:1997;

(h) The efficiency of whichever is applicable of thermoplastic resin forming characteristics or thermoset resin cure and post-cure processes for laminates are to be determined using one or more of the following methods:

    (i) Direct measurement of formed thermoplastic resin characteristics or thermoset resin degree of cure: glass transition temperature (T_g) or melting temperature (T_m) determined using differential scanning calorimetry (DSC) via ISO 11357-2:2016; or

    (ii) Indirect measurement of formed thermoplastic resin characteristics or thermoset resin degree of cure:

        - HDT via ISO 75-1:2013;

        - T_g or T_m using thermo-mechanical analysis (TMA) via ISO 11359-1:2014;

        - Dynamic thermo-mechanical analysis (DMA) via ISO 6721-11:2019:

        - Barcol testing via ASTM D2583:2013-03 or EN 59:2016.

6.9.2.7.1.3 The chemical compatibility of the liner and chemical contact surfaces of service equipment with the substances to be carried shall be demonstrated by one of the following methods. This demonstration shall account for all aspects of the compatibility of the materials of the shell and its equipment with the substances to be carried, including chemical deterioration of the shell, initiation of critical reactions of the contents and dangerous reactions between both.

(a) In order to establish any deterioration of the shell, representative samples taken from the shell, including any liners with welds, shall be subjected to the chemical compatibility test according to EN 977:1997 for a period of 1 000 hours at 50 °C or the maximum temperature at which a particular substance is approved for transport. Compared with a virgin sample, the loss of strength and elasticity modulus measured by the bending test according to EN 978:1997 shall not exceed 25 %. Cracks, bubbles, pitting effects as well as separation of layers and liners and roughness shall not be acceptable;

(b) Certified and documented data of positive experiences on the compatibility of filling substances in question with the materials of the shell with which they come into contact at given temperatures, times and other relevant service conditions;

(c) Technical data published in relevant literature, standards or other sources, acceptable to the competent authority;

(d) Upon agreement with the competent authority other methods of chemical compatibility verification may be used.

6.9.2.7.1.4   Ball drop test as per EN 976-1:1997

The prototype shall be subjected to the ball drop test according to EN 976-1:1997, No. 6.6. No visible damage inside or outside the tank shall occur.

6.9.2.7.1.5   Fire resistance test

6.9.2.7.1.5.1   A representative prototype tank with its service and structural equipment in place and filled to 80 % of its maximum capacity with water, shall be exposed to a full engulfment in fire for 30 minutes, caused by an open heating oil pool fire or any other type of fire with the same effect. The fire shall be equivalent to a theoretical fire with a flame temperature of 800 °C, emissivity of 0.9 and to the tank a heat transfer coefficient of 10 W/(m²K) and surface absorptivity of 0.8. A minimum net heat flux of 75 kW/m² shall be calibrated according to ISO 21843:2018. The dimensions of the pool shall exceed those of the tank by at least 50 cm to each side and the distance between fuel level and tank shall be between 50 cm and 80 cm. The rest of the tank below liquid level, including openings and closures, shall remain leakproof except for drips.

6.9.2.8   *Inspection and testing*

6.9.2.8.1   Inspection and testing of portable FRP tanks shall be carried out as per provisions of 6.7.2.19. In addition, welded thermoplastic liners shall be spark tested under a suitable standard, after pressure tests performed in accordance with the periodic inspections specified in 6.7.2.19.4.

6.9.2.8.2   In addition, the initial and periodic inspections shall follow the service life inspection programme and any associated inspection methods per 6.9.2.6.3.

6.9.2.8.3   The initial inspection and test shall verify that construction of the tank is made in accordance with the quality system required by 6.9.2.2.2.

6.9.2.8.4   Additionally, during inspection of the shell the position of the areas heated by heating elements shall be indicated or marked, be available on design drawings or shall be made visible by a suitable technique (e.g. infrared). Examination of the shell shall take into account the effects of overheating, corrosion, erosion, overpressure and mechanical overloading.

6.9.2.9   *Retention of samples*

Shell samples (e.g. from manhole cut out) for each tank manufactured shall be maintained for future inspection and shell verification for a period of five years from the date of the initial inspection and test and until successful completion of the required five-year periodic inspection.

6.9.2.10   *Marking*

6.9.2.10.1   The requirements of 6.7.2.20.1 apply to portable tanks with an FRP shell except those of 6.7.2.20.1 (f) (ii).

6.9.2.10.2　　The information required in 6.7.2.20.1 (f) (i) shall be "Shell structural material: Fibre-reinforced plastic", the reinforcement fibre e.g. "Reinforcement: E-glass", and resin e.g. "Resin: Vinyl Ester".

6.9.2.10.3　　Requirements of provision 6.7.2.20.2 apply to portable tank with an FRP shell.

PART 7

PROVISIONS CONCERNING TRANSPORT OPERATIONS

Introductory note

NOTE: *In general, development of the detailed provisions of this part would be left to national, modal or regional authorities. For the purposes of these Regulations, chapter 7.1 contains operational provisions that are applicable to all modes of transport. An additional chapter is provided, but generally reserved, for additional provisions applicable to the individual modes of transport that may be added by national, modal or regional authorities.*

CHAPTER 7.1

PROVISIONS CONCERNING TRANSPORT OPERATIONS BY ALL MODES OF TRANSPORT

7.1.1   Application, general provisions and loading requirements

7.1.1.1   This chapter contains provisions applicable to dangerous goods transport operations by all modes of transport.

7.1.1.2   Unless otherwise specified in these Regulations, dangerous goods shall not be offered for transport unless:

      (a)   goods have been properly classified, packed, marked, labelled and described and certified on a dangerous goods transport document; and

      (b)   goods are in a fit condition for transport as required by these Regulations, and no dangerous residue of the dangerous goods adheres to the outside of the package.

7.1.1.3   *Acceptance of dangerous goods by carriers*

7.1.1.3.1   Unless otherwise specified in these Regulations, a carrier shall not accept dangerous goods for transport unless:

      (a)   A copy of the dangerous goods transport document and other documents or information as required by these Regulations are provided; or

      (b)   The information applicable to the dangerous goods is provided in electronic form.

7.1.1.3.2   The information applicable to the dangerous goods shall accompany the dangerous goods to final destination. This information may be on the dangerous goods transport document or may be on another document. This information shall be given to the consignee when the dangerous goods are delivered.

7.1.1.3.3   When the information applicable to the dangerous goods is given to the carrier in electronic form, the information shall be available to the carrier at all times during transport to final destination. The information shall be able to be produced without delay as a paper document.

7.1.1.4   Unless otherwise specified in these Regulations, dangerous goods shall not be transported unless:

      (a)   Cargo transport units have been appropriately marked, labelled and placarded; and

      (b)   Cargo transport units are otherwise in a condition for transport as required by these Regulations.

7.1.1.5   Packages containing dangerous goods shall only be loaded in cargo transport units that are strong enough to withstand the shocks and loadings normally encountered during transport, having regard to the conditions to be expected during the anticipated journey. The cargo transport unit shall be constructed in such a way as to prevent the loss of contents. Where appropriate the cargo transport unit shall be fitted with devices to facilitate securing and handling of the dangerous goods.

7.1.1.6   The interior and the exterior of a cargo transport unit shall be inspected prior to loading to ensure that there is no damage that could affect its integrity or that of the packages to be loaded in it.

       The cargo transport unit shall be checked to ensure it is structurally serviceable, that it is free of possible residues incompatible with the cargo and that the interior floor, walls and ceiling, where applicable, are free from protrusions or deterioration that could affect the cargo inside and that freight containers are free of damages that affect the weather-tight integrity of the container, when required.

Structurally serviceable means that the cargo transport unit is free from major defects in its structural components. Structural components of cargo transport units for multimodal purpose are e.g. top and bottom side rails, top and bottom end rails, corner posts, corner fittings and, for freight containers, door sill, door header and floor cross members. Major defects include:

(a) Bends, cracks or breaks in structural or supporting members, or any damage to service or operational equipment that affect the integrity of the unit;

(b) Any distortion of the over-all configuration or any damage to lifting attachments or handling equipment interface features great enough to prevent proper alignment of handling equipment, mounting and securing on chassis, vehicle or wagon, or insertion into ships' cells; and, where applicable;

(c) Door hinges, door seals and hardware that are seized, twisted, broken, missing or otherwise inoperative.

NOTE: *For filling portable tanks and MEGCs, see chapter 4.2. For filling bulk containers, see chapter 4.3.*

7.1.1.7 Cargo transport units shall be loaded so that incompatible dangerous or other goods are segregated in accordance with this chapter. Specific loading instructions such as orientation arrows, not to be double stacked, keep dry or temperature control requirements shall be met. Liquid dangerous goods shall be loaded below dry dangerous goods whenever possible.

7.1.1.8 Packages containing dangerous goods and unpackaged dangerous articles shall be secured by suitable means capable of restraining the goods (such as fastening straps, sliding slatboards, adjustable brackets) in the cargo transport unit in a manner that will prevent any movement during transport which would change the orientation of the packages or cause them to be damaged. When dangerous goods are transported with other goods (e.g. heavy machinery or crates), all goods shall be securely fixed or packed in the cargo transport units so as to prevent the release of dangerous goods. Movement of packages may also be prevented by filling any voids by the use of dunnage or by blocking and bracing. Where restraints such as banding or straps are used, these shall not be over-tightened to cause damage or deformation of the package.

7.1.1.9 Packages shall not be stacked unless designed for that purpose. Where different design types of packages that have been designed for stacking are to be loaded together, consideration shall be given to their compatibility for stacking with each other. Where necessary, stacked packages shall be prevented from damaging the package below by the use of load-bearing devices.

7.1.1.10 During loading and unloading, packages containing dangerous goods shall be protected from being damaged. Particular attention shall be paid to the handling of packages during their preparation for transport, the type of cargo transport unit on which they are to be carried and to the method of loading or unloading, so that accidental damage is not caused through dragging or mishandling the packages. Packages that appear to be leaking or damaged so that the contents may escape shall not be accepted for transport. If a package is found to be damaged so that the contents leak, the damaged package shall not be transported but moved to a safe place in accordance with instructions given by a competent authority or a designated responsible person who is familiar with the dangerous goods, the risks involved and the measures that should be taken in an emergency.

NOTE 1: *Additional operational requirements for the transport of packagings and IBCs are provided in the special packing provisions for packagings and IBCs (see chapter 4.1).*

NOTE 2: *Additional guidance on the packing of cargo transport units can be found in the IMO/ILO/UNECE Guidelines for Packing Cargo Transport Units (CTUs) contained in the supplement to the International Maritime Dangerous Goods Code. Modal and National Codes of Practice (such as the loading guidelines in appendix II of the Agreement Governing the Exchange and Use of Wagons between Railway*

Undertakings (RIV 2000), published by the International Union of Railways (UIC) or the United Kingdom Department for Transport Code of Practice on Safety of Loads on Vehicles) may also be available.

7.1.1.11 Flexible bulk containers shall be transported within a conveyance with rigid sides and ends that extend at least two-thirds of the height of the flexible bulk container.

NOTE: *When loading flexible bulk containers in a freight container as defined in 5.4.2 particular attention shall be paid to the guidance on the packing of cargo transport units referred to in 7.1.1.10, note 2 and notably to the IMO/ILO/UNECE Guidelines for Packing Cargo Transport Units (CTUs) contained in the supplement to the International Maritime Dangerous Goods Code.*

7.1.1.11.1 Flexible bulk containers shall be secured by suitable means capable of restraining the container in the conveyance in a manner that will prevent any movement during transport which would change the orientation of the container or cause the container to be damaged. Movement of the containers may also be prevented by filling any voids by the use of dunnage or by blocking and bracing. Where restraints such as banding or straps are used, these shall not be over-tightened to cause damage or deformation to the flexible bulk containers.

7.1.1.11.2 Flexible bulk containers shall not be stacked for road or rail transport.

7.1.2 Segregation of dangerous goods

7.1.2.1 Incompatible goods shall be segregated from one another during transport. For the purposes of segregation, two substances or articles are considered mutually incompatible when their stowing together may result in undue hazards in the case of leakage, spillage, or any other accident. In this regard, detailed segregation requirements for substances and articles of Class 1 are provided in 7.1.3.1 and 7.1.3.2.

7.1.2.2 The extent of the hazard arising from possible reactions between incompatible dangerous goods may vary and the segregation arrangements required shall also vary as appropriate. In some instances such segregation may be obtained by requiring certain distances between incompatible dangerous goods. Intervening spaces between such dangerous goods may be filled with cargo compatible with the dangerous substances or articles in question.

7.1.2.3 The provisions of these Regulations are general in nature. The segregation provisions for each particular mode of transport shall be based on the following principles:

(a) Incompatible dangerous goods shall be segregated from one another so as to effectively minimize hazards in the event of accidental leakage or spillage or any other accident;

(b) Whenever dangerous goods are stowed together, the most stringent segregation provisions for any of the goods shall be applied;

(c) For packages required to bear a subsidiary hazard label, the segregation appropriate to the subsidiary hazard shall be applied when it is more stringent than that required by the primary hazard.

7.1.2.4 An overpack shall not contain dangerous goods which react dangerously with one another.

7.1.3 Special provisions applicable to the transport of explosives

7.1.3.1 *Separation of goods of Class 1 of different compatibility groups*

NOTE: *The safety of explosive substances and articles would be enhanced by transporting each kind separately, but considerations of practicability and economics preclude such an ideal. In practice, a proper balance of the interest of safety against the other relevant factors necessitates a degree of mixing in the transport of explosive substances and articles of several kinds.*

7.1.3.1.1 The extent to which goods of Class 1 may be loaded together in transport is determined by the "compatibility" of the explosives. Goods of Class 1 are considered to be "compatible" if they can be transported together without significantly increasing either the probability of an accident or, for a given quantity, the magnitude of the effects of such an accident.

7.1.3.1.2 Goods in Compatibility Groups A to K and N may be transported in accordance with the following provisions:

(a) Packages bearing the same compatibility group letter and the same division number may be transported together;

(b) Goods of the same compatibility group but different divisions may be transported together provided that the whole is treated as belonging to the division having the smaller number. However, when goods of Division 1.5, Compatibility Group D, are transported together with goods of Division 1.2, Compatibility Group D, the total of the consignment shall be treated as Division 1.1, Compatibility Group D, for the purposes of transport;

(c) Packages bearing different compatibility group letters shall not in general be transported together (regardless of the division number) except in the case of compatibility group letters C, D, E and S as explained in 7.1.3.1.3 and 7.1.3.1.4.

NOTE: *Other combinations of Compatibility Groups A to K and N may be permitted under provisions applicable to the individual mode of transport.*

7.1.3.1.3 Goods in Compatibility Groups C, D and E are permitted to be carried together in the same unit load or cargo transport unit provided the over-all classification code is determined in accordance with the classification procedures in 2.1.3. The appropriate division is determined in accordance with 7.1.3.1.2 (b). Any combination of articles in Compatibility Groups C, D and E is assigned to Compatibility Group E. Any combination of substances in Compatibility Groups C and D shall be assigned to the most appropriate of the compatibility groups shown in 2.1.2.1.1, taking cognizance of the predominant characteristics of the combined load.

7.1.3.1.4 Goods in Compatibility Group S may be transported with goods in all compatibility groups other than A and L.

7.1.3.1.5 Goods in Compatibility Group L shall not be transported with goods in other compatibility groups. Furthermore, goods in Compatibility Group L may only be transported with the same type of goods within Compatibility Group L.

7.1.3.1.6 Goods of Compatibility Group N shall not in general (see 7.1.3.1.2 (b)) be transported with goods in other compatibility groups except S. However, if these goods are transported together with goods of Compatibility Groups C, D and E the goods of Compatibility Group N shall be considered as goods having Compatibility Group D (see also 7.1.3.1.3).

7.1.3.2 ***Mixed transport of goods of Class 1 with dangerous goods of other classes in freight containers, vehicles or wagons***

7.1.3.2.1 Except where otherwise specially provided for in these Regulations, goods of Class 1 shall not be transported together in freight containers, vehicles or wagons with dangerous goods of other classes.

7.1.3.2.2 Goods in Division 1.4, compatibility group S, may be transported together with dangerous goods of other classes.

7.1.3.2.3 Blasting explosives (except UN 0083 Explosive, blasting, type C) may be transported together with ammonium nitrate (UN Nos. 1942 and 2067), ammonium nitrate emulsion or suspension or gel (UN 3375) and alkali metal nitrates (e.g. UN 1486) and alkaline earth metal nitrates (e.g. UN 1454) provided the aggregate is treated as blasting explosives under Class 1 for the purposes of placarding, segregation, stowage and maximum permissible load.

NOTE: *Alkali metal nitrates include caesium nitrate (UN 1451), lithium nitrate (UN 2722), potassium nitrate (UN 1486), rubidium nitrate (UN 1477) and sodium nitrate (UN 1498). Alkaline earth metal nitrates include barium nitrate (UN 1446), beryllium nitrate (UN 2464), calcium nitrate (UN 1454), magnesium nitrate (UN 1474) and strontium nitrate (UN 1507).*

7.1.3.2.4　Life-saving appliances (UN Nos. 3072 and 2990) containing Class 1 goods as equipment may be transported together with the same dangerous goods as contained in the appliances.

7.1.3.2.5　Air bag inflators, or air bag modules, or seat-belt pretensioners, of Division 1.4, compatibility group G, (UN 0503) may be transported with air bag inflators or air bag modules or seat-belt pretensioners of Class 9 (UN 3268).

7.1.3.3　*Transport of explosives in freight containers, road vehicles and rail wagons*

7.1.3.3.1　For free-flowing powdery substances of 1.1C, 1.1D, 1.1G, 1.3C and 1.3G and fireworks of 1.1G, 1.2G and 1.3G, the floor of a freight container shall have a non-metallic surface or covering.

7.1.4　Special provisions applicable to the transport of gases

7.1.4.1　Aerosols transported for the purposes of reprocessing or disposal under the provisions of special provision 327 shall only be transported in well-ventilated cargo transport units other than closed freight containers.

7.1.5　Special provisions applicable to the transport of self-reactive substances of Division 4.1, organic peroxides of Division 5.2 and substances stabilized by temperature control (other than self-reactive substances and organic peroxides)

7.1.5.1　All self-reactive substances, organic peroxides and polymerizing substances shall be protected from direct sunlight and all sources of heat, and placed in adequately ventilated areas.

NOTE: *Some substances which are transported under temperature control are prohibited from transport by certain modes.*

7.1.5.2　Where a number of packages are assembled in a freight container, closed road vehicle or unit load, the total quantity of substance, the type and number of packages and the stacking arrangement shall not create an explosion hazard.

7.1.5.3　*Temperature control provisions*

7.1.5.3.1　These provisions apply to certain self-reactive substances when required by 2.4.2.3.4, and certain organic peroxides when required by 2.5.3.4.1 and certain polymerizing substances when required by 2.4.2.5.2 or special provision 386 of chapter 3.3 which may only be transported under conditions where the temperature is controlled.

7.1.5.3.2　These provisions also apply to the transport of substances for which:

(a) The proper shipping name as indicated in column 2 of the Dangerous Goods List of chapter 3.2 or according to 3.1.2.6 contains the word "TEMPERATURE CONTROLLED"; and

(b) The self-accelerating decomposition temperature (SADT) or the self-accelerating polymerisation temperature (SAPT) determined for the substance (with or without chemical stabilization) as offered for transport is:

　(i)　50 °C or less for single packagings and IBCs; or

　(ii)　45 °C or less for portable tanks.

When chemical inhibition is not used to stabilize a reactive substance which may generate dangerous amounts of heat and gas, or vapour, under normal transport conditions, these substances need to be transported under temperature control. These provisions do not apply to substances which are stabilized by the addition of chemical inhibitors such that the SADT or the SAPT is greater than that prescribed in (b) (i) or (ii), above.

7.1.5.3.3　　In addition, if a self-reactive substance or organic peroxide or a substance the proper shipping name of which contains the word "STABILIZED" and which is not normally required to be transported under temperature control is transported under conditions where the temperature may exceed 55 °C, it may require temperature control.

7.1.5.3.4　　The "control temperature" is the maximum temperature at which the substance can be safely transported. It is assumed that during transport the temperature of the immediate surroundings of the package does not exceed 55 °C and attains this value for a relatively short time only during each period of 24 hours. In the event of loss of temperature control, it may be necessary to implement emergency procedures. The "emergency temperature" is the temperature at which such procedures shall be implemented.

7.1.5.3.5　　Derivation of control and emergency temperatures

Type of receptacle	SADT[a]/SAPT[a]	Control temperature	Emergency temperature
Single packagings and IBCs	≤ 20 °C	20 °C below SADT/SAPT	10 °C below SADT/SAPT
	> 20 °C and ≤ 35 °C	15 °C below SADT/SAPT	10 °C below SADT/SAPT
	> 35 °C	10 °C below SADT/SAPT	5 °C below SADT/SAPT
Portable tanks	≤ 45 °C	10 °C below SADT/SAPT	5 °C below SADT/SAPT

[a]　*i.e. the SADT/SAPT of the substance as packed for transport.*

7.1.5.3.6　　The control and emergency temperatures are derived using the table in 7.1.5.3.5 from the SADT or from the SAPT which are defined as the lowest temperatures at which self-accelerating decomposition or self-accelerating polymerization may occur with a substance in the packaging, IBC or portable tank as used in transport. An SADT or SAPT shall be determined in order to decide if a substance shall be subjected to temperature control during transport. Provisions for the determination of the SADT and SAPT are given in 2.4.2.3.4, 2.5.3.4.2 and 2.4.2.5.2 for self-reactive substances, organic peroxides and polymerizing substances and mixtures, respectively.

7.1.5.3.7　　Control and emergency temperatures, where appropriate, are provided for currently assigned self-reactive substances in 2.4.2.3.2.3 and for currently assigned organic peroxide formulations in 2.5.3.2.4.

7.1.5.3.8　　The actual transport temperature may be lower than the control temperature but shall be selected so as to avoid dangerous separation of phases.

7.1.5.4　　*Transport under temperature control*

NOTE:　　*Since the circumstances to be taken into account differ for the various modes of transport, only general guidance is provided.*

7.1.5.4.1　　Maintenance of the prescribed temperature is an essential feature of the safe transport of substances stabilized by temperature control. In general, there shall be:

(a)　Thorough inspection of the cargo transport unit prior to loading;

(b)　Instructions to the carrier about the operation of the refrigeration system;

(c)　Procedures to be followed in the event of loss of control;

(d)　Regular monitoring of operating temperatures; and

(e)　Provision of a back-up refrigeration system or spare parts.

7.1.5.4.2   Any control and temperature sensing devices in the refrigeration system shall be readily accessible and all electrical connections weather-proof. The temperature of air space within the cargo transport unit shall be measured by two independent sensors and the output shall be recorded so that temperature changes are readily detectable. The temperature shall be checked every four to six hours and logged. When substances having a control temperature of less than +25 °C are carried, the cargo transport unit shall be equipped with visible and audible alarms, powered independently of the refrigeration system, set to operate at or below the control temperature.

7.1.5.4.3   If during transport the control temperature is exceeded, an alert procedure shall be initiated involving any necessary repairs to the refrigeration equipment or an increase in the cooling capacity (e.g. by adding liquid or solid refrigerants). The temperature shall also be checked frequently and preparations made for implementation of the emergency procedures. If the emergency temperature is reached, the emergency procedures shall be initiated.

7.1.5.4.4   The suitability of a particular means of temperature control for transport depends on a number of factors. Factors to be considered include:

(a) The control temperature(s) of the substance(s) to be transported;

(b) The difference between the control temperature and the anticipated ambient temperature conditions;

(c) The effectiveness of the thermal insulation;

(d) The duration of transport; and

(e) Allowance of a safety margin for delays.

7.1.5.4.5   Suitable methods for preventing the control temperature being exceeded are, in order of increasing control capability:

(a) Thermal insulation; provided that the initial temperature of the substance(s) to be transported is sufficiently below the control temperature;

(b) Thermal insulation with coolant system; provided that:

(i) An adequate quantity of coolant (e.g. liquid nitrogen or solid carbon dioxide), allowing a reasonable margin for delay, is carried;

(ii) Liquid oxygen or air is not used as coolant;

(iii) There is a uniform cooling effect even when most of the coolant has been consumed; and

(iv) The need to ventilate the unit before entering is clearly indicated by a warning on the door(s) of the unit;

(c) Single mechanical refrigeration; provided that for substance(s) to be transported with a flash point lower than the sum of the emergency temperature plus 5 °C explosion-proof electrical fittings are used within the cooling compartment to prevent ignition of flammable vapours;

(d) Combined mechanical refrigeration system with coolant system; provided that:

(i) The two systems are independent of one another;

(ii) The provisions in (b) and (c) are complied with;

(e) Dual mechanical refrigeration system; provided that:

(i) Apart from the integral power supply unit, the two systems are independent of one another;

(ii) Each system alone is capable of maintaining adequate temperature control; and

(iii) For substance(s) to be transported with a flash point lower than the sum of the emergency temperature plus 5 °C explosion-proof electrical fittings are used within the cooling compartment to prevent ignition of flammable vapours.

7.1.6 *(Reserved).*

7.1.7 Special provisions applicable to the transport of Division 6.1 (toxic) and Division 6.2 (infectious) substances

7.1.7.1 *Division 6.1 (toxic) substances*

7.1.7.1.1 *Segregation from foodstuffs*

Substances marked as or known to be toxic (packing groups I, II and III) shall not be carried in the same railway wagon, lorry, hold of a ship, compartment of an aircraft or other cargo transport unit with substances marked as or known to be foodstuffs, feeds or other edible substances intended for consumption by humans or animals. Relaxation of this position may be allowed for substances of packing groups II and III provided the competent authority is satisfied that the packing and segregation are adequate to prevent the contamination of foodstuffs, feeds or other edible substances intended for consumption by humans or animals.

7.1.7.1.2 *Decontamination of cargo transport units*

A railway wagon, lorry, cargo space of a ship, compartment of an aircraft or other cargo transport unit which has been used to carry substances marked as or known to be toxic (packing groups I, II and III) shall, before re-use, be inspected for contamination. A railway wagon, lorry, hold of a ship, compartment of an aircraft or other cargo transport unit which has been contaminated shall not be returned to service until such contamination has been removed.

7.1.7.2 *Division 6.2 (infectious) substances*

7.1.7.2.1 *Responsibility of carrier*

Carriers and their staff shall fully understand all applicable regulations for the packing, labelling, transport and documentation of consignments of infectious substances. The carrier shall accept and expedite the transport of consignments conforming to the rules in force. If the carrier finds any error in the labelling or documentation, he shall immediately notify the consignor or consignee so that the appropriate corrective measures may be taken.

7.1.7.2.2 *Action to be taken in the event of damage or leakage*

Any person responsible for the carriage of packages containing infectious substances who becomes aware of damage to or leakage from such packages shall:

(a) Avoid handling the package or keep handling to a minimum;

(b) Inspect adjacent packages for contamination and put aside any that may have been contaminated;

(c) Inform the appropriate public health authority or veterinary authority, and provide information on any other countries of transit where persons may have been exposed to danger; and

(d) Notify the consignor and/or the consignee.

7.1.7.2.3   *Decontamination of cargo transport units*

A railway wagon, road vehicle, cargo space of a ship, compartment of an aircraft or other cargo transport unit which has been used to transport infectious substances shall be inspected for release of the substance before re-use. If the infectious substances were released during transport, the cargo transport unit shall be decontaminated before it is re-used. Decontamination may be achieved by any means which effectively inactivates the released infectious substance.

7.1.8   Special provisions applicable to the transport of radioactive material

7.1.8.1   *Segregation*

7.1.8.1.1   Packages, overpacks and freight containers containing radioactive material and unpackaged radioactive material shall be segregated during transport and during storage in transit:

(a)   From workers in regularly occupied working areas by distances calculated using a dose criterion of 5 mSv in a year and conservative model parameters;

(b)   From members of the the public, in areas where the public has regular access, by distances calculated using a dose criterion of 1 mSv in a year and conservative model parameters;

(c)   From undeveloped photographic film by distances calculated using a radiation exposure criterion for undeveloped photographic film due to the transport of radioactive material for 0.1 mSv per consignment of such film; and

(d)   From other dangerous goods in accordance with 7.1.2 and 7.1.3.2.

7.1.8.1.2   Category II-YELLOW or III-YELLOW packages or overpacks shall not be carried in compartments occupied by passengers, except those exclusively reserved for couriers specially authorized to accompany such packages or overpacks.

7.1.8.2   *Activity limits*

The total activity in a single hold or compartment of an inland waterway craft, or in another conveyance, for carriage of LSA material or SCO in Type IP-1, Type IP-2, Type IP-3 or unpackaged, shall not exceed the limits shown in table 7.1.8.2. For SCO-III, the limits in table 7.1.8.2 may be exceeded provided that the transport plan contains precautions which are to be employed during transport to obtain an overall level of safety at least equivalent to that which would be provided if the limits had been applied.

Table 7.1.8.2: Conveyance activity limits for LSA material and SCO in industrial packages or unpackaged

Nature of material	Activity limit for conveyances other than by inland waterway other than inland waterway craft	Activity limit for a hold or compartment of an inland waterway craft
LSA-I	No limit	No limit
LSA-II and LSA-III non-combustible solids	No limit	100 A_2
LSA-II and LSA-III combustible solids, and all liquids and gases	100 A_2	10 A_2
SCO	100 A_2	10 A_2

7.1.8.3 *Stowage during transport and storage in transit*

7.1.8.3.1 Consignments shall be securely stowed.

7.1.8.3.2 Provided that its average surface heat flux does not exceed 15 W/m^2 and that the immediately surrounding cargo is not in sacks or bags, a package or overpack may be carried or stored among packaged general cargo without any special stowage provisions except as may be specifically required by the competent authority in an applicable certificate of approval.

7.1.8.3.3 Loading of freight containers and accumulation of packages, overpacks and freight containers shall be controlled as follows:

(a) Except under the condition of exclusive use, and for consignments of LSA-I material, the total number of packages, overpacks and freight containers aboard a single conveyance shall be so limited that the total sum of the transport indexes aboard the conveyance does not exceed the values shown in table 7.1.8.3.3;

(b) The dose rate under routine conditions of transport shall not exceed 2 mSv/h at any point on the external surface of the vehicle or freight container, and 0.1 mSv/h at 2 m from the external surface of the vehicle or freight container, except for consignments transported under exclusive use by road or rail, for which the dose rate limits around the vehicle are set forth in 7.2.3.1.2 (b) and (c);

(c) The total sum of the criticality safety indexes in a freight container and aboard a conveyance shall not exceed the values shown in table 7.1.8.4.2.

Table 7.1.8.3.3: TI limits for freight containers and conveyances not under exclusive use

Type of freight container or conveyance	Limit on total sum of transport indexes in a freight container or aboard a conveyance
Freight container	
Small freight container	50
Large freight container	50
Vehicle	50
Aircraft	
Passenger	50
Cargo	200
Inland waterway vessel	50
Seagoing vessel[a]	
(1) Hold, compartment or defined deck area:	
Packages, overpacks, small freight containers	50
Large freight containers	200
(2) Total vessel:	
Packages, overpacks, small freight containers	200
Large freight containers	no limit

[a] *Packages or overpacks carried in or on a vehicle which are in accordance with the provisions of 7.2.3.1.2 may be transported by vessels provided that they are no removed from the vehicle at any time while on board the vessel.*

7.1.8.3.4 Any package or overpack having either a transport index greater than 10, or any consignment having a criticality safety index greater than 50, shall be transported only under exclusive use.

7.1.8.4   *Additional requirements relating to transport and storage in transit of fissile material*

7.1.8.4.1   Any group of packages, overpacks, and freight containers containing fissile material stored in transit in any one storage area shall be so limited that the total sum of the criticality safety indexes in the group does not exceed 50. Each group shall be stored so as to maintain a spacing of at least 6 m from other such groups.

7.1.8.4.2   Where the total sum of the criticality safety indexes on board a conveyance or in a freight container exceeds 50, as permitted in table 7.1.8.4.2, storage shall be such as to maintain a spacing of at least 6 m from other groups of packages, overpacks or freight containers containing fissile material or other conveyances carrying radioactive material.

Table 7.1.8.4.2: CSI limits for freight containers and conveyances containing fissile material

Type of freight container or conveyance	Limit on total sum of criticality safety indexes in a freight container or aboard a conveyance	
	Not under exclusive use	Under exclusive use
Freight container		
Small freight container	50	n.a.
Large freight container	50	100
Vehicle	50	100
Aircraft		
Passenger	50	n.a.
Cargo	50	100
Inland waterway vessel	50	100
Seagoing vessel[a]		
(1) Hold, compartment or defined deck area:		
Packages, overpacks, small freight containers	50	100
Large freight containers	50	100
(2) Total vessel:		
Packages, overpacks, small freight containers	200[b]	200[c]
Large freight containers	No limit[b]	No limit[c]

[a]   *Packages of overpacks carried in or on a vehicle which are in accordance with the provisions of 7.2.3.1.2 may be transported by vessels provided that they are not removed from the vehicle at any time while on board the vessel. In that case the entries under the heading "under exclusive use" apply.*

[b]   *The consignment shall be so handled and stowed that the total sum of CSI's in any group does not exceed 50, and stowed so as to maintain a spacing of at least 6 m from other groups.*

[c]   *The consignment shall be so handled and stowed that the total sum of CSI's in any group does not exceed 100, and stowed so as to maintain a spacing of at least 6 m from other groups. For transport under exclusive use, the intervening space between groups may be occupied by other compatible cargo.*

7.1.8.4.3   Fissile material meeting one of the provisions (a) to (f) of 2.7.2.3.5 shall meet the following requirements:

(a)   Only one of the provisions (a) to (f) of 2.7.2.3.5 is allowed per consignment;

(b)   Only one approved fissile material in packages classified in accordance with 2.7.2.3.5 (f) is allowed per consignment unless multiple materials are authorized in the certificate of approval;

(c)   Fissile material in packages classified in accordance with 2.7.2.3.5 (c) shall be transported in a consignment with no more than 45 g of fissile nuclides;

(d) Fissile material in packages classified in accordance with 2.7.2.3.5 (d) shall be transported in a consignment with no more than 15 g of fissile nuclides;

(e) Unpackaged or packaged fissile material classified in accordance with 2.7.2.3.5 (e) shall be transported under exclusive use on a conveyance with no more than 45 g of fissile nuclides.

7.1.8.5 *Damaged or leaking packages, contaminated packagings*

7.1.8.5.1 If it is evident that a package is damaged or leaking, or if it is suspected that the package may have leaked or been damaged, access to the package shall be restricted and a qualified person shall, as soon as possible, assess the extent of contamination and the resultant dose rate of the package. The scope of the assessment shall include the package, the conveyance, the adjacent loading and unloading areas, and, if necessary, all other material which has been carried in the conveyance. When necessary, additional steps for the protection of people property and the environment, in accordance with provisions established by the relevant competent authority, shall be taken to overcome and minimize the consequences of such leakage or damage.

7.1.8.5.2 Packages damaged or leaking radioactive contents in excess of allowable limits for normal conditions of transport may be removed to an acceptable interim location under supervision, but shall not be forwarded until repaired or reconditioned and decontaminated.

7.1.8.5.3 A conveyance and equipment used regularly for the transport of radioactive material shall be periodically checked to determine the level of contamination. The frequency of such checks shall be related to the likelihood of contamination and the extent to which radioactive material is transported.

7.1.8.5.4 Except as provided in 7.1.8.5.5, any conveyance, or equipment or part thereof which has become contaminated above the limits specified in 4.1.9.1.2 in the course of the transport of radioactive material, or which shows a dose rate in excess of 5 µSv/h at the surface, shall be decontaminated as soon as possible by a qualified person and shall not be re-used unless the following conditions are fulfilled:

(a) the non-fixed contamination shall not exceed the limits specified in 4.1.9.1.2;

(b) the dose rate resulting from the fixed contamination shall not exceed 5 µSv/h at the surface.

7.1.8.5.5 A freight container or conveyance dedicated to the transport of unpackaged radioactive material under exclusive use shall be excepted from the requirements of 4.1.9.1.4 and 7.1.8.5.4 solely with regard to its internal surfaces and only for as long as it remains under that specific exclusive use.

7.1.8.6 *Other requirements*

7.1.8.6.1 Where a consignment is undeliverable, the consignment shall be placed in a safe location and the appropriate competent authority shall be informed as soon as possible and a request made for instructions on further action.

7.1.9 **Reporting of accidents or incidents involving dangerous goods in transport**

7.1.9.1 Accidents and incidents involving the transport of dangerous goods shall be reported to the competent authority of the State in which they occurred in accordance with the reporting requirements of that State and applicable international law.

7.1.9.2 Information reported shall include at least the description of the goods as provided in 5.4.1.4, description of the accident/incident, date and location, estimated loss of dangerous goods, containment information (e.g., packaging or tank type, identification marks, capacity and quantity) and cause and type of any packaging or tank failure that resulted in a release of dangerous goods.

7.1.9.3	Certain types of dangerous goods, as determined by the competent authority or established under applicable international law, may be excepted from these requirements for reporting of accidents or incidents.

**7.1.10	Retention of dangerous goods transport information**

7.1.10.1	The carrier shall retain a copy of the dangerous goods transport document and additional information and documentation as specified in these Regulations, for a minimum period of three months.

7.1.10.2	When the documents are kept electronically or in a computer system, the carrier shall be capable of reproducing them in a printed form.

CHAPTER 7.2

MODAL PROVISIONS

7.2.1 Application and general provisions

7.2.1.1 This chapter requires provisions applicable to dangerous goods transport operations by individual modes of transport. These provisions are in addition to those applicable to all modes of transport as provided in chapter 7.1.

7.2.2 Special provisions applicable to the transport of portable tanks on vehicles

Portable tanks may only be transported on vehicles whose fastenings are capable, in conditions of maximum permissible loading of the portable tanks, of absorbing the forces specified in 6.7.2.2.12, 6.7.3.2.9 or 6.7.4.2.12, as appropriate.

7.2.3 Special provisions applicable to the transport of radioactive material

7.2.3.1 *Transport by rail and by road*

7.2.3.1.1 Rail and road vehicles carrying packages, overpacks or freight containers labelled with any of the labels shown in 5.2.2.2.2 as models No. 7A, 7B, 7C or 7E or carrying unpackaged LSA-I material, SCO-I or SCO-III, shall display the placard shown in figure 5.3.1 (Model 7D) on each of:

(a) The two external lateral walls in the case of a rail vehicle;

(b) The two external lateral walls and the external rear wall in the case of a road vehicle.

In the case of a vehicle without sides the placards may be affixed directly on the cargo-carrying unit provided that they are readily visible; in the case of physically large tanks or freight containers, the placards on the tanks or freight containers shall suffice. In the case of vehicles which have insufficient area to allow the fixing of larger placards, the dimensions of the placard as described in figure 5.3.1 may be reduced to 100 mm. Any placards which do not relate to the contents shall be removed.

7.2.3.1.2 For consignments under exclusive use, the dose rate shall not exceed:

(a) 10 mSv/h at any point on the external surface of any package or overpack, and may only exceed 2 mSv/h provided that:

(i) The vehicle is equipped with an enclosure which, during routine conditions of transport, prevents the access of unauthorized persons to the interior of the enclosure, and

(ii) Provisions are made to secure the package or overpack so that its position within the vehicle enclosure remains fixed during routine conditions of transport, and

(iii) There is no loading or unloading during the shipment;

(b) 2 mSv/h at any point on the outer surfaces of the vehicle, including the upper and lower surfaces, or, in the case of an open vehicle, at any point on the vertical planes projected from the outer edges of the vehicle, on the upper surface of the load, and on the lower external surface of the vehicle; and

(c) 0.1 mSv/h at any point 2 m from the vertical planes represented by the outer lateral surfaces of the vehicle, or, if the load is transported in an open vehicle, at any point 2 m from the vertical planes projected from the outer edges of the vehicle.

7.2.3.1.3   In the case of road vehicles, no persons other than the driver and assistants shall be permitted in vehicles carrying packages, overpacks or freight containers bearing category II-YELLOW or III-YELLOW labels.

7.2.3.2   *Transport by vessels*

7.2.3.2.1   Packages or overpacks having a surface dose rate greater than 2 mSv/h, unless being carried in or on a vehicle under exclusive use in accordance with table 7.1.8.3.3, footnote (a), shall not be transported by vessel except under special arrangement.

7.2.3.2.2   The transport of consignments by means of a special use vessel which, by virtue of its design, or by reason of its being chartered, is dedicated to the purpose of carrying radioactive material, shall be excepted from the requirements specified in 7.1.8.3.3 provided that the following conditions are met:

    (a)   A radiation protection programme for the shipment shall be approved by the competent authority of the flag state of the vessel and, when requested, by the competent authority at each port of call;

    (b)   Stowage arrangements shall be predetermined for the whole voyage including any consignments to be loaded at ports of call en route; and

    (c)   The loading, carriage and unloading of the consignments shall be supervised by persons qualified in the transport of radioactive material.

7.2.3.3   *Transport by air*

7.2.3.3.1   Type B(M) packages and consignments under exclusive use shall not be transported on passenger aircraft.

7.2.3.3.2   Vented Type B(M) packages, packages which require external cooling by an ancillary cooling system, packages subject to operational controls during transport, and packages containing liquid pyrophoric materials shall not be transported by air.

7.2.3.3.3   Packages or overpacks having a surface dose rate greater than 2 mSv/h shall not be transported by air except by special arrangement.

7.2.4   **Security provisions for transport by road, rail and inland waterway**

NOTE: These provisions are in addition to those applicable to all modes of transport as provided in chapter 1.4.

7.2.4.1   Each crew member of road vehicles, trains and inland waterway craft transporting dangerous goods shall carry with them means of identification, which includes their photograph, during transport.

7.2.4.2   When appropriate and already fitted, the use of transport telemetry or other tracking methods or devices shall be used to monitor the movement of high consequence dangerous goods (see table 1.4.1 in chapter 1.4.).

7.2.4.3   The carrier shall ensure the application to vehicles and inland waterway craft transporting high consequence dangerous goods (see table 1.4.1 in chapter 1.4) of devices, equipment or arrangements to prevent the theft of the vehicle or inland waterway craft or its cargo and shall ensure that these are operational and effective at all times.

7.2.4.4   Safety inspections on cargo transport units shall cover appropriate security measures.

TABLE OF CORRESPONDENCE BETWEEN PARAGRAPHS, TABLES AND FIGURES IN THE 2018 EDITION OF THE IAEA REGULATIONS FOR THE SAFE TRANSPORT OF RADIOACTIVE MATERIAL AND THE TWENTY-THIRD REVISED EDITION OF THE RECOMMENDATIONS ON THE TRANSPORT OF DANGEROUS GOODS

Correspondence between paragraphs

IAEA	Model regulations	IAEA	Model regulations	IAEA	Model regulations
101	1.5.1.1	231	1.2.1, 4.1.9.1.1	410	3.3.1 SP336
102	X	232	1.2.1	411	4.1.9.2.1, 7.1.8.2
103	1.1.1.3	234	1.5.2.1	412	2.7.2.4.3
104	1.5.1.2	235	1.2.1	413	2.7.2.3.2
105	1.1.1.4	236	2.7.1.1	414	4.1.9.2.1, 7.1.8.2
106	1.5.1.3	237	1.2.1	415	2.7.2.3.3
107	1.5.1.4	238	1.5.4.1	416	2.7.2.3.4
108	X	239	2.7.1.3	417	2.7.2.3.5,
109	X (chapter 1.4)	240	2.7.1.3	418	4.1.9.3
110	1.5.5.1, 4.1.9.1.5	241	2.7.1.3	419	2.7.2.4.5
111	X	242	1.2.1	420	2.7.2.4.5.1
201	2.7.1.3	243	1.2.1	421	2.7.2.4
202	1.2.1	244	1.2.1	422	2.7.2.4.1.1
203	1.2.1	245	2.7.1.3	423	2.7.2.4.1.3
204	1.2.1	246	2.7.1.3	423 (e)	1.1.1.6 (b)
205	1.2.1	247	2.7.1.3	424	2.7.2.4.1.4
206	1.2.1	248	1.2.1	424 (c)	1.1.1.6 (b)
207	1.2.1	249	1.2.1	425	2.7.2.4.1.5
208	1.2.1	301	1.5.2.2	426	2.7.2.4.1.6
209	1.2.1	302	1.5.2.3	427	2.7.2.4.1.7
210	1.2.1	303	1.5.2.4	428	2.7.2.4.4
211	1.2.1	304	1.5.2.5	429	2.7.2.4.4
212	1.2.1	305	1.5.2.6	430	2.7.2.4.4
213	1.2.1	306	1.5.3.1	431	2.7.2.4.6.1
214	2.7.1.2	307	Recommendations §17	432	2.7.2.4.6.2
215	2.7.1.2	308	Recommendations §18	433	3.3.1, SP337
216	2.7.1.2	309	1.5.6.1	434	2.7.2.5
217	1.2.1	310	1.5.4.2	501	4.1.9.1.6
218	1.2.1	311	1.5.2.7	502	4.1.9.1.7
219	1.2.1	312	1.3.1	503	4.1.9.1.8
220	1.2.1	313	1.3.2	504	4.1.9.1.3
220A	1.2.1	314	1.3.3	505	5.1.3.2
221	1.2.1	315	1.3.4	506	7.1.2
222	2.7.1.3	401	2.7.2.1.1	507	1.5.5.1
223	1.2.1	402	2.7.2.2.1	508	4.1.9.1.2
224	1.2.1	403	2.7.2.2.2	509	4.1.9.1.4
225	2.7.1.3	404	2.7.2.2.3	510	7.1.8.5.1
226	2.7.1.3	405	2.7.2.2.4	511	7.1.8.5.2
227	2.7.1.3	406	2.7.2.2.5	512	7.1.8.5.3
228	1.2.1	407	2.7.2.2.6	513	7.1.8.5.4
229	1.2.1	408	2.7.2.4.2	514	7.1.8.5.5
230	1.2.1	409	2.7.2.3.1.2	515	1.5.1.5.1, 1.5.1.5.2

IAEA	Model regulations
516	2.7.2.4.1.2
517	4.1.9.2.1
518	4.1.9.2.2
519	4.1.9.2.3
520	4.1.9.2.4
521	4.1.9.2.5
522	7.1.8.2
523	5.1.5.3.1
524	5.1.5.3.2
524A	5.1.5.3.2
525	5.1.5.3.3
526	4.1.9.1.10
527	4.1.9.1.11
528	4.1.9.1.12
529	5.1.5.3.4
530	5.1.5.3.5, 5.2.1.5.8, 5.2.2.1.12.5, 5.4.1.5.7.3
531	5.2.1.5.1
532	5.2.1.1, 5.2.1.2, 5.1.2.1
533	5.2.1.5.3
534	5.2.1.5.4
535	5.2.1.5.5
536	5.2.1.5.6
536A	5.2.1.5.6
537	5.2.1.5.7
538	5.2.2.1.12.1
539	5.2.2.1.12.1
540	5.2.2.1.12.2
541	5.2.2.1.12.3
542	5.2.2.1.12.4
543	5.3.1.1.5.1
544	5.3.2.1.1, 5.3.2.1.2
545	5.1.1.2
546	5.4.1.3, 5.4.1.4.1, 5.4.1.5.7.1
547	5.4.1.6.1
548	X
549	5.4.1.6
550	5.4.1.6.2
551	5.4.2.1
552	5.4.2.2
553	X
554	5.4.1.5.7.2
555	5.4.4

IAEA	Model regulations
556	5.4.1.5.7.4
557	5.1.5.1.4 (a)
558	5.1.5.1.4 (b)
559	5.1.5.1.4 (d)
560	5.1.5.1.4 (c)
561	4.1.9.1.9, 5.1.5.2.2
562	7.1.8.1.1
563	7.1.8.1.2
564	7.1.8.3.1
565	7.1.8.3.2
566	7.1.8.3.3
567	7.1.8.3.4
568	7.1.8.4.1
569	7.1.8.4.2
570	7.1.8.4.3
571	7.2.3.1.1
572	5.3.2.1.1, 5.3.2.1.2
573	7.2.3.1.2
574	7.2.3.1.3
575	7.2.3.2.1
576	7.2.3.2.2
577	7.2.3.3.1
578	7.2.3.3.2
579	7.2.3.3.3
580	1.1.1.6
581	1.1.1.6
582	X
583	7.1.8.6.1
584	5.4.1.1.1/5.4.1.1.2
585	X
586	5.4.1.1.3
587	X
588	X
601	2.7.2.3.1.3
602	2.7.2.3.3.1
603	2.7.2.3.3.2
604	2.7.2.3.3.1
605	2.7.2.3.4.1
606	2.7.2.3.6
607	6.4.2.1
608	6.4.2.2
609	6.4.2.3
610	6.4.2.4
611	6.4.2.5

IAEA	Model regulations
612	6.4.2.6
613	6.4.2.7
613A	6.4.2.8
614	6.4.2.9
615	6.4.2.10
616	6.4.2.11
617	6.4.2.12
618	6.4.2.13
619	6.4.3.1
620	6.4.3.2
621	6.4.3.3
622	6.4.4
623	6.4.5.1
624	6.4.5.1, 6.4.5.2
625	6.4.5.1, 6.4.5.3
626	6.4.5.4.1
627	6.4.5.4.2
628	6.4.5.4.3
629	6.4.5.4.4
630	6.4.5.4.5
631	6.4.6.1
632	6.4.6.2
633	6.4.6.3
634	6.4.6.4
635	6.4.7.1
636	6.4.7.2
637	6.4.7.3
638	6.4.7.4
639	6.4.7.5
640	6.4.7.6
641	6.4.7.7
642	6.4.7.8
643	6.4.7.9
644	6.4.7.10
645	6.4.7.11
646	6.4.7.12
647	6.4.7.13
648	6.4.7.14
649	6.4.7.15
650	6.4.7.16
651	6.4.7.17
652	6.4.8.1
653	6.4.8.2
654	6.4.8.3

IAEA	Model regulations
655	6.4.8.4
656	6.4.8.5
657	6.4.8.6
658	6.4.8.7
659	6.4.8.8
660	6.4.8.9
661	6.4.8.10
662	6.4.8.11
663	6.4.8.12
664	6.4.8.13
665	6.4.8.14
666	6.4.8.15
667	6.4.9.1
668	6.4.9.2
669	6.4.10.1
670	6.4.10.2
671	6.4.10.3
672	6.4.10.4
673	6.4.11.1
674	6.4.11.2
675	6.4.11.3
676	6.4.11.4
677	6.4.11.5
378	6.4.11.6
679	6.4.11.7
680	6.4.11.8
681	6.4.11.9
682	6.4.11.10
683	6.4.11.11
684	6.4.11.12
685	6.4.11.13
686	6.4.11.14
701	6.4.12.1
702	6.4.12.2
703	2.7.2.3.1.4
704	2.7.2.3.3.4
705	2.7.2.3.3.5 (a)
706	2.7.2.3.3.5 (b)
707	2.7.2.3.3.5 (c)
708	2.7.2.3.3.5 (d)

IAEA	Model regulations
709	2.7.2.3.3.6
710	2.7.2.3.3.7
711	2.7.2.3.3.8
712	2.7.2.3.4.2
713	6.4.12.3
714	6.4.12.3
715	6.4.12.3
716	6.4.13
717	6.4.14
718	6.4.21
719	6.4.15.1
720	6.4.15.2
721	6.4.15.3
722	6.4.15.4
723	6.4.15.5
724	6.4.15.6
725	6.4.16
726	6.4.17.1
727	6.4.17.2
728	6.4.17.3
729	6.4.17.4
730	6.4.18
731	6.4.19.1
732	6.4.19.2
733	6.4.19.3
734	6.4.20.1
735	6.4.20.2
736	6.4.20.3
737	6.4.20.4
801	5.1.5.2.3
802 (a) (b) (c)	5.1.5.2.1
802 (d)	7.2.3.2.2
802 (e)	2.7.2.2.2
803	2.7.2.3.3.1, 2.7.2.3.4.1, 6.4.22.5, 6.4.23.8
804	5.1.5.2.1
805	6.4.22.6, 6.4.23.9
806	5.1.5.2.1
807 (a)	6.4.22.1 (a)

IAEA	Model regulations
807 (b)	6.4.22.1 (b)
807 (c)	6.4.23.6
807 (d)	5.1.5.2.1
808	6.4.22.2
809	6.4.23.4
810	5.1.5.2.1
811	6.4.22.3
812	6.4.23.5
813	5.1.5.2.1
814	6.4.22.4
815	6.4.23.7
816	5.1.5.2.1
817	6.4.22.7, 6.4.23.10
818	5.1.5.2.1
819	6.4.24.1
820	6.4.24.2
821	6.4.24.3
821A	6.4.24.4
822	6.4.24.5
823	6.4.24.6
824	6.4.23.19
825	5.1.5.1.2
826	5.1.5.1.2
827	6.4.23.2
827A	6.4.23.2.1
828	5.1.5.2.1
829	1.5.4.2
830	6.4.23.3
831	5.1.5.2.1
832	6.4.23.11
833	6.4.23.12
834	6.4.23.13
835	6.4.23.14
836	6.4.23.15
837	6.4.23.16
838	6.4.23.17
839	6.4.23.18
840	6.4.23.20

<table>
<tr><th colspan="2">Correspondence between tables</th></tr>
<tr><th>IAEA</th><th>Model regulations</th></tr>
<tr><td>1</td><td>included in 2.7.2.1.1</td></tr>
<tr><td>2</td><td>2.7.2.2.1</td></tr>
<tr><td>3</td><td>2.7.2.2.2</td></tr>
<tr><td>4</td><td>2.7.2.4.1.2</td></tr>
<tr><td>5</td><td>4.1.9.2.5</td></tr>
<tr><td>6</td><td>7.1.8.2</td></tr>
<tr><td>7</td><td>5.1.5.3.1</td></tr>
<tr><td>8</td><td>5.1.5.3.4</td></tr>
<tr><td>9</td><td>X</td></tr>
<tr><td>10</td><td>7.1.8.3.3</td></tr>
<tr><td>11</td><td>7.1.8.4.2</td></tr>
<tr><td>12</td><td>6.4.8.6</td></tr>
<tr><td>13</td><td>6.4.11.2</td></tr>
<tr><td>14</td><td>6.4.15.4</td></tr>
</table>

<table>
<tr><th colspan="2">Correspondence between figures</th></tr>
<tr><th>IAEA</th><th>Model regulations</th></tr>
<tr><td>1</td><td>Figure 5.2.1</td></tr>
<tr><td>2</td><td>5.2.2.2.2 No. 7A</td></tr>
<tr><td>3</td><td>5.2.2.2.2 No. 7B</td></tr>
<tr><td>4</td><td>5.2.2.2.2 No. 7C</td></tr>
<tr><td>5</td><td>5.2.2.2.2 No. 7E</td></tr>
<tr><td>6</td><td>5.3.1.2.2 Figure 5.3.1 No. 7D</td></tr>
<tr><td>7</td><td>5.3.2.1.3, Figure 5.3.3</td></tr>
</table>